The Essential Sangharakshita

THE COMPLETE WORKS OF SANGHARAKSHITA include all his previously published work, as well as talks, seminars, and writings published here for the first time. The collection represents the definitive edition of his life's work as Buddhist writer and teacher. For further details, including the contents of each volume, please turn to the 'Guide' on pp. 759–63.

FOUNDATION

1   A Survey of Buddhism / The Buddha's Noble Eightfold Path
2   The Three Jewels I
3   The Three Jewels II
4   The Bodhisattva Ideal
5   The Purpose and Practice of Buddhist Meditation
6   The Essential Sangharakshita

INDIA

7   Crossing the Stream: India Writings I
8   Beating the Dharma Drum: India Writings II
9   Dr Ambedkar and the Revival of Buddhism I
10 Dr Ambedkar and the Revival of Buddhism II

THE WEST

11 A New Buddhist Movement I
12 A New Buddhist Movement II
13 Eastern and Western Traditions

COMMENTARY

14 The Eternal Legacy / Wisdom Beyond Words
15 Pāli Canon Teachings and Translations
16 Mahāyāna Myths and Stories
17 Wisdom Teachings of the Mahāyāna
18 Milarepa and the Art of Discipleship I
19 Milarepa and the Art of Discipleship II

MEMOIRS

20 The Rainbow Road from Tooting Broadway to Kalimpong
21 Facing Mount Kanchenjunga
22 In the Sign of the Golden Wheel
23 Moving Against the Stream
24 Through Buddhist Eyes

POETRY AND THE ARTS

25 Poems and Short Stories
26 Aphorisms, the Arts, and Late Writings

CONCORDANCE

27 Concordance to the Complete Works

COMPLETE WORKS 6 FOUNDATION

Sangharakshita
The Essential Sangharakshita

EDITED BY VIDYADEVI

Windhorse Publications
38 Newmarket Road
Cambridge CB5 8DT

info@windhorsepublications.com
www.windhorsepublications.com

© Sangharakshita, 2018
First published in 2024.

The right of Sangharakshita to be identified as the author of this work has been asserted by him in accordance with the Copyright, Designs and Patents Act 1988.

No portion of this book may be utilised in any form for the training, development, enhancement, or operation of any artificial intelligence technologies. This prohibition includes all forms of AI, including generative models, neural networks, and any other types of computational intelligence. This restriction extends to all methods of obtaining or utilising data, including but not limited to, data scraping, data mining, direct or indirect observation, manual entry, or any innovative data sourcing techniques that might be developed in the future.

Cover design by Dhammarati
Cover images: Front: Sangharakshita, 1970s
Back: Sangharakshita in his room at Padmaloka, 1980.
Photo Roger Jones
Both images courtesy of Urgyen Sangharakshita Trust

Typesetting and layout Tarajyoti
Printed by Bell & Bain Ltd, Glasgow

British Library Cataloguing in Publication Data:
A catalogue record for this book is
available from the British Library.

ISBN 978-1-915342-13-3 (paperback)
ISBN 978-1-915342-12-6 (hardback)

CONTENTS

A Note from the Editor xv
Preface xvii
Launch of *The Essential Sangharakshita* xxi

PART I: THE ESSENTIALS

1 Who is the Buddha? 3
   1. The Buddha's journey to Enlightenment 3
   2. The symbolic meaning of the four sights 18
   3. The characteristics of existence 20
   4. *Dukkha* as an example of conditionality 32
   5. The Buddha's victory 33
   6. Archetypal symbolism in the biography of the Buddha 48
   7. Inspiration from the Buddha's life 60

2 Going for Refuge 64
   1. 'Coming home' to Buddhism 64
   2. What Going for Refuge is 65
   3. Going for Refuge and the concept of escape 69
   4. My own Going for Refuge and Going Forth 73
   5. The rainbow road 80

3 The path to Enlightenment   85
　1. 'What is your Dharma?': the Buddha's answer to Mahāpajāpatī Gotami   85
　2. The arising of vision   90
　3. The connection between philosophy and practice   92
　4. The essence of the Dharma   95
　5. The path as a symbol   99
　6. Spiritual growth: developmental or immanent?   101
　7. What is Nirvāṇa?   105

4 Buddhism – one or many?   113
　1. Variety and unity in the Buddhist tradition   113
　2. The forms of Eastern Buddhism   123
　3. The ideal approach to Buddhism   127
　4. The nature of Tantric Buddhism   131
　5. What do all the schools of Buddhism have in common?   132
　6. Misunderstandings about Buddhism   135

PART II: BUDDHISM AND THE MIND

1 Thinking clearly   141
　1. 'The impossibility of retracting an opinion I believe to be true'   141
　2. The voice within   142
　3. Getting a clear idea of Buddhism   145
　4. Learning to think   147
　5. More and more of less and less   149

2 Mind reactive and creative   153
　1. Sonnet   153
　2. The path of regular steps and the path of irregular steps   154
　3. What do we really know?   163
　4. Mind reactive, mind creative   167
　5. The Perfection of Wisdom – the flavour of irrelevance   173
　6. The shattering nature of Reality   174
　7. 'Above me broods …'   176

3 Views and truths   177
   1. Wrong views, right views, and Perfect Vision   177
   2. No 'ready-made' Buddhist answers   179
   3. The *anātman* doctrine   181
   4. Breaking the fetters   183
   5. Life is King   187
   6. The Buddhist attitude to death   187
   7. Reflections on impermanence   189
   8. How to reflect   190
   9. Karma and rebirth   193
   10. Is it necessary for a Buddhist to believe in rebirth?   202

4 Buddhism among isms and ologies   208
   1. Realizing I was not a Christian   208
   2. Religion as revelation or discovery   209
   3. The Buddha's attitude toward the teachings of his time   212
   4. The transcendental critique of religion   216
   5. The individual and the group   219
   6. Buddhists should state their views clearly   228
   7. The ideal student of Buddhism   232
   8. A revival of paganism?   233
   9. Formulations of the Buddhist path   238
   10. Buddhism and evolution   242

PART III: ART, BEAUTY, AND MYTH IN THE BUDDHIST TRADITION

1 The place of beauty in the spiritual life   249
   1. Sangharakshita I and Sangharakshita II   249
   2. Beauty as a characteristic of life   250
   3. Early experiences of beauty   253
   4. Learning to see   254
   5. Bamboos   256
   6. The snows of the Himalayas   257
   7. The greater mandala of aesthetic appreciation   259
   8. The temple bell   262
   9. Learning to stand still   263
   10. Pauses and empty spaces   264
   11. The simple life   265

2 Buddhism and art   268
   1. The religion of art   268
   2. Music and mystical experience   269
   3. The transformative power of art   273
   4. Art as an integral part of spiritual life   276
   5. Buddhism and Western culture   278
   6. The Dharma in Western poetry   280
   7. Stretching the mind through art   281
   8. Going to Covent Garden   283

3 The creative life   285
   1. After Rilke   285
   2. The arising of the poetic state   286
   3. Entering a spiritual dimension through writing   287
   4. A creative relationship with the world   292
   5. Should Buddhists have a sense of humour?   293
   6. The playful arts   295

4 A 'Buddhist Bible'? – Buddhist scriptures and where they come from   298
   1. The sea of Buddhist literature   298
   2. The origin of the Buddhist scriptures   299
   3. How to read Buddhist texts   301
   4. Buddhist stories   302
   5. The Bible designed to be read as literature   304
   6. Pāli scriptures and Mahāyāna *sūtras*   311

5 Dreams, myths, and symbols   315
   1. The nature of Tantric Buddhism   315
   2. The value of the dream state   317
   3. What is myth?   319
   4. The emergence of myth in Buddhism   321
   5. Taking myths literally   323
   6. The Tibetan wheel of life   324
   7. The Parable of the Burning House   340
   8. The Myth of the Return Journey   352

PART IV: BUDDHISM AND THE HEART

1 Buddhism and emotional life 369
   1. Involving the emotions in spiritual life 369
   2. Being moved by the Dharma 371
   3. The difference between feelings and emotions 374
   4. Cultivating positive emotions 376
   5. Dealing with desire 379
   6. Desire for the eternal 381
   7. Renunciation: not giving up but growing up 382
   8. Remembering the retreat 383
   9. The practice of forbearance 384
   10. The importance of feeling alive 386

2 Meditation 389
   1. Meditation 389
   2. Rainy season retreat 390
   3. The five basic methods of meditation 390
   4. Finding a place to meditate 402
   5. Happiness and concentration 404
   6. Why are we so easily distracted? 406
   7. The Japanese tea ceremony 409
   8. Mindfulness and spontaneity 410
   9. How to succeed at meditation 411
   10. Meditation isn't the only way 413
   11. Tantric meditation: the *yidam* 416
   12. White Tārā 420

3 Faith, devotion, and ritual 422
   1. Visiting Ghoom Monastery with Lama Govinda 422
   2. The nature of Buddhist faith 423
   3. The necessity of dependence 426
   4. What is ritual trying to achieve? 429
   5. A vision of Amitābha 437
   6. Secret Wings 438
   7. The importance of spiritual receptivity 439
   8. 'In the woods are many more' 441
   9. Everything that lives is holy 442

10. Devotion at Lumbini   444
11. Tibetan pilgrims   444
12. Call forth as much as you can   448

4 Buddhism and the natural world   450
  1. Animism and spiritual life   450
  2. Feeling that the universe is alive   453
  3. The traditional society   456

5 Friends and teachers   460
  1. Why should a Buddha need a friend?   460
  2. The network of relationships   465
  3. The importance of spiritual friendship   473
  4. Friendship: the whole of the spiritual life?   477
  5. Is a guru necessary?   484
  6. Spiritual hierarchy   500
  7. Gratitude   509

PART V: BUDDHISM AND THE WORLD

1 Compassionate activity   527
  1. The Bodhisattva's Reply   527
  2. The attraction of the bodhisattva ideal   529
  3. Compassion: the most important virtue   531
  4. Responding to the needs of others   533
  5. Withdrawal and involvement   534
  6. Giving: the basic Buddhist virtue   538
  7. The altruistic dimension of Going for Refuge   539
  8. Is the bodhisattva ideal realistic?   542
  9. Ways of helping   545

2 Buddhist ethics   549
  1. Before Dawn   549
  2. The basis of Buddhist ethics   549
  3. The five precepts   553
  4. Natural morality and conventional morality   556
  5. Beyond 'Buddhist respectability'   563
  6. The ethics of speech   565

7. Rights and duties   573
  8. Mindfulness of purpose   576
  9. Why we conceal things   577
  10. Buddhist confession   579
  11. 'The oppression of existence'   582

3 The nature of spiritual effort   587
  1. Living with purpose   587
  2. The spiral path   588
  3. The four exertions   590
  4. What counts as laziness?   591
  5. Discipline   592
  6. A regular routine   594
  7. Certainty of success   595
  8. Encountering the *ḍākinī*   596

4 Great Buddhists of the Twentieth Century   600

5 Living in the world   622
  1. The ideal society   622
  2. The basis of ethical work   627
  3. Right livelihood businesses   634
  4. Being easy to support   636
  5. Begging in India   644
  6. The group and the individual   648
  7. The integration of Buddhism into Western society   650
  8. Getting comfortable in the Pure Land?   652

6 Buddhism and the future of the world   654
  1. Buddhism and world peace   654
  2. A Buddhist approach to world problems   669
  3. The miracle of spiritual development   676
  4. 'Coming home' to Buddhism   678

Sources   681
Notes and References   687
Index   731
A Guide to *The Complete Works of Sangharakshita*   759

A NOTE FROM THE EDITOR

My preface to the first edition of *The Essential Sangharakshita*, together with Sangharakshita's own account on the occasion of the book's launch in 2009, explain how this book came into being, so I need only say here that we are very grateful to Wisdom Publications for releasing the rights to make this new edition possible, and for the inspiration that prompted the creation of the book in the first place.

We have taken the opportunity of creating this *Complete Works* edition to reinstate Sangharakshita's appreciation of Dr Ambedkar and several other passages and extracts that were left out of the first edition, to add further explanatory notes, and to present the material in a style consistent with the other *Complete Works* volumes, while retaining some of the editorial features of the original Wisdom edition.

To enable each of the extracts to stand alone it was sometimes necessary to drop in a definition or brief explanation of a term, and to remove irrelevant or elaborative material. Some extracts were even created by combining material from different books. However, to make the volume as readable as possible, we have not encumbered the text with ellipses and square brackets. At the end of each extract is a brief reference to its source, and the Sources pages at the back of the book give more details, explaining where in the *Complete Works* the original material is to be found.

This is an unusual *Complete Works* volume in that, although it is a previously published work in its own right, almost all of its content also appears elsewhere in the *Complete Works*, so it could be thought of as an introduction to the collection as a whole. All Dharma books are 'of the nature of a personal invitation', and that is certainly true of this one. If you don't know where to start with the *Complete Works*, or know someone who is in that position, this volume would be a good place to begin.

As always, I am very grateful to the whole *Complete Works* team for the care they have taken with the production of this volume, but in particular I want to express my deep gratitude to Shantavira for all his careful work on this new edition. It couldn't have happened without him. Thank you, Shantavira.

Vidyadevi
Herefordshire
March 2024

PREFACE

In the course of his long career Sangharakshita has written a great deal, and more than fifty books are still in print: introductions to Buddhist history, thought, and practice; commentaries on texts from many parts of the Buddhist tradition; as well as several volumes of memoirs and poetry, book reviews, and essays. He has made use of many genres, from polemic and academic exposition to story-telling, poetry, and personal anecdotes. And he has written about many different Buddhist traditions, from the Theravāda to the Tantra, from Abhidharma to Zen, as well as many Western traditions viewed from a Buddhist perspective. Some of the books began life in written form; others have their origins in talks and seminars which have been edited and published.

In assembling this collection of his writings, I wanted to include as many as possible of the aspects of Buddhist life and thought on which Sangharakshita has placed special emphasis. The first challenge was to decide what to include – or rather, what must be left out, despite the generous space allowed by Wisdom Publications. Once that was done, I found myself surrounded by a glittering but muddled heap of words. All my attempts to organize them seemed just to shift the heap into another heap; and the words, taken from their contexts, kept losing their lustre. And then an idea came into my mind – or rather, an image. I decided to try organizing the collection according to a symbolic pattern to which Sangharakshita has returned many times in the course of his teaching: the mandala of the five Buddhas from the Tibetan Buddhist tradition.

The mandala is based on the Enlightened qualities of Śākyamuni, the historical Buddha who lived 2,500 years ago. In the course of the hundreds of years of Buddhism's history in India and then Tibet, the Buddha's attributes came to be visualized in archetypal form, as mandalas of Buddhas, each Buddha embodying a particular quality of Enlightenment: compassion, wisdom, energy, purity, and so on. The mandala of the five Buddhas is one of the simplest of these. To borrow from a description by Sangharakshita: in the centre is *the* Buddha – the primary Buddha you could say. To his right and left are the Buddhas of the east and west, representing respectively wisdom and compassion, or the intellectual and emotional aspects of Buddhahood. This was a development of the Mahāyāna. Then, with the Tantra, appeared the Buddhas of the north and south, representing further aspects of Enlightenment: compassionate action and beauty. So now there were five: one at the centre and one at each of the cardinal points.

It is this pattern that gives this book its shape. It is traditional to enter the mandala from the east, but here the starting point is the centre. In the Tibetan tradition, there are many Buddhas to be visualized or depicted within the pattern of a mandala, but in the simple five-Buddha mandala the Buddha at the centre is often Vairocana, who is called the Illuminator; he is white in colour and his hands make the gesture of teaching. In this first section are gathered what might be called the essentials, the central concerns of Buddhism: who the Buddha was and what he taught; what makes a Buddhist and what might move anyone to become one; what the unifying principles of Buddhism are and how the different traditions express them.

In the east is the realm of Akṣobhya the Imperturbable, the deep blue Buddha whose wisdom is described as mirror-like. This is the realm of the mind, and this section of the book covers Buddhism in its intellectual aspect: the importance of clear thinking, the nature of knowledge and the mind, key concepts such as conditionality and karma, and how Buddhism stands in relation to the other religions and philosophies of the world.

In the south is a very different world: the realm of Ratnasambhava the jewel-born one, the golden Buddha of beauty. Here are collected writings on the relationship of Buddhism with art, the Buddhist tradition as expressed in writing and scripture, the aesthetic aspect of Buddhist life, and the place of myth and symbol in the Buddhist tradition.

Continuing to move round the mandala, we come to the western realm of Amitābha, the red Buddha of infinite light. This is the realm of the heart, and one of the key themes here is the importance of the emotions to Buddhist life, and the role of faith and devotion in Buddhism. This section also explores the role of human relationships in spiritual life, especially friendship, and the nature of the relationship between teacher and disciple. Amitābha is especially associated with meditation, so this too is a theme here, as is our relationship to the natural world.

Then, in the northern realm of Amoghasiddhi, the deep green Buddha whose name means 'unobstructed success', we move into another very different aspect of Buddhist life: the life of activity. Here we will consider what it is to lead an ethical life, and how the Buddhist relates to society as a whole, focusing especially on the spirit of altruism of the bodhisattva. We will also encounter the heroic and active aspects of the Buddhist life, meet some of the most distinguished Buddhists of the last century, and look at what Buddhism has to say about the world's problems.

So that is the pattern into which the heaps of words have fallen, or been placed. I have been struck by how these different aspects of Buddhism really do seem like entirely different worlds: conceptual clarity and philosophy balanced with emotional warmth and devotional fervour, action in the world balanced with myths and dreams. Perhaps each of us will be drawn more to one of these worlds than the others, but the pattern also gives a sense of the mandala of Buddhism as a whole. As for Sangharakshita himself, it is difficult to guess in which of these realms he might feel most at home; to judge from these writings he is happy in all of them. As he himself readily admits, he is a complex person, and his teachings happily reflect this complexity. This means, incidentally, that each section of the book contains a great variety of material: even on a particular theme there are so many variations. Indeed, even in a book of these proportions it is hard to do justice to them.

While working on this project, I have thought a lot about Buddhism and about Sangharakshita's approach to it. I have thought also about my own relationship to this material, and have been glad to again bring to mind some favourite teachings, as well as persuading myself to consider some matters I would rather avoid. I have also thought about you, the reader of this book, with frank curiosity. I wonder who you are, and what you want to know. I hope that, whatever it is, you will find it here, somewhere in this collection of the ideas, practical teachings, inspirations, and exhortations that this particular Buddhist teacher has thought or felt it important to express at this particular time in history.

Vidyadevi
Herefordshire,
2008

THE LAUNCH OF *THE ESSENTIAL SANGHARAKSHITA*

The Western Buddhist Order was founded in 1968 and in the course of its history quite a lot has happened. Even quite recently quite a lot has happened, and earlier this year there was a very important development which took place in Bodh Gaya, one of the four chief holy places of Buddhism in India. In fact it is *the* holy place inasmuch as there, under the bodhi tree 2,500 years ago, the Buddha attained supreme Enlightenment. Last February the international convention of the Western Buddhist Order was held at Bodh Gaya for the first time. Several hundred Order members came from India and several hundred from various parts of the West, so we had the confluence, as it were, of these two great streams of Order members, all following and practising the same Dharma, all having the same ordination, all observing the same precepts, all going for Refuge to the Buddha, Dharma, and Sangha in the same way. That was quite a milestone in the history of the Order. I myself wasn't able to be present physically, but I was present in a way, because a few weeks before that event Mahamati interviewed me at Madhyamaloka, and the film of the interview was shown on the first day of the convention.

In the course of that interview one of the things I spoke about was what I called my legacy to the Western Buddhist Order, to the FWBO, and our whole Movement. I spoke of it as threefold: a legacy of Dharma teachings, a legacy of spiritual practices, and a legacy of institutions. Under the heading of Dharma teachings I mentioned the four noble truths, the Noble Eightfold Path, *pratītya samutpāda*, conditionality, the positive *nidānas*, the four levels of Going for Refuge, and so on, all of which over the years I've emphasized very strongly. Under the heading of spiritual practices I mentioned the *mettā bhāvanā*, the mindfulness of breathing, and the whole *satipaṭṭhāna* practice, all the dimensions of awareness, as well as the concentration on the six elements, and spiritual friendship, one of our most important practices. And under the heading of institutions I mentioned the Order itself, and the fact that the Order has chapter meetings, regional Order meetings, and international Order meetings; and also that we have the institution of the Mitra system, the Mitra study course, and so on. These are among the institutions which are part of my institutional legacy.

Had there been time, I could actually have spoken about a fivefold legacy, because there are two more. The first of these could be described as a material legacy. I'm thinking of all the Buddha images, bodhisattva images, thangkas, and other religious artefacts that I've collected over the years, some of which I acquired in India and some of which have been given to me since I returned to England. There's quite a collection, principally Buddha images, bodhisattva images, and thangkas. Some of the thangkas are quite rare and even precious. A few years ago the people at Madhyamaloka had the whole collection valued, and I was astonished at how much it was worth, especially a series of eight thangkas.

There's a story attached to those thangkas. I acquired them when I was in Kalimpong. I was living at my vihara, and one day a poor Tibetan came knocking at the door with thangkas to sell. When poor refugee Tibetans had thangkas to sell they usually came to see me, because although they needed the money, they were very concerned into whose hands those thangkas fell, and preferred to sell them to Buddhists if they could. So that morning this old man came to my door, and he had a set of eight thangkas to sell. At that time I had very little money – in those days I usually had very little money, and sometimes no money at all – so I didn't even look at the thangkas. I said, 'I'm very sorry. I just can't afford to buy any thangkas just now.' The man said, 'I'll let you have them for a hundred rupees.' I had a look at them and yes, they were good. But I said, 'I'm really sorry. I can't afford it. I don't have a hundred rupees.' So he said, 'All right, eighty rupees.' 'Very sorry, no, I don't even have eighty rupees.' 'Sixty rupees.' I said, 'No, I really mean it. I don't have the money.' So he said, 'Forty rupees.' It so happened that I had just forty rupees in the house and no more. So I said, 'All right. I'll take them,' and I took these eight beautiful old thangkas. I didn't feel happy about it, because the man clearly thought that I was just haggling, trying to get the price down, but I would gladly have given much more money for those thangkas. But forty rupees was all I had, and he was apparently pleased to get even that. He probably hadn't enough food to eat.

I unrolled the thangkas and found that I had a set of eight thangkas of the eight forms of guru Padmasambhava. I'd recently received the initiation into the Padmasambhava practice, so I was very pleased to have these thangkas, even though I was unhappy that I'd got them for such a low price. Years and years later, when the thangkas were valued, they were found to be very valuable indeed. I don't like to tell you how many thousands of pounds they're worth. They're quite old and in a quite distinctive, relatively simple style, and they form the nucleus of my material legacy.

There's another legacy I want to mention, and that is my literary legacy, the legacy of all the books that have been published, as well as unpublished material in the form of diaries, letters, notes, and so on. I've published quite a few volumes, well over forty by now, and they can be divided into two groups. First of all there are the books that I've written with my own hand, like *A Survey of Buddhism*, *The Three Jewels*, *The History of My Going for Refuge*, and all the volumes of memoirs and autobiography, as well as *The FWBO and 'Protestant Buddhism'* and *Ambedkar and Buddhism*. Usually I write everything out in longhand, or at least I used to, and then it's typed and sent to the press. But there are also a lot of volumes in the Spoken Word series. These are books based on the lectures and seminars that I've given from time to time, and they've been edited by various people, very often by Vidyadevi, who's become almost a specialist in this sort of work and knows my work very well. In this group we have books like *Wisdom Beyond Words*, *Who is the Buddha?*, *What is the Dharma?*, *What is the Sangha?*, and *Know Your Mind*. So between these two groups there's quite a lot of material.

A few years ago Windhorse Publications received a letter from Wisdom Publications, a well-known American publishing firm that publishes a lot of books on Buddhism. They had noticed that Sangharakshita had published quite a lot of books, and they thought it was high time that a *Sangharakshita Reader* was produced, so they said they were willing to bring out a selection of my writings, including the Spoken Word material. The next question was who would make the selection and arrange the excerpts that are selected? Eventually Vidyadevi undertook that responsibility. She was working on this material for about three years. I think she read and reread practically everything I'd written. She took the job very seriously indeed. In the end she had some 330 extracts, varying in length from two to three pages. She sent the material that she'd gathered and arranged to Wisdom Publications, and they were very happy indeed with what she had done.

I must mention that in the course of her work she was presented with quite a problem. She had this mass of material, all these extracts from some thirty-eight volumes of my writings, but how was she to organize them? She didn't want to put them in chronological order. She thought about this quite a bit, and we had various discussions on the telephone about it, and then one day she had a bright idea. I don't know how it floated into her mind, but she decided to arrange the material under the headings of the five archetypal Buddhas. We've got Vairocana at the centre of the mandala, Amoghasiddhi to the north, Akṣobhya to the east, Ratnasambhava to the south, and Amitābha in the west. So she arranged the material in five main groups under the patronage, as it were, almost under the inspiration of these five archetypal Buddhas. Material of central importance she put under the patronage of Vairocana. Material of a deep philosophical significance she put under the patronage of Akṣobhya. All my writings dealing with the relationship between Buddhism and the arts, like *The Religion of Art*, she put under the patronage of Ratnasambhava. Writings dealing with meditation and with spiritual friendship she put under the patronage of Amitābha. And writings dealing with right livelihood, especially team-based right livelihood, and other activities she put under the patronage of Amoghasiddhi. There were subdivisions too. The publishers were very pleased with the way she'd arranged it.

But, as I mentioned, the arrangement of the material is not chronological, which means that you've got material from various periods of my writing career juxtaposed. On the cover of the book, the publishers wrote something to the effect of 'Fifty years of writings from Sangharakshita, founder of the Western Buddhist Order'. I'd been writing for more than sixty years actually, but fifty was a good round number. That meant that extracts were plucked both from relatively early writings and also from relatively more recent writings. You may find, if you look at the extracts as a whole, that there are different emphases in different places, and that is because in the course of sixty years of writing and teaching I sometimes found it necessary to emphasize one aspect of the Dharma and sometimes another.

For instance, in India I was in contact with quite a number of Theravāda *bhikkhus*, and in correspondence also with some very well-known Theravāda *bhikkhus*, and I found that the Theravādins generally had a very low opinion of the Mahāyāna. Some of them believed that the Mahāyāna was not really Buddhist at all. I didn't agree with that, so in some of those relatively early writings, as well as in my lectures and talks, I used to draw attention to the importance of the Mahāyāna, the beauty of the Mahāyāna scriptures, their significance, their profundity, and so on. That was an emphasis that I found necessary to make at that particular time. When I got back to England, I found that a lot of people had rather Theravādin ideas and attitudes with regard to the Mahāyāna, so I continued to emphasize the importance of the Mahāyāna and its scriptures. But later on, the situation changed. I started to feel that people, even some people in the FWBO, were tending to overlook the importance of the Pāli scriptures, that is to say the *Dīgha Nikāya*, the *Majjhima Nikāya*, the *Aṅguttara Nikāya*, the *Saṃyutta Nikāya*, as well as the *Sutta-Nipāta*, the *Udāna*, the *Itivuttaka*: all these very important early Buddhist texts. So more recently I've been emphasizing the importance of our getting to know these texts. The best-known of them perhaps is the *Dhammapada*, which I translated a few years ago and which was published by Windhorse Publications. The Pāli scriptures are our principal source of information about the life and personality of the Buddha Śākyamuni, so it's very important that we should acquaint ourselves with them, especially as nowadays we have some excellent new translations. I'm thinking especially of the translation of the *Majjhima Nikāya*, the *Middle-Length Sayings*, which has been made by Bhikkhu Bodhi, an American *bhikkhu* who was trained in Sri Lanka and is now living in his native America. There's also a very useful compilation by Bhikkhu Ñāṇamoli of a series of extracts from different strata of the Pāli canon, all illustrating the life of the Buddha. This is probably the most useful work of the kind that we have at present.[1] But an Order member has been commissioned by a publisher to write a biography of the Buddha. He has been engaged on that work for the last year, and I'm hoping that it will be published next year.[2] That will surely be a great accession to our knowledge of the personal life and character, as well as the teaching, of the Buddha Śākyamuni.

So at some times of my writing and teaching life I've found it necessary to emphasize *this* aspect of the total Buddhist heritage and at other times *that*. Although over the last sixty years I haven't changed my mind in any fundamental respect with regard to my understanding and presentation of the Dharma, there have been a few minor adjustments. For instance, there is the case of the three-*yāna* model as understood in Tibetan Buddhism. In Tibetan Buddhism they classify spiritual practices and attainments under the heading of the three *yānas*: the Hīnayāna, the Mahāyāna, and the Vajrayāna. They see these three *yānas* as progressive, so you start off with the very simple, basic teachings of the Hīnayāna, you progress to the more advanced practices and teachings of the Mahāyāna, and then when you're ready you practise the most highly developed teachings and practices, that is to say those of the Vajrayāna. In recent years I've become rather critical of that presentation of the three *yānas*. I tend to see them not as successive stages on a spiritual path, but as being, as it were, all on the same level – different approaches to the understanding and practice of the Dharma but from different perspectives, not one higher than the other. I think some Tibetan lamas are beginning to realize this. In Tibet they had access to the Mahāyāna *sūtras* and many *tantras*, but they don't seem to have had access to material corresponding to the *Nikāyas* of the Pāli canon. I get the impression that what they describe as the Hīnayāna is rather undervalued, and the depth of the Hīnayāna is not appreciated. In my view the teachings contained in the Pāli canon, especially in the *Nikāyas*, are no less profound than those contained in the Vajrayāna. So that's one of the ways in which my views have changed a little over the years. I no longer see the three *yānas* as successive, but I see them as all operating on the same level, and all leading to Enlightenment.

The compilation that Vidyadevi put together covers a great deal of material, and its title was changed more than once. Originally, as I mentioned, the publishers wanted to bring out *The Sangharakshita Reader*, but as the work progressed, they decided that it should be called *The Pocket Sangharakshita*. But Vidyadevi pointed out that she'd accumulated a very large amount of material and it certainly wouldn't go into a pocket. So we've ended up with *The Essential Sangharakshita* in 800 pages and prefaced by a little biography. I'm very grateful to Vidyadevi for all those years of painstaking work.

She did something else which I was quite pleased with. As well as including material from my written books and from the Spoken Word books, she also included a few of my poems. Now, I've always had a soft spot for my own poems. I know that not everybody likes them, but I rather like them, or at least some of them, and I know that some of them are quoted and even read in pujas on various retreats. I don't think I'm giving away any secrets, but I suspect that that is more often the case on women's retreats. The women seem to have more of a feeling for my poetry than the menfolk do, though perhaps that's a bit of an over-generalization. But anyway, Vidyadevi quotes several of my poems, not necessarily my best ones, but she gives them a place, and I'm very pleased about that.

One of the poems included is, I think, one of my more popular poems within the Movement, more popular in a relative way! – not read every day in every centre. It's called 'Meditation'. I don't know many of my own poems by heart, but I think I know this one, so I'm going to attempt to recite it.

> Here perpetual incense burns;
> The heart to meditation turns,
> And all delights and passions spurns.
>
> A thousand brilliant hues arise,
> More lovely than the evening skies,
> And pictures paint before our eyes.
>
> All the spirit's storm and stress
> Is stilled into a nothingness,
> And healing powers descend and bless.
>
> Refreshed, we rise and turn again
> To mingle with this world of pain,
> As on roses falls the rain.

I can remember writing this poem, and I can remember where I was when I wrote it. I wrote it in the first half of 1947, shortly before I took up my wandering life. I was staying on my own in a Hindu ashram for a few weeks. I spent my time there meditating, and somehow this poem emerged. Many years later, when I happened to read it again, it struck me that it was a sort of summary of the whole process of meditation. I hadn't realized that before, and I hadn't written it with that intention, but as I looked at it I realized that it says everything that needs to be said, essentially, about meditation. Having realized that, when I was in Berlin once and was asked to give a talk, I decided to speak about this poem. I explained it line by line, drawing out what seemed to be the fuller meaning, of which I hadn't been conscious at the time of writing it.

What I said was something like this. The first line goes, 'Here perpetual incense burns.' We burn incense as an offering. Offering is a very basic devotional practice in Buddhism, the offering of incense, light, and flowers, so the first line is dealing with that. And it's 'here' – not elsewhere but here, here and now. Remember the slogan in the old hippie days? 'Be here now!' And here *perpetual* incense burns. A devotional practice is not something that you just do and that's it. You keep it up. It's perpetual, something you do every day, in your heart at least. And there's another association. The *Dhammapada* speaks of the fragrance of *sīla*, the fragrance of ethics, of morality, being superior to that of any other fragrance.[3] So in this first line we have the preliminary devotional practice and also the practice of ethics, laying the foundations.

So now the heart to meditation turns. You've completed your devotional practices, you've settled, and you feel like meditating. You feel a little withdrawn. You feel in a contemplative mood. You withdraw from the objects of the outside world. And it's the heart that turns: not the brain, not the head, but your heart. You feel that you want to meditate. You feel you want to expand into some higher, subtler, more beautiful state. So the heart to meditation turns, and all delights and passions spurns. It turns away from the five hindrances, and because it does so, it is able to experience the *dhyānas*, to go higher, to experience these states of superconsciousness as we sometimes call them. So this is the message, as it were, of the first verse. Here perpetual incense burns. The heart to meditation turns, and all delights and passions spurns.

What happens then? What's our experience after that? A thousand brilliant hues arise. In our meditation we may have the experience of light, colours, forms, in infinite variety. A thousand brilliant hues arise, more lovely than the evening skies – even more beautiful than anything we see in the outer, material world – and pictures paint before our eyes. Here we may be thinking of the visions we may have, visions of Buddhas, visions of bodhisattvas, especially when we do our *sādhana*. These are the pictures we may be said to paint in our minds. This is the message, so to speak, of the second verse.

And what happens then? Usually the mind is so restless, tossed by waves of passions and interests and prejudices. But when we reach this point, all the spirit's storm and stress is stilled, calmed down, into a nothingness. This word 'nothingness' is very important, because it represents the denial of the ego. It represents what I sometimes speak of as spiritual death. That's when you pass, as it were, from *śamathā* to *vipaśyanā*. That's when you think in terms of spiritual death. That's when you do the six element practice. So all the spirit's storm and stress is stilled into a nothingness. You feel ineffably peaceful, so peaceful that there's no 'you' there any more. You've gone beyond the 'I'. And healing powers descend and bless. At a certain point in our meditation, when it's not just us making an effort, there's something that seems to come from elsewhere, some healing power that descends and blesses us and others.

And in the last verse, refreshed, we rise and turn again. We don't linger in that state, because there's a job to do in the world. We recollect perhaps the bodhisattva Green Tārā, who represents active compassion, compassion operating in the world. So we don't remain seated on our meditation cushion; we get up, we go forth, maybe to try to spread the Dharma, to mingle with this world of pain, to mix with people and to do our best to relieve their sufferings. Hopefully we have on them the refreshing effect that the rain has when it falls on the roses. Maybe you don't always feel like that when you go about in the world, but that's how it should be. When I look back at this little old poem of mine, written all those years ago, I think there is much more in it than I realized at the time, and I was very pleased when I found that Vidyadevi had included it in *The Essential Sangharakshita*, along with a few other poems.

So that's *The Essential Sangharakshita*, which is one of the two books I'm launching this evening. Some of you may remember that last time I was here I spoke about some of my teachers in connection with the launch of my book *Precious Teachers*. One of the precious teachers about whom I wrote in the book was Jamyang Khyentse Rimpoche, who was one of the greatest and most famous of the Tibetan lamas of his day. He came to Kalimpong as a refugee. Some of the ordinary Tibetans who came weren't able to bring anything with them, but he managed to get out with a few possessions, and among them was a set of very beautiful thangkas. They were quite ancient, and they depicted important ancient Indian Buddhist teachers. I remember these thangkas very well. Jamyang Khyentse Rimpoche donated them to the Namgyal Institute of Tibetology in Gangtok, and I saw them there.

One of them in particular caught my eye, a thangka depicting the ocean. On the ocean there was a raft floating, and on the raft there was a seated figure. But he wasn't alone. There was another figure, a sort of mermaid coming up out of the water and presenting the figure on the raft with a big book. The figure on the raft was the great teacher Nāgārjuna, and the mermaid-like figure was a *nāgā* princess, a serpent or dragon princess, presenting Nāgārjuna with the books of the Perfection of Wisdom. Nāgārjuna is very much associated with those teachings, and according to tradition it was he who discovered them at a time when they were relatively unknown, and made them available for a wider audience.

Nāgārjuna is in some ways the most important Buddhist philosopher. He lived about 600 years after the Buddha, and he's especially famous for a work called the *Mūlamadhyamakakārikā*, the *Verses on the Middle Way*, which is the foundation of a whole school of Indian philosophy, one that flourishes still among Tibetan lamas. He also wrote what are sometimes called minor works, but which are still very important, and one of these is the *Ratnamāla*, the *Precious Garland*. Many years ago I led a seminar on this text. It has some five hundred verses, and its principal topics are ethics and wisdom.

Recently Vidyadevi extracted all the verses dealing with ethics, together with my verbal commentary on those verses, and compiled them into a new Spoken Word book called *Living Ethically*, which is the second book I am launching this evening, published by Windhorse Publications. Vidyadevi is hoping to be able to bring out a second volume, dealing with wisdom, sometime in the future.[4] *Living Ethically* deals mainly with the ten precepts, but there are discussions on other very important aspects of the ethical life, for instance gratitude and spiritual friendship.

That reminds me of something the prominent Buddhist scholar Herbert Guenther used to say. Guenther has translated a number of works from Tibetan and from Sanskrit, and he has more than once made the point that in his opinion the term *śīla* shouldn't be translated just as ethics, but as ethics and manners. I tend to agree with him. Many Buddhist texts that deal with what we call ethics also deal with what we call manners. For instance, in the Vinaya Piṭaka, the text dealing with the rules for monks, the monks are admonished not only to behave ethically, but also to be well behaved in the sense of cultivating good manners. Sometimes the text compares what the monks are not to do with what the brahmins do. There's a list of five different things that some *bhikkhus* do when they eat, and *bhikkhus* are not to do those things.⁵ And there are many other little rules or recommendations of this kind, because both ethics and good manners involve consideration for other people. I think in our modern times good manners are very often dismissed as very middle-class or not really necessary. I'm sometimes quite shocked at examples of bad manners on the radio, even when I'm listening to Radio 4. I notice that when the interviewer is interviewing someone, even a quite distinguished person, sometimes the interviewer interrupts what he or she is saying in a very rude way. That sets a very bad example to the listening public. I think that in our own Movement, and especially in the Order, we should set an example not only of ethical living but also of good manners, and of treating one another in a decent and human way. That's just one of my pet peeves at the moment.

So that's the other book I'm launching this evening. So here they are, *The Essential Sangharakshita*, which you can read straight through from cover to cover or just dip into from time to time as you please, and *Living Ethically*. Obviously you're all trying to do that all the time, but a little reminder never goes amiss.

This is the edited transcript of one of several launch talks given in the UK in 2009.

PART I
THE ESSENTIALS

I
WHO IS THE BUDDHA?

1. THE BUDDHA'S JOURNEY TO ENLIGHTENMENT

The ultimately unacceptable limitations of human life had impressed themselves upon Siddhārtha's consciousness too forcibly for him to be able to ignore them, to put them aside and just 'get on with his life'.

To contemplate the biographical details of the Buddha's early life is to be concerned not just with the spiritual path followed by a man who lived 2,500 years ago. It is to contemplate a path which one can follow here and now, a path that one is committed to following if one is a Buddhist, if one has Buddhahood as one's ultimate goal. In other words, when as Buddhists we celebrate the Buddha's Enlightenment, we are not just rejoicing in a thing of the past. We are reminding ourselves that it is high time we started to think of our own Enlightenment, if indeed we have not already done so – and if we have, to think of it more persistently, more seriously, and more deeply.

I will sketch an outline of the Buddha's early life, to get a general idea of the way to Enlightenment, and then take up for more detailed examination certain crucial episodes or features of his biography that have a definite bearing on our own process of development towards Enlightenment. Like the story of the Buddha's life as a whole, these notable elements are in substance historical, inasmuch as we know they actually did happen. However, the versions that have come down to us contain a certain amount of legendary material, and it is this legendary material that helps to bring out the universal significance, the inner spiritual dimension, of the external events. The mythical aspect makes it clear, among other things, that these events are concerned not with one man's spiritual career, but with the career of every man and woman who aspires to grow and develop as an individual.

It is very often said that Siddhārtha Gautama, who became the Buddha, was born in India, and a hundred years ago this would have been true. But owing to changing political boundaries we would have to say today that his birth took place in the southern part of what is now Nepal. He was born into a tribe called the Śākyans, who had inhabited that particular area in the foothills of the Himalayas for many centuries. Nor is it quite true – as it is, again, often said – that his father, Śuddhodana Gautama, was the king of the tribe. He did certainly hold the title of rajah at the time of Siddhārtha's birth, but today he would probably be called a president. Like other small tribes in northeastern India at that time, the Śākyans had a semi-republican form of government, with a leader elected from the clan assembly for a fixed period of twelve years. Towards the end of the Buddha's lifetime the little republics of India were swallowed up by the developing Magadha empire, but at the time of his birth they were, for the most part, in a flourishing condition.

Siddhārtha's mother, Māyādevī, was the daughter of the chief of a neighbouring tribe, the Koliyas. It was then the custom, as it still is in many parts of India, for the first child to be born in the house of the mother's parents. When she felt her time approaching, therefore, Māyādevī set off from Kapilavastu, the Śākyan capital, to make for her father's city, carried, as far as we know, in a palanquin. She was still only halfway there when, seized with the pangs of labour, she dismounted, and in a grove of sāl trees at a little place called Lumbinī gave birth to the future Buddha. She died shortly afterwards – seven days later, according to tradition.[6]

Siddhārtha was reared by his maternal aunt, Mahāprājapatī Gautamī, whom his father had also married. We know little more about his childhood, but a single authentic incident stands out, one that took place when he was 5, 6, or perhaps 7 years old, on the occasion of the annual ploughing ceremony. In primarily agricultural civilizations all over the world, the sowing of the first seed in the spring was a matter of magical and mythical significance, and the first ploughing was always undertaken by the king or chief. It was one of the duties of the old emperors of China, and until quite recently the emperor of Japan used to inaugurate the ploughing every year. It was thus one of the jobs that fell to Siddhārtha's father to carry out. Later accounts tell us that it was done with a golden plough drawn by beautiful white oxen. (Storytellers love to embroider their material.) But leaving that aside, what we can say with confidence is that Siddhārtha's father performed this ceremony and that Siddhārtha was brought along to watch.

The little boy was put on one side on a bank in the shade of a *jambu* or rose-apple tree, and it was there that he had what we would describe nowadays as a spontaneous mystical experience. According to the Buddha himself, as he reminisced to his disciples a great many years later, what he experienced beneath the rose-apple tree was a sort of superconscious state known as *dhyāna*. So deep was his absorption that he never saw the ploughing at all, and he had still not emerged from the experience when they came to take him home.

It is at this point that an interesting legendary anecdote finds its way into the episode. The legend has it that although it was noon when the ploughing started, and evening by the time the ceremony was over, the shadow of the rose-apple tree had not moved during that time. On a literal level this would be what we call a miracle, but it is perhaps more meaningful if we take it symbolically. The obvious implication is that the sun stood still; and the implication on the symbolic level is that for the young Siddhārtha time itself had stopped.[7]

Later on, as we shall see, the memory of this experience was to have a crucial bearing on the direction of Siddhārtha's spiritual career. But meanwhile, mystical experience or no mystical experience, he was a Kṣatriya, a warrior, and he would have been brought up like one. That was his caste – the caste of the whole tribe – so he was literally born a warrior, as others were born Brahmins (priests), Vaiśyas (traders and farmers), or Śūdras (labourers) – just as they are today, although these four castes are now subdivided into some 2,000 subcastes.[8]

The future Buddha spent his formative years not in the close study of philosophy or the observance of religious practices, but acquiring the arts of archery and spear-throwing, swordplay, and the skilful handling of a war-chariot. With his patrician background he would have received the best martial training available. He would also have been initiated into the various traditions, customs, beliefs, and superstitions of the tribe, and he would have learned a little history and genealogy too. Of course, whatever he learned would have been by word of mouth from the elders of the tribe. It is not clear whether the Buddha ever learned to read or write. We must imagine him as a man who was cultured, educated, and well-bred without ever having attended anything like a school. (It is, in any case, questionable whether education has really anything to do with going to school.) He led on the whole a quite comfortable, well-to-do life, had no particular responsibilities, and was doted on by his father.

Siddhārtha's upbringing was not, however, quite so simple and straightforward as all that. Shortly after his birth, his father took him to see a *rishi*, the sage Asita, to have his horoscope cast. This was common practice, as it still is in India today. There is hardly anybody, even among the Westernized so-called élite, who does not have this done for their children – especially for their sons. You want to know what is going to happen to your child, what sort of a career he or she will have, so you go to an astrologer. It is not known exactly how Siddhārtha's horoscope was cast, but we know that he was placed in the arms of Asita, and that the *rishi* made his calculations. He predicted that the child would have a remarkable future: Siddhārtha would either become a great Kṣatriya, a great warrior and ruler, or else he would give it all up and become a great spiritual master.[9]

Śuddhodana was deeply disturbed at this prognostication, of course. He liked the idea of his son becoming an illustrious conqueror – he liked it very much – but he was appalled at the idea that the lad might take it into his head to retire from the world altogether and devote his talents to the spiritual quest. The older Siddhārtha grew, the more Śuddhodana turned the matter over in his mind. He thought, 'I want him to grow up like me. I want him to be brave and strong and extend the territory of the tribe, and – if the *rishi* is right – to become a great ruler and maybe conquer all of India. He must not be allowed to waste his time over all this religious nonsense. Therefore he must be prevented from thinking too deeply about anything; he must not be introduced to the more unpalatable facts of life – at least not too early. His heart must be set firmly on worldly things.'

So Śuddhodana was determined that the young prince should want for nothing, that all he should learn about life should be how to enjoy it to the most refined pitch of sensual pleasure. The Buddha later related in one of his autobiographical discourses how his father had provided him with three beautiful mansions, one for each season, so that he should never feel discomfort from the heat or the cold or the rains. And he recounted also how these mansions were filled with alluring dancing girls and bewitching singing girls, and how his days and nights were spent in drinking, dancing, and singing, one pleasure succeeding another, with hardly a moment for sadness.[10]

At 16 he was married off to a cousin, Yaśodharā. It was an arranged marriage, of course, just as in India today a marriage is usually negotiated by the families of the bride and bridegroom rather than by the young people themselves. He settled down happily enough and in this way for many years his life went on. All the same, though, he seems to have had an underlying sense of dissatisfaction with the life he was leading. When the news was brought to him that his wife had given birth to a son his reaction was not the usual one of a proud father. Asked what the boy should be called, he said, 'A fetter has been born to me. Call him Rāhula,'[11] for this is what the name Rāhula means – 'fetter'. (A fetter is a chain or manacle used to tie down a prisoner.) It was as if he sensed what his father had been trying to do all his life. Somehow he knew that Śuddhodana was trying to bind him down: with pleasure, with property, with power, with family, with wife and child. Realizing what was happening, he neglected his martial exercises and lost interest in the amusements and distractions laid on for him. Domestic life held no joy for him.

Increasingly he took himself off for long periods in order to think, and at some point he evidently had some sort of spiritual crisis – though this is not of course how the early scriptures put it. This psychological and spiritual turning point is known among Buddhists everywhere in the form of a dramatic narrative called the four sights. Whether this is a legend, whether it is an external projection of an experience arising out of intense inner questioning, or whether it actually happened in something like the way the story has come down to us, it is impossible for us to say for sure. What is certain is that the story of the four sights crystallizes in a very powerful form some of the fundamental teachings of Buddhism, as well as throwing light on the Buddha's own early spiritual development.

The story goes that one bright morning Siddhārtha called his charioteer to harness the horses for an outing. 'Let's see what is going on in the world, see what people are up to,' he said. The charioteer shook his head. 'I'm afraid we can't do that. I'll get into trouble. You know the king has said you are not to go out among the people.' But the young prince insisted: 'Don't worry. I'll take full responsibility. If the king has anything to say about it, let him say it to me. But let's go.' So the horses were whipped up and away they went. They drove out into the village and Siddhārtha saw life going on much as he might have expected – until his attention was arrested by the sight of a very old man.

The traditional accounts give a graphic description of this old man's appearance – feeble, withered, and bent over, his bones sticking out, tottering along on a stick. He had a long white beard and the rheum was trickling from his eyes. If this seems to be laying it on a bit thick, it would not seem so in India. There, old people, even today – because of the climate and the hard life – can sometimes look very old indeed. We have to remember that according to the legend his father had deliberately secluded him from anything unpleasant about life, and this included old age. So when Siddhārtha saw this very old man, he pointed at him and said, 'Who … what … is that?'

The charioteer thought, 'Well, he'll have to find out sooner or later,' and he said, 'It's an old man.' 'But why is he like that? Why is he so bent? Why do all his bones stick out? Why is that fluid trickling out from his eyes?' The charioteer was not used to fielding this sort of question, except perhaps from children. He said simply, 'Well, he's just an old man.' Obviously Siddhārtha was not satisfied by this: 'But how has he got like that?' 'It just happens,' the charioteer explained gently. 'You don't have to do anything to get old – you just get old. It's natural, I'm afraid – everybody gets old.' The young prince felt his flesh creep. 'What, everybody?' he asked, and the charioteer said, 'Well, yes, of course. Everybody.' 'What about me? Will I become like that?' The charioteer nodded: 'The king, your father, the queen, your mother, your wife, myself, and you too – all of us – are subject to old age.'

We are told that Siddhārtha received this intelligence like an elephant struck by a thunderbolt,[12] and he broke into a cold sweat with the shock. 'What is the use of being young?' he lamented. 'What is the use of this vitality and strength, if it all ends in such emaciation and frailty?' He was sick at heart. 'That's enough for today. Let's go home,' he said, and as they rattled back to the palace he brooded over the knowledge he had been given.

This, then, is the legend of the first sight. Siddhārtha may or may not have literally clapped eyes on an old man for the first time in this way, but there is no mistaking the real significance of it. He might have seen many old men before, but somehow missed *really* seeing them. That day, perhaps, he saw an old man *as though* for the first time. This is how life is, of course. We may see a thing every day of our lives, just as we see the sun rising and the sun setting, but we don't really *see* it because we are not aware and we don't think. We see but we don't see. For example, one might work in an old people's home for years without taking in the fact of old age to any great depth. Then when we develop some awareness, some clarity, we can find that things appear to us in such a fresh light that it is as if we never saw them before. So Siddhārtha realized, truly realized for the first time in his life, that there was such a thing as old age, and that youth would be brief, even for him.

Shaken as he was by this realization, Siddhārtha went out again a few days later – so the legend has it – and again he saw something he had never seen before. What he saw was a sick man, lying by the roadside with an attack of fever or something of that sort, tossing this way and that. Again Siddhārtha asked the charioteer to explain what was going on: 'What has happened to this man? What is wrong with him? Why is he shaking and shivering? Why are his eyes rolling so wildly? Why does his face look so ghastly?' Of course the charioteer had to tell him, 'Well, he's ill.' And Siddhārtha, who had apparently enjoyed blooming health up to that time, wanted to know whether he too would be likely to suffer in this way: 'Does this happen to other people? Will it happen to me?' So again the charioteer drove the point home: 'All men, all women, are liable to sickness. It might come at any time. At any moment strength and health may go from us and then we must suffer sickness.' So again Siddhārtha had something to think about as he returned to the palace.

After a few days, they went once more in the chariot, and this time he saw four men coming towards them carrying something on a sort of stretcher, the poles of which were balanced on their shoulders. Lying on the stretcher there was a man wrapped in a yellow sheet. His face was exposed, but there was something odd about it. He didn't move a muscle. The face was quite expressionless, stiff-looking, and the eyes were closed.

Of course, you can still see this sight any day of the week in India. An Indian funeral is rather different from what most of us are used to in the West. Here, when you die you are smuggled away in a box, and that's that. You are just quietly disposed of; you're put into the incinerator or into a hole in the ground and covered over. But in India it isn't like that. In India you are laid out in the best room of the house and all your friends and relations come round to have a good look and say, 'Well, he looks quite happy, quite peaceful. Goodbye then, old fellow.' They shed a tear and throw a few flowers onto the corpse, and then it is hoisted on the shoulders of four strong men and borne through the streets with the face still uncovered. As the corpse is jolting along, crowds of people following behind in the heat, the people passing by look and say, 'Oh, there's old so-and-so – didn't know he had died.'

This sort of procession is what Siddhārtha saw, and he said to the charioteer, 'That's very strange. Why are they carrying that man like that? What's he done?' The charioteer replied in his usual laconic style, 'Well, this is a dead body.' We have to remember, of course, that death was one of those matters Siddhārtha was supposed to have been kept in the dark about, so he was mystified by this explanation. 'Dead? What do you mean?' And the charioteer again had to expatiate a little: 'Well, you can see, he's stiff, lifeless, doesn't breathe, doesn't see, doesn't hear, he doesn't feel. He's dead. They are taking him to the burning ground. They are going to burn the body. It's what happens at death.' Siddhārtha gasped with horror: 'Does this too happen to everybody? Will everybody come to this death, as you call it? Will I too come to death?' The charioteer drew a long sigh. 'Yes. Your father, your mother, your wife, your child – they must all die one day. I must die. You must die. Everybody who is born must die. There have been millions of men and women born since the world began and every single one of them has died. No doubt there will be millions more born in the future, but every single one of them will die. No one can escape the cold hand of death. Death is king of all.' More sad, more thoughtful, more anguished than ever, Siddhārtha ordered the charioteer to turn round and head back to the palace.

Over these three outings with his charioteer he had come up against what nowadays might be called existential situations: facts of existence from which you cannot escape. You don't want to grow old but you can't help it. You don't want to fall sick, but it happens. You don't want to die, but die you will, like it or not. So you start asking yourself questions: 'How do I come to be in this condition? I want to go on living for ever, young and strong and healthy, but it isn't going to be that way. How is it that I have been given this urge to live when I am given not the remotest chance of escaping death? It's a riddle. But why am I presented with this riddle at all? Why this mystery? Is it God who is responsible? Is it fate? Or is this just the way it is? Is there an explanation? Or is there no explanation?'

Siddhārtha was wrestling with the fundamental questions of life and death in this way when he took in the last of the four sights. Driving out again in his chariot he saw a man dressed not in the usual white garb, but in a yellow robe, and shaven-headed. This man was walking calmly along the village street with a begging-bowl, going from door to door. There was something in his mindful gait that Siddhārtha found quietly compelling, and he asked the charioteer, 'What manner of man is this that looks so at peace with himself and the world?' The charioteer replied, 'This is one who has gone forth.' 'Gone forth?' said Siddhārtha. 'Gone forth from what?' 'From the world,' the charioteer explained. 'Gone forth from his home, from his family. He has simply left it all behind to devote himself to the search for Truth. He's trying to find an answer to the riddle of existence. To do this he has given up all worldly ties, all domestic responsibilities, all social and political obligations. In this way he has gone forth.'[13]

You may find such people in India even today, still wearing the saffron robe. They are called sadhus, which simply means 'good people', and supporting them with alms is considered very meritorious. People give them food, invite them into their homes, and look after them. Very much the same system is still in operation after 2,500 years. And it was the sight of just such a figure that awoke in the young Siddhārtha the inspiration to go forth himself. The ultimately unacceptable limitations of human life had impressed themselves upon his consciousness too forcibly for him to be able to ignore them, to put them aside and just 'get on with his life'. You can choose not to see them, but they are there all the time, and he knew this. But now he knew also that there was a way of penetrating through to the meaning of it all. After spending a long time thinking things over, he decided that there was nothing for it but to become a sadhu himself. He felt that these questions had to be answered and that he could not rest until an answer was found.

So one full-moon night when everything was quiet, Siddhārtha bade a last farewell to his sleeping wife and child.[14] He was not happy to leave them, but there could be no alternative. He had told no one about his decision except his faithful charioteer, who saddled the horse for him to ride out of the palace as a prince for the last time. We are told that the charioteer, whose name was Channa, seized hold of the horse's tail and trotted behind,[15] and that they travelled as far as a river marking the border of the Śākyan territory. There, Siddhārtha cut off his beard and his long, flowing black hair. Just then – it was the crack of dawn – a beggar came along, and Siddhārtha offered to swap clothes with him. It did not take the beggar long to agree to this proposal, eccentric as it seemed, and he went on his way blinking with delight at the richly embroidered robes he now wore, the gold and silver buttons and buckles on them gleaming in the first rays of the sun.[16] Siddhārtha made his farewells to his faithful charioteer and his faithful horse, and watched them go. Then he plunged on into the jungle, alone.

First he went in search of teachers who he hoped might have penetrated to the ultimate mystery of existence. In those days in India, as much as in India today, there were many who illumined the ways to the attainment of Truth. He went from one teacher to another; he practised according to their instructions and mastered what they had to teach. But he was not satisfied. Good and profound as their teachings were, he knew that there was something beyond all they knew, something beyond all they had realized. He had no name for it. He did not know what it was. But he had to find it – he had to know it. He had to carry on his search.

He was grateful for all that he had learned, but he moved on. He began a programme of terrible austerities. This was a common practice in India, as it is still today, for it was thought that the thinner the veil of the flesh, as it were, the more transparent it was to the light of the spirit. For years Siddhārtha mortified the flesh, and no one in India exceeded him in self-torture. It was said that 'the fame of his great austerities had spread like the sound of a great bell hung in the canopy of the skies',[17] and he began to gather followers of his own. Eventually, however, something happened to make him wonder if perhaps he was heading in the wrong direction. He fainted and collapsed into a river, from which, not having the strength to save himself, he was fortunate to be rescued.[18] When he recovered he said to himself, 'This is ridiculous. I'm getting no nearer to the Truth, for all this asceticism. I've been wasting my time. It's all been a big mistake.'

So Siddhārtha Gautama the great ascetic started taking regular meals again. His five disciples were not at all impressed. The fact was that they were not so much disciples as admirers, hangers-on. They relied on him to make the effort, and just stayed around in the hope that his achievements would somehow rub off on them. They thought that when he achieved his goal by virtue of his austerities they would be the first to benefit. So it was obviously a great disappointment to them when he made the decision to give his body the nourishment it needed. 'He's backsliding,' they said to one another, 'He's gone back to the luxurious ways of the world. Clearly he's not the man we thought he was.' And they trooped off in disgust. Once again, Siddhārtha was on his own.

It was six years after he had left the palace when he came to the place that would mark the end of his quest. At a spot in the present-day state of Bihar called Uruvelā, now known as Bodh Gaya, he found a copse of beautiful trees beside a river. It seemed an ideal location in which to sit and meditate. Then as he sat there in the shade, with a cool breeze blowing, he remembered something that suddenly seemed to show the way forward. He recollected his experience of thirty years before, sitting beneath another tree, while his father initiated the season's ploughing. He gently felt his way back to that integrated state of concentration – not trying to force it, but just letting it come, and letting go of whatever hindered its arising. As he did so a cowherd's wife from a neighbouring village brought him some milk-rice, which he took, and he was nourished and strengthened by it. A grass-cutter also came up to provide him with a heap of *kuśa* grass to sit upon, and he made himself comfortable on it. Then he settled down and gave himself to his meditative experience. Tradition tells us that he then made the resolution, 'I will not rise from this spot until I am Enlightened.'[19]

There is a beautiful and dramatic verse which is put into his mouth by some of the early compilers of the teachings: 'Flesh may wither away, blood may dry up, but until I gain Enlightenment I shall not move from this seat.' Then he settled down and gave himself to his meditative experience. He plunged deeper and deeper into it, through level after level of superconscious states.

How long he sat there we do not know. It may have been days; it may have been weeks; it may even have been months. As he sat there he controlled and concentrated his mind, purified his mind, suppressed the mental hindrances, the defilements. And on Vaiśākha Pūrṇimā night, the night of the full moon of May, just as the morning star was rising – just as he fixed his mind on that star glittering near the horizon – full illumination, full Enlightenment, arose.

It is obviously very difficult to describe this sort of state. We can say it is the plenitude of wisdom. We can say it is the fullness of compassion. We can say that it is seeing the truth face to face. But these are only words, and they do not convey very much. So let us simply say that at that moment the 'light' dawned, and Siddhārtha Gautama became the Buddha.

In a sense this was the end of his quest. He had become the Buddha, the 'one who knows'. He had found the solution to the riddle of existence. He was Enlightened, he was Awake. But in a sense it was only the beginning of his mission. Deciding to make known to humanity the truth he had discovered, he left what we now call Bodh Gaya and walked to Sarnath, about one hundred miles away, gathered together the disciples who had left him when he gave up his austerities, and made known to them his great discovery.

Gradually a spiritual community grew up around the Buddha. He didn't stay permanently in any one place, but roamed all over northeastern India. He had a long life, gaining Enlightenment at the age of 35 and living to be 80. So he had forty-five years of work, of active life, spreading his teaching. The pattern seems to have been that for nine months of the year he wandered from place to place teaching, and then for three months he took shelter from the torrential monsoon rains. Whenever he came to a village he would, if it was time for his one meal of the day, get out his begging-bowl and stand silently at the doors of the huts, one after another. Having collected as much food as he needed, he would retire to the mango grove which, even now, is to be found on the outskirts of every Indian village, and sit down under a tree. When he had finished his meal the villagers would gather round and he would teach them. Sometimes Brahmins would come, sometimes wealthy landowners, sometimes peasants, sometimes merchants, sometimes sweepers, sometimes prostitutes. The Buddha would teach them all. And sometimes in the big cities he would preach to kings and princes. In this way he gained a great following and became in his own day the greatest and best known of all the spiritual teachers in India. And when he died, when he gained what we call *parinirvāṇa*, there were thousands, even tens of thousands, of his disciples to mourn his departure, both monks and lay people, men and women.

In outline, at least, such is the traditional biography of Siddhārtha Gautama, the Indian prince who became the Buddha, the Enlightened One, the Awakened One, the founder of the great spiritual tradition which we call Buddhism. But does this really answer the question, 'Who was the Buddha?'? It certainly gives us all the facts, but does such a biography, however well documented, really tell us who the Buddha was? Do we *know* the Buddha – and the emphasis is on the 'know' – from a description of the life of Siddhārtha Gautama? What, in fact, do we mean by knowing the Buddha? Even from a worldly point of view, we may know a person's likes and dislikes, his or her opinions and beliefs, but do we really know that person? Sometimes even our closest friends do things that we find quite out of character, quite out of keeping with the ideas we had about them. This shows how little one really knows other people. We are not really able to plumb the deepest spring of their action, their fundamental motivation. Usually, the nearer people are to us, the less we really know them. There is an old saying: 'It's a wise child that knows its own father.' It is as though familiarity, or superficial closeness, gets in the way, so that what we know and relate to is not the other person but our own preconceptions, our own projected mental states, our own quite subjective reactions to that person. In other words, our 'ego' gets in the way. In order really to know another person we have to go much deeper than the ordinary level of communication, which isn't real communication at all.

It is the same with regard to this question of knowing the Buddha. This question in its deeper sense has been asked since the very dawn of Buddhism. In fact it is a question which was put to the Buddha himself, apparently, soon after his Enlightenment: 'Who are you?'

Journeying along the high road, the Buddha met a man called Doṇa. Doṇa was a Brahmin, and skilled in the science of bodily signs. Seeing on the Buddha's footprints the mark of a thousand-spoked wheel he followed in his track along the road until he eventually caught up with the Buddha, who was sitting beneath a tree. As the Buddha was fresh from his Enlightenment, there was a radiance about his whole being. We are told it was as though a light shone from his face – he was happy, serene, joyful. Doṇa was very impressed by his appearance, and he seems to have felt that this wasn't an ordinary human being, perhaps not a human being at all. Drawing near, he came straight to the point, as the custom is in India where religious matters are concerned. He said, 'Who are you?'[20]

The ancient Indians believed that the universe is stratified into various levels of existence, that there are not just human beings and animals, as we believe, but gods and ghosts, *yakṣas* and *gandharvas*, and all sorts of other mythological beings, inhabiting a multistorey universe, the human plane being just one story out of many. So Doṇa asked, 'Are you a *yakṣa*?' (a *yakṣa* being a rather terrifying sublime spirit living in the forest). But the Buddha said 'No.' Just 'No.' So Doṇa tried again. 'Are you a *gandharva*?' (a sort of celestial musician, a beautiful singing angel-like figure). Once again the Buddha said 'No,' and again Doṇa asked, 'Well then, are you a *deva*?' (a god, a divine being, a sort of archangel). 'No.' Upon this Doṇa thought, 'That's strange! He must be a human being after all.' And he asked him that too, but yet again the Buddha said 'No.' By this time Doṇa was thoroughly perplexed, so he demanded, 'If you are not any of these things, then who are you?' The Buddha replied, 'Those mental conditionings on account of which I might have been described as a *yakṣa* or a *gandharva*, as a *deva* or a human being, all those conditionings have been destroyed by me. Therefore I am a Buddha.'

The word for mental conditionings is *saṃskāra*, which means all kinds of conditioned mental attitudes. It is these conditioned mental attitudes, these volitions or karma-formations as they are sometimes called, which, according to Buddhism, and Indian belief in general, determine the nature of our rebirth. The Buddha was free from all these, so there was nothing to cause him to be reborn as a *yakṣa*, a *gandharva*, a god, or even as a human being, and even here and now he was not in reality any of these things. He had reached the state of unconditioned consciousness, though his body might appear to be that of a man. Therefore he was called the Buddha, Buddha being as it were an incarnation, a personification, of the unconditioned mind.

The human mind proceeds by degrees, from the known to the unknown, and this is what Doṇa tried to do. Seeing the glorious figure of the Buddha, he tried to apply to it the only labels he had at his disposal – the labels of *yakṣa*, *gandharva*, etc. – but none of them would fit. This is very relevant to us because there are two of Doṇa's categories which represent mistakes that we still commit, here and now, when we try to understand who the Buddha was, or is. These are the categories of 'god' and 'man', the only two categories still available to us in the West. One school of thought says, 'The Buddha was a very good man, even a holy man, but just a man and no more than that.' This is the view taken by, for instance, some Christian writers about Buddhism. It is a rather insidious sort of approach. Though they may praise the Buddha for his wonderful love, wonderful compassion, and wonderful wisdom, they are careful to add that after all he was only a man, whereas Jesus Christ was the Son of God. The other school says, 'No, the Buddha is a sort of God for the Buddhists. Originally he was a man, of course, but after his death his followers deified him because they wanted something to worship.'

Both of these views are wrong. The Buddha was a man, yes, a human being, in the sense that he started off as every other human being starts off, but he wasn't an ordinary man, he was an Enlightened man. And such a being, or Buddha, is, according to Buddhist tradition, the highest being in the universe, higher even than the so-called gods. In Buddhist art the gods are represented in humble positions on either side of the Buddha, saluting him and listening to the teaching.

A certain amount of confusion has arisen in the West about the Buddha being a god, or God, because they see that he is worshipped – that Buddhists offer flowers to the shrine, light candles, and bow down – and if you worship someone, we think, it means that for you that person is God. But that is quite wrong. Not only Buddhists, but people generally in the East, have got quite a different conception of worship. In India the same word, 'puja', is used for paying respect to the Buddha, to one's parents, to one's elder brothers and sisters, to one's teachers, spiritual or secular, and to any senior or respectable person. So what the Buddhists are doing when they offer flowers to the Buddha-image is respecting or honouring the Buddha as an Enlightened being, not worshipping him as God.

But let us get back to the question of knowing the Buddha. We have seen that 'Buddha' means 'unconditioned mind' or 'Enlightened mind'. Knowing the Buddha therefore means knowing the mind in its unconditioned state. So if at this stage we are asked, 'Who is the Buddha?' we can only reply, 'You yourself are the Buddha – potentially.' We can really and truly come to know the Buddha only in the process of actualizing – in our spiritual life, our meditation and so on – our own potential Buddhahood. It is only then that we can say from knowledge, from experience, who the Buddha is.

We cannot do this all at once. We have to establish, first of all, a living contact with Buddhism. We have to arrive at something which goes further than mere factual knowledge about Gautama the Buddha, about the details of his earthly career, even though it falls far short of knowing the unconditioned mind, of really knowing the Buddha. This something that comes in between the two is what we call Going for Refuge to the Buddha. This does not just mean reciting *Buddhaṃ saraṇaṃ gacchāmi* ('To the Buddha for Refuge I go'), though it does not exclude such recitation. It means taking Buddhahood, taking the ideal of Enlightenment, as a living spiritual ideal, as our ultimate objective, and trying our utmost to realize it. In other words, it is only by taking Refuge in the Buddha in the traditional sense that we can really know who the Buddha is. This is one of the reasons why I have always attached such great importance to the Refuges, not only to Going for Refuge to the Buddha, but also to the Dharma (the Buddha's teaching), and to the Sangha (the community of his followers).

In conclusion, it is only by taking Refuge in the Buddha, with all that that implies, that we can really and truly answer, from the heart, from the mind, and from the whole of our spiritual life, the question, 'Who is the Buddha?'

from *Who is the Buddha?* and *A Guide to the Buddhist Path*

2. THE SYMBOLIC MEANING OF THE FOUR SIGHTS

Most of us are occupied, much of the time, with matters that are simply unworthy of the attention of a moderately aware human being.

Let us consider the four sights: Siddhārtha's seeing for the first time – or as if for the first time – an old man, a sick man, a corpse, and a holy wanderer. Up to this point his father had apparently managed to seclude him from the world by occupying him with his martial exercises by day and entertaining him with singing girls and dancing girls in one of his three mansions by night. In a sense Siddhārtha had been secluded from real life, secluded even from reality. In Buddhist mythical literature the father sometimes represents ignorance, while the mother may represent craving (one being the more intellectual poison, and the other the more emotional source of suffering). So Siddhārtha had been confined by ignorance, the universal father of those beings who live without awareness. Lacking the wider perspective, he had lived in a world of his own. He had been hardly aware that there was a world outside at all – not so as to make any difference to the way he had occupied himself, anyway. The existential reality of his situation had not yet broken in upon his little world.

The same theme is given a different treatment in the Parable of the Burning House from the *Saddharma Puṇḍarīka*, or *White Lotus Sūtra*. In a huge crumbling mansion, a lot of children are engrossed in their various childish games when a fire breaks out. But while the fire blazes merrily and gradually takes hold of the ancient fabric of the building, the children pay no attention to the acrid smell in the air, or the smoke curling up from under the door, or the crackle and roar of the flames and the creak and crash of falling timbers. They are simply not aware of the danger. They just go on amusing themselves with their toys. We are not concerned with the rest of the story here – suffice to say that the children are eventually saved.[21]

The point of the opening of this parable hardly needs labouring. The burning house is this world, blazing with old age, disease, and death, while the children, of course, represent ourselves. The cosmos, conditioned existence itself, is on fire with existential suffering, yet we remain immersed in our trivial pursuits, our distractions and amusements. Most of us are occupied, much of the time, with matters that are simply unworthy of the attention of a moderately aware human being. Though we may catch glimpses of our real situation, of a real purpose to our existence, it is only too easy to slip back into the old ruts carved by social pressures and long habit.

Even when we are passionately absorbed in trivial things, however, even as we waste our time over distractions and diversions, sooner or later something happens. One day, something catastrophic happens, and our little world is shattered or so badly cracked that we can never again be really comfortable living in it. It's as though we had, until then, never been born, like a chick in its egg; but suddenly our little world is broken open, and we find ourselves looking out into another, wider world. Reality has finally started to break in. We begin to see things as they really are. We feel as though we have grown up, and are no longer entranced by the toys and tales of childhood. Or it is as though we have woken from a dream. When we are immersed in our dreams, whatever happens seems as real, as vivid, as our waking experience. But when we wake up, the dream world rapidly fades. After a few minutes, or perhaps after a few hours, it is nothing, usually not even a memory. In the same way, when reality irrupts into our sleepy, cosy existence, we look back at our old life, all the old pursuits for which we have lost the appetite we once had, and we think, 'How could I have lived in that way? Was that really me? Was I really so foolish, so deluded?'

As a result of this sort of experience our behaviour changes, just as an adult behaves differently from a child. People may notice that we've changed. They may even wonder if there's something wrong with us. 'Is anything the matter?' they may ask, not unkindly – though privately they may think we're not quite in our right mind, because we're no longer taking any interest in the sort of things that we used to like, no longer doing the things that other people like to do.

The event which shatters one's private world is very often unpleasant – it may be a bereavement, or the loss of a job, or being dropped by a lover, or discovering the infidelity of a spouse. On the other hand the breakthrough can come about in a more agreeable fashion – you get a sudden insight through art, perhaps, or music or poetry. Then again, it can occur through an experience that is neither pleasant nor unpleasant, nor even sudden: you just become discontented and dissatisfied. But whatever serves as the trip-wire, the experience which follows tends to be painful, disturbing, and all-consuming, because the old patterns are disrupted, the old moulds are broken. This is the sort of experience that Siddhārtha had, as illustrated by the four sights.

from *Who is the Buddha?*

3. THE CHARACTERISTICS OF EXISTENCE

This is the essential religious question. How may the conditioned become the Unconditioned; how may the mortal become immortal; how may I conquer death?

The *Majjhima Nikāya*, the medium-length discourses of the Pāli canon, includes a discourse that is of rather special interest on account of its autobiographical content. This is the *Ariyapariyesanā Sutta*, in which the Buddha describes how he left home, how he became a wandering monk, how he strove for Enlightenment, and how he deliberated about whether or not to try to teach the Dharma.

What surprises some readers of this *sutta* is that there is no mention in it of the famous 'four sights', of how Siddhārtha Gautama, the future Buddha, sallied forth one fine morning in his chariot with his charioteer, and saw a sick man, and then – on successive occasions – an old man, a corpse, and finally a wandering ascetic; and thus came alive to the existence of sickness, old age, and death, and the possibility of becoming a truth-seeking wanderer.

Instead, this particular account gives a comparatively naturalistic, even humanistic, description of how Siddhārtha came to the decision to give up the household life. It is, so far as this account is concerned, a purely internal process, not connected with anything in particular that he saw or heard. Here he is represented – in his own words – as simply reflecting.

The Buddha relates how one day he was sitting at home in the palace, reflecting alone. We should imagine him perhaps under a tree in the compound; it is probably the early evening, when a cool, calm quiet descends over the Indian scene. He is there simply reflecting, 'What am I doing with my life? I am mortal, subject to old age, sickness, and death. And yet, what do I do? Being myself subject to birth, I pursue that which is also subject to birth. Being myself subject to old age I pursue that which likewise will grow old. Being myself subject to sickness and decay, I pursue that which is subject to the same decay. And being myself subject to death, I pursue that which also must die.'[22]

Then – as the Buddha goes on to relate to his interlocutor in this *sutta*, who is a Jain ascetic – there arose in his mind a different, almost a contrary train of reflection. It occurred to him, 'Suppose now I were to do otherwise? Suppose now, being myself subject to birth, I were to go in search of that which is not subject to birth, which has no origin, which is timeless? Suppose, being myself subject to old age, I were to go in search of that which is immutable? Suppose, being myself subject to sickness, to decay, I were to go in search of that in whose perfection there is no diminution? Or suppose, finally, being myself subject to death, I were to go in search of the deathless, the everlasting, the eternal?'

As a result of these reflections, shortly afterwards he left home. There is no great drama in this *sutta*, no stealing out of the palace by moonlight on muffled hooves. It simply says that although his father and his foster-mother wept and wailed, he put on the yellow robe, shaved his head, cut off his beard, and went forth from home into the homeless life.

This is the story, in brief, of the Buddha's conversion – conversion in the literal sense of a 'turning round', though in Siddhārtha's case it was not an external turning round, from one religion to another, but an internal one, from the conditioned to the Unconditioned. Siddhārtha realized that he was a conditioned being, and that he was spending all his time and energy in pursuit of conditioned things – that is, in the *anariyapariyesanā* or 'ignoble quest'. He realized, in other words, that he was binding himself to the endless round of existence, the wheel of life on which we all turn, passing from one life to the next indefinitely.

So he decided simply to turn round completely and go in search of the Unconditioned instead, to take up the *ariyapariyesanā*, the 'noble quest'. In time, he would realize this quest as the spiral path leading from the endless round to the goal of Enlightenment or Nirvāṇa. But at this point he identified the course before him with this simple but strong, pre-Buddhistic expression, found in the oldest Upanishads: *esana*, urge, desire, will, search, aspiration, quest, pursuit. He could continue with the 'ignoble quest', or he could undertake the 'noble quest' instead.

The Buddha's conversion was not easy, we can be sure of that, because here and there, in other places in the scriptures, we get indications that a terrible struggle went on in his mind before he made his final decision. But stripped of all the legends and myths that have accumulated around it over the centuries, it was as simple – almost classically simple – as this. And it is in this most simple description of the first great insight of the Buddha-to-be that the essence of the spiritual life is to be found. Here we put our finger on the spring that works the whole mechanism.

This spring is the conditioned in pursuit of the Unconditioned, the mortal seeking the immortal: seeking, that is, not immortality of the self, but a self-transcending immortality. What Siddhārtha was looking for was basically the answer to a question, one that we find asked (in the *Dīgha Nikāya*) by a young monk, Govinda, who spends a rainy season retreat – that is, a retreat of about three months – meditating on *mettā* or universal loving-kindness, and as a result has a vision of the 'eternal youth' Brahmā Sanankumāra. The question Govinda asks Sanankumāra in this *sutta* is, 'How may the mortal obtain the immortal Brahmā world?'[23]

This is the essential religious question. How may the conditioned become the Unconditioned; how may the mortal become immortal; how may I conquer death? Now it all sounds very fine put like that, but if one is going to take seriously the question of how to leave the conditioned and go in search of the Unconditioned, one will want the answer to a further question. What exactly does one mean by the conditioned? How do we identify the conditioned?

According to Buddhist tradition, that which is conditioned invariably bears three characteristics, or *lakṣaṇas*, by which it may be recognized as such. These three characteristics are sometimes called the 'three signs of being', but more properly this should be the 'three signs of becoming', as the nature of the conditioned is nothing as static as a 'state of being'.

The three *lakṣaṇas*, the three inseparable characteristics of all conditioned existence, are: *duḥkha*, the unsatisfactory, or painful; *anitya*, the impermanent; and *anātman*, the emptiness of self, of essential being.[24] All conditioned 'things' or 'beings' whatsoever in this universe possess all these three characteristics. They are all unsatisfactory, all impermanent, all devoid of self. Of these three *lakṣaṇas* the first is in some ways the most difficult for most people to come to terms with emotionally, so we shall look at it in rather more depth and detail than at the other two.

Suffering

The Sanskrit word here is *duḥkha*, and the usual translation is 'suffering', but a better one – if a bit cumbersome – is 'unsatisfactoriness'. Best of all, perhaps, is to attend to its etymology: though the traditional account of the origin of the word *duḥkha* is no longer universally accepted, it still leaves us with a true and precise image.

Duḥ- as a prefix means anything that is not good – bad, ill, wrong, or out of place; and *kha*, the main part of the word, is supposed to be connected with the Sanskrit *cakra*, meaning 'wheel'. So *duḥkha* is said to have meant originally the ill-fitting wheel of a chariot, thus suggesting a bumpy, jarring ride, a journey on which one could never be comfortable, never at one's ease.

So much for a general picture of *duḥkha*. As we look closer, though, we see that unease or suffering comes in many different forms – and the Buddha usually speaks of seven.[25] First, he says, *birth* is suffering: human life starts with suffering. In the more poetical words of Oscar Wilde, 'At the birth of a child or a star there is pain.' In whatever way it is expressed, this is a great spiritual truth; it is significant that our life begins with suffering.

Birth is certainly physically painful for the mother, and consequently it is often emotionally painful for the father, while for the infant it is, we are told, a traumatic experience. It is very unpleasant to be suddenly thrust forth from the warm, protective world of the womb out into a cold, strange world, to which one is very likely to be welcomed with a slap on the bottom.

Secondly, the Buddha says, *old age* is suffering. One of the discomforts of old age is physical weakness: you cannot get about in the relaxed, agile way you used to. Then there is loss of memory: you can't remember names, or where you put things; you are not as agile and flexible intellectually as you were. Where this degeneration becomes senility it is a tragic thing to observe, most especially in once eminent individuals. Perhaps most painful of all, when you are very old you are dependent upon others: you cannot do much for yourself, and you may even need constant looking after by a nurse or by your relations. Despite all modern comforts and amenities – and often as a result of modern advances in medicine – many of us will experience this suffering, especially if we survive to an extreme old age.

Thirdly, *sickness* is suffering. Whether it is a toothache or an incurable disease like cancer, no sickness is pleasant. It is not just the physical pain that is suffering: there is also the helplessness, the fear, and the frustration of it. Medical science may sometimes palliate the suffering of sickness, but there is no sign at all that we will ever banish it entirely. It seems that no sooner do we get rid of one disease than another comes along. As soon as one virus is defeated, a new, stronger strain of virus arises. And as soon as we feel physically quite healthy, we start to develop all sorts of mental ailments, more and more complex neuroses and mysterious syndromes, all of which involve suffering. Almost any sense of imperfection in our lives can develop into an illness of some sort: stress turns into heart attacks, fatigue turns into syndromes, habit turns into addictions. So it seems that sickness may change its appearance, but it doesn't go away.

Fourthly, *death* is suffering. We suffer when those dear to us die; we suffer as we watch the life ebbing from a physical body that we have long associated with the life of a loved one. We suffer in the knowledge that our loved ones will die, and we suffer in the knowledge of our own dissolution. Much of our suffering with regard to death, of course, is simply fear. Most of us would put up with a great deal of suffering before we would choose to die, such is our terror of the inevitable conclusion to our own existence:

> The weariest and most loathéd worldly life,
> That age, ache, penury, and imprisonment
> Can lay on nature, is a paradise
> To what we fear of death.[26]

People do not always feel ready to die. They are sorry to leave the scene of their labours and pleasures and achievements. Even if they do want to go, even if they are quite happy to pass on to a new life, or into they know not what, there is still the pain involved in the physical process of dissolution, and with this goes, sometimes, a great deal of mental suffering. Sometimes on their deathbeds, people are stricken with remorse: they remember wrongs they have done, harm and pain they have inflicted on certain individuals; and they may have, in consequence, fears and apprehensions for the future. All this makes death a horrifying experience for many people, and one which, before it comes, they do their best not to think about.

Fifthly, *contact with what one dislikes* is suffering. We all know this. It may be that even in our own family there are people with whom we just don't get on. This is very tragic, especially when it is our own parents or children whom we dislike. Because the tie – even the attachment – of blood is there, we have to put up with a certain amount of contact, and this can be painful.

The work we do can also be a source of suffering, if we do it just because we need to earn a living and it is the only work we can get. Again, we may feel that we have to put up with what we dislike, and perhaps work with people we find uncongenial, for periods of time anyway, even though we would rather do something else.

There are, as well, all sorts of environmental conditions which are unpleasant: pollution, noise, weather. It is obviously not possible for everyone to go off and live in a Greek villa. So there seems to be no way of escape – certainly no way of escaping entirely. You just have to live with people, places, things, and conditions that you don't altogether like.

Sixthly, *separation from what one likes* is suffering. This can be a very harrowing form of suffering indeed. There are people we would like to be with, to meet more often – relations, friends – but circumstances make it simply impossible. This happens often in time of war, when families are broken up – men conscripted and taken to far-off battlefields, children sent away to places of safety, and people simply disappearing as refugees.

When I was in India during the war as a signals operator, many of my friends used to get letters from home regularly every week or so; and then a day might come when the letters would stop. They wouldn't know what had happened, but they would know that there were bombs falling in England, so after a while they would start suspecting the worst. Eventually, perhaps, they would get the news, either from another relation or officially, that their wife and children, or their parents, or their brothers and sisters, had been killed in an aerial bombardment. This is the most terrible suffering – permanent separation from those we love. Some people never get over such suffering, and brood over their loss for the rest of their lives.

Seventhly, *not to get what one wants* is suffering. There is little need to elaborate upon this. When you have set your heart on something (or someone) and you fail to achieve your goal, when the prize does not fall to you, then you feel disappointed and frustrated, even bitter. We have all known short-lived experiences of this kind, when we fail to get a job we particularly wanted, or fail to be selected for something, or find that someone else has got to something (or someone) before us.

Some people experience a lifetime of disappointment, frustration, and bitterness if they feel that life has short-changed them in some way – and of course the stronger the desire, the more the suffering. But even in small ways, it is something with which we are acquainted almost every day, if not every hour – for example, when we find that all the cake has gone.

So these are the seven different aspects of *duḥkha* identified by the Buddha. The Buddha once declared, 'One thing only do I teach – suffering and the cessation of suffering'[27] – and emancipation from the bondage of suffering is indeed the keynote of his teaching. In the Pāli scriptures he compares himself to a physician who attempts to relieve his patient of a tormenting disease – the disease of conditioned existence with which we are all afflicted.[28] Of course, we are not always willing patients, as the Buddha clearly found. But on the many occasions when he spoke about suffering, and tried to get people to see it in perspective, he would apparently sum up his discourse by saying that existence as a whole is painful, that the totality of conditioned sentient experience, comprising form, feeling, perceptions, volitions, and consciousness, is unsatisfactory.

Now most people would say that this is going a bit far, that it is a pessimistic, if not morbid, view of life. They would say that human existence can by no means be said to be unsatisfactory and painful all the way through. They will admit to birth being painful, they will agree that sickness, old age, and yes, death, are indeed painful. But at the same time they are reluctant to accept the conclusion that follows from all this, which is that conditioned existence itself is suffering. It is as though they admit all the individual digits in the sum, but they won't accept the total to which those digits add up. They say that yes, there is a certain amount of suffering in the world, but on the whole it's not such a bad place. Why be so negative? There's plenty to smile about. While there's life, there's hope.

And there is, of course. We have pleasant experiences as well as painful ones. But the Buddhist view is that even the pleasant experiences are at bottom painful. They are really only suffering concealed, glossed over, deferred – a whistling in the dark. And the extent to which we can see this, see the suffering behind the gilding of pleasure, 'the skull beneath the skin', depends on our spiritual maturity.

Edward Conze has identified four different aspects of concealed suffering.[29] Firstly, something that is pleasant for oneself may involve suffering for other beings. We don't tend to consider this, of course. If we are all right, if we're having a good time, we don't worry too much or too often about others. The most common example of this is the frank enjoyment with which people eat the flesh of slaughtered animals, without consciously thinking about the suffering of the animals.

But the unconscious mind is not so easily fooled. You can shut out some unpleasant fact from the conscious mind, but unconsciously you notice everything and you forget nothing. You may never be consciously aware of that unpleasant fact, but it will exert an influence on your mental state that is all the more powerful for being unseen. In this way we develop an 'irrational' feeling of guilt, because in the depths of ourselves we know that our own pleasure has been bought at the expense of the suffering of other living beings. This kind of guilt is the source of a great deal of uneasiness and anxiety.

Conze gives the example of wealthy people, who are nearly always afraid of becoming poor. This is, he says, because unconsciously they feel that they don't deserve to have their money. Unconsciously they feel that it *ought* to be taken away from them, and consciously they worry that perhaps it *will* be taken away from them. By contrast, you notice that poor people who may not know where next week's food is coming from are rarely racked with anxiety over it. They are generally much more relaxed and cheerful than the rich.

Wealthy people may suffer from unconscious guilt feelings because they know, however much they may deny it consciously, that the acquisition of their wealth has brought suffering to other people, directly or indirectly. Consequently, they feel a constant need to justify themselves. They say, 'I earn my money, I contribute to the well-being of the community, I offer a service that people want, I provide employment....' Or else they say, 'If I'm rich and other people are poor, it's because I work harder, I take risks – at least I don't ask to be spoon-fed....'

If the feeling of guilt gets too much then drastic measures are required to relieve it, and the most drastic measure of all is to give away some of that wealth – to the church, or to a hospital or whatever. Hospitals are a favourite option because you can compensate for the suffering you have caused in acquiring the wealth by giving some of it to alleviate suffering. It is called 'conscience money'. If one has anything to do with religious organizations, one soon learns to recognize this sort of donation. Sometimes it is just put through the letter box in an envelope inscribed 'from an anonymous donor'. Then you know that someone's conscience is really biting.

Conze's second kind of concealed suffering is a pleasant experience that has a flavour of anxiety to it because you are afraid of losing it. Political power is like this: it is a very sweet thing to exercise power over other people, but you always have to watch your back, not knowing if you can trust even your best friend, or the very guardsmen at your door. All the time you are afraid of losing that power, especially if you have seized it by force and others are waiting for their chance to get their hands on it. In such a position you do not sleep easily.

The traditional Buddhist illustration of this kind of experience is that of a hawk flying off with a piece of meat in its talons. What happens, of course, is that dozens of other hawks fly after it to try and seize that piece of meat for themselves, and they do this by tearing and stabbing not at the meat itself but at the possessor of the meat, pecking at its body, its wings, its head, its eyes.[30] The highly competitive world of finance and business and entertainment is like this. Any pleasure that involves any element of power or status is contaminated by an element of anxiety, by the sense that others would like to be able to replace you at the top of your own particular dunghill.

The third concealed suffering indicated by Dr Conze is something that is pleasant but which binds us to something else that brings about suffering. The example he gives is the human body. Through this we experience all sorts of pleasurable sensations that make us very attached to it; but we experience all sorts of unpleasant sensations through it as well. So our attachment to that which provides us with pleasant sensations binds us also to that which provides us with unpleasant sensations. We can't have the one without the other.

Lastly, Conze suggests that concealed suffering is to be found in the fact that pleasures derived from the experience of conditioned things cannot satisfy the deepest longings of the heart. In each one of us there is something that is *un*conditioned, something that is *not* of this world, something transcendental, the Buddha-nature – call it what you like. Whatever you call it, you can recognize it by the fact that it cannot be satisfied by anything conditioned. It can be satisfied only by the Unconditioned.[31]

Whatever conditioned things you may enjoy there is always a lack, a void, which only the Unconditioned can fill. Ultimately, it is for this reason that – to come back to the Buddha's conclusion – all conditioned things, whether actually or potentially, are unsatisfactory, painful. It is in the light of the Unconditioned that suffering, *duḥkha*, is clearly seen as characteristic of all forms of conditioned existence, and of sentient conditioned existence especially.

Impermanence

The second fundamental characteristic of conditioned existence, *anitya*, is quite easily translated. *Nitya* is 'permanent', 'eternal', so with the addition of the negative prefix you get 'impermanent', 'non-eternal'. It is also quite easily understood – intellectually at least. It can hardly be denied that all conditioned things, all compounded things, are constantly changing. They are by definition made up of parts – that is, compounded. And that which is compounded, made up of parts, can also be uncompounded, can be reduced to its parts again – which is what happens, of course, all the time.

It should really be easier to understand this truth nowadays than it was in the Buddha's day. We now have the authority of science to assure us that there's no such thing as matter in the sense of actual lumps of hard solid matter scattered throughout space. We know that what we think of as matter is in reality only various forms of energy.

But the same great truth applies to the mind. There is nothing unchanging in our internal experience of ourselves, nothing permanent or immortal. There is only a constant succession of mental states, feelings, perceptions, volitions, acts of consciousness. In fact, the mind changes even more quickly than the physical body. We cannot usually see the physical body changing, but if we are observant we can see our mental states changing from moment to moment.

This is the reason for the Buddha's (at first sight) rather strange assertion that it is a bigger mistake to identify yourself (as a stable entity) with the mind than with the body.[32] But this is the Buddhist position. Belief in the reality of the 'self' is a bigger spiritual mistake than belief in the reality of the body. This is because the body at least possesses a certain relative stability, but there is no stability to the mind at all. It is constantly, perceptibly changing.

Broadly speaking, the *lakṣaṇa* of *anitya* points to the fact that the whole universe from top to bottom, in all its grandeur, in all its immensity, is just one vast network of processes of different types, taking place at different levels – and all interrelated. Nothing ever stands still, not even for an instant, not even for a fraction of a second.

We do not see this, though. When we look up we see the everlasting hills, and in the night sky we descry the same stars as were mapped by our ancestors at the dawn of history. Houses stand from generation to generation, and the old oak furniture within them seems to become more solid with the passing of the years. Even our own bodies seem much the same from one year to the next. It is only when the increments of change add up to something notable, when a great house is burnt down, when we realize that the star we are looking at is already extinct, or when we ourselves take to our deathbed, that we realize the truth of impermanence or non-eternity, that all conditioned things – from the minutest particles to the most massive stars – begin, continue, and then cease.

Emptiness of self

The third *lakṣaṇa*, *anātman*, encapsulates the truth that all conditioned things are devoid of a permanent, unchanging self. So what does this mean exactly? When the Buddha denied the reality of the idea of the *ātman*, what was he actually denying? What was the belief or doctrine of *ātman* held by the Buddha's contemporaries, the Hindus of his day?

In the Upanishads alone there are many different conceptions of *ātman* mentioned.[33] In some it is said that the *ātman*, the self – or the soul, if you like – is the physical body. Elsewhere the view is propounded that the *ātman* is just as big as the thumb, is material, and abides in the heart. But the most common view in the Buddha's day, the one with which he appears to have been most concerned, asserted that the *ātman* was individual – in the sense that I am I and you are you – incorporeal or immaterial, conscious, unchanging, blissful, and sovereign – in the sense of exercising complete control over its own destiny.

The Buddha maintained that there was no such entity – and he did so by appealing to experience. He said that if you look within, at yourself, at your own mental life, you can account for everything you observe under just five headings: form, feeling, perception, volitions, and acts of consciousness. Nothing discovered in these categories can be observed to be permanent. There is nothing sovereign or ultimately blissful amongst them. Everything in them arises in dependence on conditions, and is unsatisfactory in one way or another. These five categories or aggregates are *anātman*. They don't constitute any such self as the Hindus of the Buddha's day asserted. Such a self exists neither in them nor outside of them nor associated with them in any other way.

The three liberations

Seeing conditioned existence, seeing life, in this way, as invariably subject to suffering, to impermanence, to emptiness of self, is called *vipaśyanā* (Sanskrit) or *vipassanā* (Pāli), which translates into English as 'insight'.

Insight is not just intellectual understanding. It can be developed only on the basis of a controlled, purified, elevated, concentrated, integrated mind – in other words, through meditative practice. Insight is a direct intuitive perception that takes place in the depths of meditation when the ordinary mental processes have fallen into abeyance. A preliminary intellectual understanding of these three characteristics is certainly helpful but, ultimately, insight is something that transcends the intellectual workings of the mind.

So in meditation, through insight, you see that without exception everything you experience through the five senses and through the mind – everything you can feel and touch and smell and taste and see and think about – is conditioned: subject to suffering, impermanent, and empty of self. When you see things in this way, you experience what is called revulsion or disgust, and you turn away from the conditioned. It is important to note that this is a spiritual experience, not just a psychological reaction; you turn away not because you are personally repelled by things as such, but because you see that the conditioned is not, on its own terms, worth having. When that turning away from the conditioned to the Unconditioned takes place decisively, it is said that you enter the 'stream' leading to Nirvāṇa.

from *What is the Dharma?*

4. *DUKKHA* AS AN EXAMPLE OF CONDITIONALITY

People often conclude that Buddhism is suffering-oriented, inward-looking, and self-centred, as though the idea was to become immersed in one's own suffering and how to alleviate it. But this is not what the Buddha is saying.

Buddhist tradition makes a distinction between those teachings that require interpretation and those that do not. The Buddha's statement in the *Dhammapada* that hatred never ceases by hatred is literally true, and the truth of it can be seen quite clearly in everyday life (except, of course, by those who are blinded by the desire for revenge). There are other teachings, however, that require us to go beyond the literal meaning, demanding a prior knowledge of the Dharma before we can understand them. A good example is that of one of the Buddha's most famous teachings, the four noble truths, to which the *Satipaṭṭhāna Sutta* now directs our attention. It is not often realized that when the Buddha speaks of suffering, its origin, and its cessation, he is using that as an *example* of how things arise and cease. It is not a definitive statement; in terms of another traditional distinction, it is method rather than doctrine.

It is worth giving careful thought to this. Hearing these truths, people often conclude that Buddhism is suffering-oriented, inward-looking, and self-centred, as though the idea was to become immersed in one's own suffering and how to alleviate it. But this is not what the Buddha is saying. What is usually translated as 'suffering' is the Pāli term *dukkha*, which points to the fact that conditioned existence, taken as a whole, is unsatisfactory and frustrating. But this does not mean that Buddhists view life as unremittingly painful and unpleasant, which it obviously is not. On the other hand, we can be sure that the Buddha did not choose this example of the workings of conditionality at random. It is salutary to reflect on the inherent unsatisfactoriness of things; like reflecting on the loathsomeness of the body, it is an example of 'bending the bamboo the other way'. We are not being asked to stop finding life agreeable, if that is our experience, but to acknowledge that however agreeable it may be, it is never wholly so. *Dukkha* is pain and sickness, but it is also lack of complete fulfilment; it is anxiety and loss, bitterness and cynicism, a sense of lengthening shadows. It is also the truth that even pleasant circumstances cannot last for ever, inasmuch as they arise within conditioned existence.

from *Living with Awareness*

5. THE BUDDHA'S VICTORY

According to the Buddha, the spiritual life is an active life, a strenuous life. We might even say that it is a militant *life.*

Although very few people in the West have so far had the opportunity to study or practise Buddhism to any great depth, most of us will have formed some sort of impression of it. We will have formed, too, some sort of impression of the Buddha. We meet people or we hear of people who have espoused Buddhism, we read articles about Buddhism in the newspapers, we hear people talking on the radio or the television about Buddhism – we may even, if we go to the cinema, see film stars impersonating the Buddha. Some of these impressions may be quite positive, even in some degree accurate, but inevitably there will be others which are very misleading. And, once established, misconceptions are notoriously difficult to eradicate. The most persistent misconceptions derive, in fact, from the earliest Western interpreters of Buddhism, who naturally saw it from the standpoint of their own religious tradition, a Victorian version of Christianity. They naturally tended to see him as a sort of oriental Jesus, and the popular Victorian conception of Jesus was a rather weak version of the real thing. It has been said that for the Victorians Christ was a ghostly figure in a white sheet gliding around Galilee and gently rebuking people for not believing in the Nicene Creed. So a Victorian Buddha was likewise installed in the popular imagination as a ghostly figure in a yellow sheet gliding around India and gently rebuking people for not being kind to animals.

In this way, Buddhism began to be perceived as a rather passive, negative, or gutless teaching and tradition. This impression, unfortunately, can only be reinforced, perhaps unconsciously, by any acquaintance one may have with later Buddhist art, in which decadent phase the Buddha is depicted as a sweet, dreamy, effeminate figure. As for the mass-produced representations of the Buddha that are turned out today, their attempts at the smile of Enlightenment leave the Buddha with a kind of coquettish simper. Such images are sure to influence the way we see the Buddha in our own minds.

In order to redress this imbalance we need to take a fresh look at what Buddhism is about, and in the process perhaps we will have to rethink our whole attitude to the spiritual life. The aim of Buddhist teaching is the attainment of Enlightenment, or Buddhahood, a state of moral and spiritual perfection, and this ideal calls for the exercise, on the moral and spiritual plane, of heroic qualities. When we speak of the heroic ideal in Buddhism, we are not speaking of anything distinct from – much less still opposed to – the spiritual ideal. We are speaking of the spiritual ideal itself – an ideal that is not just about meekly refraining from this, that or the other, but requires heroism in the highest degree.

Of course 'hero' is an unfashionable word in English these days, but it accurately translates one of the titles by which Siddhārtha Gautama was known after his Enlightenment. We know him as 'the Buddha', or sometimes 'the Compassionate One', but the Pāli and Sanskrit texts also apply to the Buddha the epithets Mahāvīra, which means 'Great Hero', and Jina, which means 'Conqueror'. In fact, the title Jina is almost as common in the earliest Buddhist texts as the one we are so familiar with, 'the Buddha'. He is the Conqueror because he has conquered the whole of conditioned existence within himself. He has conquered the world by conquering himself. According to the *Dhammapada*, 'Though one should conquer in battle thousands upon thousands of men, yet he who conquers himself is (truly) the greatest in battle.'[34] Later, medieval Buddhism produced the idea of the Trailokya Vijaya, 'the conquest of the three worlds' – conquest, that is, of the world of sensuous desire, the world of archetypal form, and the world of no form.[35] So the Jina's victory is over these three inner worlds.

Victory usually implies victory *over* someone or something. Who or what, then, could this have been in the Buddha's case? The answer is simple: the Buddha conquered Māra, the 'Evil One', and after conquering Māra, attained Enlightenment. In a sense, his conquest of Māra, his *māra-vijaya* as it is called, *was* his attainment of Enlightenment.

It is possible that you have already encountered descriptions of the episode of the conquest of Māra. Perhaps you have seen it depicted in Buddhist art. If so, you will have seen the Buddha-to-be sitting on a heap of *kuśa* grass beneath the spreading branches of the *ficus religiosus*, or sacred fig tree – subsequently known, in honour of the Buddha, as the bodhi tree, or 'tree of Enlightenment'. He is surrounded on all sides by thousands of fearsome figures, all horribly misshapen and deformed. Some of them are whirling enormous clubs; some are spitting fire; some are in the act of hurling great rocks, even whole mountains that they have torn up by the roots; some again are discharging arrows. These are the forces of Māra. Māra himself stands to one side directing his terrible army in its onslaught on the Buddha. But the Buddha himself takes no notice. He is completely surrounded by an aura of golden light. As soon as the various missiles touch this aura they turn into flowers and fall to the ground at the Buddha's feet as though in unintentional worship. The

Buddha is undisturbed and carries on meditating. He does not take any notice even when Māra summons his three daughters and orders them to dance in the most seductive manner. So Māra retires defeated, his forces disappear, and his three daughters withdraw in confusion. The Buddha is left alone beneath the bodhi tree on his heap of *kuśa* grass, and carries on meditating. Sitting there in that way he attains Enlightenment.

Such is the well-known episode. But like other well-known episodes in the Buddha's life it is open to misunderstanding. We might of course realize that the episode is symbolic, but we may not understand that the episode of the *māra-vijaya* was not the only victory, but a culmination of an entire series of victories. This is only to be expected, because spiritual life is like that. Just as one does not develop the fullness of wisdom all at once or the fullness of compassion all at once. One does not develop the fullness of energy and heroism necessary to defeat Māra and his forces all at once. One does not develop any spiritual quality all at once; one develops it gradually. As the Buddha himself said in the *Dhammapada*: 'As a pot becomes full by the constant falling of drops of water, so, little by little, does a man fill himself with good.'[36] Before the Buddha's great victory there will have been many lesser victories, victories without which the great victory could hardly have taken place. We shall now consider some of those lesser victories – victories that are such only in relation to the *great* victory over Māra. In themselves, these lesser victories are such as we might find hard even to imagine.

The Buddha's first victory, so far as we know at least, is generally described as the 'Going Forth' from home into homelessness. We may not be accustomed to considering this as a victory, but that is what it was. Just suppose that you were the son or daughter of wealthy parents, with high social position and great prestige. Suppose you were young, healthy, and good looking. Suppose too that you were happily married, perhaps with a child.... Would *you* have found it easy to give it all up? Would you have been able to 'go forth' for the sake of you knew not what – for the sake of the 'truth', for the sake of something 'higher', something beyond anything you had yet experienced or imagined? This is exactly what Siddhārtha, the Buddha-to-be, actually did.

There are several accounts of what happened on that occasion, some of them very colourful and romantic. They describe, for instance, how Siddhārtha drew aside a curtain in the inner apartments of his palace and took his last long, lingering look at his peacefully sleeping wife and infant son. They describe how the gods of the various heavens silently opened the gates so that he could depart unseen and unheard. And they describe how those same gods supported the hooves of his horse on the palms of their hands so that there would be no noise.... But the oldest account is actually very simple. Reminiscing in his old age, the Buddha simply said to his disciples:

> Then I, monks, after a time, being young, my hair coal-black, possessed of radiant youth, in the prime of my life – although my unwilling parents wept and wailed – having cut off my hair and beard, having put on yellow robes, went forth from home into homelessness.[37]

Whether the description is elaborate or simple, what actually happened is sufficiently clear. The Buddha-to-be left home. He left his family, left the *group*. But in what sense was this a victory? What was it a victory *over*? It was a victory over the family, or rather, over the *group* as represented especially by his parents. The Buddha himself once said that he went forth 'against the wishes' of his weeping parents. But this was also a victory in a deeper sense. It was a victory over his *attachment* to the group. It could not have been easy for Siddhārtha to leave his family; his actual departure must have been preceded by a long internal struggle. But in the end he broke free from the group. This did not just mean leaving the group physically: it meant overcoming group attitudes and group conditioning; it meant taking the initiative, doing something that he wanted to do; it meant thinking for himself, experiencing things for himself; it meant living his own life; it meant being an *individual*. Thus the 'Going Forth' from home into homelessness was a victory over the 'internalized' group.

Having gone forth from home into homelessness, Siddhārtha approached two famous spiritual teachers. These teachers, who seem to have been good and noble men, taught the Buddha everything they knew, taught him what they believed to be the highest truth. Siddhārtha was a very good pupil, and learned what they had to teach. Whatever they taught him, he experienced for himself, very quickly becoming their equal. Realizing this, they offered to share with him the leadership of the communities they had founded. But he refused and, leaving them, returned to his solitary wanderings.

This too was a victory, a victory over spiritual complacency and spiritual ambition. Siddhārtha had experienced for himself everything that his teachers had to teach, but he knew that there was still something 'beyond', something higher which he had not yet realized – and which he wanted to realize. He knew that he was not yet fully Enlightened, despite what his teachers were telling him. In other words, he did not settle down with a limited spiritual experience – even though by ordinary standards it was quite a high experience. It was not the highest, and Siddhārtha *knew* that it was not the highest. In this way he overcame spiritual complacency. Moreover, his teachers had offered to share with him the leadership of their communities. What an opportunity was this for a young man! But Siddhārtha refused. He was not concerned with leadership. He was concerned with *truth*, he was concerned with *Enlightenment*. In this way he overcame spiritual ambition.

It is interesting to note that Siddhārtha overcame spiritual complacency and spiritual ambition at the same time. The two are actually closely connected. If you are spiritually ambitious, in the sense of seeking a position of spiritual leadership, you are likely to become spiritually complacent. Similarly, if you are spiritually complacent, you will tend to seek a position of spiritual leadership by way of compensation for your lack of real spiritual effort.

Continuing his quest alone, Siddhārtha decided to live in the depths of the forest, far from any human habitation. He lived somewhere where it was very difficult to live, even for those committed to the spiritual life. Furthermore, he stayed in what we would call 'haunted' places, places inhabited, at least according to popular belief, by ghosts and spirits – places in which feelings of fear and terror were likely to arise. And those feelings of panic, fear, and terror *did* arise in his mind. So what did Siddhārtha do on these occasions? If the fear and terror arose while he was walking to and fro, he continued walking to and fro until he had overcome them. He did not run away, did not try to escape from those feelings. Similarly, if they arose while he was sitting still, or while he was lying down, then that is where he faced and overcame them. In this way he was victorious over fear.

Even today, of course, many people have this experience of fear and terror, panic and dread – or of anxiety at least – especially when they are alone. But howsoever and wheresoever we have this sort of experience, it is important to face it. It is important not to run away, whether literally or metaphorically. If we face it we will eventually overcome it, as Siddhārtha did.

Even though Siddhārtha had overcome fear, he had still not attained Enlightenment. He now embarked upon a course of extreme 'self-mortification'. The Buddhist scriptures give us full details of the various torments that he inflicted upon himself. Suffice it to say that he subsequently asserted that no one had gone to such extremes of self-mortification as had he. Indeed, he very nearly died. But there were compensations. He became famous. In those days it was popularly believed that you could attain Enlightenment by means of self-mortification – the more extreme the better. He therefore attracted, in particular, five close disciples, who intended to remain with him until, as a result of his self-mortification, he attained Enlightenment.

But Siddhārtha did not attain Enlightenment in this way. Apparently, he remained as far from Enlightenment as ever. He therefore gave up self-mortification, even though he had been practising it for years, and – to the shock of his disciples – started taking solid food again. The five disciples left him immediately, deeply disappointed that he was not the man they had thought him to be. He had weakened, they thought, and had returned to a life of luxury. Once again Siddhārtha was left alone.

On the face of it this might look like a defeat, but it was actually a great victory. On this instance Siddhārtha had overcome the very human tendency to refuse to admit that one has made a mistake, that one has been on the wrong path, and that one must now retrace one's steps and start all over again. After all, when one has invested a great deal of energy, not to speak of time, money, and all sorts of other things, in making that mistake, one does not like to admit, even to oneself, that all the effort has in a sense been wasted. But Siddhārtha did not mind doing this. He did not mind losing his disciples, he did not mind being on his own again. It would have been easy, in comparison, to continue with his self-mortification, easy to become more and more famous, easy to attract great numbers of disciples. But instead he admitted that he had made a mistake, and continued his quest.

Eventually, his quest took him to the foot of the bodhi tree. There he sat down, as we have seen, and was attacked by Māra and his forces. But who, or what, is Māra? I have already described this episode as it is depicted in Buddhist art, but I must now pay some attention to its *significance* – even though the symbolic terms in which the episode is described do actually communicate their own message. If we do not understand what Māra represents, we will not be able to understand the true significance of the Buddha's *māra-vijaya*, his victory over Māra.

The word *māra* means 'killing', 'destroying', it means bringing death and pestilence. Māra is therefore the principle of destruction. Sometimes this principle is personified, and thus it happens that the Buddhist texts mention no less than *four* Māras. These are (in Pāli) *maccu-māra*, *khandha-māra*, *kilesa-māra*, and *devaputta-māra*. We will look at each of them in turn.

First of all, comes *maccu-māra*. Here, Māra simply means 'death' or 'destruction'. Death, of course, is usually very unwelcome. Sometimes people are really surprised when it comes, even though they should have known it was coming all the time. Because death is so unwelcome, people tend to regard it as an evil. But in itself death is neither good nor evil: it is just a fact of existence and has to be recognized. That is what *maccu-māra* actually represents.

Secondly, rather more metaphysically, there is *khandha-māra*. This Māra represents a sort of extension of *maccu-māra*. Here we remember that death is not just an abstraction, not just a word. Death is a concrete reality. Death means that there are *things* and *beings* which die, which are destroyed. And these things and beings which die between them constitute a world. In other words, there is a world which is under the sway of death. This is the world of what are called in Sanskrit the *skandhas* (Pāli *khandhas*). These *skandhas*, or 'aggregates', as the word is often translated, are five in number. First of all there is *rūpa*, or material form, then *vedanā*, or feeling, then *saṃjñā*, or perception, then *saṃskāra*, or volition, and finally *vijñāna*, or consciousness. These five *skandhas* are well known; if you know anything at all about Buddhism you will be familiar with them. Between them these five *skandhas* represent the whole of conditioned existence, the whole of mundane existence, the whole of 'relative reality', or, in more traditional terms, the whole of *saṃsāra*. That is what *khandha-māra* represents.

Thirdly, there is *kilesa-māra*. The Pāli word *kilesa* (Sanskrit *kleśa*) comes from a root meaning 'to adhere' or 'to stick to', and is cognate with the word for 'slime'. *Kleśa* means 'stain', 'soil', or 'impurity'. In an ethical sense it means 'depravity', 'lust', or 'passion'. Broadly speaking, *kleśa* corresponds to what is otherwise called *akuśalacitta* or *akuśalacittāni*, or 'unskilful mental states'. The five principal *kleśas*, or 'defilements', as they are generally called in English, are usually enumerated as craving, aversion, ignorance, conceit, and distraction. The first three of these – craving, aversion, and ignorance – correspond to the three *akuśala-mūlas* or 'roots of unskilfulness', which are represented by the cock, the snake, and the pig that we see at the centre of the Tibetan wheel of life. It is these three that keep the wheel turning. In other words, it is because our minds are dominated by the *kleśas* that we are reborn within *saṃsāra*, reborn in the world of conditioned existence, the world that is under the sway of death. This is what *kilesa-māra* represents.

And then there is *devaputta-māra*. *Deva* means 'god', with a small 'g', and *putta* means 'son'. So *devaputta* means 'son of a god', which is to say, a god – just as 'son of man' means a man. *Devaputta-māra* is Māra as an actually existent being or person. He is the being who appears in the episode of the Buddha's *māra-vijaya*. Sometimes *devaputta-māra* is regarded as being simply a personification of the *kleśas* or defilements, but *devaputta-māra* cannot really be reduced in this way. Naturally he is dominated by the defilements, just as are most beings within *saṃsāra*; but at the same time he has his own being and position in the universe. He has his own place in Buddhist mythology.

Buddhism sees the universe as consisting of various planes and worlds. These are the objective counterparts – or correlatives – of mental states, both positive and negative. Just as there is a 'world' of human beings, according to Buddhist cosmology, so also is there a 'world' of animals, a 'world' of gods, a 'world' of demons, and so on. Māra belongs to one of these worlds, in fact to one of the lower heaven worlds. Low though it is, however, Māra rules over this world; indeed, he rules over all the worlds belonging to what is called the *kāmaloka*, or 'realm of sensuous desire', which includes our own human world. In a wider sense, of course, Māra rules over the entire universe, the whole of conditioned existence – because it is subject to *death*, which Māra primarily represents. But he rules particularly over the *kāmaloka*, or realm of sensuous desire.

In order to understand why this should be we must first realize that above the realm of sensuous desire there is the *rūpaloka* or 'realm of archetypal form'. This realm corresponds to the various mental states of higher meditative consciousness. From these states, from the *rūpaloka*, it is possible to gain Enlightenment – which it is not possible to do from the *kāmaloka*. Māra is therefore particularly anxious to stop people reaching the *rūpaloka*, that is, stop them escaping from the *kāmaloka*. This is why Māra, with the help of his forces and his daughters, tried to interrupt the Buddha's meditation beneath the bodhi tree. Perhaps he sometimes tries to interrupt *your* meditation. Perhaps that little distraction which arises in your mind, perhaps even that little tickling sensation that distracts you, is none other than Māra.

Perhaps I have said enough about Māra to place us in a better position to understand what it was that the Buddha actually conquered. We can now return to the *māra-vijaya* itself. As we have seen, there are four *māras*: *maccu-māra*, *khandha-māra*, *kilesa-māra*, and *devaputta-māra*. The Buddha overcame all four of them; his victory was therefore a fourfold victory. Let us look at each of them in turn.

How did the Buddha overcome *maccu-māra*? How did he overcome death? He overcame death by overcoming *birth*, for where there is birth there will inevitably be death. He overcame birth by overcoming the unskilful mental states that lead to birth – that is to say to *rebirth*. In other words, the Buddha overcame death by attaining what in Sanskrit is called the *amṛtapada*, the 'deathless state', the state that is free from death, free from birth – that is, Nirvāṇa. He overcame death by attaining Enlightenment, a state which is above and beyond conditioned existence. It is not that after attaining Enlightenment the Buddha could not be reborn in the human world if he wanted to be. But he would not be reborn there *out of compulsion*, as a result of previous karma that he had committed. He would be reborn – if he was reborn at all – out of compassion, in order to continue to help ordinary, unenlightened human beings.

How did the Buddha overcome *khandha-māra*? How did he overcome conditioned existence? He overcame conditioned existence by overcoming the *kleśas*, the defilements, which lead one into conditioned existence. He overcame the *kleśas* at the time that he attained Enlightenment. In a sense, the two things were synonymous. According to tradition, however, the Buddha did not finally overcome the *skandhas* until his *parinirvāṇa* forty-five years later. At the time of his *parinirvāṇa* he severed all connection with the physical body, severed all connection with the *khandhas*. For this reason the *parinirvāṇa* is also known as *skandha-nirvāṇa*, or *anupādisesa-nibbāna*, that is to say, 'Nirvāṇa without remainder in the form of a physical body'.

But how *did* the Buddha overcome the *kleśas*? So much depends upon this. As we have seen, there are five principal *kleśas*: craving, aversion, ignorance, conceit, and distraction. The Buddha overcame craving by means of tranquillity, aversion by means of friendliness and compassion, ignorance by means of wisdom, conceit by means of selflessness, and distraction by means of awareness, or mindfulness. Naturally, it was not easy even for the Buddha to do this. Tranquillity, friendliness, compassion, and so on do not just appear – not even when one is seated beneath the bodhi tree! They have to be developed. But they *can* be developed. Indeed, the fact that they can be developed is one of the central teachings of Buddhism. It is one of the central teachings of Buddhism that our mental states are in our own power and can be changed. Furthermore, Buddhism not only exhorts us to change them, but also tells us just *how* to do this; it gives us specific meditation 'methods'.

Tranquillity is developed by means of the three 'contemplations': the contemplation of the repulsiveness of the physical body, the contemplation of death, and the contemplation of impermanence.

The first of these, the contemplation of the repulsiveness of the physical body, is the most extreme, and generally takes the form of actually contemplating the ten stages in the progressive decomposition of a corpse. Perhaps I should add that it is usually taught only to those who are psychologically and spiritually mature. The other two are less extreme and are therefore taught more widely. But whichever method we practise, whether the contemplation of death or the contemplation of impermanence, or even the contemplation of the repulsiveness of the physical body, we can succeed in developing tranquillity. And by developing tranquillity we overcome craving.

We develop friendliness and compassion by means of *mettā bhāvanā*, or the 'cultivation of universal loving-kindness'. This practice consists in the systematic development of goodwill towards oneself, towards a near and dear friend, towards a 'neutral' person, towards an 'enemy', and, finally, towards all living beings. The *mettā bhāvanā* is one of the best known and most popular of all Buddhist meditation methods. By practising it we can succeed in developing friendliness and compassion, and by developing friendliness and compassion we overcome aversion.

We can develop wisdom by means of the contemplation of the twelve *nidānas*, or 'links'. For a detailed discussion of these, I must refer readers to my other writings (in particular *A Survey of Buddhism* and *The Three Jewels*).[38] Broadly speaking, we develop wisdom by reflecting on the conditionality of mundane existence, on the fact that whatever mundane phenomenon arises or comes into existence does so in dependence on certain definite causes and conditions. Reflection on the conditionality of mundane existence is also roughly tantamount to reflecting on *śūnyatā* or 'voidness'. In these different ways we develop wisdom, and by developing wisdom we overcome ignorance.

We develop selflessness by reflection on the six 'elements'. The six elements are earth, water, fire, air, space, and consciousness. In this practice we reflect that there exists in our own physical body the element *earth* in the form of flesh, bone, and so on. We then further reflect that the earth element in our physical body does not really belong to us. We may point to our bodies and say 'this is me', 'this is mine'. But it does *not* belong to us; the earth element within our physical bodies has been borrowed, literally borrowed, from the earth element in the universe. One day we shall have to give it back. If we see a corpse – even the corpse of a little bird – in the process of decomposition, we can actually see this happening, especially if the corpse is lying on the earth. We can see the flesh and bone that once belonged to the body returning to the soil, returning to the earth, returning to the earth element in the universe from which it came. Similarly, one day, we too shall have to give our body back to the earth element. We should therefore not be attached to it. We should not identify with it by saying 'this body belongs to me'. We then continue to reflect in this way with regard to all of the six elements. As we do so, we develop selflessness, and by developing selflessness we overcome conceit.

Finally, we develop mindfulness, or awareness, by means of *ānāpānasati*, or the mindfulness of breathing. Here we simply 'watch' our breath, without interfering with it in any way, allowing our minds to be increasingly focused, increasingly concentrated on the breath. By practising *ānāpānasati* we develop mindfulness, and by developing mindfulness we overcome distraction, overcome the wandering mind.

Thus the five principal *kleśas* are overcome by these methods of meditation. This is how the Buddha overcame them. He overcame craving by means of tranquillity, aversion by means of friendliness and compassion, ignorance by means of wisdom, conceit by means of selflessness, and distraction by means of mindfulness, or awareness. In this way the Buddha overcame *kilesa-māra*.

There is one Māra left. How did the Buddha overcome *devaputta-māra*, or 'Māra the son of a god'? To understand this we must return to the episode of the *māra-vijaya*, or victory over Māra, as depicted in Buddhist art. In the traditional representations of this incident we see the Buddha seated beneath the bodhi tree, his eyes closed, or half closed, and we see Māra with his forces and his daughters. The Buddha is not paying Māra any attention at all. We could therefore say that the Buddha overcame *devaputta-māra* simply by ignoring him.

In ordinary life, of course, to ignore someone usually means that we have a rather negative attitude towards them. But the Buddha could not possibly have had a negative attitude towards anyone – not even towards Māra. So we must try to put things a little more positively. It is not so much that the Buddha ignored Māra: rather, he overcame Māra simply *by being himself*. He overcame him by being the Bodhisatta, by being the Buddha. According to the medieval Indian commentator Mallinātha, the word *jayati*, or 'to conquer', means to surpass everything else by means of one's own excellence.[39] It means to be the 'highest'. Thus the Buddha's victory over Māra was not the result of a fight *on Māra's terms*; he defeated Māra simply by being himself, by virtue of the sheer excellence of his moral and spiritual qualities.

Thus the Buddha's victory over Māra was complete. Because it was complete he attained Enlightenment. One would have thought, therefore, that there was nothing left for him to do, nothing left for him to overcome. In a sense this is true, but after the *māra-vijaya* there is in fact another episode, an episode that represents yet another victory, perhaps the ultimate victory. This is the episode of Brahmā's request. Let us now witness it in our mind's eye:

The Buddha has attained Enlightenment; he is enjoying the freedom and bliss of Enlightenment. He is also reflecting that the truth he has discovered is very deep indeed, and therefore very difficult to understand. As he reflects in this way he is inclined not to try to communicate this truth – the Dharma – to other human beings: it will be just too difficult. After all, he reflects, beings are deeply immersed in worldly pleasures, they will not be able to understand the Dharma he has discovered. Just then, Brahmā Sahāmpati, another figure from Buddhist mythology, the 'Lord of a Thousand Worlds', appears. He pleads with the Buddha, pointing out that there are at least a few beings who *will* understand. He implores that for their sake the Buddha should communicate the truth he has discovered. In the end the Buddha agrees, saying: 'Opened for those who hear are the doors of the Deathless, Brahmā, let them give forth their faith.'[40]

Here, the Buddha has overcome the temptation to keep his Enlightenment to himself, or even to think that he *could* keep it to himself. He has overcome spiritual individualism. The Buddha has overcome the Buddha – and has therefore become truly the Buddha. This is the last and greatest of all his victories. He has overcome the group, including the internalized group. He has overcome spiritual complacency and spiritual ambition. He has overcome fear. He has overcome the tendency to refuse to admit that he has made a mistake. He has overcome all four Māras. Now, finally, he has overcome spiritual individualism. He has been victorious all along the line. He is not only the Buddha, not only the Enlightened One, but he is also the Jina, the 'Victorious One'.

In the West we are accustomed to using the title 'Buddha'. But we should not forget that the Buddha is also commonly known as the Jina. Similarly, followers of the Buddha are usually called 'Buddhists', but perhaps they could just as easily be called 'Jinists': followers of the Jina, the Victorious One. The Buddha did in fact once tell his disciples that they were *kṣatriyas*, or 'warriors', fighting for *śīla*, fighting for *samādhi*, fighting for *prajñā*. They were fighting to live an ethical life, fighting for higher states of consciousness, and fighting for transcendental wisdom.[41] According to the Buddha, the spiritual life is an active life, a strenuous life. We might even say that it is a *militant* life. We have to take the offensive against Māra. We should not wait for him to come and tap us on the shoulder. Attack is the best method of defence, prevention is better than cure.

For this reason, Western Buddhists should beware of taking too soft a view of the spiritual life. Perhaps we do not meditate hard enough, study hard enough, work hard enough, even play hard enough. Perhaps we have not committed ourselves to the Three Jewels with sufficient depth and intensity. Perhaps we do not really want to spread the Dharma. Perhaps we are just playing at being Buddhists. If that is the case then we will not get very far: we will not be truly successful or genuinely happy. We will not be real Buddhists, and we certainly won't be real *Jinists*, real spiritual warriors.

Nowadays there is so much to be overcome, both in ourselves and in the world. There is so much to be transformed by the 'golden light'. As the life of the Buddha reminds us, we have to overcome the group; we have to overcome spiritual complacency and spiritual ambition; we have to overcome fear; we have to overcome that very human tendency to refuse to admit that we have made a mistake; we have to overcome Māra; and we have to overcome spiritual individualism. In short, we have to overcome everything that the Buddha overcame so that we can attain Enlightenment just as he did, and benefit the world just as he benefited it.

This is certainly not easy, and no real Buddhist has ever said that it was. But a human being should be ashamed not to attempt that which is difficult rather than easy. A human being should be ashamed not to attempt that which is the most difficult of all. A human being should be ashamed not to be fighting against the odds. Sometimes we may feel that we are being overwhelmed. We may feel that we are having to hack our way through a dense jungle: the jungle of *saṃsāra*, the jungle of conditioned existence. The Buddha must have felt like that too at times. After his Enlightenment he gave some of his disciples the following parable:

> Just as if, brethren, a man travelling in a forest, along a mountain height, should come upon an ancient road, an ancient track, traversed by men of former days, and should proceed along it: and as he went should come upon an old-time city, a royal city of olden days, dwelt in by men of bygone ages, laid out with parks and groves and water tanks, and stoutly walled about – a delightful spot.
>
> Then suppose, brethren, that this man should tell of his find to the king or royal minister, thus: 'Pardon me, sire, but I would have you know that while travelling in a forest, along a mountain height, I came upon an ancient road, an ancient track, traversed by men of former days, and proceeded along it. And as I went I came upon an old-time city, a royal city of olden days, dwelt in by men of bygone ages, laid out with parks and groves and water tanks, and stoutly walled about, a delightful spot. Sire, restore that city.'

Then suppose, brethren, that king or royal minister were to restore that city, so that thereafter it became prosperous, fortunate, and populous, crowded with inhabitants, and were to reach growth and increase.

Even so, brethren, have I seen an ancient Path, an ancient track traversed by the Perfectly Enlightened ones of former times. And what is that Path? It is this Ariyan Eightfold Path.[42]

This parable tells us a number of things. It tells us that the Buddha was a pioneer. It tells us that the state of Enlightenment is like a wonderful city inhabited by innumerable people. It tells us that there is a way to that city, a way to that state. Above all, however, the parable reminds us that the Buddha's teaching is something that can be lost. The Three Jewels can be lost. Values can be lost. Fortunately, we are living at a time and in a place where the Dharma is still known, and can still be practised. We can still tread the ancient road to the city. But the jungle has started to encroach. Fewer people now live in the city; parts of the city are in a derelict condition, and entire sections of the road are overgrown.

Even though we are not being called upon to be pioneers in the way that the Buddha was, there is still a lot for us to do. We have to hack away at the jungle; we have to be spiritual warriors; we have to be not just Buddhists, but *Jinists*: we have at least to make an effort to overcome what the Buddha overcame.

from *Who is the Buddha?* and *The Buddha's Victory*

6. ARCHETYPAL SYMBOLISM IN THE BIOGRAPHY OF THE BUDDHA

In the course of our spiritual life, especially as we practise meditation, these archetypes tend to emerge in various ways into consciousness.

If we look below the rational, conceptual surface of the human mind, we find vast unplumbed depths which make up what we call the unconscious. The psyche in its wholeness consists of both the conscious and the unconscious. The unconscious, non-rational part of us is by far the larger part of our total nature, and its importance is far greater than we generally care to recognize. Consciousness is just like a light froth playing and sparkling on the surface, while the unconscious is like the vast ocean depths, dark and unfathomed, lying far beneath. In order to appeal to the whole person, it isn't enough to appeal just to the conscious, rational intelligence that floats upon the surface. We have to appeal to something more, and this means that we have to speak the language of images, of concrete form. If we want to reach this non-rational part of the human psyche, we have to use the language of poetry, of myth, of legend.

This other, no less important, language is one which many modern people have forgotten, or which they know only in a few distorted and broken forms. But Buddhism does very definitely speak this language and speaks it no less powerfully than it speaks the language of concepts, and it is through the latter that we are going to approach our subject, changing over from the conceptual approach to the non-conceptual, from the conscious mind to the unconscious. Here, we shall be beginning to descend into this language, encountering there some of what I have called the 'archetypal symbolism in the biography of the Buddha'. To allow for this encounter, we have to be receptive, to open ourselves to these archetypal symbols, to listen to them and allow them to speak in their own way to us, especially to our unconscious depths, so that we do not realize them just mentally, but experience them and assimilate them, even allowing them eventually to transform our whole life.

The language of Buddhism

Some people are under the impression that Buddhism speaks only the language of concepts, of reason; that it is a strictly rational system, even a sort of rationalism. When they hear the word Buddhism, they expect something very dry and abstract – it is as though they almost heard the skeleton rattle! Such a misunderstanding is in a way quite natural in the West. After all, ninety percent, if not ninety-nine percent, of our knowledge is derived from books, magazines, lectures, television programmes, and so on, so that, although we may not always be aware of this, our approach is in terms of intellectual understanding. It addresses our rational intelligence, our capacity to formulate concepts. In this way we get a very one-sided impression of Buddhism. But if we go to the East we see a very different picture. In fact, we may even say that in the Eastern Buddhist countries they tend to the other extreme. They tend to be moved and influenced by the divinities and images all about them without easily being able to give a mental formulation of what they actually believe. When I first went to live in Kalimpong, up in the Himalayas, I was surprised to find that many of my Tibetan, Sikkimese, and Bhutanese friends who were ardent practising Buddhists had never heard of the Buddha! – or, if they had heard of him, they thought he was a very unreal, distant historical figure. Archetypal forms such as Padmasambhava, or the five *jinas*, or Maitreya, were real to them, but not the historical facts and figures.

So far as Buddhism in the West is concerned, much more attention has been given to the conceptual, analytical, intellectual approach. We now have to give much more time and much more serious attention to the other type of approach, to begin to try to combine both these approaches, unite both the conceptual and the non-conceptual. In other words, we need a balanced spiritual life in which both the conscious and unconscious mind play their part.

But let us define our key terms. What do we mean by archetypal symbolism? What is an archetype? Broadly speaking, an archetype is the original pattern or model of a work, or the model from which a thing is made or formed. In Jung's psychology – and it was Jung who familiarized this term in the modern psychological context – the term is used in a much more specialized sense. I must say, I find it rather difficult to elucidate the precise sense in which Jung uses this word; his use of it is very fluid and shifting. The meaning is not always conceptually clear and he tends to rely on examples, which he cites profusely. In doing this, he no doubt proceeds deliberately. Perhaps it is better to follow him in this and make the meaning of this term clear by citing examples.

And what do we mean by symbolism? A symbol is generally defined as a visible sign of something invisible. But philosophically and religiously speaking it is more than that: it is something existing on a lower plane which is in correspondence with something existing on a higher plane. Just to cite a common example, in the various theistic traditions, the sun is a symbol for God, because the sun performs in the physical universe the same function that God, according to these systems, performs in the spiritual universe: the sun sheds light, sheds heat, just as God sheds the light of knowledge, the warmth of love, into the spiritual universe. One can say that the sun is the god of the material world, and in the same way God is the sun of the spiritual world. It is the same principle manifesting on different levels in different ways. This is, of course, the old Hermetic idea: 'As above, so below.'[43]

Two kinds of truth

Various Western scholars in modern times have tried to write full, detailed biographies of the Buddha. There is quite a lot of traditional material available. Quite a number of biographies were written in ancient India, for instance the *Mahāvastu* (which means 'great relation'). This is essentially a biography of the Buddha, though it does contain a great deal of other matter, especially *Jātakas* and *Avadānas*.[44] It is a bulky work – three volumes in the English translation, altogether about 1,500 pages – which contains some very ancient and interesting material. Then there are the *Lalitavistara* and the *Abhiniṣkramaṇa Sūtra*, both Mahāyāna *sūtras*. The *Lalitavistara* is a highly poetic work and has great devotional appeal and literary value. In fact, Sir Edwin Arnold's famous poem, *The Light of Asia*, is primarily based on it. These works are in Sanskrit, but we also have in Pāli the *Nidāna*, Buddhaghosa's introduction to his own commentary on the *Jātaka* stories. Then again, we have Aśvaghoṣa's *Buddhacarita* (which means acts of the Buddha), a beautiful epic poem in classical Sanskrit.

Western scholars have explored this abundant material thoroughly, but having gone through the various episodes and incidents, they divide them into two great 'heaps': on one side, they put whatever they consider to be a historic fact – that the Buddha was born into a certain family, that he spoke a certain language, that he left home at a certain age, etc. On the other side, they put what they consider to be myth and legend. This is all right so far as it goes, but most of them go a step further and start indulging in value judgements, saying that only the historical facts – or what they consider to be the historical facts – are valuable and relevant. As for the myths and legends, all the poetry of the account, they usually see this as mere fiction and therefore to be discarded as worthless.

This is a very great mistake indeed. There are two kinds of truth: there is what we call scientific truth, the truth of concepts, of reasoning; and in addition to this – some would even say above this – there is what we may call poetic truth, or truth of the imagination, or the intuition. Both are at least equally important. The latter kind of truth is manifested, or revealed, in what we call myths and legends, as well as in works of art, in symbolic ritual, and also quite importantly in dreams. The archetypal symbolism of the biography of the Buddha belongs to this second category – it is not meant to be historic truth, factual information, but poetic, even spiritual, truth. We may say that this biography – or partial biography – of the Buddha in terms of archetypal symbolism is not concerned with the external events of his career, but is meant to suggest to us something about his inner spiritual experience and, therefore, to shed light on the spiritual life for all of us.

This archetypal symbolism is often found in Buddhist biographies, for example, in the life of Nāgārjuna,[45] of Padmasambhava,[46] of Milarepa.[47] In all these so-called biographies there are many incidents which are not based, and are not supposed to be based, on historical facts, but which have an archetypal symbolic significance pointing to inner experience and inner realization. Sometimes it is difficult to distinguish between the two categories, to make up one's mind whether something belongs to the historical or to the symbolic order. Very often we find that the Buddhist tradition itself does not clearly distinguish between the two. It usually seems to take the myths and legends just as literally as the historical facts, as though in early times people almost didn't possess the capacity, or perhaps even the willingness, to distinguish in this way. Everything was true, everything was fact, of its own kind, in its own order. There is no harm in our trying to make up our minds what constitutes the factual, historical content of the Buddha's biography, and what represents its archetypal and symbolic content, but we should be careful not to undervalue the mythical and the legendary elements.

Buddhist symbolism

The Buddha, according to the traditional account, gained Enlightenment at the foot of a peepul tree. It is significant that, from a historical, factual point of view, we don't really know whether he sat under a tree or not: the oldest accounts don't mention this. We may assume quite naturally that he did because, after all, he gained his Enlightenment in the month of May, which is the hottest time of year in India; so it is more than likely that he was sitting under a tree, just for the sake of shade and shelter from the heat. But we don't know. Gradually, it seems, as the legendary and mythical element grew in the biographies, the Buddha came to be more and more associated at the time of his Enlightenment with sitting at the foot of a tree. A tree's roots go deep down into the earth, but at the same time its branches tower high into the sky. So the tree links heaven and earth, is a symbol of the union, or harmony, of opposites.

The World Tree is found in most mythologies. For instance, we have the Norse Yggdrasil, which is the World Ash – roots deep down, branches right up in the heavens, all the worlds as it were suspended on the branches. And one often gets this identification of the Christian cross with a World or Cosmic Tree. I have seen a representation of the crucifixion where branches were growing out of the sides of the cross, and the roots went deep down into the soil. The cross also, like the World Tree, links heaven and earth cosmically in the same way that Christ unites the human and the divine natures 'psychologically'.

Closely associated with the idea of a tree is the image of the central point. In all the traditional legendary accounts of the Buddha's gaining Enlightenment, he is represented sitting on what is called the *vajrāsana*, which literally means the diamond seat, or diamond throne as it is sometimes translated. The diamond, the *vajra*, the *dorje*, in Buddhist tradition always represents the transcendental element, the metaphysical base.[48] According to tradition, the *vajrāsana* is the centre of the universe. One can compare this with the corresponding Christian tradition that the cross stood on the same spot as the Tree of Knowledge of Good and Evil, from which Adam and Eve had eaten the forbidden fruit, and that this spot represents the exact centre of the world. This centrality in the cosmos of the *vajrāsana* suggests that Enlightenment consists in adopting a position of centrality.

I could go on in this way almost indefinitely – the traditional biographies are full of material of this sort. But now I want to look at a whole sequence of symbols that are connected with the most important event in the Buddha's whole career, his attainment of Enlightenment. These symbols are represented by certain incidents usually regarded as historical, or partly historical, though their actual significance is much deeper.

The first of these incidents is traditionally known as the victory over Māra,[49] the Evil One, the Satan of Buddhism. According to some of the later legendary accounts, the Buddha – or the Bodhisattva (Pāli *bodhisatta*), the Buddha-to-be – was seated in meditation at the foot of the tree when he was attacked by terrible demon hosts, by all sorts of foul, unsightly, misshapen figures, led by Māra. These hosts and their attack are vividly depicted in Buddhist art as well as in poetry. They were partly human, partly animal, hideously deformed, with snarling, leering, angry, and wrathful expressions, some of them lifting great clubs, others brandishing swords, all very menacing and frightful indeed. But all the stones, arrows, and flames, on reaching the edge of the Buddha's aura of light, turned into flowers and fell at his feet.

The significance of this is obvious and doesn't need to be explained, only to be felt. The Buddha wasn't touched, wasn't moved, by this terrible attack. His eyes remained closed, he remained in meditation, with that same smile on his lips. So Māra sent against the Buddha his three beautiful daughters, whose names are Lust, Passion, and Delight. They danced in front of the Buddha, exhibiting all of their wiles, but the Buddha didn't even open his eyes. They retired discomfited.

All this represents the forces of the unconscious in their crude, unsublimated form. The demons, the terrible misshapen figures, represent anger, aversion, dislike, and so on. As for the daughters of Māra, they represent, of course, the various aspects of craving and desire. Māra himself represents primordial ignorance or unawareness, on account of which we take birth again and again. Incidentally, the literal meaning of the name Māra is simply 'death'.

The second incident is known as the calling of the Earth Goddess to Witness.[50] After he had been defeated, after his armies had returned discomfited, Māra tried another trick. He said to the Buddha-to-be, 'You are sitting on the central point of the universe, on the throne of the Buddhas of old. What right have you, just an ordinary person, to sit on that diamond throne where the previous Buddhas sat?' So the Buddha said, 'In my past lives I have practised all the *pāramitās*, all the perfections, that is to say, the perfection of giving, perfection of morality, perfection of patience, perfection of energy, perfection of meditation, perfection of wisdom.[51] I have practised all these, and I have reached a point in my spiritual evolution where I am ready now, where I am about to gain Enlightenment. Therefore I am worthy to sit on this diamond throne like the previous Buddhas when they gained Enlightenment.'

Māra wasn't satisfied. He said, 'All right, you say that you practised all these perfections in your previous lives, but who saw you? Who is your witness?' Māra takes on the guise of a lawyer; he wants a witness, he wants evidence. So the future Buddha, who was seated on the diamond throne in the position of meditation, with his hands resting in his lap, just tapped on the earth – this is the famous *bhūmisparśa mudrā*,[52] the earth-touching or earth-witnessing *mudrā*, or position – and up rose the Earth Goddess, bearing a vase in her hand. She bore witness, saying, 'I have been here all the time. Men may come and men may go, but the earth always remains. I have seen all his previous lives. I have seen hundreds of thousands of lives in which he practised the perfections. So I bear witness that on account of his practice of these perfections he is worthy to sit in the seat of the Buddhas of old.'

This scene is also often depicted in Buddhist art – sometimes the Earth Goddess is shown as dark green in colour, sometimes a beautiful golden-brown, always half-emerged from the earth, very much like the figure of Mother Erda in Wagner's *Ring*. (Erda of course means 'the earth', and Erda and the Earth Goddess are the same as Hertha, as in Swinburne's famous poem of that name.) The significance of the Earth Goddess is a whole subject in itself and there is a whole literature on it. Basically, she represents the same forces as those represented by Māra's daughters. But whereas Māra's daughters represent them in their crude, negative, unsublimated aspects, the Earth Goddess, as she bears witness, represents them in their tamed, subdued, even in their sublimated aspect, ready to help, not hinder.

The third incident is known as Brahmā's request.[53] After his Enlightenment, the Buddha was inclined to keep silent. He reflected, 'This Truth, this Reality, which I have discovered, is so abstract, so difficult to see, so sublime, that ordinary people, their eyes covered with the dust of ignorance and passion, are not going to see it, to appreciate it. It is better to remain silent, to remain under the bodhi tree, better to remain with eyes closed, not to go out into the world and preach.' But then another great apparition arose. A great light shone forth, and in the midst of the light an ancient figure, the figure of Brahmā Sahāmpati, Brahmā the Great God, Lord of a Thousand Worlds, appeared before the Buddha with folded hands. He said, 'Please preach, preach the Truth. There are just a few with only a little dust on their eyes. They will appreciate it, they will follow it.' The Buddha opened his divine eye and looked forth over the universe. He saw all beings, just like lotuses in a pond, in various stages of development. And he said, 'For the sake of those with just a little dust over their eyes, those who are like lotuses beginning to blossom, I will preach the Dharma.'

We shouldn't of course take this incident literally in the historical sense. The Buddha was Enlightened; he didn't need to be asked to preach. Brahmā's request represents the manifestation within the Buddha's own mind of the forces of compassion which eventually compelled him to make known the Truth he had discovered.

The fourth and last episode is the Mucalinda episode.[54] For seven weeks after his Enlightenment, the Buddha sat at the foot of the bodhi tree and other trees in its vicinity, and in the middle of the seventh week there arose a great storm. The Buddha was Enlightened in the month of May, so seven weeks takes us to the middle of July, the beginning of the rainy season. In India, when the rainy season begins, in a matter of instants the whole sky becomes black and rain descends not in bucketfuls but in absolute reservoirfuls. The Buddha was out in the open, under a tree, with just a thin robe – he couldn't do much about it. But another figure arose out of the undergrowth, out of the shadows: a great snake, King Mucalinda, the serpent-king. He came and wrapped his coils around the Buddha and stood with his hood over his head like an umbrella, and in this way protected him against the downpour. This episode is often depicted in Buddhist art, sometimes almost comically: you see a coil, like a coil of rope, with the Buddha's head just poking out, and the hood like an umbrella over him. Then the rain disappeared, the storm-clouds cleared up, and the serpent-king assumed a different form, that of a beautiful youth about 16 years of age, who bowed before the Buddha.

Some scholars try to take this episode literally, try to force some factual meaning from it, saying, 'Oh yes, it is well known that in the East snakes are sometimes quite friendly with holy men, and come and sit near them, and this is what must have happened.' But we cannot accept this pseudo-historical type of explanation. We are on a different plane, a different level of meaning altogether. All over the world, water – or the sea, or the ocean – represents the unconscious. And in Indian mythology – Hindu, Buddhist, and Jain – the *nāgas*, that is to say, the serpents or the dragons, live in the depths of the ocean. So the *nāgas* represent the forces in the depths of the unconscious in their most positive and beneficent aspect – and Mucalinda is the king of the *nāgas*.

The falling of the rain, the torrential downpour after seven weeks, represents a baptism. All over the world, pouring water on someone or something represents the investiture of that person or that object with all the powers of the unconscious mind. For example, in Christianity there is a baptism with water and with fire, an investiture with the forces of the unconscious mind and with the forces of the spirit.

The rain, we saw, falls at the end of the seventh week, and Mucalinda wraps his coils seven times around the seated figure of the Buddha. This repetition of the figure seven is no coincidence. Mucalinda also stands for what the Tantras call the *caṇḍālī*, the fiery power, or the fiery one, which the Hindus call the *kuṇḍalinī*, or the coiled-up one, or the serpent power. This represents all the powerful psychic energies surging up inside a person, especially at the time of meditation. The seven coils, or the winding seven times round the Buddha, represent the seven psychic centres through which the *kuṇḍalinī* passes in the course of its ascent.[55] Mucalinda's assuming the form of a beautiful youth represents the new personality which is born as a result of this upward progression of the *caṇḍālī* or *kuṇḍalinī*. Mucalinda in the new form bows to the Buddha: this represents the perfect submission of all the powers of the unconscious to the Enlightened mind.

It is obvious from all this that these four incidents all have a deep psychological and spiritual significance. They are not just pseudo-history, and they are not just a fairytale (though even fairytales have a significance). They are invested with a powerful symbolic and archetypal meaning.

The four principal archetypes

Going a little further, we may say that the four main figures with which we have been concerned form a very definite set: Māra the Evil One, Vasundharā the Earth Goddess, Brahmā, and Mucalinda, in that order. Now I am going to draw what some people may feel is a bold analogy, but I think it has great significance and suggestiveness. It seems to me that these four figures are to some extent analogous to the four principal archetypes according to Jung and that their appearance in this order represents an integration of these contents into the conscious mind – in other words, it represents, on a higher level, what Jung calls the individuation process. Māra corresponds to what Jung calls the Shadow, that darker side of ourselves of which we are ashamed, which we usually try to keep hidden. The Earth Goddess represents the Anima. (In Jung's analytic psychology, the Anima is the inner feminine part of the male personality, while the Animus is the inner masculine part of the female personality. The Buddha, being a man, had an Anima – in the case of a woman it would be an Animus.) Brahmā represents the archetype of the Wise Old Man. He is seen in Buddhist art with white hair and a beard, a sort of God-the-Father figure. And Mucalinda is the archetype of the Young Hero.

There is also a correspondence with the principal figures of Christian mythology, Māra corresponding to Satan, the Earth Goddess to the Virgin Mary, Brahmā to God, and Mucalinda to Christ. I don't think this is too far-fetched. If we study these matters carefully, go into them deeply, we should see the analogy. In Tantric Buddhism, there is a similar set: the Guardian (or Protector, as he is sometimes called), the *ḍākinī*, the guru, and the *yidam*.

Though I have drawn these analogies, there is a great difference of principle between the Buddhist and the Christian approaches to, or attitudes toward, the archetypes of their respective traditions. In Buddhism, it is always clearly, even categorically, stated that all these appearances, all these archetypal forms, are ultimately phenomena of one's own true mind, or projections from one's own unconscious, and that they are all to be integrated. But in Christianity the corresponding archetypes are regarded as objectively existing beings. One cannot really resolve an archetype in the sense of incorporating it as representing unconscious contents into one's conscious mind, one's conscious attitudes, or one's new self, unless one realizes that, in the last analysis, it isn't something objectively existing, but something that one has projected from some depths, from some hidden source within oneself.

On account of this limitation, in the Christian tradition – with the exception perhaps of a few heretical mystics – there is no full resolution of the archetypal figure, whereas in Buddhism, on account of a more deeply metaphysical and spiritual background, such a resolution is possible. In Buddhism all the archetypes can be dissolved, can be drawn back into one's own conscious attitude and integrated there so as to enrich, perfect, and beautify it. In other words, the individuation process can be carried to its absolute conclusion: Enlightenment.

We have only touched on a few of the archetypal symbols occurring in the biography of the Buddha. I would have liked to mention many more, for instance the Buddha's begging-bowl. There are many legends about it, some of them very interesting indeed. In fact, we may say without any exaggeration that it occupies in Buddhist legend and history a position analogous to that of the Holy Grail in Christianity, and carries much the same significance.

The archetypes are not just of historic or literary interest, not something foreign to us. Each and every one is present within us all; or we can say that we are all present in them. We share them, we have them all in common, or they share us, have all of us in common. And in the course of our spiritual life, especially as we practise meditation, these archetypes tend to emerge in various ways into consciousness. Sometimes they show themselves, at least by way of a glimpse, in dreams, in meditation, or in waking fantasies. We all have to encounter the Shadow, for instance. This is the dark, unpleasant side of ourselves which appears in dreams, for example, as a dark snarling hound snapping at our heels which we want to get rid of, but cannot; or as a dark man, perhaps. We have to face the Shadow, come to terms with it, even assimilate this darker side of ourselves, just as the Buddha faced and overcame Māra and his hosts. And here, just as in the case of Māra, repression is no solution. The Shadow, or the content represented by the Shadow, must be saturated with awareness and resolved. The Buddha himself didn't start emitting flames to counteract the flames of Māra's hosts; but when the flames touched his aura, they were transformed into flowers, transmuted. This is also the sort of thing we have to do with our own Shadow – just see it, recognize it, accept it, and then transform and transmute it into what Tantric tradition calls a guardian, or protector.

We too have to call up the Earth Goddess, which means in psychoanalytical language that we have to face, and free ourselves from, the Anima – in the case of a man – that is to say, we have to bring and integrate into our conscious attitude our unconscious femininity, just as a woman has to bring up and integrate her unconscious masculinity. If this is done, there will no longer be any question of projecting these unconscious, unrealized contents onto members of the opposite sex, and the 'problem', as it sometimes called, of sex will have been resolved. This is a very important aspect of the spiritual life.

Next, we all have to learn from the Wise Old Man. Sometimes we may quite literally have to sit at the feet of a teacher, or at least have some ideal image to which we owe allegiance. Then, perhaps after many years, we have to incorporate into ourselves the qualities which that figure represents – wisdom, knowledge, and so on.

And then, finally, each one has to give birth within himself or herself to the Young Hero; in other words, create the nucleus of a new self, a new being, or in traditional Buddhist language, give birth within ourselves to the Buddha.

If we face our own Shadow, call up our own Anima or Animus, learn from our Wise Old Man, and give birth within ourselves to our own Young Hero, we shall live out, we shall recapitulate within ourselves in our own lives, at all levels, in all aspects, the archetypal symbols which appear in the Buddha's biography.

from *Aspects of Buddhist Psychology* (Lecture Series)

7. INSPIRATION FROM THE BUDDHA'S LIFE

After all those years, in which he had heard so much, the overall impression the Buddha had made upon Ānanda is summed up in those few words: 'He who is so kind.' Half of Buddhism is in that remark.

When the Buddha died, it was as though Enlightenment itself had disappeared from the universe. Some people exclaimed, 'The Eye of the World has disappeared!'[56] And although this wasn't really true – a cloud had moved across the face of the sun, but the sun was still shining – it *felt* true, and they were devastated. According to tradition, even the animals were affected.

But even though the disciples felt that the light of the world had gone out, still, slowly, they recovered from their grief, as we all have to recover on these occasions, and started to take stock of the situation. Unbelievable as it seemed at first, the Buddha was gone and they had to settle down to life in a Buddhaless world – which, especially for those who had lived in his presence for many years, was a terrible change. But eventually they started trying to understand what they were left with. And some – perhaps the intellectuals among them – said, 'Well, we've got the teachings the Buddha gave us: the doctrines, the rules of behaviour, and so on. That's enough, surely.' (One can imagine that these were the kind of people who went on to spend their lives happily analysing and classifying the teachings, and later began the tradition that became what is known as the Abhidharma.)[57] But there were many among the disciples of the Buddha who, while they had nothing against the teachings or the rules, felt there was something missing from their lives now that the Buddha had gone. We can imagine that even when they were supposed to be thinking of the teachings and committing those long lists of terms to memory, they couldn't help thinking of the Buddha, and recalling incidents in his life that exemplified his personal qualities.

For instance, some of them no doubt remembered the occasion when the Buddha was going round from one hermitage to the next and found in one hut an elderly monk lying on the floor in a terrible condition; he had dysentery. It was obvious that he had been lying there for days without receiving any help at all. The Buddha asked the old man why the other monks weren't looking after him, and he said, 'Well, I'm useless to them now. Why should they bother to look after me?' So the Buddha sent his companion, Ānanda, to fetch warm water, and together they lifted the old monk on to a bed, washed him, and made him comfortable. Then the Buddha called all the monks together and said, 'Monks, you have neither father nor mother, brother nor sister. You've given up the world. You must be brother and sister, mother and father, to one another. He who wishes to serve me, let him serve the sick.'[58]

Incidents like this, incidents which show the Buddha's practical compassion, must surely have remained in the minds and hearts of many of his disciples. Some of them, especially the lay disciples, might also have remembered the story of Kisāgotamī. In India in those days, as now, infant mortality was very high, and the story goes that a young woman called Kisāgotamī lost her only child when he was only a few years old. Unable to believe he was dead, crazed with grief, she took his body in her arms from house to house, asking for medicine to make him well again. Eventually someone had the good sense and kindness to suggest that she should go to the Buddha for help, so she went to him and asked him to bring her baby back to life.

He didn't refuse. He didn't give her a sermon – he knew that would be useless, grief-stricken as she was. In fact, he didn't answer her question directly at all. He just said, 'Bring me just a few grains of mustard seed – but bring them from a house where no one has died.' So off she went, going from one house to another. Everywhere she went, the people were more than willing to give her some mustard seed. But when she asked, 'Has anyone died in this house?' they said, 'Do not remind us of our grief. The dead are many, but the living are few.' At every house she learned the same lesson: death comes to all. Eventually she laid her child's body to rest in the jungle, came back to the Buddha, and sat quietly at his feet. She didn't say anything for a long time. Then at last she said, 'Give me a refuge,' and she became a nun.[59]

Such incidents added to the general stock of stories and anecdotes which must have been fresh in the hearts and minds of his disciples. Many of them must have felt that these stories communicated something of tremendous importance, something the formal teachings did not convey: the effect the Buddha had on those with whom he came in contact, the direct impact of an Enlightened being, which is above and beyond all words.

No one could have been a better judge of this than the Buddha's cousin Ānanda, who for more than twenty years was the Buddha's personal attendant, and went with him everywhere. If the Buddha was invited to lunch, Ānanda went too. If the Buddha went to give a sermon, Ānanda went along. If the Buddha received visitors, or answered questions, Ānanda was present. He was always there, like the Buddha's shadow. And the Buddha, we gather, was all in all to him. When the Buddha was about to die, Ānanda, understandably, felt it more deeply than anybody. According to the *Mahāparinibbāna Sutta*, as the Buddha lay in the *sāl* grove, Ānanda left him and went to a nearby lodging-house. There he stood at the door of the hut and leaned against the doorpost. As he stood there, he tried to realize that the Buddha was going to die in a matter of days or even hours. Weeping bitterly, he said to himself, 'The Master is about to pass away from me: he who was so kind.'[60]

These words are of the greatest significance. In the course of the twenty years Ānanda had spent with the Buddha he must have heard the Buddha deliver hundreds of discourses, including many abstruse, philosophical, deeply mystical teachings. He had heard him answer thousands of questions. He must have admired his brilliance, his affability, the easy way he handled difficult questions. No doubt he had witnessed all sorts of supernormal happenings. But it was not the Buddha's wisdom or his understanding of philosophy, his skill in debate or his ability to work miracles, his courage or his tireless energy, that stood out. For Ānanda the Buddha's outstanding quality was his kindness. After all those years, in which he had heard so much, the overall impression the Buddha had made upon Ānanda is summed up in those few words: 'He who was so kind.'

Half of Buddhism is in that remark. And – here we return to our theme – it also gives us the origin of the bodhisattva ideal. The Buddha's wisdom is revealed in his doctrinal teachings, but his love, his compassion, which so deeply impressed Ānanda, is revealed in his personal example. This is what those disciples who could not identify Buddhism exclusively with the verbal teaching of the Buddha were getting at. They were saying that Buddhism was not just wisdom, as represented by the teaching, but also love and compassion, as exemplified by the Buddha's life; and in any formulation of Buddhism, both should be taken into consideration. Yes, we should try to attain Enlightenment, to awaken, to see the Truth; this is the wisdom aspect. But we should try to attain wisdom for the sake of all sentient beings; this is the compassion aspect. These two together form the bodhisattva ideal.

from *The Bodhisattva Ideal*

2
GOING FOR REFUGE

1. 'COMING HOME' TO BUDDHISM

The system of spiritual teaching and training that we call Buddhism is, in reality, neither Eastern nor Western, any more than we ourselves, in the depths of our being, are either Eastern or Western.

On the occasion of their first contact with Buddhism, whether that contact takes the form of reading a Buddhist book, seeing an image of the Buddha, or paying a visit to a Buddhist spiritual community, many people experience a paradoxical feeling of absolute newness and, at the same time, complete familiarity. They feel not just that they have gained something infinitely precious but that they have *re*gained it. They feel that, after many wanderings, they have not only arrived at last at the gates of a glorious palace but also that, incredible as it seems, they have 'come home'. Some of them seek to account for this feeling of complete familiarity by saying that to them Buddhism represents what they have, in fact, always believed, though without fully realizing it. Others seek to account for it by saying, with varying degrees of conviction, that they must have been Buddhist in a previous existence. However they may account for the feeling, or even if they choose not to account for it at all, such Western Buddhists are naturally astonished when somebody tells them, as somebody occasionally does, even today, that he – or she – is unable to understand how it is possible for one born and brought up in the West, as a member of Western society and in the midst of Western culture, to accept an Eastern religion like Buddhism or, in other words, to accept a religion that is foreign and exotic. But such a thing *is* possible, as daily is becoming more evident, and the reason why it is possible is that the system of spiritual teaching and training that we call Buddhism is, in reality, neither Eastern nor Western, any more than we ourselves, in the depths of our beings, are either Eastern or Western. When we accept the so-called Eastern religion of Buddhism we accept it, even as we encounter it, on a level where the terms Eastern and Western no longer have any meaning.

If a few words of personal confession may be permitted, this was very much my own experience forty-five years ago when, at the age of 16, I had my first real contact with Buddhism. That contact took place when I read two short but exceptionally profound Buddhist scriptures of great historical and spiritual significance. These were the *Diamond Sūtra*, a work belonging to the 'Perfection of Wisdom' corpus, and the *Sūtra of Wei Lang*, a collection of discourses by the first Chinese patriarch of the Chan or Zen school, who is better known as Huineng. Reading these two works and realizing that, although in one sense the truth they taught, or the reality they disclosed, was new to me, in another sense it was not new at all but strangely familiar. I certainly did not feel that I was accepting an Eastern religion, or a religion that was foreign and exotic. Rather I felt that contact with Buddhism was, at the same time, contact with the depths of my own being: that in knowing Buddhism I was knowing myself, and that in knowing myself I was knowing Buddhism.[61]

from *The Priceless Jewel*

2. WHAT GOING FOR REFUGE IS

We too are capable of gaining Enlightenment. This is what committing oneself to the Buddha means.

A Buddhist is one who 'goes for Refuge' to the Buddha, the Dharma, and the Sangha, is one who *commits* himself to the Buddha, the Dharma, and the Sangha, and who commits himself to them totally, with body, speech, and mind. There are many stories to illustrate what this means in the ancient Buddhist scriptures. When we read those scriptures, especially the Pāli scriptures, we encounter the Buddha as he wanders from place to place, begging his food as he goes. In the course of his wanderings, he might meet somebody under a tree, or in a village, and the two of them get into a conversation. Maybe it's a Brahmin priest, or a farmer, or a well-to-do merchant, or a young man about town. Maybe it's a wandering ascetic, maybe it's a housewife, maybe it's a prince,... but in one way or another they get talking.

Sooner or later, this person asks the Buddha a question, perhaps about the meaning of life, or about his teaching, or about what happens after death. The Buddha might reply at considerable length, giving a detailed discourse, or he might reply in just a few words. If he is very inspired he might reply in verse, 'breathing out' what is called an *udāna*. He might even give one of his famous 'lion roars', a full and frank, almost defiant, declaration of his great spiritual experience and the path that he teaches; or he might reply with complete silence – a wordless communication that says so much more than words.[62] But whatever the Buddha says or does not say, if the listener is receptive, the result is the same. He or she feels deeply affected, deeply moved, deeply stirred. They are so stirred, so thrilled, in fact, that their hair might stand on end, or they might shed tears, or be seized by a violent fit of trembling. They feel as if they are seeing a great light; they have a tremendous sense of emancipation; they feel as if a great burden has been lifted from their back, or as though they have been suddenly let out of prison. At such a moment, the listener feels spiritually reborn. And at that extraordinary turning point they respond to the Buddha and to the Dharma with a cry that breaks spontaneously from their lips. According to those ancient Pāli texts, they say; '*Buddhaṃ saraṇaṃ gacchāmi, Dhammaṃ saraṇaṃ gacchāmi, Saṅghaṃ saraṇaṃ gacchāmi*,' which means, 'To the Buddha for Refuge I go, to the Dharma for Refuge I go, to the Sangha for Refuge I go.'[63] This is their response: they go for Refuge, commit themselves, because the Buddha has shown them a vision of inner truth, of existence, of life itself in all its depth and complexity. This vision is so great that all one can do is give oneself to it completely, live for it, and if necessary die for it.

But what does one actually mean when one says, 'To the Buddha for Refuge I go; to the Dharma for Refuge I go; to the Sangha for Refuge I go'? The English word 'refuge' is not very satisfactory. It is a literal translation of the Pāli and Sanskrit word *saraṇa*, but does not give its real meaning. There is certainly no question of running away from anything when one goes for Refuge, no question of taking shelter with anyone. Going for Refuge really means commitment: committing oneself to the Buddha, committing oneself to the Dharma, committing oneself to the Sangha. So what does this mean?

Committing oneself to the Buddha does not mean handing oneself over to the Buddha or blindly obeying the Buddha. It means taking the Buddha as one's ideal, taking *Buddhahood* as an ideal. The historical Buddha, Gautama, was a human being. By his own human efforts he developed higher and ever higher states of being, states that eventually culminated in what we call 'Enlightenment', the highest conceivable state of moral and spiritual perfection, a state of supreme wisdom, of infinite compassion, and absolute purity. We too are human beings; we too, therefore, according to Buddhism, are capable of developing higher and higher states of being and consciousness. We too are capable of gaining Enlightenment. This is what committing oneself to the Buddha means. It means recognizing the Buddha as the living embodiment of the highest conceivable state of human perfection. It means recognizing Buddhahood as a practical ideal for all human beings, and actually devoting all one's energies towards the realization of that ideal.

What is meant by 'committing oneself to the Dharma'? The Dharma is the teaching of the Buddha, and it is concerned mainly with two things: with the goal of Enlightenment, or Buddhahood, and with the path leading to that state. Committing oneself to the Dharma therefore means actually following the path in order to realize the goal. The path consists of several steps and stages which are variously enumerated according to the particular point of view adopted. One popular enumeration of the stages of the path is that of the three stages of morality, meditation, and wisdom. Another enumeration is that of the Noble Eightfold Path. This is not really a path of eight stages, as is generally thought, but a path of two stages: a stage of vision and a stage of transformation. The stage of vision represents an actual vision of the goal – not just a theoretical idea but an actual spiritual experience – and the stage of transformation represents the gradual transformation of all aspects of one's being, from the highest to the lowest, in accordance with that vision. There is also the path of the six perfections of generosity, morality, patience, vigour, meditation, and wisdom. So committing oneself to the Dharma means following the path in any of these various ways. It means committing oneself to the process of one's development as an individual by whatsoever means.

The Sangha is the spiritual community – that is, the community of the spiritually committed. The Dharma, as we have seen, is a path that consists of various steps and stages. Naturally, different individuals are on different steps and at different stages. Some are more advanced than we are, some are less advanced, and some are equally advanced. What, then, is our attitude towards these people? We reverence those who are more advanced, we are receptive to their spiritual influence, and assist them in their spiritual work. We help those who are less advanced than we are, giving advice and moral support as and when we can. And we enjoy spiritual friendship with those who are as advanced as ourselves. Indeed, we can enjoy spiritual fellowship with all members of the Sangha in different ways and in differing degrees. This is what we mean by committing ourselves to the Sangha.

Certainly each individual must develop for himself or herself, by his or her own efforts, but we will develop more easily and more enjoyably if we do so in spiritual fellowship with others. We could even say that spiritual fellowship is necessary to individual development. In the spiritual community all help each, and each helps all. In the end, all narrow, pseudo-religious individualism is transcended, there is only a spiritual community of individuals who are, as it were, transparent to each other, individuals through whom the light of Enlightenment shines.

So this is how one can know who is a Buddhist. A Buddhist is one who goes for Refuge in response to the Buddha and his teaching. A Buddhist is one who gives him- or herself to the Buddha and the Dharma and the Sangha. This was the criterion in the Buddha's day 2,500 years ago, and it remains the criterion today.

In many traditionally Buddhist countries this profound change of heart is institutionalized in the form of a ceremony called 'taking the Refuges'. In this form it tends to get trivialized. Any public meeting, even a political meeting, it is sad to say, will start with everyone 'taking' the Refuges and Precepts – that is, reciting them – just to show that they are all good Buddhists. Another way that Going for Refuge gets diminished is when it is taken as something you do once and for all, like baptism in Christianity, so that it is assumed that when you have 'taken the Refuges' from a monk, you are safely a Buddhist.

As a committed Buddhist one goes for Refuge – or tries to – all the time. As one's appreciation of the Three Jewels grows, one's Going for Refuge becomes correspondingly more profound, and this can sometimes have surprising results. It may mean that what brings you to Buddhism in the first place becomes not more but less important, as your deepening understanding comes to displace the comparatively superficial appreciation of Buddhism that was sufficient to get you going in the first place.

For instance, one may have heard it said that whereas Christianity is a religion of faith, Buddhism is a religion of reason, and one may be drawn to Buddhism on that basis. As one goes more deeply into it, one finds that while reason is given an honoured place in Buddhism, it is by no means enthroned as its governing principle, but one remains a Buddhist because one has gone deep enough not only to be able to put reason in its proper place, but also to find other aspects of Buddhist practice profoundly meaningful.

Thus Going for Refuge is an experience that is deepening and growing more multidimensional all the time. One accepts the ideal of Enlightened humanity, exemplified by the historical Buddha, as being more and more relevant to oneself personally; one takes that ideal as one's personal goal in life more and more to heart; and one tries to practise the Dharma in such a way as to realize that ideal more and more effectively.

from *New Currents in Western Buddhism* and *What is the Sangha?*

3. GOING FOR REFUGE AND THE CONCEPT OF ESCAPE

The fact that the word saraṇa, *refuge, is so firmly embedded in Buddhist tradition makes it extremely important to bring out its positive implications, otherwise we get a one-sidedly negative picture of the spiritual life, like talking about escape from the bud without mentioning the flower.*

One of the commonest criticisms of the spiritual life is that it is escapism, and that those who try to practise some such thing as Buddhism are escapists. What people mean by this probably comes quite close to the dictionary definition of escapism: 'the tendency to seek distraction and relief from reality'. As we shall see, nothing could be less like a description of Buddhism.

But escape – 'to get away, as by flight or other conscious efforts; to break away, get free, or get clear, from or out of detention, danger, discomfort or the like, as to escape from prison' – *is* quite a good description of the spiritual life, at least as looked at from a certain point of view. It may not be the whole truth about spiritual life, but it is a substantial part of it. When one sets out to live a spiritual life, one is – or one should be – making a conscious effort to break away, to get free, to get clear of all sorts of entanglements, involvements, and complicated murkiness. Or, to put it another way, one is trying to make the transition from lower to higher states of being and consciousness, trying to develop, trying to evolve. This is what the spiritual life is substantially about.

So why might we try to do this? What makes us want to escape, to develop, to rise from a lower to a higher state of being and consciousness? We are impelled, even *com*pelled, to do it because we experience our present state as restrictive, cramped, limiting, confined, unsatisfactory, even dangerous. In our present state and circumstances, we feel only too often as though we are imprisoned, even caged, on a treadmill. Naturally we have the urge to get out, to *break* out if necessary, to get free and clear.

The Pāli canon contains a passage attributed to the Buddha in which he tries to explain to some of his disciples what it feels like to be Enlightened. Obviously they are very curious to know how it feels when you've got there. What does it feel like to be liberated? What does it feel like to be a Buddha? In his attempt to put across the inner content of the experience rather than offer a conceptual explanation, the Buddha chose to use three similes.[64] He said suppose that on a hot and dusty day you've been carrying an enormous burden for many miles; and suppose that after you've been staggering along with it for mile after mile, hour after hour, you are at last able to lift that load off your shoulders and put it down, free from that tremendous, oppressive weight. Becoming Enlightened, he said, is like that. You feel as though you have set down all your burdens. There's no weight for you to carry, nothing oppressing you. You are light and buoyant; you can float free.

Then again, he said, suppose you've been engaged in some trade, and suppose as the result of your business enterprise – or lack of enterprise – you've got heavily into debt. You owe a lot of money to a lot of people and you have no idea how you are going to pay them back. Your creditors are knocking on your door, following you about, wanting their money. Before you is the prospect of going to prison. Then one day, by some miracle, you suddenly acquire a large sum of money and can discharge all your debts. At last you can look everybody in the face again, free from that terrible anxiety. Becoming Enlightened, the Buddha said, is a bit like that.

Then a third image: becoming Enlightened, the Buddha said, is like being released from prison. Imagine how it might feel to have been shut up in prison for years on end. Then, one day, the door is flung open. Suddenly you are free to walk out into the sunlight and go wherever you please. Being Enlightened is just like that – you've escaped from the prison of the world itself.

Through these three similes, the Buddha tried to express something of how it feels to become Enlightened. You feel light, buoyant, carefree. You may even strike unenlightened people as being rather irresponsible, as not taking life seriously enough. You feel completely unconcerned about the past, because there is nothing left over that you have to deal with, and you are not concerned about the future either. Above all, you feel free, absolutely free, because you have at last escaped in the fullest possible sense.

It is therefore quite appropriate to describe the spiritual life as being, at least from one point of view, about escape. As for escapism, that is something else entirely. If an escapee is one who breaks out of prison, an escapist is one who tries to forget that he is in prison at all, who pretends to himself that the prison is not a prison, and that he is really free. Broadly speaking, this kind of escapism takes two forms: the non-religious and the religious. Of these two, non-religious escapism is probably the more common these days. It consists in trying to forget that one is in prison by becoming absorbed in whatever activities can be carried on within the prison walls. Religious escapism, on the other hand, consists in trying to forget that one is in prison by becoming absorbed in books on how to escape from prison.

Closely related to the idea of escape in Buddhism generally, and much more familiar, is the idea of 'refuge', which the dictionary defines as 'that which, or one who, shelters, protects from danger, distress, calamity etc, a place inaccessible to the enemy'. In Buddhism, refuge – a means of escape and a place to escape to – is provided by the Three Jewels, or Three Refuges: the Buddha, the Enlightened teacher, the Dharma, the teaching, and the Sangha, the more highly developed members of the spiritual community. Between them the Three Refuges represent not only the means of escape from lower to higher levels of consciousness; they also represent what we escape to, those higher levels themselves. The act of Going for Refuge to the Buddha, the Dharma, and the Sangha is the central act of the whole Buddhist life; it is Going for Refuge that makes one a Buddhist. For the Buddhist tradition, therefore, Going for Refuge is identical with the following of the spiritual path itself.

All of this finds expression in the very earliest Buddhist texts, most famously in the *Dhammapada*, in which the Buddha is recorded as making a clear distinction between what could be called false refuges and true refuges, the main point being that no mundane thing can give refuge in an absolute sense. He says:

> Many people, out of fear, flee for refuge to sacred hills, woods, groves, trees, and shrines. In reality this is not a safe refuge. In reality this is not the best refuge. Fleeing to such a refuge one is not released from all suffering. He who goes for refuge to the Enlightened One, to the Truth, and to the Spiritual Community, and who sees with perfect wisdom the Four Ariyan Truths – namely, suffering, the origin of suffering, the passing beyond suffering and the Ariyan Eightfold Way leading to the pacification of suffering – for him this is a safe refuge, for him this is the best refuge. Having gone to such a refuge, one is released from all suffering.[65]

Just to clear up possible misunderstanding, it should be observed that the idea of Going for Refuge in the sense of escaping from all that is unsatisfactory does not do full justice to the ideals and practice of the spiritual life. The spiritual life also involves committing oneself to all that is truly satisfactory, and the point of escaping is to leave yourself free to make that commitment. There is nothing wrong in escaping if there is something to escape from, but to escape is not the be-all and end-all of the spiritual life any more than it is of worldly life. The fact that the word *śaraṇa*, refuge, is so firmly embedded in Buddhist tradition makes it extremely important to bring out its positive implications, otherwise we get a one-sidedly negative picture of the spiritual life, like talking about escape from the bud without mentioning the flower.

from *Creative Symbols of Tantric Buddhism*

4. MY OWN GOING FOR REFUGE AND GOING FORTH

Once I realized that I was a Buddhist it seemed that I had always been one, that it was the most natural thing in the world to be one, and that I had never been anything else.

The experience with which the history of my Going for Refuge begins took place in the late summer or early autumn of 1942, when I was 16 or 17, and it took place as a result of my reading the *Diamond Sūtra* and the *Sūtra of Wei Lang* (Huineng), especially the former. I have described this crucial experience in my memoirs of the period, written in the late fifties, and since I am unable to improve upon the account I then gave I shall simply quote from the first part of it. Speaking of my initial response to the *Diamond Sūtra*, I wrote,

> Though this book epitomizes a teaching of such rarified sublimity that even *arahants*, saints who have attained individual Nirvāṇa, are said to become confused and afraid when they hear of it for the first time, I at once joyfully embraced it with an unqualified acceptance and assent. To me the truth taught by the Buddha in the *Diamond Sūtra* was not new. I had known and believed and realized it ages before and the reading of the *Sūtra* as it were awoke me to the existence of something I had forgotten. Once I realized that I was a Buddhist it seemed that I had always been one, that it was the most natural thing in the world to be one, and that I had never been anything else.[66]

After offering two possible explanations for my feeling that I had always been a Buddhist I went on to describe my experience of the *Sūtra of Wei*

Lang which, I wrote, threw me into 'a kind of ecstasy' whenever I read it. The truth taught by the Buddha in the *Diamond Sūtra* and to a more limited extent by the Sixth Patriarch in the *Sūtra of Wei Lang* was, of course, the highest truth of Buddhism (so far as that truth can be expressed in words), the truth of *śūnyatā* or 'Voidness' – the truth, that is to say, that the phenomena of existence are ultimately non-different from absolute reality and absolute reality ultimately non-different from the phenomena of existence. Such being the case, the fact that I had responded so positively and unreservedly to this teaching meant that my Dharma Eye had been opened, at least to some extent, and that as a result of my reading of the *Diamond Sūtra* and the *Sūtra of Wei Lang* I had in fact gone for Refuge to the Dharma, the second of the Three Jewels.

Whether I also went for Refuge to the first and third of the Three Jewels as a result of my reading the two *Sūtras*, and, if so, whether I went for Refuge to them in the same way that I did to the second, is another question. I was certainly aware that the truth taught in the *Diamond Sūtra* had been taught by the Buddha and that, although its immediate recipient was the *arhat* Subhūti, it had in fact been addressed to an assembly of monks and Bodhisattvas representing the spiritual community or Sangha. I was even aware that in the *Sūtra of Wei Lang* the sixth Patriarch had exhorted his listeners to take refuge in the Three Jewels of their 'essence of mind' (as Wong Mow Lam translated the expression). Nevertheless, so overwhelmed was I by what the *Diamond Sūtra* itself calls 'the impact of the Dharma' that for the time being I was virtually oblivious to the existence of the Buddha and the Sangha. Indeed, were it not for the fact that both the Buddha and the Sangha are ultimately non-different from *śūnyatā* it might be said that, so far as I was concerned, the first and third of the Three Jewels had both been swallowed up by the Void!

But though for the time being I was oblivious to the existence of the first and third Jewels, I had long been fascinated by the life and personality of the Buddha. Three or four years before my encounter with the *Diamond Sūtra* and the *Sūtra of Wei Lang* I had, in fact, written a 'Life of Siddhartha Gautama the Buddha', as I called it. This little work I compiled mainly from the *Children's Encyclopaedia* and H. G. Wells's *A Short History of the World*, and it is perhaps significant that, apart from school essays, it was my first completed piece of writing. At about the same time I bought, at a curio shop in Brighton, a small brass Kamakura Buddha in which – the top of its head being perforated for the purpose – I regularly burned joss sticks. This act of devotion did not in itself amount to Going for Refuge, of course, any more than did the writing of my 'Life of Siddhartha Gautama the Buddha', but at least it showed that I had a feeling for the Buddha that I certainly did not have for the Sangha or spiritual community. After my realization that I was a Buddhist nearly two years, in fact, were to pass before I made personal contact with other Buddhists and two years and a few months before I formally went for Refuge to all Three Jewels.

These other Buddhists with whom I made personal contact, in the winter of 1943–4, were the members of the Buddhist Society, founded in London in 1924 by Christmas Humphreys as the Buddhist Lodge of the Theosophical Society. By the time I made contact with them, I had been conscripted into the army, but I attended meetings whenever I could and struck up acquaintance with a few people. At one of these meetings (it may have been a Wesak meeting, but I cannot be sure) I found myself 'taking *pansil*', as it was called, from an orange-robed figure seated behind a table at the far end of the room. '*Pansil*' was the Sinhalese corruption of the Pāli *pañcasīla* or 'five precepts', and one 'took *pansil*' by repeating the five precepts, preceded by the Three Refuges, after whoever happened to be conducting the ceremony. Though many of the circumstances of that meeting have long faded from my mind, I have vivid recollections of myself and some fifteen or twenty other people standing in our places with our *pansil* cards in our hands as, with varying degrees of uncertainty with regard to the pronunciation of the unfamiliar Pāli words, we followed a clear-voiced and confident Christmas Humphreys as he led us in the chanting of the responses. Most vivid of all is the recollection of looking down at the *pansil* card I held in my own two hands. Even now I can see the oblong of shining white card, on which the Refuges and Precepts were printed in both Pāli and English. Even now I can hear the voice of Christmas Humphreys pronouncing the *dutiyampis* and *tatiyampis* of the Refuge-going formula in a way that, to my unaccustomed ear, seemed to bear little relation to the words as printed.

The orange-robed figure from whom I had 'taken *pansil*', and whose guttural tones had been too low for me to catch, was the Burmese monk U Thittila. He was the first Buddhist monk I had seen, and in view of some of the developments which, many years later, took place in my own life and thought as a Buddhist, it was significant that it was he, rather than a more 'orthodox' representative of Eastern Buddhism, who conducted the ceremony whereat I recited for the first time the formula which, publicly repeated after a leading Buddhist, constitutes 'conversion' to Buddhism and formal acceptance into the Buddhist community. It was significant that it was U Thittila who conducted the ceremony because, though on this occasion he wore the robes of the branch of the Theravāda monastic order to which he belonged, he did not always wear them. On less formal occasions, as when he was out with the ARP (Air Raid Precautions), he wore whatever form of Western dress was appropriate. Years later, when I was myself 'in the robes', I learned that this 'unorthodox' behaviour had not met with universal approval. As I wrote in my memoirs,

> Narrowly formalistic Burmese Buddhists had severely criticized him for his supposed misconduct in wearing ordinary European clothes when not actually performing his religious duties. English Buddhists saw the matter in quite a different light. Throughout the Blitz U Thittila had worked as a stretcher-bearer, on several occasions risking his life to rescue people trapped under fallen masonry. Finding that the voluminous drapery of his robes hampered his movements he sensibly exchanged them for more practical garments. People who knew him said he practised what he preached.[67]

For my own part, I have always been glad that I first took the Refuges and Precepts from this quiet and unassuming man for whom, as we now say, commitment was primary and lifestyle secondary – a man who, whether wearing orange robes or a blue boiler-suit, was at heart neither monk nor layman but simply a Buddhist.

Between my taking *pansil* from U Thittila and my 'Going Forth' there was an interval of more than three years. During that period the signals unit to which I belonged had been ordered overseas, I had been stationed in Delhi, Colombo, Calcutta, and Singapore, had made contact with Chinese and Sinhalese Buddhists, had returned to India (for good, as I then thought), had been associated with various religious organizations and groups, both Buddhist and Hindu, and had taken up the regular practice of meditation. Now I was ready to enter upon the next of the various stages by which the meaning, the significance, and the importance of Going for Refuge became clear to me and accordingly, on 18 August 1947 (three days after the Union Jack ceased to flutter over the Indian subcontinent and eight days before my twenty-second birthday), in Kasauli in East Punjab, I renounced the household life and went forth into the life of homelessness. The immediate cause of my taking this drastic step was disillusionment with worldly life, especially with worldly life as represented by organized religion. Together with the Bengali friend with whom, on my return to India, I had joined forces, I had worked for the Ramakrishna Mission Institute of Culture and for the Maha Bodhi Society. More recently, I had been involved in a project for the revival of the Dharma Vijaya Vahini, an organization for the propagation of Buddhism in India that had been started, many years earlier, by an old scholar whom I happened to meet at an inter-religious gathering in Ahmedabad. With all these organizations, as well as with the group that had formed round a well-known female ascetic, I had been deeply disappointed, as had my friend. Working with such bodies was, it seemed, a hindrance rather than a help to spiritual development. They had a natural tendency to degenerate and the only course open to us was to sever our connection not just with them but with the world. As related in my memoirs, we therefore dyed our clothes the traditional ochre, disposed of our worldly possessions, said goodbye to our friends, and the following morning set out on foot down the road that led from Kasauli to the plains.

In 'Going Forth' in this way we were of course following an ancient Indian tradition, a tradition which the Buddha himself had followed some twenty-five centuries earlier. Indeed, both before and after my companion and I took our plunge into the ocean of the spiritual life instead of sitting hesitating on the shore (to vary the metaphor), I was very conscious that in exchanging the household life for the life of homelessness we were following the personal example of the Buddha, as well as that of many of his closest followers, and the consciousness that we were so doing inspired and uplifted me. The Buddha's own 'Going Forth' had terminated at the foot of the bodhi tree, when he attained the Supreme Enlightenment that, for the last six years, had been the object of his 'noble quest'. So far as his followers were concerned (i.e. those of them who had 'Gone Forth' either before meeting him or after Going for Refuge to the Three Jewels as a result of hearing his teaching), some attained Enlightenment while others did not, depending on how faithfully they had followed the path he had shown. As time went on, and especially after the Buddha's *parinirvāna* or 'great decease', Going for Refuge, 'Going Forth', and even 'becoming a monk' in the later narrow, more formalistic sense, came to be more and more closely identified (just as the Sangha or Spiritual Community and the monastic order came to be more and more closely identified). The story of how this happened is a long one. I mention it here only because I want to make the point that at this stage in the history of my Going for Refuge I had not sorted these things out. Despite having taken *pansil* from U Thittila I had not realized that Going for Refuge was the central and decisive, indeed the definitive, act of the Buddhist life (one did not go for Refuge because one was a Buddhist but was a Buddhist because one went for Refuge), and that 'Going Forth' and 'becoming a monk' were spiritually of significance and value only to the extent that they were expressions of one's Going for Refuge. I had not realized that 'Going Forth', far from being simply a matter of renouncing the household life, in fact consisted in the emergence of the individual – in the sense of the self-aware, emotionally positive, and responsible human being (to name only a few of his or her characteristic qualities) – from the matrix of group or merely-collective existence.

Because I did not realize this latter point, for me, as for many Eastern Buddhists, the next step after 'Going Forth' (which in any case had been formalized as *śrāmanera* or 'novice' ordination) consisted not, as it should really have done, in finding and being accepted into a (spiritual) community of those who had both gone for Refuge and 'Gone Forth', but in taking *bhikṣu* ordination and in this way entering into full membership of the monastic order. Thus it was not surprising that my companion and I, having 'Gone Forth', should not only want to study Buddhism but should also want to take ordination as *bhikṣus*. Our original plan had been to study and, if possible, to take ordination, in Ceylon (now Sri Lanka), and on reaching Delhi we had accordingly lost no time in heading south. On our arrival in Colombo, however, we were refused entry into Ceylon and were forced to return to South India where, after some interesting adventures, we eventually settled in a deserted ashram on the outskirts of the town of Muvattupuzha, in the state of Travancore, where we stayed for fifteen months.

Looking back over the years, it is difficult not to feel that the failure of our original plan was an instance of the proverbial blessing in disguise, since it is extremely unlikely that we should have found in Ceylon the right conditions for our spiritual development. During the period of our stay in Muvattupuzha the greater part of my time was spent in study, meditation, and reflection, and in this way I came to have a clearer understanding of the Dharma, especially of the Dharma as represented by the teachings of dependent origination (conditioned co-production), the Four Noble Truths, and the three characteristics of conditioned existence, as well as a keener awareness of the fact that I was a Buddhist. This keener awareness of my spiritual identity, as it may be termed, was due in part at least to the fact that throughout our stay in South India I was surrounded by Hindus of various castes and sects (the few Indian Christians did not really count) and had no contact with Buddhists whatever, for my companion, though in some respects appreciative of Buddhism, was by birth a Brahmin and had not yet completely freed himself from his Hindu conditioning. Indeed, I had had no contact with Buddhists of any kind since my departure from the Maha Bodhi Society nearly two years earlier. Despite this prolonged spiritual isolation, my allegiance to Buddhism remained unshaken. If anything it was more firmly and deeply rooted than ever, so that by the time our stay in Muvattupuzha came to an end I was again thinking of ordination and thinking of it more seriously than ever, as indeed was my companion. Nevertheless, though I was again thinking of ordination, I still thought of it not in terms of finding and being accepted into a spiritual community but in terms of taking *bhikṣu* ordination and joining the monastic order. In other words, I had not understood that for the Buddhist, at least, the act of 'Going Forth' was a transition from group or merely-collective existence as represented by the household life to supra-collective but associated existence as represented by the spiritual community. I had not understood this because I did not, at this stage, have a clear understanding of the difference between the group, consisting of those who are merely group-members, and the spiritual community, consisting of those who are individuals in the sense I have indicated. Because I did not have a clear understanding of this vitally important difference, I was unable to envisage the possibility that in becoming a monk and joining the monastic order I might become, not a 'member' of a spiritual community, but only a member of another kind of group – not a secular group but a religious or even an ecclesiastical group.

For my failure to understand the difference between the group and the spiritual community, the group-member and the individual, I was not altogether to blame, for, as I came to appreciate only years later, it was a failure common to virtually the whole Buddhist world, many parts of which were sunk in monastic or pseudo-monastic formalism of an extreme kind. As I trace the early stages of this history of my Going for Refuge, therefore, I must be careful not to be too hard on my younger and less experienced self and careful not to expect too much of him. More important still, I must be careful lest I forget, or lose touch with, or even start underestimating, the mood of spiritual exaltation with which I renounced the household life and went forth into the homeless life. Our past selves underlie our present self, even as the catacombs underlie modern Rome, or rather they live on in our present self and in a sense actually form part of it. This is certainly the case with my 'Going Forth' in Kasauli and the period of seclusion at Muvattupuzha that followed. Indeed, despite the fact that I did not, at the time, understand the full significance of the step I was taking, I regard my 'Going Forth' as being not only one of the most important stages in the history of my Going for Refuge but one of the principal turning-points in my life.

from *The History of My Going for Refuge*

5. THE RAINBOW ROAD

We would renounce the household life and go forth into the life of homelessness as wanderers in search of Truth. For the last few months we had only sat hesitantly on the shore of the vast ocean of the spiritual life. Now, casting aside all fear, we would plunge boldly in.

There was only one way out. Religious societies, organizations, and groups, far from being a help to spiritual development, were only a hindrance. However lofty the ideals with which they were founded, they had a natural tendency to degenerate, in the hands of selfish human beings, into instruments for the acquisition of money, position, power, and fame. Instead of trying any longer to work with them we would follow the example of the Buddha and sever at one stroke our connection with an incorrigible world. We would renounce the household life and go forth into the life of homelessness as wanderers in search of Truth. For the last few months we had only sat hesitantly on the shore of the vast ocean of the spiritual life. Now, casting aside all fear, we would plunge boldly in.

Having made this resolution, we lost no time putting it into effect. With the help of a handful of *gerua-mati*, the reddish-brown earth used since time immemorial by Indian ascetics, we dyed our shirts and sarongs the traditional saffron of the world-renunciant. Suitcases and watches were sold, trousers, jackets, and shoes given away, identification papers destroyed. Apart from the robes that we were to wear we kept only a blanket each and our books and notebooks. As for the last three months hair and beard had been allowed to grow we did not need shaving tackle.

Next morning, after joyfully donning our saffron robes, we walked, feeling shy and rather conspicuous, through the bazaar to Dr Gurukipal Singh's house. Lalla Pyarelal and other friends, though regarding our aspirations with sympathy, did not feel at all happy about our decision, which in their opinion was rash. Only Dr Singh wholeheartedly approved. With him, therefore, we had agreed to take breakfast before leaving Kasauli. Apart from one of his sons, a stalwart youth who accompanied us part of the way, our worthy Sikh friend, whose deep emotion when he wished us success in our quest both humbled and heartened us, was the last person to whom we spoke before setting out on foot along the ten-mile road that led to the plains.

Tibetan Buddhists believe that the appearance of a rainbow is one of the most auspicious of signs, and the biographies of their saints and yogis are replete with references to this phenomenon. Whether our 'going forth' on 18 August 1947 may be considered an auspicious event I cannot say, but it was certainly signalled by the appearance not of one but of scores of rainbows.

As we left Kasauli it was raining, but, as in the course of our descent we emerged from the clouds into the bright sunshine below, we saw arching the road, at intervals of a few dozen yards, not only single but double and triple rainbows. Every time we turned a bend we found more rainbows waiting for us. We passed through them as though through the multicoloured arcades of some celestial palace. Against the background of bright sunshine, jewel-like glittering raindrops, and hills of the freshest and most vivid green, this plethora of delicate seven-hued bows seemed like the epiphany of another world....

The concluding stages of our journey were the worst, and had it not been for the hope that every step was bringing us nearer to the goal of our desires it might have been difficult for us to carry on. It was still early May, and the heat, having risen in fiery crescendo to its terrific climax, now seemed likely to remain there indefinitely. Not a drop of rain fell. Day by day the hot dry wind from the desert, laden with dust, blew more strongly and more scorchingly than ever upon the hard, sun-baked earth, which by this time had become criss-crossed with a network of innumerable cracks and fissures, some of them several inches wide. Travelling during the less hot hours of the day, and taking advantage of every scrap of shade, grimly and wearily Satyapriya and I plodded on from temple to temple and from ashram to ashram, mile after mile across the heat-stricken land. In some of the temples and ashrams at which we halted we were given a cordial welcome, in others our reception was more reserved. Towards the end of our journey our stops became more and more frequent. At one place we took our bath in a pond full of lotuses. At another, where we came across an unusually well-kept ashram standing within a secluded mango grove, a friendly Nanak Panthi, or follower of Guru Nanak, not only put us up for the night but treated us with exceptional kindness.

On our last morning we were less fortunate. Indeed, this was the least fortunate part of the whole journey. We had intended to halt for an hour or two at the Buddhist Rest House which had been built, so the Nanak Panthi had informed us, not half a dozen miles from our destination. On our arrival there we found that the Rest House had been converted into a school, and the headmaster received us in a very unfriendly fashion. We had no alternative but to set off again at once. Before long we were heartened by the sight of the dome of the Mahaparinirvana Stupa rising majestically from behind a cluster of trees in the far distance, and leaving the road we cut straight across the fields towards it. I could not help thinking with what exultation, only ten or twelve days earlier, we had seen the pinnacle of the Mulagandhakuti Vihara rising above the treetops of Sarnath. Did Kusinārā hold a similar disappointment in store for us? Or were we destined to receive here the ordination on which we had set our hearts?...

Our heads had already been shaved the previous day. The robes for which we now exchanged the informal saffron of the last two years were of the regulation size, shape and colour, and along with the rest of the permitted articles – girdle, water-strainer, needle, and razor – had been presented to us by Mother Vipassana and the other *anagārikās*, who in order to have them ready in time for the ceremony had, in fact, sat up stitching the complicated seams until late at night. U Chandramani himself had presented us with our begging-bowls. On our returning to the Chapter House, duly 'robed and bowled', as the texts have it, we were made to squat on our heels with our elbows resting on our knees and our hands joined together at our foreheads. This was an extremely difficult and uncomfortable position. Indeed, after a few minutes the pain in various parts of my body became excruciating. As I afterwards realized, the position we were made to adopt was that of the child in the womb, for the ordination represented the process of spiritual rebirth, and 'at the birth of a child or a star, there is pain'.

Having to remain in such a position throughout the ceremony was by itself ordeal enough, but for me at least the difficulties of ordination were by no means over. The Three Refuges – the Refuges in the Buddha, the Dharma, and the Sangha – had not only to be repeated thrice each but repeated in both Pāli and Sanskrit. This was to make sure that the novice monk was able to distinguish between the two kinds of pronunciation, for in the early days of Buddhism, when the Buddha's Message was preserved and transmitted exclusively by oral means, the slightest carelessness in matters of phonetics could in the course of time result in a serious distortion of the letter of the teaching leading, perhaps, to eventual loss of its spirit. Try as I might, however, my English tongue could not manage to reproduce the elusive Indian sounds. U Chandramani, for his part, was determined that the requirements of tradition should be scrupulously respected. Time and again he intoned the sacred formulas, patiently coaching me in the production of aspirated consonants, nasalized terminations, and palatal sibilants. After much effort on my part, and much exercise of patience on his, I eventually succeeded in repeating the Refuges to his complete satisfaction in both Pāli and Sanskrit and we were able to pass on to the next part of the ceremony, which consisted in the taking of the ten *śrāmaṇera* precepts. This time reciting in Pāli only, and with less regard to pronunciation, Satyapriya and I undertook to abstain from injury to living beings, from taking the not-given, from unchastity, from false speech, and from intoxicants, as well as from untimely meals, from song, dance, instrumental music and indecent shows, from garlands, perfumes, unguents and other worldly adornments, from large and lofty beds, and from handling gold or silver. All these precepts we were already observing, but the kindly, simple, and good-humoured manner in which U Chandramani explained each one gave them a fresh significance, and we felt that we would die rather than be guilty of the smallest infringement. The more formal part of the proceedings ended with the Mahāthera solemnly adjuring us in the last words which the Buddha had addressed to his disciples, as he lay on his deathbed in the Sāl Grove, only a few hundred yards away: 'With mindfulness strive on!'

from *The Rainbow Road from Tooting Broadway to Kalimpong*

3
THE PATH TO ENLIGHTENMENT

1. 'WHAT IS YOUR DHARMA?': THE BUDDHA'S ANSWER TO MAHĀPAJĀPATĪ GOTAMI

The Dharma is whatever helps us to rise from wherever we are now, and from whatever we are now.

There are many different versions of Buddhism, and many interpretations. After all, the word 'Buddhism' itself represents an interpretation. Buddhism was not originally called Buddhism at all. It was certainly never called Buddhism in India, and it was certainly never called Buddhism by the Buddha. It was called *Dharma* in Sanskrit, or *Dhamma* in Pāli. The word *Dharma*, or *Dhamma*, means Reality, or Truth; it means law, doctrine, or teaching. Or, one may say, it represents reality or truth as communicated in the form of a teaching from the Enlightened to the unenlightened mind. The originator of this Dharma, this vision of reality as a teaching, is, of course, Gautama the Buddha. He communicates to his followers a reality, a truth, which he has personally experienced – the experience of which constitutes Enlightenment. Therefore, the Buddha is the best spokesman, the best interpreter, of Buddhism. So what does the Buddha himself say that the Dharma is? In this connection we can refer to an episode in the Pāli scriptures, for the Buddha himself was once asked this very question, namely: 'What is your Dharma? What is your teaching?'

The person who asked this was Mahāpajāpatī Gotami, the Buddha's aunt and foster-mother. She had brought him up since childhood, since the death of his mother when he was just a few days old. In later years Mahāpajāpatī Gotami had not only become a follower of his teaching, but had 'gone forth', as we say, after hearing those teachings from his own lips. She had been so impressed by them that she had wanted to give up all her other interests, connections, and ties, so as to be able to devote her entire life to practising the Dharma. She had therefore gone forth, leaving her home, leaving her family, leaving her husband, leaving the city of Kapilavastu, and wandering from place to place, meditating and seeking to practise the Dharma.

At the time of our episode, Mahāpajāpatī Gotami had passed a period of time without any direct contact with the Buddha, and so there was a certain amount of confusion in her mind. She wanted to practise the Dharma, but she was not quite sure what the Dharma was. This is not such an uncommon thing. Sometimes, at least, many of us may find ourselves in the position of wanting to practise the truth, without being quite sure, or even at all sure, what the truth actually is.

Although Mahāpajāpatī Gotami was in contact with some of the Buddha's disciples and was able to ask them what it was that the Buddha taught, the interpretations they gave her were often very different; they each had their own point of view. In the end she decided to go and ask the Buddha himself what it was that he did fundamentally teach. She therefore made the journey to the place where the Buddha was staying and asked, point blank, as it were, 'What is your Dharma? How can we know what you actually do teach? What is the criterion?' Here is a translation of what, according to the tradition, the Buddha said to Mahāpajāpatī Gotami on that occasion:

> Gotami, those things of which you know, 'These things lead to passion, not to dispassion; to attachment, not to detachment; to amassing, not to dispersal; to ambition, not to modesty; to discontent, not to content; to association [association with the group, that is], not to seclusion [from the group)]; to idleness, not to energy; to luxury, not to frugality,' of them, you can quite certainly decide. 'This is not the Dharma, this is not the Vinaya, this is not the Master's teaching.'

But those things of which you know, 'These things lead to dispassion, not to passion; to detachment, not to attachment; to dispersal, not to amassing; to modesty, not to ambition; to content, not to discontent; to seclusion [from the group], not to association [with the group]; to energy, not to idleness; to frugality, not to luxury,' of them you can quite certainly decide, 'This is the Dharma, this is the Vinaya, this is the master's teaching.'[68]

So here in the Buddha's own words is the criterion; this is the principle. The Dharma is whatever contributes to the spiritual development of the individual. It is whatever the individual finds, in his own experience, does actually contribute to his own spiritual development.

In this passage, as in others, individuals are clearly seen to be living, growing, and developing. And in this connection we may also remember the Buddha's 'vision' of humanity immediately after his Enlightenment. At that time, the Buddha was undecided as to whether or not he should actually teach the truth he had discovered. It was, he knew, something very deep, very difficult and abstruse. But he eventually decided that he would go out and teach, he would communicate the truth he had discovered to other beings. And at that moment, we are told, he opened his eyes and looked out over the world to see those living beings as a bed of lotus flowers.[69] It was as if he could see just a vast bed of lotuses spreading in all directions, as far as the eye could reach. This was humanity. This was the human race. Some of these 'flowers' – some of these people – were clearly sunk in the mud. Others had risen just a little way out of it and were struggling free. Others still had broken out of the mud altogether and their heads were rising above the surface of the water so that their petals could open out to receive the light of the sun.

This is how the Buddha saw humanity at that moment. He saw all beings as individuals, and he could see that they were all at different stages of development, all growing but needing the sunlight of the Dharma in order to grow and develop further.

In another passage, in the great Mahāyāna *sutra* called the *Saddharma Puṇḍarīka* or *Lotus Sūtra*, there is another very beautiful comparison. Here, individuals are compared not just to lotuses emerging from the mud and slime, but to many different kinds of plants. They are compared to grass, trees, flowers, and shrubs, while the Buddha's teaching is compared to a great rain cloud.[70] During the winter and summer in India it is very hot and dry for many months. Everything becomes very withered and parched. But then, suddenly, at the beginning of the rainy season, a great black cloud arises in the midst of the sky. There is thunder, lightning, and then the rain falls, very heavily and very steadily, day in and day out, sometimes for weeks on end. And as it rains, everything grows. Everything that was so parched and dry becomes green again and starts springing up. All the leaves, all the grass, trees, flowers, and shrubs, start to grow again. And everything grows in its own way. The tree grows as a tree, the shrub grows as a shrub, the grass grows as grass, the flower grows as a flower; each grows in its own way. This is important to the Buddha's analogy, for the Dharma is just like that rain cloud: it gives us just the nourishment we each need. It leads us from where it finds us, its starting point – so far as we are concerned – being where we are now, because everyone needs the Dharma in his or her own way. The Dharma is whatever helps us to rise from wherever we are now, and from whatever we are now. The Dharma is therefore defined as whatever contributes to the development of the individual. That is the criterion.

This may sound rather broad and general, but it is not really so. The Dharma – the Buddha's teaching – is embodied in a number of actual spiritual practices. This is made clear in another episode from the Pāli scriptures. In this particular episode we are reminded that there were a number of spiritual teachers in India during the Buddha's time. One of the best known of these was Nigaṇṭha Nāthaputta, as he is called in the Pāli texts, who is usually identified with Mahāvīra, the founder of Jainism. Nigaṇṭha Nāthaputta died shortly before the Buddha, and after his death his monk followers split into two factions. These factions disagreed so vehemently about what their master had taught that they almost came to blows. Ānanda, who seems to have been something of a gossip, told the Buddha about this, adding that he hoped there would be no such disputes after the Buddha himself had gone.

The Buddha replied that such a thing would be impossible. He was confident that there were not even two monks among his followers who would describe his teachings discordantly. He then reminded Ānanda what those teachings were. There were the four foundations of mindfulness: mindfulness of the body, of the feelings, thoughts, and of reality. There were the four right efforts: the effort to prevent the arising of unskilful mental states that have not arisen; the effort to abandon unskilful mental states that have arisen; the effort to develop skilful mental states that have not arisen; and the effort to maintain in existence those skilful mental states that have already arisen. He reminded Ānanda about the four bases of success, the five spiritual faculties, the five powers, the seven factors of Enlightenment, the Noble Eightfold Path... All these things constituted the Dharma that he had taught and about which he was confident there would be no dispute after his death even between two of his disciples.[71]

The immediately noticeable thing about this list of teachings is that they are all practical. They are all actual *practices*. There is nothing theoretical here; the Buddha says nothing about Nirvāna, nothing about *śūnyatā*, nothing about the mind. He does not even mention 'dependent origination'. It is as if he is saying that the teachings he has given his disciples are all practical teachings and cannot therefore really be described differently by different people. After all, practical teachings involve actual practice so the experience would be the same for all who practised. It is much the same in ordinary life; we may disagree about theory, but we do not very often disagree about practice. We may disagree, for example, about the nature of electricity, but we are unlikely to disagree about how to replace a fuse. Similarly, the Buddha's disciples might disagree about theoretical teachings, but they could hardly disagree about practical teachings, provided of course that they had actually practised them. So the Dharma is embodied primarily in spiritual practices, in things that you actually do.

There is another interesting point which arises in connection with this episode. Despite the Buddha's answer, Ānanda was not satisfied. He now said, 'Well, even though they may all agree about the teaching, there might still be disputes about livelihood, or there might be disputes about the code of rules'.[72] The Buddha's reply to this was very important. A dispute over livelihood, or a dispute over the code of rules, he said, would be a 'trifling matter'. It is only disputes over the path, or disputes over the way of practice, that would be disastrous.

from *New Currents in Western Buddhism*

2. THE ARISING OF VISION

The aim of this great Buddhist teaching of the Path of Vision and the Path of Transformation is to enable us to bring the whole of our life up to the level of its highest moments.

According to the Indian Buddhist tradition the Noble Eightfold Path falls quite naturally into two great divisions. The first of these is known as the Path of Vision (*darśana-mārga*), the second as the Path of Transformation (*bhāvanā-mārga*).[73] Thus the Noble Eightfold Path comprises two lesser 'Paths', in the sense of two successive stages. The Path of Vision corresponds only to the first *aṅga*, or so-called step, Perfect Vision. The Path of Transformation corresponds to the seven remaining 'steps': Perfect Emotion, Perfect Speech, Perfect Action, Perfect Livelihood, Perfect Effort, Perfect Awareness, and Perfect Meditation. The significance of this division is that Perfect Vision represents the phase of initial spiritual insight and experience, whereas the rest of the Eightfold Path represents the transformation of one's whole being, in all its heights and depths, in all its aspects, in accordance with that initial insight and experience. The Path of Transformation represents a complete and thoroughgoing transformation of one's emotional life, speech, communication with others, livelihood, and so on. One may transform one's livelihood, which is the fifth 'step', before one's speech, which is only the third; but eventually, in one way or another, the whole being is to be transformed, in its heights and in its depths, conscious and unconscious.

This initial spiritual experience – this Perfect Vision or Path of Vision – may arise in different ways for different people. There is no uniform pattern. Indeed the great variety that exists among people also shows itself in the spiritual life generally, and in the way people enter upon the spiritual path. For some people the Path of Vision arises as the result of personal tragedy, bereavement, or loss. Their whole existence is disturbed and upset as though by a great earthquake in which everything they had cherished or held dear is laid low. In this wreck, this ruin of their lives, they start questioning, start looking deeper, and start wondering about the meaning and purpose of existence.

For others, Perfect Vision may arise by way of a spontaneous mystical experience. ('Mystical' is not really the right word. For many people it is redolent of mystery and mystery-mongering. But we don't have a better one.) One can find a number of such mystical experiences described in Bucke's *Cosmic Consciousness*, a book published in 1901, which is still worth reading.[74] It is surprising how many people have had an experience of this kind, some rare moment of ecstasy, or insight, or tremendous love, which apparently without any preparation possessed them, swept them away, lifted them up into a new dimension, and completely altered their outlook on life. Also under the heading of mystical experience we can include our experience of nature, as when we are overwhelmed by the sight of some wonderful sunset, or when in the midst of the countryside we experience a great, all-pervading peace, stillness, and tranquillity.

Sometimes the Path of Vision can arise as a result of looking at a beautiful painting, or listening to music. On such occasions we can be carried away into a new dimension of existence. Sometimes it can arise as a result of deep and prolonged thought. Some people endeavour to reach out and grasp the truth by means of the intellect. They try to plumb the depths of being with reason and logic. This is the way of the thinker, the philosopher, the sage. Some people actually *think* their way through to reality, to the Path of Vision.

For others it may arise in quite a different way, as the result of the practice of meditation. When the mind has been systematically stilled, and when, although thoughts have been banished, clear consciousness still persists, then under these conditions also Perfect Vision may arise.

Sometimes it may arise for those who are engaged in altruistic activities, such as nursing the sick and looking after the old. For those who are sacrificing themselves and their personal interests, and who are completely selfless on the plane of work and action, even in the midst of their activity Perfect Vision may arise.

Finally, it may arise, for some people at least, out of their whole experience of life – especially as they grow older and, it is to be hoped, more mature. When all the different threads seemingly come together, and the pattern of their lives seems to make some kind of sense, to reflect some glimmer of meaning, then out of the depths of their simple human maturity Perfect Vision may arise. This is not to suggest that wisdom comes automatically with age. Far from it! If such were the case we need not take the trouble to acquire wisdom when young. But certainly for those who have led a truly human life, as they mellow and perhaps sweeten a little, and as their experience clarifies, the Path of Vision may sometimes arise.

Thus the Path of Vision may arise for different people in all these different ways. For some it has even arisen in a dream. But however it does arise we should be very careful not to lose it, not to forget it. This happens very easily, for as the poet says, 'the world is too much with us'.[75] We may have an experience so wonderful that we might think we will never forget it. But after a short time, after a few days or weeks, it is no longer there. It is as though it had never been. So we should cherish it, cultivate it, dwell upon it – try to deepen it, clarify it, develop it – all the time. We should eventually try to allow it to permeate and transform our whole being, our whole life.

To sum up we may say that the aim of this great Buddhist teaching of the Path of Vision and the Path of Transformation is to enable us to bring the whole of our life up to the level of its highest moments. This is what it means to evolve spiritually. This is what it means to follow the Noble Eightfold Path. It means to achieve Perfect Vision by one means or another, and then transform our whole being in accordance with that vision.

from *The Buddha's Noble Eightfold Path*

3. THE CONNECTION BETWEEN PHILOSOPHY AND PRACTICE

Buddhism is not a system of abstract thought, and it does not attempt to satisfy mere intellectual curiosity by giving a rationally coherent account of the universe.

About a century ago Schopenhauer, who, more deeply than any other Western thinker, was influenced by and imbued with the spirit of ancient Indian philosophy, ventured to predict that the renaissance that would be brought about by the discovery, in the nineteenth century, of the treasures of oriental literature, would be incomparably more glorious than that which had been ushered in during the fifteenth and sixteenth centuries by the rediscovery of the classics of Greece and Rome. This bold prediction of the nineteenth century is being fulfilled, or at least beginning to be fulfilled, in the twentieth. What was merely political and commercial contact between the nations of the East and the West has begun to deepen into cultural exchanges and interreligious fellowship. Throughout every Western land, men and women are now to be found – few in number, indeed, but increasingly influential – who are convinced that, now as ever, light comes from the East: *Ex Oriente lux*.

Of the rays into which that light, shooting through the spectrum of human understanding, is broken up, none confronts occidental eyes with a steadier radiance, or shines forth with a more blindingly brilliant effulgence, than the hitherto unknown splendour to which the West, startled into awareness of a whole new world of values, has given the name 'Buddhism'. Yet often is that splendour dimmed by the opacity of the medium through which it is transmitted. Even today, when the Pali Text Society of London and other bodies, as well as distinguished scholars working independently in the field of Buddhist studies, have between them published a small library of Pāli, Sanskrit, Chinese, and Tibetan Buddhist texts and their translations, the writers of articles and compilers of popular handbooks on Buddhism, ignoring this mass of authentic material, are frequently found repeating the same old misunderstandings about Nirvāṇa and other points of Buddhist doctrine.

Such misunderstandings, when they are not due to ineradicable religious prejudice, such as still animates many Christian writers on non-Christian religions, may be traced to a misconception of the very nature of Buddhism. This misconception has its roots deep down in the history of Western thought. Briefly stated, it consists in regarding Buddhism as a system of philosophy in the modern academic sense.

To the ancient Greeks and Romans, philosophy was not merely an opinion, but a passion; it meant not only loftier thinking, but nobler living. A philosopher was expected to leave his hair and beard untrimmed, to wear but one long simple garment, to sleep on the bare ground, and to eat sparingly. With the irruption of Christianity into the Graeco-Roman world, the old classic ideals of moderation, balance, and harmony were destroyed. Wisdom was replaced by faith, while for the harmless and helpful philosophic life was substituted one of aggressive good works (which included the conversion of the heathen, by force, if necessary, and the burning of heretics). Between faith and works some kind of harmony was indeed sought to be maintained, but, covering as these did only a small part of the scale of human potentialities, this harmony was not rich or full enough to be long sustained, and, before many centuries had passed, the shrill note of faith first dominated and then drowned all others.

The modern scientific attitude of mind developed in part as a protest against the unverifiable dogmas of medieval Christianity, and every advance in scientific knowledge was made in the teeth of determined ecclesiastical opposition; for the schoolman, no less than the scientist, was aware that the victory of science spelled the defeat of faith. With the abandonment of Christian doctrine came the tacit repudiation of the Christian way of life, and, though individual thinkers continued to conform to Christian ethical standards and even, in some cases, professed to accept the Christian revelation, Western thought came more and more under the influence of science and developed with increasing freedom from religious preconceptions. The introduction of psychological and epistemological interests strengthened still further the theoretical and speculative tendencies in modern thought, and, by the time Schopenhauer arose to challenge the academic and professorial conception of philosophy, despite artificial attempts at reconciliation, the divorce between religion and philosophy had been made absolute.

A division between concrete living and abstract thinking continues to characterize modern Western culture. Philosophy is taught at universities as a purely theoretical subject; it does not demand from its votaries the adoption of a distinctive mode of life, neither does it have as a whole any bearing upon practical affairs. For the philosophic life, as it was understood by the Greeks and Romans in even their most degenerate days – the passionate pursuit of beauty, truth, and goodness, and the endeavour to reflect them in one's own life – has been substituted the detached and barren study of the history of philosophical opinions.

When the star of Buddhism first rose above these icy academic horizons, its dependence on reason rather than faith, its freedom from credulity and superstition, not unnaturally caused it to be regarded as an ethico-philosophical system rather than as a religion in the Christian sense of the term. Owing to the congenitally abstract proclivities of Western thought, the close connection between the practical and the theoretical aspects of Buddhism was gradually ignored, and topics such as the nature of Nirvāṇa came to be discussed as though they had a simply theoretical import that could be determined by the exercise of the speculative reason. The fact that Buddhism is, above all, a way of life was forgotten.

Most of the problems, and many of the misunderstandings, that have arisen in connection with Buddhism may be traced to this wrong habit of considering the significance of its profoundest teachings in complete dissociation from their pragmatic consequences in the actual Buddhist way of living. It therefore becomes necessary to stress the fact that Buddhism is not a system of abstract thought, and that it does not attempt to satisfy mere intellectual curiosity by giving a rationally coherent account of the universe. Buddhism is a way of life that leads to a spiritual experience; in fact, to a number of experiences. These experiences link up into a series that culminates in the supreme experience of Nirvāṇa.

from *The Religion of Art*

4. THE ESSENCE OF THE DHARMA

The Buddha compares the state of mind of one gaining Enlightenment to that of someone who has come safely out of a dangerous jungle, or been freed from debt, or released from prison.

Many students of Buddhism are at first staggered by the vastness of the field before them and bewildered by the abundance of material. This is natural. Like Christianity and Islam, Buddhism is not only a teaching but a culture, a civilization, a movement in history, a social order, in fact a whole world in itself. It comprises systems of philosophy, methods of meditation, rituals, manners and customs, clothes, languages, sacred literature, pagodas, temples, monasteries, calligraphy, poems, paintings, plays, stories, games, flower-arrangements, pottery, and a thousand other things. All this is Buddhist, and often immediately recognizable as such. Whether it be a stone Buddha seated cross-legged in the jungles of Anuradhupura, a Tibetan sacred dance, a cup of tea between friends in Japan, or the way in which a *bhikṣu* answers a question in London, everything is invisibly signed with the same mysterious seal. Sometimes it floats with the clouds between heaven and earth, shines in the rainbow, or gurgles over pebbles in the company of a mountain stream.

Looked at, it cannot be seen; listened to, it cannot be heard.[76]

Sooner or later, however, the student tries to identify it. He wonders what it could be that gives unity to all these diverse expressions, so that however remote in space and time, and however different their respective mediums, one perfectly harmonizes with another, creating not the dissonance that might have been expected but 'a concord of sweet sounds'. Eventually a question shapes itself in his mind, and at last he enquires, 'What is the essence of the Dharma?'

The best answer to this question would be the 'thunder-like silence' with which Vimalakīrti, in the Mahāyāna *sūtra* that bears his name, answered the bodhisattva Mañjuśrī's question about the nature of reality.[77] Can we describe even the colour of a rose? But this apparently negative procedure the student would not find very helpful. Concessions must be made. Buddhism is essentially an experience. 'An experience of what?' Before answering this second question let us try to explain why, of all the words in the dictionary, 'experience' is the first term on which one falls back when compelled to abandon the 'thunder-like silence'. Unlike thought, experience is direct, unmediated; it is knowledge by acquaintance. Hence it is characterized by a feeling of absolute certainty. When we see the sun shining in a clear sky we do not doubt that it is bright; when a thorn runs beneath our fingernail we do not speculate whether it is painful. In saying that Buddhism is essentially an experience we do not suggest that the object of that experience in any way resembles the objects of sense-experience, nor even that there is an object at all. We simply draw attention to its unique unconceptualized immediacy. The relation between sense-experience and the one with which we are now concerned is merely analogical. For this reason it is necessary to go a step further and complete our definition by saying that the essence of the Dharma, of Buddhism, consists in a *spiritual* or *transcendental* experience. This is what in traditional terminology is called Enlightenment-experience.

Apart from conveying an impression of the subject having now been lost sight of in the clouds, the mere addition of these adjectives is inconclusive. They themselves need definition. But inasmuch as this will involve the use of terms even more abstract, more remote from concrete experience, such definition will set up a process of conceptualization as a result of which the reflection of Enlightenment-experience in our minds will be in danger of complete distortion, like the moon's reflection in a pond the surface of which the wind has chopped into waves. Concepts had therefore better be treated as symbols, the value of which lies not in their literal meaning so much as in their suggestiveness. They should be handled in the spirit not of logic but of poetry; not pushed hither and thither with grim calculation like pieces on a chessboard, but tossed lightly, playfully in the air like a juggler's multicoloured balls. Approaching the subject in this spirit we may define Enlightenment-experience as 'seeing things as they are (*yathābhūta-jñānadarśana*)'. This is the traditional definition. Here also, it will be observed, the use of the word 'seeing' (*darśana*) – which primarily denotes a form of sense-perception – emphasizes not only the directness and immediacy of the experience but also its noetic character. Enlightenment-experience is not just a blind sensing of things, but, as the English word suggests, the shining forth of a light, an illumination, in the brightness of which things become visible in their reality. Such expressions should not mislead us into thinking that there is any real difference between the subject and the object of the experience, between the light and the things illuminated (which disposes of the second question raised above). Were it not for the fact that all words indicative of existence have for Buddhism a disagreeable substantialist flavour, it might even be preferable not to speak of Enlightenment as an experience at all but as a state of being. Fortunately other ways of surmounting the difficulty are available. The *Avataṃsaka Sūtra*, for instance, depicts the world of Enlightenment-experience as consisting not of objects illuminated from without but entirely of innumerable beams of light, all intersecting and intersected, none of which offers any resistance to the passage of any other.[78] Light being always in motion, this striking similitude has the additional advantage of precluding the notion that Enlightenment is a definite state in which one as it were settles comfortably down for good, instead of a movement from perfection to greater perfection in a process in which there is no final term, the direction of movement alone remaining constant.

If spiritual or transcendental experience is a state of seeing things as they are, its opposite, mundane experience, wherein all unenlightened beings are involved, must be one of seeing them as they are not. The cause of this blindness is twofold. Being creatures of desire, we are concerned with things only to the extent that they can be made to subserve our own ends. We are interested not in truth but in utility. For us things and people exist not in their own right but only as actual or possible means of our own gratification. This is the 'veil of passions' (*kleśāvaraṇa*). Usually we do not like to acknowledge, even to ourselves, that our attitude towards life is often no better than that of a pig rooting for acorns. Motives are therefore rationalized. Instead of admitting that we hate somebody, we say he is wicked and ought to be punished. Rather than admit we enjoy eating flesh, we maintain that sheep and cows were created for our benefit. Not wishing to die, we invent the dogma of the immortality of the individual soul. Craving help and protection, we start believing in a personal God. According to the Buddha, all the philosophies, and a great deal of religious teaching, are rationalizations of desires.[79] This is the 'veil of (false) assumptions' (*jñeyāvaraṇa*). On the attainment of Enlightenment both veils are rent asunder. For this reason the experience is accompanied by an exhilarating sense of release. The Buddha compares the state of mind of one gaining Enlightenment to that of someone who has come safely out of a dangerous jungle, or been freed from debt, or released from prison.[80] It is as though an intolerable burden had at last been lifted from one's back. So intense is this feeling of release from pain, suffering, conflicting emotions, and mental sterility and stagnation that many of the older canonical texts speak of the Enlightenment-experience exclusively in terms of freedom or emancipation (*vimukti*). One of them represents the Buddha himself as saying that even as the great ocean had one taste, the taste of salt, so his teaching had one flavour, the flavour of emancipation.[81] Besides a psychological aspect, *vimukti* has an intellectual and an existential aspect. In the first place it is a freedom from all theories and speculations about reality; and in the second, from any form of conditioned existence whatever, including 're-becoming' as a result of karma. The freedom into which one breaks through at the time of Enlightenment is not limited and partial, but absolute and unconditioned.

This introduces an aspect of Enlightenment-experience which is not always properly understood. Freedom, to be really unconditioned, must transcend the distinction between conditioned and unconditioned, *saṃsāra* and *nirvāṇa*, bondage and liberation, all of which are really mental constructions and, as such, part of the 'veil of assumptions'. Therefore there can in the ultimate sense be no question of escaping from the conditioned to the Unconditioned as though they were distinct entities. To speak paradoxically, in order to be truly free one has to escape not only from bondage but from liberation, not only from *saṃsāra* into *nirvāṇa* but from *nirvāṇa* back into *saṃsāra*. It is this 'escape' or descent that constitutes the *mahākaruṇā* or 'Great Compassion' of the Buddha, which is in reality his realization of the non-duality of the conditioned and the Unconditioned as that realization appears from the viewpoint of the conditioned. The Enlightenment experience is therefore not only one of illumination and freedom but also of infinite and inexhaustible love, a love which has for object all sentient beings, and which manifests as uninterrupted activity in pursuit of their temporal and spiritual welfare.

from *The Three Jewels*

5. THE PATH AS A SYMBOL

One is not following the Buddhist path if one feels that one is being driven along it like a sheep, rather wishing one could stray off and have a nibble on some succulent wayside shrub or flower.

According to Buddhism our predicament arises out of our ignorance. Ignorance (Sanskrit *avidyā*) is traditionally likened to drunkenness, while the volitions (*saṃskāras*) that arise from ignorance are compared to actions committed whilst in a state of drunkenness. This perception of the human condition may seem extreme, but it is no more than sober fact. Sometimes we don't realize the extent of the damage we do simply because we don't know what we are doing. We initiate things, we say things, we get involved with people, and in doing so we inevitably set up problems. Although we sometimes become aware that our lives are more or less made up of the problems we create in this way, very often we don't even see them as problems – and this is a problem in itself.

Of course, there is no question of trying to stay on the safe side by putting off doing anything at all until we are Enlightened; to live, we must act, and we are therefore bound to make mistakes. But if we can understand what we are doing, we can break the reactive patterns that cause us to create the same problems over and over again. And the way to break those reactive patterns that bring us so much suffering is to set up different patterns of thought, feeling, and behaviour.

When you see your predicament clearly, when you know where you are starting from, you are in a position to perceive the choices before you, which gives you a certain degree of freedom. It isn't absolute freedom—you can't choose your starting point—but you are free to choose what you make of your situation. Where you are is less important than whether or not you *know* where you are. There is a freedom which arises out of knowing oneself and knowing the possibility of evolving beyond one's present condition.

That freedom is, however, double-edged. The mind is not a thing; it is not, as Guenther puts it in the introduction to his translation of *Mind in Buddhist Psychology*, 'a static entity or a mere state or function of consciousness'.[82] It consists solely in its activities. 'It' is therefore always changing, always moving. But it can move either creatively or reactively. At every moment the mind is confronted with the choice of repeating old patterns and going round in circles or rearranging the pattern and setting up more positive conditions for spiritual growth. At every moment there is the possibility of moving forward and also the possibility of just moving round and thus not really moving at all. We are free to develop our awareness of the spiritual path, to look for solutions; and we are also free to sink back into unconsciousness and stop asking questions. Furthermore, mental states cannot be compartmentalized. Painful and harmful states of mind cannot be shut away somewhere while we develop mindfulness, joy, and kindness. At any one time we are either encouraging positive mental states or reinforcing negative ones.

If one makes the effort to develop in a positive direction, one's life assumes a more serious meaning as one takes responsibility for it. One realizes for oneself the necessity, almost, of a certain way of living. This is what it means to follow the Buddhist path. Buddhism is presented as a path or way, but this is only a manner of speaking. The path is a symbol, representing the fact that we can change, we can develop. If we know what we are now and what we can become, we can take steps to effect that transition. We have the capacity, and the freedom, to perceive and to realize our best interests.

According to the Pāli idiom, we *develop* the path.[83] It is not 'something out there', an objective thing. We *are* the path. If we think of it as something out there, like a road or track, we may get stuck with an unhelpful notion of the spiritual discipline required in order to follow it. One is not following the Buddhist path if one feels that one is being driven along it like a sheep, rather wishing one could stray off and have a nibble on some succulent wayside shrub or flower.

There is certainly an objective criterion of development which one has to understand and act upon, but the path itself is not out there; it is in here. There is no question of forcing yourself to follow a particular track or go in a particular direction. The path simply represents the individual solution to one's own particular predicament. If you know and understand yourself as you are now, that puts you in a position to develop in your own way. The path is you in the process of organizing your mental states in such a way that growth and development will take place in a positive direction.

from *Know Your Mind*

6. SPIRITUAL GROWTH: DEVELOPMENTAL OR IMMANENT?

There is no point in saying that one believes in the Buddha, even if the Buddha can be demonstrated to have lived, if one makes no effort to close the gap between oneself and the Buddha.

It is only too easy to think of the bodhisattva's path in a very literal way, as though it leads up to Buddhahood just as the garden path leads to the door of a house. We think that following the path will mean going along step by step until one day we reach the wonderful gateway of Nirvāṇa, all glistening and golden. There it is, and we go in. It is very natural for us to think in this way – but it isn't really like that. When you come to the end of the bodhisattva path, you don't find a gate or doorway, or any sort of celestial mansion waiting for you. You don't find anything at all. There's nothing there. The path just ends – and there you are at the end of it.

In fact, you find yourself – to use another metaphor, which is also not to be taken literally – at the edge of a precipice. The path has gone on nicely, step by step, stage by stage, mile after mile. You have counted all those milestones, and you were expecting to arrive in comfort at the entrance to a great house. But no – you find that the path ends right at the edge of a precipice. So there you are, standing on the edge, and the drop goes down not just a few feet, but what seems like miles. Somehow you know that it's bottomless, infinite. What are you going to do?

The Zen people put it another way. They say that the spiritual life is like climbing a high and greasy flagpole.[84] When, after a great deal of effort, you get to the top, you find that there's nowhere to go. You obviously can't go any further up – and you can't come down, because at the bottom there's a Zen master with a big stick. Nor is there a cosy little platform at the top of the flagpole on which you can settle down like St Simeon Stylites.[85] There's nothing there but empty space. And, of course, you're too high up to jump. You can't go up, you can't go down, you can't stay there, and you can't jump off. What are you to do? Well, it is quite impossible to say.

This predicament arises out of the fact that 'path' and 'goal' are discontinuous. Contrary to our usual metaphorical mode of description, Enlightenment is not reached by following a path. But this doesn't mean that the path should not be followed. Paradoxically enough, you follow the path knowing that it doesn't lead anywhere.

Not even the 'right' path will take us to Enlightenment. The path, one may say, is in the dimension of time, while the goal is in the dimension of eternity. We will never reach eternity by going on and on in time. That is, one does not arrive at eternity by an indefinite prolongation of time, any more than one can arrive at a two-dimensional figure by the prolongation of a one-dimensional line. The two – eternity and time, the goal and the path – are by definition discontinuous, discrete. The bodhisattva represents the dimension of time because the bodhisattva path is followed in time. It's something that happens – it has a past, a present, and a future – and it doesn't go beyond time. But the Buddha represents the dimension of eternity. The Buddha represents the goal, and the goal is attained out of time. One reaches the end of the path within time, but one shouldn't think that one attains the goal in time: one attains the goal out of time or, to put it another way, the goal is eternally attained.

There are two ways of looking at spiritual development. It can be seen in terms of advancing from stage to stage, but it can also be seen in terms of deepening one's experience of what is already there. We need both. If one thinks one-sidedly of the spiritual life as a progression from stage to stage, one is liable to become too goal-oriented. But if one thinks only in terms of deepening one's present experience, unfolding from a deep centre within oneself, one may become rather inert. It is perhaps best to think of operating in both modes at the same time, or alternating between them at different periods of one's life.

We have said that one follows the path knowing that it doesn't lead anywhere. One also follows it with no guarantee that it is the *right* path. However, it is possible to resolve this contradiction and uncertainty by balancing the model of the path with the model of unfolding. Sometimes people are over-concerned that they have got exactly the right teacher, the right mantra, the right book – that they are doing the right thing that will get them to the right Enlightenment. In a sense, it isn't possible to know. If someone came along and said, 'You are on the wrong path. You are definitely going to hell,' what could you say? You couldn't prove they were wrong. You don't 'know' in that logical, demonstrable fashion. But is that sort of knowledge applicable or appropriate to Enlightenment, and the path to Enlightenment?

If it is possible to know that one is on the path to Enlightenment, it can only be because there is something within one already, however embryonic, that corresponds to what is fully developed in the Buddha. Without that consonance, one could never follow the path or gain Enlightenment. An unenlightened human being and an Enlightened human being are both human beings; so one has something in common with the Buddha, and the Buddha has something in common with oneself. What one is trying to do is increase what one has in common so that there will be less and less difference between the Buddha and oneself. When there is no difference at all, one will oneself be Enlightened.

All we can do is say, 'Here I am, and there is the Buddha – or at least we have what purport to be records of a being of that sort. When I examine those records I can see that I have certain things in common with the Buddha, and although he had those qualities to a much greater degree than I do, the teachings suggest that I can develop them. So, provisionally accepting that there might be something in these teachings, I will see if I can. For instance, this text says that the Buddha was extremely kind. I can be kind myself on occasion, but I can see that I could be a lot kinder. Is it possible for me to develop more kindness?' So we try, and we find that, yes, it is possible. Then we conclude, 'Well, if I can develop a bit more kindness, I can surely develop a lot more.' And so we go on.

It all comes down to one's own practice. There is no point in saying that one believes in the Buddha, even if the Buddha can be demonstrated to have lived, if one makes no effort to close the gap between oneself and the Buddha. It is a continuous refinement through which one becomes progressively happier and more integrated. And there will be something in oneself which insists that when one becomes more emotionally positive and more mindful, one is on the right path. When you feel healthy, no one can say, 'Ah no, you're very ill.' You *know* that you're in a state of health, at least if it lasts for a little while. In the same way, if you are full of friendliness and compassion and mindfulness, no one can convince you that you are on the wrong path. The naturally self-transcending nature of the conscious being means that when you are all the time transcending yourself, you know that you are on the right path, because such a path corresponds to your innermost nature.

Sometimes you may feel as though you are unfolding like a flower; at other times spiritual life may feel more like climbing a mountain. The two modes correspond to the nature of the *bodhicitta*. The absolute *bodhicitta* is Enlightenment itself, while the relative *bodhicitta* is the *bodhicitta* everlastingly in the process of attaining Enlightenment. The two together are the ultimate realization. Thus in our spiritual life we are trying all the time to achieve that which we already have. We have to do both: realize that we already have it, but at the same time go all out to achieve it. One without the other leaves us out of balance.

We can get a sense of the possibility of combining the two from our dream life. Say, for example, you wake up with a memory of having been dreaming about travelling in India. At the same time, you are aware that this dream was really about painting a picture of a flower. Somehow you have to accept that the same dream was about both things. To your waking consciousness they seem like two alternatives, but the dream experience was both, in a mysterious way that the waking consciousness cannot apprehend. The spiritual life is rather like that. You have to have a sense of racing forward all the time, moving from stage to stage, climbing that mountain. At the same time, you have to be absolutely still, just realizing more and more deeply where you are now.

from *The Bodhisattva Ideal*

7. WHAT IS NIRVĀṆA?

The question we should be asking is not 'What is Nirvāṇa?' but 'Why am I interested in Nirvāṇa? Why am I reading this book rather than another, or rather than, say, watching television?'

The first question Buddhists get asked when they meet non-Buddhists is, as likely as not, 'What is Nirvāṇa?' Certainly, when I was a Buddhist monk travelling about India, I used to find on trains that no sooner had I taken my seat than someone would come up to me (for in India people are by no means bashful when it comes to getting into conversation) and say, 'You seem to be a Buddhist monk. Please tell me – what is Nirvāṇa?'

Indeed, it is a very appropriate question to ask. The question is, after all, addressing the whole point of being a Buddhist. You may see Buddhists engaged in all sorts of different activities, but they all have the same overall purpose in view. You may see shaven-headed Japanese monks in their long black robes sitting in disciplined rows, meditating hour after hour in the silence and tranquillity of a Zen monastery. You may see ordinary Tibetans going in the early morning up the steps of the temples, carrying their flowers and their candles and their bundles of incense sticks, kneeling down and making their offerings, chanting verses of praise to the Buddha, the Dharma, and the Sangha, and then going about their daily business. You may see Sri Lankan monks poring over palm-leaf manuscripts, the pages brown with age. You may see layfolk in the Theravādin countries of South-east Asia giving alms to the monks when they come round with their black begging-bowls. You may see Western Buddhists working together in right livelihood businesses.

When you see unfolded this whole vast panorama of Buddhist activities, the question that arises is: Why? What is the reason for it all? What is the moving spirit, the great impulse behind all this activity? What are all these people trying to do? What are they trying to achieve through their meditation, their worshipping, their study, their alms-giving, their work, and so on?

If you asked this of any of these people, you would probably receive the traditional answer: 'We're doing this for the sake of the attainment of Nirvāṇa, liberation, Enlightenment.' But what then is this Nirvāṇa? How is it to be understood or explained? How is it to be fitted in to one's own particular range of mental furniture? One naturally gropes after analogies. If one has a Christian background one will try to envisage Nirvāṇa as a sort of eternal life in heaven after death. If one takes it outside the usual religious framework altogether, one may even think of it as a state of complete annihilation or extinction.

But in fact there is no excuse for these kinds of badly mistaken views. It is not difficult to give a clear account of Nirvāṇa, because the ancient canonical texts are quite clear as to what it is and what it isn't. If one has the job of presenting the topic of Nirvāṇa, one will probably need to begin by discussing the etymology of the word Nirvāṇa – whether it means a 'blowing out' or a 'cooling down'. And one will no doubt go on to explain that, according to the Pāli texts at least, Nirvāṇa consists in the extinction of all craving, all hatred, and all ignorance of the true nature of things.[86]

At some point it is customary to say that Nirvāṇa is a state of incomparable bliss, to which the bliss of this world cannot be compared.[87] And if one wants to get a bit technical one may want to describe the two kinds of Nirvāṇa: the *kleśa nirvāṇa*, consisting in the extinction of all passions and defilements; and the *skandha nirvāṇa*, consisting in the extinction of all the various processes of psychophysical existence, an event that takes place upon the death – as we call it – of someone who has already gained *kleśa nirvāṇa* during their lifetime.[88]

One may then go on to the different interpretations of Nirvāṇa in the various different schools of Buddhism – the Theravāda, the Madhyamaka, the Yogācāra, the Tantra, Zen, and so on. Finally, it is always necessary to emphasize that Nirvāṇa is neither eternal life in the Christian sense, nor annihilation or extinction in the materialist sense – that here, as elsewhere, one has to follow the middle path between two extreme views.

So this is how Nirvāṇa is traditionally delineated. Above all, perhaps, Nirvāṇa is conventionally defined as the *goal* of Buddhism. And it is in respect of this particular way of positioning the concept that my approach here will appear to some people – mistakenly, in my view – to be perhaps rather unorthodox.

The psychology of goal-setting

There are all kinds of groups of people in the world – religious groups, political groups, cultural groups, charitable groups, and so on – and each of these groups has its goal, be it power, or wealth, or some other satisfaction, and whether it is for their own good or the good of others. And it would seem that Buddhists likewise have their own particular goal that they call Nirvāṇa. So let us look at what is meant by this idea of a goal to be attained or realized, and then establish to what extent it is applicable to Nirvāṇa.

It should be clear at once where this procedure is going to lead us. The fact is that whenever terms are used rather loosely, without any lucid consideration of what they mean, you get the beginnings of serious misunderstandings. This is particularly the case when we transfer terms and expressions derived from mundane experience, like 'goal', to spiritual or transcendental experience, like 'Nirvāṇa'. If they don't quite fit, we need to be aware of this, and if they don't fit at all, we need to think through the whole question afresh.

With this in mind, let us examine the idea of a 'goal' a bit more closely. A goal is an objective, something you strive for. You could, if you like, draw a distinction between striving to *be* and striving to *have*, but actually, the two come to the same thing: 'having' is a sort of vicarious 'being'. A goal is in the end something that you want to *be*. Suppose, for instance, your goal is wealth: you can say that your goal is to *possess* wealth, or that your goal is to *be* wealthy, but obviously the possessing, the having, is reducible to the being, the existing.

There is one really crucial (if obvious) precondition for setting a goal: it must represent something you are not. You don't want to have or to be what you already have or are. You can only want to be what you are not – which suggests, obviously, that you are dissatisfied with what you are. If you're not dissatisfied with what you are, you will never strive to be what you aren't.

Suppose, just by way of example, your goal happens to be money and material possessions. You will have made these things your goal because you are dissatisfied with being poor. Or if, say, you make knowledge your goal, if you want to add to your understanding, investigate fundamental principles, and so on, you want to do this because you are dissatisfied with your present state of being ignorant.

We don't always see it in quite these stark terms, but this is the basic pattern or procedure involved in setting ourselves goals, and it is a quite appropriate way of proceeding on its own level. But we get into a tangle when we extend it into the spiritual life – and by this I don't mean some elevated sphere of experience far removed from everyday concerns. By the spiritual life I mean something very close to home.

Any complex of problems we may have can be boiled down to the most basic problem of all, which is unhappiness in one form or another. A case of bad temper, for example, is a problem because it makes us miserable, and one could equally well say the opposite: that being miserable makes us bad-tempered. Even though we don't usually think of the problem we have as one of unhappiness, that is what it really is.

So we try to get away from unhappiness and attain happiness. The way we go about this is to try to ricochet, as it were, from that experience of feeling miserable or discontented into an opposite state or experience of feeling happy; and this usually involves grasping at some object or experience that we believe will give us the happiness we seek.

When we feel unhappy, what we do is set up this goal of happiness, which we strive to achieve. And as we all know, we fail. All our lives through, in one way or another, we are in search of happiness. No one is in search of misery. Everyone is in search of happiness. There's no one who could possibly say they're so happy that they couldn't imagine themselves being a little happier. Most people, if they're honest with themselves, have to admit that their life consists of a fluctuating state of unease and dissatisfaction, punctuated by moments of happiness and joy which make them temporarily forget their discomfort and discontent. So this possibility of being happy becomes everybody's goal – a goal which can never be realized because happiness is by its nature fleeting. We all continue to set up this phantom goal, however, because the alternative – which is simply to be aware – is too challenging for us.

The setting up of goals – which means trying to get away from one's present experience – is really a substitute for awareness, for self-knowledge. Even if we do develop a measure of self-knowledge, we don't tend to maintain it because to do so would be just too threatening. We always end up setting up goals rather than continuing to be aware.

To take a simple example, suppose I have something of a problem with my temper: I get irritated, even angry, rather easily – even a small thing can spark me off – and this bad temper of mine makes life difficult, and perhaps miserable for myself and others. And suppose that I wake up one day and decide that enough is enough, that it's time it came to a stop. So I set up a goal for myself – the goal of being good-tempered. I think, 'I'm undeniably bad-tempered: my goal, however, is to be sweet-tempered and amiable, always returning the soft answer, always ready to turn the other cheek.'

What actually happens, though? One almost invariably fails. The intention – even the degree of self-knowledge – is admirable. But after a while one's resolve falters. In the face of the same old provocations, one is back again in the same old rut – and probably blaming the same old people and the same old external circumstances for it. So why is this? Anybody who has ever begun to recognize that their problems are, at least to a degree, of their own making will also recognize that this is what happens. But why does it happen?

The reason is that we are continuing to tackle the symptoms rather than the disease. If we try to get away from our unhappiness simply by trying to be good-humoured, we are still unaware of the fundamental cause of our being bad-tempered. And if this isn't resolved, if we don't know why we are bad-tempered, if we don't know what is prompting the angry answer or the violent reaction, then we can't possibly hope to become good-tempered.

Whatever our problem, we automatically – almost instinctively – set up a goal of being happy in order to get away from our unhappiness. Even if a little awareness, a little insight, does arise, it is not sustained. We revert automatically to setting up a goal of one kind or another rather than continuing to be aware and trying to understand very deeply why that problem arises. Setting up goals is an automatic reflex to short-circuit the development of awareness and self-knowledge – in short, to get away from ourselves.

How then do we change this? To start with, we need a change of attitude. Rather than trying to escape from ourselves, we need to begin to acknowledge the reality of what we are. We need to understand – and not just intellectually – why we are what we are. If you are suffering, don't just reach out for a chocolate. Recognize the fact that you are suffering and look at it more and more deeply. If you're happy, recognize it, take it in more and more deeply. Instead of running from happiness into guilt, or into some sort of excitable intoxication, try to understand what the true nature of that happiness is, where it really comes from. Again, this isn't just intellectual; it's something that has to go very deep down indeed.

For some people this sort of insight will come in the course of meditation. Meditation isn't just fixing the mind on an object, or revolving a certain idea in the mind. Meditation really involves – among other things – getting down to the bedrock of the mind, illuminating the mind from the bottom upwards, as it were. It is about exposing to oneself one's motives, the deep-seated causes of one's mental states, one's experiences, one's joy and one's suffering, and so on. In this way real growth in awareness will come about.

But where is all this leading? What has all this to do with Nirvāṇa? It may seem that we have strayed rather from our subject, but in fact we have been doing some necessary preparing of the ground. With some things, if one tackles them too directly, one can easily miss the mark. What we can now do is open up some kind of perspective on the way Nirvāṇa is traditionally described – or rather on the effect on us of these traditional descriptions.

Suppose, for example, I have been going through rather a difficult, upsetting period, and I'm feeling rather miserable. Then one day I pick up a book in which it is stated that Nirvāṇa is the supreme happiness, the supreme bliss. What will be my reaction? The likelihood is that I will think, 'Good – that's just what I want – bliss, happiness.' I will make Nirvāṇa my goal. And what this means is that effectively I will be making lack of awareness my goal. I will be latching on to Nirvāṇa – labelled as the supreme bliss – because it happens to fit in with my subjective needs and feelings at this particular time. Such a reaction has of course nothing to do with being a Buddhist, but it is the way that a lot of us approach Buddhism, and indeed use Buddhism, in a quite unaware, almost automatic way. Unconsciously we try to use Nirvāṇa to settle problems that can only really be resolved through awareness.

We do not succeed in banishing unhappiness by pretending to ourselves that we are happy, by shoving our misery out of sight. The first step is to acknowledge the reality of our condition: if there is an underlying unhappiness to our lives, we must face up to the fact. It is certainly good to be cheerful and positive, but not at the expense of fooling ourselves. One has only to look at the faces of the people you see in any city to see the 'marks of weakness, marks of woe'[89] that William Blake saw in London two hundred years ago, and yet few people will admit to their misery even in their own minds.

No progress can be made till we come to terms with our actual experience, till we get to know our unhappiness in all its comings and goings, till we learn to live with it, and study it. What is it, at bottom, that makes us unhappy? What is its source? We will get nowhere by looking for a way out of our misery, by aiming for the goal of happiness, or even Nirvāṇa. It is a mistake to postulate the goal of Nirvāṇa too quickly or too unconsciously. All we can do is try to see more and more clearly and distinctly what it is in ourselves that is making us unhappy. This is the only way that Nirvāṇa will be attained.

In this sense Nirvāṇa cannot be seen as an escape from unhappiness at all. It is by trying too hard to escape from unhappiness that we fail to do so. The real key is awareness, self-knowledge. A paradoxical way of putting it would be to say that the goal of Buddhism consists in being completely and totally aware at all levels of your need to reach a goal. We can also say, going a little further, that Nirvāṇa consists in the full and complete awareness of why you want to reach Nirvāṇa at all. If you understand completely why you want to reach Nirvāṇa, then you've reached Nirvāṇa. We can go further even than this. We can even say that the unaware person is in need of Nirvāṇa, but is unable to get a true idea of it. An aware person, on the other hand, is quite clear about this goal, but doesn't need it. That's really the position.

So there we have the basic drawback to conventional accounts of Nirvāṇa as being this or that. We simply accept or reject this or that aspect of Nirvāṇa in accordance with our own largely unconscious needs. If the underlying – and therefore unconscious – drive of our existence is towards pleasure, then we will find ourselves responding to the idea of Nirvāṇa as the supreme bliss. If on the other hand we are emotionally driven by a fundamental need to know, to understand, to see what is really going on, then almost automatically we will make our goal a state of complete illumination. And again, if we feel oppressed or constrained by life, if our childhood was one of control and confinement, or if we have a sense that our options in life are restricted by our particular circumstances – by poverty, by being tied down to a job or a family, or looking after elderly relatives – then we will be drawn to the idea of Nirvāṇa as freedom, as emancipation.

In this way there takes place a half-conscious setting up of goals based on our own psychological or social conditioning, instead of a growing understanding of *why* we feel dissatisfied, *why* we feel somehow 'in the dark', or *why* we feel tied down. Nirvāṇa becomes simply a projection of our own mundane needs. Hence when we consider the subject of Nirvāṇa, the goal of Buddhism, the question we should be asking is not 'What is Nirvāna?' but 'Why am I interested in Nirvāna? Why am I reading this book rather than another, or rather than, say, watching television?' Is it curiosity, is it duty, is it vanity, is it just to see how Sangharakshita is going to tackle this thorny topic? Or is it something deeper?

Even these questions will not settle the matter. If it is curiosity, why are we curious about Nirvāna? If it is duty, towards what or whom do we feel dutiful? If it is vanity, why do we want to preen ourselves in this particular way? What is underneath our interest? If there is something deeper in our motivation, what is it?

This line of questioning might appear unconventional or unorthodox, and in pursuing it we may not learn much about Buddhism or Nirvāna in the purely objective, historical sense. But we will learn a great deal about what the ideas of Buddhism represent. If we follow this particular line, constantly trying to penetrate to the depths of our own mind, we may even get a little nearer to the goal of Nirvāna itself.

from *What is the Dharma?*

4
BUDDHISM – ONE OR MANY?

1. VARIETY AND UNITY IN THE BUDDHIST TRADITION

Divergences in both institutional religion and personal religion being so numerous, and in many cases so radical, are we justified in speaking of Buddhism at all?

As even the most superficially interested visitor cannot fail to observe, the Dharma assumed in every land in which it took root a distinct, unique, and unmistakable national form and local colouration. The history of the stupa, as it evolves from its spheroid Indian original into the bell-shaped beauty of its Sinhalese type, the waisted *chortens* of Tibet, the almost Gothic perpendicularity of the graceful gilded Thai *chedis*, the streamer-swathed *chaityas* of Nepal, each of their four sides alive with a pair of hypnotically staring eyes, the city-like formations of Java and Cambodia, and the many-storeyed pagodas of China and Japan, may be taken as an architectural illustration of the richness and diversity of the Dharma on the institutional side. Of India one does not speak: though later systems incorporated a number of its teachings, here Buddhism as an institutional religion no longer exists. Let us go southward to Sri Lanka, for centuries the stronghold of Theravāda, where even now are to be found the most intelligent and cultured exponents of this ancient school. The sky is an abyss of cloudless blue, and our eyes are almost blinded by the sunlight reflected from the dazzling white walls of squat, bungalow-like viharas, each with red-tiled roofs and deep verandas, and of the larger and grander temple buildings nearby: the *dagobas* are so white that they seem flat rather than round, shapes cut out of enormous sheets of white paper and pinned onto the landscape. Coconut palms are everywhere – in groves, in clumps and clusters, and singly. Their trunks are bent at angles of various degrees of acuteness towards the earth, and when silhouetted against the sky seem to be interlaced; their plumes sweep the ground; the green nuts are high up, hanging in clusters, and seem quite small until we see a tiny turbaned figure scramble up and start hurling them to the ground. It is still early morning. Slowly and quietly there comes along the road – so slowly and so quietly that at first there seems to be only a patch of colour in almost imperceptible motion – a figure draped in brilliant yellow with bowed and shaven head. He clasps in his two hands a large black bowl. His countenance is impassive. His eyes seem to be shut, for they are fixed upon the ground in front of him. With dignity and deliberation he moves from door to door, and is received with respectful salutations. Halting for a moment, he lifts the lid of the bowl to receive the alms of the faithful, who, from their reverential demeanour, evidently feel that they are indebted to him rather than he to them. More and more yellow figures as it were materialize on the scene, appearing in the alternate bars of brilliant sunshine and purple shadow lying along the dusty road like the silent unfolding of yellow flowers. They are not seen for long, though, and as the sun mounts and the shadows shorten no human figures are visible save a few Tamil coolies whose blue-black bodies, glistening with sweat, stagger along under enormous loads. The rickshaw puller sleeps between the shafts of his vehicle in a scrap of shade. Earth and sky begin to vibrate with heat. Presently a haze flickers in front of the eyes, blurring the landscape, which now jumps and dances as though seen through a tongue of flame … perspiration … exhaustion … prostration…. The click of the fan above the bed … then unconsciousness.

When we awake the land is steeped in deep, cool shadows. A light breeze brings unimaginable refreshment. The palm trees rustle above our heads, and looking up through the fronds we see that the unclouded sky is ablaze with stars. The tom-toms begin to throb from the temple nearby; the clarinets wail; the air, that had vibrated all day with the intensity of heat, now vibrates with the fury of sound. Already white figures are flitting through the shadows of the trees. Each one bears a tray on which is a heap of five-petalled temple flowers – ah! the incredible sweetness of their fragrance as it floats through the dusk – a few sticks of incense, and a tiny lamp. Let us follow them to the temple. We shall bow down together at the feet of the Exalted One. Squeezing in, we find that the shrine is densely packed with white-clad worshippers, and the air oppressive with the fumes of thousands of brightly burning lamps of coconut oil. Progress is slow; the men and women are either silent or muttering prayers; there is no impatience, no pushing. Inch by inch, we move forward with the crowd; at last the pressure relaxes; we find ourselves standing with waist pressed against the edge of the great altar. Flowers are everywhere; the smell of the incense is overpoweringly sweet; thousands of candles splutter and burn. Lifting our eyes we see behind the altar, clad in robes of the same brilliant yellow, a dozen or so serene figures who smile benignly at the worshippers. Above and beyond them towers the brightly painted image of the Buddha, upon its face the smile of eternal peace. But our contemplation cannot last long. A gentle pressure from behind reminds us that it is time to give place to others, and before many minutes have passed we find ourselves outside in the cold night air. We stand beneath the palm trees watching the streams of worshippers passing through the temple gates. A line of elephants, gorgeously caparisoned and surrounded by troops of excitedly shouting boys, comes swaying through the darkness, their triumphal progress illuminated by flaring torches. Parties of strongly built male dancers, with black oil-bright bodies that reflect the ruddy glare of the torches and fantastic headdresses, pirouette on either side, their bare feet stamping upon the hard ground in time with the rhythm of the tom-toms. The tumult is deafening. But only for a few moments. As swiftly as it had come the procession disappears from sight. In an hour's time the last worshippers have left the temple and gone home. Silence reigns. But hour after hour, and even long after we have gone to bed, we can still hear the faint insistent beat of the tom-tom ... *tom-tom ... tom-tom....*

Geographically speaking, the distance between Sri Lanka, the Theravādin stronghold, and Tibet, the inmost citadel of Mahāyāna tradition, is only 2,000 miles. But on the spiritual plane, at least so far as the institutional aspect of religion is concerned, the gulf dividing them is seemingly immeasurable. Crossing the snow-clad peaks of the Himalayas, the largest and the loftiest mountain barrier in existence, we find ourselves on the Roof of the World. An icy wind blows furiously, cutting through quilted garments and furs; lightly but steadily comes the snow, driven almost horizontally by the wind. Soon our eyes are sore with looking at the blinding whiteness of the earth and the pitilessly brilliant blueness of the sky. Every now and then the tempest shrieks suddenly past, giving mighty buffets as though it were a legion of devils seeking to send us rolling from our horses down the 5,000-foot precipice yawning beneath our feet. We cling on tightly, gripping the horse's mane with numbed fists. At last we feel the animal between our knees slithering down the stony slopes of the mountain-side ... our three-week-long journey to the Land of Religion is nearing its end. Painfully we open our gummed lids with the help of our fingers. Around us the unbroken circle of the horizon makes a sharp edge against the sky. We realize that we had never known before the meaning of space. Here and there are patches of light green colour; but no trees, hardly a shrub. Only a vast expanse of waving grass as smooth and flat as a billiard table, with what look like specks of stone but are really Tibetan homesteads, and the black dots of grazing yaks and nomad tents scattered over it at enormous intervals: they are so small that at first sight the landscape seems deserted.

As we ride forward, and as the days pass, what at first had seemed a slight corrugation of the horizon becomes a long low range of mountains blue-black in the far distance. Gradually, as we approach, they thrust themselves higher and higher into the sky, and eventually the central peak towers above our heads seemingly halfway up to heaven. Saddle-sore, we dismount at the foot of a flight of stairs hewn as though for the feet of a giant out of the rock. Slowly we ascend. Each turn of the path reveals a fresh flight and each flight contains thousands of steps. We dare not look down. At last, on the next ridge, only a few hundred feet above our heads, we see red and white striped walls and gilded roofs. Where the mountain ends and the monastery begins is difficult to say, though, for they are built of the same material and on the same colossal scale. The black mouth of an enormous door yawns before us. Stalwart figures are mounting guard on either side, their bulk prodigiously increased by swathings of maroon-coloured woollen cloth, their already exceptional stature heightened by yellow headgear shaped like the helmet of Achilles, and yet more terrible; in their hands are enormous staves studded with brass. As we approach their eyes narrow suspiciously in their grimy faces;

but they say nothing, and we are allowed to pass. The iron door slams shut behind us; there is a rattling of chains. After a full half-minute has passed the sound is echoed as though from the very heart of the earth. Slowly we grope our way forward through the pitch darkness, tripping and stumbling over the uneven ground. We are aware of flittings to and fro on either side of us; suddenly a hand seizes hold of our arm, and we are pulled roughly along. A misty light shines forth; a door has opened. With the sudden lifting of a curtain the mist becomes a blaze and a deep roaring and groaning noise of trumpets, inexpressibly moving, that had been hitherto muffled by the thickness of the stone walls, blares mournfully in our ears.

We find ourselves in an enormous chamber. On the floor sit rows and rows of maroon-coloured figures: there must be thousands of them. From the ceiling hang huge cylinder-shaped banners of victory, every flounce of a different colour. Before each monk is a bowl of steaming tea; some are sipping, some adding their voices to the deep-throated rumbling chorus that the assembly sends rolling wave-like from one end of the long chamber to the other. Armed with a whip, a figure resembling those we saw at the main entrance strides up and down the central aisle. A few vertical shafts of misty sunshine, penetrating from some aperture above, illumine the faces of the celebrants, some of whom are obviously very old, others astonishingly youthful; but all, despite bent backs and rounded shoulders, are sturdily built and all are shaven-headed. In the far distance, ranked on a long narrow table running almost the entire width of the room, hundreds of golden butter-lamps are steadily burning. Behind them is the shrine whereon have been arranged various artistically moulded offerings. To the left, high above the heads of the worshippers, is a magnificently carved, painted, and gilded throne. In front of this, a white silken scarf in our hands, we now find ourselves. Cross-legged upon its brocade cushions sits an old man, magnificently clad in garments of dark red silk. The smile with which he looks down at us as we make our obeisance is not of this earth; it is the smile of Enlightenment. Far more brightly than any ray of earthly sunshine it penetrates our heart. Within his small, twinkling eyes all knowledge seems to dwell, and we are aware that not even our most secret thoughts are hidden from him; yet we do not feel afraid.

When, a few minutes later, we stand in front of the main altar, it is the same smile which, as though from the moon itself, calmly and tenderly shines from the central face of the eleven-headed white image behind the glass doors of the tabernacle. A thousand arms, each ending in a hand which either bears an emblem or makes with tapering fingers a graceful symbolical gesture, radiate from its shoulders like spokes from the hub of a wheel. We are face to face with Universal Compassion.

Five minutes later we are face to face with Death. After being hurried through dimly lit corridors, the noise behind us receding further and further into the distance, we are ushered into a small black hole. A single lamp is burning. Fearfully, as though in unwilling obedience to a command, a monk lifts the heavy curtain of iron rings that hangs before the inmost shrine. Involuntarily we recoil from the sight. The figure that stares down upon us with bulging eyeballs is full of menace. His huge, powerful body, deep blue in colour, is festooned with garlands of skulls. His four arms are raised threateningly, and his hands grasp various weapons. One brawny knee is uplifted as he tramples upon the enemies of the Dharma. His face is that of a horned beast, and his red tongue lolls out from between his rows of gleaming fangs as though thirsty for blood. Round his waist is a tiger-skin. Clinging to his bosom, her slender arms clasped tightly round his bull-neck, her legs wrapped round his thighs, and her mouth strained passionately to his, is the small white figure of his consort. They are locked in sexual embrace. Round them roars a halo of flames. Terrible but strangely fascinating, vibrant with power incalculable, are the Father and the Mother, the transcendental pair whose union symbolizes the inseparability of wisdom and compassion, of doctrine and method – or, returning to the much more limited point of view wherefrom we started, the metaphysical unity of the institutional and personal aspects of religion – as they tower in all their preternatural vigour before us until, with a ringing clash, the curtain falls, and we are left with the smoky lamp throwing against the ceiling the fantastic shadows of the huge stuffed animal carcasses suspended there.

Two strikingly dissimilar pictures indeed! Could a greater contrast be imagined, the reader may wonder, than that between the Buddhism of Sri Lanka and the Buddhism of Tibet? For though we may freely own up to a deliberate heightening of colour, a calculated distribution of lights and shades, the diptych we have painted is nevertheless a faithful illustration of the differences prevailing at the institutional level between the various distinct and mutually independent branches of Buddhist tradition. No wonder, then, that those who have been born or brought up within an environment dominated, from the religious point of view, by any one form of institutional Buddhism, to the exclusion of the rest, should find it difficult to avoid falling into the pitfall of thinking that the form with which they have been familiar since childhood is the one true form, while less familiar forms are false. For although there does exist a Basic Buddhism which is the common foundation of all schools, the doctrines by which one line of tradition is distinguished from another are almost always placed, by those belonging to that line, at the very centre of their picture of Buddhism, and receive the highlight, while the remainder, their shapes hardly discernible in the gloom, are distributed towards the circumference, some in fact being cut in half owing to the necessity of having a frame. It is hardly astonishing, therefore, that even a conscientiously impartial student of the Buddhist schools should discover, more often than not, mutual opposition and contradiction rather than agreement and harmony. Differences regarding doctrine, no less than a variety of institutions, do exist: the fact cannot be ignored; and of those who become aware of them without having transcended the intellectual standpoint what can we expect but a violent reaction towards an even more bigoted belief in the exclusive truth and authenticity of the traditions of their own school?

Modern Theravādins, insisting that progress upon the path depends solely upon one's own efforts, wax eloquent over the fact that we are each our own saviour, that we ourselves are the architects of our fortunes, the captains of our souls, and the masters of our fates, and that heavens and hells are the creations of our own good and evil deeds. The Buddha is simply a guide pointing out to us the path which, whether we like it or not, we must perforce tread with our own two feet. He is like a schoolmaster (a comparison for which several exponents of this school exhibit a special fondness) who can explain to us a difficult algebraical problem on the blackboard but who cannot, unfortunately, give us the intelligence with which to do our own sums. One of their favourite texts is *Dhammapada* verse 165, which says:

> Evil is done by self alone, by self alone is one stained; by self alone is evil left undone, by self alone is one purified. Purity and impurity depend on one's own self. No man can purify another.

This individualistic doctrine the Jōdo Shinshū school repudiates as dire heresy. Emancipation, it believes, depends not on our own efforts but entirely upon the grace of Amitābha Buddha; attempting to save ourselves is as ridiculous as trying to hoist ourselves up into the air by tugging at our own bootlaces. Good deeds, far from being of any help, only intensify the feeling of individual selfhood, thus obstructing the operation of the saving grace or 'other-power' of Amitābha. Hence the paradoxical saying, no less popular with Jōdo Shinshū followers than the *Dhammapada* verse is with Theravādins, 'Even the good man will be saved. How much more so the evil man!'[90] Instead of striving to win Enlightenment in this world and in this life by means of our own unaided efforts, we should, with a heart full of love and faith, simply invoke the name of Amitābha and pray to be reborn in Sukhāvatī, the Land of Bliss he has established in the West.

No less extreme is the difference which exists between certain Tantric schools, on the one hand, and the non-Tantric schools, on the other, regarding the importance of morality. Though both parties agree in recognizing the instrumental function and relative value of ethical observances, the recognition is accorded from positions so wide apart as in effect to amount to a radical divergence of views. To the non-Tantric schools, the fact that morality is a means to Enlightenment adds to, rather than detracts from, its importance; for in the absence of the proper means, the desired goal becomes impossible of attainment. Morality is not only the means, but the indispensable means to Enlightenment; hence it is an absolute value. Some of these schools therefore strive for a rigid observance not only of the major precepts of morality but even of the minor monastic obligations which, though many of them are in reality without ethical significance, are all comprehended in the traditional Buddhist conception of morality.

Against this view, which can so easily harden into a petrified ethical formalism, the followers of various Tantric schools contend that the fact of morality being only a means to an end instead of proving its absoluteness demonstrates its relativity. The sole absolute value is compassion; even wisdom is only a means for the realization of that supreme end. However indispensable at the time of sickness, medicines may be emptied down the drain when we are restored to health; the Perfected Ones, having by means of ethical observances attained full Enlightenment, thereafter have personally no further use for them, and henceforth may act according to circumstances either in an 'ethical' or in an 'unethical' manner. Their sole concern is with the welfare of all sentient beings, for the sake of which they are prepared to sacrifice every other consideration. If by their merely apparent violation of the ethical precepts they can assist in his progress along the path a single pilgrim soul they do not shrink from committing what, in the case of an unenlightened person, would be a deadly sin, even though they thereby forfeit their own reputation for sanctity (one of the subtlest fetters, this) and incur the disapprobation of society. The biography of more than one Tantric teacher is replete with episodes in which he deprives animals and even human beings of life, appropriates to his own use the property of others, freely indulges in sexual intercourse, tells lies, and partakes of strong drink to the point of inebriation. We appear far indeed from the sobriety and restraint, the almost pathetic eagerness to 'keep up appearances' in the eyes of the world, even though not always in the mirror of one's own conscience, which characterizes ordinary practitioners! Where even the major ethical precepts are treated with so little ceremony, the minor monastic obligations, indeed the very idea not only of monasticism but of any formally religious life at all, can expect nothing but a rude dismissal. All pretences to respectability are abandoned; dignity, decorum, and even ordinary decency are flung to the winds. In place of the noble bearing and refined manners of the true monk we see the reckless demeanour and hirsute behaviour of the outcasts of society. Among non-Tantric schools, the appearance of saintliness is easily achieved even by those who are in reality furthest from saintliness; in some Tantric schools, however, the opposite is the case: the saintliest appear as the least saintly. It is not difficult to see that the doctrine of ethical relativism is fraught with grave dangers; the frailty of human nature is only too willing to believe that since the Perfected Ones may, upon occasion, act 'unethically', one who acts unethically is a Perfected One, and that the easiest and the quickest way of gaining Enlightenment is by breaking, one after another, all the moral laws. In the Tantric schools, too, may be found those who follow the letter rather than the spirit of tradition. Whatever our own attitude towards ethical relativism may be, the fact is that, in the extreme form we have described, the doctrine is far from being upheld by all Tantric schools, the majority of which are as exacting in their ethical demands as any of the schools belonging to the non-Tantric group.

Differences of this kind are by no means rare in Buddhism; the two somewhat extreme cases we have described, far from being exceptional, are only illustrative of a hundred divergences of opinion on doctrinal issues – some of them of fundamental importance. Ere long the student of the Dharma discovers, rather to his amazement, that whereas the *dharmas* are for one school realities, for another they are merely words; on the one hand he is exhorted to work out his own salvation with diligence, on the other to dedicate his life to the emancipation of all sentient beings; for *this* school the Buddha is merely a man who attained Enlightenment, while for *that* he is the wholly transcendental and eternally enlightened reality itself in human form; one party tells us that meditation and wisdom are inseparable, and that with the attainment of the former the latter is attained automatically, but this view the opposite party denies, saying that meditation is not necessarily associated with wisdom; *here* we see vegetarianism upheld, *there* meat-eating permitted; one school defines reality as absolute consciousness, another as complete emptiness; in some teachings *nirvāṇa* and *saṃsāra* are identical, in others an irreducible duality; on one side we see a celibate monastic order, on the other an association of married priests. And so on. The catalogue is without end.

Divergences in both institutional religion and personal religion being so numerous, and in many cases so radical, are we justified in speaking of Buddhism at all? Or are we not rather concerned with a number of practically independent religious movements, all more or less nominally Buddhist? Is Buddhism one or many? Obviously, there is no external uniformity. There is not always even unity of doctrine. What, then, constitutes the fundamental ground of unity in Buddhism?

The unity of Buddhism consists in the fact that, through differences and divergences of doctrine innumerable, all schools of Buddhism aim at Enlightenment, at reproducing the spiritual experience of the Buddha. The Dharma is therefore to be defined, not so much in terms of this or that particular teaching, but rather as the sum total of the means whereby that experience may be attained. Hence it can even be considered as being in principle and function, though not always in institutional form and specific intellectual content, identical for all schools of Buddhism.

from *A Survey of Buddhism*

2. THE FORMS OF EASTERN BUDDHISM

There is no harm in dressing up as an Indian, or pretending to be Japanese, or imagining that you are a Tibetan. It is quite harmless – except to the extent that it represents an alienation from your own culture. But it has nothing to do with being a Buddhist.

Historically speaking at least, Buddhism is an Eastern religion. It originated in India, and for 2,500 years it has been virtually confined to the East. It is only quite recently, in the course of the last hundred years in fact, that it has become known in the West at all. So what is the relation between Western Buddhists and Eastern Buddhism?

In attempting to answer this question, the first thing that has to be said is that there is no such thing as Eastern Buddhism. What we actually have is a number of Eastern Buddhisms, in the plural. Broadly speaking there are four of these now extant in the Eastern Buddhist world. There is South-east Asian Buddhism, Chinese Buddhism, Japanese Buddhism, and Tibetan Buddhism.

South-east Asian Buddhism is found in Sri Lanka, Burma, Thailand, and in Cambodia – as well as, here and there, in Singapore and Malaysia. This form of Buddhism belongs to the Theravāda school, whose scriptures are contained in the Pāli Tipiṭaka – in some forty-five volumes in the Royal Thai edition.

Chinese Buddhism is found mainly in China, Taiwan, Korea, Vietnam, and, again, in parts of Singapore and Malaysia. (I am of course ignoring recent political developments which have certainly altered the situation.) Chinese Buddhism belongs to what we may call 'general', or non-sectarian, Mahāyāna, and its scriptures are contained in the *Sānzàng*, or 'Three Treasuries', corresponding to the Tipiṭaka, in fifty-five volumes. These volumes are very much bigger than the volumes of the Pāli Tipiṭaka. In this particular collection there are no less than 1,662 independent works, a few of which are almost as long as the Bible.

Japanese Buddhism is found, of course, in Japan, but also in Hawaii, and among Japanese immigrants in mainland USA. It comprises various schools of what may be described as 'sectarian' Mahāyāna. The best known of these are Zen and Shin. There are also various modern schools developed even in the present century. The scriptures of Japanese Buddhism are the Chinese *Sanzàng* plus various Japanese works according to sect – which may in practice sometimes displace the *Sānzàng*.

Tibetan Buddhism is found in Tibet, Mongolia, Sikkim, Bhutan, Ladakh, parts of China, and even in parts of the former USSR. It consists of four main traditions, all of which follow all three of the *yānas* – that is, Hīnayāna, Mahāyāna, and Vajrayāna. The differences between these four traditions occur mainly in respect of Vajrayāna – that is to say Tantric – lineages. Their scriptures are all contained in the Kangyur, which means the 'Buddha-word', in 100 or 108 (according to the edition) xylographed volumes, plus special collections like the *Rinchen-Terma* for the Nyingmapas, or the *Milarepa Grubum* in the case of the Kagyupas.

These are the four extant Eastern schools of Buddhism. There are many intermediate forms, and sub-forms, and sub-sub-forms, but for the sake of simplicity I have ignored them. For practical purposes Western Buddhists find themselves confronted by four Eastern Buddhisms rather than by just one monolithic Eastern Buddhism with complementary unitary features.

Perhaps I could just add here that they do not find themselves confronted by an Eastern mind, or by an Eastern psychology either. Some writers speak of the Western mind and the Eastern mind as though they were two completely different minds, and it is suggested that it is very difficult for the Eastern mind to understand the Western mind, and vice versa. Buddhism of course is supposed to be a product of the Eastern mind, which is why, we are sometimes told, it is difficult for Westerners to understand Buddhism. Speaking from experience, however, I have found no evidence for any such belief. Wherever I went during my twenty years in the East, whether I was associating with Indians, Tibetans, Mongolians, Thais, or Sinhalese – or even Europeans, I found that I could understand them, and they could understand me. Buddhism is admittedly difficult to understand, but not because it is a product of the 'Eastern mind'. It is difficult to understand because it is a product of the *Enlightened* mind, a mind which transcends the conditionings of both the East and the West.

Another popular myth which I might as well mention in this connection is that there is a 'spiritual' East, and a 'materialistic' West. This really is another myth. The West is no more materialistic than the East. One might say that the West is simply more 'successful' in its pursuit of materialism.

However, to return to the theme of Western Buddhists and the four Eastern Buddhisms, these four Eastern Buddhisms are differentiated from each other in two main ways. They are differentiated, first of all, according to the doctrinal school of Buddhism to which they belong. Secondly, they are differentiated according to the regional or national culture with which they are associated.

From a practical point of view, at least, the regional, cultural association is probably the more important since, as a consequence, the Buddhism that most people come across in the West, whether in content or in practice, is not really Buddhism. We could even say that many Western Buddhists never really encounter Buddhism at all. What they encounter is a particular school or sub-school of Buddhism associated with a particular national or regional culture. They may encounter the Theravāda, for instance, which is associated with South-east Asian – specifically Sinhalese – culture. Or they may encounter Zen, which is associated with Japanese culture, and so on.

But the situation is even more complicated than that. Buddhism arose in India, a country with a very rich and ancient culture. From its very beginning, from the moment it emerged from the Buddha's mouth, so to speak, Buddhism was associated with Indian culture, indeed with Indian cultures, because in the course of the 1,500 years during which Buddhism was alive in India, Indian culture went through several different phases of development, each with very strongly marked characteristics.

When Buddhism went on from India to China, what actually 'went' was Buddhism plus Indian culture. Then, in China, Buddhism assumed certain Chinese cultural characteristics before going on to Japan. In Japan, of course, Buddhism assumed certain Japanese characteristics. So today, Japanese Buddhism consists of Buddhism plus Indian culture plus Chinese culture plus Japanese culture. *That* is the Buddhism which is coming to the United States of America, to Britain, to Australia, and so on. Sometimes, of course, the Buddhism succeeds in penetrating all those layers of culture which are superimposed upon it, but sometimes it does not.

Confronted by these different Eastern Buddhisms, the first thing that the Western Buddhist has to do is learn to distinguish what is really Buddhism from what is actually South-east Asian, or Chinese, or Japanese, or Tibetan, or even Indian culture. It is not that there is anything wrong with any of those cultures; they are often very beautiful indeed. But they are not the same thing as Buddhism, not the same thing as the Dharma.

However, some Western Buddhists are unable to make this distinction between Buddhism and Eastern culture. They think that they are attracted by Buddhism when in reality they are attracted to an exotic oriental culture. Sometimes they think they are trying to be Buddhists when in reality they are just trying to copy Indians, Japanese, or Tibetans – or at least to look like them. This is quite harmless of course. There is no harm in dressing up as an Indian, or pretending to be Japanese, or imagining that you are a Tibetan. It is quite harmless – except to the extent that it represents an alienation from your own culture – but it has nothing to do with actually being a Buddhist.

In some parts of the West we now have a very strange situation indeed. All four of the main Eastern Buddhisms have now been introduced. They have their Western followers, all of whom are supposedly Buddhists; but because they follow different Eastern cultures they are unable to live together or to practise Buddhism together.

I remember an example of this sort of thing from the very early days of the FWBO. Not far from London lived a group of English Zen Buddhists. They decided that they would like to join one of our FWBO communities, and, after some discussion, we agreed – even though I had my own misgivings. Almost as soon as they had moved in, a difficulty arose: they refused to join in the puja – that is, the evening devotions. The reason for this was that our puja was recited in Pāli and English, and their guru (who was, incidentally, an English woman who had spent some time in Japan) had told them that they should do their puja only in Japanese.[91] So while some members of the community performed their puja in English and Pāli these English Zen Buddhists waited outside the shrine-room; they would not even sit in the room and listen.

Another example comes to mind in connection with this same guru. Japanese culture is what sociologists call a 'shame culture'. In Japanese culture shame is used as a technique of social control. (Our Western Christian culture is probably a 'guilt culture'.) In traditional Japanese society, when a young person misbehaves, an older person will proceed to imitate him – but greatly exaggerating the misdemeanour. If the young person has been noisy, the older person will be four or five times as noisy. If he has slammed a door the older person must go and slam it three or four times very, very loudly. The young person then feels ashamed; he realizes that he has been corrected and desists from that particular misbehaviour out of shame. At some stage this technique of control through shame was transferred to the Japanese Zen temple. If the disciple misbehaved the master would imitate him. If the disciple slouched during meditation the master would immediately slouch right over; the disciple would notice, feel ashamed, pull himself up straight, and in that way he would learn. The technique was known as 'mirroring'.

Now this English/Japanese Zen guru happened to pass through London some years ago. It seems that she did not very much like what some of the English Buddhists, who had not been to Japan, were doing. So she started mirroring them. Her head monk, an American who was accompanying her, started mirroring them as well. For example, thinking that English Buddhists ate far too much while on retreat, he started mirroring them, and took a second helping of everything, just to show them how greedy they were. However, the English Buddhists, not being Japanese, did not understand what was going on. They thought the poor fellow must be hungry, and gave him a third helping of everything. The guru, I heard, was quite annoyed. She said that English Buddhists were stupid because they could not appreciate her mirroring technique. But really it was she who could not understand that mirroring was part of Japanese culture; it had nothing to do with Buddhism, and it was not appropriate in the West.

from *New Currents in Western Buddhism*

3. THE IDEAL APPROACH TO BUDDHISM

To identify Buddhism with one particular version, on whatever grounds, is ridiculous.

In the *Udāna* the Buddha relates the Parable of the Blind Men and the Elephant.[92] A number of men, blind from birth, are asked to feel the body of an elephant and then describe the beast. Those who felt the head declared it to be a pot, those who grasped the ear said it was a winnowing-basket, those who handled the tusk opined it was a ploughshare, and so on. Eventually, each one vehemently maintaining his own opinion, they began to quarrel and fight. The parable illustrates not only the one-sidedness of the sectarian teachers of the Buddha's own time, in connection with whom it was originally told, but also the wide divergences that can be noticed between the different approaches to Buddhism adopted by modern writers.

Until very recently three approaches were most common. They may be termed respectively the sectarian, the fundamentalist, and the encyclopedic. The basic error of the sectarian approach is that it mistakes the part for the whole. Quite early in the history of Buddhism, perhaps within a century of the *parinirvāṇa*, there arose within the Buddhist community circumstances which eventually led to the formation of different schools. Though differing on various doctrinal and disciplinary points, these schools shared a common tradition which united them to a far greater extent than their points of difference divided them. As time went on, however, and they started occupying different geographical centres, not only in India but throughout Asia, their differences gradually grew more pronounced. The result is that instead of consisting of one version of the Dharma only, Buddhism now comprises a number of different versions laid as it were side by side and overlapping in varying degrees. To identify Buddhism with one particular version, on whatever grounds, is ridiculous. As Dr Edward Conze says,

> The doctrine of the Buddha, conceived in its full breadth, width, majesty and grandeur, comprises all those teachings which are linked to the original teaching by historical continuity, and which work out methods leading to the extinction of individuality by eliminating the belief in it.[93]

Unfortunately, some corners of the Buddhist world have not yet awoken to the truth of these words. Books, pamphlets, and articles continue to be produced which naively present a single branch as the whole tree. This is not to say that the branch is not a noble branch, nor that individual accounts of the different Buddhist schools are not needed. We refer to something quite different: the practice of presenting, as complete accounts of Buddhism, what are in fact expositions of the tenets of one school based on a highly selective reading of a single branch of the canonical literature, usually the Pāli Tipiṭaka. Some writers go to the extreme of explicitly repudiating as 'not the pure Dharma' all Buddhist traditions but their own.⁹⁴ Despite occasional absurdities of this kind, however, the sectarian type of approach to Buddhism is fortunately on the wane. Throughout the Buddhist world the conviction is steadily gaining ground that so far as the Dharma is concerned the truth, to apply the Hegelian dictum, is the whole.⁹⁵

The fundamentalist approach is concerned with what the Buddha 'really' said. It has two forms. The first to some extent coincides with the sectarian approach which, in one of its forms, maintains even in the face of abundant internal evidence to the contrary that the Pāli Tipiṭaka consists entirely of the *ipsissima verba* of the Buddha. The second, the intellectually respectable form, is a product of modern scholarship, largely non-Buddhist. By means of textual criticism, comparison with archaeological and epigraphical evidence, etc., it endeavours to separate the passages belonging to earlier from those belonging to later strata of the canonical literature. Broadly speaking, this attempt has met with some success. The fundamentalist desires, however, a greater degree of certainty than the nature of the subject allows. Even if it is possible to isolate the most ancient texts, the problem of the relation of these to the oral tradition which preceded them and of this to the Buddha's own utterances remains insoluble. It is doubtful whether any known Buddhist text contains a line which preserves the Dharma in the same language or dialect in which it was originally expounded by the Buddha. The more strictly scientific methods are applied, the greater likelihood there seems to be that the fundamentalist will eventually be left with nothing but the Buddha's 'noble silence'. Some, indeed, horrified by the void confronting them, have sought to fill it with their own arbitrary constructions of what they imagine the Buddha 'really' taught. Both forms of fundamentalism commit the mistake of assuming that the teaching is bound up with a certain form of words, and that unless these are known it cannot be properly understood.

The encyclopedic approach emphasizes breadth rather than depth of knowledge. It tends to confuse knowledge *about* Buddhism with knowledge *of* Buddhism. It is concerned more with facts than with principles, tries to see from without instead of feeling from within. For a century it has profoundly influenced, if not dominated, the world of non-traditional Buddhist scholarship. Since it is not an isolated phenomenon, but has its roots deep in the soil of the modern scientific outlook, whose general tendencies it exemplifies within its own special field, this approach is likely to remain important for some time to come. Provided its limitations are understood, and any mischief to which they might give rise guarded against, this is not necessarily a bad thing for Buddhism. Such scholarship has accomplished much useful work. Moreover, during the last decade it has been leavened and enlivened, in the case of one or two well-known writers, by elements of sympathy and understanding which were originally lacking. Nevertheless, this does not alter the basic fact that, owing to the vast extent of Buddhist literature, which includes thousands of works regarded as canonical, besides innumerable non-canonical works, its aim of achieving complete factual knowledge about Buddhism and from this inferring its nature is impossible of attainment.

The ideal approach to Buddhism incorporates elements from the sectarian, the fundamentalist, and the encyclopedic approaches, shorn of their imperfections. It has for basis an insight into the Dharma derived from the actual practice of a system of spiritual discipline which, owing to the specialized nature of such techniques, is necessarily that of a particular school – Japanese Zen, Tibetan Mahāmudrā, or the Thai 'sammā arahaṃ' method. Despite this fact, it will be vividly aware and warmly appreciative of the multiple richness of the Buddhist tradition, and however firmly it may grasp a particular thread will never lose sight of its connection with the whole fabric. While accurately distinguishing earlier formulations of the teaching from later ones, and even preferring the former for introductory purposes, it will not commit the mistake of treating the age of a formulation as the sole criterion of its spiritual authenticity, nor consider the Dharma to be limited to its verbal expressions. Depth will not, however, exclude breadth. Besides keeping abreast of developments in the field of non-traditional Buddhist studies, the ideal approach to Buddhism will not only take all Buddhism for its province but will enforce its conclusions by drawing upon as wide a range of scriptural reference as possible. Above all, it will be concerned to exhibit the living spirit of Buddhism.

from *The Three Jewels*

4. THE NATURE OF TANTRIC BUDDHISM

Tantric Buddhism is concerned not with theories or speculations, not with formal religiosity or external piety, but with the direct experience, in the depths of one's being, of what one truly and essentially is.

I well remember my early impressions of the Tantra. As I tried to penetrate a little into it, to see what it was about and how it connected with other forms of Buddhism and with modern thought (psychology, comparative symbolism, and so on) I felt more and more that it was a jungle – a jungle in which one could very easily get lost. There seemed to be so many different traditions within it. There were so many meditation methods and forms of ritual observance, so many kinds of offerings, even so many kinds of ceremonial robe – and, indeed, ceremonial hat.

I used to tell my Tibetan friends that I found the Tantra far too vast and complicated to study as a whole, and that I was therefore going to confine myself to the study of one little corner of it. My chosen field of study, I said, would be the hats, some of which were very weird and wonderful indeed. I would make a collection of at least a hundred kinds of Tantric hat, and then write a book about them. Of course, I never did. But even when I began to study the Tantra in earnest, there were so many images in the temples, so many scroll paintings, so many figures of Buddhas and bodhisattvas and gurus, and *ḍākas* and *ḍākinīs* and *dharmapālas*, that for a long time I continued to feel that the Tantra was truly a vast jungle.

This is likely to be the experience of any Westerner beginning to investigate the Tantra. The impression one gets of richness and variety, growth, fertility, and abundance is quite bewildering to begin with. But a feeling of being lost among the creative symbols of Tantric Buddhism is no cause for alarm. Indeed, to become *intellectually* lost in the context of the Tantra is quite a positive thing. One may find oneself moved or stirred by the symbols without being able to say exactly how or why. With more experience, one comes to discover that the Tantra is not really the jungle it appears to be. It is more like a garden or, rather, a complex of gardens. Despite the richness of the Tantra, despite its incredible profusion, its superabundance of material, and its exuberance, there is a pattern running through it, or a number of interlocking patterns.

These patterns are not intellectual but spiritual. They are not imposed on the Tantra from the outside, but unfold from within it, expressing its innermost nature and essential purpose.

What is that purpose? Tantric Buddhism is concerned not with theories or speculations, not with formal religiosity or external piety, but with the direct experience, in the depths of one's being, of what one truly and essentially is. It seeks to reveal to us our essential nature – not just psychologically but existentially, metaphysically, even transcendentally. So far as the Tantra is concerned, this experience cannot be mediated by concepts. In fact, concepts give no idea of it at all, do not lead to it or point to it in any way. It is beyond words, beyond thought, beyond the conscious mind and personality. But this direct experience can be evoked, conjured up, or at least glimpsed, with the help of symbols. The whole Tantric path to Enlightenment is strewn with symbolic images, mantras, and rituals. You stumble over them at every step; indeed, the Tantric path largely consists of them. And they are all intended to reflect, or lead to, or give a glimpse of, this direct experience.

from *Creative Symbols of Tantric Buddhism*

5. WHAT DO ALL THE SCHOOLS OF BUDDHISM HAVE IN COMMON?

A clue through the labyrinth, a switch that, when turned on, will light up the whole edifice – in short, a principle of unity that will enable us to see the schools as all 'parts of one tremendous whole' which is Buddhism – does exist.

Like almost all productions of the Indian mind Buddhism is characterized by richness, profusion, amplitude, and diversity. In the course of fifteen centuries of uninterrupted development on Indian soil its inherent spiritual vitality has found expression in a multitude of forms. Organizationally, it consists of an immense number of schools, all of which are branches of, or divisions within, the one sangha, and all of which besides sharing in the common heritage have their own distinctive doctrines and practices, their own lineages of teachers, and their own literatures. Pluralistic realism, absolutism, and idealism all flourished in turn, each being regarded by men of the highest philosophical genius as the correct interpretation of

Buddhist thought. Now wisdom is recommended as the principal means to deliverance, now meditation, and now faith and devotion. One great spiritual movement proclaims emancipation of self alone as the goal of the religious life, another Supreme Enlightenment for the sake of all sentient beings. And so on and so on. These differences, amounting sometimes to logical contradictions, give to Buddhism an appearance not only of multifariousness but of confusion. Like a traveller lost in some enormous, architecturally complex Indian temple, the student tends to be so overwhelmed by the lavish abundance of the ornamentation as to be incapable of appreciating the simplicity and grandeur of the design. Since there is an almost complete absence of historical records, Chinese pilgrims and Tibetan historians being sometimes the sole available sources of information for crucial periods, the student moreover finds himself alone in the temple at night – its immensities dimly lit by lamps that allow him, as he gropes his way around, no more than a glimpse of a column here and an archway there.

A clue through the labyrinth, a switch that, when turned on, will light up the whole edifice – in short a principle of unity that will enable us to see the schools as all 'parts of one tremendous whole' which is Buddhism – does however exist. The unity of Buddhism consists in the fact that, through differences and divergencies of doctrine innumerable, all schools of Buddhism aim at Enlightenment, at reproducing the spiritual experience of the Buddha. This unity is not rational but transcendental. That is to say, the doctrinal and other differences between the schools are not resolved by being reduced on their own level one to another or all to a conceptual denominator, but transcended by referring them to a factor which, being supra-logical, can be the common object of contradictory assertions. According to the Prajñāpāramitā *sūtras*, indeed, recourse to paradoxes or propositions involving a logical oppugnancy, as when the bodhisattva is urged to deliver sentient beings who do not exist,[96] is inevitable if justice is to be done to the non-conceptual nature of Reality and of the spiritual experience which has Reality for its 'objective' counterpart. The specific differences between the schools are due to the fact that the schools approach the transcendental factor, Enlightenment or Nirvāṇa, from opposite directions.

This can be made clearer by a reference to the five spiritual faculties (*pañca-indriya*), a set of 'cardinal virtues' figuring prominently in the early literature. The five are faith (*śraddhā*), vigour (*vīrya*), mindfulness (*smṛti*), concentration (*samādhi*), and wisdom (*prajñā*). All these the disciple develops equally, counterbalancing, by means of mindfulness, faith and wisdom, and vigour and concentration, in such a way as to attain a state of perfect psychological and spiritual equilibrium (*indriya-samatta*). Soṇa Koḷivisa is rebuked for developing vigour at the expense of concentration. In a famous simile, the Buddha tells him that, just as a lute is unfit for playing when the strings are either too taut or too slack, so does too much output of vigour conduce to restlessness and too feeble a vigour to slothfulness. He should, therefore, determine on evenness of vigour.[97] Full development of the five spiritual faculties makes one an *arhant*.[98] After the Buddha's *parinirvāṇa*, or 'final passing away', however, different schools tended to specialize, as it were, in one particular faculty and to approach Enlightenment from that 'direction'. Thus, for example, the Abhidharmikas and the Mādhyamikas developed wisdom, the Yogācārins concentration, the popular devotional movements faith, and the esoteric Tantric traditions vigour.

The five spiritual faculties can also be cultivated one after another.[99] It is also possible, therefore, to regard them as representing so many successive stages of spiritual development. Explaining how those unworthy beings who are hard to tame are brought to subjugation, the Lord says in the *Hevajra Tantra*:

> First there should be the public confession (*poṣadha*), then
> they should be taught the ten rules of virtuous conduct, then
> the Vaibhāṣya teachings, and then the Sautrāntika, after that
> the Yogācāra and the Madhyamaka. Then when they know all
> mantra-method, they should start upon Hevajra.[100]

Usually, however, when arranged according to the order of their spiritual progression, the schools are subsumed under the three *yānas*, that is to say the Hīnayāna, the Mahāyāna, and the Vajrayāna, representing the three phases of the Buddha's personal teaching and the three stages of its historical development. By cultivating each *yāna* in turn, taking the earlier as the basis for the understanding and practise of the later, the disciple attains Supreme Enlightenment. The *triyāna* system is, therefore, not just a philosophical synthesis, but the most practical possible expression of the unity of Buddhism.

Inasmuch as all were regarded as aiming, in one way or another, at the same goal, it is not surprising that between the different schools of Buddhism there was a relationship of mutual respect and tolerance. This is not to say that doctrinal differences were not keenly felt and vigorously debated, or that sectarian feeling did not sometimes run high; but such differences were always settled peacefully, by means of discussion, no attempt ever being made to enforce conformity. Persecution, or 'arguing by torture', was unknown. Neither was anyone ever consigned to hell by his opponent for holding unorthodox views. The Pudgalavādins, who believed in the real existence of the Person, were constantly refuted by other schools; but no one ever questioned their ability to gain Enlightenment. Such, indeed, was the harmony that prevailed, that monks of different schools sometimes occupied the same monastery, observing a common rule and sharing in the same corporate monastic life, but devoting themselves, in addition, each to his own special studies and meditations.

from *A Bird's-Eye View of Indian Buddhism*

6. MISUNDERSTANDINGS ABOUT BUDDHISM

Confusing Buddhism with any one of its specific forms is like identifying an entire oak tree with a single branch or even a single acorn.

Buddhism has been known now in Europe and North America for considerably more than a hundred years, and one might have thought that, at least in some quarters, it would have become fairly well known. Unfortunately this is by no means the case. Even after all this time and so much scholarship, it is still relatively unknown and often misunderstood. Some people, for example, still classify Buddhism as one of the various 'religions' of the world – which it is not, if the word 'religion' is taken to mean (as it almost always is) 'religion as revelation' or 'revealed religion'. For other people Buddhism is some sort of exotic oriental cult. For others again, Buddhism is a system of abstract philosophical ideas, quite remote from ordinary life, something in fact that does not impinge on life at any point. Another misunderstanding that used to be very widespread is the view of Buddhism as simply a code of ethics that tells you what you should or should not do – merely a system of rules and prohibitions. Yet others see Buddhism as a form of asceticism – at least, this was the case when I returned to England from India in 1964. In those days, when people came to visit me in the vihara, or small monastery, where I was staying, they were surprised to find that there were no high walls or barbed wire surrounding the building and that everybody could enter freely and talk to whomever they chose. They seemed to expect that we would be completely secluded from the world, and living in perpetual solemn silence (despite the fact that the vihara was in the middle of Hampstead). This used to be quite a prevalent impression of Buddhism then, that it was something negative, repressive, and life-denying.

In addition to these general misunderstandings, many people identify Buddhism with one or another of its specific forms. For example, they encounter the Buddhism of Thailand or the Buddhism of Sri Lanka and think that this, and only this, is Buddhism. Or they come into contact with the colourful and rich tradition of Tibetan Buddhism, and they are carried away by their feelings for lamas, thigh-bone trumpets, thangkas, and all the rest of the Tantric tradition, and think that this is Buddhism – just this and nothing more. Others read books by Japanese masters, start trying to solve koan, and think, 'Zen! Zen is Buddhism. All the other schools, all the other teachings, are not Buddhism at all. Zen is the real thing!' Perhaps the most damaging identification of this kind is to confuse Buddhism with Nichiren Buddhism, a sect that is so far from the central Buddhist tradition as to exhibit some of the characteristics of a 'revealed religion', including an infallible book (the *White Lotus Sūtra*), a prophet (Nichiren), and an intolerant and dismissive attitude towards other forms of Buddhism. Confusing Buddhism with any one of its specific forms in this way is like identifying an entire oak tree with a single branch or even a single acorn.

In view of such misunderstandings – and I've just touched upon some of the more prominent, popular ones – it is reasonable to say that Buddhism is not really known in the West. Sometimes it is actually dangerous to be slightly acquainted with something, because we tend to overlook the fact that we do not really know it. As Pope puts it, 'A little learning is a dangerous thing.'[101] In some cases, it might be better to have no knowledge at all, better to wipe the slate clean of all our misunderstandings and misinterpretations and make a completely fresh start. And this is the purpose for which the Friends of the Western Buddhist Order (FWBO) was founded in 1967 – to make a completely fresh start at Buddhism.

from *Buddhism for Today and Tomorrow*

PART II
BUDDHISM AND THE MIND

I
THINKING CLEARLY

1. 'THE IMPOSSIBILITY OF RETRACTING AN OPINION I BELIEVE TO BE TRUE'

I became aware of the existence within me of a rock bottom of obstinacy that made it utterly impossible for me to retract or disown any opinion which I genuinely believed to be true even to save my life.

Satyapriya, the friend with whom I travelled and was ordained in India, was so morbidly sensitive, and so quick to take offence, that he seemed to imagine differences where none existed. It was as though he had to create a difference in order to give himself an excuse for losing his temper. Something of this sort happened two or three days after we had stopped observing silence. We were bathing in the icy waters of the pool, eight or ten feet across and very deep, that lay beneath an overhanging fragment of rock, a few yards along the cliff face from the temple. Something I said, which he interpreted as expressing a difference of opinion, upset him, and despite all my efforts to calm him down he succeeded in gradually working himself up to a pitch of murderous fury such as I had never before witnessed. He had had enough of me, he hissed, his eyes bloodshot with rage. He had allowed me to torment him with my unreasonable behaviour too long already. Now he was going to kill me. He would drown me in the pool. No one would ever know. He would tell them that I had died accidentally. Looking at him,

I knew that he meant it. For the first time in my life I was actually face to face with death. Strange to say, though I was frightened, I had no intention whatever of withdrawing the offending remark. On the contrary, I became aware of the existence within me of a rock bottom of obstinacy that made it utterly impossible for me to retract or disown any opinion which I genuinely believed to be true even to save my life. How the episode ended I no longer recollect.

from *The Rainbow Road from Tooting Broadway to Kalimpong*

2. THE VOICE WITHIN

Buddhism has been described as 'the proudest assertion ever made of human freedom' because it stands up boldly, even defiantly, against the ponderous brute mass of externality that threatens to grind out of existence the moral and spiritual life of humanity.

Human beings are today less free to think and feel simply, naturally, and spontaneously than at any other period in history. The pitiless pressure of education and environment tends to grind down even the feeblest manifestation of independent and original thought or feeling. Our ideas and emotions are manufactured for us by those to whose advantage it is that we should think or feel as they hypocritically tell us it is good for us to think and feel. Lurid hoardings scream at us that this or that particular beverage will give us vitality and strength. Newspaper advertisements assure us with expressions of the fondest solicitude that yet another undreamed-of article is indispensable to our well-being. Political columnists tell us with an air of infallible authority which nation is right and which wrong, while popular orators inform us which ideological group we ought to love and which to hate. The propaganda machines of governments and political parties pour out an incessant stream of ready-made opinions on every possible subject, from the latest international crisis to the most recent scientific discovery. Critics of literature and art, with their 'book of the month' and 'picture of the year', save us the trouble of having to judge for ourselves which books and paintings deserve our attention and which do not. The synthetic emotion of the latest popular song renders deep and genuine feeling superfluous. Cinemas and radios, newspapers and school textbooks, billboards and public speeches, together with a thousand other devices for the mass-production and wide dissemination of prefabricated thoughts and emotions, opinions and ideas, are doing our thinking and feeling for us. We no longer create, but passively receive the cartoned products of mechanical efficiency. And that which does not create does not live. Stunned and deafened by the clamorous pressure of the external, we are no longer masters of ourselves, and therefore no longer masters of our environment. Our heads are full of ideas which we do not truly think, our hearts of emotions we do not sincerely feel. A thousand voices from the world without beat upon our ears as relentlessly as the surf upon the sea-beach. The Voice Within is silent.

Not only in the sphere of politics and commerce, literature and art, education and journalism, but in the sacred sphere of religion, also, the same intolerable weight of the external is felt. Here, in fact, it has been felt longer than that of almost anything else. The tyranny of cinema and radio, of popular slogan and newspaper advertisement, is a thing of yesterday and today; but the tyranny of religion dates back three or four millennia at least, to the time when divinely-inspired scriptures, infallible prophets, and mediatorial priesthoods made their first attempt to smother the nascent spiritual life. As advertisements tell us what to buy, and stump-orators how to vote, so do the Vedas, Bibles, and Korans tell us what to believe, and the prophets and priests who manipulate them, how to invest our money in celestial stocks and shares so as to obtain the largest possible dividends. When the poor investor eventually realizes who really profits from the whole transaction, he may be pardoned if he doubts equally the good faith of his political, commercial, and ecclesiastical advisers! Religious life, instead of being a voyage of spiritual self-discovery, thus becomes an uncritical acceptance of creeds and dogmas which subserve the selfish interests of some particular class or community. Independent thought and unbiased investigation are discouraged and, if possible, suppressed by force, while blind faith (the blinder the better!) is heaped with superlatives and extolled as the one infallible means of obtaining salvation. Divinely-revealed sacred books, infallible prophets, mediatorial priesthoods, and irrefragable dogmas have thundered so loud and long in the ear of humanity that it has been almost deafened by the sound. Once again, the Voice Within is silent or, if not silent, at least unheard.

Buddhism has been described as 'the proudest assertion ever made of human freedom'[102] because it stands up boldly, even defiantly, against the ponderous brute mass of externality that threatens to grind out of existence the moral and spiritual life of humanity. It not only teaches us that our first duty is to understand things as they really are, but gives us the courage necessary to make the attempt. It exhorts us never to allow ourselves to be overwhelmed by the flood of thoughts and emotions which come pouring in upon us from all sides, but to weigh and test each one of them in the light of our own knowledge and experience. We should be equally critical of the claims of an advertisement, an election poster, and a religious teaching. That which we find wrong and harmful we should at once reject, while that which we find true and good we should accept and endeavour to put into practice. We should in all circumstances think clearly and feel sincerely, then we will act rightly, too. For Buddhism does not take up such an independent attitude towards the external world simply for the sake of display, but in order to make room for the full development of our latent spiritual-creative powers. Pressure from without is wrong and bad only because it crushes the life which is struggling to flower forth from within.

This does not mean that we should allow free play to whatever instincts and impulses happen to spring up within us, but that the purpose of external discipline should be understood before its restraints are accepted. The Buddha said that his disciples should try his words as gold is tried by fire. They were neither to accept them nor reject them without examination. Their confidence in him should be like that of a patient in his doctor, or of a student in his teacher. The books in which his words have been recorded are not, therefore, regarded by his followers as a revelation in which they must blindly believe, but as a guide to practice with which they may experiment. For this reason Buddhism does not lend itself very easily to the manipulations of priestcraft, and wherever it has remained pure has contributed to the liberation of the creative forces of the human spirit.

When the eyes and ears are blinded and deafened by the very multiplicity of the sights and sounds which come surging in upon them, the mind grows bewildered and independent thought on the situation impossible. The Buddha therefore taught us that if we want to see things as they really are, if we desire to act nobly and powerfully in the affairs of life, we must first learn to retire within ourselves and hear, or rather feel, the whisper vibrating through the silence there. We must be our own island of refuge, our own light; we should not look to any external refuge. We should be deaf to all the voices that thunder at us from without so that we can listen to the Voice Within. Then only will we be the masters of ourselves, and masters of our environment. Then only will we be able to see and tread the path that will lead us, one day, even to the heart's Enlightenment.

from *Crossing the Stream*

3. GETTING A CLEAR IDEA OF BUDDHISM

The reason we so often fail to put in the commitment required to realize our ideals is that we have not addressed our underlying doubt and indecision about them.

Doubt and indecision lie at the root of our difficulties with the spiritual life, and that is where we have to bring clear thinking to bear. If one doesn't really believe that it is possible to develop as an individual, one won't be able to put into that development the energy that will enable one to develop. If one is unsure about the value or effectiveness of meditation, so that one does it with an attitude of just seeing how it will turn out, hoping something will come of practising it, one probably won't get very far. One can't start off with no doubts whatsoever, but there must be at least some sort of willing suspension of disbelief; one must have a degree of conviction sufficient to fuel one's practice with the requisite energy and decisiveness and thus produce a result tangible enough to confirm the rightness of the original decision. In this way there is a possibility of something tentative and provisional being proven on the anvil of experience.

For example, perhaps one believes that psychological development is possible but one is not sure about the whole idea of spiritual development – or vice versa. Either way, one has to be clear about what these notions actually amount to before one decides to commit oneself to them. The reason we so often fail to put in the commitment required to realize our ideals is that we have not addressed our underlying doubt and indecision about them.

Does one, for instance, really believe in the non-reality of the self? What *is* the self? In what sense is it unreal? And has one thought out one's position as regards oriental Buddhism and Buddhism in the West? As regards the three *yānas* – the Hīnayāna, the Mahāyāna, the Vajrayāna? As regards the *arhant* ideal and the bodhisattva ideal? Is one trying to be an *arhant*, or a bodhisattva? Or has one vaguely kept the two ideas (which are supposed to be ideals) in different compartments of one's mind, unsure how they might hang together – except that one day one somehow feels that it's time to get down to being an *arhant*, while the next it's the bodhisattva spirit that seems the thing.

One probably feels it's hardly worth thinking about, but inasmuch as one cares about these ideals at all, one hopes that in the long run they'll turn out to be more or less the same thing. Perhaps one likes to be pragmatic: perhaps one thinks that abstract theorizing and metaphysics are all right if you like that sort of thing, but they butter no parsnips. One has perhaps picked up the idea that the truth of things is not to be approached through the rational mind at all, but that it will suddenly vouchsafe itself while one is muddling along, and then everything will become clear.

But it is not going to be like this. One penetrates beyond the rational by way of exhausting the resources of the rational mind. The thing is not going to be achieved except through the tension of the rational mind stretching itself to its limit. Even more immediately practical matters require more clear thinking than we generally like to afford them. Why exactly should one be a vegetarian, for instance – what are the principles involved? Or why does one meditate – what actually is the point? You can't just say, 'If you're a Buddhist, these are the things you do.' Well, you can, but you won't thereby make much of an impression on a sceptical non-Buddhist.

It may be true that not everything one does as a Buddhist is fully susceptible to rational analysis. The Dharma does point towards something beyond the grasp of the rational mind. But there are rational considerations that certainly do arise, and which may be communicated in response to enquiries about why you do what you do. There can be a false humility in admitting that you have no clear idea about what you are doing.

from *Know Your Mind*

4. LEARNING TO THINK

From the point of view of learning to think clearly, argument is better than agreement.

To reflect on the Dharma is to reflect on the expression of fundamental truth in terms only barely accessible to human thought; without intellectual clarity we will be unable to grasp the essence of the teaching in all its subtlety and depth. If we are to practise Buddhism effectively, in short, we will need to learn to reflect.

It is not easy, however, to concentrate the mind and direct one's thoughts undistractedly for sustained periods. When you are engaged in a discussion or absorbed in a book, you might be able to hold your mind to a train of thought, but if you leave it to its own devices you are likely to find your attention wandering and your concentration starting to flag. You might set yourself to reflect undistractedly for an hour on, for instance, the three *lakṣaṇas* (Pāli *lakkhaṇas*), but it takes a lot of practice to manage more than a few minutes. (Anyone who doubts this should try it and see what happens.)

Thinking should be under one's control, and when it isn't objectively necessary one just shouldn't engage in it. The Buddha used to exhort his disciples to maintain a noble silence (Pāli *ariya-mona*) rather than indulge in unprofitable talk, and one could say that the same should go for thought-processes. The alternative to clear and mindful thinking should not be idle mental chatter; one should be able to maintain inner silence. Again, it is obviously a lot easier to say this than to do it – but it is possible.

One way to improve one's ability to think in a directed way is to plan time for thinking. One can learn to take up and put down one's thinking according to one's own needs, not just circumstances. Why not plan thinking time just as you schedule other activities? This is in effect a practice of *samprajanya*, mindfulness of purpose. We all have plenty to think about but our trains of thought seldom reach a conclusion. We are forever dropping one thing and picking up another, then when we sit down to meditate, unfinished business resurfaces and hinders our concentration. Such muddled mental activity is an obstacle to action of any kind and means that we often end up making decisions on the spur of the moment rather than thinking them through. If it is necessary to make a decision it is best to sit down, apply oneself to the matter in hand, and come to a well-considered conclusion. But if we sit down to reflect at all, we often turn the matter over in our mind in such a half-hearted way that quite soon our thoughts have wandered away to irrelevant topics. Unable to come to any clear conclusion, we just make the decision on the basis of how we happen to be feeling at the time, or in response to some quite incidental external pressure. We cannot afford to do this if our decisions are going to count for anything.

We should think about things when we have time to do them justice. Just as mealtimes, meeting friends, and making time for exercise and meditation involve making definite arrangements, mental activity can also be planned. You could apportion, say, an afternoon each week for thinking about things that really matter, things that are of much more consequence than day-to-day practicalities, although they might not be so pressing. If you keep yourself free of thinking about your deeper problems until the appointed time, you might also find everyday difficulties easier to deal with. If you try this out, though, make sure you are going to be free from interruption for however long you need – half an hour or an hour, or even weeks or months together. A chain of sustained and directed thinking can be very subtle, and to have it snapped by untimely and trivial interruptions is painful. The idea of planning in a period of thinking at two o'clock on Tuesday afternoon might come as a shock, but anyone with a busy life already has to do this to some extent. There are always urgent matters to attend to, but these should not be allowed to push the really important questions to the margins of our consciousness.

Whether planned or not, the best way to improve one's directed thinking is simply to think more. Just as physical exercise is the way to become fit, so thinking is the way to improve the capacity for thought. It is a good idea to take any opportunity you get to consider views and opinions with a logical, questioning attitude. Reasoned discussion with a friend or in a small group – the smaller the better – gives different angles on an issue and brings an enjoyable stimulus to thinking. Because our views tend to be emotionally based, if you are thinking about something on your own, there is always the temptation to come to a premature conclusion and resist thinking along lines that run counter to that conclusion. Collaborative thinking forces you to be more objective, to look for a truth that does not necessarily suit you. There is something about the physical presence of another person that generates interest and a keenness to get at the truth, and if you are talking with someone whose intellect is quite active, you might find that you have to get used to organizing and articulating your thoughts more carefully, to avoid non-sequiturs and short-cuts in your argument. Your friends might convince you, or you them. You might even end up convincing yourself, if you were not sure at the outset of the discussion what you really thought. Writing also helps to develop clear thinking – your argument has to be more rigorous than when you are speaking to people you know, and you have to be more careful to make logical connections between the ideas you present.

From the point of view of learning to think clearly, argument is better than agreement. If you only ever have discussions with people whose views you share and read books you agree with, you will never be obliged to address any faulty reasoning that might underpin your view of things. A valid conclusion does not guarantee the logic of any and every argument used in its support. A statement based on a poor line of argument – or no argument at all – might go unchallenged because everyone agrees with the conclusion anyway, regardless of how it is reached. It can therefore be a good idea to seek out a bit of opposition: there is nothing like meeting criticism for improving one's ability to frame a logical argument and make it watertight. Even though sound arguments are unlikely to win over someone with a deep emotional investment in the views they hold, trying to win that person over can make you aware of the strength or weakness of your logic. On the other hand, if your arguments do hold water, the confidence this gives you will help you to be more open to new ideas, because you will know that you have the ability to sift through them without getting muddled or feeling threatened.

from *Living with Awareness*

5. MORE AND MORE OF LESS AND LESS

'The books and letters which you do not practise – give them up!'

On an intellectual level, Buddhism, historically, is characterized by clarity, honesty, and rigour of thought. The problem from our point of view is that most of us aren't accustomed to analysing situations and propositions, to rigorously drawing conclusions from evidence properly adduced. We tend to go on hunches, bits and pieces of information, and little scraps of knowledge, from which we draw all sorts of weird and wonderful conclusions.

As Buddhists, therefore, we need to challenge one another to think more clearly. We don't have to be nit-picking or unnecessarily controversial, but we do need to make sure that we know what we are talking about. For example, what do the words we use really mean? If they are translations from, say, the Pāli or Sanskrit, do we know how accurate they are? Indeed, are we really clear about the meaning of the terms we use in our own language? Dictionaries are full of interesting surprises.

We don't all have to be intellectuals, but whenever we use language we can try to use it clearly and precisely; otherwise it will give us vague and inaccurate ideas. One does not avoid the undoubted dangers of intellectualism by being sloppy; and sloppy thinking may even hinder one's spiritual development. It is true that transcendental insight itself is independent of conceptual thought, but it doesn't just appear out of nowhere. It arises on the basis of the conceptual expression of the Dharma. It is on the basis of thinking about the concept of impermanence, say, that you develop *insight* into the truth of impermanence. Intellectual understanding comes first; it's a sort of springboard.

Intellectual clarity is not attained by becoming better educated, reading more books, or becoming an intellectual. Indeed, becoming engrossed in theory is as unhelpful as woolly thinking. Wanting to know more and more about the theory and philosophy of Buddhism in a vain attempt to consume as much Buddhism as we can as fast as we can will just give us intellectual indigestion.

Some modern expositions of Buddhism deal so much in concepts, talk so much about Buddhist thought, Buddhist philosophy, and so on, that one can get the impression of something one-sidedly, even overwhelmingly, intellectual. It can seem as if to understand it you have to undergo a rigorous course in logic, metaphysics, and epistemology. But in ancient India, when spiritual teaching was entirely a matter of oral transmission, people were given exactly what they needed at the time. You couldn't read a book describing the stages of the path to Enlightenment. Perhaps you would be completely ignorant of the very idea of Enlightenment. You would go along to a teacher and he would say, after a bit of conversation or just looking you up and down, 'Go away and do this practice.' You would go away and do it, perhaps for several years, and when you had mastered it thoroughly he would give you some further teaching to practise. You certainly wouldn't be given a theoretical preview.

These days we are constantly being given theoretical previews. We know the path, we know all about the different stages, we know all about *prajñā*, we know all about the different degrees and levels of *śūnyatā*. Because we are so familiar with this material theoretically, it is hard for us to distinguish between theoretical knowledge and the kind of knowledge that comes only from experience. And to recognize the difference, we may have to *un*know what we know and *un*learn what we have learned.

What are we to do, given the amount of Buddhist theory by which we are surrounded? The key, probably, is more and more of less and less: in other words, to focus on a very few texts or teachings or approaches to the Dharma, and deepen our experience of them through reflection and practice and questioning. Indeed, that reflection and questioning itself should be real. Our reflections and questions should be our own – not just a game of rearranging concepts. A real question springs out of one's own experience, even one's own conflict. 'The books and letters which you do not practise – give them up!' is the robust statement of the great Buddhist teacher Padmasambhava.[103]

Western culture being what it is, we are probably going to want to make at least a rapid survey of the whole field. But having made it we should get back to where we actually are, and practise and study accordingly. The Buddha used the language of clear conceptual analysis, but the purpose of that analysis was never merely theoretical.

Sometimes the Buddha made this point by using a completely different language to communicate the Dharma – as when, according to the Zen tradition, on one occasion, in the midst of a gathering of monks, he spoke no words, but simply held up a golden flower. Of all the disciples gathered there just one, Mahākāśyapa, understood what was being communicated, and responded with a smile. And that, they say, is how Zen began. That great spiritual movement, which spread throughout the Far East and produced hundreds of Enlightened masters, sprang not from a system of philosophy, not from a lengthy discourse, but from that one simple action: the holding up of a golden flower, in whose petals all the wisdom of the Buddhas was to be discerned.[104] That is what Mahākāśyapa understood, and that is why he smiled. He probably thought to himself that the Buddha had never done anything more wonderful in his whole life than to hold up that golden flower, which even now is continuing to transmit its beauty.

The language of symbolism is a language that we too have to learn to speak. We may be ready, even glib, with the language of ideas and concepts – we may discuss Buddhist philosophy endlessly – but this must be complemented by the language of images. This dimension of communication may be comparatively unfamiliar to us, but by immersing ourselves in legends, myths, and symbols, we can learn to understand and even speak that language.

from *The Bodhisattva Ideal*

2
MIND REACTIVE AND CREATIVE

1. SONNET

Reading some books, you'd think the Buddha-Way,
As though macadamized, ran smooth and white,
Straight as an arrow, bill-boards left and right,
And that the yellow buses, thrice a day,
Whirled past the milestones, whose smug faces say,
'Nirvāṇa 15 miles.... By 10 tonight
You'll all be there, good people, and alight
Outside the Peace Hotel, where you're to stay.'

But those who read their own hearts, inly wise,
Know that the Way's a hacked path, roughly made
Through densest jungle, deep in the Unknown....
And that, though burn a thousand baleful eyes
Like death-lamps round, serene and unafraid,
Man through the hideous dark must plunge alone.

from *Complete Poems*

2. THE PATH OF REGULAR STEPS AND THE PATH OF IRREGULAR STEPS

Western Buddhists tend to pick and choose from the material available and to select not according to their real spiritual needs but according to quite subjective and superficial whims and fancies.

The distinction between the Path of Regular Steps and the Path of Irregular Steps is a very ancient one. It goes back to sixth-century China, to the great Chinese teacher Zhiyi, who was the virtual founder of one of the greatest of all Buddhist schools – though so far rather neglected by Western Buddhists – the Tiantai school.[105] Besides producing important works of scholarship, Zhiyi founded monasteries and preached the Dharma widely. By reason of his profound spiritual attainments he was able to attract an extraordinarily large number of disciples, and these he addressed from time to time, commenting upon the scriptures, speaking about the spiritual life, and especially, it seems, giving instruction on meditation. In the course of his discourses on meditation, many of which have come down to us, Zhiyi spoke of meditation by regular steps, of meditation by irregular steps, and also of meditation without any steps at all.[106]

On the present occasion we are concerned only with regular steps and irregular steps, and we are concerned with them because Zhiyi's distinction between meditation by regular steps and meditation by irregular steps is applicable not only to the practice of meditation but to the practice and experience of the whole spiritual path, in all its stages and all its aspects.

What then is the path of regular steps? What is the path of irregular steps? In attempting to answer these questions I propose to be a little irregular myself and deal with the second path first.

The path of irregular steps

In order to understand what the Path of Irregular Steps is, we must first look at Buddhism as it exists in the Western world today, whether in Britain, in continental Europe, or in the Americas. When we look, the first thing that we see is books – hundreds of books – about Buddhism. This is the most conspicuous feature of Buddhism in the West.

If we are young and enthusiastic, and have lots of time, we start trying to read these books – all of them if possible, or at least as many as we can of the better-known ones. Usually we read quite a lot – some of us may even get around to reading the Buddhist scriptures themselves. In this way, by virtue of our miscellaneous reading, we start getting an impression of Buddhism and even start forming ideas about it. These ideas are usually very confused. They are so confused that in many cases we do not even begin to realize how confused they are until years afterwards. In some cases we may never realize it. But meanwhile, we think we understand Buddhism because we have read about it.

The position is, however, that we do not understand Buddhism *at all*. When I say 'at all' I mean this quite literally. It is not that we have a little understanding of Buddhism, that we have grasped just a portion of it. The position is that we do not understand Buddhism *at all*. But we think we do. From this a very important consequence follows.

When we understand a thing – whether we really understand it or just think we do – we become in some sense superior to that thing. Understanding means appropriating; it means taking the subject of one's knowledge into oneself, making it part of oneself, making it one's own. Thus we speak in terms of 'mastering' a subject: mastering accountancy, or mastering mathematics. And so we speak – or at least think – of mastering Buddhism. So because we have, as we think, understood Buddhism – because we have appropriated it, and made it part of ourselves – we start feeling superior to Buddhism, because we have 'mastered' it. Because we feel superior to Buddhism we do not look up to it; we do not feel toward Buddhism any real devotion or reverence. We are in fact devoid of any such feelings. We have simply 'mastered' the subject.

This kind of attitude is not new, and it is by no means confined to modern Western Buddhists. It has been widespread in the Western world for quite a long time. We find Samuel Taylor Coleridge, the great poet and thinker, complaining about it 150 years ago (of course, within a Christian context) in the following terms:

> There is now no reverence for any thing; and the reason is
> that men possess conceptions only, and all their knowledge
> is conceptional only. Now as to conceive is a work of the
> mere understanding, and as all that can be conceived may be

comprehended, it is impossible that a man should reverence that to which he must always feel something in himself superior. If it were possible to conceive God in a strict sense, that is, as we conceive of a horse or a tree, even God himself could not excite any reverence.

And reverence, Coleridge goes on to say,

> is only due from man, and, indeed, only excitable in man, towards ideal truths, which are always mysteries to the understanding, for the same reason that the motion of my finger behind my back is a mystery to you now – your eyes not being made for seeing through my body.[107]

At about the same time as Coleridge was delivering himself of these sentiments, an even greater poet and thinker was saying much the same thing, though rather more briefly. In his *Maxims and Reflections* Goethe writes:

> The finest achievement for men of thought is to have fathomed the fathomable, and quietly to revere the unfathomable.[108]

It is this quiet revering of the unfathomable, of that which, in Buddhist terminology, is *atakkāvacara* or beyond the reach of thought – beyond the reach of understanding and conception – that until recently has been so lacking among Western Buddhists. We have been much too quick to 'understand', much too ready to speak, even about the unfathomable – in fact, *especially* about the unfathomable.

This is not altogether our fault. To a great extent it is the result of the situation in which we find ourselves. Amongst the mass of published material available to us – amongst so many translations of ancient Buddhist texts – there is much that is extremely advanced. Some of the great Mahāyāna *sūtras*, for example, are addressed to disciples of a high degree of spiritual development, as is made evident in their opening scenes. They begin with the Buddha seated in the midst of a great concourse of disciples, perhaps in some heaven or archetypal realm. All around him are *arhants* and great bodhisattvas, even irreversible bodhisattvas, that is, bodhisattvas who cannot regress from the ideal of supreme Buddhahood and who have, as it were, Nirvāṇa in the palm of their hand. The sublime teachings that the Buddha proceeds to give are addressed to such beings as these – beings who exist on a level of spirituality beyond all that we can conceive or imagine.

Many of these Mahāyāna *sutras* have now been translated and thus, in a sense, made available to us. So we read this or that *sūtra*, and we think we have mastered its contents, and thinking we have mastered it we tend to adopt a cool, superior, even patronizing attitude toward Buddhism. So much is this the case that some of us may even think it unnecessary to call ourselves Buddhists at all – after all, we have 'gone beyond' all that – and may even look down somewhat on those simple-minded folk in the West who do choose to call themselves Buddhists, who pay their respects to images, who offer flowers and light candles, and who try to observe the precepts. We may think our attitude more advanced, but the truth is that it is purely theoretical, purely mental, and devoid of any deep and genuine feeling of reverence and devotion.

Because of this lack of all 'quiet revering of the unfathomable,' until recently Western Buddhism has tended to be a rather shallow and superficial thing. Western Buddhists tend to pick and choose from the material available and to select not according to their real spiritual needs but according to quite subjective and superficial whims and fancies. Thus you find people saying 'I like this bit, but I do not like that bit. I am happy with the idea of karma, but I do not like the idea of rebirth.' Or you find people being drawn by the doctrine of *anātman* (Pali *anattā*). For some reason or other, the idea that they do not have a soul or a self seems rather to attract some people – though at the same time they find the thought of Nirvāṇa rather depressing. Thus people tend to pick and choose, and to select – and of course their likes and dislikes change. For a while one may be into Zen, because one rather likes the idea that one is already a Buddha, already 'there', and that there is nothing to do. It seems to make life a lot easier: one does not have to practise anything, apparently! One does not have to give up anything. So you rather like Zen – for a while. But eventually you get rather bored with being a Buddha, so you start getting into the Tantra, and Tantra, of course, immediately conjures up visions of sex, and you start getting into the yoga of sex (theoretically, of course!). In this way the average Western Buddhist has been browsing and dabbling for all these years.

Even so, despite all these difficulties – and they are difficulties that every one of us has experienced – some Western Buddhists do get around to practising Buddhism. On the basis of my personal experience, seeing so many people coming and going, I would say that perhaps, at a liberal estimate, one in twenty Western Buddhists gets around to trying to practise Buddhism. Eventually it dawns on them that Buddhism is not just a collection of interesting ideas – not just a philosophy, not just something to think about. It dawns on them that Buddhism is something to be applied, even something to be experienced. So they start trying to practise it; start trying to put it into operation. But, unfortunately, so strong is the force of conditioning and habit that even when they start trying to practise Buddhism the same old pattern, derived from their previous theoretical approach, persists. Their attitude is still shallow and superficial. They still tend to pick and choose.

Not so long ago there was very little Buddhism in the West in any form, books or otherwise. Now the situation is different. We could even say that there is too much Buddhism around. There are so many books, so many practices, so many teachers, so many schools represented! There is such a bewildering confusion and profusion of forms of Buddhism. In our excitement and greed we snatch first at this and then at that, sampling a bit here and a bit there, like a greedy child in a sweet shop. We are in the transcendental sweet shop of Buddhism, with all these beautiful spiritual goodies around us, and so we grab this and grab that: Zen, Tantra, Theravāda, ethics, meditation of one sort and another. But nonetheless, we do make some progress. The path of irregular steps is a path, and it does give us some experience of Buddhism.

But only up to a point. As we follow the path of irregular steps we find, sooner or later, that we are slowing down. We seem to be up against an invisible obstacle. Apparently in a sort of spiritual doldrums, we are going through the motions, but nothing is happening: we don't seem to be getting anywhere. At this point a radical change is called for. We need to make not just another change of direction within the path of irregular steps, but a more fundamental transition: a transition from the path of irregular steps to the path of regular steps.

The path of regular steps

What is the path of regular steps? How does it differ from the path of irregular steps, and why does further progress depend on our making a transition from the one to the other? To answer these questions we must first understand the nature of the path in general, the path which leads from *saṃsāra*, the round of mundane, conditioned existence, to Nirvāṇa, the 'realm' of unconditioned being, the path from unenlightened humanity to the Enlightened humanity of the Buddha.

The Buddhist path is traditionally divided into three successive stages: the stage of *śīla* or morality, the stage of *samādhi* or meditation, and the stage of *prajñā* or wisdom. Though there are other ways of dividing – and even subdividing – the path, this threefold division remains the most important and the most fundamental.

Śīla, morality, is simply skilful action: action which benefits oneself, which helps one to grow and develop; and action which benefits others too, which helps them also to grow and develop. Not that *śīla* is a matter of external action divorced from mental attitude; it is both the mental attitude and the mode of behaviour in which that attitude naturally expresses itself. Thus *śīla* is skilful action in the sense that it is action arising from certain skilful mental states, especially states of love, generosity, peace, and contentment. It is, indeed, everything one does out of these skilful mental states. That, essentially, is what morality or ethics in Buddhism comprises: actions expressive of skilful mental states.

Samādhi, usually translated 'meditation', is a word with many different meanings on a number of different levels. First of all, it consists in the gathering together of all one's scattered energies into a single focus. Most of the time our energies are divided; they take different directions; they are unintegrated. So first of all we have to integrate them. This does not mean forcibly concentrating on a particular point; it means bringing together all our energies, both conscious and unconscious, and harmonizing them in a natural and spontaneous manner. Thus concentration, in the sense of the complete unification of one's psychospiritual energies, is the first grade or level of *samādhi*.

Next, *samādhi* consists in the experience of progressively higher states of consciousness – states extending into what are called the *dhyānas* or superconscious states. In these states we transcend the body (in the sense of physical awareness) and also, eventually, the mind (in the sense of discursive mental activity). We also experience bliss, peace, joy, and ecstasy (but not transcendental insight, since we are still within *saṃsāra*, still within the realm of the mundane). Finally, *samādhi* includes the development of such supernormal powers of the mind as telepathy, clairvoyance, clairaudience, and the recollection of one's previous existences. However, 'supernormal' does not mean 'supernatural': when these powers arise in the course of meditation, they do so quite naturally and spontaneously.

The last stage of the threefold path is *prajñā* or wisdom. This consists in direct insight into, or personal contact with, the truth or reality. At first it occurs only momentarily, like a sudden flash of lightning that, on a dark night, lights up the landscape just for an instant. As the flashes of insight become more frequent, however, and more continuous, they eventually become a steady beam of light that is capable of penetrating as it were into the very depths of reality. When fully developed, this wisdom or insight is what we call *bodhi* or Enlightenment – though at that level it is not to be spoken of in exclusively cognitive terms. At that level we also have to speak of it in terms of love and compassion or, rather, in terms of the transcendental counterpart of the emotions which we usually designate by those names.

This division of the path into three stages is not arbitrary: the stages are no mere chalk marks, but are inherent in the path itself, and represent natural stages in the spiritual and transcendental growth of the individual. As such they resemble stages in the growth of a plant: from the seed comes forth a little shoot, which grows into a stem, from which leaves and finally buds and flowers are produced. Of course we must not push an analogy of this sort too far. The whole process of the flower's growth is unconscious. The flower does not have to decide whether to grow or not; nature 'decides' for it. But in the case of a human being spiritual development is conscious and deliberate, and by its very nature must be so. We are dependent for our further growth on our own individual, personal effort – though this is not a one-sided, egoistic, straining wilfulness, but the growth and development, in awareness, of the whole being.

A more satisfactory analogy for spiritual development from this point of view (though it doesn't work so well as an illustration of a development from within) is that of the construction of a house or any multistorey building. First you lay the foundation, then build the first storey, then the second, and so on, and finally you put on the roof. You cannot reverse the sequence, because it is determined by the nature of the structure itself.

The stages of the path of regular steps correspond to various Buddhist teachings; and different teachings pertain to different stages of the path, that is, to different stages of spiritual and transcendental development. When we practise the Dharma we should therefore practise those teachings that correspond to the stage of development we have actually reached – and reached not mentally or theoretically but with our whole being. This is the traditional method, or at least the predominant traditional method.

So first you practise morality: you observe the precepts. In doing so, you gradually become a thoroughly ethical individual, both inwardly and outwardly; this may take several years. Then, when your ethical individuality has been established relatively firmly, you take up the practice of concentration: you learn to tame the unruly wandering mind, and to concentrate at will on any object for any length of time – which may take several more years. Then, very slowly, you start raising your level of consciousness. You experience the first *dhyāna*, the second *dhyāna*, and so on, gradually training yourself not just to touch them but even to dwell in these superconscious states. Finally, perhaps after many years of endeavour, you direct your purified, elevated, and sublimely concentrated mind, together with the integrated energies of your whole being, to the contemplation of reality itself. This is the path of regular steps. Progress is systematic; you consolidate each stage of the path before proceeding to the next one.

By contrast, in treading the path of irregular steps one starts practising on the basis of a more or less mental or theoretical grasp of the Dharma (and a confused and incomplete grasp at that). Usually, I am afraid, in the West, one begins without a teacher; and one does not start practising those teachings which correspond to the stage of development one has actually reached, because one does not know what stage one is at anyway. One starts practising in a way that is immediately and superficially appealing – one starts practising, perhaps, what appeals to one's vanity. One might, for instance, start practising the Perfection of Wisdom.

Now it is not absolutely impossible, even for an absolute beginner – even on the basis of a purely theoretical understanding of the subject – to practise the Perfection of Wisdom. After all, the seed of Buddhahood is there, however deeply hidden. Deep down, an affinity with the Perfection of Wisdom is there. One may succeed, to a very slight extent, by sheer force of the egoistic will, in holding oneself, just for an instant, at a level of concentration where one gets just a glimpse of the Perfection of Wisdom, an experience, however fleeting, of the Void.

However, one will not be able to keep it up. One will sink back from it, and there will even be a reaction – a reaction from one's whole being or consciousness, which is, as a whole, simply not at that level and not ready to practise the Perfection of Wisdom. So one has to go back. One has to practise ethics and meditation, develop higher states of consciousness, and, in this way, create a firm basis from which to practise the Perfection of Wisdom effectively.

Going back to go forward

Following the path of irregular steps usually involves forcing the process of spiritual development. It is like trying to make a plant grow by forcibly opening the buds with one's fingers, or like building a house without foundations. Sooner or later we discover that it cannot be done. Instead of pulling open the buds one has to water the roots. One doesn't start building anything until one has dug the foundations. As Buddhists, the flower that we want to see blooming is the thousand-petalled lotus itself, so plenty of water is needed. The tower we want to build is the tower that reaches up into the very heavens, so a very firm foundation is required.

To state the matter axiomatically, we may say that a higher stage of the path cannot be developed even to a moderate extent before a lower stage of the path has been developed in its fullness. This is the basic principle. If we want to experience the higher stage, or higher level, with any intensity or any permanence, we must first perfect the lower stage. There is no other way. This is why, sooner or later, we have to make the transition from the path of irregular steps to the path of regular steps. And this transition means, basically, going back in order to go forward.

But how far back do we have to go? One could say: back to morality – back to basics. Or one could say: back to the individual path. But in fact we have to go back to something even more fundamental than morality, even more basic than the Hīnayāna. We have to go back to the Three Jewels. We have to sit or kneel with hands together, and go for Refuge, saying '*Buddhaṃ saraṇaṃ gacchāmi, Dhammaṃ saraṇaṃ gacchāmi, Saṅghaṃ saraṇaṃ gacchāmi.* To the Buddha for Refuge I go, to the Dharma for Refuge I go, to the Sangha for Refuge I go.' This is where Buddhism really begins. This is the root, the foundation, the absolute bedrock of our spiritual life. This is how we really start practising the path – by Going for Refuge.

from *The Taste of Freedom*

3. WHAT DO WE REALLY KNOW?

We have to learn the value of silence, not only physical silence but the silence of thoughts, the silence of the mind.

We say we know this or know that. But what do we really mean? We mean, surely, that we have read it somewhere, or heard about it, or seen it on television. We have no *direct* knowledge. It is all based on hearsay, on second-hand, third-hand, and tenth-hand information, on conjecture and gossip. We consider, for instance, that we know what is going on in the world at large, what is happening in distant places – India, Rhodesia, Indonesia, etc. But whence is our 'knowledge' derived? From words and letters. From the radio and the newspapers, from snatches of conversation overheard on the Tube, from chance remarks at parties. How great is our dependence! The thought is quite a horrifying one. Suppose there were no radios, no newspapers, we would 'know' very little of what went on in the world. We would have fewer thoughts, fewer ideas. Being less cluttered up mentally, we would be better able to concentrate on things near at hand. We would be able to live more intensely. Perhaps we would be closer to Reality.

This was, of course, the condition of our ancestors in bygone days, even as it is still the condition of many people in the 'undeveloped' countries. Compared with us, our ancestors knew very little of what was going on in the great world that lay outside the gates of their own village or township. Vague rumours reached them from the distant capital, and usually that was all. Sometimes, of course, they saw armies marching past, and sometimes armies devastated with fire and sword, but despite beating drums and flying colours ordinary folk did not understand what the war was about or who was fighting whom. Occasionally men were conscripted. Otherwise, apart from natural calamities, the stream of life flowed on placid and undisturbed from year to year and from generation to generation. I am not trying to idealize the past. I am only trying to point out how much our knowledge depends upon words and letters and how little on direct personal experience, and that this dependence is, moreover, both proportionally and absolutely, greater now than ever before in history.

This is true in all fields. Take any subject that we think we 'know'. Take botany, or the history of art, or any other branch of human knowledge, from astronomy to zoology. By far the greater part of our knowledge of these subjects, if not the whole of it, is second-hand. Hardly any of it is original, the result of our own independent thought and discovery. Inheriting as it were a great stockpile of knowledge from the past, we go through life, for the most part, without adding to it so much as a single grain of our own. Originality would seem to be the prerogative of genius.

In everyday life all this, though perhaps regrettable, does not matter very much. We manage to get along somehow. From the Zen point of view, however, it is nevertheless important to realize what is actually happening. It might be interesting to perform an experiment. As you sit here, fold your hands and close your eyes, just as you do for meditation. Forget all you have ever learned from books, newspapers, magazines, radio, television, and advertisements. Forget even talks, lectures, and discussions. How much knowledge would you then have left? Very little indeed. If we were to perform the experiment regularly the experience would be a very salutary one. We should then realize how little we really know. To know that we do not know is the beginning of wisdom.[109]

From our general dependence on words and letters let us now turn to our dependence on them where spiritual things are concerned. We have, let us assume, a certain amount of religious knowledge. We know about Buddhism. We know about the Four Noble Truths and the Noble Eightfold Path; about karma and rebirth, Nirvāṇa and dependent origination; about *śūnyatā*, bodhisattvas, and the Pure Land. What a lot we know! We even know about Zen. Now where has all this knowledge come from? From books and lectures. Ultimately, of course, it comes from the scriptures, which consist of words and letters. On words and letters, therefore, is our knowledge of Buddhism dependent. Hence it is all second-hand, not based on direct, personal experience and perception.

Let us perform another experiment. Let us put aside all knowledge of Buddhism that depends on words and letters, all that we have not experienced and verified for ourselves. Probably we shall have to discard quite a lot. Do we really *know* what Nirvāṇa is? What about *śūnyatā*? Put them aside too if necessary. At the end of the experiment how much real knowledge is left? Perhaps none at all.

We should not think we have lost anything, however. In fact there is a great gain. As we saw last week, Zen is concerned with the experience of the living spirit of Buddhism, and with the transmission of that spirit. For Zen nothing else matters. Nothing must be allowed to stand in the way. This is what makes Zen so 'ruthless'. Zen has no hesitation about burning holy Buddha images or tearing up sacred books if these get in the way. But what is it that gets in the way more than anything else? What is it that most of all prevents us from having a real knowledge of Buddhism, based on our own experience? Can anybody tell me?... You are all silent. Surely the greatest obstacle is *to think that we know*. Until this obstacle has been removed, no progress is possible. Here, more than anywhere else, is the beginning of wisdom. It is also the beginning of Enlightenment, the beginning of progress: *to know that we do not know*.

Such knowledge involves distinguishing between what we know at second-hand, from the scriptures, and what we know from experience. This is what Zen means when it urges us not to confuse the two kinds of knowledge. If we do confuse them no spiritual progress is possible. Unfortunately we are guilty of this confusion all the time. It is, in fact, part of our general psychological conditioning. Having failed to distinguish thoughts from things, we then fail to distinguish words from thoughts. We think that if we can label a thing we have understood it. Take, for example, Nirvāṇa. This is essentially a spiritual principle, or transcendental reality, and can be thought of in various ways. For instance, it can be thought of in terms of the complete cessation of craving. Since we understand what is meant by the words 'cessation of craving' we think that we know what Nirvāṇa is! When, therefore, in some non-Buddhist work, we come across the idea of freedom from craving, we at once triumphantly exclaim, 'Ah yes, Nirvāṇa!' At once we slap on the label. We think we 'know' that the state of freedom from craving mentioned in the non-Buddhist work and the Buddhist Nirvāṇa are one and the same. All that we have in fact done is to equate thoughts and words. We are not dealing directly with things, with realities, at all. At best we are dealing with thoughts about things, or often with just words.

Conceptualizing and verbalizing activity of this sort is only too common in the West. People talk far too much. They always want to affix ready-made labels to their experiences. It is as though they were unable to enjoy the beauty of a flower until they had given it its correct botanical classification and a Latin name. We have to learn the value of silence, not only physical silence but the silence of thoughts, the silence of the mind. In this connection I remember an anecdote told me, many years ago, by an Indian friend of mine, an elder brother in the Order. Some years previously this friend had paid a visit to Germany, where he gave some lectures on Buddhism. One morning a German Buddhist lady came to see him. As he was in the middle of writing a letter, and wanted to catch the post, he asked her to wait in an adjoining room. He had only been writing for a few minutes, however, when the door suddenly burst open, and the German lady violently exclaimed, 'I shall go mad if I stay here much longer. *There's no one to talk to!*' As he came to the end of the story my friend threw up his hands in mock despair, as if to say, 'What hope is there of spreading Buddhism among such people?' And, of course, such people are to be found in all countries, Western and Eastern.

Some things there are which can be experienced and also thought about and described in words. Others, though capable of being experienced, transcend thought and speech. At best they can only be indicated, or suggested, or hinted at. Such are the realities, or aspects of reality, of which we speak in such terms as 'Enlightenment', 'Nirvāṇa', 'Buddhahood'. All these terms are used only provisionally. They give us a certain amount of practical guidance, some idea of the quarter in which to look, the direction towards which we have to orient our spiritual strivings, but their validity is only relative. They do not really define the Goal. In using them we say, therefore, in the absolute sense, nothing at all. Hence in the *Laṅkāvatāra Sūtra* the Buddha declares that from the night of his supreme Enlightenment to the night of his final passing away he did not utter a single word.[110] Between the two events lay forty-five years of untiring earthly ministry. During that period he had taught thousands, perhaps hundreds of thousands, of people. Hardly a day had gone by without discourses, dialogues, answers to questions. Yet in reality nothing had been said because nothing can be said about reality. All his words had been pointers to what is beyond words. As Aśvaghoṣa says, 'We use words to get free from words until we reach the pure wordless Essence.'[111]

from *The Essence of Zen*

4. MIND REACTIVE, MIND CREATIVE

The creative mind loves where there is no reason to love, is happy where there is no reason for happiness, creates where there is no possibility of creativity, and in this way 'builds a heaven in hell's despair'.

Taking a bird's-eye view of human culture, we see that there exist in the world numerous spiritual traditions. Some of these are of great antiquity, coming down from the remote past with all the authority and prestige of that which has been long established; others are of more recent origin. While some have crystallized, in the course of centuries, into religious cults with enormous followings, others have remained more of the nature of philosophies, making few concessions to popular tastes and needs. Each one of these traditions has its own system, that is to say, its own special concatenation – its own network – of ideas and ideals, of beliefs and practices, as well as its own particular starting-point in thought or experience out of which the whole system evolves. This starting-point is the 'golden string' which, when wound into the ball of the total system, will lead one in at 'heaven's gate, built in Jerusalem's wall'[112] of the tradition concerned.

Like other traditions Buddhism possesses its own special system and its own distinctive starting point. The system of Buddhism is what is known as the 'Dharma', a Sanskrit word meaning, in this context, the 'doctrine' or the 'teaching', and connoting the sum total of the insights and experiences conducive to the attainment of Enlightenment or Buddhahood. Its starting-point is the mind.

That this, and no other, is the starting-point, is illustrated by two quotations from what are sometimes regarded as the two most highly antithetical, not to say mutually exclusive, developments within the whole field of Buddhism: Theravāda and Zen. According to the first two verses of the *Dhammapada,* an ancient collection of metrical aphorisms included in the Pāli canon of the Theravādins,

> Experiences are preceded by mind, led by mind, and produced by mind. If one speaks or acts with an impure mind, suffering follows even as the cart-wheel follows the hoof of the ox.

> Experiences are preceded by mind, led by mind, and produced by mind. If one speaks or acts with a pure mind, happiness follows like a shadow that never departs.[113]

The Zen quotation is if anything more emphatic. In a verse which made its appearance in China during the Tang dynasty, Zen itself, which claims to convey from generation to generation of disciples the very heart of the Buddha's spiritual experience, is briefly characterized as:

> A special transmission outside the Scriptures.
> No dependence on words and letters.
> Direct pointing to the mind.
> Seeing into one's own nature and realizing Buddhahood.[114]

From these quotations, representative of many others which could be made, it is clear that the starting-point of Buddhism is not anything outside us. In the language of Western thought, it is not objective but subjective. The starting-point is the mind.

But what do we mean by mind? In the *Dhammapada* verses the original Pāli word is *mano*; in the Chinese Zen stanza it is *xīn*, corresponding to the Sanskrit and Pāli *citta*. As both these terms can be quite adequately rendered by the English 'mind' there is no need to explore etymologies and we can plunge at once into the heart of our subject.

To begin with, mind is twofold. On the one hand there is absolute mind; on the other, relative mind. By absolute mind is meant that infinite cosmic or transcendental awareness within whose pure timeless flow the subject–object polarity as we ordinarily experience it is forever dissolved. For mind in this exalted sense Buddhism employs, according to context, a number of expressions, each with its own distinctive shade of meaning. Prominent among these expressions are the One Mind, the Unconditioned, Buddha-nature, the Void. In the more neutral language of philosophy, absolute mind is Reality. It is the realization of absolute mind through the dissolution of the subject–object polarity – the waking up to Reality out of the dream of mundane existence – which constitutes Enlightenment, the attainment of Enlightenment being, of course, the ultimate aim of Buddhism.

By relative mind is meant the individual mind or consciousness, functioning within the framework of the subject–object polarity, and it is with this mind that we are now concerned. Like mind in general, relative mind or consciousness is of two kinds: reactive and creative. While these are not traditional Buddhist expressions, neither of them rendering any one technical term in any of the canonical languages, they seem to express very well the import of the Buddha's teaching. In any case, the distinction which they represent is of fundamental importance not only in the 'system' of Buddhism but in the spiritual life generally and even in the entire scheme of human evolution. The transition from 'reactive' to 'creative' marks, indeed, the beginning of spiritual life. It is conversion in the true sense of the term. What, then, do we mean by speaking of 'reactive mind' and 'creative mind'?

In the first place, we should not imagine that there are literally two relative minds, one reactive, the other creative. Rather should we understand that there are two ways in which relative mind or the individual consciousness is capable of functioning. It is capable of functioning reactively and it is capable of functioning creatively. When it functions in a reactive manner, it is known as the reactive mind; when it functions in a creative manner, it is known as the creative mind. But there is only one relative mind.

By the reactive mind is meant our ordinary, everyday mind, the mind that most people use most of the time, or, rather, it is the mind that uses them. In extreme cases, indeed, the reactive mind functions all the time, the creative mind remaining in complete abeyance. People of this type are born, live, and die animals; though possessing the human form they are in fact not human beings at all. Rather than attempt an abstract definition of the reactive mind let us try to grasp its nature by examining some of its actual characteristics.

In the first place, the reactive mind is a *re*-active mind. It does not really act, but only *re*-acts. Instead of acting spontaneously, out of its own inner fullness and abundance, it requires an external stimulus to set it in motion. This stimulus usually comes through the five senses.

We are walking along the street, an advertisement catches our eye, its bright colours and bold lettering making an instant appeal. Perhaps it is an advertisement for a certain brand of cigarette, or for a certain make of car, or for summer holidays on the sun-drenched beaches of some distant pleasure resort. Whatever the goods or services depicted, our attention is attracted, arrested. We go and do what the advertisement is designed to make us do, or make a mental note to do it, or are left with an unconscious disposition to do it as and when circumstances permit. We have not acted, but have been activated. We have *re*-acted.

The reactive mind is, therefore, the conditioned mind. It is conditioned by its object (e.g. the advertisement) in the sense of being not merely dependent upon it but actually determined by it. The reactive mind is not free.

Since it is conditioned the reactive mind is, moreover, purely mechanical. As such it can be appropriately described as the 'penny-in-the-slot' mind. Insert the coin, and out comes the packet. In much the same way, let the reactive mind be confronted with a certain situation or experience and it will react automatically, in an entirely mechanical, hence predictable, fashion. Not only our behaviour but even much of our 'thinking' conforms to this pattern. Whether in the field of politics, or literature, or religion, or whether in the affairs of everyday life, the opinions we so firmly hold and so confidently profess are very rarely the outcome of conscious reflection, of our individual effort to arrive at the truth. Our ideas are hardly ever our own. Only too often have they been fed into us from external sources, from books, newspapers, and conversations, and we have accepted them, or rather received them, in a passive and unreflecting manner. When the appropriate stimulus occurs we automatically reproduce whatever has been fed into our system, and it is this purely mechanical reaction that passes for expression of opinion. Truly original thought on any subject is, indeed, extremely rare, though 'original' does not necessarily mean 'different', but rather whatever one creates out of one's own inner resources regardless of whether or not this coincides with something previously created by somebody else. Some, of course, *try* to be different. This can, however, be a subtle form of conditionedness, for in trying to be different such people are still being determined by an object, by whatever or whoever it is they are trying to be different from. They are still *re*-acting, instead of really acting.

Besides being conditioned and mechanical, the reactive mind is repetitive. Being 'programmed' as it were by needs of which it is largely unconscious, it reacts to the same stimuli in much the same way, and like a machine therefore goes on performing the same operation over and over again. It is owing to this characteristic of the reactive mind that 'human' life as a whole becomes so much a matter of fixed and settled habit, in a world of routine. As we grow older, especially, we develop a passive resistance to change, preferring to deepen the old ruts rather than strike out in a new direction. Even our religious life, if we are not careful, can become incorporated into the routine, can become part of the pattern, part of the machinery of existence. The Sunday service or the mid-week meditation become fixed as reference points in our lives, buoys charting a way through the dangerous waters of freedom, along with the weekly visit to the cinema and the launderette, the annual holiday at the seaside, and the seasonal spree.

Above all, however, the reactive mind is the unaware mind. Whatever it does, it does without any real knowledge of what it is doing. Metaphorically speaking, the reactive mind is asleep. Those in whom it predominates can, therefore, be described as asleep rather than awake. In a state of sleep they live out their lives; in a state of sleep they eat, drink, talk, work, play, vote, make love; in a state of sleep, even, they read books on Buddhism and try to meditate. Like somnambulists who walk with eyes wide open, they only appear to be awake. Some people, indeed, are so fast asleep that for all their apparent activity they can more adequately be described as dead. Their movements are those of a zombie, or a robot with all its controls switched on, rather than those of a truly aware human being. It is with this realization – when we become aware of our own unawareness, when we wake up to the fact that we are asleep – that spiritual life begins. One might, indeed, go so far as to say that it marks the beginning of truly human existence, though this would imply, indeed, a far higher conception of human existence than the word usually conveys – a conception nearer to what is usually termed spiritual. This brings us to the second kind of relative mind, to what we have termed the creative mind.

The characteristics of the creative mind are the opposite of those of the reactive mind. The creative mind does not *re*-act. It is not dependent on, or determined by, the stimuli with which it comes into contact. On the contrary, it is active on its own account, functioning spontaneously, out of the depths of its own intrinsic nature. Even when initially prompted by something external to itself it quickly transcends its original point of departure and starts functioning independently. The creative mind can therefore be said to *respond* rather than to react. Indeed, it is capable of transcending conditions altogether. Hence it can also be said that whereas the reactive mind is essentially pessimistic, being confined to what is given in immediate experience, the creative mind is profoundly and radically optimistic. Its optimism is not, however, the superficial optimism of the streets, no mere unthinking reaction to, or rationalization of, pleasurable stimuli. By virtue of the very nature of the creative mind such a reaction would be impossible. On the contrary, the optimism of the creative mind persists despite unpleasant stimuli, despite conditions unfavourable for optimism, or even when there are no conditions for it at all. The creative mind loves where there is no reason to love, is happy where there is no reason for happiness, creates where there is no possibility of creativity, and in this way 'builds a heaven in hell's despair'.[115]

Not being dependent on any object, the creative mind is essentially non-conditioned. It is independent by nature, and functions, therefore, in a perfectly spontaneous manner. When functioning on the highest possible level, at its highest pitch of intensity, the creative mind is identical with the Unconditioned; that is to say, it coincides with absolute mind. Being non-conditioned the creative mind is free; indeed, it is Freedom itself. It is also original in the true sense of the term, being characterized by ceaseless productivity. This productivity is not necessarily artistic, literary, or musical, even though the painting, the poem, and the symphony are admittedly among its most typical, even as among its most strikingly adequate, manifestations. Moreover, just as the creative mind does not necessarily find expression in 'works of art', so what are conventionally regarded as 'works of art' are not necessarily all expressions of the creative mind. Imitative and lacking true originality, some of them are more likely to be the mechanical products of the reactive mind.

Outside the sphere of the fine arts the creative mind finds expression in productive personal relations, as when through our own emotional positivity others become more emotionally positive, or as when through the intensity of their mutual awareness two or more people reach out towards, and together experience, a dimension of being greater and more inclusive than their separate individualities. In these and similar cases the creative mind is productive in the sense of contributing to the increase, in the world, of the sum total of positive emotion, of higher states of being and consciousness.

Finally, as just indicated, the creative mind is above all the aware mind. Being aware, or rather, being Awareness itself, the creative mind is also intensely and radiantly alive. The creative person, as one in whom the creative mind manifests may be termed, is not only more aware than the reactive person but possessed of far greater vitality. This vitality is not just animal high spirits or emotional exuberance, much less still mere intellectual energy or the compulsive urgency of egoistic volition. Were such expressions permissible, one might say it is the Spirit of Life itself rising like a fountain from the infinite depths of existence, and vivifying, through the creative person, all with whom it comes into contact.

from *Buddha Mind*

5. THE PERFECTION OF WISDOM – THE FLAVOUR OF IRRELEVANCE

It's refreshing to have something which in a way you understand, but which in another way you don't understand at all.

As seriously practising Buddhists we do need to be able to relate traditional teachings to our own personal experience. We need to work out how the Dharma bears upon our own lives, how it applies to the world we live in, and how to interpret ancient texts so as to be of practical and immediate concern to the situation in which we find ourselves. But on another level we should not be over-concerned with what is relevant to 'me', interesting to 'me', applicable to 'my' situation in the West. It is all very well to expect Buddhism to be meaningful to where we are, here and now – but where is here and when is now? Is our conditioned existence all we are? In the end there needs also to be some element of the Dharma which is not relevant to our spiritual development at all. When it comes to transcending conditioned existence, the last thing we need is something useful. In fact it takes something quite irrelevant to transcend conditions – and then the pointless becomes the most relevant thing of all.

So in the *Diamond Sūtra* we are still concerned with the Dharma, but we are not concerned with any of the things that we usually think of as constituting the Dharma – the things that we settle down and feel comfortable with. We are taking a rest from looking at ethics or meditation or impermanence; instead we are getting a breath of nonsense, a touch of Lewis Carroll or Edward Lear (without suggesting by this analogy that *'Alice in Wonderland'* is some kind of Zen text, of course).[116]

The Perfection of Wisdom is like salt. An exclusive diet of it probably wouldn't do you much good, but you need a pinch of it in your spiritual diet all the time. It gives it a little flavour – the flavour of irrelevance. Otherwise, if it all becomes too relevant, well, you take it all too seriously – you think too much in terms of yourself as you are now. It's refreshing to have something which in a way you understand, but which in another way you don't understand at all.

What we have in the *Diamond Sūtra* is a comprehensible but irrelevant meaning, with a further significance or purport that *is* relevant but is *not* comprehensible. It is not difficult to get at the meaning of the sentences, but to get at what I am calling the purport, the direction in which the words are pointing above and beyond the verbal meaning, is much more difficult. It may also sometimes be difficult to explain the connection between the meaning and the purport. What we may be sure of is that we can only get at the purport by constantly bearing the meaning in mind. One way to do this is to recite the words constantly, as one does in some visualization practices, repeating certain short verses over and over again. If we repeat the comprehensible but irrelevant words often enough, as monks have been doing for hundreds of years in the monasteries of Japan and the lamasaries of Tibet, something of the purport will begin to dawn on us.

from *Wisdom Beyond Words*

6. THE SHATTERING NATURE OF REALITY

The experience of reality in what the Tantras call its 'nakedness' can be a shattering experience.

The Perfection of Wisdom is one of the most important themes of the Mahāyāna, and it is dealt with principally in the group of scriptures known as Prajñāpāramitā *sūtras*. There are more than thirty-five of these, some of enormous length and some very short indeed. One of the best known and most important of them is the *Vajracchedikā Prajñāpāramitā sūtra*, the discourse on the transcendental wisdom that pierces like the thunderbolt or cuts like the diamond.[117] What transcendental wisdom pierces or cuts is our illusions, our wrong ideas, our false notions, our projections. We can even go so far as to say that it is destructive. It destroys our intellectual assumptions, usually adopted so unthinkingly. It destroys the psychological conditionings in which we are enmeshed. It destroys the emotional hang-ups to which we are so attached. It destroys, in short, ourselves as we are at present.

It is not always understood that wisdom, the *experience* of reality, is destructive. It is tempting to think of it as a pleasant extra, something comfortably added on to what we already are. But it isn't like that at all. The experience of reality in what the Tantras call its 'nakedness' can be a shattering experience. One can even go so far as to say that *any* shattering experience has an element of reality in it. If an experience shatters, it is real – and if it doesn't shatter us, its authenticity may be questioned. This is not to say that this experience of breaking through or shattering needs to be traumatic – it can be very joyful.

Whether one can expect to have this kind of experience oneself all depends on the way one goes about one's spiritual practice. If you meditate for half an hour or an hour a day over a period of years, you will get results, but they will be slow in coming. However, if you meditate for ten or twenty hours a day, and keep that up, you can expect something much more dramatic to happen. Breaking through depends not so much on the kind of meditation you do as on the intensity with which you do it. And, of course, most people tend to take things quite easily. There is certainly room for a great deal more intensity in the spiritual practice of most western Buddhists. This includes, of course, concentrated attention upon the views that direct that intense practice, and a robust faith with which to meet the strong reactions and inner resistance that such intensity tends to provoke.

from *Creative Symbols of Tantric Buddhism*

7. 'ABOVE ME BROODS...'

Above me broods
A world of mysteries and magnitudes.
I see, I hear,
More than what strikes the eye or meets the ear.

Within me sleep
Potencies deep, unfathomably deep,
Which, when awake,
The bonds of life, death, time and space will break.

Infinity
Above me like the blue sky do I see.
Below, in me,
Lies the reflection of infinity.

from *Complete Poems*

3
VIEWS AND TRUTHS

1. WRONG VIEWS, RIGHT VIEWS, AND PERFECT VISION

... the total vision of the total human being ...

Traditionally Buddhism distinguishes two kinds of view: wrong view and right view. We may understand in general terms the difference between the two kinds of 'philosophical' view or vision by making a simple analogy with ordinary physical vision. With good vision we see clearly and for a great distance. Good vision is unblinkered: we can see all around us. Good vision is also undistorted; nothing clouds or colours or refracts it. Conversely, poor vision may be weak in that we do not see very far or distinctly; it may be blinkered, restricted to a narrow field so that we see only what is straight in front of us; or it may be distorted, as when we look through a thick fog or through coloured glass or bottle-glass.

Wrong view is very much like poor vision. First of all, it is weak. Our mental vision is weak when it lacks the concentrated energy to be derived from meditation. It is this energy that transforms a purely conceptual understanding of the truth into direct experience. If this energy is not there, then we do not see deeply into the true nature of things. We do not see things clearly or distinctly; we do not see them as they truly are.

Secondly, wrong view is blinkered. It is limited to a narrow range of experience, to what can be experienced through the five physical senses and the rational mind. It is to have just this narrow viewpoint from which to draw conclusions, to be simply unaware of other possibilities of perception or experience. On a very basic level this kind of wrong view is exemplified by the poverty of outlook of someone who is interested only in their job, their family, football scores, and television programmes. Having no interest in world affairs, the arts and sciences, or personal development, they see life simply in terms of their own limited existence.

Thirdly, wrong view is distorted. Vision can be distorted by our mood – whether we are feeling happy or gloomy. It can be distorted by our likes and dislikes. If we dislike someone we see all sorts of faults, whereas if we like someone we may see in them all sorts of perfections that they do not really possess. Our vision may be distorted, too, by prejudices regarding race, class, religion, or nationality. Thus wrong view is weak, limited to a narrow range of experience, and distorted by personal feelings and prejudices.

Right view, obviously, is the opposite of this. Right view is powerful. Based on the concentrated energy of meditation, it gives rise not just to conceptual understanding but also to direct experience of the truth. For this reason, it does not remain on the surface, but penetrates deep into the heart of things, and sees everything clearly and distinctly. Secondly, right view is unlimited. It ranges over the whole field of human experience; it is not confined to what can be experienced through the physical senses or the rational mind. If it generalizes at all, those generalizations are made from the entire range of human experience in all fields, at all levels. Lastly, right view is not distorted by emotion or prejudice; it sees things as they are.

The distinction between wrong view and right view is of supreme importance in Buddhism. A view does not, after all, exist in the abstract, somehow apart from people. It belongs to someone. So if we can identify two kinds of view, we may also identify two kinds of people. People whose view of existence is limited, restricted, and distorted are known in Buddhism as *pṛthagjanas* – the 'many-folk' – and as the name implies, they constitute the majority of people. Most people have not worked to develop themselves at all and consequently are just as nature made them, so to speak. On the other hand, there are those whose view is unlimited in extent, unrestricted in scope, and without any distortion whatsoever. These are known as *āryas*, the 'spiritually noble'. Such individuals, having worked to attain some degree of personal development, have remodelled themselves, at least to some extent. Of course, the crucial point about these categories is that it is possible to move from the one to the other – by developing awareness, by cultivating positive emotions, by raising the level of consciousness, and, above all, by discarding wrong views and developing right ones.

So these two – wrong view and right view – are what we have to work with, practically speaking. However, there is actually a third kind of view – Perfect View, or rather Perfect Vision. Perfect Vision is right view developed to the fullest possible extent. It is the total vision of the total human being at the highest conceivable level of development. It is the unconditioned vision of the unconditioned reality. It is the vision that does not just look beyond space and time but is totally unconditioned by it, that totally transcends the ordinary framework of perception. Perfect Vision is the vision of the Enlightened One, the Buddha, the one who sees with wisdom and compassion.

For the most part, our own view is wrong view. Moreover, we tend to rationalize our wrong views, presenting them in systematic conceptual form. These rationalizations are the worldly philosophies, the various isms and ologies. Only occasionally do we have a flash of right view – and such sparks of right view derive ultimately from Perfect Vision. They become available to us through the Perfect Vision of the Buddha. If we can attend to what the Buddha has communicated of his vision of existence, we can momentarily rise to that level, at least in imagination, and see exactly where we stand. We will have a true philosophy that will enable us to understand the general principles that underlie the whole process of personal development, and that will give meaning and purpose to our lives.

from *Buddhism for Today and Tomorrow*

2. NO 'READY-MADE' BUDDHIST ANSWERS

On the whole, people want to know what to think, which means something black and white. They want certainty. What they are certain about is less important to them than the certainty itself.

Most people put their faith and trust in someone who makes a strong impression, someone who is very emphatic and certain and self-confident. If you try to be careful about what you are saying, introducing qualifications where appropriate and suggesting that yours is only a certain way of looking at things, that there are other ways, and that one will have to make up one's own mind, you will make a comparatively feeble impression. On the whole, people want to know what to think, which means something black and white. They want certainty. What they are certain about is less important to them than the certainty itself. They will believe any farrago of nonsense as long as they have permission to believe in it absolutely. It is not clarity but certainty they are looking for. Certainty is security; and being exposed to the difficulties and confusions of having to think seriously is to be thrown into insecurity.

Many people seem to want to rush to take up views where, one may say, angels fear to tread. I have noticed this in, for example, Hindus with a smattering of religious knowledge. I remember on one occasion when I took the public jeep from Kalimpong to Siliguri, I was sitting in the front next to the driver when there was a hold-up of some sort, and the Bihari policeman who was controlling things, seeing there was a sadhu in yellow robes – i.e. myself – waiting there, and having nothing better to do for the moment, strolled up and started asking the usual questions: 'Are you a holy man?' and so on. Then he began to tell me all about how the universe had evolved from Brahman, and how it was all unreal, and how the soul was the same as God. He held forth in this way for about fifteen minutes and then strolled off again. There was a Tibetan Buddhist sitting behind me who had observed all this with mounting horror: 'That man was talking about the Dharma,' he said at last, as if he couldn't believe his ears. That someone with a few undigested religious notions rattling around in his head should shoot his mouth off about them, in public, to a total stranger, had left him almost speechless.

As a Buddhist one finds that one has to resist a tendency in people to look for absolutist views. They might ask about a certain gifted but wayward Buddhist teacher, 'Is so-and-so a bodhisattva or is he a total fake?' Of course, the fact is that such a person is a complex human being and worthy of more than a snap judgement either way – or even somewhere precisely in between. Or someone might say, 'What's the

Buddhist view on such and such: hanging, abortion, astrology, extra-marital sex?' What they want is a definite, simple answer to take away with them.

But there is no 'Buddhist view' as such; there is no hierarchy of authority from which to draw one's views. One can have one's own view as a Buddhist, but it will not have the stamp of authority that Christians have from God or the Bible or the Pope. And people generally want the kind of security one gets from a source of authoritative judgements. As a Buddhist, the best one can do sometimes is to say, 'Here are the four noble truths. Do what you can with these.'

By looking for ready-made 'Buddhist' answers – the party line – people also want to be able to categorize one as a Buddhist. Just as people say, 'He's an Aries,' or 'She's a greed type,' or 'He's an accountant,' and think they've got that person dealt with, classified, docketed; likewise, if they can categorize Buddhism, then they can put one in the Buddhist category. Again, one needs to resist this tendency. It's a way of dismissing you, disposing of you, not being concerned with you as an individual. What to think of you has been settled by the fact that you are a Buddhist. This is not to say that one should be afraid of saying that one is a Buddhist – or an accountant, for that matter – but that one should not imagine (or hope) that being a Buddhist puts one as an individual in a category.

from *Know Your Mind*

3. THE *ANĀTMAN* DOCTRINE

The idea that the doctrine of no-self declares life to be worthless, meaningless, and in fact non-existent, is simply not Buddhist.

Traditionally, the extreme views which are held to be representative are eternalism and nihilism: the view that the self is eternally existent, and the view that the self is totally non-existent.[118] In ancient India these two views concerned whether or not the self survived death in some form. The eternalist view was that the self persisted unchanged from life to life; this is akin to the Christian view of the soul, that it survives death intact and goes on to heaven, hell, or limbo. The nihilistic view was that the whole psychophysical organism was totally annihilated at the moment of death – which is of course the common, modern, secular view.

Such is, we may say, the psychological aspect of these two extreme views. They may also be put in a more metaphysical context. This version offers the view that mundane existence, in terms of the five *skandhas*, is ultimately real in some way, and at the other extreme the view that it is completely unreal and illusory at every level.

Thirdly, in ethical terms, nihilism and eternalism may be interpreted as the two extremes of self-indulgence and self-torture. It is possible to see self-indulgence – in the philosophy of 'eat, drink, and be merry, for tomorrow we die' – as a form of nihilism. And it is possible to see self-torture – for the purpose of releasing the eternal soul from its prison – as a form of eternalism. However, this is just from the viewpoint of the traditional idea of the two extremes as representing attitudes to the possibility of life after death. It is probably more true to the psychological reality to say that self-indulgence expresses a belief in the absolute reality of mundane existence, while self-torture expresses self-hatred, and thus a desire for self-destruction and, by extension, for the destruction of mundane existence.

The Buddhist doctrine of *anātman*, no-self, is unfortunately sometimes interpreted in such terms as to appeal to this tendency towards self-destruction. If this teaching is interpreted as a total negation of the self, it will be very attractive to people who want to express their own self-hatred. Quite a few people seem to have this sort of attitude: a fascination with the *anātman* doctrine as an essentially life-denying principle. But the idea that the doctrine of no-self declares life to be worthless, meaningless, and in fact non-existent, is simply not Buddhist.

The *anātman* doctrine can also be used as a way of avoiding personal responsibility, or of sitting on one's natural energies. Anything one decides to do, particularly in an energetic or wholehearted way, becomes an expression of ego and thus doctrinally suspect. Again, this is a wrong view. The goal of Buddhahood is to go beyond the individual self, not to regress from the achievement of individual selfhood.

The ego is no more than the tendency to absolutize one's present state of being. It is not a thing, but a faulty interpretation. One is seeing something that just isn't there. The individual is there in a process of continuous change and therefore of ever-present potential development; delusion may also be there, in the form of a belief in a fixed, unchanging self or essence or soul. But that fixed, unchanging self or essence or soul or ego is not there; it never was, and it never will be. And because it isn't there, one can't do anything with it – get rid of it, go beyond it, or whatever. The best thing to do as far as the ego is concerned is just to forget about it.

We are not just an absence of self; we are an absence of *fixed* self, a flow of ever-changing components, physical and mental. The Buddha himself was evidently a powerfully distinct individual, with a very clear idea of who or what he was. To have self-view means to identify oneself with a sort of cross-section of the flow of *skandhas* and imagine that one can arrest the flow at that point. It is just a state of arrested development, like being a child who says, 'When I grow up I'm going to fill my house with toys and eat sweets all day,' unable to imagine the transformation involved in growing up.

from *Know Your Mind*

4. BREAKING THE FETTERS

We could even say that each one of us is simply a habit – probably a bad habit.

According to Theravāda teaching, Stream Entry is achieved by breaking the first three of the ten fetters that are said to bind us to the wheel of life. These three fetters are usually described as, firstly, the fetter of belief in an essential, unchanging self; secondly, the fetter of doubt and indecision with regard to the Dharma; and thirdly, the fetter of attachment to religious observances as ends in themselves. Here, however, we are going to approach them in very general, even basic – or down-to-earth – terms, as: firstly, the fetter of *habit*; secondly, the fetter of *vagueness*; and thirdly, the fetter of *superficiality*.

The fetter of habit

A habit is something we are said to *have*. We have 'the tendency or disposition to act in a particular way'. However, as this dictionary definition makes clear, a habit consists of actions, and action is an essential part of us, not just something added on, something we have. In fact according to the *Dharma-Vinaya* we *are* our actions. And this is the way we usually think of, and refer to, a person: someone is the sum total of his or her actions of body, speech, and mind, and doesn't exist apart from these.

The fact that we have a 'tendency or disposition to *act* in a particular way' means, therefore, that we have a tendency or disposition to *be* in a particular way. We are not just the sum total of our actions: we are the sum total of our habits. We *are* our habits. We could even say that each one of us is simply a habit – probably a bad habit. The person we think of as George or Mary, and recognize as acting in a particular way, is simply a habit that a certain stream of consciousness has got into.

But since it has got into it, it can get out of it. It is like a knot tied in a piece of string: it can be untied. Breaking the fetter of habit means, essentially, getting out of the habit of being a particular kind of person. It is only a habit you have got into. You don't *have* to be the way you are. There is no necessity about it. Breaking the fetter of habit means, therefore, getting rid of the old self, the past self. It means becoming a true individual; that is, becoming continually aware and emotionally positive, continually responsible, sensitive, and creative – continually creative of one's own self.

This is the meaning of the Buddhist doctrine of *anātman* (Pāli *anattā*) or 'no-self'. It is not so much that we never have a self as that we always have a *new* self. And if each new self is a better one than the last, then we can say that spiritual progress is taking place.

It is not easy to get out of the habit of being the kind of person that we are. It is not easy to get rid of the old self and become a true individual. One of the reasons for this is other people. Not only have we ourselves got into the habit of being in a particular way, but other people have got into the habit of experiencing us as being in the habit of being in a particular way.

The people who experience us as what we *were* rather than as what we *are* – or what we are in process of becoming – represent a collective way of thinking, feeling, and acting. They represent the group as opposed to the individual. The group is the enemy of the individual – of the true individual – inasmuch as it will not allow the true individual to emerge from its ranks. It insists on dealing with you not as you are but as you were, and to this extent it tries to deal with someone who no longer exists. This tends to happen, for example, when one visits one's family after some time.

Becoming free of the group does not, of course, necessarily mean actually breaking off relations with the group. What it means is breaking away from the influence – the habit-reinforcing influence – of the group.

The fetter of vagueness

'Vague' means 'indistinct, not clearly expressed or identified, of uncertain or ill-defined meaning or character'. So why should anyone *be* vague? The fact is, we are vague when we are undecided, vague when we don't *want* to decide, and, above all, vague when we don't want to commit ourselves. Our vagueness is, therefore, a dishonest vagueness.

After all, spiritual life is very difficult. Growth and development is often a painful process (even though it is always enjoyable). Therefore we tend to shrink back. We keep our options open. We keep a number of different interests, or a number of different aims, on which we can fall back, and allow ourselves to oscillate between them, even to drift between them. At all costs we remain vague: woolly, foggy, shapeless, indistinct, unclear.

Breaking the fetter of vagueness means being willing to think clearly. It means giving time to thinking things out, having the determination to think things through. It means being prepared to look at what the alternatives really are, and to sort out one's priorities. It means being ready to make up one's mind. It means making a decision to choose the best and then to act wholeheartedly upon that choice. It means not postponing the moment of decision.

The fetter of superficiality

To be superficial means to act from the surface of ourselves and, in consequence, to act without thoroughness or care; it is about acting in outward appearance rather than genuinely or actually. Now why should we do this? Why should we act superficially?

The reason is that we are divided. More often than not, the conscious rational surface is divided from the unconscious emotional depths. We act out of intellectual conviction but do not succeed in carrying the emotions with us. Sometimes, of course, we do act out of the fullness of our emotions but then, only too often, the rational mind holds back, and even, perhaps, does not approve. In neither case do we act totally, wholeheartedly. We do not act with the whole of ourselves and, therefore, in a sense, do not really act at all.

This state of affairs is very general. Superficiality is one of the curses of the modern age. Matthew Arnold, more than a hundred years ago, spoke of our 'sick hurry', our 'divided aims' – and that just about describes the situation.[119] We are neurotically busy, without any real focus, any singleness of purpose. We don't truly, authentically, do anything. We don't do anything with the whole force of our being. When we love we don't really love, and when we hate we don't really hate. We don't even really think. We half do all these things.

It is the same, only too often, when we take up the spiritual life and try to follow the *Dharma-Vinaya*. When we meditate, it is only with part of ourselves. When we communicate, or when we work, again it is only with part of ourselves. Consequently we don't get very far: we don't really grow; we don't really develop. We don't carry the whole of our being along with us, so to speak. A small part of us is prospecting ahead, but the greater part is lagging far behind.

Breaking the fetter of superficiality therefore means acting with the whole of oneself: acting with thoroughness and care; acting genuinely and actually. It means, in a word, commitment. It means committing oneself to the spiritual life, committing oneself to being a true individual.

Creativity, clarity, and commitment

The three fetters – of habit, of vagueness, and of superficiality – are broken by means of insight, that is, by means of knowledge and vision of things as they really are. In less traditional terms, they are broken by our becoming creative (in the sense of self-creative or creative of our own new self), by becoming clear, and by becoming committed. When insight arises, one enters the Stream, the Stream that leads directly to Enlightenment: one becomes a Stream Entrant and, being a Stream Entrant, one becomes a true individual. And as a true individual, one can experience *vimukti* (this being the Pāli term for 'freedom', 'release', describing the state of mind of the Stream Entrant), one can enjoy the taste of freedom. Two key points emerge from all this. The first is that only the true individual is really free; the second, that one becomes a true individual only by developing insight: that is, by breaking the three fetters and thereby becoming creative, clear, and committed. This is freedom.

from *The Taste of Freedom*

5. LIFE IS KING

> Hour after hour, day
> After day we try
> To grasp the Ungraspable, pinpoint
> The Unpredictable. Flowers
> Wither when touched, ice
> Suddenly cracks beneath our feet. Vainly
> We try to track birdflight through the sky trace
> Dumb fish through deep water, try
> To anticipate the earned smile the soft
> Reward, even
> Try to grasp our own lives. But Life
> Slips through our fingers
> Like snow. Life
> Cannot belong to us. We
> Belong to Life. Life
> Is King.

from *Complete Poems*

6. THE BUDDHIST ATTITUDE TO DEATH

After all, death is just as natural as life.

Everything is impermanent. From the solar system to one's own breath, from instant to instant everything is changing, flowing, transient. When one remembers this, one can view things as being like clouds passing through the sky. One can't hang on to anything very determinedly when one knows that sooner or later one will have to give it up.

Every day the newspapers are full of reports of fatal accidents, and this gives, as well as the occasion for compassion, an opportunity for reflection. Human life is liable to unexpected termination; one may not live to a ripe old age. As Pascal said, just a grain of dust is sufficient to destroy us if it gets into the wrong place.[120] Life is very precarious. Such reflections can be sobering and fruitful; but they will be counter-productive if what they produce is a kind of neurotic timidity. One has to be sensitive to one's own nature in this regard.

A skull or a few bones, preferably human ones, can also be useful objects of reflection. It might sound strange or even amusing – we are sometimes inclined to laugh at death to cover up our fear of it – but this is standard practice among Tibetan Buddhists. (Of course, we have a precedent for it in the Western tradition, in Hamlet's contemplation of Yorick's skull in Shakespeare's play.) In fact, Tibetans tend to surround themselves with all kinds of things made of human bone: bone rosaries, thigh-bone trumpets, skull-cups. They take a common-sense view of death; they don't think there's anything morbid or macabre about it.

In the West, though, the very word 'death' is supposed to send a shiver down one's spine. Not that the Christian tradition avoids the straightforward facts of death. Many ancient tombstones bear representations of skeletons and skulls, in some burial places bones are kept for visitors to see, and monks practise the constant recollection of death. Corpses are laid out for friends and relations of the dead person to come and have a look – and of course there is the tradition of the wake. Indeed, if we sweep death under the carpet in our modern culture, perhaps it is partly because the Christian tradition is less important to us than it used to be. The problem in our culture is not really denial but the tendency to identify the total self with the body, even when the soul has departed. According to some kinds of popular Christianity, the teaching of the resurrection of the body means the literal resuscitation of the corpse. It follows that when a man is buried the worms are eating *him* – not just his body, but him. This identification of the decomposing corpse with the deceased person gives death a peculiar sort of horror mixed with fascination.

But this is not the Buddhist way of looking at death – nor, come to that, the Hindu or Muslim way of looking at it. After all, death is just as natural as life. Tagore, the great modern Bengali poet, says, 'I know I shall love death, because I have loved life.'[121] Life and death are opposite sides of the same thing. If you love life, you will love death; and if you can't love death, you haven't really loved life. It sounds paradoxical, but it is deeply true.

from *The Bodhisattva Ideal*

7. REFLECTIONS ON IMPERMANENCE

Impermanence is what makes the path possible, for without it there could be no transformation or creativity.

Reflecting on impermanence is so important because through it we begin to break down the tendency to over-identify with the body, and thus the delusion of a fixed self is weakened. This is the heart of the matter. An experience of bereavement, for all its pain, is a precious opportunity to grow. If everything changes, indeed must do so, then you can change too. You can develop and grow; you need not be confined to what you are at present, or have been in the past. Impermanence is what makes the path possible, for without it there could be no transformation or creativity. You would be stuck with your old self for ever, with no hope of release. Think how terrible that would be! You might be able to put up with it for quite a while, but eventually life would become truly unbearable. Yet, paradoxically, here we are, clinging to this fixed view of self for all we are worth.

Impermanence is what enables us to turn our whole lives towards the ideal of Enlightenment. To speak of death is not necessarily to lapse into pessimism – it is just being realistic. Old age, grief, lamentation, and death are after all just facts. But life can still be positive, even though it sometimes involves having to face things we find unpleasant. If we are to grow, we will need to face those things, acknowledge them, and go beyond them. The overall process is positive, and the Buddhist vision expresses that positivity without seeing everything through a rosy mist or refusing to face unpleasant facts.

The recollection of death should therefore be as familiar to the Buddhist as it is strange to the person who hasn't given any thought to the fact that they will one day die. If you have never reflected on impermanence in any serious way, you will be in a difficult position when the time of your own death draws near. You won't suddenly be able to intensify your mindfulness if you haven't already developed sufficient momentum in your practice of it. This is when you will need to call your spiritual friends around you, to give you help and moral support. But although they will be able to help you to some extent, the best and wisest thing is to keep up your spiritual practice as an integral part of your life when you are free from sickness and danger. Do not leave it too late. One does not wish to be morbid, but we are reminded sometimes that we never know when we are going to be run over by the proverbial bus. The best policy is to concentrate your energies and pour them wholeheartedly not just into your practice of meditation or study, but into the whole of your spiritual life.

from *Living with Awareness*

8. HOW TO REFLECT

Simply taking note of certain objective facts about existence is crucial to the process of growing up, of maturing in a truly human way.

The so-called corpse meditations are traditionally recommended for people of the greed type, the passionate type of person, because if you have always concentrated on the bright, agreeable, pleasant side of human life, you must remind yourself that there is another side. You may be very much attached to someone physically, for example, but if you are going to be truly aware of what you are attached to, you must ask yourself what is going to happen to it in ten, fifteen, thirty, a hundred years' time. The point of cultivating a deeper awareness of the more challenging aspects of human experience is not to take the sparkle out of life, but to help detach yourself from an over-preoccupation with the kind of beauty that is bound up with craving, and thus make yourself free to experience a more refined beauty.

But if you are of the hate type, it might not be good for you to practise these meditations because you already see life as essentially disagreeable, or even disgusting. You will need rather to remind yourself that life, and especially the aspect of life that concerns other people, has a bright side, an agreeable aspect. In such a case, the *mettā bhāvanā*, the development of loving-kindness, will be a more suitable meditation practice.

Even if you are of the greed type, going out in search of corpses to meditate on is not necessarily the best approach. If you are so greedy by temperament that you are completely obsessed with material things and with other people on the purely physical level, then a visit to the cemetery, or a burning ground if you could find one, might be salutary (though with such a temperament you would be unlikely to go out of choice). But if you aren't of that extreme type, you can reflect upon death or even just upon impermanence. It will not have the kind of dramatic effect that trying to force oneself into an awareness of death may have. However, simply taking note of certain objective facts about existence is crucial to the process of growing up, of maturing in a truly human way. If you apply what you understand and experience to yourself, you will gradually deepen that awareness of impermanence to allow real insight to emerge.

Merely taking in one's natural surroundings can help with this exercise. It is easier in the countryside than in the city, but even in the city you can see impermanence as an immediate reality. When I lived in the East End of London there was a tree outside my window which I used to enjoy looking at, noticing its annual flourishing and withering: in the spring covered in blossom, in the summer in full leaf, and in the winter with no leaves at all. Even where there is no turning of the seasons to observe, one can still catch striking glimpses of the same reality. When I visited New Zealand, for example, although the native bush was virtually all evergreen, in the midst of the green I noticed skeletons of trees, bleached white by the sun. That was quite odd, a real memento mori, a skeleton at the feast. It was as if you were to go down to a beach full of healthy, bronzed people sunbathing and see at intervals human skeletons, bleached white, reclining among the sunbathers.

The Romans allegedly had skeletons at their feasts, dressed up with garlands of roses, to remind them that the feasting was going to end one day, for everybody. To us this would no doubt seem an unnecessarily morbid addition to our guest list. We don't even keep flowers in our rooms once the petals have begun to fall. But if you live in the countryside, you cannot pick and choose from its seasons, and that does give you a sense of the evanescence of things, if you are observant. You can also nourish this sense with the arts: reflections on transitoriness are of course the constant theme of both English nature poetry, and Chinese and Japanese Zen Buddhist poetry.

In all these different ways one may deepen one's awareness of one's own existence, becoming more alert to the shortness of one's life, and learning to see things more constantly from this truer perspective. Nor is such a perspective at all negative – rather the opposite. As you start recognizing the impermanence of things, you realize that change is not just about decay and deterioration – things can also change for the better. Indeed, you can *make* them change for the better, so that change becomes not just change but transformation. This is symbolized by the Hindu figure of the dancing Shiva: although Shiva is apparently a violent, destructive figure, the symbolism is essentially positive because it represents the potential for transformation. Likewise, in Buddhist tradition, the bodhisattva Avalokiteśvara who appears in all the six realms of existence of the wheel of life reminds us that the possibility of transformation exists in every one of those realms.

Facing up to impermanence before old age forces us to do so helps us to make the most of life. Whereas many people start to take full advantage of life only when they get older and a bit wiser, if you are fortunate enough still to have youth on your side, you can reflect, while you are still young, 'Here I am, alive, and with luck I will live for a few more years. In that time, I can really do something with my life, make it something worthwhile, so that at the end of it I can look back and think, "Well, I have had a wonderful opportunity, and thank heaven I have been able to take advantage of it."'

The corpse meditation is therefore only the most hair-raising way of contemplating impermanence. There are many other practices concerned with the same basic theme and purpose that are better suited to most people's spiritual needs. It is said that one should do the corpse meditation in the full manner only if one has strong nerves – and indeed one should approach any version of the practice with caution and seriousness and a firm foundation of mindfulness and *mettā* – especially *mettā* towards oneself.

from *Creative Symbols of Tantric Buddhism*

9. KARMA AND REBIRTH

From the Buddhist point of view the universe is an ethical universe.

Old age, sickness, and death were the spurs to Siddhārtha Gautama's quest, and what he realized when he became the Buddha somehow put an end to these things. It was not just that he came to terms with death, or looked forward to death. He *realized* something – not intellectually but by way of direct perception – that transformed him into a new species of being to whom birth and death simply did not apply. The Buddha doubted at first the possibility of communicating this alchemical insight – what he called 'the truth of *pratītya-samutpāda*' – to anyone else. But communicate it he did, deep and subtle as it was. And though his seminal formulation of *pratītya-samutpāda* engendered, over the years, a vast and rich array of teachings, it remains the basis, the very foundation, of all of them. In philosophical terms, at least, it is the realization of this truth of universal conditionality which constitutes the essence of the Buddha's Enlightenment. Hence we describe it as the fundamental principle of Buddhism.

It originally took the form in his mind of a laconic, even bleak statement: 'This is conditioned by that. All that happens is by way of a cause.' However, the most renowned version of this principle derives, perhaps significantly, from an occasion when it was being *communicated* – and with dramatic success. In this instance it was communicated not by the Buddha himself, but by one of his disciples, and it was imparted to a seeker after the truth who was to become the Buddha's chief disciple.

It was a few months after the Buddha's Enlightenment. A young Brahmin from Bihar called Śāriputra had gone forth from home, just as the Buddha had, along with his childhood friend Maudgalyāyana. He was now on his own because the two of them had agreed that they would go off in different directions, and that whichever of them found an Enlightened teacher first would tell the other, thus doubling their chances, so to speak.

In the course of his travels, Śāriputra happened to meet one of the Buddha's first five disciples, called Aśvajit, who had by this time become Enlightened himself and gone forth to teach the Dharma. Very much impressed by the appearance of this wandering monk, who radiated tranquillity and happiness, Śāriputra approached him, greeted him, and asked, 'Who is your teacher?' This might seem to us a rather direct way of addressing a total stranger. In Britain we generally open a conversation with a remark like 'Nice weather we're having,' or 'Looks like it's beginning to clear up a bit now.' But in India they tend to come straight to the point. So Śāriputra asked the question that people in India still sometimes ask each other, and Aśvajit answered, 'My teacher is Śākyamuni, the Sage, the Wise One of the Śākya tribe, the Buddha.' Śāriputra then put to Aśvajit the second standard question – standard, but in this case momentous: 'What does he teach?' Aśvajit said, 'Frankly, I'm a beginner. I really don't know much about the Dharma. But I can tell you in brief what it's about.' And what he then said has since become famous throughout the Buddhist world in the form of a short Pāli verse of just two lines. He said:

> Of all those things that proceed from a cause, the Tathāgata[122] has explained the cause, and also its cessation. This is the teaching of the great *śramaṇa*.[123]

It seems that this stanza made a shattering, and at the same time liberating, impression on the mind of Śāriputra. He had an instantaneous glimpse of the truth that it embodied, Transcendental insight arose in him, and he became a Stream Entrant on the spot. Obviously, the ground had been so well prepared that this most compressed exposition of the Dharma was enough to tell him his quest was at an end. He could go to his friend, Maudgalyāyana, and tell him with confidence that he had found the Enlightened teacher they were looking for.[124]

This verse of Aśvajit's is recorded, honoured, and worshipped all over the Eastern Buddhist world. In Tibet, China, Japan, Thailand, and Sri Lanka, it is found carved on stone monuments and clay tablets, printed on strips of paper to be stuffed inside images, and inscribed on plates of silver or gold. It is, we may say, the credo of Buddhism. If it seems rather dry and abstract, academic, uninspiring even, it certainly did not seem so to Śāriputra. And when you really think about the principle of *pratītya-samutpāda* – in whatever form it is expressed – when you meditate on it, when you really follow through its implications, you begin to understand the extraordinary impact it has had on the world. Whatever comes into existence, on whatever level, does so in dependence on conditions, and in the absence of those conditions it ceases to exist. This is all it says. But if anything is Buddhism, this is Buddhism.

What it is saying is that, from the viewpoint of the Enlightened mind, the outstanding feature of all phenomena, whether physical or psychical, is that they are conditioned. The unceasing flux of things, both material events and states of mind, is a process of interdependent stages, each of which comes about through the presence of conditions and, in its turn, conditions the stages succeeding it. Rainfall, sunshine, and the nourishing earth are the conditions from which arises the oak tree, whose fallen leaves rot and form the rich humus from which the bluebell grows. A jealous attachment will have consequences that may lead to murder. Nothing phenomenal is spontaneously produced without preceding conditions, or itself fails to have consequences. And it is the process of becoming aware of this law of conditionality that gradually liberates us from all conditions, leading to the freely functioning, spontaneous creativity of Enlightenment.

If we are reasonably clear about what it was that constituted the Buddha's realization, we can move on to look at how it actually dealt with the questions that Siddhārtha originally set out to answer. What about old age, sickness, and death? Where do the immutable facts of our physical decay fit into the whole process of conditionality? Does this 'unceasing flux of things' continue beyond death – or is death the end? These questions, of course, are not abstract or theoretical for us. The mystery of death which so troubled primitive humanity is still a mystery. Even these days, when we apparently know so much, you only need to give a talk called 'The Tibetan Book of the Dead' or 'What happens after death' or 'Where you go when you die' to draw record crowds, and there is always a healthy market for books about death and dying. We may think things have changed immeasurably since primitive times, but they haven't changed much when it comes to our understanding of death. Indeed, if anything, the 'problem' of death has become more pressing.

We are not, however, talking about one single problem of death common to everyone. The way we feel about death, and the way we personally come to terms with death, or fail to do so, is not exactly the same as the way other people feel about it, and people's feelings and ideas about death have changed over time, over the centuries, as well. Putting the problem of death into some kind of historical perspective, we may say that it all really began when mankind first started growing crops, in the age of the great river valley civilizations. This was perhaps ten or fifteen thousand years ago. At that time the world began to take on an aspect that was less hostile and mysterious, but people were still in the dark about the greatest of all mysteries – death. The mystery, in fact, grew deeper and darker, and it seemed to weigh on people's minds more oppressively than ever before. And there was a reason for this. People no longer lived a nomadic life; they lived in villages and towns, even in great cities. Civilization had begun. Life had become more secure and comfortable, and people enjoyed it more. And having begun to enjoy it, they wanted to go on enjoying it. They didn't want to leave their wives or husbands, their children, their houses and their neatly cultivated fields, their singing and their dancing, their games of chance and their religious rites – but one day they would have to leave it all, and they knew it. The thought of death threw a shadow over the sunlight of their lives. What was life for, if it had to end so soon? You had just a few short years of youth, pleasure, and prosperity, and after that, just a blank, a void, with nothing apparently surviving – perhaps some ghostly wraith twittering in the darkness, but nothing more.

What could you do about it? It seemed that you could do nothing at all. Most people just tried to forget about it and enjoy life as much as possible while they could. 'Eat, drink, and be merry, for tomorrow we die,' expressed the substance of their philosophy. A few who were made of sterner stuff immersed themselves in action. They performed heroic deeds – went about slaying monsters, fighting battles, conquering kingdoms. They tried to make a name for themselves so that even though they might perish – probably sooner rather than later – their names would live on after them, so they hoped, for ever. But even these heroes, in their more reflective moments, saw that this was all a bit pointless.

Human life, it seemed, was not just a mystery, but a tragedy. This mood is reflected in the traditions and tales of ancient cultures, which were eventually written down to become the earliest examples of literature. We find it in the Babylonian epic of Gilgamesh, from around 3000 BCE, and in Homer's account of the fall of Troy, the *Iliad*, composed over 2,000 years later. It is there in the Anglo-Saxon epic poem *Beowulf*, dating from the eighth century, and it is even more powerfully and bitterly expressed in the Bible, in the Book of Ecclesiastes, the 'Book of the Preacher'. The vanity of human ambition in the face of death, the great leveller, is a favourite theme in ancient literature, and has inspired the same sort of thing in more recent times:

> The boast of heraldry, the pomp of pow'r,
> And all that beauty, all that wealth e'er gave,
> Awaits alike th'inevitable hour:
> The paths of glory lead but to the grave.[125]

But this was not the whole story. It was only half the story – the western half. Further east, people had started to take a different attitude, and had, in fact, arrived at some sort of solution to the mystery of death, which of course also meant some sort of solution to the mystery of life. What they perceived was that death was not the end. Human beings did not just vanish. After a time, they came back in a new body, in accordance with the nature of the deeds they had performed in their previous life. This perception made its first appearance in India at about the time of Homer (c.800 BCE), and from India thereafter spread widely. The first clear reference to it is found in the Hindu *Brihadaranyaka Upanishad*, in which the idea is represented as a highly esoteric teaching, to be communicated only to the chosen few. But as the idea spread, it became known, in a more organized, systematized form, as the teaching of karma and rebirth.

When people in the West go flocking along to a lecture on karma and rebirth, or the *Tibetan Book of the Dead*, what they really want to know is: 'What is going to happen to me when I die? Is death the end, the absolute full stop, or not?' The fact is, if we could be assured that death was not the end, there would be no problem at all. If people knew with absolute certainty that they weren't going to just disappear when they died, they would be a lot less inclined to go and hear a lecture on karma and rebirth. For us, death is the problem. But in the East, especially the Hindu and Buddhist East, it is rather different. People are not so bothered about death there. For them, death is natural and inevitable – and so is rebirth. You die and you are reborn, you die again and you are reborn again – that's just the way it is. It's not a matter for speculation at all. In the East it is not death that is the problem. The problem is how to escape from the whole process of birth and death. How can you reach a state in which you will no longer be subject to birth and death? The problem is dying and being born time and time again, through endless ages. So the question is carried a stage further: what for the West is a solution of the problem is for the East a problem in itself, requiring a further solution. And this is where the Buddha's discovery of the universal principle of conditionality comes in.

When, in the course of the Enlightenment experience, the Buddha surveyed the whole vast range of conditioned existence, he saw that everything, from the lowest to the highest, was subject to the universal law of conditionality.[126] And he also saw that this universal law operates – as we have already seen from the point of view of our evolutionary model – in two distinct modes: a cyclical mode and a spiral mode. In the cyclical mode, there is action and reaction between opposites. We experience pleasure and pain, vice and virtue, birth and death – and usually what happens is that we swing back and forth between them. Life is followed by death, which is in turn followed by new life. Pain is followed by pleasure which is again followed by pain. At all levels of life – physical, biological, psychological, sociological, historical – this same cyclical process can be found to be operating. Empires rise only to fall; growth must be succeeded by decay; health, wealth, fame, and status have old age, sickness, death, loss, and oblivion as their inevitable outcome.

In the spiral mode of conditionality, on the other hand, there is the possibility of real and permanent growth. Each factor in this process, rather than reversing the effect of the previous one, increases its effect. For example, instead of an oscillation between pleasure and pain, you go from pleasure to happiness, then from happiness to joy, from joy to rapture, from rapture to bliss, and so on indefinitely. And this spiral mode can be applied to life and death just as much as to anything else. The Buddha saw that as well as being subject to the endless round of birth and death, it was possible for human beings to enter the spiral path of spiritual development, which was 'the way to the door of the Deathless', the way beyond the opposites of life and death.

When applied to the process of life and death, the principle of conditionality gave rise to one of the most famous and important – and most frequently misunderstood – of Buddhist teachings: karma and rebirth. The first thing to understand about karma is that it is simply an application of the principle of conditionality. Nothing mysterious, nothing odd, nothing strange, nothing occult. Karma, in the most general terms, represents the law of conditionality at work on a certain plane of existence. This has to be emphasized because one major source of confusion seems to be the idea that karma *is* the Buddhist teaching of cause and effect, and that it is universal – which is not the case. The universal principle is conditionality, and karma is only one of the ways in which conditionality operates. This point may be clarified by referring to a Buddhist teaching which dates from considerably later than the Buddha's own lifetime. It comes, in fact, from the analytical and systematizing philosophical tradition of the Abhidharma, and it is the teaching of what is called the five *niyamas*. These five *niyamas* are a very useful formulation because, as is the way with the Abhidharma, they draw together strands which are otherwise rather loose and disconnected as we find them in the original *suttas*.[127]

The word *niyama* is a term common to Pāli and Sanskrit meaning a natural law, a cosmic order. According to this teaching there are five of them, showing the law of cause and effect at work on five different levels. The first three are straightforward enough, as they can be related to Western sciences. Firstly, there's *utu-niyama*. *Utu* means non-living matter. Nowadays people are beginning to doubt whether there is any such thing as non-living matter, but let's call it that for the time being. In other words, this is the physical, inorganic order of existence. *Utu-niyama* is therefore the law of cause and effect as operative on the level of inorganic matter. It very roughly embraces the laws of physics and chemistry and associated disciplines.

The second *niyama* is *bīja-niyama*. *Bīja* means 'seed', so *bīja-niyama* deals with the world of living matter, the physical organic order whose laws constitute the science of biology.

Then there is *citta-niyama*. *Citta* is 'mind', so *citta-niyama* is conditionality as operative in the world of mind. The existence of this third *niyama*, therefore, implies that mental activity and development are not haphazard, but governed by laws. It is important that we understand what this means. We are used to the idea of laws operating on the level of physics, chemistry, and biology, but we are not so used to the idea that similar laws might govern mental events. We are more inclined, in the West, to the view that mental events just happen, without any particular causation. To some extent and in some quarters, the influence of Freud has begun to shift this assumption, but the idea that mental phenomena arise in dependence on conditions is not one that has yet penetrated deeply into popular thinking. It is there in Buddhism, however, in this teaching of *citta-niyama*, the law of cause and effect as operative in the world of mind – and we may say that it is a concept which corresponds to the modern science of psychology.

Fourthly: *kamma-niyama*. *Kamma* (Pāli) is of course more popularly known in its Sanskrit form, *karma*, and it means 'action', but in the sense of deliberately willed action. So it is traditionally, and paradoxically, said sometimes that karma is equivalent to *cetanā* (volitional consciousness), that is that action equals volition: 'for as soon as volition arises, one does the action, whether by body, speech, or mind.'[128] *Kamma-niyama* therefore pertains to the world of ethical responsibility; it is the principle of conditionality operative on the moral plane.

It is perhaps difficult for those of us with a background of Western thought on morality to understand how this works. In ordinary social life, if you commit a crime, you are arrested and brought before the judge or magistrate, tried and convicted, sentenced, and sent to jail or fined. Committing the crime and being punished are quite separate events, and there is someone or something – society, the police, the judge, the law – who punishes you. Our tendency is to apply this legal model when it comes to morality as a whole. We think of sin and the *punishment* of sin, virtue and the *reward* of virtue. And traditionally we have tended to think in terms of a judge too: somebody who sees what you do, and punishes or rewards you accordingly – the judge being, of course, God. People imagine God as holding a sort of tremendous courtroom trial, with everybody hauled up in front of him, and the angels and demons standing around like police witnesses. It is still official Christian doctrine that when you die you face your judge, and this is a terrible thought for the orthodox Christian – that you are going to be put in the dock before the Transcendental Judge and then bundled off wherever he sends you. The dramatic possibilities inherent in the doctrine have made for some terrific literature, music, drama, and art – Michelangelo's tremendous painting of the Last Judgement in the Sistine Chapel is just one notable example. But it also makes for rather poor philosophy, and a mode of thinking from which we are still suffering a ghastly hangover.

The Buddhist point of view is totally different, and it may seem distinctly odd to us, with our approach to ethics – almost whether we like it or not – tending to be underpinned by Christian theology. In Buddhism there is a law but no lawgiver, and no one who administers the law. I have heard Christian missionaries arguing with Buddhists and insisting that if you believe in a law, there must be a lawgiver – but this is quite specious. After all, there is a law of gravity, but there isn't a god of gravity pushing and pulling things. The law of gravity is just a generalized description of what happens when objects fall. In the same way we don't have a god of heredity, or a god of sexual selection. These things just happen; they work themselves.

It is much the same on the moral plane, according to Buddhism. The law administers itself, so to speak. Good karma naturally results in happiness, and bad karma naturally results in misery. There is no need for anybody else to come along, look at what you've done, and then fit the punishment or the reward to the deed. It happens of its own accord. 'Good' and 'bad' are built into the structure of the universe. This might sound dreadfully anthropomorphic – and I am putting it rather crudely here – but what it really means is that from the Buddhist point of view the universe is an ethical universe. Putting it more precisely, the universe functions according to conditionality, and this operates at the karmic level in a way which we could describe as ethical, in that it conserves ethical values. This is *kamma-niyama*.

The fifth and last *niyama* is *dhamma-niyama*. Dhamma (*dharma* in Sanskrit) is a word with a number of different possible applications, but here it means simply spiritual or transcendental as opposed to mundane. So the principle of conditionality operates on this level too. Exactly how it works, however, has not always been made very clear, and some of the more popular traditional explanations of this *niyama* are a bit childish and superficial. For example, many legends report that when the Buddha gained Enlightenment, and also when he died – and indeed on other momentous occasions – the earth shook and trembled in six different ways; and this, according to some commentators, was due to the operation of *dhamma-niyama*.

In fact we do not have to look very far in order to locate a more sensible and helpful interpretation. The obvious key, it seems to me, is in the distinction between the two types or modes of conditionality. The first four *niyamas*, including *kamma-niyama*, are all types of conditionality in the cyclical sense, in the sense of action and reaction between pairs of opposites. But *dhamma-niyama* corresponds to the spiral type of conditionality. As such it constitutes the sum total of the spiritual laws which govern progress through the stages of the Buddhist path.

Thus karma is not the law of conditionality in general, but only that law as operating on the ethical level, the plane of moral responsibility. This means we cannot assume that what befalls us necessarily does so as a result of our past actions, because karma is only one of the five levels of conditionality. What happens to us may be a result of physical, biological, psychological, ethical, *or* spiritual factors. In all likelihood, it will involve a complex *combination* of factors, bringing several of the *niyamas* into play.

from *Who is the Buddha?*

10. IS IT NECESSARY FOR A BUDDHIST TO BELIEVE IN REBIRTH?

The very survival of human life on this planet seems to many of us more pressing than any consideration of future rebirths.

There is no need to assent to the idea of karma and rebirth in order to be a practising Buddhist. Any account of Buddhism as traditionally handed down tends to bring it in at some point, but there are plenty of texts and teachings which present the path simply as the path, making no reference to karma and rebirth at all. If the Buddhist tradition holds good, then as one's understanding deepens the truth of karma and rebirth will presumably become clearer. After all, Buddhists have disagreed over many things, but no teacher of any school or sect has ever suggested that belief in karma and rebirth might be a wrong view – except in the sense that time itself, mundane existence itself, is not ultimately real. The idea of rebirth, one could say, follows logically upon the fundamental tenet of Buddhism that actions have consequences. However, one doesn't have to be completely logical in order to follow the Buddhist path, and it is possible to draw motivation for one's practice by considering the operation of karma in this life without necessarily taking rebirth into account.

Of course, however logical belief in it may be, rebirth is not the only possible answer to the universal question 'What happens when we die?' For many people the Buddhist conception of rebirth seems more or less self-evident. But there are, obviously, other views on the matter. In fact there are three, or possibly four, views to choose from. The first view is that one will exist after death – in heaven or elsewhere, though not again on earth – but that one did not exist before this life. This is the Christian view, or, at least, that is the view which has been held almost universally throughout Christian history. One or two of the early Greek Christian scholars, like Origen, did believe in some sort of pre-existence before physical birth. Their idea was that the soul, which one inherited from one's parents, ultimately came from Adam. This belief – which amounted to a belief in a sort of group soul of which one's individual soul is a part – was known as Traductionism (because one's soul is 'traduced' or conveyed from Adam).

Christian opinion is more divided on what happens after death. Some believe that the soul created by God is immortal, and that it eventually goes to heaven or hell – or, in the case of unchristened babies, to Limbo – for all eternity. Others take the view that the soul is created mortal and dies with the death of the body until it is revived, either shortly after death or – according to, for example, Seventh Day Adventists and Jehovah's Witnesses – at the time of the Last Judgement. Then one goes either to heaven or to hell – though the Seventh Day Adventists replace eternal torment with a much kinder final solution for the condemned, which is that God simply annihilates them.

The second possible view is the strictly materialist one: the belief that there is just this life with no kind of existence whatsoever before or after. There is, theoretically speaking, also a third possibility which would be the view that there is just this life and a succession of previous lives, but no next life – but no one, to the best of my knowledge, actually holds this view. Finally, the fourth possible view is that there is a past life or lives, a present life, and a future life or lives.

Most people find that one of these views seems more satisfactory than the others. No one view is altogether free from difficulties; but I have come to the conclusion that the idea of rebirth fits best. And the most telling confirmation of this lies not in some objective intellectual demonstration but in a feeling – a quite definite and powerful feeling – that develops through one's life.

This is something one can't appreciate when one is young, unless one is rather exceptional. But as one gets older, one starts seeing that one's whole life has had a certain clear direction or tendency which cannot fully be accounted for by any accumulation of circumstances within this present life, but which definitely seems to originate from what one can only assume is a previous life. Furthermore, one gets a strong feeling that this trend isn't just going to stop, but will continue after one's death. If one is relatively observant and reflective I think one cannot but entertain quite seriously the idea that one has come into this life with a propensity, even an agenda, already in place and that one will project it – project oneself – beyond the conclusion of one's life.

One can get a sense of this from telling one's life story to a friend or friends. This is a useful and powerful practice which often brings to the surface half-forgotten aspects of one's life and allows one to discover patterns in one's experience. And one theme that frequently emerges as one tells one's life story is a sense that in the business of growing up something important has been lost along the way. Quite a number of people have this feeling, that when they were young, before they got caught up in worldly responsibilities, they really did have a sense of what life was all about, before it all got overlaid by the dense complex of adult experience. It's as though we lose contact with our true feelings, our true self, even – not just in a psychological way that requires some psychotherapeutic solution, but in a definitely spiritual way.

In our early years many of us have experiences or feelings that seem to belong not to this world but elsewhere – or that even seem to indicate that we *belong* elsewhere. A few years later, when one starts to think and feel as an individual without yet being weighed down with responsibilities, one wants to find one's way back to one's origins, back to a truer, more innocent experience, and take that as one's starting point.

All this is not to suggest that there is some kind of primeval innocence about a child, or that children are in some way in touch with the Absolute. Unfortunately, one can get a sentimental and mistaken impression of this sort from some of the English poets: Vaughan, for example: 'Happy those early days when I / Shined in my Angel-infancy'; or Wordsworth: 'trailing clouds of glory do we come / From God who is our home'. Wordsworth himself is a very clear, though unusual, example of someone who achieved a true vision in early adolescence which he managed to sustain well into his thirties. William Blake is another – indeed, he never really lost contact with his childhood. Though he was a very mature person he never grew up at all in the sense of becoming corrupted with (in Traherne's phrase) 'the dirty devices of the world'.

There will always be people who say that it is a necessary part of one's development to taste something of the dirty devices of this world, but this is a wrong view. Ideally, one should try to remain an adolescent in this positive sense for as long as possible. One should seek to deepen one's vision, to mature it – but not to lose it. To return to the idea of rebirth, it's as though when we are young we are in touch with something from a previous life. One may not be aware of it as a small child, but as one comes up to adolescence one becomes old enough to have a sense of it – though not, perhaps, old enough to appreciate how precious it is, or how easily it is lost.

Such experiences lead many people to see the idea of rebirth as quite reasonable, even obvious. However, if we find it difficult to take it to heart as our Tibetan author would like us to, we do not thereby lose our motivation for the spiritual life – at least, not necessarily. In fact, in some Buddhist countries the doctrine of karma and rebirth sometimes provides an excuse for postponing any real spiritual effort. It is even said that it isn't possible to gain Enlightenment any longer – the Buddha lived so long ago and there aren't any Enlightened teachers around any more – so our best bet is to accumulate merit, hope for good rebirths, and wait a few thousand years for the next Buddha to reappear, in the hope that we will get a chance to become his disciples. That will be the time to make an effort to gain Enlightenment. So some people believe – but it is a disastrously wrong view. It is better to disbelieve in karma and rebirth and follow the path anyway than to believe in karma and rebirth and make that one's excuse for not following the path here and now.

The traditional assumption that it is concern for one's future rebirth that motivates one to take up Buddhism is simply not the way most people think in the West today. People tend to become interested in Buddhism, or start practising meditation, because it seems to offer a solution to psychological problems, or an intellectually respectable alternative to a purely materialist philosophy. Many practising Buddhists may be said to take a frankly agnostic or even sceptical attitude to the idea of rebirth. The very survival of human life on this planet is an issue that seems to many of us more pressing than any consideration of future rebirths.

Nowadays we can see things happening much more quickly than people could in more traditional and stable societies. It seems as though the whole process of life has speeded up, so that we can see the results of karma in this life itself. We are continually made aware through the media that we are teetering on the edge of global catastrophe, and this deepens our sense of responsibility. Never mind future lives; if we don't act now something terrible will happen in *this* life. (Of course, one can also think in terms of the consequences of our actions for future generations.) On a more personal level, too, one may conclude that only through some kind of spiritual development will one be able to transcend one's immediate painful conditions in this life. In these ways it is possible to accept the principle of karma within the much narrower context and more limited timescale of a single lifespan. Some people derive sufficient inspiration from thinking in terms of transforming their lives and the world around them, without needing to consider a long view of futurity at all.

Alternatively, one can take a completely opposite, more positive, perspective to that recommended by our author. Within the framework of karma and rebirth, one is usually thinking in terms of escaping from something. Some Tibetan lamas teaching in the West make a point of describing in vivid detail all the different hells and heavens that await us – what will happen to you if you do this, what will happen to you if you do that – and this uncompromising, even dogmatic laying down of traditional doctrine evidently has a strong effect. But many western Buddhists see this approach as unnecessarily fundamentalist. For them the spiritual life has its own intrinsic appeal which overrides the fear of any unpleasant contingencies attendant upon the worldly life, whether here and now or in the future. This innate love for the spiritual life should be encouraged. There are people who do not need to be told that they will suffer if they follow the worldly life, because they see spiritual development as good in itself.

Of course, the doctrine of karma and rebirth need not be intimidating. Some people are positively invigorated by the prospect of practising the spiritual life for life after life after life, gathering momentum over aeons of time and visiting all sorts of Buddha-worlds as described in the Mahāyāna *sūtras*. That others will find the mind-boggling duration of three *asaṃkhyeyas* of lifetimes simply depressing testifies to the necessity of developing an appropriate motivation of one's own.[129]

But whatever we think about rebirth, we can still take karma seriously. Karma, it should be noted, is only one of the five levels on which conditionality operates. This is an aspect of the teaching that is not always made explicit in the Mahāyāna, although it is standard

Theravādin teaching.[130] (Indeed, not all Mahāyāna Buddhists would even agree that conditionality is multifaceted in this way; in some Mahāyāna traditions karma has become very dominant indeed.) But taking the Theravādin line on this, we can say that everything that happens does so as the result of a network of conditions, involving causal links which can be of a physical, biological, psychological, karmic, or transcendental nature. While karma – the level on which our skilful actions bring happiness for us and our unskilful actions bring suffering – is a causal factor in our lives, it does not follow that everything that happens to us is a result of our karma. Nonetheless, an understanding of the karmic level of conditionality is crucial to us because it is something on which we can rely. If we act skilfully, joy is sure to follow; if we act unskilfully, we are letting ourselves in for suffering we could have avoided.

This insight can be traced back to the very earliest Buddhist teachings, to the first two verses of the *Dhammapada*, which state:

> Unskilful mental states are preceded by mind, led by mind, and made up of mind. If one speaks or acts with an impure mind suffering follows him even as the cart-wheel follows the hoof of the ox.

> Skilful mental states are preceded by mind, led by mind, and made up of mind. If one speaks or acts with a pure mind happiness follows him like his shadow.[131]

As these verses make clear, there is a connection between our mind and the nature of our future life or lives. According to the doctrine of karma and rebirth, our actions have a direct effect on our own being by modifying the patterns of habit, the conscious and unconscious volitional drives, which constitute the most essential part of us. This 'essential nature' is not unchangeable; on the contrary, it can change in any direction at any time. It carries on through death and into another rebirth, in accordance with the karma that has accumulated during the previous life.

from *Know Your Mind*

4
BUDDHISM AMONG ISMS AND OLOGIES

1. REALIZING I WAS NOT A CHRISTIAN

This realization gave me a sense of relief, of liberation as from some oppressive burden, which was so great that I wanted to dance and sing for joy.

One Saturday afternoon, as I was changing books, I noticed on a door in the Reference Room the words 'Moyse Collection'. On my application to the librarian the door was unlocked and I found myself in the midst of the biggest and richest collection of books I had yet seen. Resisting the very strong temptation to describe in detail the excursions into the Greek and Latin classics, Old English texts, and Elizabethan drama which I thenceforward made on Saturday afternoons (for the books belonging to this collection had to be read on the spot), I shall confine myself to two volumes which were my stepping-stones to higher things. The first of these was Hartmann's *Paracelsus*. Though the work interested me deeply, I was still more interested by its constant references, usually in footnotes, to *Esoteric Buddhism*, a work of which I had never heard. Coming upon it one afternoon not far from *Paracelsus*, I promptly read it. Much more vividly than the vague sense of widening horizons which it gave me do I remember its constant references, also in footnotes, to another work of which I had never heard: *Isis Unveiled*. This was not available in the Moyse Collection, but I discovered it soon afterwards in the Lending Department and bore the two bulky volumes back with me to St Marychurch.

How shall I describe their effect upon me? Though in itself almost entirely negative, it proved to be more far-reaching in its consequences than any book I had previously encountered. Within a fortnight I had read both volumes twice from cover to cover. Impressed, bewildered, thrilled, excited, stimulated as I was by their staggeringly immense wealth – their 'inexhaustible truckloads', as Maeterlinck called them – of information on every conceivable aspect of philosophy, comparative religion, occultism, mysticism, science, and a hundred other subjects, the realization which dawned most clearly upon me, and which by the time I had finished stood out with blinding obviousness in the very forefront of my consciousness, was the fact that *I was not a Christian* – that I never had been, and never would be – and that the whole structure of Christian doctrine was from beginning to end thoroughly repugnant to me. This realization gave me a sense of relief, of liberation as from some oppressive burden, which was so great that I wanted to dance and sing for joy. What I was, what I believed, I knew not, but what I was not and what I did not believe, that I knew with utter certainty, and this knowledge, merely negative though it was as yet, gave me a foretaste of that freedom which comes when all obstacles are removed, all barriers broken down, all limitations transcended.

from *The Rainbow Road from Tooting Broadway to Kalimpong*

2. RELIGION AS REVELATION OR DISCOVERY

Religion-as-Discovery would envisage the Dharmic or normative life not as the engraftment of some exotic blossom on the barren stock of humanity but as the flowering forth of its native perfection from the seed within.

The problem of whether religion is essentially a revelation of truth *to* humanity or a discovery of truth *by* humanity is in fact the intellectual formulation of a spiritual difficulty which each one of us experiences in the course of his or her quest for Reality. The most obvious and natural grouping of the various religious sects of the world is, therefore, into those for whom religion consists in revelation, and those for whom it consists of discovery, of the Truth. This division is not simply theoretical, since each of these definitions of religion has exercised a profoundly modifying influence upon the entire body of the beliefs and practices of the religions which were, whether consciously or unconsciously, dominated by it. Perhaps it was with the thought of some such division in his mind that Stanislaw Schayer wrote of Buddhism as 'the most profound and most fundamental antithesis to Christianity'.[132] Nor is this division wholly new. Far-Eastern Buddhists have long been familiar with the classification of religions into those depending on 'self-power', in Japanese *jiriki*, and those depending on 'other-power', or *tariki*. And in India religious aspirants are sometimes spoken of as displaying the characteristics of the young monkey, which clings fast to the hair of its mother's belly, and of the kitten, which is simply carried about helpless in her mouth.

Religion-as-Revelation holds that the existence of religion in the world, and therefore the possibility of the attainment of Salvation or Emancipation by man, is ultimately dependent on the Object, the Other, and that the initiative in the matter belongs wholly to it or him. It conceives the spiritual life not as the progressive actualization of a perfection potentially present in human beings but as the acceptance of something which we would never have been able to acquire by means of our own unaided efforts. Consequently, it tends to stress the weakness and sinfulness of human nature and to emphasize the necessity of extra-terrestrial intervention in the affairs of humanity. It is therefore only natural that Reality should be conceived as personal, and that the founders of the various religions and sects should be regarded as prophets or messengers sent from, or as full or partial incarnations of, him. The written record of the message, teaching, or life of each such founder is invariably regarded as the word of God himself, and to doubt, question, or criticize it is considered not only to preclude all possibility of salvation but even to run the risk of eternal damnation. Religion-as-Revelation therefore places the strongest possible emphasis on faith in God, faith in his prophet, messenger, or incarnation, faith in his infallible Word, faith in his Church, faith in his priest. Unfortunately, the beliefs of the various founders, scriptures, and churches which are included in this group of religions often disagree not only among themselves but also with those that are included in the other group. Hideous fanaticism and ferocious persecution thus ensue. Since each such religion regards its own particular revelation as the supreme and incontrovertible source of Truth the possibility of an appeal to reason and experience is automatically precluded. Obviously God would not wittingly contradict himself. One revelation must therefore be true, and the remainder false, that is to say, not revelations at all but simply human fictions and inventions. Moreover, Religion-as-Revelation's house is divided not only against itself but against many other houses as well – against science, for instance, which has succeeded in demonstrating the fallibility of many an infallible scripture.

Religion-as-Discovery, on the other hand, holds that religion is essentially a manifestation of the human spirit, that as human beings we are able to discover the Way to Truth ourselves by means of our own unaided human efforts, that the attainment of liberating knowledge depends upon the subject or self, and that the initiative in the matter rests ultimately within the abysm of one's own volition. It would envisage the Dharmic or normative life not as the engraftment of some exotic blossom onto the barren stock of humanity but as the flowering forth of its native perfection from the seed within. Consequently, it is inclined rather to inspire us by appealing to our innate strength and goodness than to discourage us by dwelling upon our mistakes and failures. Instead of imagining an arbitrary divine intervention to be the most important event in history it asserts the supremacy of natural law and maintains that the aspiration towards emancipation must, like every other process, proceed in accordance with an eternal and universal order (*sanātana dharma*). It is therefore hardly surprising that Religion-as-Discovery conceives Reality as a suprapersonal principle of knowledge or state of consciousness or that it regards the religious founder simply as one who, after realizing that principle or state, teaches humanity the way thereto. The records of his life and teachings are only a map describing the Way, a raft to cross the stream, or a finger pointing to the moon. They demand not blind faith but clear-sighted understanding, they appeal not to some infallible authority but to reason and experience. Religion-as-Discovery is therefore not only tolerant of all other religious beliefs and practices, howsoever divergent from its own, but is able to join hands with earnest seekers after truth in every sphere of human activity. It sees science not as an enemy but as a friend and fellow worker.

from *Crossing the Stream*

3. THE BUDDHA'S ATTITUDE TOWARD THE TEACHINGS OF HIS TIME

He knew that a positive method of teaching was more appealing, more likely to find entrance into the hearts and minds of his auditors, than a purely negative and destructive one, however correct and logical the latter might be.

> Now, Kālāmas, do not ye go by hearsay, nor by what is handed down by others, nor by what people say, nor by what is stated on the authority of your traditional teachings. Do not go by reasoning, nor by inferring, nor by argument as to method, nor from reflection on and approval of an opinion, nor out of respect, thinking a recluse must be deferred to. But, Kālāmas, when you know, of yourselves: 'These teachings are not good; they are blameworthy; they are regarded with contempt by the wise: these teachings, when followed out and put in practice, conduce to loss and suffering' – then reject them.[133]

The real import of this oft-quoted but much misunderstood passage should be carefully noted. It was not intended as a vindication of 'free thought'; neither does it give *carte blanche* to rationalistic scepticism. Rationalism is in fact explicitly rejected. The Kālāmas were no more disposed to question the possibility of a transcendental attainment than the Buddha himself was; but they were confused by the impossibility of reconciling the claims made on behalf of one method of reaching the goal with the claims made on behalf of other methods. All the rival teachers could not be speaking the truth. If one was right, the others must be wrong. The Buddha's reply is not an invitation to question the existence of a transcendental state, nor an encouragement to doubt whether the realization of such a state is within the reach of human effort. It simply affirms that we are to decide between the rival claims of religious teachings, firstly, on the basis of their results as revealed in our own experience and secondly, (a statement which is almost always ignored) in accordance with the testimony of the Wise. Who the Wise are, and how we may recognize them, is told elsewhere. One of their characteristics is that, unlike the recluses and Brahmins who had disturbed the minds of the Kālāmas, they do not indulge in acrimonious disputes.

The Buddha's reply to Mahāpajāpatī, the Gotamid, who had asked him to show her a teaching, hearing which from the lips of the Exalted One she might dwell 'alone, solitary, zealous, ardent, and resolved', formulates in much more positive terms, and in a more definitely Buddhist context, the general principle that was the burden of his discourse to the Kālāmas:

> Of whatsoever teachings, Gotamid, thou canst assure thyself thus: 'These doctrines conduce to passions, not to dispassion: to bondage, not to detachment: to increase of (worldly) gains, not to decrease of them: to covetousness, not to frugality: to discontent, and not content: to company, not solitude: to sluggishness, not energy: to delight in evil, not delight in good': of such teachings thou mayest with certainty affirm, Gotamid, 'This is not the Norm. This is not the Discipline. This is not the Master's Message.'

> But of whatsoever teachings thou canst assure thyself (that they are the opposite of these things that I have told you), – of such teachings thou mayest with certainty affirm: 'This is the Norm. This is the Discipline. This is the Master's Message.'[134]

These well-known passages from the Pāli canon make perfectly clear the nature of the principle by which the Buddha's attitude towards contemporary teachings was governed. He was prepared neither to accept nor to reject them absolutely. With complete intellectual detachment and freedom from preconception, he surveyed them all from the standpoint of Enlightenment – just as one who has ascended a mountain height can look back and see clearly that, of the numerous paths winding up from the valley below, some come to an end at the edge of a precipice or a foaming torrent, while others lead safely to the summit – and followed the Middle Path of accepting as part of his own teaching whatever was conducive to the attainment of the beyondless heights of Liberation, and rejecting as false and wrong whatever hindered, or retarded, or even merely did not help, in the process of spiritual ascent.

Thanks to the unexampled intellectual fertility of the Indian mind in that age, and to the unrestrained exuberance of its religious imagination, which ran riot through a thousand brilliantly coloured forms and fancies, as well as to the fanatical enthusiasm with which a thousand zealots experimented with the most fantastic methods of salvation, there was no lack of material for the Buddha to work upon. What he himself described as the 'jungle of views', which flourished so richly and so rankly in those days, seems to have produced the sublime and the ridiculous, the more than divine and the hardly less than bestial, in the way of religious ideals, with the same perfect indifference with which the great subtropical forests of the Himalayan region produce at the same time the marvellous blossoms of the rare and lovely orchid, and the monstrous growth of the common poisonous *datura*. This luxuriant crop of ideas the Buddha had partly to uproot, partly to prune, and partly to train to grow in the right direction. One has only to read the *Brahmajāla Sutta*, the opening discourse of the *Dīgha Nikāya* (collection of 'long discourses') with which the Sutta Piṭaka, the first of the three great divisions of the Pāli canonical scriptures, begins – where no fewer than sixty-two contemporary 'false views' are classified – to realize the immensity of the work of religio-philosophical criticism accomplished by the All-knowing One. It may, in fact, be said that it was he who laid down the main lines for the development of Indian spirituality, not only in its Buddhist but in its non-Buddhist forms, for thousands of years to come.

Though the Buddha rejected in the most categorical manner a great many of the beliefs and practices current in his time, references to which will be found scattered all over the pages of the scriptures, it should not be concluded that his attitude towards contemporary trends of thought was entirely negative, much less still unsympathetic or hostile – words which have no meaning in relation to a Fully Enlightened and Wholly Compassionate One. He was as ready to accept as to reject; in fact, more ready. For he knew that a positive method of teaching was more appealing, more likely to find entrance into the hearts and minds of his auditors, than a purely negative and destructive one, however correct and logical the latter might be. Consequently we find the Buddha constantly putting – if we may be permitted a metaphor which he probably would not have used, even if he had known it – the new wine of his teaching into old bottles. He does not condemn the practice of ceremonial ablution, for instance, so much as insist that real purification comes by bathing, not in the Ganges as people thought, but in the cleansing waters of the Dharma. He does not ask the Brahmin to give up tending the Sacred Fire, with which so many ancient traditions and so much religious emotion were bound up, but to remember that the true fire burns within, and that it feeds not on any material object but solely on the fuel of meditation. These examples of the Buddha's capacity to utilize Indian traditional practices for the purposes of his own teaching could be paralleled by a hundred others from the same canonical sources. Though self-torture had been definitely rejected as a means to Enlightenment, he permitted thirteen ascetic practices, called *dhutāṅgas*, out of hundreds of similar ones, to the members of his Order, not because he considered them necessary, but because there was a popular demand for them and because they were in any case not positively harmful.

This spirit of adaptation and assimilation was one of the causes which enabled Buddhism to spread so rapidly and easily, and with the minimum of opposition, among races and peoples whose traditions and cultural background were in many ways quite different from those of India. The Dharma, while remaining in essence changeless, was capable of assuming a thousand forms, because, as we have already seen, it is in principle simply the means to Enlightenment. With this criterion constantly in view, Buddhism, both in India and abroad, was able not only firmly to reject beliefs, customs, and observances that hindered the living of the holy life, but also freely to accept those by which it was helped, regardless of their origin. The illustration by means of which we sought to elucidate the relation of Buddhism to contemporary teachings may here be of further service to us. In the soil of the pot, there are found not only particles of earth which contain various nutritious elements, but also potsherds and fragments of stone containing none. Among the doctrines current in north-eastern India during the life of the Buddha, there were some which could provide materials for the growth and development of the seed of the Dharma, and others which could not provide such materials. The former were of course utilized, and not so much incorporated into the Buddha's teaching as recognized as being in truth already a part of it. The latter were simply picked out and thrown away.

What we need most of all to remember is the fact that whatever the part played by the contents of the pot may be, the seed out of which grew up the mighty spreading banyan tree of the Dharma came not from inside but from outside it. Only if we grasp this idea will it be possible for us to comprehend the traditional conception of the Buddha and his teaching.

from *A Survey of Buddhism*

4. THE TRANSCENDENTAL CRITIQUE OF RELIGION

We need to grow, we need to become free, and we need something to help us do so. If we agree to call that thing 'religion', how are we to make sure that religion does not become a means of enslaving or stultifying, even of crushing, the individual?

Once our basic needs for food, clothing, shelter, and leisure have been met, what do we need more than anything else in life? What is our essential need as human beings? Surely it is freedom. The real meaning of human life is to develop our distinctively human characteristics: awareness, emotional positivity, responsibility for ourselves and others, and creativity. But we cannot develop, we cannot grow, unless we have space – both literally and metaphorically – to grow into. We need freedom: freedom from all that restricts us, both outside us and within us, freedom from our own conditioning, even freedom from our old self.

And what helps us to be free – apart from our own efforts – is, or at least is considered to be, religion. We have seen that in Buddhism the spiritual life is frequently described in terms of freedom, but Buddhism is not alone in this. The followers of other religions, at least the universal religions, would probably also say that their religion stands for the freedom of the individual. The Christian might quote from the New Testament the words: 'You shall know the truth, and the truth shall set you free.'[135]

But if we consider what it is that stops us from becoming free – apart from our own sloth and torpor, laziness, neglect, forgetfulness, and so on – we encounter a tremendous paradox. Strangely enough, religion, rather than helping us to become spiritually free, only too often helps to keep us enslaved, and even adds further shackles to our chains. To many people, the very idea that religion has anything to do with freedom sounds like an absurd contradiction in terms. Some people, and I must confess that I am among them, feel uncomfortable using – in a sense being obliged to use – the word 'religion' at all.

We find it so difficult to associate religion with freedom, not because of what religion is in principle, but rather because of its historical record. Take, for example, the record of Christianity over the last 1,600 years, since it was declared the official religion of the Roman Empire. It is fairly obvious that we cannot develop as individuals unless we are free at least to think for ourselves. But organized Christianity – certainly in the form of its major churches – has hardly ever allowed the individual that freedom. People in Christian countries have been obliged to think as the Church thought, to toe the theological line – or face the consequences. Even today, what the Church calls blasphemy is still a criminal offence in Britain.[136]

Not only has organized Christianity refused to allow individuals to think for themselves; it has made them think in ways actually detrimental, actually inimical, to their own personal development. It has made them think of themselves as miserable sinners, as weak and powerless, made them think that being independent and taking the initiative is wrong, if not positively sinful.

So what went wrong? How is it that religion has become not a liberator but a jailer? The short answer is that religion has become an end in itself. The forms which religion takes – doctrines, rituals, institutions, rules – have all become ends in themselves. It has been forgotten that religion is a means to an end – that end being the individual's development from ignorance to Enlightenment, from mundane consciousness to transcendental consciousness.

What are we to do in this situation? We need to grow, we need to become free, and we need something to help us do so. If we agree to call that thing 'religion', how are we to make sure that religion does not become a means of enslaving or stultifying, even of crushing, the individual? We need something that will constantly remind us of the limitations of religion, something that will constantly remind us that religion is only a means to an end. In other words, we need a transcendental critique of religion.

This critique has always been part of Buddhism. The Buddha said, 'I teach the Dharma under the figure of a raft.'[137] In other words, just as a raft is useful for getting you across the water, but you wouldn't carry it with you once you had reached dry land, so the Buddha's teaching is useful for carrying us across the waters of *saṃsāra*, but we will have no need for it when we have reached the other shore of Enlightenment. This sort of emphasis is particularly strong in the Mahāyāna, and strongest of all, perhaps, in Zen. You get Japanese and Chinese pictures of the Sixth Patriarch tearing up the *Diamond Sūtra*. There is the story of the travelling monk who needed fuel because he was cold, and chopped up the wooden Buddha images in the temple at which he was staying. And there is the master who famously said to his disciple, 'If you meet the Buddha on the road, kill him!'

These are all rather extreme, rather bizarre ways of underlining the same message: that Buddhism is only a means to an end. It is because Buddhism has always been aware of the difference between means and ends that down the centuries it has remained spiritually alive. For the same reason, it has not on the whole been dogmatic or intolerant. It has never persecuted the followers of other religions, and the followers of one form of Buddhism have rarely persecuted the followers of another.

Some people think that one should not criticize religions other than one's own, or even that one should not criticize religion at all. But such criticism is essential in revealing obstacles to one's development as an individual. It is only by means of a critique that we can ensure that the means to the development of the individual remains a means and does not harden into an end in itself.

We should therefore apply this critique, even this criticism, to everything that presents itself to us as religion. We should apply it to Christianity, apply it to Buddhism, apply it to the Hīnayāna, apply it to the Mahāyāna, apply it to the Vajrayāna.

We need, of course, to make sure that we apply our critique appropriately; sometimes it is more appropriate to express appreciation. A guiding principle might be to apply the critique first and foremost to oneself. If we all applied this transcendental critique to our own spiritual practice, there would hardly be any need for a transcendental critique of religion in general, or of our own religion in particular. We must be careful not to knock away the very ladder by which we are climbing – not, at least, until we are ready to do without it. We need to apply the critique to whatever practices we undertake – whether it is meditation or devotional practice, reading books or attending lectures, living in a community or working in a right livelihood business. We need to stay alive to the crucial question: is it helping me to develop? We should never allow any of these things to become ends in themselves; they are all means to an end.

from *The Inconceivable Emancipation*

5. THE INDIVIDUAL AND THE GROUP

For the person who is essentially a member of the group, an individual – who does not belong to the group, whose being is not totally submerged in the group – is rather difficult to conceive.

The world today has certain special problems, problems that did not exist in the past quite in the way that they exist now. These problems are not entirely new, but they happen to be more acute now, and confront us in a more urgent form – which means that their solution has become more urgent. You may immediately think of economic problems, or ecological problems, according to your particular interest, but the biggest problem of all, at least in human or spiritual terms, is the problem of the *individual*: the survival of the individual.

It is very difficult for the individual to survive nowadays. It is very difficult for the individual to grow and develop. And that which threatens the survival of the individual is clearly, in one word, the *group*. We could therefore say that the FWBO is Western in the sense that it is a spiritual movement of Buddhist origin which is concerned with the protection of the individual from the group.

That the individual – as such – needs to be protected might be a new idea to some people. We are familiar with the idea that children should be protected; we are even familiar with the idea that animals should be protected. But what about the individual? We sometimes forget that, nowadays, the individual too needs to be protected. The individual is threatened by the group, is threatened, even, with extinction. By now you will have realized that I am using the terms 'group' and 'individual' in a rather special way. To explain what I mean I will have to go back a little in history, even into pre-history, and attempt a few definitions.

The group, of course, came before the individual, before the 'true individual'. Anthropologists tell us that human beings have always lived in groups; the group was necessary to survival. This was true not only of humans but of all our pre-hominid ancestors as well: they all lived in groups of various sizes, containing anything from a dozen to two or three dozen members of various ages, and of course of both sexes. In this way they formed a sort of extended family group. This pattern was followed by human beings, but with the difference that in our case the group gradually became bigger. Extended families merged to form tribes, tribes merged to form nations, nations founded states, and states even merged to form empires. This process extended over a period of many hundreds of thousands of years, gradually accelerating towards the end when we reach the period of recordable, datable history, which begins around 8000 BCE.

Whether the group was large or small, in principle it remained unchanged. We can therefore define the group as a collectivity organized for its own survival, in which the interests of the individual are subordinated to those of the collectivity. The group, or collectivity, is also a power structure in which the ultimate sanction is force. The group did not just make survival possible for its members; in the case of humans, it made it possible for them to enjoy higher and higher levels of material prosperity and culture. It made possible the emergence of folk art and ethnic religion; it made possible the emergence of civilization. But there was a price to be paid by the proto-individual, and that price was conformity with the group. The individual was regarded as being essentially a *member of the group*. The individual had no existence separate from the group, or apart from the group.

Let me give you an illustration of this from my own experience. Living in India for twenty years, I made many Hindu friends. Some of them, being very orthodox and rather old fashioned, used to be rather puzzled by the fact that I did not have a caste. Sometimes they would ask me, 'What is your caste?' because, in their view, I *had* to belong to a caste. When I told them that I did not have a caste, first of all, because I was born in England, where we don't have caste, and secondly, because I was a Buddhist, and in Buddhism we do not recognize the system of hereditary caste, they would say, 'But you *must* have a caste! Every human being must have a caste.' They could not conceive of someone who did not belong to one of the 2,000 or so castes of Hinduism. They could not conceive of someone who did not belong to a group of some kind. There is something a little parallel to this in the West in that we cannot conceive of someone who is not of a particular nationality. But caste is even harder, even stricter, than that.

For the person who is essentially a member of the group, an individual – who does *not* belong to the group, whose being is not totally submerged in the group – is rather difficult to conceive. Because such a person is essentially a member of the group, he does not think for himself, he thinks and even feels just as the group does, and acts as other members of the group act. It does not even *occur* to him that he can do anything else. It does not *occur* to an orthodox Hindu that you need not have a caste. Whether we are talking about prehistoric times or nowadays, a group member, as such, is perfectly content with this state of affairs, because the group member is not an individual – not in the sense of being a *true* individual. He or she may have a separate body, but there is no really independent mind, no independent consciousness. The group member shares in the group consciousness, so to speak. We can call this sort of individual a 'statistical individual'. He can be counted, he can be enumerated, but he doesn't really exist as an individual in the true sense. He is simply a group member.

However, at some stage in human history, something remarkable happened. A new type of consciousness started to develop, a type of consciousness that we usually call reflexive consciousness, or self-consciousness, or self-awareness. Reflexive consciousness can be contrasted with 'simple consciousness'. With simple consciousness, you are aware of sights, you are aware of sounds, you are aware of trees, houses, people, books, flowers, and so on, but you are not aware of *being aware*. But in the case of reflexive consciousness, consciousness as it were doubles back upon itself, and one is *aware of being aware*.

When one is aware of being aware, one is conscious of oneself as an individual, conscious of oneself as separate from the group. One is conscious of one's ability to think and feel and act differently from the group, even against the group. An individual of this type is a true individual. Such a person is not only self-aware but is emotionally positive, full of good will towards all living beings. He or she is also spontaneous and creative because he or she is not determined in their thinking, feeling, or acting, by previously existing mental, emotional, and psychological patterns – whether their own or those of other people. The true individual is also responsible, aware of his or her own needs, aware of others' needs, and prepared and willing to act accordingly.

True individuals started appearing on the stage of history in relatively large numbers in the course of what we call – to use Karl Jaspers's term – the Axial Age.[138] This Axial Age, a sort of crucial turning point in human history, was a 300-year period extending very roughly from around 800 BCE to around 500 BCE. The true individuals who started to emerge during this period appeared in Palestine, Greece, Persia, India, and China, in fact in most of the great centres of civilization. Some of them were great thinkers, others were prophets and mystics; others again were poets, sculptors, and founders of religions. In Palestine we have such figures as the prophets Isaiah, Jeremiah, and Amos, as well as the unknown author of the *Book of Job*. In Greece, we have Pythagoras and the great philosopher Plato; we have the Attic dramatists, the great poet Pindar, the sculptor Phidias, and so on. In Persia we have the prophet Zoroaster. In India we have the Upanishadic sages like Yagnavalkya; we have Mahāvīra, the founder of Jainism, and we have the Buddha. In China we have Confucius and Laozi, the two most important individuals to arise in the whole history of Chinese culture. Of course, some of these individuals went far beyond the stage of mere self-consciousness. At least some of them developed what I have called 'transcendental consciousness', and even 'absolute consciousness'.

In this way, the Axial Age was a period of efflorescence of the true individual. Indeed, from this time onwards we can see two factors at work in human cultural, religious, and spiritual history. On the one hand there is the individual, and on the other hand there is the group.

Between the true individual and the group there was always a certain creative tension, the group pulling one way – in the direction of conformity – and the individual pulling the other – in the direction of nonconformity, of freedom, of originality, of spontaneity. In this dialectical relationship, the group provided the individual with his raw material. We find this, for example, in Greek drama. Here, certain myths and legends, themselves a product of the collective unconscious, provided the dramatists with stories which they adapted in such a way as to give expression to their own highly individual vision of existence. In this way the individual influenced the group, reacted upon the group, raising the statistical individuals who still belonged to the group, at least momentarily, to a higher level, bringing them closer to true individuality.

This relationship was in force for about 2,000 years. On the whole it was a lively and a healthy one. Sometimes it broke down, as when the medieval Catholic Church started persecuting those 'heretics' who dared to think differently from the Church. (By this time, of course, the Church was no longer a spiritual community, as it had once been to some extent, but simply a religious group, a sort of ecclesiastical power structure.) But on the whole the relationship between the true individual and the group continued fairly healthy for about 2,000 years. Generally speaking, the group at least tolerated the individual – provided he or she did not impinge too uncomfortably upon the group. During the last 200 years, however, a change has taken place to such an extent that a serious imbalance now prevails between the individual and the group. There are various reasons for this, but I will only summarize some of the more important ones.

To begin with, the population of practically every country in the world has greatly increased in recent years. Because we have so many more people in the world, almost everywhere, it has become much more difficult to get away from one's fellows, much more difficult to get away from the group. This is especially the case in small, densely populated countries like Holland and the United Kingdom, and in some parts of the bigger countries.

Secondly, there is the increase in the power of the corporate state. Today's corporate state, we may say, is the group *par excellence*, and it controls so many aspects of our lives. In most countries, this control is increasing rather than decreasing. These corporate states now divide the whole world between them. There is no portion of the Earth's land surface that is not controlled by one or another corporate state, and they have even started staking out claims to the sea. There used to be some nice empty spaces of *terra incognita* between them, where you could go if you wanted to get away from the state, but those spaces no longer exist; there are no spaces anywhere in the world where no state exercises any authority. Every individual has to belong to a state, whether they like it or not. From time to time we hear about a few miserable people who have been declared stateless. Their condition is considered a terrible calamity because, these days, you just have to belong to a state. You have to have a passport, for without one you cannot travel from one state to another. This is a fairly recent development; passports came into general use only after the First World War. Before that it was not so necessary to have one. Now they are really indispensable.

Thirdly, there is the growth of modern technology. This is in many ways a helpful development, but it has its disadvantages. It means that, among other things, the corporate state can now keep track of its citizens far more efficiently. A computer system can be set up to tell its operators a person's date of birth, when he or she last paid taxes, how many parking offences they have ever committed, where they spent their holiday last year, whether they have ever had measles, and so on. With this information at its fingertips, the state finds it much easier to exercise control over the individual.

Fourthly, there is our higher standard of living. This too is a blessing up to a point, but it does make us dependent on the group. We are dependent on the group for such good things of life as cars and televisions, not to speak of petroleum and electricity, since it is very doubtful whether we could produce these things by ourselves. Generally, we are so helpless, so dependent, that we cannot even grow our own food or make our own clothes. The general principle would therefore seem to run thus: the higher our standard of living, the bigger and more complex the state to which we have to belong – and, therefore, the more control it exercises over our lives and the less freedom we have. There is something a little paradoxical about this. If we have a car, for instance, we have greater freedom in the form of more personal mobility. But that freedom is taken away from us in certain other respects by the fact that, in order to possess and to drive a car, we have to be part of a society that is geared to the production of cars – which may not necessarily be the best kind of society. For these reasons we can now see that there is an imbalance between the individual and the group.

Now I have said that the corporate state is the group *par excellence*. But within the corporate state there are many other smaller groups. The corporate state is in fact a sort of interlocking system of groups, some of which are very powerful indeed when set against the individual. There is the political party, the trade union, the chamber of commerce, the church, the bank, the school. Some of these impinge on us in certain respects more strongly and more directly than does the corporate state itself. The result is that we are left with a virtually powerless individual in a virtually all-powerful state. The group has practically overwhelmed the individual, who feels, very often, that he is quite unable to influence the group, even in those matters which most closely concern his own life.

This is the state of affairs in the world today, especially in the Western democracies, in the old Communist states, and in various military dictatorships. It is a state of affairs that is becoming more and more widespread, and the result is that the true individual is dissatisfied. The 'statistical individual', very often, is not dissatisfied; very often he or she is happy with what the group provides, whether it is bread and circuses, as in the case of ancient Rome, or motor cars and television sets as is the case today. Such people's only complaint is that they would like to have more of them more frequently! But the true individual is frustrated. In extreme cases, his frustration may sometimes find expression in violence. We know that violence is on the increase in our cities – and I am certainly not saying that frustration of the kind I've mentioned is the sole cause of this violence – but it is certainly one factor. What, then, are we to do?

To begin with, and above all, we have to restore the balance between the individual and the group. This means that we need a philosophy, a way of looking at things, that can provide the perspective within which we will be able to see the possibility of restoring the balance. We need a philosophy that recognizes the value of the individual, a philosophy that shows the individual how to grow, how to be a true individual. This is where what nowadays we call Buddhism (but which calls itself, in its own habitat, the *Dharma*) comes in.

Buddhism places the individual in the very forefront of its teaching. The Buddha's teaching is concerned solely with the individual, both alone and in free association with other individuals. It shows the individual how to grow, shows him or her, by means of actual methods, how to develop awareness, how to develop emotional positivity, how to live spontaneously and creatively, how to accept responsibility for oneself and for others, how, in other words, to be more and more of a true individual.

Gautama the Buddha, the original teacher, was and is an example of a true individual. He was an individual of the highest kind: an *Enlightened* individual. He was an individual who had developed not only reflexive consciousness, but also 'transcendental' consciousness and 'absolute' consciousness. If we take even a cursory glance at the Buddha's life we can see how the Buddha's individuality demonstrated itself right from the start. Quite early in his life he cut himself off from the group; that was the first step he took of any significance. He left his parents, left his wife and child, left his city, left his tribe, and gave up his social position to wander alone from place to place. Occasionally he joined various religious groups and cults, but in the end he cut himself off from them too. They too were hindrances, they too were groups. He was left entirely alone – in a way that perhaps no one had ever been alone before. Being alone, he was able to be himself; being himself, he was able to be an individual; being an individual – looking at things as an individual, seeing things as an individual – he was able to see the Truth for himself, able to experience it for himself. Being able to see the Truth, he was able to become what we call a Buddha, an Enlightened individual. And having become an Enlightened individual, he was able to help others to become such. From that moment, we may say, the power of the group, the power of Māra – the power of the gravitational pull of conditioned existence – was diminished.

In the Buddha's day the power of the group was perhaps not so great as it is today, but the Buddha's teaching and example were needed all the same. It is needed, we may say, whenever and wherever the survival of the individual is threatened, wherever there is an imbalance between the individual and the group, especially when that imbalance is as extreme as it is in the world today. There is no political or economic solution to such a problem. There is only a *spiritual* solution, a solution which takes the individual into account. If put into operation, that solution will of course have political and economic implications and consequences, but it has to be a solution that respects and emphasizes the value of the individual.

This is a radical view of things. After all, how many people respect the individual? You can meet so many people who do not respect you as an individual, who don't even *see* you as an individual. You can go into a shop or into a government office and try to deal with the people there. They do not see you as an individual; they see you as a sort of public zombie who has just drifted in. But the solution we need is a solution that *sees* the individual, that respects the individual, that allows the individual, even, to make his own mistakes, that does not hold the individual's hand all the time. This attitude is very well illustrated by an incident in the Buddha's life.

A Brahmin once came to see the Buddha and asked whether he taught all his disciples the way to Nirvāṇa *equally*. When the Buddha affirmed that he did, the Brahmin asked, 'But do they all, equally, *attain* Enlightenment?'

When the Buddha replied that some did, while others did not, the Brahmin was again rather puzzled and asked, 'Well, why is this? If they all get the same teaching, why don't they all realize Nirvāṇa?'

The Buddha therefore gave him the following example: 'Over there', he said, 'is the city of Rājagaha. Now you know the city of Rājagaha; you know the way to the city of Rājagaha. So suppose two men come to you and both ask, "Please tell me the way to Rājagaha." And suppose you give quite detailed instructions: "Go along this road, turn that corner, go through that grove of mango trees, and then you'll get to the city." Suppose you give both of them these directions, and suppose one follows your directions and arrives, but the other does not follow your directions and does not arrive because he makes a mistake, would it be your fault? Would you be to blame for that?'

'No,' said the Brahmin. 'If, after I had given the proper directions, one of them found the way but the other did not, it wouldn't be any fault of mine. I wouldn't be to blame. I am only the shower of the way. I only give directions.'

'It is the same in my case', said the Buddha, 'I am only a shower of the way.'[139]

The Buddha is only the one who shows the way, but it is up to the individual to follow that way, to decide for himself whether he is going to follow that way or not. We may say that this attitude shows tremendous respect for the individual. It shows great confidence in the potential of the individual. It shows an appreciation of the fact that the individual cannot be forced. He must *want* to change; he must *want* to develop. All that one can do is show him *how*, show him an example, encourage him, and, if one can, inspire him. But one can do no more than that. You can't force him, you can't bribe or threaten him; you can only show him the way. That is to say, if you are an individual, and are trying to deal with him as an individual, then you can only show him the way and leave it to him to follow or not to follow.

This attitude is the basis for Buddhism's well-known spirit of tolerance. Buddhism is deeply conscious of human differences, deeply conscious of the fact that we are not all the same. We each have our own temperaments, characters, and our different ways of looking at things. We therefore have to be allowed to develop, each one of us, in our own manner. This is why, in the whole of its 2,500-year history, Buddhism has never persecuted anybody for their beliefs. There is no such thing as heresy in Buddhism. There are such things as 'wrong views', views that hold us back and prevent us from developing, but these wrong views are to be corrected – if they are to be corrected at all – by discussion and not by force. Force has absolutely no place in Buddhism, no place in the spiritual life.

Buddhism recognizes the value of the individual. Buddhism shows the individual how to grow, how to become more and more of an individual; it allows him or her to develop in their own way. It also gives us an inspiring example of the Buddha and the support of the sangha, or spiritual community, of other *individuals* with whom we are in direct personal contact.

from *New Currents in Western Buddhism*

6. BUDDHISTS SHOULD STATE THEIR VIEWS CLEARLY

We must be completely honest about what we believe; otherwise, what is our so-called freedom of speech worth?

Although Buddhism teaches tolerance, not only towards all forms of Buddhism but towards all other religions, it isn't vague. Its tolerance is not the woolly kind that simply blurs distinctions. Buddhist tolerance is not pseudo-universalist. But while it is clear about the truth of things, it does not impose its truth-teachings on others. It is perhaps tempting to think that the more confident one is in the truth of what one believes, the more right one has to impose one's views on other people, and the greater their stupidity if they won't accept what one says. But Buddhist faith does not work like this. Buddhists should have a clear understanding of such precise, well thought-out teachings as the Four Noble Truths, the Eightfold Path, conditioned co-production, *śūnyatā*, and so on. But perfect freedom is extended to other people to think differently. Buddhists don't – or shouldn't – become upset or feel threatened or undermined at the thought that elsewhere in the world, even in their own environment, there are people who don't accept what they accept, who don't believe that the Buddha was Enlightened, who don't believe that the Noble Eightfold Path leads one to Nirvāṇa, who reject all that.

At the same time, it is important that Buddhists should state their views clearly, and this in itself may seem to present a challenge or even a threat. One doesn't want to attack anyone's beliefs for the sake of it; but teaching the Dharma traditionally has two aspects – propagating the truth and dispelling error – and sometimes the two are closely connected. You can't express a non-theistic point of view without rejecting, and giving reasons for rejecting, belief in a personal God. Of course, that will be taken by some people as an attack on the notion of God, or on God himself. Buddhists in the West are sometimes afraid, or at least reluctant, to emphasize points of difference.

One can't help feeling disappointed when Buddhist teachers prevaricate on the question of God. They know perfectly well that Buddhism is a non-theistic teaching, that belief in an Iśvara, a creator God, is rejected in all the Buddhist sources. But – perhaps out of concern to make some sort of common cause with Christianity – they sometimes not only play down the non-theistic character of Buddhism, but even let it appear that Buddhism is not in fact non-theistic. That is very unfortunate. To insist on this point may create antagonism, but as a Buddhist one has to take that risk. We must be completely honest about what we believe; otherwise, what is our so-called freedom of speech worth? We don't have to be aggressive or provocative; we can say what we have to say in a reasonable and positive and friendly way. One should never indulge in purely negative, destructive criticism, but one shouldn't prevaricate or conceal one's views.

It is difficult for people with a Christian background to understand the nature of Buddhism. It is difficult to overcome one's tendency to see things in a particular way, and one needs to make a very definite effort to do so. In 1840 the Scottish philosopher Thomas Carlyle wrote that at the time he was writing it was difficult for people to understand or imagine the seriousness with which people in the seventeenth century took the Christian religion, and the conviction with which they believed that God was personally intervening in national politics, military campaigns, and so on. It would have been very difficult for a person of the seventeenth century in England to imagine a social order that was not solidly based on the rock of the Word of God. They honestly believed, if they considered it at all, that if people ceased to believe in God – or the Trinity, or the Incarnation – society would immediately fall apart.

Christians approaching Buddhism are in a similar position. Even if they make a sincere attempt to understand it, they are likely still to be operating with their own assumptions and concepts and trying to accommodate Buddhism within those. For instance, there is the hoary old chestnut of how it is that Buddhists, who do not believe in God, can worship the Buddha. People think they'll have you wriggling on a pin trying to explain this awful contradiction in your religion. When you lay out the reasoning step by step, the explanation is usually quite clear to them, but it represents a point of view that they had simply been unable to conceive of before.

It works the other way round too. There are Buddhists in Thailand who find it impossible to understand how any sensible human being could believe in a God who created the world. The idea makes them fall about laughing. They don't even have a word in their language for God, and it takes Christian missionaries a great deal of time and trouble to explain to them the weird notion of a personal God who has made the heavens and the earth. We have to try always to transcend the limitations of our own point of view, and at least try to imagine the possibility that someone believes something we don't. We can still reject it, but at least we won't find it incredible that someone should believe in that particular idea.

While the kind of tolerance of religious diversity which allows everyone the freedom to choose which spiritual path to follow is clearly crucial, it is equally important to speak out against views that are spiritually harmful, 'wrong views', as the Buddha called them (the Pāli term is *micchā-diṭṭhi*). A wrong view that needs to be addressed these days – perhaps rather more urgently even than belief in a personal God – is one that is often linked, and sometimes confused, with tolerance: pseudo-egalitarianism.

One way of thinking about pseudo-egalitarianism is that it is the denial of the superior achievements of certain individuals and even groups. True egalitarianism is the faith that all beings everywhere have an infinite capacity to develop as individuals, and to cultivate particular positive qualities of their own humanity to an infinite degree. Pseudo-egalitarianism is the unthinking assumption that everybody is quite literally equal and to be treated accordingly. This has become more or less a form of orthodoxy – neo-orthodoxy, one could say.

In the Middle Ages and even later it was considered unthinkable to question such doctrines as the divinity of Christ and the Trinity of the Godhead. So far as most people were concerned, if you did question them, you were so clearly flying in the face of an obvious truth that you must be either utterly stupid or inconceivably wicked. All decent, right-thinking people would automatically react against you. They might even want to imprison you or burn you at the stake. There was no question of sitting down and talking with you about it – you were so obviously just plain wrong. This is orthodoxy: the belief that somebody is so obviously wrong that they cannot be reasoned with, but only disposed of. And what I am calling neo-orthodoxy is like that too – not a belief in this or that particular doctrine, but the attitude that if someone holds a certain view, there is no point in entering into discussion with them. In fact, it is almost impossible nowadays to say what one thinks, even in our Western 'democracies'. We don't have freedom of speech; in practice there are certain 'politically correct' things that one is allowed to say and certain things that one is not.

How does a tolerant belief or teaching or organization protect itself from an intolerant one? This is an extremely difficult question. Usually people who believe in tolerance also believe in non-violence; there is no question of defending oneself by violent means. So what can one do? Is one to allow oneself to be completely overwhelmed?

The only answer that presents itself – and it may not be a complete one – is that one must be far-sighted, diplomatic, even cunning. One must see the danger coming and take steps to counteract it before it reaches a point where only violent means would be effective. One must not hesitate to take full advantage of the law when it is on one's own side. And one must engage freely and vigorously in debate, presenting and arguing one's point of view, not letting one's case go by default. It is particularly important to protest against any misrepresentation of the Dharma. The Buddha himself corrected misunderstandings of his teachings, there's no doubt about that. And one can make such protests without becoming irate or hysterical.

from *The Bodhisattva Ideal*

7. THE IDEAL STUDENT OF BUDDHISM

One of the most original contributions of the Buddha to human knowledge is the discovery that theories are rooted in desires.

Nowadays Buddhism has more often to pray for protection from its friends than from its enemies. The number of those who like Buddhism for the wrong reason, or who, more correctly, are attracted by what they wrongly imagine is Buddhism, is increasing, and by reason of their very sincerity they constitute a growing threat to the purity and integrity of the doctrine that they profess to support. Such people will generally be found to have developed strong religious convictions prior to their study of Buddhism. These convictions they do not wish to have unsettled, and although genuinely attracted by certain aspects of the Dharma they do not hesitate to challenge, misinterpret, or simply 'explain away' whatever other aspects of the teaching are in conflict with their preconceived ideas. One of the most original contributions of the Buddha to human knowledge is the discovery that theories are rooted in desires, and the very tenacity with which, in the face of the clearest textual evidence to the contrary, such students persist in clinging to their erroneous interpretations of the Dharma, is an unmistakable indication of the extent of their emotional commitment. Theories of a personal God and an immortal soul are so deeply rooted in the soil of the human heart that belief in them has often been regarded as synonymous with religion itself. Such belief is not synonymous with the Dharma. The Buddha in fact taught that belief in a personal God and an immortal soul were rationalizations of desires, of our craving for love and protection, our attachment to our own personalities, and our thirst for life. Enlightenment can be attained by the renunciation not only of selfish desires but of the religious theories or 'views' (*dṛṣṭi*) that are based on those desires. Belief in a personal God and immortal soul are not helps but hindrances to one who would follow the Dharma, and the student who is strongly attached to such beliefs and who feels at the same time attracted by certain aspects of Buddhism, or who shrinks from the suggestion that so distinguished a tradition should deny his most cherished convictions, will be compelled by his emotional needs to blunder into misunderstandings and misinterpretations of the Dharma. 'The Buddha *must* have believed in God,' cry some such people, 'He *could not* have denied the existence of the *ātman*,' protest others; but unfortunately for them the Buddha did do both 'shocking' things. The wisdom of the Tathāgata is not to be measured by the yardstick of human intelligence, nor limited by the cravings of the human heart.

The ideal student of Buddhism would be one who, whether scientifically trained or not, was prepared to admit the possibility of a spiritual experience which would transcend the physical senses and the rational mind, and who would be willing to give unprejudiced consideration to the Buddha's claim that he had achieved this experience himself and that by following his teaching others might achieve it for themselves too. Such a person would not commit the mistake of thinking that the intellect, though capable of performing useful preliminary work, was able to penetrate the inner meaning of Buddhism, or that Truth would reveal itself to any faculty save to intuition awakened by spiritual practice. He or she would be free from beliefs which, though they pass for religious doctrines in the world, are in fact born of fear, craving, and other egocentric emotions. Resolved fearlessly to pursue, frankly to examine, and faithfully to accept and follow whatever the truth about Buddhism might turn out to be, such an ideal student could be said to be fairly well equipped for the study of Buddhism, and to approach the Dharma with at least an approximation to right motive in the specifically Buddhist sense.

from *A Survey of Buddhism*

8. A REVIVAL OF PAGANISM?

I have sometimes thought that Buddhism will only become widespread in the West after a revival of paganism.

Orthodox Christian ideas and ideals, which are not necessarily those of the Gospels themselves, but which are underpinned by the doctrine of original sin, have been responsible for generating such intense feelings of sinfulness and guilt in many people as to ruin their lives. All of us who have been brought up in the West are to some extent influenced by these attitudes. Even those who consciously reject Christianity, whether they are atheist, humanist, agnostic, or indeed Buddhist, are often still deeply influenced by Christian ethical assumptions. As a Buddhist one needs to understand this; otherwise, one will unconsciously carry Christian attitudes into one's Buddhist life, which will result in confusion, especially in the sphere of ethics.

While the old moral order has to some extent broken down, a new one has not yet been established. So far we haven't even cleared the ground. In any case, we can't completely abolish the old moral order and establish a new one from scratch; the two will always overlap.

And we can draw inspiration from the past – not the recent past, but the dim and distant pre-Christian past, the past of pagan times. Today we can look back through 1,500 years of religious history, to the Oxford Movement of the nineteenth century, the Methodist revival before that, Puritanism before that, the medieval church, the beginnings of the Church, right back to the introduction of Christianity. But before that, nothing: only an abyss of darkness in which we see hideous shapes vaguely swarming, an abyss from which we have been taught to shrink back in horror, the pre-Christian dark abyss of paganism. We can't feel our own roots deep down in that darkness; we feel no continuity with the past. A site like Stonehenge, that great circle of stones that has stood on Salisbury Plain for 4,000 years, is very impressive; but for us it may be no more than an archaeological monument. We don't necessarily feel any continuity with the religious and cultural life of the people who put those great stones there.

Usually we are not aware that we have been deprived of this continuity, but we can see it if we compare our situation with that of modern Hindus. They can look back thousands and thousands of years – back to the great saints and reformers of the nineteenth century, the medieval mystics, the early medieval philosophers, back to Buddhism, back to brahminical Hinduism, Vedic Hinduism, the primitive cults before that, back and back – one single uninterrupted process, right back into the dawn of history, the mists of the past. Modern Hindus can feel their continuity with the Vedic *rishis* living hundreds, even thousands, of years before Christ. This surely is a wonderful feeling, to be able to feel that one's religious roots go so deep, like a flowering plant rooted deep in the earth.

But in any Christian country, one is more like a flower without roots, a flower in a glass of water, even an artificial flower, because continuity with the past, with our own religious past, has been lost. The continuity of Western religious life was disrupted by the advent of Christianity.

Wherever Christianity went, first within the Roman Empire and then outside it, paganism was ruthlessly destroyed. Pagan images were smashed, stone circles were damaged, sacred groves were cut down, priests were killed. Virtually nothing of paganism survived in Britain; it was destroyed root and branch. If it survived at all, it did so in somewhat distorted forms, such as what is popularly called witchcraft. Official Christianity no longer includes much that is in any sense pagan or ethnic. Perhaps traces have survived in the churches of the Mediterranean area, in which certain practices are performed in the name of Christianity but are really remnants from earlier pagan times, in the same way that some saints were created by baptizing pagan gods and heroes.

But essentially our own special brand of paganism has been lost; our link with the past has gone. And this link must be restored. People are beginning to recognize that it is important that the old myths and legends, beliefs and practices, should be studied – not just as so much grist for the academic mill, but so that we can feel our way back into the old myths and legends of our native land. It is important that all of us, including Buddhists, should try to establish contact with our pre-Christian past. Indeed, I have sometimes thought that Buddhism will only become widespread in the West after a revival of paganism. Perhaps Buddhism will have to put down roots in the West before it can start producing flowers.

In what would such a renewed paganism consist? First of all, we need to be careful not to romanticize pagan culture. There were very positive elements in it, elements on which we can draw, but it would be a mistake to paint a glowing picture of a noble paganism, contrasted with a dark picture, say, of medieval Christianity. That would be neither fair nor historically correct. Also, although it would be nice to think that as people freed themselves from unhelpful ethical attitudes their natural straightforward humanity would simply blossom, it would be naive to suppose that the demise of Christianity would leave us with a pure clean sweet-smelling humanity. The Nazis were pagan in a sense – some of them professed to look to the old pagan gods, and even revived some pagan festivals – but what sort of paganism was that?

In any case, pre-Christian pagans were by no means perfect. One reads truly horrible things about the morals of ancient Rome. Perhaps one shouldn't attach too much importance to the *Satires* of Juvenal – he was making a few points of his own in a rather heavy-handed way

– but it certainly wasn't all sweetness and light before the advent of Christianity. Pagan culture wasn't all beautiful Greek statues and people walking around in flowing white garments. Quite dreadful things went on – slavery, for example, and the gladiatorial contests at the Colosseum. In certain respects Christianity was a definite improvement on all that. (And, of course, the Romans themselves were responsible for the near-destruction of Celtic paganism.)

So in contemplating a revival of paganism, I am not thinking of paganism in any specific cultic sense – not Classical paganism or Teutonic paganism – but something more like 'unspoiled human nature' or 'healthy, happy, human nature'. This, though, as far as we are concerned, is something to be cultivated, to be developed. The happy, healthy, human individual, living free and independent of the attitudes of the surrounding society, is a figment of the imagination. One doesn't encounter anybody who has not been conditioned in some way, positively or negatively, by the society in which he or she has been brought up.

In the eighteenth century people liked to speculate about what would happen if you put a child on a desert island and let him grow up by himself. What sort of human being would he become? Well, we will never know, because we cannot bring up a child in that way. The concept of the human individual who has not been conditioned by any sort of culture is a hypothetical construct. However, one can certainly become a happy, healthy human being as a result of spiritual life and training.

Personally I would be happy to see a combination of Celtic paganism and Buddhism – the one for the majority, the other for the minority, and each tolerant towards the other, so that it would be easy to pass from one to another. It was rather like that in the Buddha's time: most people followed the old ethnic cults, but the Buddha was free to recruit followers from their midst.

We can't put the clock back. It is difficult to get away from Christian influences in the West. Some people are brought up without Christianity impinging on them very much, but there is no healthy pagan substitute, no ready-made paganism to make use of as an alternative to the missing ethnic element in Christianity. A truly pagan attitude has not so far developed in our Western post-Christian culture to any degree, although some people would like to think it has.

So how can we bring into our Buddhist life those elements of paganism that are especially helpful? There are two fundamental aspects of paganism, which are especially important to a happy, healthy human life: first, a sense of our connectedness with nature, and second, a more natural morality.

One of the characteristics of paganism is a sense of connectedness with the life of the earth. Official Christianity teaches that the earth was cursed as a result of the fall of man. If you see the earth through Christian spectacles, it has fallen, just as mankind has. The earth is evil because nature is evil, bound up with the devil. This is the orthodox Christian attitude, although it is sometimes left unformulated: everything natural is of the devil. God created the earth good, but it has become corrupt due to man's fall. People may say they don't believe that doctrine any more, but that sort of feeling about nature is still around, as well as the idea that nature is to be exploited, which also derives from the Old Testament.

Paganism, conversely, is a feeling of oneness with nature, a feeling that one is part of nature, and that nature is healthy and good – 'natural' in a word, innocent. And because one is part of it, one is oneself also natural, healthy, and innocent. This is the essence of paganism, and if the study of ancient ethnic religions or pagan mythology helps one to experience that, it is worth engaging in such study; otherwise, it has little spiritual value.

We could gain a more direct experience through celebrations and rituals. We could celebrate the seasons, for example: we could have a midwinter festival and a spring festival. We might feel self-conscious at first, but we would get used to it: bonfires, dancing round the maypole, all that sort of thing. There is something analogous in the Tibetan tradition, in the form of their New Year festival. Tibetans make a big thing of this. They give it Buddhist colouring, but it definitely comes from their pre-Buddhist pagan roots. For example, horses were very important to the pre-Buddhist nomadic peoples of Tibet, and to this day horse-racing is a big part of the New Year celebration – interpreted as helping to speed the coming of Maitreya, the future Buddha!

The second area in which we could benefit from a revival of paganism is the sphere of morality. A more pagan attitude, dropping the less helpful ethical attitudes of Christianity, should not, of course, mean the complete absence of any ethical code, but it would be a more natural morality, something closer to the realities of human life and experience.

from *The Bodhisattva Ideal*

9. FORMULATIONS OF THE BUDDHIST PATH

Travelling on a path implies a journey, and it is of a journey that both the scriptures and history often speak.

Speaking in the clearest and most general terms then, Buddhism is a path or way. It is a path leading from the impermanent to the permanent, from sorrow to happiness, from the darkness of ignorance to the light of perfect wisdom. This is the path for which the Buddha himself, in the days before his Enlightenment, is represented as searching. For the sake of this path he went forth from home into homelessness. For the sake of this path he sat at the foot of the bodhi tree. This is the path he discovered at the time of his Supreme Enlightenment, this is the path which, after initial hesitation, he made known to mankind. In his own words, as recorded in the *Dhammapada*,

> Walking this path you shall make an end of suffering.
> This is the path made known by me when I had learnt to remove all darts.[140]

This path it was that, for the forty-five years of his teaching life, in one formulation or another made up the principal content of the Buddha's message. The formulations were indeed very numerous. Perhaps the most basic was that of the path as consisting of the three great stages of right conduct (*śīla*), meditation (*samādhi*), and wisdom (*prajñā*).

> Great becomes the fruit, great the advantages of meditation, when it is set round with (i.e. supported by) upright conduct. Great becomes the fruit, great the advantage of wisdom, when it is set round with meditation.[141]

Such was the gist of the 'comprehensive religious talk' which the Buddha delivered in eleven out of the fourteen places he visited in the course of the last six months of his life. No less important, and even better known, is the formulation of the path as eightfold, that is to say, as consisting in the gradual extension of Perfect Vision – the vision of the transcendental – successively to one's emotional attitude, one's communication with other people, one's actions, one's means of livelihood, one's energy, one's recollection, and one's overall state of being and consciousness. Much rarer is a formulation which in fact occurs only once in the Pāli canon. This is the formulation of the path in terms of the seven stages of purification – ethical, emotional, intellectual, and so on.[142] Together with right conduct, meditation, and wisdom, this formulation provides the double framework of Buddhaghosa's great exegetical work the *Visuddhimagga* or 'path of purity', the standard work of Theravāda Buddhism, i.e. of the Pāli-Buddhism of Sri Lanka, Burma, Thailand, Cambodia, and Laos.

In the Mahāyāna scriptures many other formulations are found. Some of these are extremely comprehensive in scope, so that with them the path begins to take on a more universal character. Among these more comprehensive formulations the most important, both historically and spiritually, is that of the path of the ten perfections, the ten perfections being generosity, right conduct, patience and forbearance, vigour, meditation, wisdom, skilful means (= compassion), salvific vow, strength or power, and knowledge or transcendental awareness. This path of the ten perfections is, of course, the path of the bodhisattva, 'he whose nature or essence is *bodhi*' (interpretations vary), the great spiritual hero who instead of aiming at the inferior goal of individual Enlightenment, i.e. Enlightenment for oneself alone, out of compassion seeks to attain the universal Enlightenment of a Buddha, so as to be able to deliver all sentient beings from suffering. For the accomplishment of this sublime purpose he practises the ten perfections not for one lifetime only but for an unthinkable number of lifetimes, being reborn in many different worlds, and on many different planes of existence. In this way he traverses the ten great 'levels' (*bhūmis*) of spiritual progress – another formulation – from that called 'the Joyful' right up to 'the Cloud of Dharma', at which stage he becomes a Buddha.[143] Thus he fulfils the bodhisattva ideal, as it is called – an ideal which the Mahāyāna regards the historical Buddha as himself exemplifying. Yet another formulation of the path found in the Mahāyāna scriptures is that of the thirteen 'abodes' (*vihāras*)[144] which are also stages of spiritual progress traversed by the bodhisattva, and which coincide to some extent with the ten 'levels'. Perhaps the most comprehensive of all formulations of the path is that of the Nyingma school of Tibetan Buddhism, according to which the total path consists of nine 'ways' (*yānas*) which between them cover all the three major *yānas*, i.e. the Hīnayāna, the Mahāyana, the

Vajrayāna, conceived not only as stages in the historical development of Indian Buddhism but as stages in the spiritual evolution of the individual Buddhist.

The number and importance of these abstract formulations of the path should not blind us to the fact that the path also finds vivid concrete embodiment in actual human lives, whether as depicted in the scriptures or as recorded by profane history. The path in truth *is* the pilgrim, and the pilgrim the path, so that 'Thou canst not travel on the Path before thou hast become the Path itself.'[145] Travelling on a path implies a journey, and it is of a journey that both the scriptures and history often speak. Thus in the *Gaṇḍavyūha Sūtra* the youth Sudhana, in order to achieve what the text calls 'the highest knowledge of Enlightenment', goes on a journey that takes him to various parts of India and in the course of which he visits more than fifty spiritual teachers.[146] Similarly, in the *Prajñāpāramitā* or 'Perfection of Wisdom' *Sūtra* (the version in 8,000 lines), the bodhisattva Sadāprarudita or 'Ever-Weeping', advised by a divine voice, goes east in search of the perfection of wisdom, encountering many adventures on the way until, in the city of Gandhavatī, he meets with the bodhisattva Dharmodgata and hears his demonstration of the Dharma.[147] On a more mythic level, in the *Saddharma Puṇḍarīka* or 'White Lotus of the True Dharma' *Sūtra* the journey is a *return* journey not unlike that of the king's son in the Gnostic 'Hymn of the Pearl'.[148] In more strictly geographical terms there is Xuanzang's and Monkey's famous pilgrimages from China to the West, i.e. to India. There is also Bashō's 'Journey to the Far North'.[149]

Though the promised picture of Buddhism has now been drawn, and though the rough outline of the path has been filled in with details of abstract formulations and concrete embodiments in actual human – and animal – lives, this is by no means enough for our purpose. If we are really to understand what Buddhism is we must understand what the path is *in principle*, i.e. must understand what it is that makes the path the path. In order to understand this, we shall have to go back, so to speak, to the fundamental principles of what, in the absence of any more suitable term, we are obliged to call Buddhist philosophy. This will bring us close to the very essence of Buddhism.

Philosophy takes for its object all time and all existence. It is the science which, as metaphysics, investigates the most general facts and principles of reality (the dictionary definition). The fundamental principles of Buddhist philosophy, from which all its other principles derive, are therefore principles that embody its understanding of the nature of existence in the most general sense – though in the case of Buddhism this understanding is the product not of systematic reflection on sense experience but of direct spiritual vision. According to Buddhism the nature of existence is best described in terms of change, or becoming. This does not mean that existence changes, in the sense of being subject to change but distinct from it, but that existence itself *is* change, *is* becoming. One of the fundamental principles of Buddhism, therefore, is that which finds embodiment in the well-known equation 'Existence (or Reality) = Change (or Becoming)'. This change or becoming is not fortuitous, but takes place in a certain fixed manner, in accordance with a certain definite law. (Not that the law really exists apart from the changing physical and mental phenomena it is said to govern. The law simply describes the way in which physical and mental phenomena behave in accordance with their inherent nature.) The general formula for this law, a formula which according to the Pāli scriptures goes back to the Buddha himself, is that 'This being, that becomes; from the arising of this, that arises. This not being, that does not become; from the ceasing of this, that ceases.'[150] The law is thus a law of conditionality or, in more specifically Buddhist language, it is a law of dependent origination or conditioned co-production, as the term *pratītya-samutpāda* is variously translated. Just as existence is change, so change is conditionality. The vision that Buddhism sees – the vision that the Buddha saw on the night of his Enlightenment – is a vision of existence in terms of an infinitely complex, constantly shifting network of physical and mental phenomena, all arising in dependence on certain conditions and ceasing when those conditions cease.[151]

Universal though it is in scope, however, the law of conditionality is not uniform in operation – not all of one same kind, so to speak. Within the infinitely complex, constantly shifting network of physical and mental happenings – within the totality of existence – it is possible to distinguish two distinct trends or types of conditionality. In the one case there arises, in dependence on the immediately preceding factor in a 'dependently originating' series, a factor which is the opposite of the preceding one, as when good arises in dependence on evil (or vice versa), happiness in dependence on suffering, death in dependence on birth. In the other case there arises, in dependence on the preceding factor, a factor which far from being the opposite of the preceding one, and thus negating it, is what may be termed its positive counterpart, so that it actually augments it, as when joy arises in dependence on happiness, rapture in dependence on joy, bliss in dependence on rapture. One trend or type of conditionality consists in a rotary movement between pairs of factors which are opposites, and the order of conditionality is therefore said to be cyclical in character. The other consists in a cumulative movement between factors which are counterparts or complements, and the order of conditionality is therefore said to be progressive. The first trend or type or order of conditionality Buddhism sees as a wheel endlessly turning round – a wheel of birth and death. The second it sees as a spiral constantly ascending – a spiral of spiritual development. We are now in a position to understand what the path is in principle, and therefore what Buddhism really is. *The path is in principle identical with the progressive order of conditionality.* The path is essentially an ascending series of mental factors or mental states.

from *The Bodhisattva Principle*

10. BUDDHISM AND EVOLUTION

Our project as Buddhists must be to replace a mechanistic universe with one that has meaning, one that carries throughout its fabric intimations of spiritual values.

Buddhism is a vast subject. Although in this context I want to consider it in relation to a concept which is familiar to the modern Western mind, this is not like finding a big box into which we can fit a smaller box. It is a matter rather of laying out the Buddhist system of thought as a whole in terms that should be sufficiently familiar to all of us as a way of looking at the world as not to require much explanation. And the idea that functions most comprehensively in this way is the principle of evolution, derived from the biological sciences. The fact that the Christian faith in particular has become reconciled to this principle only with the greatest difficulty makes it also a useful tool in highlighting some of the more distinctive features of the Buddhist vision. Nothing like the kind of *tour de force* we meet with in the works of the Catholic thinker Teilhard de Chardin is required to bring Buddhism and modern evolutionary ideas together.[152]

We now know that the theory of evolution was anticipated by a number of thinkers, by Kant, Hegel, and others – and even, according to some, by Aristotle himself.[153] But Darwin was the first to trace the operation of evolution in detail within the field of biology. To attempt to refute the principle of evolution in that field today would be like saying the earth is flat. It is the given basis for all the biological sciences. If anything, the idea has invaded all sorts of other disciplines, from politics to astronomy, so that one could fairly say that just as the Elizabethan age was dominated by the concepts of order and hierarchy, so the modern world is dominated by the concept of evolution.

In taking up an idea that is generally understood in scientific or at least academic applications and applying it in a spiritual context, we have, of course, to draw some precise boundaries. Scientific knowledge depends on the evidence of the senses – but, just because Buddhism has never tried to resist the evidence of the senses, that does not make it a 'scientific religion'. It is certainly true that Buddhism's appeal in the West owes much to the spirit of empirical, open-minded inquiry which the Buddha laid down as axiomatic to the spiritual quest – and this lack of dogmatism does align Buddhism in some important respects with the Greek scientific spirit rather than with the dominant religious traditions in the modern West. Equally axiomatic to the Buddhist notion of the spiritual quest, however, is the recognition of a transcendental Reality – which is not, of course, a provable scientific hypothesis. As a practising Buddhist one starts, in accordance with the Buddha's advice, from the evidence of one's own experience, and this will tend to support more and more the idea of a spiritual order of evolution. It is on the basis of this evidence that biological evolution carries conviction – not the other way round. If we see human beings as in any way constituting some kind of key to the universe, then on the basis of our own experience of progression we may fairly conclude that progression is in some way inherent in the universe.

In this respect, at least, Buddhism inclines more towards a traditional, pre-scientific viewpoint. If we look at a traditional civilization, we find that everything, every activity, every piece of knowledge, is linked with ideas of a metaphysical order. Ordinary things, ordinary events, accepted ideas, are not just of practical use. They have a symbolic value, they point beyond themselves, they have meaning. Amidst our own fragmented, 'specialist', economically defined culture we may find it difficult to appreciate this attitude, but it is the basis for the Tantra, and it was the world-view of our own society until comparatively recently. According to this view everything is interconnected and nothing can ever really be ordinary – in the sense of being without a deeper meaning – at all. Rather than look for scientific proof of spiritual realities, we may say, paraphrasing G. K. Chesterton, that it is because we no longer believe in the gods that we no longer believe in ourselves.[154] Our project as Buddhists must be to replace a mechanistic universe with one that has meaning, that carries throughout its fabric intimations of spiritual values.

Buddhism therefore looks at the rational knowledge derived from the senses in the light of a knowledge that is derived not from the senses and reason alone, but from a fusion of reason with emotion in a higher faculty of archetypal knowledge which we may call 'vision', 'insight', or 'imagination'. It is not a question of justifying Buddhism in scientific terms, but rather of understanding sense-derived knowledge by means of knowledge that is not sense-based. In other words, the knowledge that is derived from the senses fits into a much larger pattern of knowledge that is not derived from the senses. From a Buddhist point of view, there is a hierarchy of levels of being and consciousness, a hierarchy of degrees of spiritual attainment, which seems to be reflected in, or as it were anticipated by, the whole process of biological evolution. It seems to make sense, therefore, to regard both biological evolution and the hierarchies of spiritual development as being – from the Buddhist point of view – in their separate spheres, exemplifications of a single law or principle.

It is clear that according to the principle of evolution life is not just existence. It is a process – a process of becoming – and humankind is not something apart from the rest of nature, as the theistic religions usually teach. Humankind itself also comes under the operation of this great process of becoming. It too is evolving and developing, not just towards new forms of existence and organization, but towards new and higher levels of being.

Of the two general scientific theories of evolution, that it is a mechanistic, random process, and the opposite view, that it could not have taken place without some kind of purpose or direction, the

Buddhist approach is more akin to the second view. It is very broadly 'vitalist' in that it recognizes a will to Enlightenment somehow present in all forms of life and manifesting in any gesture of consideration or act of intelligent good will. With the beginning of the evolutionary process you get the impression of a sort of fumbling, with a lot of false starts – it seems a bit hit-or-miss. But then as you follow it further, whatever it is that stands behind the evolutionary process seems to become surer of itself, as it were, and to define itself more clearly as time goes by. And with the emergence of the aware individual human being undertaking the spiritual path it becomes fully conscious of itself, thereby speeding up the whole process.

The Buddhist has to tread very lightly in this area to avoid misunderstanding. Evolution is just a metaphor or model for Buddhism, a temporal model. If we speak in terms of developing from one stage to another, that is to look at reality in temporal terms. But if we speak of what is there all the time, the absolute reality which is always here and now, that is to speak in spatial terms. So this is the function of the 'will to Enlightenment' or *bodhicitta*, in this context – to transcend these spatio-temporal models. It is not the life-force of the universe, or any kind of causative first principle, but rather a liberation principle, a will to transcend the universe or *saṃsāra*.

We may say, in fact, that self-transcendence is what the whole of evolution, from the amoeba upwards, is about. We can say further that this evolutionary principle of self-transcendence is expressed in its highest and most fully self-conscious form in the figure of the bodhisattva, the one who, according to Mahāyāna Buddhism, dedicates himself or herself to the cause of helping all sentient existence to Enlightenment. The will to Enlightenment of a bodhisattva is a fully committed volition to perpetual self-transcendence. And from the bodhisattva to the Buddha there is only, as it were, a step.

It is from this perspective, seeing spiritual development in terms of perpetual self-transcendence, that we can best appreciate the often half-understood Buddhist concept of *anātman*, or 'no-self'. This is sometimes interpreted as meaning that we don't really exist, that there's a sort of hole where one imagines one's self to be. In fact, the point of this teaching is that we have no substantial unchanging self, no soul. Indeed, putting it more dynamically and experientially, we can say that for radical change, radical development, to take place –

for a fully conscious self-transcendence to be possible – there *can* be no unchanging self.

We may look at Buddhism from a purely academic perspective as just an activity or philosophical position of a number of individuals calling themselves Buddhists. On the other hand, we can take the vast and awe-inspiring perspective of the Buddha's teaching itself. From this latter perspective, we are all frail, impermanent beings, born into the world and passing out of it with apparently little to show for our trouble – but at the same time we embody the universal possibility of Enlightenment. Just as the scientific concept of evolution involves a progression towards new biological organisms through periods of time that are practically unimaginable, so, according to Buddhism, our own lives take their place in a context of literally unimaginable temporal duration, in which, however, they are of literally cosmic importance. For among all the life-forms in the universe, from the amoeba to the highest realms of the gods, it is only the kind of sentient life to which human beings conform that can be, in the words of Lama Govinda, 'the vehicle for the rediscovery of the transcendental and inconceivable nature of mind or consciousness'[155] – that can become, in short, a Buddha.

from *Who is the Buddha?*

PART III
ART, BEAUTY, AND MYTH IN THE BUDDHIST TRADITION

I
THE PLACE OF BEAUTY IN THE SPIRITUAL LIFE

1. SANGHARAKSHITA I AND SANGHARAKSHITA II

Sometimes Sangharakshita I was victorious, sometimes Sangharakshita II, while occasionally there was an uneasy duumvirate.

Sangharakshita I wanted to enjoy the beauty of nature, to read and write poetry, to listen to music, to look at paintings and sculpture, to experience emotion, to lie in bed and dream, to see places, to meet people. Sangharakshita II wanted to realize the truth, to read and write philosophy, to observe the precepts, to get up early and meditate, to mortify the flesh, to fast and pray. Sometimes Sangharakshita I was victorious, sometimes Sangharakshita II, while occasionally there was an uneasy duumvirate. What they ought to have done, of course, was to marry and give birth to Sangharakshita III, who would have united beauty and truth, poetry and philosophy, spontaneity and discipline; but this seemed to be a dream impossible of fulfilment. For the last two and a half years Sangharakshita II had ruled practically unchallenged. Aided and abetted by Buddharakshita (the friend with whom I wandered in India and sought Buddhist ordination), who strongly disapproved of poetry, he had in fact sought to finish off Sangharakshita I altogether, and but for the timely intervention of Swami Ramdas, who firmly declared that writing poetry was *not* incompatible with the spiritual life, Sangharakshita I might well have died a premature death in Muvattupuzha.

However, despite the bludgeoning that he had received he had not died, and after leading a furtive existence in Nepal he was now coming into his own again at Buddha Kuti. Kashyap-ji's dealings were of course mainly with Sangharakshita II (the Venerable Jagdish Kashyap was the learned Buddhist monk with whom I studied Pāli, Abhidhamma, and logic at Benares), but he had no objection to Sangharakshita I being around, and even spoke to him occasionally. Soon Sangharakshita I was feeling strong enough to demand equal rights. If Sangharakshita II devoted the afternoon to *The Path of Purity*, Sangharakshita I spent the evening immersed in the poetry of Matthew Arnold, which for some reason or other exerted a powerful influence during this period. When the former wrote an article on Buddhist philosophy, or edited the second edition of Kashyap-ji's *Buddhism for Everybody*, the latter composed poems. Sometimes, while one self was busy copying out extracts from the books he had been reading, the other would look idly out of the window and watch the falling of the rain. One day there was a violent clash between them. Angered by the encroachments of Sangharakshita I, who was reading more poetry than ever, and who had written a long poem which, though it had a Buddhist theme, was still a poem, Sangharakshita II suddenly burned the two notebooks in which his rival had written all the poems he had composed from the time of their departure from England right down to about the middle of their sojourn in Singapore. After this catastrophe, which shocked them both, they learned to respect each other's spheres of influence. Occasionally they even collaborated, as in the completion of a blank verse rendition of five *paritrāṇa sūtras* that had been started in Nepal. There were even rare moments when it seemed that, despite their quarrels, they might get married one day.

from *The Rainbow Road from Tooting Broadway to Kalimpong*

2. BEAUTY AS A CHARACTERISTIC OF LIFE

Life is fleeting, life is transient, but life is also beautiful.

> As stars, a fault of vision, as a lamp,
> A mock show, dewdrops, or a bubble,

A dream, a lightning flash, or cloud,
So should one view what is conditioned.

These comparisons are taken from a well-known Buddhist text, the *Diamond Sūtra*, and they are meant to illustrate the impermanence of all conditioned things. The lightning flash doesn't last very long, the dewdrop doesn't last very long, the cloud drifts by, the dream comes and goes. All these things are evanescent, impermanent. Life is like that.

But there is something else to notice about these comparisons: they are all beautiful. They may be illustrating impermanence, but they also illustrate the beauty of the world. The cloud is beautiful as it floats through the sky. The dewdrop is beautiful as it glistens in the early morning sunlight. The lightning flash is beautiful in its brief, awesome power. The bubble on the stream, reflecting myriad hues – like a rainbow sometimes – is also beautiful. So to my mind there is a twofold message in that particular verse: life is fleeting, life is transient, but life is also beautiful.

In the early Buddhist scriptures – those, that is, which can be said to reflect the historical circumstances under which the Buddha taught – there is evidence of a very great sensitivity to the natural world. The Buddha himself, as also his immediate disciples, lived close to nature. He was actually born in an orchard – his mother holding onto the branch of a tree. He gained Enlightenment at Bodh Gaya sitting underneath a tree. He died in the *sāl* tree grove of the Mallas, stretched out between two *sāl* trees. And of course he spent much of his time wandering from place to place, from village to village, in the open air.

So Buddhism had its origins in the open air, and this open air background to the scriptures inevitably affected the way the Dharma was taught by the Buddha and experienced by his disciples. For instance, there is a set of verses in the *Theragāthā* ('Verses of the Elders'), attributed to one of the Buddha's senior disciples. In it he describes a cloud – a heavy, black, or rather, dark blue, cloud – and how a white bird flies across the dark cloud. The beauty of this sight seems to send him into a sort of ecstasy.

Scholars have a tendency, perhaps, to overlook this aspect of Buddhism in their intent to present Buddhism as a *teaching*, sometimes, even, as quite a dry, methodical, analytical teaching. But if you look at the *life* of the Buddha, the life of his close companions, you see the natural world very much *there* in their lives, in their practice of the Dharma. And there is therefore a close connection, I would say, between early Buddhism and the natural environment.

The most common symbol in Christianity is the cross, even the crucifix. But the most common symbol in Buddhism is the lotus flower. It goes right back to the time immediately after the Buddha's Enlightenment, when he was wondering whether or not he would ever be able to communicate his experience to others. He looked out over the world and saw human beings as lotus flowers growing in a pond. Some were deep down in the mud, some had just raised their petals above the water, and some were standing completely free of the water, opening their petals to the sunlight.[156] This was the Buddha's vision of humanity. And through it he knew that human beings could grow and expand and open up to receive the sunlight of the Dharma – and that like blossoms, some individuals were more developed and mature – and therefore more receptive to the Dharma – than others.

So it does seem that the Buddha himself was not just conscious of the natural environment but felt deep sympathy with it. The Buddhist scriptures are full of references to nature spirits – spirits of the trees, spirits of the ponds, spirits of the streams, even spirits of flowers. There's a story in one of the scriptures of a monk who goes and smells a lotus flower growing in the water, and the spirit of the flower comes out and says, 'Why are you stealing my scent?' – which obviously gives the monk something to think about.[157] In future he won't thoughtlessly take from nature without asking permission in some way. He won't even think to smell a lotus flower without the flower's permission. After all, it isn't *his* scent – it's the flower's scent.

This does, perhaps, convey to us some kind of environmentalist message about the way we exploit nature. The idea that we shouldn't so much as smell a flower without seeking the flower's permission might seem a bit sentimental, but there is a philosophy underlying it which has some quite far-reaching implications for us today, and this is that there can be a sort of imaginative identification between man and nature.

from *In the Realm of the Lotus*

3. EARLY EXPERIENCES OF BEAUTY

My experience was predominantly one of being caught up into a world of images and archetypes of overwhelming beauty and profound significance.

I first read *The Divine Comedy* when I was 13 or 14, in a copy of the Cary blank verse translation, with Flaxman's illustrations, that I had borrowed from the Tooting Public Library. About the same time, or a little later, I also read Maria Francesca Rossetti's *The Shadow of Dante*, borrowed from the same invaluable institution, and a year or two after that I read the *Convitio* and Dante Gabriel Rossetti's classic version of the *Vita Nuova*, second-hand copies of both of which I had been able to acquire. But in fact my acquaintance with Dante went back a long way before any knowledge of his works. In the passage between my own room and my parents' bedroom, in our upstairs flat at 23 Selincourt Road, hung small reproductions of two well-known Pre-Raphaelite paintings: Holiday's *Beatrice Refuses Dante Her Salutation* and Rossetti's *Dante's Dream*. I must have looked at these hundreds of times, and the latter, in particular, with its rich hues and mysterious personages, was among the most familiar objects of my childhood. Who knows what part it may have played in my lifelong admiration for Rossetti, both as a painter and as poet?

So far as I remember, I did not again accompany Dante on his celebrated journey through Hell, Purgatory, and Paradise until the eighties, when I read I. C. Wright's version of *The Divine Comedy* while on retreat in Tuscany. Like the original it was in *terza rima*,[158] and like the Cary version I had read forty or more years earlier it was illustrated by the engravings after Flaxman. Some of these were admirable, but this time, at least, I felt Flaxman's neo-classical style was incompatible with the medieval spirit of Dante's great poem. What kind of impression *The Divine Comedy* made on me when I first encountered it, at 13 or 14, it is now impossible for me to say. Perhaps I could never say. At that time of my life I did not clearly distinguish between poetry and religion, and in *The Divine Comedy*, as in Milton's *Paradise Lost* and Aeschylus' *Oresteia* trilogy, I sought as much for spiritual enlightenment as for aesthetic enjoyment. Reading them, my experience was predominantly one of being caught up into a world of images and archetypes of overwhelming beauty and profound significance. Doctrinally, they were all on much the same level. I no more believed in the objective truth of Dante's vision than I believed in that of Milton or Aeschylus. Beatrice and the Virgin Mary were no more – and no less – real to me than were the figures of Satan and Messiah, the Eumenides and Pallas Athene. Beauty was Truth, Truth Beauty – though the Truth in question was not that of science or even philosophy in the usual sense of the term. When I reread *The Divine Comedy* in Tuscany I had long been aware that ordinarily poetry and religion, symbol and fact, history and legend, were distinguishable the one from the other, but I was still able to experience the work as though the seamless garment had not been rent, albeit I experienced it with, perhaps, a lesser degree of intensity. Of the three parts of the poem it was the second, the Purgatorio, over which I lingered with the keenest feelings of admiration and delight. Even though what I was reading was not the original but a translation, it seemed I had hardly ever encountered anything so beautiful.

from *Through Buddhist Eyes*

4. LEARNING TO SEE

We have to learn to look at things themselves, for their own sake, untainted by any trace of subjectivity, personal preference, or desire.

Most of the time we are only vaguely conscious of the things around us, and have no more than a peripheral awareness of them. We are not really aware of our environment, not really aware of nature, not really aware of the cosmos, and the reason for this is that we seldom or never really stop and look at them. How many minutes of the day – not to speak of hours – do we spend just looking at something? Probably we do not even spend seconds in this way, and the reason we usually give is that we have no time. This is perhaps one of the greatest indictments of modern civilization that could possibly be made – that we have no time to stop and look at anything. We may pass a tree on the way to work, but we have no time to look at it, or even to look at less romantic things such as walls, houses, and fences. This makes one wonder what this life, and this modern civilization of ours, is worth if there is no time to look at things. In the words of the poet:

> What is this life if, full of care,
> We have no time to stand and stare.[159]

Of course the poet has used the word 'stare' for the sake of the rhyme, and what he really means is not staring in the literal sense but just looking and seeing. The fact that we have no time for this is something of which we need to remind ourselves. Yet even if we do have time to stop and look and try to be aware we hardly ever see things in themselves. What we usually see is our own projected subjectivity. We look at something, but we see it through the veil, the curtain, the mist, the fog of our own mental conditioning.

Some years ago, in the Himalayan region of India, I went for a walk with a Nepalese friend, and we happened to stop at the foot of a magnificent pine tree. As I looked up at the smooth trunk and the mass of deep green foliage I could not help exclaiming, 'Well, isn't that a beautiful tree!' My Nepalese friend, who was standing beside me, said, 'Oh yes, it is a beautiful tree. There's enough firewood there for the whole winter.' He did not see the tree at all. All he saw was a certain quantity of firewood. Most of us look at the world of material things in just this way, and it is an attitude from which we have to free ourselves. We have to learn to look at things themselves, for their own sake, untainted by any trace of subjectivity, personal preference, or desire.

This attitude or approach is much emphasized in Far Eastern Buddhist art, that is in the art of China and Japan. In this connection there is the story of a certain apprentice painter who once asked his master, a celebrated artist, how to paint bamboos. The master did not, however, say that you take your brush and make certain strokes on the silk or the paper. He did not say anything about brushes or pigments, or even about painting. He only said, 'If you want to learn to paint bamboos, first learn to see bamboos.'[160] This is a sobering thought – that one might rush to paint something without having even looked at it – but this is what many artists actually do, or at least what many amateurs in art do. So the disciple, we are told, just looked. He went about looking at bamboos. He looked at the stems, and he looked at the leaves. He looked at them in the mist, and in the rain, and in the moonlight. He looked at them in spring, in autumn, and in winter. He looked at large bamboos, and he looked at small bamboos. He looked at them when they were green, and when they were yellow, when they were fresh and springy, and when they were dry and decayed. In this way he spent several years just looking at bamboos. He became genuinely aware of the bamboos. He really saw them. Seeing them, being aware of them in this way, he became at one with the bamboos. His life passed into the life of the bamboos. The life of the bamboos passed into his life. Only then did he paint bamboos; and of course you may be sure that it was real bamboos that he painted. In fact we might say that it became a question of a bamboo painting bamboos.

According to Buddhism, at least according to Far Eastern Buddhism – the traditions of China and Japan and, above all perhaps, the traditions of Chan and Zen – this should be our attitude towards all material things. This should be our attitude towards the whole of nature: not only towards bamboos, but towards the sun, the moon, the stars, and the earth; towards trees and flowers and human beings. We should learn to look, learn to see, learn to be aware, and in this way become supremely receptive. Because of our receptivity we shall become one with, or at least fused with, all things; and out of this oneness, this realization of affinity and deep unity, if we are of artistic temperament we shall create, and truly create.

from *The Buddha's Noble Eightfold Path*

5. BAMBOOS

Among all branched things, I for beauty choose
The yellowness and slimness of bamboos,
Whose bunched leaves twinkle on a gusty day
And back and forth the clattering branches sway.

And when from frozen skies the pure snows fall
In large white flakes that softly mantle all
The loaded branches stoop without a sound
Till their green leaf-tips almost touch the ground.

Then, when they seem a kind of crystal tree
Sparkling with diamond buds and silvery
Shoots, by the snowflakes' overburdening
And their own patience freed, the lithe boughs spring

Up, and in powdery showers the white snow flies
Flung by the wind across the freezing skies,
While, as the bamboos dance in wind and rain,
Like stars the bunched leaves twinkle forth again.

Hence, among branched things I for beauty choose
The yellowness and slimness of bamboos,
Which taught me, more than what in books is writ,
That life is conquered when we yield to it.

from *Complete Poems*

6. THE SNOWS OF THE HIMALAYAS

Contemplating them in this way ... I could begin to understand why the Himalayas had such a hold on the imagination of the people of the subcontinent and why they occupied so prominent a place in the religious and cultural life of Hindus, Buddhists, and Jains alike. I could understand why Kalidasa, in an oft-quoted phrase, had described the Himalayas as 'the congealed laughter of Shiva'.

The snows were not visible from the Hermitage, but as one walked up the road, in the direction of the bazaar, they gradually hove in sight. By the time one reached the Dharmodaya Vihara, which was situated half a mile from the Hermitage, there was the dazzling white mass of Kanchenjunga, with its twin peaks, piled up on the horizon at an unbelievable height. For the best view of the snows one had to climb up to Dailo, the skull-shaped hill beyond Dr Graham's Homes, and one day, with three companions, Sachin and I did just that. The three companions were Jungi, Dawa, and Omiya, the cheerful Bengali proprietor of a small watch-repair business in Darjeeling with whom Sachin had become acquainted and who was now spending a few days with him. As agreed the night before, we met at Sachin's house after breakfast and from there set out. The climb was a stiff one, especially towards the end, and it was not until nearly midday that, having emerged from the pine forest, we found ourselves on the bare top of Dailo Hill. The sun was shining brilliantly. Below us was the River Ranjit, winding through silver sands towards the plains, while around us, and stretching away into the distance, rose innumerable hills, all covered in soft blue haze. Aloft on the horizon, and extending in an unbroken line from farthest east to farthest west, were the snow peaks of the eastern Himalayas. There must have been hundreds of them. Except for Kanchenjunga and Lama Yuru, a pyramidal mountain so called from its resemblance to a meditating monk, I did not know their names. Nor did I care to know them. For me it was enough to sit there in that intense stillness, 5,000 feet above sea level, simply contemplating those silent white forms. Contemplating them in this way – taking *darshan*, as my Indian friends would have said – I could begin to understand why the Himalayas had such a hold on the imagination of the people of the subcontinent and why they occupied so prominent a place in the religious and cultural life of Hindus, Buddhists, and Jains alike. I could understand why Kalidasa, in an oft-quoted phrase, had described the Himalayas as 'the congealed laughter of Shiva',[161] and why the author of the *Skanda Purāṇa* had gone so far as to personify the Himalaya or Himachala, in the singular, and extol him as a deity, saying:

> He who thinks of Himachala, even though he should not behold Him, is greater than he who performs worship at Kashi. And he who contemplates upon Himachala shall have pardon of all sins. All things that die on Himachala, and in dying think of His snows, are freed from evil. In a hundred years of the gods I could not tell you of the glories of Himachala, where Shiva lives and where the Ganga falls from the feet of Vishnu like the slender thread of the lotus flower. Truly, as the dew is dried by the Sun so are the sorrows of mankind dried up by the sight of Himachala.[162]

I had contemplated Himachala, and though I did not feel that my sins had been pardoned I could well believe that my sorrows had dried up, at least for the time being.

from *Facing Mount Kanchenjunga*

7. THE GREATER MANDALA OF AESTHETIC APPRECIATION

We usually think of 'aesthetic appreciation' as a little separate part of life within a much larger area that is utilitarian and 'practical', but really it needs to be the other way around.

The Enlightenment of the Buddha was not a cold, detached knowledge. He saw with warmth; he saw with feeling; what is more, he saw everything as being pure, or *śubha*, which also means beautiful. The Buddha saw everything as pure beauty because he saw everything with compassion – just as, conversely, when you hate someone, they appear ugly. When, out of *maitrī*, you see things as beautiful, you naturally experience joy and delight. And out of that joy and delight flow spontaneity, freedom, creativity, and energy. This flow from *maitrī* to joy to freedom and energy is the constant experience of the bodhisattva. The bodhisattva's wisdom in the fullest sense therefore includes *maitrī*. In a sense, we could even say that *maitrī is* wisdom, *is prajñā*.

We may further dispel any impression a superficial look at the Perfection of Wisdom literature, the Prajñāpāramitā, may give that the bodhisattva is a sort of glorified logic-chopper by looking at another word used to describe the bodhisattva's experience: *vidyā*. *Vidyā* is the opposite of *avidyā*, 'ignorance', and is usually translated as 'knowledge'. However, Guenther renders it as 'aesthetic appreciation' (like *prajñā* but without the element of analysis), which comes much closer to its true meaning. *Vidyā* is a sort of relishing of things, a harmony with the world; and its opposite, *avidyā*, conveys a sense of alienation and conflict – certainly not an absence of *knowledge* in the usual sense of the word.

When one is said to *know* something, this carries the suggestion that the knowledge is utilitarian. One knows what the thing is good for; one knows what one can do with it. If what we see is the utilitarian value of something, we are relating to it from a need, which becomes desire, which turns to craving for the object conceived as fulfilling that desire. The tree is seen not as existing in its own right, for its own sake, but as something to fulfil our need. If, however, we have no desires to be fulfilled, there is no subject and no object. That is the state of the bodhisattva – empty of any desire to use things for any particular purpose. All that is left is aesthetic appreciation. If you are a bodhisattva you enjoy the world much as you enjoy a work of art or an artistic performance – with the difference that you do not experience a division between yourself and something 'out there'. Normally – though less so in the cinema – people in an audience retain a sense of themselves as subjects separate from what they are experiencing as an aesthetic object, and to that degree remain alienated from it. But the bodhisattva's experience of the world is more like

> Music heard so deeply
> That it is not heard at all,
> But you are the music
> While the music lasts.[163]

And unlike the experience of the woman in the stalls who forgets it is 'only' a play and shouts to Othello that Desdemona is innocent.

The 'purpose' of a bodhisattva, if one may speak in that way at all, is in no degree passive, however. It is not unlike the function of the artist – except that a painter, say, can rarely just enjoy the world without starting to think of how to make a picture out of it. What the bodhisattva creates is something different. The bodhisattva, quite unpurposefully, rearranges the whole universe and turns it into a gigantic mandala.

What does this mean? What is a mandala? Putting aside the more conventional descriptions, let us take this short definition by a Tibetan teacher, Rongzom Chökyi Zangpo: 'To make a mandala is to take any prominent aspect of reality and surround it with beauty.'[164] Why you should select one particular aspect of reality over another will be a matter not of attraction as a form of craving, but of spiritual affinity. It will be a facet of reality that you value and appreciate enough to want to surround it with a harmonious pattern of beautiful images. You take, say, a particular Buddha figure – one that you find particularly appealing, sublime, or precious – as the aspect of reality you want to focus on, and you decorate it with, for instance, other Buddha figures at the points of the compass. Then you might place the four elements in between, and use all the other things in nature as materials with which to fill the spaces so as to make a harmonious and pleasing configuration.

The bodhisattva creates a mandala through a response to the world that is aesthetic and appreciative rather than utilitarian. To sustain life you have to engage in a certain amount of practical activity – you have to think about things and understand how the world works – but if you are a bodhisattva all this takes place within an overall context of aesthetic appreciation. We usually think of 'aesthetic appreciation' as a little separate part of life within a much larger area that is utilitarian and 'practical', but really it needs to be the other way around. Our overall attitude, our overall response to life, should be purely aesthetic. We should not seek to use things, but just enjoy them, appreciate them, feel for them. We don't have to think of our mandala of aesthetic appreciation as something the size of one of those Tibetan thangkas sitting in a corner of the great big real world of important practical business. Instead, we can think of ourselves as living *within* a 'greater mandala' of aesthetic appreciation, of which all our practical mundane affairs, and the fulfilment of all our (non-neurotic) needs and wants, occupy just a tiny corner. The real values are aesthetic, not utilitarian.

There is a story of a Taoist sage who was sitting by a river with a fishing rod when someone came along and asked him how he could reconcile trying to catch fish with being a Taoist sage. He replied, 'It's all right, I'm not using any bait.' He was just enjoying the fishing; he didn't need to try and catch anything. We don't *really* have anything to do – well, do we? Most of the time we could just be sitting back, as it were, and enjoying the universe. That's our major occupation. That's our real work – not to work. We need to get food to eat, clothing, a roof over our head, healthcare, a few books, transport of some kind ... but the rest of our time and energy we can just devote to the contemplation of the universe, simply enjoying it all. This is how a bodhisattva lives, anyway.

I am not talking about some lotus-eating, day-dreaming, navel-gazing ideal here. The bodhisattva is the greatest worker of all, constantly responding to the objective needs of a situation, but at the same time he or she operates within the greater mandala of aesthetic appreciation. It is not even as though the sphere within which the bodhisattva operates is a sphere of 'practical activity' that exists apart from the greater mandala. Bodhisattvas do not absent themselves from the mandala of aesthetic appreciation when they carry on their practical activities. The greater mandala interpenetrates that limited sphere, so that those practical activities are an expression of the values of the greater mandala within a certain context and for the sake of certain people.

from *Wisdom Beyond Words*

8. THE TEMPLE BELL

Between the hill and the bell, between the anvil and the hammer, I was being reshaped, was being beaten into something, I knew not what. I was being changed.

Long before dawn, as well as at intervals throughout the day and night, we heard the temple bell. Perhaps it was my imagination, but I seemed always to hear the temple bell. It was not really one bell but two bells that I heard, the first being higher in pitch than the second, but the twin strokes came so close together, and were at once so well contrasted and so well harmonized, that they constituted for me a single experience. As a single experience I referred them to a single origin, and thought of the sound as being produced by one bell, or rather by a kind of double bell which was struck, perhaps, either by two hammers in one place or in two places by one hammer. The bell sounded louder than any of the instruments that accompanied the evening worship, louder than all of them combined. It was so loud that it penetrated rock as easily as air, so loud that it made no difference whether we were inside the cave or outside it. When we were inside the cave, indeed, it was as though the great bell swung not somewhere inside the temple but up in the air, directly outside the cave. Sometimes I heard it in my dreams. Hour after hour it seemed to toll, incessant and insistent, wave after wave of brazen sound breaking upon me like the repeated thunder of surf on the sea shore. Sometimes it was as though the bell, swinging outside, was striking against the hill, and that the hill was the bell and the bell itself the hammer that struck the bell. Again, the hill was not bell but anvil, and the bell the hammer that, stroke after sonorous stroke, smote upon the anvil. The point of impact, the point where the hill and bell met, where hammer smote anvil, was the cave, was me. Between the hill and the bell, between the anvil and the hammer, I was being reshaped, was being beaten into something, I knew not what. I was being changed.

from *The Rainbow Road from Tooting Broadway to Kalimpong*

9. LEARNING TO STAND STILL

We have to listen to the exhortation of the Buddha – to the voice of our own immanent Buddhahood – and learn simply to 'stand still' at all levels of our being, both physical and mental.

What is the effect of this acceleration of the speed at which we can travel – indeed of the pace at which we now live – on the general human consciousness? Physical speed and the sense of duration being intimately related, the more quickly we are able to do anything the less time there appears to be in which to do it. Conversely, the less time there appears to be in which to do a thing, the more quickly we desire to do it, whether the action concerned be that of travelling or anything else. Such is the vicious circle in which a rapidly increasing section of the human race now finds itself involved. In the expedience of time, there would seem to operate a principle analogous to the law of diminishing returns in economics, in accordance with which the more time-saving devices are placed at one's disposal the more pressed for time one becomes. Under such conditions the activities of twentieth-century humanity are increasingly characterized by a feverish haste which eventually results in physical exhaustion, nervous strain, and mental breakdown.

Aṅgulimāla the bandit, pursuing the Buddha along the jungle path with drawn sword, found himself in a similar predicament. However fast he ran he was unable to catch up with the Enlightened One, though the latter was walking at a slow, dignified pace. Eventually, exhausted by his efforts and terrified by the inexplicable phenomenon, he called to the Master to stand still. Back came the reply, 'I am already standing still (i.e. have attained Nirvāṇa); it is you who are running (i.e. round and round in *saṃsāra*, impelled by the force of ignorant desire).'[165]

The more desperately we try to catch up with the future the more it eludes our grasp. Like Aṅgulimāla, we have to listen to the exhortation of the Buddha – to the voice of our own immanent Buddhahood – and learn simply to 'stand still' at all levels of our being, both physical and mental. This can be done, initially, only by becoming aware that we are running. Awareness of speed, of duration, of the three tenses, eventually enables us to realize that past and future are concepts only. With this realization comes about a subsidence, a calming down and dying away, of all those emotions – desires and fears, anxieties and regrets – that are based on those concepts. We begin to live in the present in the true spiritual sense, and thus living in the present, unobsessed by the passage of time, find that we have time enough in which to do all things. Having reached such a state of awakened *prajñā*, we shall be able to board a jet-propelled Boeing, if circumstances so require, or even go for a weekend on the moon, with the same unruffled composure, the same freedom from all sense of haste, with which we walk at night in our garden among the fragrance of tranquil flowers.

from *Beating the Drum*

10. PAUSES AND EMPTY SPACES

Truly did a Chinese sage say that it is only because of empty space that the wheel is able to revolve, and houses to be made use of.

When the composer Mozart was asked what was the most important part of his music, he did not reply that melody, or harmony, or counterpoint, or even orchestration was the most important, but simply 'the pauses'.

As in the music of Mozart, so in the paintings of the Far Eastern – Chinese and Japanese – masters of the art of landscape. It is the empty spaces which are the most important parts of the picture. The vast empty spaces of sky, or snow, or water are not only themselves charged with mysterious significance as a cloud with lightning, but they somehow infuse that significance into the single blossomless branch, or tiny floating boat, or solitary human figure, which stands almost lost at the edge, or in the centre, of the huge blank expanse of paper, or faintly tinted silk.

And just as the pauses are the most important part of music, and the empty spaces the most important part of a picture, so are silence and emptiness the most important part of life. A life which consists of a frantic stream of external activities, without one moment of inward recollection, is like music which is an uninterrupted succession of sounds, or a picture which is crammed with figures: all three are not only meaningless, but positively painful.

As music is born of silence, and derives its significance therefrom; and as a painting is born of empty space, and derives its significance therefrom; so are our lives born of silence, of stillness, of quietude of spirit, and derive their significance, their distinctive flavour and individual quality, therefrom. The deeper and more frequent are those moments of interior silence and stillness wherein, transcending all sights and sounds, tastes and touches, we experience Reality as it is, the more rich in significance, the more truly meaningful, will our lives be.

It has been said that there is a silence of words, a silence of desires, and a silence of thoughts. Only when the egoistic will itself is 'silent', that is, no longer operative, will be heard the True Sound. Only when our hearts are utterly empty of all self-will shall we behold the True Form. And since this Silence and Emptiness are not states of mere negation, but dynamic and full of life, our thoughts and words and deeds, even the most insignificant, will be charged with a mysterious potency, like two or three notes of a flute sounding in the midst of a great pause in a symphony, or a few delicate twigs sketched in the corner of an else empty scroll.

Truly did a Chinese sage say that it is only because of empty space that the wheel is able to revolve, and houses to be made use of.

It is the pauses which make beautiful the music of our lives. It is the empty spaces which give richness and significance to them. And it is stillness which makes them truly useful.

from *Crossing the Stream*

11. THE SIMPLE LIFE

The truly simple life glows with significance, for its simplicity is not the dead simplicity of a skeleton but the living simplicity of a flower or a great work of art.

Men and women bewildered by the ever-increasing complexity of modern civilization cry out for the simple life as a drowning man gasps for air. Visions of cool trees and quiet cottages arise before eyes almost blinded by the glare of neon lights; and ears well nigh deaf with the thunder of traffic and shriek of machinery seem to catch, during brief interludes of silence, the sound of white surf as it sweeps hissing up the beach or the song of a bird as it floats sweet and clear through the moonlight from the darkness of distant trees.

But the simple life is by no means one of ease and idleness, as the town-dweller, with his sentimental 'idealization' of life in the country, is apt to suppose. Nor is it necessarily associated with lonely hermitages wreathed in mountain mist or gleaming coral beaches fringed with languorous palms, although the relative freedom from 'external' distractions and irritations which such places enjoy may make them more helpful to the leading of a simple life than others less fortunate. For the simple life is also a strenuous one, being the product of a process of simplification, a reduction of life to its barest essentials; and the successful accomplishment of this process is, amidst the monstrous jungle-growth of the complexities of modern living, a task calling for unremitting endeavour and inflexible resolve. Nor does it involve merely the simplification of the external mode of one's existence, but something far more fundamental upon which hinges not only this but every other mode of existence as well.

But before we can reduce life to its essentials we must determine what those essentials are, otherwise the expression remains a mere gaudy flower of rhetoric barren of all fruition in experience. And before we can determine what are the essentials of life and what its adventitious trappings we must ask ourselves the question, essential to what? For life as we ordinarily live it is obviously not an end in itself, but only a means to an end, and until we know what that end is it is impossible for us to judge what in our lives is essential, and what inessential, to the attainment of it.

Buddhism posits *bodhi*, or the realization of transcendent wisdom, as the ultimate goal not only of every human being but of every other form of sentient existence as well. Life is for the sake of Enlightenment. The essentials of life are those things which are helpful to the attainment of Enlightenment, and it is back to these naked boughs that the luxuriant foliage and innumerable buds of our life-tree must be ruthlessly stripped and pruned if ever it is to bear its loveliest blossoms and most ambrosial fruit. The truly simple life is that which is dedicated solely to the attainment of Supreme Wisdom, and wherein each thought, word, and deed is integrated to the achievement of that end. Killing, stealing, wrong means of livelihood, and all other forms of unskilful bodily action must be given up until those actions alone remain the performance of which abounds in spiritual significance. Thus bodily action is simplified into *mudrā*. The use of false, frivolous, abusive, and obscene speech must be gradually restricted until no word is uttered without some background of spiritual recollection behind it. Thus speech is simplified into *mantra*. Greedy, malicious, and deluded thoughts must be eliminated until the concentrated mind admits only thoughts that are pure, compassionate, and illumined. Thus thought is simplified into *samādhi*. As the bodhisattva disciplines himself in this way his body, speech, and mind gradually become as it were transparent, and through each thought, word, and deed streams into the world the effulgence of Great Compassion, just as the beams of the rising sun leap through the windows of a room and disarm the darkness within. The truly simple life glows with significance, for its simplicity is not the dead simplicity of a skeleton but the living simplicity of a flower or a great work of art. The unessential has melted like mist from life and the Himalayan contours of the essential are seen towering with sublime simplicity above the petty hills and valleys of the futilities of mundane existence.

Far Eastern aesthetics make extensive use of a term which may be interpretively translated as 'aesthetic impoverishment'. This kind of art finds its highest expression in ink drawings which reveal a whole world of significance with three strokes of the brush, and tiny verses which seem almost to exhaust the possibilities of poetic expression within the compass of thirty-seven syllables, although the principle on which it is based is not peculiar to the realm of art but penetrates every phase of the life and culture of the Far Eastern peoples. In fact, it is an aesthetic application of the principle on which the simple life, in the sense of the bodhisattva career, is founded – the principle that the more rigorous the simplicity of the outward form the more clearly is the significance of the inner spirit revealed.

It is the presence of this parallelism which makes it possible to speak of the spiritual life as a work of art, as the greatest of all works of art, and which perhaps explains the aesthetic pleasure with which we contemplate the bodhisattva ideal, an ideal which seems not only good and true but also incomparably beautiful. For the simple life is in fact all three, and where goodness, truth, and beauty abound happiness is of a surety not far to seek.

from *Crossing the Stream*

2
BUDDHISM AND ART

1. THE RELIGION OF ART

If it is true that the arts have taken the place of religion, this is because they form an integral part, not of religion in the narrow sense, but of the spiritual life.

Enjoyment of great works of art broadens and deepens our own consciousness. When we listen to a great piece of music, see a great painting, read a great poem – when we really experience it, allow it to soak into us – we go beyond our ordinary consciousness. We become more generous in our sympathies; our whole life is subtly but deeply modified. If we persist in pursuing an interest in the arts, our whole mode of being may be affected, and our lives may even be transformed.

Today, traditional religion – in the form of Christianity, at least – has lost its unquestioned hold on the minds of people in the West. The astonishing architectural monuments to Christianity are still around us, but however glorious some of them may be, for most people they are empty shells. For the vast majority of people, orthodox religion is no longer a means of grace. We don't get anything from it. It means nothing to us. It no longer uplifts us, or moves us, or transforms us, much less still transfigures us. People aren't even against it any more.

As the title of my own book on art is meant to suggest,[166] for many people the place and function of religion has been taken over by art.

This is one of the reasons, I think, for the immense popularity today of all the fine arts – for despite all the grumbling one hears about the decay of culture, the fine arts are hugely popular as they have never been before. Formerly the enjoyment of works of art was the privilege of a few. Five hundred years ago in England, most of us would have been living in miserable hovels. We would never have seen any paintings except perhaps one or two in the local church, and we would have heard little music of any quality. As for reading, hardly anyone read for pleasure, or even at all. Enjoyment of high culture was the privilege of no more than a few wealthy ecclesiastics and noblemen. Even as late as the eighteenth century, how many people heard the works of Bach, Haydn, or Mozart performed? A few tens of thousands at the very most – and sometimes only a few hundred bored aristocrats.

But nowadays the artistic heritage of the ages is within the reach of practically everyone. The music of the great composers may be heard and enjoyed over and over again, by millions of people throughout the world. High culture is being disseminated on an unprecedented scale. What results this is likely to have we can only guess, but there must be some possibility that the sudden mass availability of high culture will start to exert a slow and steady refining influence on a considerable and influential section of the population.

If it is true that the arts have taken the place of religion, this is because they form an integral part, not of religion in the narrow sense, but of the spiritual life. And if I am right in this analysis, we should encourage all the fine arts, as an integral part of the spiritual life and the evolution of our humanity.

from *What is the Sangha?*

2. MUSIC AND MYSTICAL EXPERIENCE

The objective world, though again visible, seemed strangely unreal, as if it had no business to be there and might disappear at any second.

The two and a half years which followed my return from Torquay were among the most important of my present existence. Every aspect of my being, from the lowest to the highest, sought eagerly for the fullest possible unfoldment and expression, so that my life was during this whole period a chaos of conflicting impulses. My love of art, of literature, of music, already sufficiently ardent, became a ruthless passion. Books, never chewed or merely tasted, were now indiscriminately swallowed whole in a fruitless attempt to satisfy an appetite frightful in its ravenousness. My senses, practically dormant until then, suddenly awoke and clamoured for satisfaction. For the first time in my life came psychical and mystical experiences. Though heights were touched, existence for me consisted not in progress but in a perpetual violent oscillation between extremes. Small wonder that the heroes of this period were stricken, tormented, demoniacal figures – Strindberg, Nietzsche, Beethoven....

With Father on duty at the ARP headquarters, in the evenings Mother and I were generally alone. As she sat silently mending socks and shirts hour after hour there would sometimes escape from her a sigh of sheer weariness which, though it pierced me to the heart, I ignored and went on reading. If she ventured a remark I answered with a grunt. After leaving England I bitterly regretted this selfish behaviour, the memory of which filled me with grief and shame. Never in my life was the aesthetic so inimical to the ethical. If she wanted to listen to the Forces Programme I curtly told her that it would disturb me; but if I wished to listen to Bach or Beethoven, which gave her a headache, I switched on the radio without caring for her feelings. Later on, Joan and I always quarrelled about the radio, which I took into the sitting-room, where there was an extra plug-in, whenever I wanted to listen to the Promenade Concerts. Since Joan was good-natured and I bad-tempered she usually gave in to me, but if one of her favourite crooners was on the air she insisted on her rights. On such occasions I did sometimes give in, though with a very bad grace; but if a symphony or concerto which I particularly wanted to hear was being broadcast over another wavelength I would go to any lengths of rudeness and ill-temper to get my own way. With Mother there was never any dispute. Besides being accustomed to me having my own way, she was naturally of a gentle, patient disposition. Once, in a moment of exasperation, she exclaimed, 'You're just like your father – obstinate as a mule!' But such outbursts were rare. Thus it was that she submitted to evenings of sheer boredom without a word of complaint, darning socks and turning the wrists and collars of shirts with war-time economy, while I read philosophy and religion or listened to classical music on the radio.

Though I had responded to classical music ever since that afternoon I had heard *Fingal's Cave* at the Methodist Central Hall, only after my return from Torquay did it become an addiction. Bach's *Toccata and Fugue in D Minor*, which seemingly explores the heights and depths of the universe, occupied in my experience of music a place analogous to that of *Paradise Lost* in my experience of poetry. Stunned, overwhelmed, annihilated by those majestic chords, I went about for several days in a kind of waking trance. As soon as I came to my senses I tried to translate my experience of the music into poetry. Later on, in fact, I wrote in imitation of Baudelaire's 'Les Phares' a poem on all the great composers from Bach to Delius, as well as a dramatic idyll on Beethoven.

My enjoyment of music was far more intense than that of poetry had ever been. This was partly due to the very nature of music, which unlike poetry is pure feeling devoid of all cognitive content, and partly to the fact that at this period I craved constant emotional intoxication. My two favourite composers, that is to say those by whom I was most strongly stimulated, were Beethoven and Tchaikovsky. When the violence of my feelings had subsided I preferred Mozart and Haydn, while Bach remained a constant favourite.

Whether the intensity of my enjoyment of music contributed to my first mystical experience, which came at about this time, I am unable to say. But a Beethoven overture or a symphony by Mozart used to affect me so powerfully that for several days I would hear the music ringing again and again in my ears. So intense, indeed, would my concentration on these inner sounds be, that not only did they sound as loud and clear as when I had heard them with my physical ears over the radio, but I would practically lose consciousness of my body. This state of semi-trance which music sometimes induced in me seemed to be of the same order as the two experiences which, appropriating a conveniently vague term, I have called mystical.

Both occurred several times. The first had indeed come to me, though not very intensely, even before my evacuation. Like most of my other mystical experiences, it is associated in memory with the place at which it occurred. One day, on my way to the Tooting Public Library, I as usual had to cross the road at Amen Corner – so called because in ancient times, when the choir of the parish church performed the annual ceremony of 'beating the bounds', they broke up at this spot, which marked the boundary of the parish, with a loud 'Amen'. As I crossed from one side of the street to the other I suddenly awoke to the complete absurdity of the mind being tied down to a single physical body. Why could I not look at the world through the eyes of the man standing on the opposite pavement? Why could I not know his thoughts as easily as I knew my own? As these questions flashed upon me I felt my consciousness desperately struggling to free itself from the body and project itself into all the bodies walking round Amen Corner. Though its efforts were unavailing and it sank back exhausted I thereafter had a feeling of being imprisoned. When years later I read in the *Śūraṅgama Sūtra*, a famous text of Buddhist idealism, the dialogue in which the Buddha makes his disciple Ānanda realize, step by step, that his consciousness is neither inside the body nor outside it, nor yet somewhere between, being in its true nature universal, I felt I was treading on familiar ground.

The other experience was even more striking. As I was walking down the main road towards Tooting Broadway, it suddenly seemed as though I was moving in a world of ghosts. The whole street with its houses, shops, and people suddenly receded into the infinitely remote distance. The roar of the traffic faded into an intense silence. My own body felt light, airy, insubstantial, and it seemed I no longer walked on the solid pavement but floated, clearly conscious, through an immense void. This void was simultaneously coterminous with my own consciousness, so that it also seemed that I was floating through myself. Though this experience, which was much more vivid than the first, generally lasted for the time it took me to walk a hundred yards, its after-effects persisted much longer; for upwards of an hour the objective world, though again visible, seemed strangely unreal, as if it had no business to be there and might disappear at any second. My subsequent study of Buddhist literature confirmed this experience too. When I read in the *Laṅkāvatāra Sūtra* and other works that one must meditate on the world as being in reality like a dream, I at once understood what was meant.

from *The Rainbow Road from Tooting Broadway to Kalimpong*

3. THE TRANSFORMATIVE POWER OF ART

Buddhism and art are both indispensable to a balanced spiritual life.

From the dual viewpoint of subject matter and quality of inspiration, four categories of art can be distinguished. The first is neither religious in form nor spiritualizing in effect. Tabloid newspapers, pulp magazines, and the majority of popular films may be mentioned in this category. The second category of art is that which is formally, but not essentially, religious. Such are the lithographed pictures of gods and saints and religious teachers which one finds in the possession of devout people all over the world. Though religious in theme, they are either technically inept or executed in mechanical fashion, without feeling, and do not produce an expansion of consciousness so much as condition a devotional reflex. Thirdly, we have a type of art that is essentially, though not formally, religious. Chinese landscape painting springs at once to mind as the almost classic example of this category of art. Though devoid of any formally religious content, such paintings are in the deepest sense spiritual, the extraordinary sense of liberation and infinite expansion of consciousness that they produce in the spectator being sufficient proof of the tremendous height of inspiration whence, like a cataract that 'smokes upon the mountainside', they descend through brushes and black ink onto rolls of silk.

The fourth and last of our categories includes works of art that are both formally and essentially religious. Enough has been said of the three previous categories to make clear, without need of further explanation, the nature of this one, the crown and flower of them all. The ancient Buddhist art of India and Sri Lanka, China and Japan, Tibet and Cambodia, may without reproach of partiality be allowed the honour of representing this supreme class. Though it is difficult, even impossible, to single out any one type of Buddhist art as being more typical of the whole group than are others, it will no doubt be conceded that the image of the Buddha seated in meditation is the most popular and widely known of all. Here the meaning of Buddhism and the value of art coalesce upon the lips of the Buddha into a smile that expresses what is, perhaps, the greatest expansion of consciousness that it is possible for the plastic arts to mediate.

From how high a quality of inspiration the work of art issued, we hardly dare to guess. How tremendous an effect it can have upon the whole character may be understood from a story that we heard a few weeks ago from a French lady, a scholar in Sanskrit and poetess in her own language, now a Buddhist nun in India, who had received so deep an impression – a spiritual shock of such high voltage – from an image of this kind that she had seen in the Musée Guimet in Paris that she resolved to consecrate her whole life to the study and practice of Buddhism, so as to experience for herself, to however small an extent, that liberation of consciousness, that wisdom and compassion, which shone through those stone features as though they had been transparent to a light within.[167]

An archaic torso of Apollo that the poet Rilke saw in a museum seems to have produced a similar transformation in his consciousness; but the transformation was not so much reflected in his life as registered in his art. Not that he was unaware of the spiritual significance of deep aesthetic experience. He was, perhaps, more conscious of the inner relations between the experience of the saint and the experience of the artist than any other modern poet, and this consciousness makes him, in an age when external contact between religion and art has been broken off, an artist whose work is of very special significance and value. If the first twelve and a half lines of his sonnet, 'An Archaic Torso of Apollo', show how deep, how heartfelt, was his experience of beauty, the concluding one and a half lines, which mark an abrupt, almost a violent, transition from the descriptive to the reflective mood, reveal how clearly he understood the ethical and spiritual demands of that experience, and how little afraid he was to meet and grapple with them. His meaning is unmistakable, as feeling abruptly deepens into insight and he cries out,

> ... for here is no place
> That does not see you. You must change your life.

This change of life, this transformation of character and attitude, constitutes not only the message of the Buddha image and of the archaic torso of Apollo, but, as we have tried to show, the essence and meaning of Buddhism and the real value of art as well.

Buddhism and art both effect an expansion in consciousness; the practical results that they achieve are of the same kind, however greatly such results may vary in degree, and however dissimilar may be the methods employed by Buddhism, on the one hand, and art, on the other, to bring them about. Buddhism effects an expansion of consciousness by acting directly on the understanding and the will. Art produces a change of life indirectly, by appealing to our sense of beauty. Since we possess an emotional as well as an intellectual and a volitional nature, and are capable of response to beauty no less than to truth and goodness, it is necessary for us to develop and expand simultaneously the emotional, intellectual, and volitional aspects of our personalities. Buddhism and art, therefore, are both indispensable to a balanced spiritual life. Not that we intend to suggest an absolutely exclusive distribution of functions between them, allotting to Buddhism the sole responsibility for developing the mind, and to art the sole responsibility for developing the emotions. Every thought possesses emotional colouring, however obscure. Buddhism, though acting primarily on the intellect, certainly makes a powerful secondary appeal to the emotions, especially to the devotional feelings, which are developed as fully, though not so one-sidedly, in members of the Buddhist community as in people belonging to religions that appeal more to the heart than to the head, to faith rather than to reason. Art, though it operates on the imagination directly, does not fail to influence the understanding. In poetry especially, it is impossible to dissociate the emotional impact of a work of art from the framework of objective reference to which it is attached and which constitutes its 'meaning' for the intellect.

Whether the life of any particular person will be dominated more by interests pertaining to Buddhism, or more by interests pertaining to art, is a question that will be determined by the relative strength in him or her of reason and of emotion. We are concerned only to insist, first of all, that the meaning of Buddhism coincides with the value of art; and secondly, that the development of understanding and insight through the one, and of imagination and sensitiveness to beauty through the other is, for modern men and women, in whom the emotional life and the intellectual life are of almost equal vividness and vigour, not only a need, but almost a necessity.

from *The Religion of Art*

4. ART AS AN INTEGRAL PART OF SPIRITUAL LIFE

Art and meditation are creative states of the human mind.

When one has looked forward to meeting two people as much as I had been looking forward to meeting Lama Govinda and Li Gotami – and as they, apparently, had been looking forward to meeting me – there is always the possibility of mutual disappointment. In the event, this was far from being the case. Within half an hour of their arrival at the Hermitage a definite rapport had been established between us and we were talking as freely as though we had known each other for years. As might have been expected, I felt a greater rapport with Lama Govinda than I did with Li Gotami, who in any case had only a fraction of the wisdom and insight that was manifest in almost every word that Lama Govinda spoke. Nevertheless, I appreciated Li Gotami for her liveliness and intelligence, as well as for her delightful outspokenness, which at times bordered on the outrageous. Though her religious affiliations were by no means exclusively Buddhist, she knew enough about Buddhism to be able to take a serious interest in the subject and there was, therefore, no question of her being excluded from the lengthy discussions in which Lama Govinda and I soon became involved.

What these discussions were about it would be difficult to say. It was as though in the course of the five days that my two guests spent with me in Kalimpong, as well as the seven days that I spent with them in Ghoom immediately afterwards, Lama Govinda and I ranged over practically the whole field of Buddhist thought and practice. On whatever topic we happened to touch, we found ourselves in agreement to an extent that would have been surprising had we not been familiar with each other's writings and had we not already exchanged ideas in a number of letters. Indeed, as the cloudless autumn days went by, my feeling that we were kindred spirits received more abundant confirmation than I had dared to hope, and I was left in no doubt whatever that despite the fact that he was a married lama and I was a celibate monk I had more in common with Lama Govinda than with any other Buddhist I had ever met.

One of the most important topics on which we touched, and in fact touched more than once, was that of the relation between Buddhism and the spiritual life, on the one hand, and literature and the fine arts, on the other. Besides being a Buddhist by conviction, Lama Govinda was himself an artist and poet of no small repute. He had held exhibitions of his paintings in a number of major Indian cities, and had brought out two small volumes of poetry in his native German.[168] For my part, I had written poetry since the age of 11 or 12, and was even now thinking of putting together some of my more recent poems for publication in book form. A few of these poems had already appeared in the pages of the *Illustrated Weekly of India*, which had financed Lama Govinda's expedition to Tsaparang in Western Tibet and afterwards serialized Li Gotami's account of their experiences, and from the nature of these poems he was well aware that I was no more indifferent to the claims of Beauty than I was to those of Truth or Goodness.

The fact that Lama Govinda and I cultivated literature and the fine arts did not, however, mean that he painted pictures or that I wrote poems *in addition to* doing such specifically Buddhist things as observing the precepts, meditating, studying the Dharma, and giving lectures. For him as for me the painting of pictures and the writing of poems was an integral part of the spiritual life itself. The relation between Buddhism and the spiritual life, on the one hand, and literature and the fine arts, on the other, was not, therefore, one that was merely external, as between different material objects. On the contrary, there was a deep inner connection between them. For this reason there could be no question of the cultivation of literature and the fine arts being inconsistent with the practice of Buddhism and the living of the spiritual life, as I had for a time supposed (or had been led to suppose), much less still of the one being actually inimical to the other. Thanks largely to his intimate acquaintance with Tibetan Buddhist art in all its forms, Lama Govinda's understanding of this important truth was at that time much clearer and more explicit than my own. In particular he had a deep appreciation of the relation between art and meditation. 'Art and meditation are creative states of the human mind,' he had written in a little book on the subject that he afterwards gave me,

> Both are nourished by the same source, but it may seem that they are moving in different directions: art towards the realm of sense-impressions, meditation towards the overcoming of forms and sense-impressions. But the difference pertains only to accidentals, not to the essentials. First of all, meditation does not

mean pure abstraction or negation of form – except in its ultimate illimitable stages – it means the perfect concentration of mind and the elimination of all unessential features of the subject in question until we are fully conscious of it by experiencing reality in a particular aspect or from a particular angle of vision. Art proceeds in a similar way: while using the forms of the external world, it never tries to imitate nature but to reveal a higher reality by omitting all accidentals, thus raising the visible form to the value of a symbol, expressing a direct experience of life. The same experience may be gained by a process of meditation. But instead of creating a formal (objectively existing) expression, it leaves a subjective impression, thus acting as a forming agent on the character or the consciousness of the meditator.[169]

from *Facing Mount Kanchenjunga*

5. BUDDHISM AND WESTERN CULTURE

Just because something is labelled 'Buddhist' does not mean that you can call it an expression or even a part of Buddhist culture.

Can Buddhism be separated from Eastern culture? Well, not only can it be separated; it *must* be separated, or at least distinguished. Buddhism is not Eastern culture, however beautiful Eastern culture may be. Buddhism is not culture at all. The Dharma is not culture. The golden light is not culture. Culture is only the medium. Unfortunately, many Eastern Buddhists, including those who come to the West hoping to teach, do not understand this. Sometimes they think they are preaching the Dharma when they are only propagating their own national culture, and this causes great confusion in the minds of at least some Buddhists in the West.

Second question: Is an acquaintance with Eastern culture necessary to the understanding of Buddhism? Yes and no. Historically, Buddhism has found expression in terms of Eastern culture, and if we want to approach the Dharma we therefore need to have some acquaintance with Eastern culture, at least to begin with. In the *Sūtra of Golden Light*, for example, the Dharma is expressed very much in terms of Indian culture, so that unless one has some understanding of Indian culture, the message of the *sūtra* remains more or less inaccessible. An acquaintance with Eastern culture can be dispensed with only if one is in personal contact with a spiritual teacher who does not have to rely on Eastern culture as a medium of communication.

There is, I think, very little purely 'Buddhist' culture. In my view there are very few cultural forms or artefacts which can be said purely to express the spirit of Buddhism. Just because something is labelled 'Buddhist' does not mean that you can call it an expression or even a part of Buddhist culture. At the same time you need, generally speaking, a cultural context of some kind for the practice of Buddhism. So, although a Western Buddhist practising in the West does not have to adopt Eastern culture in principle, until Western Buddhist cultural equivalents have emerged we shall have to use or adapt some elements of Eastern Buddhist culture, for instance in such matters as robes, style of chanting, and iconography. In the East it is probably best for the Western Buddhist to conform completely to the local Buddhist culture – while being careful not to mistake that culture for the Dharma. However, it is becoming less and less necessary for the Western Buddhist to go East at all. Now we have everything we need at home.

Third question – and this is quite a complex one: how can Western culture place itself at the service of Buddhism? Western Buddhists can at least make a start by establishing points of contact with great artists, and other great Western creative figures, who, at least at times and to a limited extent, have made some approach to the Dharma: people like Goethe, Schopenhauer, Nietzsche, Blake, Wordsworth, and even D. H. Lawrence. I certainly hope that one day a Western Buddhist culture will be developed, and there are signs that beginnings are being made. But you can only really hope to create a Western Buddhist culture if you are deeply imbued with the spirit of Buddhism. In a sense, Buddhism comes first and Buddhist culture follows. However, it can work the other way round as well. Involvement with culture in the best sense helps to refine the emotions, and the refinement of the emotions is important, even essential, for one's spiritual development as an individual. The practice of Buddhism and the development of Buddhist culture must go together.

from *Transforming Self and World*

6. THE DHARMA IN WESTERN POETRY

In explaining a poem ... I was in fact teaching Buddhism.

We studied each poem word by word and line by line, appreciating the appropriateness of an adjective and exploring the implications of a metaphor or simile, yet trying at the same time not to lose sight of the poem as a whole. Nor was that all. Whether it was a poem by Wordsworth, or Keats, or Shelley, or any other poet, as winter gave way to spring and bamboo orchids were succeeded, in the garden of the Hermitage, by camellias and gardenias, Sachin and I (Sachin was a Nepali student to whom I gave tuition in Kalimpong) went through each poem not once but many times and I dictated to him not paraphrases – one cannot really paraphrase a poem – but extensive critical notes. The greater the number of times we went through a poem the more deeply we were able to penetrate into its meaning – a meaning that seemed, in the case of some poems, to coincide with the meaning of Buddhism itself. Once again I realized what I had first realized three years earlier, namely, that in explaining a poem – a poem such as Shelley's 'The Cloud' or one of Keats's Odes – I was in fact teaching Buddhism, especially when I was explaining it to, or studying it with, a dear friend. It was therefore not surprising that at the time when Sachin and I were together going through the poetry selection that he was studying for his exams that I should have been impressed by Rilke's idea that poetry is not *about* existence but *is*, itself, a new kind of existence, or that I should have thought of writing an article on what I called 'the metaphorical nature of reality', as well as an article on the Buddhist element in the plays of Sophocles. (Next to Yeats, Rilke was my favourite poet at this time, and Sophocles I was rereading with great enjoyment after a lapse of some years.) Neither of the two projected articles was ever actually written, but the kind of ideas I had intended to express in them were henceforth to be a permanent part of my thinking.

from *Facing Mount Kanchenjunga*

7. STRETCHING THE MIND THROUGH ART

Time and again the literalness and abstractness of philosophic and religious terminology introduce confusions which vitiate the spiritual strivings of humanity.

In his book *The Meaning of Art*, Herbert Read says that 'art *stretches* the mind'. How difficult it would be to find a more appropriate verb! It connotes a continuity, and, at the same time, a progressive development, of experience through higher and higher levels of subtilization not suggested by cruder and more abstract terms such as 'transcend', or even by concrete ones like 'overstep' and 'pass beyond', all of which imply that the mind is somehow lifted up bodily over the 'limits of the rational', like a small boy over a fence, and dumped down safely on the other side. The rational is not external to the mind, but is the mind itself at one stage of its development, and to transcend the rational does not mean to transfer the mind unchanged from the rational to the super-rational plane (such transferrals are possible only for physical bodies), but to continue changing it until a complete transformation takes place and it enters the super-rational stage of its development by becoming itself super-rational.

Time and again the literalness and abstractness of philosophic and religious terminology introduce confusions which vitiate the spiritual strivings of humanity. Most of these confusions, like that from which Herbert Read saves himself by speaking of stretching the mind, arise from the misconception that the mind, or soul, or whatever else it may be called, is not a flux, a process – a *santāna*, as the expressive Pāli word has it – in a state of continuous change and development, but an inert, unchanging *thing* subject only to external changes of time and place, and therefore differing from a stone in no observable particular. From this fatal misconception, which is in fact the rationalization of ordinary human egoism, the Religion of Art, no less than other forms of spiritual culture, promises to deliver us. If within the sphere of art itself the delusion that the mind is an immutable non-material 'substance' arises, the possibility of transforming the mind through art is precluded, and works of art are regarded not as engines of delight but solely as instruments of selfish pleasure, with the consequence that the pseudo-aesthetic life depicted by Tennyson in 'The Palace of Art', together with the ruin which inevitably overtakes such a life, of necessity ensues in place of the train of lofty consequences set in motion by the Religion of Art.

We should do well, therefore, to think of the function of art as being quite literally to stretch the mind (the implied comparison with a piece of elastic is far less objectionable than a covert comparison with a stone) further than the limits of its own rationality into the 'distance beyond' of Beauty, as this will enable us to see more clearly in what consists the value of the Religion of Art to its average devotee. Works of art are valuable to him because they stretch his mind. Usually, his mind is stiff and unyieldingly rigid; changes take place in it, but there is no development. The egoistic pattern of his life remains the same, though the elements composing it may vary from time to time. To a 'tough' mind like this, conventional religion nowadays often appeals in vain. Tug and pull as she may, it stubbornly refuses to be stretched or, even if she does succeed in stretching it for just a fraction of an inch, the minute her grip is relaxed it flies back to its former position more obstinately than ever. Then along comes the artist. Gently, very gently, he takes hold of the reluctant mind; slowly, oh so slowly, he starts drawing it out of itself, caressing and coaxing it all the time. Then, little by little, with infinite patience and inexorable firmness, he stretches and stretches it until it passes, no longer coarse and thick but delicate as the thread of a spider's web, over the limits of selfhood into that realm of selflessness which is the homeland of true art no less than of true religion.

At first the mind shrinks from the artist's touch; but it soon discovers that to be stretched is, after all, not such an unpleasant experience as it had supposed. Eventually, the experience becomes a positive delight, dearer, perhaps, and more rewarding, than any hitherto known. The spiritual life claims another devotee. So irresistible are the charms of Art. As Irwin Edman has written, 'Values translated into immediately loved images have a powerful suasion on the imagination.'[170] A single smile of Beauty can bring about greater transformations of character than all the frowns of Righteousness.

from *The Religion of Art*

8. GOING TO COVENT GARDEN

We must have been an odd-looking pair. The first time we made our way to the Royal Opera House, through Covent Garden market, one of the porters called out to his companion, with true cockney wit, 'Look, mate, 'ere comes Julius Caesar and Cleopatra!'

As a teenager I had been passionately fond of music, and had listened to symphony concerts on the radio whenever I had the opportunity. For me music was not the brandy of the damned but the ambrosia of the blessed, and swept me up to heights of ecstasy in a way that even poetry could not do.[171] In India I was rarely able to listen to music – that is, Western classical music. Such music was not easy to come by, and in any case, as a (Theravādin) Buddhist monk I was expected to observe the rule of abstaining from 'dance, song, instrumental music, and improper shows'. This rule I had long understood as applying only to music of the cruder and more vulgar kind, such as must have been no less popular in the Buddha's day than it is in our own, and I was therefore able to listen to Mozart and the rest of my – and Terry's – favourites with a clear conscience. The School of Philosophy, which Terry had recently left, indeed regarded the music of Mozart, in particular, as having a positive, spiritualizing effect on the mind.

What the 'School' thought of Wagner I do not know. The composer was by no means a favourite of mine, though as a teenager I had enjoyed the overtures to *Lohengrin* and *Tannhäuser*, but when a member of the Sangha Association offered, that autumn, to take me to see all four constituent parts of *The Ring* cycle at Covent Garden I was glad to accept.[172] Wendy was a tall, angular woman of thirty or thereabouts who worked at Coutts in the Strand and was a keen practitioner of judo. Her angularity was not only physical but mental. There were all sorts of sharp corners and edges to her personality, and while she could be warm-hearted and generous (as her offer to me demonstrated) she was morbidly quick to take offence and was, in truth, of so prickly, indeed so spiky, a disposition, and so extremely sharp-tongued, that I called her – to her great amusement and delight – Kūṭadanta or 'Sharp Tooth', after an old brahmin mentioned in the Pāli scriptures.[173] Had I then been as familiar with modern psychology and its jargon as I afterwards became, I would probably have said that Wendy-Kūṭadanta found it difficult to accept herself as a woman (in India the women had appeared to experience no such difficulty). She certainly resented being treated as a woman, and the fact that I accepted her offer to take me to see *The Ring* cycle pleased her immensely, for since monks were not supposed to go out and about with women my acceptance meant I was not treating her as a mere woman but as a man. So pleased was she that she dressed for our opera-going in a striking, Chinese-style outfit of yellow satin, heavily embroidered, which besides giving her a distinctly oriental look made her appear much more feminine. I of course had on, over my robes, the long fawn-coloured cloak I always wore outside the Vihara. We must have been an odd-looking pair. The first time we made our way to the Royal Opera House, through Covent Garden market, one of the porters called out to his companion, with true cockney wit, 'Look, mate, 'ere comes Julius Caesar and Cleopatra!' Neither of us could help laughing, and Wendy, strange to relate, seemed not at all displeased to think that she looked like the royal Egyptian *femme fatale*. As for me, for a moment it was as though Caesar's laurel wreath encircled my brow.

from *Moving Against the Stream*

3
THE CREATIVE LIFE

1. AFTER RILKE

    The poet is the world's interpreter,
    At least to his own self. He recreates
    In his own heart the things he contemplates,
    And brings them forth transformed from what they were
    Into a beauty-truth that cannot err,
    That cannot fade or die. Though dull ingrates
    May mock, no vile disparagement abates
    The benefits the poet's words confer.

    A tree is not a tree, unless within
    The poet's all-transmuting mind it grows
    Refined, reborn, – by his own power redeemed
    Into a truer life. The poet's kin
    Are Memnon, Orpheus, Merlin. History shows
    The best but live what once the poet dreamed.

from *Complete Poems*

2. THE ARISING OF THE POETIC STATE

Whatever I allowed my mind to rest on became a poem.

Whether because of the more relaxed routine that I was still following, or on account of the peace and silence with which the retreat was increasingly pervading the house, I felt my more 'creative' energies beginning to rise to the surface, displacing – to some extent – the 'executive' energies. Indeed, as the retreat, and the year 1979, started coming to an end, and as the Christmas season stole upon us, I found myself in a more strongly, and more exclusively, 'poetic' mood than I had known for quite a number of years.

It is difficult to describe this mood, which lasted for several weeks. First of all came a period of 'silence', both internal and external, during which there were no objective demands made upon me and no 'needs' to meet. This meant that I could allow the responses that usually arise in connection with such demands and needs to die down, so that whatever mental processes then went on were, on the whole, self-originating. Next, out of the silence, which was also a kind of creative rest, there arose a certain rhythm, or a poem without words – a poem that went on and on, without interruption. This rhythm, or wordless poem, seemed to blend with whatever I saw, or rather, with whatever it was to which I directed my attention, or on which I allowed my mind to dwell. It could blend with it because, whether it was a natural object like a tree, a realm of existence, or a figure from ancient Egyptian mythology, its rhythm was the same as the rhythm that had arisen out of my own silence, my own creative rest. As they blended, the two rhythms gave birth to words, words which were descriptive of the particular object on which I had allowed my mind to dwell and which formed, in some cases, complete poems, in others, only fragments of poems – perhaps a line or a couplet. At one stage it was as though the rhythm that arose within me was the same as, or at least in accordance with, the rhythm that arose within the depths of external nature and found expression in trees, flowers, houses, and human beings – in the whole objective order of existence. Whatever I allowed my mind to rest on became a poem, just as whatever Midas touched turned to gold. The whole world was material for poetry. In fact, the whole world was a poem. It was a poem, to the extent that the 'observer' was a poet.

I recollected that, when I was in my teens, I used to remain in this kind of 'poetic' state for months on end: it was my normal state. In that state, it was far easier for me to write poetry than not write it, and I wrote hundreds of poems. (The nature of the process, of course, tells us nothing about the value of the end result, i.e. the poem, considered from a purely 'artistic' point of view.) On this occasion, even, I managed to produce a couple of dozen poems, more than I had written in the previous half dozen years, though not all of them were as easy to produce as the account I have given might suggest. At any rate, I did produce a handful of poems, among them six sonnets on the six realms of sentient existence – one sonnet for each realm.[174] Reflecting on the whole episode afterwards, I came to the conclusion that the 'poetic' state of mind is, as I had sometimes felt before, a state in which the subject assimilates the object in such a way that the duality between them is to some extent mitigated and that this mitigated duality finds expression in the 'poem', or work of art generally, which is both subject and object, or in which the subject–object duality finds expression on a higher, more refined level. Poetry is thus the mediator between the 'real' and the 'Ideal', the mundane and the Transcendental: it is the angel; it is the *deva*; it is the archetype.

from *Travel Letters*

3. ENTERING A SPIRITUAL DIMENSION THROUGH WRITING

Concentration, truthfulness,... and self-knowledge are all entrances to a spiritual dimension or realm, and as writing ... can involve all three, writing itself can be an entrance to that dimension.

The request to write on the theme of 'What is your entrance/access to a spiritual dimension/realm' did not evoke an immediate response. As a Buddhist, my principal 'entrance' to the dimension or realm in question has been through Buddhism or, perhaps I should say, through being a Buddhist, in the sense of being one who goes for Refuge to the Three Jewels: the Buddha or perfectly Enlightened teacher, the Dharma or principial means to Enlightenment, and the Sangha or spiritual community of all Buddhists, past, present, and future. Basically, my 'entrance' has been the act of Going for Refuge, as that deepens from provisional to effective Going for Refuge, and from effective to real.

Nonetheless, the theme on which I had been invited to write must have remained at the back of my mind, for two days ago I had a kind of *eureka* experience, as it may be called. The thought struck me that besides Buddhism and Going for Refuge I had another entrance to a spiritual dimension – an entrance which had in fact been under my nose all the time and on which it might be possible for me to offer a few reflections. This other entrance was the experience of writing – the experience of transferring ideas and emotions to the written and, eventually, the printed page.

After all, writing had long been an important part of my life. Over the years I must have spent thousands of hours at my desk, and the written and printed word had been, with the spoken word, the principal means by which I had communicated the Dharma – the Buddha's teaching – to hundreds of thousands of people in both the East and the West. Let me, therefore, try to explain how it is that, for me, writing is an entrance or access to a spiritual dimension or realm.

Before that, I would like to explain what I understand by spiritual, as well as by dimensions or realms. Though the word 'spiritual' is widely used, its meaning is not very clear. According to the dictionary it means, primarily, 'relating to the spirit or soul and not to physical nature or matter; intangible'. This leaves us none the wiser, as we are not informed what the spirit or soul (apparently the two terms are synonymous) is in itself. In my own usage, standardized over many years, the word 'spiritual' has two meanings, one narrower than the other. In its narrower sense, 'spiritual' corresponds to the Buddhist term *kuśala*, literally, skilful (sometimes translated as 'wholesome') which means characterized by the mental states of freedom from craving, freedom from aversion, and freedom from delusion or, more positively, by contentment, (non-erotic) love, and wisdom. Thus the spiritual life is a life devoted to the cultivation of such states, a spiritual practice one that conduces to their development, and a spiritual teaching one that is concerned with them either theoretically or practically or both.

In its broader sense 'spiritual' corresponds, in my personal usage, not only to the term *kuśala* but also to the still more important term *lokuttara*, literally, '(the) beyond-world' or, as we may say, the transcendental or nirvāṇic. When the word spiritual is taken in this broader sense, the spiritual life is one that is devoted not only to the cultivation of skilful mental states but also to the attainment of the transcendental or nirvāṇic state. For Buddhism it is axiomatic that there is no attainment of the transcendental or nirvāṇic state except on the basis of a mind dominated by the skilful mental states of freedom from craving, freedom from aversion, and freedom from delusion.

In what way, then, does writing, for me, constitute an entrance into a spiritual dimension or realm? Nowadays a distinction is often made, at least implicitly, between 'creative writing', as it is called, and writing that is not creative. I doubt very much if the distinction is a hard and fast one. Creative writing does not form a distinct genre, as a piece of writing in any genre may be either creative or non-creative. Nonetheless certain genres undeniably give greater scope to pure creativity than do others. Such, for example, are the poem, the novel and short story, and the drama. Others, like the scientific treatise and the business letter, give it minimal scope. As for genres such as history and biography (including autobiography and memoirs), these come somewhere in the middle, for though all are concerned with facts the author has a good deal of freedom in the arrangement and presentation of those facts. Here I shall draw principally on my experience of writing my most recent volume of memoirs, an experience which lasted, on and off, for three years.

In the first place, writing involves concentration. By concentration I do not mean the forcible fixation of one's attention on a single object but, rather, the gradual mobilization of one's energies around a single point, which for me as a writer is the point where pen meets paper and inner experience is transformed into outer expression. My usual practice is to write in the morning, starting immediately after breakfast. Especially when I have been writing daily for several weeks, I find that I become concentrated as soon as I sit down at my desk and take up my pen, or rather my biro, having not yet succumbed to the blandishments of modern technology in the form of the word processor.

Here there is a definite parallel with my experience as a meditator, for especially when I have been meditating regularly I find, more often than not, that I become concentrated as soon as I sit down on my cushion, cross my legs, and close my eyes. The parallelism illustrates the fact that writing, like meditation, is able to form an entrance to a spiritual dimension by virtue of the element of concentration it involves, though it should be emphasized that for writing, as for meditation, the concentration in question is 'skilful' concentration, i.e. concentration that is associated with the mental states of freedom from craving, freedom from aversion, and freedom from delusion. The writing of a pornographic novel, for instance, would not be an entrance to a spiritual dimension inasmuch as the concentration involved would be associated with unskilful mental states.

My life has consisted of a series of incidents and experiences, and writing my memoirs means writing about these incidents and experiences. But first they have to be recalled. This I do not find too difficult, at least in certain respects; for instance I have a good visual memory, and can recall the way certain people and places looked, even though I saw them forty and more years ago. What I cannot recall so easily are conversations. I can recall the substance of what was said, whether by myself or others, but very rarely can I recall the actual words that were spoken, much less still a whole series of verbal exchanges. My memoirs therefore contain no conversations, which from a purely literary point of view is a serious defect. On the few occasions when I do place my own or another person's remarks within quotation marks the reader may be sure that the words quoted were spoken exactly as given, and that I must have remembered them because they made a deep impression on me at the time.

Autobiographies and memoirs often contain conversations. A few of them consist of little else. In some cases the author may have had a good memory for conversation, or have made notes or kept a diary; in others, I suspect, he or she simply invented the conversations and dialogue, thus doing with real life characters what the novelist does with imaginary ones. In writing my own memoirs I was determined to include nothing that was not factual even if that meant leaving some unsightly gaps in my narrative. I was determined not to usurp the function of the novelist. With regard to each incident and experience I asked myself, 'What actually happened?' and only when this was clear did I describe it. In other words I was concerned that my memoirs should be strictly truthful, and truthfulness is an entrance to a spiritual dimension. Certainly there can be no entry to such a dimension without it.

But truth is subjective as well as objective. One can be truthful not only with regard to outer events but also with regard to inner feelings. In writing my memoirs I therefore had to ask myself not only what actually happened, but also what I actually felt on a particular occasion, or in a certain situation. Sometimes this was obvious. Sometimes, however, it was not, and I had to recall the occasion or situation in detail, dwell upon it, and coax forth into present consciousness the feeling I had then experienced. Only when I had done this did I seek to describe the feeling.

Occasionally it so happened that I was able to coax forth feelings of which I had not been fully cognisant at the time or to which I had been unwilling to admit. For example, I saw that there were occasions when my real feeling had not been just one of mild annoyance, as I then thought, but actually one of anger. I was also able to see more deeply into the motives that had led me to adopt a particular course of action or behave in a certain way. I saw how I had missed opportunities and failed to take full advantage of favourable circumstances. All this meant that in writing my memoirs I got to know myself better, at least as I had been in the past; and that self-knowledge is a means of entrance to a spiritual dimension there can be little doubt.

As I described incidents and experiences, seeking to ascertain feelings and exploring motives, and as I got to know my past self better, I began to see my life more as a whole or at least to see more as a whole the part of it covered by my third volume of memoirs. Seeing it as a whole I was able to see it more objectively and, in a way, even to distance myself from it. Distancing myself from it I could see how one thing had led to another and how in dependence on events which were, in themselves, seemingly insignificant, there had arisen others that were of considerable importance.

In a word I saw my life as conditioned, and to the extent that one truly sees the conditioned as conditioned one is free from the conditioned, in the sense of being free from attachment to it, and has access to the Unconditioned. The Unconditioned being synonymous with the spiritual in the broader sense of the term, seeing one's life as a whole and as wholly conditioned is an entrance to a spiritual dimension. Not that one can see one's life as a whole only if one writes an autobiography or memoirs, or that writing these will necessarily enable one to see one's life as a whole and as conditioned, but writing them certainly enables one to focus on one's life in a sustained and systematic way that otherwise is hardly possible outside meditation.

Concentration, truthfulness both objective and subjective, and self-knowledge are all entrances to a spiritual dimension or realm, and as writing, including the (semi-creative) writing of memoirs, can involve all three, writing itself can be an entrance to that dimension. I for one have certainly found it to be so.

from *Dharma Life*

4. A CREATIVE RELATIONSHIP WITH THE WORLD

Creativity is not limited to the exercise of the fine arts; everyone is creative.

One often hears people saying – sometimes apologetically, sometimes defiantly, sometimes wistfully, sometimes ironically – 'I'm not very creative.' What they usually mean by this is that they cannot paint pictures, write poetry, compose music, or throw pots. Artistic creativity seems to be in vogue these days; everyone is supposed to be creative. But what do we mean by being creative? Is it just a matter of being able to paint pictures?

Creativity involves a distinction between subject and object. On the one hand there is you, the artist; on the other, the material out of which you create your work of art, as well as the 'idea' in accordance with which you create it, an idea that may be more or less conscious. And the 'material' out of which the artist creates may be of several kinds. There's the obvious physical stuff out of which a work is made – clay, paint, sound, language, or whatever. Then there's the involvement of the artist's own person: the voice, the physical body, the mental and emotional states. And other people also become 'artistic material', either as merely passive material for the artist's creativity (like a sculptor's model), or actively cooperating with it, themselves creative in relation to the artist's creativity (like an orchestra or a cast of actors). In the latter case, there is no absolute distinction between the artist and the 'material' – the people – from which they create.

Generally we experience ourselves as subjects in relation to the 'object' of the whole external world in the broadest sense. But we are not passive in relation to the external world. We do not merely register impressions. The world impinges on us, and we also impinge on the world, on our own environment, or a part of it. We impinge on our own selves, on ourselves considered as objects to ourselves (that is, considered reflexively), and we also impinge on other people. Not only do we impinge on the world; we affect it in various ways. We alter it, we arrange it, we *re*-arrange it – at least to some extent, however slight. And not only that. There is a pattern to the way in which we impinge on the world. We don't impinge on it at random, but in accordance with a certain idea, a certain pattern, image, gestalt, or myth, within ourselves – even, we could say, a pattern which *is* ourselves.

It is rare for us consciously to realize this, but what it means is that our relationship with the world is essentially creative. We are creating all the time. Creativity is not limited to the exercise of the fine arts; everyone is creative. It is only a question of the quality of our creativity – greater or lesser success, greater or lesser clarity, greater or lesser positivity. We are creative when we speak, when we decorate a room, when we write a letter. This is the basic principle of what we may call 'applied Zen' – Zen applied to the art of living itself.

from *The Inconceivable Emancipation*

5. SHOULD BUDDHISTS HAVE A SENSE OF HUMOUR?

It is important to cultivate a sense of proportion with regard to oneself and one's own achievements and affairs.

It has been said that to worldly people, 'spiritual' people appear frivolous because they don't care about the things that matter to worldly people. If you are spiritually-minded and you lose something, or you are not given something you were expecting, you tend to take it quite lightly, whereas a more worldly-minded person would take it very seriously indeed. In the same way, the spiritually-minded person regards as a joke things that worldly people don't find at all funny, because he or she has a greater sense of proportion. It has been said that one of the elements of humour is a sense of proportion, a sense of relative fitness. For instance, one might see a politician delivering a speech so pompously and with such self-importance that one can't help laughing, because one can see that he is not as important as he thinks he is, or as he is trying to appear.

According to the Pāli canon, the Buddha did say on one occasion that to laugh in such a way as to show the teeth is to be mad,[175] but perhaps one shouldn't take this too literally. Perhaps he was thinking of uncontrollable laughter – just abandoning oneself to it, throwing oneself around and laughing in a raucous, crude, unmindful way. The Buddha himself is almost always represented with a gentle smile; and even the Abhidharma – and you can't get much more austere than that – lists 'the smile of the *arhant*' among its classifications.[176] So the Abhidharma itself has a place for something like *līlā*, something spontaneous, just for its own sake – for the smile of the *arhant* is said to be without karmic significance. Perhaps the Buddha's smile arises from his perception of the incongruity between the conditioned and the Unconditioned; or perhaps he smiles a little at the mess unenlightened human beings get themselves into, though at the same time he responds to them with deep compassion.

Does a sense of humour have a part to play in the life of a Buddhist? Here one has to be very careful. Humour is often negative, and sometimes cruel, even sadistic or cynical. Cynicism can represent a fear of positive emotion, including one's own positive emotion, and a fear of being taken in; and sometimes it can be a more or less refined expression of basic negativity and anger. People are often unaware of this; it can be interesting to examine more closely the things that one finds oneself laughing at. There is also a certain style of humour that goes with one's nationality; one needs to be aware that what one thinks is funny may be simply unintelligible to people from another culture.

But humour can be a good thing. Freud speaks of wit in terms of energy release;[177] sometimes if you really let yourself go, notwithstanding the Buddha's dim view of extravagant laughter, innocent merriment can have an energizing and freeing effect. At its most innocent, humour has to do with not taking oneself too seriously. It is easy to fall into an attitude of regarding some trivial aspect of one's own life or work as being of world-shattering importance. It is important to cultivate a sense of proportion with regard to oneself and one's own achievements and affairs. You need be no less serious or hard-working, but you won't be taking yourself seriously in that self-absorbed, egoistic way.

This idea of spiritual life as a playful bubbling up of transcendental energy is a prominent feature in Indian thought and religious life. Some people take religion very seriously, even to the extent of feeling that it is somehow blasphemous to laugh in church – but the bodhisattva's life isn't like that. It's a game, a play, a sport. That is, it is an end in itself, uncalculating, natural, and enjoyable.

from *The Bodhisattva Ideal*

6. THE PLAYFUL ARTS

You haven't come into existence after all these millions of years of evolution just to sit down in front of a typewriter, or to keep accounts.

The difference between work and play is that play is not necessary. It is not harnessed to any goal; it serves no purpose. In Sanskrit the fine arts are called *lalitakalā*, the 'playful arts', because they're of no earthly use. You can live without the arts: no one ever dropped dead from lack of art. It is quite superfluous – which is why it's so necessary. Likewise, the bodhisattva's life – the life that is depicted in the Prajñāpāramitā – is behovely because it is the useless life. All that meditation and study and right livelihood culminates in the experience of being happy just being yourself, with nothing in particular to do. You might just be dancing around the room, aimlessly, unselfconsciously – not trying to be playful or spontaneous, but just being yourself. Some busybody will then turn up, of course, and say, 'Come on, what are you wasting your time like that for? There's work to get on with.' But that's putting the cart before the horse (or rather, harnessing the horse to the cart).

Someone came to me once and said that he did not feel that he could be very useful because he had no particular talent. I told him, 'Think of yourself as an unspecialized human being.' People think that if they can't make themselves useful in some way – they can't type, they can't keep accounts, they can't cook, they can't write or give a talk or paint or play a musical instrument – there's something wrong with them. But consider: this apparently useless human being is the product of millions upon millions of years of evolution. You are the goal; you are what it has all been for. You don't have to justify your existence by being useful. You yourself are the justification for your existence. You haven't come into existence after all these millions of years of evolution just to sit down in front of a typewriter, or to keep accounts. *You* are the justification of that whole process. You are an end in yourself. All that you can really be said to be here for is to develop into some higher form of human life – to become a bodhisattva, to become a Buddha. So don't be ashamed of sitting around and doing nothing. Glory in it. Do things spontaneously, out of a state of inner satisfaction and achievement. It is a virtue to be ornamental as well as useful.

If you take this seriously, you have to be watchful for people trying to work on your feelings of guilt. How can you be spontaneous if you're riddled with guilt? So don't let people get at you with any kind of emotional blackmail. If someone starts saying to you, 'Look how hard I'm working for the Dharma! Don't you feel bad just sitting there doing nothing, letting me do it all?' you should just say, 'No, I feel fine. I'm really enjoying watching you do it all.' It is important not to give in to this sort of emotional arm-twisting; it is highly unskilful, appealing to negative emotions in order to get things done instead of arousing an enthusiasm to work for the joy of it. Don't take your Buddhist activities too earnestly. I am not advocating irresponsible frivolity or a frittering away of energy in unmindful hilarity. But even while you are doing your best to succeed at whatever you are doing, remember that you are essentially at play – and you don't lose sleep over a game; it isn't worth it. Being serious doesn't mean being solemn, just as practising puja in front of a shrine does not call for long faces and a 'dim religious light'.[178]

There is something further to take into account when we look at the spirit in which we approach Dharmic activities: the question of psychological types or temperaments. For example, there are people who are 'organized', and there are others who are 'non-organized'. Organized types tend to do the organizing, and non-organized types are the people the organized types organize, often whether the non-organized like it or not. But just because you don't function in that organized way, it doesn't necessarily mean that you are lazy or less committed, or even that you are doing less than those who *are* organized. It is possible to function positively and creatively and energetically in a way that is anathema to the organized type.

Unfortunately, any kind of collective Buddhist activity nearly always caters for those who like being organized – and those with the opposite sort of temperament tend to get roped in willy-nilly. But why not cater for the non-organized person occasionally? Why not a have a non-organized retreat, with no programme to it at all? Call it a 'Dharma holiday' – all the retreat facilities would be there, but it would be up to you how you went about benefiting from them. Some people might want to get together, elect a leader, and organize a programme, but others would go their own way and still have a very productive retreat. Some might even decide – in the most mindful, objective, responsible, and positive way – that the best thing to do with this Dharma holiday would be to get up late and sit in the garden doing nothing. For some people this could be quite a challenge; even on a retreat it is possible to fill up the day with useful activities in such a way as to lose sight of the greater mandala.

The bodhisattva has resolved this opposition or antithesis between aesthetic contemplation on the one hand and practical activity on the other, and feels no conflict. But so long as we have to switch over from the one to the other, and so long as the presence or experience of the one implies the absence or non-experience of the other, there will always be some difficulty in the transition. All we can do is somehow try to carry the aesthetic experience into the practical activity – which is exactly what the bodhisattva does, as represented in the Perfection of Wisdom – a very difficult process. We can make a start by adopting a more light-hearted attitude towards practical things. By all means be useful, but only within the much larger context of complete uselessness. Taoism is quite good on this whole theme. Taoists say that the man of Tao is like a great tree, which is so big that it is good for nothing – the branches are too thick for making axe-handles, and so on.[179] One should try to be too big to be useful. However important the work a bodhisattva does, he or she sees, in the Perfection of Wisdom, that it takes place in a tiny circle within the greater mandala of quite pointless appreciation.

from *Wisdom Beyond Words*

4
A 'BUDDHIST BIBLE'? – BUDDHIST SCRIPTURES AND WHERE THEY COME FROM

1. THE SEA OF BUDDHIST LITERATURE

The essence of the Dharma is not a limited quantity which becomes diluted, as it were, with each successive addition to Buddhist literature.

It is true that Buddhist literature is a sea, and we freely admit that none save the most laborious scholars will ever be able to wade through the oceanic extent of all the Buddhist books in Sanskrit, Pāli, Tibetan, Chinese, and Japanese. We emphatically deny, however, that it is necessary for the ordinary Buddhist even to attempt such a feat. Far from there being any need for a person who wants to know the essence of Buddhism to study whole libraries of volumes, all that such an enquirer has to do is to understand and thoroughly assimilate a single one out of the numerous chapters or even verses, into which that essence has been concentrated.

For the essence of the Dharma is not a strictly limited quantity which becomes diluted, as it were, with each successive addition to Buddhist literature (as a small amount of milk might be diluted by liberal additions of water), so that one who wishes to know it has to master an ever increasing number of books. Such a way of thinking is an example of the fantastic literalness into which a purely rational and 'practical' intelligence may sometimes be betrayed. If any comparison were needed, the essence of Buddhism might be more fittingly, though still imperfectly, represented by the flame of a lamp, which is able to kindle the flames of other lamps without the least diminution of its own brilliance.

A contributory source of the erroneous notion that a Buddhist ought to make himself acquainted with the whole enormous bulk of Buddhist sacred literature is to be found, perhaps, in the Protestant Christian belief that, since the Bible is the Word of God, the believer should acquaint himself with every single word of it, as ignorance of a single letter, even, might prejudice his chance of salvation.

It is hardly necessary to point out how utterly foreign such conceptions are to Buddhism, or to emphasize how serious is the mistake of trying to import them into it. The fundamental principles of the Dharma are few in number, and these can be explained in a very few pages well enough for most practical purposes. The multiplicity of Buddhist scriptures is due to the desire of generations of writers to elaborate these principles to the furthest possible extent, to pursue their implications into the remotest fields of thought and, above all else, to their eagerness to adapt them to the understanding and temperament of inconceivably numerous classes of sentient beings – an eagerness which has its origin in Compassion, in the aspiration that every birth-and-death-doomed creature should one day open the Door of the Immortal.

from *Crossing the Stream*

2. THE ORIGIN OF THE BUDDHIST SCRIPTURES

The words 'Thus have I heard', with which almost every Buddhist scripture begins, represent Ānanda's personal testimony that what follows is a reliable account of what the Enlightened One actually said.

The Buddha himself, the historical Śākyamuni, never wrote anything. It's not even certain that he *could* read and write at all. In his day, writing was not a very respectable occupation. Businessmen used it for keeping their accounts, but the idea of committing anything as sacred as spiritual teachings to writing was simply unthinkable. The Buddha taught, therefore, not by writing spiritual best-sellers, but by talking to people, passing on his teachings through conversation, discussions, and discourses. For their part, his disciples made a point of remembering what he said. Sometimes, indeed, his words were so memorable that no one within earshot could possibly forget them. But even if some disciples did forget, there were others who remembered and in due course passed on the teachings they had heard to their own disciples. In this way the Buddha's teaching was orally transmitted in India for many, many generations, spanning hundreds of years.

Not only did the early disciples remember hundreds and thousands of teachings, they also managed to arrange, edit, and even index them orally, without even beginning to put pen to paper – or rather stylus to palm leaf: surely a tremendous feat. The key figure in this whole extraordinary process was Ānanda, who was the Buddha's cousin and his constant companion for the last twenty years of his life. Wherever the Buddha went, Ānanda went. If the Buddha went for alms, Ānanda would be just a few paces behind him. If the Buddha accepted an invitation, Ānanda was naturally included. And if the Buddha gave a discourse, Ānanda was present in the audience. For twenty years the Buddha was very rarely to be seen without Ānanda in tow, committing everything his master said to a prodigiously retentive memory.

I must confess to having harboured doubts about Ānanda's superhuman memory, until I actually met someone with comparable powers of recollection: a man who could remember everything he had ever heard me say word for word – together with where I had said it, when, and even why I had said it. This was enough to satisfy me that such an individual as Ānanda is unusual, but no chimera.

It was shortly after the Buddha's death – his *parinirvāṇa* – that Ānanda's gift really came into its own. This was when the Buddha's followers gathered together in a great cave near Rājagṛha in modern Bihar for the purpose of what has since become known as the First Council. But this name for it comes nowhere near evoking the true nature of the occasion. The Sanskrit word used to describe this gathering is *saṅgīti*, which literally means 'a chanting together' or even 'a singing together'. The monks – and there are supposed to have been 500 of them – chanted or sang together whatever they could remember of the Buddha's teaching. The *saṅgīti* was dominated, however, by Ānanda's contribution to what might be called the collective memory of the spiritual community.[180]

So the words 'Thus have I heard', with which almost every Buddhist scripture begins, represent Ānanda's personal testimony that what follows is a reliable account of what the Enlightened One actually said. They mean that Ānanda had been there, or that if he had not been present the Buddha had repeated it all to him afterwards. They are believed to guarantee the authenticity of that text. 'Thus have I heard at one time' is used like a general imprimatur, so to speak, for the content of any scripture.

from *Transforming Self and World*

3. HOW TO READ BUDDHIST TEXTS

Sūtras can be approached as sources of inspiration and enjoyment, not as texts that you have to slog your way through because you happen to be a Buddhist.

The Buddhist scriptures – as we call them in English – do not, like the Bible, constitute some infallible revelation from God. They are a record of the life and teaching of a supremely and perfectly Enlightened human being, a human being who was the living embodiment of absolute wisdom and infinite compassion. Nonetheless, some people probably do read a *sūtra* as though it *were* Holy Writ, and feel that they have no choice but to accept whatever the Buddha says in it, whether they like it or not; and such a projection of authority may create in them some resistance to the *sūtra*'s message.

But if a particular text is not actually labelled a *sūtra*, we can avoid the mistake of regarding it as 'spiritually authoritative'. We can read it, in fact, more or less as we would read any other work of the imagination – a novel, a poem, or a short story. If we can read Buddhist texts as literature rather than dogma, as poetry rather than scientific fact or philosophical truth, we may perhaps be more open to their spiritual message. We may even allow ourselves to be captivated – at least a little – by their atmosphere and their magic. (Conversely – this is just a thought – we might try reading works of imagination as though they were *sūtras*, and in this way open ourselves to their real spiritual content.)

What I am getting at is that *sūtras* can be approached as sources of inspiration and enjoyment, not as texts that you have to slog your way through because you happen to be a Buddhist. You may have to put in some additional study and reflection – it may take some time and many readings to understand a *sūtra* deeply and really appreciate it – but some phrases or images may affect you quite powerfully straight away. It is true that we may well feel more at home with Western literature. Most of it is easier to read because it has been written by unenlightened people like ourselves – with all sorts of little glimmers of insight here and there – and it deals generally with ordinary human predicaments with which we can easily identify. But human frailty is not the only possible subject for literature; it is certainly not always the most inspiring and uplifting one. We can also read literature which takes us away from our ordinary human life and its frailties. And this is what the Mahāyāna *sūtras* are all about – to take us away from the ordinary, to give us a taste of the magical.

Obviously it is difficult to rise to that level of experience, so it's going to be difficult to read *sūtras*, just as it is to read some of the great works of Western literature. Any work of literature has an effect commensurate with the effort one makes to understand it. It is really a matter of getting into the habit of stretching oneself a bit. If you have a strong enough desire to understand, you will make the effort.

from *The Inconceivable Emancipation*

4. BUDDHIST STORIES

Whether told by monk or minstrel, or enacted in dramatic form, the story of Vessantara is as well known to the Tibetan nomad as to the Burmese farmer, and moves both equally to tears.

Humanity has ever loved a story, and the people of India have been, perhaps, even more addicted to this form of entertainment than those of other lands. Dialogues and anthologies could hardly be expected to vie with them in popularity. Quite early in the history of the religion, therefore, the followers of the Buddha lighted, either by design or by accident, on the happy idea of appropriating the entire wealth of ancient Indian folklore, including fables, proverbs, fairy tales, anecdotes, ballads, riddles, humorous stories, jokes, novels, romances, moral narratives, and pious legends, and incorporating them *en bloc* in their own rapidly growing oral-cum-literary tradition as the simplest and most effective means of propagating the truths of the Dharma among the common people. In this way the *Jātakas* and *Avadānas* came into existence.

The stories themselves are of numerous types. Among the animal fables of the first *nipātas*, which contain the shorter *Jātakas*, there are several that parallel those of Aesop – the stories of the ass in a lion's skin; and the jackal who, to get some fruit, praised the crow for her fine voice, are examples. Who borrowed from whom we do not know. The fairy tales, of which there are many genres, include tales of grateful animals and ungrateful human beings, of strange adventures with ghostly women and lovely cannibal demonesses, of superhuman beings of various types, both quaint and monstrous, as well as tales of mystery and magic. Humorous sketches, satires, and tales in which the Bodhisattva, as hero, exhibits his ready wit, good judgement, cleverness, and skill by answering riddles, resolving dilemmas, and accomplishing all kinds of seemingly impossible tasks, are also plentiful. Of great interest from a sociological, and even from a literary, point of view, are the picaresque tales in which robbers, vagabonds, gamesters, and courtesans play the principal roles, as well as the sometimes coarse, but evidently highly popular, stories dealing with all manner of sexual improprieties.

Besides material of this sort, the connection of which with Buddhism is at times obscure, the *Jātaka* book contains, as might be expected, a good number of patently didactic moral tales. Much the greater part of the work, however, especially in its later sections, is taken up by various types of legend. These are often of great beauty. Some of them occur in that ancient Indian epic-cum-encyclopaedia the *Mahābhārata*. They inculcate the old grave moral virtues, such as service to one's parents, truthfulness, and chastity, and teach the impermanence of all worldly things and the happiness of renunciation. These latter themes often feature in the purely Buddhist stories among the *Jātakas*, especially those illustrating the practice of the *pāramitās*. As Winternitz observes, they are characterized by 'exceeding kindness and gentleness, and self-sacrifice transcending by far the bounds of what is natural.'[181] King Sivi sacrifices his eyes (*Jātaka* 499); Prince Kaṇha, renouncing all he possesses, goes to the Himalayas as a hermit (*Jātaka* 440); Khantivādin, the 'Preacher of Patience', remains free from anger even when barbarously mutilated by an enraged potentate (*Jātaka* 313); Prince Vessantara gladly gives away not only the palladium of his father's kingdom but his wife and two young children (*Jātaka* 547). The superiority of the golden rule is also inculcated. In spirit if not in form, some of the tales of grateful or heroically virtuous animals belong to the same category. The monkey-chief, in order to save his retinue, makes himself into a bridge (*Jātaka* 407); the Banyan deer, moved by the plight of the pregnant doe, offers his own life to the king as a ransom for hers (*Jātaka* 12).

Popular as the whole of the *Jātaka* book undoubtedly is, it is the legends of sublime self-abnegation and absolute altruism that have most deeply and decisively influenced the religious outlook of the Buddhist peoples of South-east Asia. So much might be said, indeed, of China, Japan, and Tibet; for, as we are about to see, there exist Sanskrit collections of *Jātakas* which, in translation, are no less familiar to the followers of the Mahāyāna. Whether told by monk or minstrel, or enacted in dramatic form, the story of Vessantara is as well known to the Tibetan nomad as to the Burmese farmer, and moves both equally to tears. Most of the finest Bodhisattva stories are, in fact, the common heritage of the entire Buddhist world, and one of its greatest unifying influences.

from *The Eternal Legacy*

5. THE BIBLE DESIGNED TO BE READ AS LITERATURE

The possibility of fundamentalism exists wherever a canonical literature exists.

In 1940 I was in Torquay, to which I was sent as a teenager to avoid the bombing in London. It was the time when, as a result of reading *Isis Unveiled*, I had realized I was not a Christian.[182] One day, in the window of a bookshop in the main street, I saw a new publication on sale: *The Bible Designed to be Read as Literature*. It was a large, thick volume, and since it lay there open I could see that it was printed like an ordinary book, the text not being divided into the usual numbered verses. At that time the idea that the Bible could be read as literature was comparatively new, at least to the wider reading public. It was certainly new to me. From school and church I had imbibed the idea that the Bible was essentially a repository of texts. Texts lay side by side in the Bible like bullets in a bandolier, and these bullets could be fired off at anyone with whom one happened to be having an argument, whether about religion or about anything else. To quote a text – or texts – from the Bible settled the matter. This kind of attitude still prevails, of course, among fundamentalist Christians of all denominations. But reading the Bible as literature meant, so far as I remember, reading it in much the same way as one would read the works of Shakespeare, and the layout of the volume that I saw in the window of my Torquay bookshop was intended to facilitate this process. It was intended to encourage one to think of the Bible as a book rather than as a collection of bullets, and to approach it accordingly. Thus *The Bible Designed to be Read as Literature* was the Bible designed to be read for enjoyment. It was the Bible designed to be read as a whole – or rather as a series of wholes – rather than as chopped up into bits in the form of numbered 'verses'. It was the Bible designed to be read, in the case of some of its books, as poetry rather than as prose. It was the Bible designed to be read for its own sake rather than for the sake of some ulterior purpose. To the fundamentalist, reading the Bible in this way was irreverent, even blasphemous. How could one possibly read the Bible as one read the works of Shakespeare? The Bible was the Word of God. How could one possibly compare profane literature, however great, with literature that had been inspired, even dictated, by the Holy Spirit?

In Buddhism there is no such thing as fundamentalism in the full-blown Christian sense. Buddhists have never chopped up the Buddhist canonical literature into bits and used the bits as bullets. Nevertheless, it has to be admitted that in some Buddhist circles there exists a sort of quasi-fundamentalism that could, if it were allowed to develop, be as much of a hindrance to our approaching Buddhist canonical literature *as literature* as Christian fundamentalism is to the appreciation of *The Bible Designed to be Read as Literature*. This quasi-fundamentalism takes the form of appealing to the authority of the canonical literature in support of a particular belief or practice but only in a general way, i.e. without actually citing any individual text or texts. An appeal of this sort is usually couched in such language as 'the Buddha says', or 'according to the Tipiṭaka', or 'it is stated in all the *sūtras* and tantras'. This quasi-fundamentalism is strengthened by the fact that in many parts of the Buddhist world the beautifully written and richly bound volumes of the canonical literature are often ceremonially worshipped rather than read – even in the case of those very *bhikkhus* and lamas who appeal to their authority in this manner. This is not to say that there is anything wrong in making the volumes of the Buddhist canonical literature an object of ceremonial worship. Such is far from being the case. But ceremonial worship of the volumes of the Buddhist canonical literature is no substitute for the actual reading of that literature. Unless we read the canonical literature we cannot understand and practise the Buddha's teaching and – what is of particular relevance to the present discussion – unless we read the canonical literature there can be no question of our approaching it as literature.

Even the quasi-fundamentalism that exists in some Buddhist circles is not easy to eradicate, however. Indeed, it may be said that despite the fact that in Buddhism there is no such thing as fundamentalism in the full-blown Christian sense, the possibility of fundamentalism exists wherever a canonical literature exists, irrespective of whether that literature is regarded as the Word of God or as the written record of the utterance of a supremely Enlightened human teacher. Such being the case, it should be possible for us to apply the same general principles that were responsible for the appearance of the large, thick volume of *The Bible Designed to be Read as Literature* in the window of that Torquay bookshop to the Buddhist canonical literature, in such a way as to enable us to understand what it actually means, in practical terms, to approach Buddhist canonical literature as literature. Thus to approach Buddhist canonical literature as literature means, in the first place, reading the canonical literature *for enjoyment*. This does not mean reading it for the sake of amusement, or simply to while away the time. Reading the canonical literature for enjoyment means reading it because, in so doing, we find ourselves immersed in an emotionally positive state of being such as – outside meditation – we hardly ever experience. Reading the canonical literature for enjoyment means reading it without any sense of compulsion. We do not *have* to read it. Whether as represented by the *Dhammapada* or the *White Lotus Sūtra*, the *Middle Length Sayings* or the *Perfection of Wisdom in Eight Thousand Lines*, the Buddhist canonical literature is not a sort of prescribed text on which we are going to be examined at the end of the year and rewarded or punished in accordance with how well – or how badly – we have done. Reading the canonical literature for enjoyment means reading it because we want to read it. It means reading it because we have an affinity for it, and are drawn to it naturally and spontaneously. Having said this, however, I must add that I always find it a little strange when someone who professes to be a committed Buddhist does not read at least some parts of the canonical literature for enjoyment, especially if he or she enjoys reading other kinds of literature.

To approach the Buddhist canonical literature as literature also means reading it *as a whole*. This does not mean reading the whole of that literature (it is in any case fifty times more extensive than the Bible) but rather reading this or that item of canonical literature as a whole. Reading the *Sutta-Nipāta*, or the *Vimalakīrti-nirdeśa*, for example, in this manner, means reading it not piecemeal, not concentrating on the parts at the expense of the whole, but reading it in such a way as to allow oneself to experience its total impact. Only if we read it in this kind of way will we be able to grasp the fundamental significance of the work or, if one likes, its gestalt. This is particularly the case, perhaps, where the work in question possesses a definite artistic unity and where it has been cast in poetic form. In the latter case, to approach the Buddhist canonical literature as literature means, of course, reading it *as poetry*. It was one of the special features of *The Bible Designed to be Read as Literature* that it printed the poetical books of the Old Testament as poetry, which gave them a rather Whitmanesque appearance, instead of chopping them up into numbered bits as though they were prose. (Not that even prose should really be treated in this way.) In the case of Buddhist canonical literature there is no danger of works, or parts of works, that are in poetic form being chopped up into numbered bits – at least, not when they are printed in the original. The danger is that when they are translated into a modern language they will be translated not into poetry but into prose and read accordingly. I shall be returning to this point later on.

Finally, and perhaps most importantly, to approach the Buddhist canonical literature as literature means to read it *for its own sake* rather than for the sake of some ulterior purpose. The ulterior purposes for the sake of which it is possible to read the canonical literature are very numerous. I shall mention only a few of them, leaving you to think of the rest for yourselves. Buddhist canonical literature can be read simply for the sake of the languages in which it has come down to us, that is, it can be read with a view to furthering our knowledge of linguistics. Similarly, it can be read for the sake of the light it sheds (particularly in the case of the *Āgamas/Nikāyas* and the Vinaya Piṭaka) on the political, social, economic, and religious condition of India at the time of the Buddha and his immediate disciples. Buddhist canonical literature can also be read for the sake of its contribution to comparative religion and mythology and to the intellectual history of mankind. It can even be read for the purpose of refuting Buddhism, as when a Christian missionary reads it before going off to work in a Buddhist country. With the possible exception of the last, there is nothing actually wrong in reading the Buddhist canonical literature for the sake of any of these purposes. But the fact remains that they are all ulterior purposes – ulterior, that is, to the purpose that the Buddhist canonical literature itself exists to subserve and for the sake of which, therefore, it should really be read.

The purpose that the Buddhist canonical literature exists to subserve is the happiness and welfare – the highest happiness and highest welfare – of all sentient beings, and we read that literature for its own sake when we read it with this in mind. The Buddhist canonical literature is, after all, the *Buddhavacana*, the word or utterance of the Enlightened One. It is a communication from the heart and mind of an Enlightened human being to the hearts and minds of those who are as yet unenlightened. It is a communication from the Buddha to ourselves. Reading the canonical literature for its own sake therefore means reading it in order to listen to what the Buddha has to say to us – which means listening seriously. Indeed, we cannot really listen in any other kind of way. Some of you know that I have more than once said of the poets – especially the great poets – that far from merely indulging in flowery language they in fact mean exactly what they say, and that they are trying to communicate to us something which they think worth communicating. How much more so is this the case with the Buddha, and how much more seriously, therefore, ought we to listen to the words of the *Buddhavacana*! How much more seriously ought we to read the Buddhist canonical literature!

This, then, is what it actually means, in practical terms, to approach the Buddhist canonical literature as literature. It means reading the Buddhist canonical literature for enjoyment, reading it as a whole, reading it – wherever appropriate – as poetry rather than as prose, and reading it for its own sake rather than for the sake of some ulterior purpose. When I speak of approaching Buddhist canonical literature as literature I do not mean to imply that it is all equally literature, or all literature in the same sense of the term. A distinction made by De Quincey will be useful here. According to De Quincey, there are two kinds of literature. There is first the literature of knowledge, and secondly, the literature of power. The function of the former is to teach, the function of the second is to move; the first is a rudder, the second an oar or a sail. The first speaks to the mere discursive understanding; the second speaks ultimately, it may happen, to the higher understanding of reason.[183]

In another place De Quincey goes so far as to suggest that the literature of knowledge is not really literature at all. 'All that is literature seeks to communicate power: all that is not literature seeks to communicate knowledge.' In the last analysis the difference between the two kinds of literature, or two kinds of communication, would seem to be one of degree rather than one of kind. Literature is not all equally literature, nor all literature in the same sense of the term, in that some works of literature communicate more power – and therefore move us more – than do others. In the case of the Bible, the *Book of Job* moves us more than the *Book of Leviticus*, even though the *Book of Leviticus* contains a great deal more information about the ancient Jewish sacrificial system. Thus the *Book of Job* belongs to the literature of power. It is literature proper. It is 'great literature'.

Applying this to the Buddhist canonical literature, we may say that the narrative power of the *Mahāparinibbāna Sutta*, which describes the Buddha's last days, moves us more than does an (to some) abstruse philosophical work like the Abhidhamma *Dhātukathā* (I am taking extreme examples to make the distinction clear); the imaginative sweep of a Mahāyāna *sūtra* like the *Vimalakīrti-nirdeśa* more than the subtle logic of a Perfection of Wisdom text like the *Suvikrāntavikrāmi-paripṛcchā*; and the stirring confession chapter of the *Suvarṇaprabhāsa Sūtra* more than the hard-to-fathom *śūnyatā* chapter. Thus the *Mahāparinibbāna Sutta*, the *Vimalakīrti-nirdeśa*, and the confession chapter of the *Suvarṇaprabhāsa Sūtra* all belong to the literature of power, while the

Dhātukathā, the *Suvikrāntavikrāmi-paripṛcchā*, and the *śūnyatā* chapter of the *Suvarṇaprabhāsa Sūtra* all belong to the literature of knowledge. Since it is the literature of power that constitutes literature in the real sense, or great literature, reading the Buddhist canonical literature as literature therefore means reading such works as the *Mahāparinibbāna Sutta* rather than such works as the *Dhātukathā*. Indeed, we might even go so far as to say that just as literature is not all equally literature so canonical literature is not all equally canonical literature, and that it is the more truly canonical the more deeply it moves us. This is not to say that, from the Buddhist point of view, there is a real distinction between *teaching*, which according to De Quincey is the function of the literature of knowledge, and *moving*, which according to De Quincey is the function of the literature of power. From the point of view of Buddhism, the Buddha teaches by moving, because his teaching is addressed not to what De Quincey calls 'the mere discursive understanding' or what we might call the alienated intellect, but rather to what De Quincey calls 'the higher understanding of reason' or what we might call the heart, in the sense of the deepest part of our being, or the spiritual intuition, or the whole person.[184] Reading the Buddhist canonical literature as literature therefore means reading it as the literature of power and allowing ourselves to be moved by that power to the fullest possible extent.

One last point. I have said that when works, or parts of works, of Buddhist canonical literature that are in poetry are translated into a modern language there is the danger that they will be translated into prose and read accordingly. The danger consists in the fact that poetry is the literature of power *par excellence*, which is the reason why poetry is capable of moving us to a far greater extent than prose, so that when poetry is translated into prose it loses much of its original power and, therefore, much of its capacity to move. In reading works of Buddhist canonical literature in translation we should be careful to read them, wherever possible, in translations that do justice to their poetic quality, otherwise we shall be unable to read them as literature in the fullest sense and thus will not be moved by them to the extent that we might have been.

If we are able, however, to read poetry as poetry, if we are able to understand the real nature of literature, if we are able to see to what extent we are justified in approaching Buddhist canonical literature *as literature*, and able to see what it actually means, in practical terms, to approach it in this way, if we allow ourselves to feel the power of works like the *Mahāparinibbāna Sutta* and the *Vimalakīrti-nirdeśa*, then we shall obtain at least a glimpse of the glory of the literary world, and gain a better understanding of the real nature of Buddhist canonical literature.

from *The Glory of the Literary World*

6. PĀLI SCRIPTURES AND MAHĀYĀNA *SŪTRAS*

If we really allow ourselves to become absorbed in a Mahāyāna sūtra, we become part of it. We join the great assembly and experience ourselves right in the midst of it, taking part in the events of the sūtra as they unfold.

If you read the Pāli scriptures and then the Mahāyāna scriptures – say two or three volumes of each, enough to give you a taste of them – you will notice that you get something from the Mahāyāna scriptures that is completely missing from the Pāli texts. This is not by any means to dismiss the unique historical and spiritual importance of the Pāli scriptures. They give us a vivid and deeply moving picture of the life and teaching career of the human historical Buddha. They contain all the basic spiritual principles and practices from which all the subsequent forms of Buddhism developed. They are rich in content and full of inspiration. We cannot possibly dispense with the Pāli scriptures; as Buddhists, we are enormously indebted to them. Humanity, in fact, is indebted to them. They cannot be praised enough and we cannot be sufficiently grateful for them.

They do not, however, contain everything that everybody needs. There is an element missing, and it is this element that we find in the Mahāyāna scriptures. Reading the Mahāyāna scriptures, we are emancipated from the contingent and the determinate, from time, space, and causality, from historical reality. We experience archetypal reality, myth, the realm of undefined meanings. In technical terms, we encounter the *sambhogakāya*. That is, we encounter the Buddhas and bodhisattvas of the Mahāyāna in their archetypal forms. Through this experience we contact something within us of which we were not previously aware.

Something is sparked off that even the Pāli scriptures were unable to spark off. And this happens because the realm of archetypal reality, of myth, of undefined meanings, corresponds to something within us.

According to the *Tibetan Book of the Dead*, we experience this realm directly when we die. In the intermediate state between death and rebirth we experience all sorts of visions, including visions of Buddhas and bodhisattvas in both their peaceful and their wrathful forms. And the Buddhist tradition tells us not to be afraid, but to recognize all these visions, all these Buddhas and bodhisattvas, as our own thought forms, as phenomena of our own true mind. If we can do this, we attain liberation on the spot.

As a writer, one inevitably notices a difference in feeling between the experience of composing passages of conceptual prose and the experience of writing something more creative, more inspired or poetic. It is this kind of shift we feel when we make the transition from the prose of the Pāli scriptures to the poetry of the Mahāyāna scriptures, the transition from history to myth on a grand scale.

Unfortunately, some people cannot make this transition. Take the well-known case of Charles Darwin. As a young man Darwin loved poetry and literature, especially Shakespeare, but for the greater part of his life he immersed himself in scientific research. When as an old man he tried to get back to Shakespeare, he found to his dismay that poetry held no meaning for him any more; he had lost his capacity to enjoy it. In the course of his years, even decades, of scientific research a whole side of him had withered and died.[185] Much the same happened to John Stuart Mill, at least for part of his life. Even as a small boy his favourite subjects were logic and political economy; and as he grew older he found that he became more and more cut off from poetry. It is not just that he was cut off from poetry in the literary sense; he was – to put it rather poetically – cut off from the poetry of life.

Today we are all exposed to this sort of danger. We all suffer from this sort of deprivation, at least to some extent. We have been suffering from it, in fact, since the Industrial Revolution, at the beginning of which William Blake warned against the loss of what he called 'the divine vision'. He criticized Bacon, Newton, and Locke so vigorously because he felt that they tended to limit humanity to the realm of historical reality, the realm of time, space, and causality.[186] In his own literary and visual creative work Blake, of course, was not limited in this way. In his Prophetic Books especially he explores the deeper levels of human experience. Blake's profound concern with archetypal forces and forms must explain why he continues to hold such a great fascination for so many people today.

Our desire to contact the realm of the archetypal also explains the popularity of tales of myth and fantasy, whether traditional, like the stories of King Arthur, or modern, like *The Lord of the Rings* and some forms of science fiction. Such works explore facets of humanity's quest for meaning, and in reading them we are trying, perhaps unconsciously, to break out of the prison of merely historical reality, seeking to experience a deeper meaning to our existence.

Meaning is not a thing that you can grasp by looking in a dictionary. Meaning must be meaning *for you*, something that you personally experience. Our quest for meaning is therefore our quest for ourselves, our quest for the totality, the wholeness, of our own being. On one level we belong to the realm of historical reality; but on another, we belong to the realm of spiritual reality. The Mahāyāna scriptures reveal this world to us. So does myth; so does poetry. And they reveal it to us not as something external to ourselves, but as our own world, as a world in which we ourselves actually live, usually without knowing it.

It was a maxim of the Neoplatonists that the eye could not behold the sun unless it had within its nature something sun-like, something akin to the sun.[187] Similarly, we can experience the archetypal realm only because we ourselves are, on another level, archetypal beings. If we really allow ourselves to become absorbed in a Mahāyāna *sūtra*, we become part of it. We join the great assembly and experience ourselves right in the midst of it, taking part in the events of the *sūtra* as they unfold.

But although we can make the transition to the realm of archetypal reality, this does not mean that we leave the realm of historical reality behind. We cannot – must not – opt for myth and discard history. We need both – because we exist in both realms. We exist in them both all the time, whether or not we are aware of it. And of course a lot of the time we are not aware of it. Our relation to the archetypal realm is analogous to our relation to the dream state. When we are asleep and dreaming, we exist, one might say, in the dream realm, and we have all sorts of experiences. When we wake up, we are no longer in the dream state, but the emotions we experienced while we were dreaming continue. It's just like an underground river that we descend into from time to time through a hole in the ground. Just as the river is flowing all the time, so there is continuity between dreams. You can even have a dream, wake up, and then fall asleep again and continue with the same dream, as though it has been going on all the time.

So in a sense we are living in that dream realm all the time. And we can extend that to the realm of archetypal experience. Just as a very strong dream continues to have its effect when we have woken up, so the archetypal realm continues to affect us, whether or not we are conscious of it.

from *The Inconceivable Emancipation*

5
DREAMS, MYTHS, AND SYMBOLS

1. THE NATURE OF TANTRIC BUDDHISM

Tantric Buddhism is concerned not with theories or speculations, not with formal religiosity or external piety, but with the direct experience, in the depths of one's being, of what one truly and essentially is.

I well remember my early impressions of the Tantra. As I tried to penetrate a little into it, to see what it was about and how it connected with other forms of Buddhism and with modern thought – psychology, comparative symbolism, and so on – I felt more and more that it was a jungle – a jungle in which one could very easily get lost. There seemed to be so many different traditions within it. There were so many meditation methods and forms of ritual observance, so many kinds of offerings, even so many kinds of ceremonial robe – and, indeed, ceremonial hat.

I used to tell my Tibetan friends that I found the Tantra far too vast and complicated to study as a whole, and that I was therefore going to confine myself to the study of one little corner of it. My chosen field of study, I said, would be the hats, some of which were very weird and wonderful indeed. I would make a collection of at least a hundred kinds of Tantric hat, and then write a book about them. Of course, I never did. But even when I began to study the Tantra in earnest, there were so many images in the temples, so many scroll paintings, so many figures of Buddhas and bodhisattvas and gurus, and *ḍākas* and *ḍākinīs* and *dharmapālas*, that for a long time I continued to feel that the Tantra was truly a vast jungle.

This is likely to be the experience of any Westerner beginning to investigate the Tantra. The impression one gets of richness and variety, growth, fertility, and abundance is quite bewildering to begin with. But a feeling of being lost among the creative symbols of Tantric Buddhism is no cause for alarm. Indeed, to become *intellectually* lost in the context of the Tantra is quite a positive thing. One may find oneself moved or stirred by the symbols without being able to say exactly how or why. With more experience, one comes to discover that the Tantra is not really the jungle it appears to be. It is more like a garden or, rather, a complex of gardens. Despite the richness of the Tantra, despite its incredible profusion, its superabundance of material, and its exuberance, there is a pattern running through it, or a number of interlocking patterns. These patterns are not intellectual, but spiritual. They are not imposed on the Tantra from the outside, but unfold from within it, expressing its innermost nature and essential purpose.

What is that purpose? Tantric Buddhism is concerned not with theories or speculations, not with formal religiosity or external piety, but with the direct experience, in the depths of one's being, of what one truly and essentially is. It seeks to reveal to us our essential nature – not just psychologically but existentially, metaphysically, even transcendentally. So far as the Tantra is concerned, this experience cannot be mediated by concepts. In fact, concepts give no idea of it at all, do not lead to it or point to it in any way. It is beyond words, beyond thought, beyond the conscious mind and personality. But this direct experience can be evoked, conjured up, or at least glimpsed, with the help of symbols. The whole Tantric path to Enlightenment is strewn with symbolic images, mantras, and rituals. You stumble over them at every step; indeed, the Tantric path largely consists of them. And they are all intended to reflect, or lead to, or give a glimpse of, this direct experience.

from *Creative Symbols of Tantric Buddhism*

2. THE VALUE OF THE DREAM STATE

Marvellous to relate, we are alive.

These days most of us imagine we have so many things to do that we can't afford to spend much of our precious time sitting about reflecting on life. But if we do happen to find time to turn things over in our minds a little more seriously than usual, we may well have to acknowledge certain things about ourselves, things that we may not find altogether pleasant or creditable to accept. And one of the things that on reflection we may be forced to acknowledge is that as human beings we take quite a lot for granted. There are certain things which we know we possess, we know we experience, but the value and significance of which we are totally unaware – so unaware, indeed, that we might as well not possess them at all.

Suppose that when you were a baby, you had been given a pebble to play with, and suppose you kept that pebble and played with it every day, every hour, so that it became as familiar to you as your own hand. You would gradually become so used to the pebble that you would probably not take any particular care of it or attach any particular value to it. You might never realize, in fact, that the 'pebble' was not a pebble at all, but a priceless precious stone.

One of the things we tend to treat as a pebble, instead of the precious stone it really is, is life itself. We fail to understand the significance of the bare fact that we are alive. But it *is* significant. After all, we might just as easily be dead, or never have existed at all. But we do exist. There was, we could say, some unique, unrepeatable combination of circumstances, and here we are. It may have been a billion to one chance, but it has come off. Marvellous to relate, we are alive. We are sitting here. How wonderful!

This is surely what the old Zen monk was celebrating when he cried out 'How wonderful! How miraculous! I draw water and I carry fuel.'[188] He had realized that until then he had taken his ordinary, everyday life for granted, utterly failing to realize its value and significance.

Another thing that we take for granted is our 'ordinary' human consciousness, the normal waking state. We take it for granted that we can see and hear. We take it for granted that we can think. We take it for granted that we can be aware. More often than not, we simply fail to realize the unaccountable singularity of it all.

In the same way, we take sleep for granted – such a wonderful, refreshing thing as sleep – unless of course we are unfortunate enough to have to resort to sleeping tablets. We even, most of us, take our dreams for granted. You get bad dreams – this is what our grandmothers used to tell us – if you eat too much cheese at night, and that's all there is to it. Or else – this is another popular theory – dreams are just a jumbled reminiscence of the events of the previous day.

But if you think about it, the dream state is a rather strange thing. In the dream state, the physical sense organs are not functioning, but nonetheless we see, we hear, we even smell and taste. In the dream state we're oblivious to the physical body, but we do seem to have a sort of body. We are free to move about, free to go places – in fact, we have more freedom than we do when we are awake. We can go anywhere, by any method. Sometimes we can even fly.

In dreams we experience a different kind of time, a different kind of space – even a different kind of world. Usually the dream world is a recognizable extension of the world of everyday waking consciousness, but not always. Sometimes it's a completely different world, a world of which we have had no previous experience in any form. It's almost as though we have passed through the dream state into quite another state of consciousness, quite another mode of being – even into a higher state of consciousness, a higher mode of being. To suppose that higher states of consciousness are accessible only from the waking state is pure assumption. It's just another of those things that we take for granted. The fact is that we certainly can have access to these higher states from or through the dream state.

In Buddhism, especially in the Mahāyāna and the Vajrayāna, the value of the dream state is recognized as being twofold. In the first place, it shows us that it is possible to experience a state of consciousness other than the waking state. This is quite an obvious point, but no less profound for that. Secondly, certain dreams show us that we can experience states of consciousness which are not only different from the waking state but higher than it. For this reason, dreams play an important role, sometimes even a crucial role, in the transformation of the individual.

from *Transforming Self and World*

3. WHAT IS MYTH?

How as Western Buddhists will we engage in the creation of myth?

The word myth, in the sense I intend it, does not mean something false or imaginary. A myth, one might think, is a story about gods and goddesses, and in a way this is so – but we have to ask what those gods and goddesses are, or what they represent. They are beings or powers or forces that exist on some other level, some other plane of being. When our life is inspired by a mythic dimension, we are working out on the historical plane something that is of archetypal significance. The *bodhicitta*, one could say, is the myth that inspires the Buddhist spiritual community.

Whatever the rational, conceptual, historically-oriented consciousness may comprehend, there is an imaginative or archetypal dimension to life that will always elude that rational consciousness. An analogy can be drawn here with our dream life. We may have a rich and vivid dream life – more vivid, sometimes, than our waking life. If we are to give a complete account of ourselves, we must describe not only our waking life but also our dream life; but this, significantly, is for most of us very difficult to do. We often don't remember our dreams; and when we are dreaming we rarely remember our waking life. They go along more or less separately, occupying their different planes. Likewise, if one does a lot of meditation, not much may be happening on the material plane – one may be on retreat and therefore not 'doing' very much at all – but a lot will be happening on that other plane of existence which is meditative consciousness.

If one's inner experience finds a collective expression in some kind of spiritual movement, one could think of that movement as having a dream life, or a mythic life, of its own. Perhaps it does have an existence on another level. Indeed, if it did not, if it was merely an organization on the material plane, it would wither away very quickly. It needs to have very deep roots – roots in the sky.

A myth comes into being when people have very strong feelings about something, feelings which are not adequately supported by the existing state of affairs. The Mahāyāna Buddhists, it seems, felt a need to create a myth able to reflect not only their positive emotions but also the higher truths of Buddhism. Unable to nourish themselves on the dry bread – as they saw it – of the Abhidharma, they *had* to believe in the sort of Buddhism those myths represented. So one isn't to think that the Mahāyānists decided on rational grounds that it was about time there was a bit of myth in Buddhism. Their myths emerged out of spiritual necessity. The creation of these myths was, as with all myths, a collective rather than an individual process. And the myths were not created out of thin air; there were elements in the teachings going right back to the time of the Buddha that the myth-makers could build on. The Pāli canon is very rich in mythical and legendary material, although the modern Theravāda tends to ignore that aspect of its literature.

Indeed, in the Pāli canon one may even see myths in the process of emerging. There is an episode in the *Mahāparinibbāna Sutta* of the *Dīgha-Nikāya* in which Ānanda asks the Buddha if he is really going to gain *parinirvāṇa* in the little wattle-and-daub township of Kusinārā. Couldn't he choose a more distinguished place? But the Buddha says, 'Don't say that, Ānanda. Formerly this was the capital of a very great kingdom.'[189] Then another *sutta* of the *Dīgha-Nikāya*, the *Mahāsudassana Sutta*, gives what is clearly an amplified version of this same episode, including a lot of imagery along almost Mahāyānistic lines.[190] The *Sukhāvatī-vyūha sūtras* of the Mahāyāna may be said to carry on from where this Pāli *sutta* leaves off; certain references to rows of jewel trees, for example, are very similar indeed.[191]

The question for us now is how we may renew this mythical dimension. How as Western Buddhists will we engage in the creation of myth? On the one hand we have the whole Buddhist tradition, together with the mythology of Western culture, to inspire us. On the other, we have so much theoretical knowledge getting in the way of that inspiration. The creation of myths will depend on our own very deep feelings and profound aspirations, feelings that go beyond our present personal situation, and even the existing world situation. If we have these feelings and aspirations, eventually there will be a need for them to be projected in an objective form, as myth. In the meantime it is important to recognize myths like the *bodhicitta* for what they are, and to appreciate what their mythical status means.

from *The Bodhisattva Ideal*

4. THE EMERGENCE OF MYTH IN BUDDHISM

The Buddha is clearly a historical figure who is concerned with teaching individuals how they may develop as human beings. It is only later on, especially in the Mahāyāna and then in the Vajrayāna, that myth appears.

To contemporary Buddhists it might seem that myth, by which I mean not 'untruth' but something that is deeply true, an expression (through image or story) of truths beyond the direct grasp of our intellect, is an integral part of Buddhism, but in fact it was quite a late development. By contrast, in the historical development of Christianity the myth came first – the myth of the saviour, the son of God who is slain by his enemies, then comes back to life and returns to his father in heaven, taking his worshippers with him. The strength – and the weakness – of Christianity is that it is based on a myth of this kind. As time went on, the myth was gradually turned into history; ethical and spiritual teachings were incorporated into it, but the myth came first. Then, the myth being firmly established as history, came the teaching. This is reflected in the Apostles' Creed, which is still recited today: the striking thing about it is that it is nothing but myth. The teaching, a certain amount of which evidently did take place, according to the Gospels, is just passed over, apparently regarded as being of no significance. A Christian is not someone who believes in the Sermon on the Mount – after all, such teachings are found in other religions too – but someone who believes in the Virgin Birth, the Crucifixion, the Resurrection, and the Ascension – in other words, someone who believes in myths.

In Buddhism it is the other way round: first teaching, then myth. The Buddha is clearly a historical figure who is concerned with teaching individuals how they may develop as human beings. It is only later on, especially in the Mahāyāna and then in the Vajrayāna, that myth appears. This is illustrated by the development of the mandala of the five Buddhas. First of all, you simply have the Buddha Śākyamuni, in the different phases of his career: in meditation under the bodhi tree, then calling the earth to witness, then teaching, then reassuring his disciples, then offering the gift of the Dharma to his disciples and to the world. From this naturalistic basis developed specific Buddha icons, each Buddha making a gesture or *mudrā* to illustrate each situation. If the Buddha was depicted with his hands folded in his lap, that would represent him meditating under the bodhi tree; and if the tips of his fingers were touching the earth, that would represent calling the earth to witness; while if he was displaying a *mudrā* as though turning a wheel, that would represent the turning of the wheel of the Dharma.

In this way there emerged a set of five episodes with five *mudrās*, and these gradually became almost like five different Buddhas. The whole idea of Buddhahood was gradually raised to a more ideal or archetypal level, giving a richer and more multifaceted – even multidimensional – expression to the content of the original, historically embodied Buddha ideal. Thus was formed the mandala of the five Buddhas. In the centre was *the* Buddha – the primary Buddha, you could say. (Over the course of time, as different traditions developed, this central position could be occupied by whichever Buddha was central to a particular tradition, or even to a particular practitioner.) To the right and left of the central Buddha were the Buddhas of the east and west representing respectively wisdom and compassion, or the intellectual and emotional aspects of Buddhahood. This was a development of the Mahāyāna. Then, with the Tantra, appeared the Buddhas of the north and south, representing further aspects of Enlightenment – compassionate action and beauty. So now there were five: one at the centre and one at each of the cardinal points.

The five Buddhas are sometimes referred to as the *Dhyāni* Buddhas, but this is not a truly Buddhist term, and never occurs in Buddhist texts. It was coined by someone writing about Nepalese Buddhism in the nineteenth century, and then taken up and popularized by the Theosophists.[192] The five Buddhas are more correctly spoken of as the five *Jinas* – that is, the five Conquerors – or the five *Tathāgatas*. Each *Jina* or Buddha can be regarded as having an active aspect, personified in the form of his attendant bodhisattva, or even two attendant bodisattvas, representing his compassion and his wisdom, or his wisdom and his activity, or his activity and his compassion. These were sometimes split up into further aspects, each of which was separately represented. In the Vajrayāna a major development was the introduction of female counterparts to all these aspects.

All these developments represent a gradual filling out of the original Buddha ideal. It is as though you had an uncut diamond: its surface would not catch and reflect the light, and consequently its true beauty would easily be missed. But worked upon by a master jeweller, its facets would sparkle with reflected light and iridescent colour, and its beauty would be revealed. That is how the mandala of the five Buddhas gradually took shape.

The five Buddhas represent an attempt to communicate something of the multifaceted nature of Enlightenment. If you define Buddhahood as 'the wisdom of reality', this description may be true, but it is hardly very beautiful or inspiring. What kind of wisdom is it, what kind of reality? To illuminate this, as we have already seen, the wisdom of the Buddha is described as having four principal aspects – the mirror-like wisdom, the wisdom of equality, the discriminating wisdom, and the all-performing wisdom – and this gives a fuller and richer idea of what Buddhahood is like, bringing out its nature more explicitly so that it can be seen more clearly.

Many of the Buddhas and bodhisattvas within the mandala became the objects of cults; they were visualized and meditated upon, and their mantras were recited, until in Vajrayāna Buddhism, and Tibetan Buddhism especially, they became the foundation of a vast range of spiritual practices and experiences, as if refracting rainbow light from the thousands of facets of the mandala.

As for dividing each Buddha into masculine and feminine, into a Buddha and his consort, this helped to bring out the passionate engagement that is part and parcel of transcendental wisdom. If the wisdoms of the Buddhas seem a bit cold, the Buddhas themselves, with their consorts, counteract that feeling. The attendant bodhisattvas who also appear in the mandala have their own effect too, each bringing out a specific aspect of the activity of the Buddhas. The *dharmapālas*, the guardians of the Dharma, bring out further aspects still. And then, in a rich and complex mandala, there may be wrathful as well as peaceful Buddhas to bring out more and more aspects of Enlightenment.

from *Creative Symbols of Tantric Buddhism*

5. TAKING MYTHS LITERALLY

The whole point about the realm of myth is that it is a realm not of clearly defined meanings, but of undefined, even indefinable, meanings.

If you take a myth in the modern, sophisticated sense, it has its effect on you, but if you are able to believe that the myth is literally true, it has a much greater effect. For instance, if you are a Christian and you believe that the resurrection of Christ has a deep symbolical significance, even though he didn't literally rise from the dead, the resurrection is a very meaningful symbol for you. But if as an orthodox Christian you believe that Christ literally rose from the dead because he was the son of God and he had that power inherent in him, your belief will have much deeper foundations, or at least you will be more strongly motivated. The nature of our approach to 'myth' is one of the basic questions that have to be faced nowadays, not only by Christians but by Buddhists as well.

For Buddhists, however, it is not such a key issue, because in Buddhism, especially early Buddhism, the taking of myth as literal truth doesn't occupy such an important place. If you read, for example, that the Buddha walked up and down in the air emitting water and fire at the same time, you can believe that quite literally and no doubt find it inspiring.[193] But taking that myth literally doesn't occupy the kind of central place in Buddhism that belief in the resurrection of Christ occupies in Christianity. There is no doubt, however, that if you are able to take myth as being literally true, you are likely to practise your religion more zealously and energetically. Of course, such literal belief can go to the undesirable extreme of fanatical fundamentalism. But in avoiding that, perhaps we need to take care not to fall into too sophisticated or rational an approach to myth. The whole point about the realm of myth is that it is a realm not of clearly defined meanings, but of undefined, even indefinable meanings. It is the same realm to which belong such things as symbols, archetypal images, the imagination itself, and poetry.

from *The Inconceivable Emancipation*

6. THE TIBETAN WHEEL OF LIFE

In fact the wheel of life is not a picture at all. It is a mirror, in which we see – what else? – ourselves.

The Tibetan wheel of life did not originate in Tibet; it is described in early Buddhist scriptures and in Mahāyāna *sutras*, and those traditions were preserved in the Tantric context, while at the same time the symbol was imbued with a distinctively Tantric spirit.[194] In fact, the wheel is only partly symbolic. While some parts of its complex structure are true symbols (that is, they stand for certain things without actually depicting them), others are only illustrative, representing in pictorial form teachings that can be expressed in other terms. Here we shall be dwelling more on the symbolic than on the illustrative elements of the wheel.

Starting with a simple description, what do we see when we look at the wheel? Basically, we see a lot of little pictures. The wheel consists of four concentric circles – that is, four circles of different sizes, one inside the other. Within the innermost circle, at the hub of the wheel, are to be seen three animals: a cock, a snake, and a pig. They appear head-to-tail in a sort of triangular relationship, each animal biting the tail of the one in front.

The circle surrounding the hub is divided into two halves, one light, the other dark. In the light segment are human beings moving upwards as though on a sort of celestial escalator. They have peaceful, joyful expressions, and they are decently clad. In the dark segment there are what seem to be human beings too – but are they really human? They are plunging headlong as though into a pit, naked and chained together, with expressions of fear and horror on their faces.

Moving outwards, the next circle is divided into six equal segments. In the first segment, right at the top of the circle, we see the world of the gods. Heaven opens before our eyes: a world of pleasures and delights where the gods live in beautiful palaces among trees and gardens, a world where every wish is instantly gratified. As soon as the desire for something floats – however vaguely – into your mind, that thing instantly appears in front of you, or in your hands, or your mouth, or on your body. This is how the gods live.

In the second segment, moving clockwise, is the world of the *asuras*, the anti-gods, the Titans. These are fierce, war-like beings – usually depicted as well-muscled, not to say heavily built – and they are engaged in perpetual warfare with the gods, fighting especially for the possession of the *kalpataru*, the magic tree that grants all wishes and fulfils all desires.

The third segment depicts the world of the *pretas*, the hungry ghosts. These beings are naked and horribly deformed: they have enormously swollen bellies, very thin necks, and mouths no bigger than the eye of a needle. Suffering all the time from ravenous hunger, they grasp at food and drink, trying desperately to cram it into their needle-eye mouths, but as they do so, the food and drink turns into excrement and liquid fire.

In the fourth segment, right at the bottom of the wheel, is the world of tormented beings: hell. At the centre of this world is a fearsome figure sitting enthroned. This is Yamarāja, the King of Death, dark blue in colour, clad in a tiger skin and surrounded by flames. In his hand he holds a mirror – the mirror of karma – and as beings are dragged before him, beings who have just died, he looks into the mirror and sees everything they have done, everything they have said, everything they have thought. If they have done more evil than good in the course of their preceding life, he orders that they should be taken away and punished. It should be said that this world is more of a purgatory than a hell, because it isn't a permanent state – but even so, in it we see guilty people suffering torments so terrible that it is painful to think about them, let alone describe them. The air is full of the sound of wailing and roaring and lamentation.

In the fifth segment is the world of animals, both wild and domesticated. They are shown in pairs, male and female, and they seem to be living a peaceful, idyllic existence – almost like the lion and the lamb in the biblical story. It isn't a very Darwinian picture, at least as depicted in Tibetan Buddhist art. There's no nature red in tooth and claw – the animals all seem very placid. Perhaps it is intended to show the animal's life from the animal's point of view, because, after all, animals don't worry about what's going to happen tomorrow.

The sixth and last segment is the world of human beings, and there men and women buy and sell, read, talk, work in the fields, meditate under the trees, and are finally carried as corpses to the cremation ground.

There is one important feature in each realm that hasn't yet been mentioned. In each of the six worlds there appears a Buddha figure of a particular colour, offering to the beings in that world something they need. In the world of the gods there appears a pure white Buddha holding a stringed musical instrument – usually in the paintings it's an Indian vina, which is rather like a medieval lute. This Buddha plays to the gods a sweet, penetrating melody: the melody of impermanence.

Nothing lasts, the tune is saying; everything changes. In the world of the *asuras*, there appears a Buddha of a beautiful emerald green colour, holding in his right hand a flaming sword. It is on fire because it is the sword of transcendental wisdom, and he brandishes it at the *asuras* as they're fighting. In the world of the *pretas*, the hungry ghosts, there appears a ruby red Buddha who showers upon the *pretas* food and drink that they are able actually to consume. In the world of tormented beings there appears a Buddha the colour of smoke, bluish-grey, and he regales the beings in hell with *amṛta*, the food or drink of the gods known in the western tradition as nectar or ambrosia. In the world of the animals there appears a dark blue Buddha who is showing something to the animals: a book. And in the human world there appears a golden yellow Buddha, bearing the twin insignia of the spiritual life in ancient India: the begging-bowl and the staff with three rings. These six Buddhas represent the introduction into the symbolism of the wheel of life of a Mahāyānistic element, the element of great compassion, which, conjoined with wisdom, sees and responds appropriately to the needs of all beings.

The outermost circle of the wheel is divided into twelve segments, in each of which is a tiny picture. Clockwise from the top, these are: (1) a blind man with a stick, (2) a potter with a wheel and pots, (3) a monkey climbing a flowering tree, (4) a boat with four passengers, one of whom is steering, (5) an empty house with five windows and a door, (6) a man and woman embracing, (7) a man with an arrow stuck in his eye, (8) a woman offering a drink to a seated man, (9) a man gathering fruit from a tree, (10) a pregnant woman, (11) a woman in childbirth, and (12) a man carrying a corpse to the cemetery.

The whole wheel is gripped by a monstrous, demoniacal figure: his face peers over the top of the wheel, his clawed hands and feet grip the sides, and his scaly reptilian tail coils below. He is impermanence personified, and he wears a crown made of five human skulls, a Tantric touch that hints at radical transformation.

Above the wheel and to the right is the figure of Śākyamuni Buddha, floating on clouds and stretching out his arm to point out the path to Enlightenment. On the left is the full moon, in which can be discerned the figure of a hare.

This is the Tibetan wheel of life as it is – or used to be – depicted on the walls of temples and monasteries, and on painted scrolls, all over

Tibet and the adjacent Himalayan region. But what does it all mean? As to that, much of it – the symbols, at least – cannot, as we have said, be explained at all. The main thing for us to do is just look at the wheel: not only at it, but into it – because in fact the wheel of life is not a picture at all. It is a mirror, in which we see – what else? – ourselves. Perhaps we could say that the wheel of life is made up not of four concentric circles, but of four mirrors. Or we could say that we look into the mirror four times, each time seeing more and more of ourselves, experiencing more of ourselves, realizing more of ourselves. The wheel of life is a sort of magic mirror or crystal ball into which we can gaze.

So let us look now into that mirror – not just four times but as many times as may be necessary – and let us have the courage to see ourselves in it. Some courage, indeed, will be needed. The very first time we look into the mirror, we see the three animals: the cock, the snake, and the pig. Usually it is said that they represent greed, hatred, and ignorance and that these three poisons are present in our own hearts, but this explanation is letting us off far too lightly; it is a kind of defensive rationalization. It is much more of a shock to look into the mirror and see not the human face we expected, but the face of an animal – a bird, a reptile, a pig. That's us, and uncomfortable as it may be, indeed should be, we should take a long look. This reflection is giving us a direct experience of our own animal nature. We see that we are not quite so human, so civilized, as we had thought. We're just an animal, a beast. And this realization is the beginning of spiritual life. We see ourselves as we are on the most basic level, we accept ourselves, and we go on from there.

Going on from there means taking another look in the mirror: once we have recovered from the shock of seeing that animal face, we take a second look. This time we see two paths, one going up, the other going down, one light, the other dark. So we are faced with two alternatives: up or down. It's as simple as that. We can either evolve or regress; the choice is before us. And this choice is before us every minute of the day, in every situation in which we find ourselves. Shall we go up or shall we go down? Shall we follow the light path or the dark path? It's up to us to decide.

If we do decide, after thinking it over, to follow the light path, the next question is, how? What must we do to grow spiritually? What is the next step? This clearly depends on where we are now. And to find that out, we need to look into the mirror a third time. This time we see one of the six worlds: the world of the gods, the world of the *asuras*, the world of the hungry ghosts, the world of tormented beings, the world of animals, or the world of human beings. In other words, we see where we are at any given moment or over any given period of time. Sometimes when we look into the mirror we see a happy, peaceful, cheerful face: the face of a god. Sometimes we see the angry, aggressive face of an *asura*. Sometimes we see a famished, hollow-eyed face, with a pinched mouth and a dissatisfied expression: the face of a hungry ghost. Sometimes we see the miserable, tormented face of someone in hell. Sometimes we see a face with a long snout and whiskers or big sharp teeth: the face of an animal. And sometimes we see just an ordinary human face. But whatever we see, we see ourselves.

The six segments into which this circle of the wheel of life is divided can be considered literally as realms of existence into which living beings are reborn as a result of their karma and in which they live until that karma has been exhausted. But this is only half the truth that the symbol represents. The segments can also be seen as representing states of mind that we can experience here and now, in the course of our everyday human existence. Sometimes our experience of these states of mind is so strong that for the time being we seem actually to be living in heaven or in hell or among the hungry ghosts. In other words, we experience them almost as states of being rather than just states of mind.

Viewed in this light, the world of the gods represents a happy state of mind, a state of relaxation, content, and repose. It's a state in which everything seems to flow smoothly, and there are no obstacles or problems. It is a state of aesthetic experience and artistic enjoyment as well as of meditation in the sense of deep concentration or *śamatha*, though not in the sense of insight into reality or *vipaśyanā* (Pāli *vipassanā*).

The world of the *asuras*, by contrast, represents an aggressive, competitive state of mind. Here there is a lot of energy – perhaps too much – and it all turns outward. There is restlessness, suspicion, jealousy. Just as the *asuras* fight for possession of the wish-fulfilling tree, the *asura*-like state of mind is one that strives for an ever higher standard of living, more and more money, and so on. It is a state of assertive egotism, a state in which one wants to be better or more distinguished than other people, and even to control and exercise power over them.

The world of the hungry ghosts is the state of neurotic desire. Desire is neurotic when it seeks from its object more than that object can give, or even something quite different from what it can give. An obvious example is the neurotic desire for food. Sometimes people gobble down huge quantities of food, especially sweet things, but they don't really want food at all. It's a substitute for something else – for affection, very often, psychologists tell us. Neurotic desire in this sense is very often present in personal relationships, especially those of the more intimate kind – to such an extent in some cases that the two people involved are like hungry ghosts trying to devour each other.

The world of the tormented beings is the state of acute mental suffering, nervous frustration, mental breakdown, even insanity. This state is brought about in various ways: by the long-continued frustration of natural human impulses, by sudden bereavement, by unconscious mental conflicts, and by many other conditions and causes.

The world of the animals represents the state of purely sensual indulgence, the state in which one is interested only in food, sex, and material comforts, all the pleasures of life. When these needs are satisfied, one is quite gentle and tame, but when they are frustrated, one becomes snappy and even rather dangerous.

Finally, the world of human beings is the state of distinctively human consciousness, the state which is neither ecstatic nor agonized, neither fiercely competitive nor mindlessly sensual nor yet neurotically desirous. It's a state in which we are aware of our own self and aware of other people, a state in which we satisfy our objective human needs but at the same time see that they have their limitations, a state in which we devote ourselves to spiritual development. We call it the human realm, but in reality the truly human state is one that most 'human beings' only intermittently – or perhaps never – experience.

Our third look into the mirror has shown us where we are, whether we are – for the moment – a god or an *asura*, a hungry ghost or a tormented being, an animal or a human being. When we have seen where we are, we know the next step we have to take – and that draws us to the six Buddhas appearing in the midst of the six worlds. According to the Tibetan Buddhist teaching, these Buddhas are all manifestations of Avalokiteśvara, the bodhisattva who embodies the compassion aspect of the Enlightenment experience. Each of these six Buddhas holds, as we have observed, a particular object, something needed by the beings of the world in which he appears. As we shall see, the nature of the object the Buddha holds gives us a clue as to how to move on from that world, or that state of mind.

In the world of the gods the white Buddha holds a lute upon which he plays the melody of impermanence. This suggests that when we are in a state of aesthetic enjoyment, the next step is to remind ourselves that it won't last and also that aesthetic pleasure, however great, is not to be mistaken for the supreme bliss of Enlightenment. Although things may be going well now, we still have a long way to go. The Buddhist tradition stresses that prolonged happiness can be spiritually dangerous, if not disastrous. If we are happy and contented all the time, if things go easily and we have our own way, we meet no problems or obstacles, we tend to become self-satisfied, complacent, and even careless. We tend to forget that we are mortal, that life is short and time is precious. This applies even to the enjoyment of meditation, as well as to the appreciation of the fine arts. We need to make the transition from the heights of mundane experience to the experience of the Transcendental.

Notice that the white Buddha doesn't stand up among the gods and deliver a lecture on impermanence; he conveys his message by playing a melody on a lute. Nor is this just a symbolic notion, if we are to believe a story told about Aśvaghoṣa, to whom tradition ascribes the seminal text called *The Awakening of Faith in the Mahāyāna*. As well as being a great philosopher and spiritual teacher, Aśvaghoṣa was also a great musician, and he travelled throughout the India of his day playing his lute.[195] The Chinese traveller Xuanzang, who followed in his footsteps a few centuries later, in the seventh century CE, reports in his account of his sojourn in India that the effect of Aśvaghoṣa's music was still remembered all those years later. Apparently, when people heard it, they immediately got a sense of the impermanence of things. Somehow the melody conveyed the message that everything conditioned is unsatisfactory, all worldly things are unreal and insubstantial, Nirvāṇa is the only reality. Just listening to Aśvaghoṣa's music gave people that direct understanding. The music played by the white Buddha in the realm of the gods has the same effect. It wakes up those who are in this complacent and self-satisfied state, making them aware of higher truths and realities, not through philosophy, religion, or intellectual discussion, but through music.

In the world of the *asuras*, a green Buddha appears, brandishing a flaming sword, the sword of wisdom, transcendental wisdom – not just intellectual knowledge, but penetration into reality as a spiritual experience. This suggests that when we are in a state of competitiveness and aggressiveness, the next step is to develop intellectual insight into truth and reality. The battle, in other words, is relocated to the intellectual front. But why is wisdom symbolized by a sword? In an essay on 'Hate, Love, and Perfect Wisdom', the great Buddhist scholar Dr Edward Conze asserts that there is an affinity between hatred and wisdom.[196] If you experience a lot of anger and hatred, he says, you should be able to develop wisdom fairly easily.

This sounds odd at first, but a little thought shows the sense of it. The characteristic of hatred is to seek to destroy the hated object. If you hate something or someone, you want to finish them off, to smash them to smithereens, to make just one big nothing where they used to be. We may not always admit it to ourselves, but this is what we would like to do. And the characteristic of transcendental wisdom is also to destroy: to destroy conditioned existence itself, to reduce to dust everything that isn't reality, isn't truth, isn't Buddhahood. This is why transcendental wisdom is symbolized by the *vajra*, the thunderbolt, which is said to smash and destroy all obstacles.

Thus there is this affinity between hatred and wisdom, although the one is highly unethical and the other entirely ethical. It is noticeable that a hot temper and a highly developed intellect often go together, even when that intellect is applied to Buddhism, which should be the epitome of equanimity. Scholars specializing in Buddhist studies can be bad tempered and quarrelsome to a remarkable degree, especially among themselves – an example being Dr Conze himself, who was celebrated not only for his tremendous scholarship and intellectual penetration, but also for his peppery temper. It is as though the destructive force that expresses itself in hatred can be diverted into intellectual channels and used to fuel the discovery and realization of truth.

Dr Conze points out that the Perfection of Wisdom tradition is associated with the Buddha Akṣobhya, called the Imperturbable, one of the set of five archetypal Buddhas. Akṣobhya is said to be the patron Buddha of people of predominantly choleric temperament. In this way the Tantric tradition seems to recognize an affinity between hatred and wisdom. It seems that an *asura*-like person has a natural ability not only to fight with the gods, but also to conquer truth itself, at least intellectually, more effectively than other people who may be easier to get on with.

Having said this, one must be careful not to make a necessary connection out of a mere correspondence between two quite separate spheres, between an aspect of psychological conditioning and an aspect of reality. This suggestion of an affinity between hatred and wisdom originates with Buddhaghosa, the great commentator on the Pāli canon who lived in the sixth century CE. But what he actually said – as near as we can make it out – was that just as hatred seizes upon the negative aspects of things, in the same way wisdom seizes upon the faults of conditioned existence.[197] He draws an analogy between hatred and wisdom, but no more than that. In other words, someone with a critical, intellectually aggressive mind may have a greater potential to follow the path of wisdom, but without actually doing so they are no closer to true wisdom than anyone else. By the same token, someone who is warmly affectionate is not, without taking steps to realize their potential, any closer to developing true compassion than less demonstrative people.

In the world of the hungry ghosts there appears a red Buddha who showers the suffering denizens of that state of existence with food and drink that they can actually consume. Now what does this mean for us in practical terms? It means that when we are in a state of neurotic desire, the next step is to get back to an accurately objective perception of the situation, which also means getting back to the present moment. We must see what the desired object can give us and what it cannot. We also need to discover what we really desire, and where that desire is coming from. Once we have done so, we can either give our desire its proper satisfaction, if that is possible, or – if it is inappropriate or unskilful – do our best to let go of it.

The *amṛta* or nectar with which the smoke-coloured Buddha regales the beings in hell can be interpreted in at least two – rather contradictory – ways. Most obviously it signifies that when we are in a state of intense mental suffering, the next step is simply to gain a respite from it, some ease and relaxation. That is often the best we can do in the circumstances. But at another level of meaning, this nectar is both more challenging and more profound. *Amṛta* is usually translated as 'nectar' or 'ambrosia', but in many Buddhist texts it is a synonym for Enlightenment itself: the *amṛtapada*, the state of nectar, the deathless, eternal state. So the smoke-coloured Buddha gives the beings in hell not just nectar but Nirvāṇa. The suggestion – which in a way seems quite outrageous – is that when we are in a state of intense suffering, the next step is to gain Enlightenment. But it does make sense. There's nothing else for us to do. All worldly hope has foundered. All we can do is head straight for Enlightenment. It's as though there were another strange affinity between a supremely negative state and a supremely positive one – this time between intense mental suffering and an aptitude for the highest spiritual attainment.

In the world of animals, the blue Buddha shows the animals a book. Surely this suggests that when we are in a state of barbarism and savagery, our next step is to become civilized, to acquaint ourselves with the arts and sciences, with the cultural life of mankind, because these things have a refining influence. It is difficult, if not impossible, to go from a barbaric state straight into a life of spiritual development. This is one of the reasons why Buddhism has always been a bearer of culture. As well as spiritual teachings, Buddhists took Indian higher culture all over Asia, because that refined, humanistic culture provided a foundation for the spiritual life. Hence the bodhisattva, the ideal Buddhist, is presented in Mahāyāna texts as a master of arts, sciences, and even handicrafts – quintessentially in the figure of Mañjughoṣa, the great Bodhisattva of Wisdom, who is said to preside over the arts and sciences.

Finally, the yellow Buddha who appears in the world of human beings carries the begging-bowl and three-ringed staff that are the insignia of the religious mendicant and therefore of the spiritual life in general. The point of this is clear: when we find ourselves in a truly human state, the next step is to devote ourselves wholeheartedly to the task of spiritual development. Once we have reached the truly human state, this should be our main interest in life.

The general message from the presence of the different Buddhas is that within each of these realms or states of existence there is the potential for development. There is always a next step. One of the fundamental teachings of Buddhism, especially Mahāyāna Buddhism, is that all sentient beings are capable of Buddhahood. Indeed, above and beyond the world of time and phenomenal particularity, all beings *are* Buddha, *are* Enlightened. And within time all beings are capable – eventually – of gaining Enlightenment.

But beings are not all equally capable of becoming Enlightened from their present state, whatever it is. In the Chinese Mahāyāna tradition it is said that some people are endowed with more 'Buddha seeds' than others. According to this tradition, there are three kinds of seed, three kinds of potentiality, in sentient beings. There are good seeds (red seeds, as they are sometimes called), bad seeds (black seeds), and Buddha seeds (yellow or golden seeds). Buddha seeds represent potentialities for spiritual growth. The distinction between good seeds and Buddha seeds is a reminder that being good does not necessarily make you a Buddha, although if you are a Buddha you can't help being good, presumably. All three kinds of seed are present in all beings, in all six realms, in varying – and sometimes rather surprising – proportions.

In the world of the gods, there are no bad seeds. The gods have no potentiality for evil – and you do get people like that, people who wouldn't hurt a fly. Almost all the seeds in the god realm are good seeds because the gods really are very good – happy, holy, contented, peaceful, and kind. But what is perhaps surprising is the fact that they possess very few Buddha seeds; the potentiality of the gods for Enlightenment is very limited.

The seeds in the world of the *asuras* are two thirds bad, one third good, with only a single Buddha seed. In the world of hungry ghosts there are no good seeds at all and a predominance of bad seeds, but quite a lot of Buddha seeds. It's almost exactly the same in the world of tormented beings, except that there are even more Buddha seeds. In the world of the animals there are very few good seeds – so they don't have a very happy time of it after all, it would seem – a predominance of bad seeds, and a few Buddha seeds, about twice as many as the good seeds there. And in the world of human beings the three kinds of seed are present in roughly equal proportions.

Some of the conclusions that follow from all this are quite obvious. The *asuras* – warlike, competitive people – have the least potential for Buddhahood. By analogy, if you are in a highly competitive environment – big business, for example, or politics – you will have only the very smallest potential for Enlightenment, it would seem. This is not to say that all competition must be removed from the spiritual life. Competitiveness can be negative and destructive, but it can also be healthy and positive. It is possible to use the competitive spirit as a means of getting oneself to make more spiritual effort without having any antagonistic feeling towards the person with whom one is competing. For example, you might feel competitive with a friend about the relative consistency of your meditation practice. But if he or she manages to get up early to meditate more often than you do, you don't in the end mind being bested, because you have got the best out of yourself in the process, and that is what matters.

The competitiveness of the *asuras*, though, is completely antithetical to the spiritual life. It is not just using competitiveness in a playful way to get yourself to make more effort; it is aimed at victory, conquest, doing the other person down. This does sometimes occur even among those trying to live a spiritual life. It manifests most frequently in a reluctance to cooperate, but it can be expressed just through talking and joking. If we come to realize that we tend to be uncooperative, we need to make the effort to be more willing to go along with what other people want, and not to have very strong views about very small things. Bitter disputes so often arise over trivialities – because, of course, the issue isn't really whether to do this or that, but whether I have my way or you have your way. It is a good practice to be very slow to take a stand on anything other than a real matter of principle. Very often the situation isn't worth arguing about, but the *asura* element in one's nature whispers, 'Why should I do what he wants? Why should I always be following him?' It is a mistake to listen to that little voice. In most situations, the more wholehearted and warm the cooperation, the better it is for everyone.

It is sobering to observe that the gods have a smaller potential for Enlightenment than either the hungry ghosts or the tormented beings. It is very difficult, unfortunately, to gain Enlightenment from a state of unadulterated happiness and pleasure. It is much easier, though still extremely difficult, to make spiritual progress from a state of intense suffering. Suffering acts as a catalyst, it makes us more aware. People undergoing serious illness, going through physical changes and pain, or suffering intense distress, sometimes have spiritual experiences of a depth and intensity that do not occur so readily under more pleasant circumstances. We are more sensitive at such times, and thus more susceptible to spiritual influences. Self-inflicted suffering is, of course, another matter – the Buddha was clear that self-mortification takes one as far from the middle way, the path to Enlightenment, as self-indulgence, which is the other extreme.[198]

So has life in the god realm nothing to recommend it from a spiritual point of view? Is it just a waste of time? Not necessarily. It is analogous to sleep, which we know is not mere time wasting, but necessary to our good health and indeed our very existence. If you have led a healthy, positive life, a period in the god realm represents a rest from mundane existence, an opportunity to assimilate and digest experience. Then, as a residue of the skilful deeds that have caused you to be reborn among the gods, you may have a happy and positive human rebirth – like someone waking refreshed from a good sleep – and you can make another positive spiritual effort. But while you are actually in the realm of the gods, as in dreams, it is difficult (though not impossible) to make any effort at all.

Contentment is, of course, perilously close to complacency, and this is the fatal flaw of life in the god realm. In *The Jewel Ornament of Liberation*, the Tibetan teacher Gampopa says:

> How is it that we have not already obtained Buddhahood? The fault lies in people like ourselves having come under the power of four obstacles by which the attainment of Buddhahood is prevented. They are: attachment to sensuous experiences during this life, to sensual pleasures in this world, to self-complacency, and to ignorance about the means of realizing Buddhahood.[199]

Hindered by the first of these obstacles, you take it for granted that your particular world will continue. Hindered by the second – taking pleasure as the highest value – you seize the pleasure of the moment and forget your long-term interests. And in the grip of the third – self-complacency – you are satisfied with yourself as you are, and what could be a greater obstacle than that? You say, 'Well, I'm all right, I'm quite happy, I'm doing well, I meditate every day,' – and you lose your sense of urgency with regard to spiritual development.

It is crucial to understand this obstacle *as* an obstacle. Once you feel established on the spiritual path, once you are meditating, going on retreat, and associating with people who share your values, you naturally and rightly feel very pleased about the state of affairs. But that is the time to say to yourself, 'I must beware of complacency. I must keep on growing.' You have to keep asking yourself if the situation you are in is helping you to keep growing spiritually.

At the same time you can't overcome complacency simply by making life difficult for yourself. It is also possible to be complacent about being someone who has to struggle and make a lot of effort in life. One is not necessarily growing just because one is struggling, especially if you feel quietly pleased with yourself because you are always the one who is making the effort. So while in general greed types are more prone to complacency than hate types, hate types are also susceptible to it in their own way.

If the teaching of the seeds is anything to go by, our best bet, if we want to make spiritual progress, would seem to be to seek rebirth in the human realm, where 'joy and pain are woven fine', as Blake says.[200] But this is not easy either. In the *Dhammapada*, the Buddha says, 'Difficult is the attainment of the human state.'[201] One can look at this statement in two ways, one traditional and the other more contemporary. The traditional view is that it is literally difficult to attain a human birth, and this view is illustrated by means of a simile. The chances of being born human are likened to the chances that a blind turtle who only emerges from the depths of the ocean once every hundred years will happen to put his head through a wooden yoke floating on the surface.[202]

This is probably not to be taken literally. No doubt the statistical probability that any living being will be born human is remote, given how many billions of insects, fish, and all sorts of other creatures there are – one could perhaps look at human birth as being rare in that way. But it is unlikely that those who have been human beings in previous existences will not be reborn human. In approaching this idea that it is difficult to attain the human state, it is more fruitful to ask what it really means to be a human being. This brings us to the more contemporary interpretation of the statement. What is the human state? Are you necessarily a human being because you bear a remote resemblance to the higher apes? What *is* a human being?

To speak of being *born* as a human being is clearly to refer to being human in the ordinary biological sense. But to speak of *attaining* the human state is to suggest that it is not enough to be human merely in the biological sense. You have to develop certain qualities to qualify as a human being. The process of becoming human consists in the full development of such qualities as self-awareness, emotional positivity, responsibility, fidelity, and cooperativeness. So it isn't easy to be human; the human state is, as the Buddha says, 'difficult of attainment'.

We have to ask ourselves the purpose of this teaching of the seeds. It is not saying that there are literally so many red, black, and yellow seeds in an animal, so many in a human being, and so on. It is not meant to be scientific. It is simply a reminder that as human beings we have great potential for spiritual development, and that we should therefore make the effort to develop whatever potential we have. Whether the six realms of existence are taken literally, or whether they are regarded as being contained within human life, the whole teaching is meant to be encouraging, meant to remind us that there is always some potential for Enlightenment. If you are a *human* human being, the potential is greater. But even if you are in a hellish or *preta*-like state of mind, even if you are neurotic or aggressive, your potential for spiritual development is not altogether obscured – you can still make progress. Inasmuch as you are a human being, Buddha seeds are there.

Having taken our third long look into the mirror, we have seen where we are, the mental state we are in, and the next step to be taken. Now we must look into the mirror again. This time we see the images depicted around the rim of the wheel of life: the blind man with his stick, the potter with his wheel and pots, the monkey climbing the flowering tree, and so on. These are the twelve *nidānas* or links that show how it all happens, how we pass from one state of existence to another, one state of mind to another.[203] This is the process of what I have termed the reactive mind.[204] And seeing it, really seeing it, we are free of it. We have seen through the reactive mind and we pass beyond it. And after a while, we look into the mirror again.

This time we see the monster in whose grip the wheel is tightly clutched. We come face to face with death, with the fact of universal, cosmic impermanence. We see that conditioned existence – that is to say, existence that comes into being in dependence on causes and conditions – is not only impermanent but also ultimately unreal. But we see at the same time, in the depths of the unreality of conditioned existence, gleaming like a pearl at the bottom of the sea, the real, the ultimately, absolutely real. It is not even really separate from the unreal, but constitutes another dimension of it.

When we look into the mirror once more, we see the Buddha – this time not up in the corner of the picture, but right in the centre of things. We see, in short, Enlightenment itself. In Zen terms, we see our own original face. We experience directly what we truly and essentially are, in the depths of our being. And then we see the Bodhisattva. This is what the hare in the full moon represents: the Bodhisattva – that is, the Buddha in one of his previous lives. According to the traditional *Jātaka* stories, the Buddha-to-be was reborn as a hare, and sacrificed his body in a fire to provide a meal for a hungry guest. As so often in legends of this sort, the guest turned out to be a king in disguise – in this case Indra, the king of the gods. He restored the hare to life and drew his picture on the full moon as an everlasting testimony to his spirit of generosity and self-sacrifice.[205] This is why, according to Indian legend, you see the hare in the moon (not the man in the moon, as our legend is in the West), even today. Every time you look up at the hare in the moon, you are reminded of the Bodhisattva's generosity and self-sacrifice.

The Bodhisattva does not represent just one individual. Seeing the Bodhisattva means seeing the spirit of Enlightenment at work in the cosmos, and seeing ourselves as participating in that work. Having seen the Buddha, our own original face, outside time, we see that same Buddha principle at work within time, through time, in the activities of the Bodhisattva.

Looking in the mirror for the last time, we don't see anything at all. In fact, the mirror disappears. There's nothing to see and nobody to see it. And yet at the same time, mysteriously, everything is seen. Everything is heard. Everything is understood. Everything is realized. The symbolism of the Tibetan wheel of life has been transcended – and fulfilled.

from *Creative Symbols of Tantric Buddhism*

7. THE PARABLE OF THE BURNING HOUSE

Today the burning house is burning more merrily than ever; we only have to open our newspapers or turn on the television any day of the week to know that.

Once upon a time there was a great elder, a very rich old man who lived in a huge mansion with his hundreds of servants and his many children. The story does not speak of wives or mothers, but we know that the elder had as many as thirty children, and they were all quite young. The house in which they lived had once been magnificent, but now it was old and tumbledown. The pillars were decaying, the windows were broken, the floorboards were rotting, and the walls were crumbling. And in the nooks and crannies of this tumbledown house there lurked all sorts of ghosts and evil spirits.

One day the house suddenly caught fire. Because it was so old and the timbers were so dry, the whole building was burning merrily in no time. As it happened, the elder was safe outside the house when the fire started, but his children were playing inside. Too young to realize that they were in danger of being burned to death, they just carried on playing and made no effort to escape.

The elder was very afraid for his children, of course, and wondered how on earth to save them. At first he thought of carrying them out of the house one by one, for he was strong and able, but he soon realized that it would be impossible to get them all out in time. Instead, he decided to try calling out to the children. He shouted, 'The house is on fire! You're in terrible danger! Come out quickly!' But the children had no idea what their father could mean by danger. They just carried on playing their games, glancing at the elder occasionally as they ran to and fro, but taking no serious notice of him at all.

The elder saw that there was no time to lose, for the house would crash to the ground at any minute. In desperation he hit upon another plan. He would try to trick the children into coming out of the house. Knowing the different nature of each child, he knew that they liked different kinds of toys, some liking one kind and some preferring another. So he called out to them, 'Come and look at the toys I have brought for you! There are all kinds of carts, some drawn by deer, some drawn by goats, and some drawn by bullocks, and they are all standing just outside the gate. Come quickly and look!' And although the children had been deaf to all his warnings, this time they heard him. They all came rushing and tumbling helter-skelter out of the burning house, pushing and shoving each other in their eagerness to get the new toys.

When the elder was sure that all the children were safely out of the house, he sat down with a great sigh of relief; and at once, of course, the children came clamouring round him demanding the toys he had promised them. The elder was extremely fond of his children, and wanted to give them whatever their hearts desired. And, fortunately, he was extremely wealthy – in fact his wealth was infinite – so he could afford to give them the best of everything. Instead of the carts of different kinds which he had promised them, therefore, he gave to each of them a magnificent bullock-drawn cart, bigger and better than they could have imagined in their wildest dreams. Although he had promised them one thing and gave them something else, this was not deceitfulness on his part, because it was motivated by his desire for the welfare and the safety of his children.

So this is the Parable of the Burning House.[206] In a way there is no need to say any more, because a parable speaks directly in its own symbolic language. It means just what it says it means, and we simply have to let it all sink in. It can be useful, however, to dwell on the events of the story and see what significance they have for us.

The elder, of course, is the Buddha, the Enlightened One, and the mansion in which he lives is the world – not just this earth, but the whole universe, the whole of conditioned existence, all worlds. The mansion – the universe – is inhabited by many beings – not just human beings, according to Buddhism, but beings of all kinds, some less developed than mankind and some even more developed. And just as the mansion is old and decayed, this universe is subject to all kinds of imperfections. For a start, it is impermanent, changing all the time. We cannot stay in it for long; it is more like a hotel than a home. The mansion has ghosts in the corners too, which suggests that this world of ours is haunted. Haunted by what? By the past. We like to think that we live in the present, but more often than not the ghosts of the past are all around us. We may think that we are experiencing objectively existing beings and situations, but often they are really the projections of our unconscious minds, the ghosts of the past that we carry along with us all the time.

In the parable the mansion catches fire at a certain time, but in reality the mansion of the world is constantly blazing and burning. The use of fire as a symbol is very common in Buddhism, and in Indian religion generally. The Buddha used it in a teaching known as the Fire Sermon which he gave not long after his Enlightenment, on an occasion when he was speaking to a company of his disciples who had previously been 'matted-hair' ascetics and whose main religious practice had been fire-worship. No doubt the Buddha was alluding to their previous practice when he led a thousand of them to the top of a hill and said to them, 'The whole world is ablaze. The whole world is burning. Burning with what? It is burning with the fire of craving and neurotic desire. It is burning with the fire of anger, hatred, and aggression. It is burning with the fire of ignorance, delusion, bewilderment, and lack of awareness.'[207] This was surely not just an *idea* of the Buddha's, not just a concept he happened to think up. He surely saw the world, as though in a vision, just like this. Perhaps before he spoke he had been looking down from the hilltop into the jungles below, and had seen a forest fire burning in the distance. Then he may have seen, in his spiritual vision, that not only was the forest burning, but the houses were burning, people were burning, the mountains were burning, the earth was burning, the sun, moon, and stars were burning – everything conditioned was burning with the threefold fires of craving, hatred, and delusion.

Fire, incidentally, far from being just a negative symbol in Buddhism, has many positive associations. It is associated with change – in fact fire, the process of combustion, *is* change, and not just change but transformation. In Indian spiritual life fire is therefore a symbol not just of destruction but also of renewal and spiritual rebirth. In Vedic times, long before the Buddha, people placed offerings on a fire altar to ascend in the subtle form of smoke to the realms of the gods. The rite of cremation involves a similar transformation, reducing the physical body to ashes but – or so the ancient Indians believed – sending the subtle aspect of being, the 'soul', to the moon or to the sun, to the world of the fathers or to the world of the gods. In Hinduism the cremation ground is the domain of Shiva (Śiva) the Destroyer, who is the god not only of destruction but also of spiritual rebirth, because before you can build up you must break down. And the flames which surround the wrathful deities of Tibetan Buddhism also symbolize a transformation by fire – the fiery breaking through of the spirit of Enlightenment into the darkness and ignorance of the world.

But fire is a threat to the children in the mansion; in fact they are in danger of burning to death. Who do the children represent? Obviously they represent living beings, especially human beings – that is to say, especially ourselves. In the context of the *sūtra* they represent the Hīnayāna disciples, those who are following lower spiritual ideals. More generally speaking, we can say that they represent all those who have evolved only up to a certain point and have some distance – maybe a great distance – still to go.

The children in the parable are in danger of being burned to death. The implication is that human beings are in danger – *we* are in danger.

What does this mean? It could mean that we are in danger of remaining within the world, within the process of conditioned existence, the cycle of birth, death, and rebirth as illustrated by the Tibetan wheel of life.[208] The danger is that if we carry on turning round and round within the wheel we must inevitably suffer, at least sometimes. But the symbolism could also mean that we are in danger of getting stuck at a lower level of development. Unfortunately this happens to very many people, and it isn't always entirely their own fault. The human organism, biologically, psychologically, and even spiritually speaking, has a natural tendency to grow. In fact, to grow is the nature of life itself. Life in all its forms wants to unfold its inner potentialities, and if any living thing cannot do this it feels miserable, or at least uneasy and dissatisfied. People are often so restricted by their circumstances that they simply cannot grow – indeed, they sometimes feel that they cannot even breathe. All sorts of unpleasant and uncontrollable factors press in on them from all sides. They strangle them, stifle them, and make them feel that they are not developing as they should and could, so that they feel not only frustrated and restricted, but miserable, resentful, and unhappy in every way.

In the parable, of course, the person trying to rescue the children from danger is their father. If the 'father' here meant the begetter of the children, this might seem to imply that the Buddha is a kind of creator god, the creator of the world, of men and women, and all living beings. But this 'father' simply stands for someone older, more experienced, and more highly evolved. He is like the 'cultural father' of some so-called primitive cultures where you have both a biological father, who begot you, and a cultural father – usually your mother's brother – who is responsible for educating you and bringing you up. (In modern societies the biological father fulfils both roles, but this is not an invariable rule.) So there is no implication of theism here.

The elder's first impulse when the fire starts is to rush into the house and carry the children out – he would be strong enough to do that – but on reflection he dismisses the idea. This goes to show that however willing and able you may be, you just cannot save people, spiritually speaking, by force. You could conceivably drag someone out of a burning building against their will, but it is impossible to make anybody evolve against their will. Yes, you can drag them to meditation classes, you can drag them into church. You can force them to recite the Creed and read the Bible. You can intimidate them into not doing this or not doing that. But you cannot make them evolve against their will. By its very nature the Higher Evolution is a voluntary process, something *you* do because *you* want to do it.

Unfortunately, this is sometimes forgotten. Some religious teachers hold the view that what people really need to make them grow spiritually is discipline – and these teachers are only too willing to dish it out, and give their disciples a very tough time indeed. Of course, there is no shortage of people who are ready to accept this sort of discipline. It is not difficult to find ways of conditioning people along certain lines. This kind of conditioning, however, is a very different thing from real spiritual development. So Buddhism does not force, it does not compel, it does not intimidate, and it doesn't have recourse to discipline in this almost military sense of the term, because trying to force people to develop is self-defeating. Throughout the history of Buddhism, therefore, Buddhist teachers have been very tolerant. Buddhism has never tried to force anybody to do anything.

So in the end the elder gives up the idea of rescuing the children and instead tries calling out to them. Now this call is full of meaning. It represents the call of Truth, the call, if you like, of the divine. Turning to the Hindu tradition again, we find the symbolism of the call beautifully expressed in the medieval Hindu story of Krishna (Kṛṣṇa) and his flute. Krishna is one of the great spiritual figures of Hinduism, a demigod said to be an incarnation of Vishnu (Viṣṇu) the Preserver, and he is surrounded by all sorts of myths and legends. The story of Krishna's flute is set in an Indian village called Vrindavana where the people live by herding cows. Just imagine the scene. It is a dark night with no moon and the whole village is sound asleep. The cows are all shut in their stalls for the night, and everywhere – the little thatched mud-walled huts, the fields, and the forest – is absolutely still. Then, suddenly, in the midst of the darkness, in the midst of the silence, from the depths of the forest there comes a sound, faint but sweet and shrill, a sound that seems to come from an infinitely remote distance – the sound of a flute. Even now in India you can sometimes have this experience. You can be all by yourself in the midst of the countryside, with no one for miles around, and all of a sudden, out of the dark and the silence, there comes the sound of a flute.

Now although the sound of the flute is very faint and distant, it does not go unheard in the village of Vrindavana. Almost as though they have been expecting to hear it, the wives of the cowherds – the *gopīs* – wake up, and know at once that Krishna is calling them. Without making a sound, without telling anybody, they get up and steal out of their houses, along the streets of the village, and into the forest. Leaving their husbands and their children, their pots and their pans, their cows and their goats, they all go stealing away, rushing away as soon as they are at a safe distance, to dance with Krishna in the heart of the forest.[209]

In this story Krishna is a symbol of the divine, and the *gopīs* represent the human heart, or the human soul if you like; and the sound of Krishna's flute is the call of the divine, sounding from the very depths of existence. In fact, most of us hear such a call at some time in our lives. It may come in a moment of quietness when we are out in the country, or through an experience of great art, literature, or music. Perhaps we may hear it after some tragic event, or perhaps when we are just rather weary of life. At such a time we may hear the call, the call which is sometimes termed the voice of the silence,[210] the voice of something beyond. But even if we have heard this call very clearly, what usually happens is that we ignore it. Indeed, the very idea that there might have been a voice vaguely worries us. We don't know where it came from, or what mysterious region it might be calling us to. And if we follow it into unknown territory, we are afraid that we will have to give up all sorts of things that we are attached to. So we tell ourselves that we were imagining things, or that it was just a dream, and go on living and working and enjoying ourselves as though we had never heard anything at all.

Quite often, of course, we are much too busy enjoying ourselves even to hear the call, like the children in the parable. They almost completely ignore their father's calls because, the Buddha says – and we can imagine him saying this with a smile – they are absorbed in their games. We are absorbed in our games – the psychological games, spiritual games, and cultural games that we play almost all the time. We are so fascinated by our little games of success, prestige, popularity, ego-tripping dressed up as self-fulfilment, and so on, that even though we hear the call of the divine, the voice of the Buddha, we just go on playing.

And like the children in the burning house, we are not only playing our games, but running to and fro from one game to another. We are restless, anxious, incapable of staying anywhere for long. We constantly want to change the game we are playing or to change our partner – in more ways than one – so we end up running backwards and forwards in desperation. Just one thing occasionally stops us in our tracks. In the story, you may remember, the children just occasionally glance at their father as they run past. Similarly, as we run to and fro playing our little games, we do give the odd glance in the direction of religion.

So what is the elder to do? Force is out of the question and the children will not respond to a direct appeal. In the end his only alternative is to have recourse to a stratagem – in plain words, to play a trick. This kind of 'trick', which benefits the person on which it is played, is known in Buddhism as *upāya-kauśalya* – 'skilful means'.[211] The elder knows that the children are very fond of toys, so he decides to persuade them to come out of the burning house by promising them carts of different kinds to play with: deer carts, goat carts, and bullock carts. These three different kinds of cart represent, technically speaking, the three 'vehicles', the three *yānas* – the *śrāvakayāna*, the *pratyekabuddhayāna*, and the *bodhisattvayāna* – that is, the *arhant* ideal, the ideal of private Enlightenment, and the bodhisattva ideal.[212] Less technically, the carts stand for different formulations of the Buddha's teaching, or even different sectarian forms of Buddhism adapted to the needs of different temperaments.

Although the children take no notice of their father's warnings of danger, as soon as he promises them all these marvellous toys, out they come rushing. Their eager response to being promised their favourite kind of toy says something very perceptive about how religions appeal to people. It seems to suggest – bearing in mind what the toys represent – that a subjective and sectarian approach to the truth is much more attractive for many people than a more objective, universal approach. And this does seem to be the case in practice. It is certainly the more exclusive forms of religion that exert the most powerful emotional appeal. If your opening gambit is, 'Well, look, this is how I see it. Other people see things differently, but we're maybe all right from our own point of view. Let's go forward together,' that is no way to convince the average person. The way to get a following is to put it about that yours is the only true religion and all the others are just plain wrong. This explains why it is that the forms of Buddhism which in the course of history have become the most exclusive – that is, exclusive by Buddhist standards – have become the most popular in the West.

A sectarian approach may be more popular, but does this mean that it is necessary? Do we have to follow a particular path believing it to be the only true way, and only later on in our spiritual experience come to a broader outlook. If we look at our situation it is really questionable whether this is actually possible for us. In the Buddha's day no doubt it *was* possible. His disciples would have been able to learn and practise one teaching at a time. There was no writing in those days, at least not for religious purposes, so the Buddha did all his teaching orally. The disciples couldn't just pick up books about religion, and they certainly didn't go to other teachers, so they knew only what the Buddha taught them.

Even in more recent times, different forms of religion existed independently in different parts of the world – even in different parts of the same country – so it was perfectly possible to stick to one teaching or sect and ignore all the others completely. Until comparatively recently you could be a Christian in the West and never have heard of Buddhism or Hinduism, and you could be a Buddhist in the East and never hear the name of Christianity from one year to the next.

The world is now a very different place. Nowadays, everybody can study everything. All the spiritual teachings are available in written form – 'Who runs, may read,' as John Keble said[213] – so it is no longer possible to keep people away from a teaching for which they are not ready. This means that people get hold of all sorts of teachings which, because they are not spiritually developed enough, they can only misunderstand and misinterpret. This just can't be helped. With improved communication and transport, the world is becoming a smaller place all the time. All religions, even all sects, are increasingly to be found everywhere, so it's no longer possible to follow any one and ignore all the others – at the very least we'll know about them from books or hearsay.

In this situation, the only thing to be done is for religions to try to see the Parable of the Burning House in its universal perspective. We all need to try to recognize that all the ways are different aspects of one and the same path, the path to perfect Buddhahood, the path to Enlightenment. Of course differences of temperament still exist, but sectarianism is no longer needed to cater for them. It is quite enough to choose a method of spiritual practice appropriate to our needs – for example, an appropriate method of meditation. We don't need to belong to a sectarian organization that excludes all the others. We don't need to be 'Theravādin' or 'Zen' or 'Mahāyānist' – why not just be Buddhist? And Buddhism itself can be interpreted very broadly. According to the Buddha's own criterion, Buddhism is whatever conduces to the Enlightenment of the individual. The Buddha alone among religious teachers seems to have understood that religion is really the process of the evolution and development of the individual. Sectarian organizations tend to lose sight of this, and in fact many of them express, for the most part, merely negative emotions, and we would be better off without their exclusivity and intolerance.

You notice that, in their eagerness to get their own particular carts, the children come out of the house pushing and shoving one another. In the same way, in our rush to get out of the house and grab the toy we want, instead of going out side by side or hand in hand, we jostle and shove all the others who are doing the same thing. We may not actually persecute anybody – at least not if we are Buddhists – but at the same time we may not exactly radiate positive feelings towards other people following other paths. This, as we have seen, needs to change, and in fact the parable goes on to show that as you progress on your chosen path it does change. Once the children are all outside, the elder gives each of them the very best kind of cart – or even one and the same cart – bigger and better than anything they could ever have imagined. Here is the indication that the closer people come to the goal, the more their paths converge.

People get into the spiritual life in different ways – some through music, art, or poetry, some through social service, some through meditation, some through the desire to resolve pressing psychological problems. Some people are attracted to Zen, others to the Theravāda. We all have our own personal idiosyncrasies, so we are naturally attracted by different things in the beginning. But as we get more and more deeply into our chosen approach, we realize that it is changing us. We begin to notice that our idiosyncrasies of temperament – even those which led us to this particular approach – are being resolved. In the end we come to realize through our own experience that all forms of art, all forms of religion, are means for the Higher Evolution of humanity. By participating in any of them we ourselves are evolving, and other people are also evolving, even though their interests and preoccupations are different from our own. We are all evolving together, all participating in the same process of the Higher Evolution, the process – in Buddhist terms – of cosmic Enlightenment; this is really the message of the Parable of the Burning House.

So does this mean that the parable is teaching universalism? It is, after all, saying that the distinction between the different *yānas* is illusory, that in reality there is only one *yāna*. But is this universalism? Well, I understand universalism as saying that all religions teach the same thing and that there is therefore no difference between them.[214] The doctrines may appear to differ, but universalists would say that this is only a matter of words – the substance is the same – and they would back this up by trying to equate doctrines from different religions. For example, they would say that the Christian Trinity – Father, Son, and Holy Ghost – corresponds to the Buddhist *trikāya* (*dharmakāya, sambhogakāya, nirmāṇakāya*) and the Hindu *trimūrti* (Brahmā, Viṣṇu, Maheśvara). This kind of wholesale system of equations – the very substance of universalism – often leads to very forced interpretations.

It is clear enough that the Parable of the Burning House does not teach universalism in this sense. It doesn't say that all religions teach the same thing; they obviously teach different things. Moreover, some religions are more advanced than others – universal religions, for example, being more advanced than ethnic religions. And whereas the universalist would claim that all religions are totally true in all respects, the Buddhist would say that there are some teachings which pass currency as religious but – because they are not true – are not really religious at all. The orthodox Christian doctrine of eternal punishment is an example of such a teaching.

The parable is not even saying that all the *yānas* of Buddhism teach the same thing. What it does maintain very definitely is that all the different ways are part of the same 'stream of tendency', to use an expression of Matthew Arnold's.[215] Everyone is trying to get out of the same burning house. Indeed the parable emphasizes movement, escape; it is dynamic, unlike the static teaching of universalism. The universalist fixes systems of belief into patterns which have to rely heavily on intellectual resemblances, whereas the Parable of the Burning House can rely on the unity of the evolutionary process.

Another general consideration arising out of this parable, and one which must be addressed as it constitutes the main theme, is the idea of escape as a model for the spiritual life. The elder's sole concern is that the children should escape from the burning house. Does this mean that the parable is teaching escapism? Well, obviously enough, it is – in a sense. A lot of people would say that this is typical of the way religions encourage us to run away from the problems of the world, and even from our own problems. And, they would say, this is particularly true of Buddhism. After all, look at the Buddha – leaving his wife and child like that, ducking out of his responsibilities and obligations! Some would say that Christians stay in the world and try to make it into a better place, try to help the sick and care for the needy, whereas Buddhists just sit around meditating, ignoring the sins and sufferings all around them. Pure escapism!

But is escape morally wrong? Suppose you were literally trapped in a burning house. There you would be, standing at the upstairs window, surrounded by smoke and flames. Along would come the fire brigade, and you would escape, either by jumping into a net or by being carried down a ladder. Would your friends say afterwards, 'You shouldn't have done that. That was sheer escapism'? Buddhism simply sees that our situation is one of pain and suffering – or at least limitation, imperfection, frustration – and says, 'Get out of it.' This is just acting realistically, like escaping from that burning house.

Perhaps the word 'escape' is the wrong one. The word traditionally means 'to gain one's liberty by flight', 'to get safely out of', and so on, but in the nineteenth century it gained a new usage – 'mental or emotional distraction from the realities of life' – and it is this which has given birth to the notion of escap*ism*: 'the tendency to seek or practice of seeking such distraction'. The burning house in the parable represents the predicament in which we find ourselves as human beings. Given the connotations of the language of escape, it would perhaps be better to speak of *transcending* this human predicament rather than escaping from it. The parable is showing us how we can transcend our present state, how we can grow from a lower, less satisfactory state of existence to a higher, more satisfactory state.

This is not to say, of course, that there is no such thing as escapism, but we need to understand what escapism really is. Not everybody is prepared to make the kind of effort that the process of growth and development requires – *that* is what we try to escape from. When we try to avoid situations which demand that we go beyond ourselves, when we try to forget our human predicament, when we try to secure an easy life – these are the times when we are really being 'escapist'. Escapism is stagnation, even regression. Sometimes, it is true, religious activity – of the kind which involves lip service but no effort towards personal change – is escapism, though there is less of this these days simply because fewer people are involved in religion of any kind. Nowadays it is more usually non-religious activities that provide outlets for escapism. For many people work is escapism, politics are escapism, even the arts are escapism. Reading is escapism. Watching television is escapism. Sex is escapism. In short, any kind of life that involves no positive, deliberate effort to evolve is escapism – which means, if you think about it, that escapism is the rule rather than the exception. And of course, escapism of this kind is the last thing that the Parable of the Burning House teaches. It is concerned above all with growth, development, evolution.

Today the burning house is burning more merrily than ever; we only have to open our newspapers or turn on the radio any day of the week to know that. So the whole question of escape – or rather the whole question of transcendence, growth, and development into a higher state – becomes more urgent than ever, both for the individual alone and for the individual as part of a spiritual community.

But we need not despair. If we take heed of the message of the Parable of the Burning House, even here, even now, we can transcend the human predicament.

from *The Drama of Cosmic Enlightenment*

8. THE MYTH OF THE RETURN JOURNEY

Religion, when properly understood, is not remote from life, not just a dull, churchy little backwater, but life become conscious of its own upward tendency, its own tendency to grow and develop. And whether we know it or not, we are all involved, directly or indirectly, in this upward tendency of life.

The Parable of the Burning House gives us the metaphor of life as predicament, or even as trap, but this is of course only one way of looking at it. Human existence is multifaceted, deep and mysterious, difficult to understand. 'Wonders are many, and none is more wonderful than man' chants the chorus of Sophocles' play *Antigone*.[216] Throughout history, facets of the nature and purpose of human life have been reflected by symbols and similes from which have arisen myths, legends, and stories – and these in turn have crystallized into epic poems, novels, dramas, and parables. The mystery of human life always having been the compelling preoccupation of humanity, the great works of ancient and modern literature which concern some aspect of human existence are read and reread, even after hundreds and thousands of years.

Some of these great works see human life in terms of conflict, or even warfare. Homer's *Iliad*, for example, tells the story of the battle between the Greeks and the Trojans over Helen of Troy, a battle involving not just men and women but even gods and goddesses. Two or three hundred years after the *Iliad* another epic was written, perhaps not so eminent from a literary point of view, but very, very much longer: the *Mahābhārata*. This was composed by the Indian poet and sage Vyāsa, and gives an account of the battle between the Kauravas and their cousins the Pandavas for possession of their ancestral kingdom. Northern Europe produced the anonymous eighth-century Anglo-Saxon epic *Beowulf*, which recounts the battles of the hero Beowulf against three terrible adversaries: the fiendish monster Grendel, Grendel's still more fiendish mother, and the dragon. Even from comparatively modern times we have one of the very greatest of all epic poems, Milton's *Paradise Lost*, whose main theme is the War in Heaven, the battle between Satan and the Messiah. In all these works life is seen in terms of conflict. Life is a battle – between right and wrong, between light and darkness, between heaven and hell, between conscious and unconscious – and the battleground is the human heart.

But human existence can also be seen as a riddle, a mystery, or even a problem, and this is how the *Book of Job* in the Bible sees it. Job has been brought up to believe that God rewards the good for their virtue – and punishes the wicked – here in this very life. But although Job is conscious of no evil in himself, he suffers, and it seems that his suffering is the punishment of God. Why should the just man be ground into dust while the unjust man 'flourishes like the green bay tree'? To make sense of life Job needs to know the answer. The same kind of question plagues Shakespeare's Hamlet, confronted with the murder of his innocent father by his villainous uncle. When Hamlet asks his famous question, 'To be or not to be?', life itself has become a problem.

There are many other ways of viewing human existence. However, of all the symbols and similes for life, perhaps the most popular and significant is that of the journey or pilgrimage. Life is not only a battle, not only a problem. It is a journey: a journey from the cradle to the grave, from innocence to experience, from the depths of existence to the heights, from darkness to light, from death to immortality. We find life seen as a journey in a great number of works: the *Odyssey*, the *Divine Comedy*, *Monkey*, *Pilgrim's Progress*, *Wilhelm Meister*, *Peer Gynt*, and countless others.

The *White Lotus Sūtra* gives its own account of human life as a journey. The Parable of the Return Journey, which occurs in chapter 4, is related not by the Buddha but by four great elders. They have heard the Buddha tell the assembly that Śāriputra is now so far advanced on the path that he is sure to reach the highest goal of all – not just emancipation from his own individual sin and suffering but Buddhahood itself. Amazed and delighted to learn that the spiritual life has a higher aim, the existence of which they had not hitherto suspected, the four great elders say they feel as though they have quite unexpectedly acquired a priceless jewel, and in chorus they give expression to their feelings in a parable.[217]

They say that once upon a time there was a man who left his father and went away into a distant country. He lived there for a long time – perhaps as long as fifty years – and during all that time he was miserably poor. Roaming around, doing a job here and a job there, he lived from hand to mouth, and all he ever possessed were the clothes he stood up in.

Meanwhile, his father was leading a very different kind of life. He was a businessman, and he met with such success in his various trading ventures that he became extremely rich. His trade took him from place to place until he finally settled in another country, where he continued to heap up riches – gold, silver, jewels, and grain. He had slaves and workmen and journeymen, horses and carriages, cows and sheep. He even had elephants – and in the East if you possess elephants you really are rich. He also, inevitably, had dozens of dependants and followers clustering around him in the hope of some reward. His influence in business – money-lending, agriculture, commerce – spread far and wide, and he lived the life of a merchant prince.

But despite his growing wealth and all his business activities, the rich man never stopped missing his son. How was the boy? Would they ever meet again? Sorrowful at their long separation, his one hope was that one day his son would come home to inherit the wealth due to him. 'After all,' the rich man thought, 'I am getting old, and one day I must surely die.'

All this time his son continued to roam from one town to the next, from one kingdom to the next, until one day, quite by chance, he came to the place where his father was living – although of course he had no idea that he was anywhere near his father. As he was passing, or rather skulking, through the streets keeping a lookout for odd jobs which would earn him a few coppers for food, he saw an enormous house, and sitting in the doorway he saw what seemed to be a very rich man. He was surrounded by an enormous company of people, all waiting on him, or waiting for him. Some had bills in their hands and others had great bundles of money that they wanted to give him. Others had presents, and maybe some had bribes.

The rich man was sitting in the gateway on a magnificent throne – even his footstool was ornamented with gold and silver. He was handling scores of gold pieces, just running his fingers through them, and someone was standing behind him fanning him with a yak's tail. In India a yak's tail is one of the symbols of royalty and divinity, so you would only be fanned with one if you were very, very rich indeed, and had been exalted almost to the plane of divinity. Not only that, he was sitting under a magnificent silk canopy which was inlaid with pearls and flowers, and hung all round with garlands of jewels. He really was a magnificent sight.

When the poor man saw this rich man seated there on his throne, in all this state, he was absolutely terrified. He thought he must have come upon the king, or at the very least some great nobleman. 'I'd better be off,' he said to himself. 'I'm much more likely to get work in the streets of the poor. If I stay here they might make me into a slave.' And he hurried away, without the faintest idea that the rich man was his own father.

But the rich merchant no sooner saw that wretchedly poor man at the edge of the crowd of followers than he knew that this was his son, come back after all these years. What a relief! Now he would be able to hand over his wealth to its rightful inheritor and die happy. Joyfully he called a couple of servants and told them to run after the poor man and bring him back. But when they caught up with the poor fellow he was more terrified than ever. 'They've been sent to arrest me. I'm probably going to have my head cut off!' he thought – and he was so afraid that he fell to the earth in a dead faint.

His father was rather surprised at this, but he began to see that all those years he had been living in riches, his son had been living in poverty, and this had created a great psychological difference between them. The boy was obviously not used to being in contact with the rich and powerful. But the faithful father thought, 'Never mind. However low he may have sunk, he is still my son,' – and he resolved to find a way of restoring their relationship. In the meantime, things being as they were, he decided that it would be better to keep his son's identity secret. He therefore called another servant and instructed him to tell the poor man that he was free to go. Hardly believing his luck, the poor man went off with all speed to seek work in the poorest quarter of the town.

But he was followed by two of his father's men, chosen for their humble appearance. When they caught up with him, the men offered him work, as the rich man had instructed them to do. The job would be to clear away a huge heap of dirt that had accumulated at the back of the mansion, and the wages would be double the normal rate. The poor man accepted this proposal at once, and went off to work with the two men. Day after day he shovelled the heap of dirt and removed it in baskets to a distant place. He found lodging in a straw hovel right next to the mansion, so close that the rich man could see it from his window. The rich man would often look out and think how strange it was that he should be living in a beautiful mansion while his son lived in squalor so near by.

One day, when the poor man had been working at the mansion for quite some time, the rich man put on dirty old clothes and, taking a basket in his hands, managed to have a talk with his son. 'Don't think of working anywhere else,' he said, 'I'll make sure you've got plenty of money. If there's anything you need – a pot, a jug, some extra grain, anything like that – just ask me. I've got an old cloak in the cupboard; you can have that if you like. Just don't worry about a thing. You've been working well and I'm pleased with you. You seem honest and sincere, not like some of the rogues I've got working for me. In fact – well, I'm an old man – you look to me as your own father, and I'll treat you just like my own son.'

So for a number of years the poor man carried on clearing away the heap of dirt, and he got into the habit of going in and out of the mansion without thinking twice, although he continued to live in his old straw hovel. Then it happened that the old man became ill, and knew that he was soon going to die. He called the poor man and said, 'I feel that I can trust you completely now, just as I would my own son, so I'm going to hand over to you the management of all my affairs. You'll do everything on my behalf.' And from that day onward the poor man was the rich man's steward, and looked after all his investments and transactions. As before, he went freely in and out of the mansion but continued to live in his old hovel. Even though he was handling all this wealth, he continued to think that he was poor, for as far as he knew the money was not his, but his master's.

But as time went on, the poor man changed. His father, who watched him constantly, saw that he was gradually becoming accustomed to handling riches, and feeling ashamed that in the past he had lived so miserably. It became obvious that the poor man had begun to want to be rich himself. By this time the rich man was very old and weak indeed, and he knew that his death was near. So he sent for all the people in the city – the king's representative, the merchants, his friends, his distant relations, ordinary citizens, and country folk from round about – and when they were all gathered, he presented his son to them and told them the whole story. When he had finished, he handed over all his wealth to his son, who, of course, could hardly believe his good fortune.

In the context of the *White Lotus Sūtra*, this parable has a specific meaning which the four elders explain as soon as they have finished telling the story. Until now, they confess, they have been contented with an inferior spiritual ideal. Now, in his kindness and generosity, the Buddha has revealed to them the ideal of attaining supreme Enlightenment not for themselves alone but for the benefit of all sentient beings, and in this way has made them heirs to all his spiritual treasures. Like the son in the parable, the four elders feel overjoyed at the wealth which they have so unexpectedly gained.

The four elders' explanation takes us quite a long way, but with a little imagination we can go much further, even much deeper. We can start by reflecting on the strangely familiar ring of this story. You may well be thinking, 'I'm sure I've heard that story somewhere before.' Thinking back, you may be pretty sure that you haven't read the *White Lotus Sūtra* – it isn't the sort of thing you can read one weekend and then forget about – so why does the parable of the return journey seem so familiar? The reason, as you may have realized, is that it resembles a much more widely known parable: Jesus' parable of the prodigal son.[218] This parable is told by Jesus of Nazareth to elucidate a different point, and it has a different ending, but in general outline the two stories are the same. In both parables there is an affectionate father and a son who runs away; in both parables the runaway son lives miserably for a while before returning to the bosom of his father; and in both parables the position of servant is contrasted with the position of son.

These are the similarities between the parables; there are also significant differences between them. Perhaps the most important of these differences is that in the gospel parable the prodigal son appears to be guilty of wilful disobedience, whereas in the *White Lotus Sūtra* the son seems to go astray just through carelessness and forgetfulness. This illustrates a crucial difference between Christianity and Buddhism, Christianity seeing the human condition in terms of sin, disobedience, and guilt while Buddhism sees it more in terms of forgetfulness, unmindfulness, and ignorance.

Another parable about a father and a son, belonging to roughly the same period as the Parable of the Return Journey, constitutes an even more interesting parallel. It occurs in the apocryphal *Acts of Thomas*, an essentially Gnostic work extant in Greek translation as well as in the original Syriac. Modern translators call the story the 'Hymn of the Pearl', but the text gives it the title 'Song of the Apostle Judas Thomas in the Land of the Indians'.[219] Saint Thomas, one of the twelve Apostles, is traditionally known as the Apostle to India because he is supposed to have visited India soon after the death of Jesus, and this parable is said to have been composed while he was imprisoned there. Whether he had much contact with Buddhism, and whether the 'Hymn of the Pearl' owes anything to the Parable of the Return Journey, we can only speculate.

The parable says that in the East there live a father and his son. The son is quite happy living in the wealth and splendour of 'the kingdom of his father's house', but one day his father sends him on a mission to the land of Egypt, to bring back the one pearl which lies, encircled by a great dragon, in the midst of the sea. When he reaches Egypt, the son finds the dragon and waits for him to go to sleep so that he can take the pearl. But the Egyptians become suspicious of this stranger, even though he is disguised in Egyptian garments, and they give him a drugged drink which causes him to lose his memory. Forgetting that he is the son of a king, forgetting all about the pearl, he enters the service of the king of Egypt. And eventually, living with the Egyptians, eating their food and drinking their drink, he becomes more and more like them. In the end, we are told, he falls into a deep sleep. His father in the East, who knows what is happening, becomes anxious, and sends his son a letter – in the form of a bird – reminding him of his mission. As soon as he receives the letter, the son comes to his senses, enchants the dragon, and seizes the pearl. He returns home in triumph, and his father receives him with great joy.

Each of these parables, the return journey, the prodigal son, and the 'Hymn of the Pearl', has its own wealth of symbolism, but they all share the same central symbol. They all begin with a separation between a father and a son; this is the event from which everything else follows. So what is meant by this separation of father and son? Who or what are the father and the son?

We could say that the father represents what may be called the higher self (although we need to be careful not to take the expression too literally), and the son is the lower self. And just as the son is separated from his father, the lower self is separated – or, in more contemporary language, *alienated* – from the higher self. Here, by the way, is another metaphor for the human condition: alienation. We are alienated from our own higher selves, our own better natures, our own highest potentialities. We are alienated from Truth, from Reality. And just as the son went not just a short distance away from his father, but to an altogether different part of the world, so the alienation between the higher self and the lower self is severe. Indeed, the schism between the two is complete; there is no contact of any kind between them.

We may say that the condition of the human race is one of alienation from Truth, but when did this condition begin? The son lives in a distant country for many years, which suggests that the alienation is of long standing. But if we take the parable literally, the implication is that although it may have happened a long time ago, it did happen at a certain point in time. This is the view of orthodox Christianity, which teaches that Adam and Eve lived happily in the garden of Eden, in harmony with God and in obedience to his commands, until Adam took a bite of the forbidden fruit, at which point mankind fell from grace and became alienated from God.

Buddhism holds a different view. According to the Buddha you can go back and back in time for millions of years, millions of ages, but you will never come to an absolute first beginning of things. However far back you go, you can still go further. You will never get back to a point before the point at which time begins. So the beginning of the parable is not in time at all, but completely outside time. This means that the 'return journey' is not a journey back into the past, but a journey out of time altogether, a journey which transcends time. It is very important to understand this.

In the books about Zen which people are so fond of reading, there are all kinds of strange and wonderful – and apparently meaningful – expressions, all kinds of appealingly snappy little *mondos* and koan. One of these Zen sayings – which is of course absolutely true – speaks of 'your original face before you were born'. The Zen masters are apparently rather fond of asking their disciples, at a moment's notice, to show them their original face before they were born. 'Come on!' they demand, 'Show it to me. I want to see it.' Of course the hapless disciple usually fails miserably, as hapless disciples tend to in these stories, written as they apparently are by the masters. The disciple tends to tackle the problem by sitting down and thinking about yesterday, the day before, the week before, a month ago, two months ago, a year ago, two years ago, twenty years ago, thirty years ago – until they get back to the day they were born. If they can get back past *that*, they think, they will encounter their original face.

This is all wrong. To think that before a certain point in time there was the original face and after that there was no original face is a complete misunderstanding. The expression may seem to mean this, but if we go trying to track down the original face in the past, if we take this expression 'original' or the word 'before' literally, we are not really practising Zen, but just regressing in the psychoanalytical sense. The past is no nearer to Enlightenment than the present or the future, because time has nothing to do with Enlightenment. We are 'born', in the Zen sense, out of time, and our original face also exists out of time, so the Zen expression 'seeing your original face' has nothing to do with going back in time, or with going forward in time, or with standing still at the present moment of time. When Zen speaks of seeing your original face before you were born, it means going outside time altogether, rocketing through time and coming up on the other side in a dimension where there is no time at all, no past, present, or future. That is where the original face is to be seen, and nowhere else. That's where it 'is' all the time.

So there is no question of going back in time to enquire into the beginning of our state of alienation. We are alienated from reality here and now, and all we have to do is overcome this alienation from reality. And we can't do that just by going back and back into the past because we are still running on the rails of the alienation itself. We have to take a leap, a crosswise leap – a jump from the top of the pole, to use another Zen expression – to land, if we're lucky, in the absolute.

This is the point of the Buddha's famous Parable of the Poisoned Arrow – another parable connected with war – which is told in the Pāli canon.[220] The Buddha says that a soldier was wounded in battle by a poisoned arrow. Fortunately there is a surgeon on hand, but when he tries to take the arrow out, the wounded man says, 'Just a minute! Before I let you take out that arrow I want to ask a few questions. Who shot this arrow? Was he a Brahmin, a Kṣatriya, or a Vaiśya? Was he dark or fair? Was he young or old? What sort of bow was he using? And what sort of arrow is it? – A wooden one? An iron one? If it's wood, what sort of wood is it made from? – Oak? Cedar? Where does the feather come from? Is it a goose feather or a peacock feather? Answer all these questions, and then you can take out the arrow.'

Long before his questions were answered, of course, the soldier would be dead from the poison in the arrow. The important thing is to get rid of the arrow, not to enquire where it came from. In the same way, if we try to go back and back all the time – 'How did the world begin? How did we get into such a mess? What was I in my last birth? What are the roots of my neurosis?' – there is no end to it. We could go step by step back into the past and still be walking in millions of years. What we need to do is just see our present alienated, neurotic, conditioned, negative state, and rise above it, go soaring up into eternity, into a spiritual dimension. This is the message of the poisoned arrow. Likewise, the 'return journey' of the son is not about going back in time, but about going beyond time.

The son, who represents the lower self, wanders from place to place looking for work, for the simple reason that he needs food and clothing. He has no higher ideals. He has none of his father's ambitions of succeeding in trade and commerce. Translating this into modern terms (borrowed from Abraham Maslow's book *Toward a Psychology of Being*),[221] the lower self is 'need-motivated'. Everything the son does is out of his subjective need, out of his craving. By contrast, the father – the higher self – is 'growth-motivated'. The parable expresses this in terms of his accumulation of riches, but this is in no way to imply that it is glorifying capitalism or anything like that; as a parable, its meaning is symbolic. The father, the higher self, accumulates wealth until he possesses all conceivable spiritual riches and qualities.

Although he is so rich, the father is not happy because he is thinking of his son *all the time*. What can we infer from this? It tells us that the higher self never loses its awareness. It's conscious all the time. Although we may completely forget the higher self, the higher self never forgets us. But at the same time – this is the mystery – we are it. An image may help to make this clear. Imagine an enormous subterranean chamber all lit up from within. We are living in a tiny chamber next to – indeed part of – the big one. A pane of glass which is transparent only from one side separates the two chambers, so that although someone in the large illuminated chamber could see everything going on in the little chamber, from the little chamber we can see nothing at all of what is going on in the large chamber. In fact, we have no idea that there *is* a large chamber. But although cramped in our little chamber we may forget, even be oblivious to, the existence of the large chamber, the large chamber always has a window onto the little chamber. Even though the lower self forgets the higher self, the higher self is the higher self *of* the lower self.

The parable says that the poor man roams from one town to another and one country to another until he eventually reaches the place where his father is living. So he is already on his way back to his father, although he does not know it. It is his need for food and clothing, his craving, which drives him from place to place and brings him almost to his father's door. What are we to make of this?

Let's look at an example. A man has a certain psychological problem. He's so worried about it that he just can't sleep, and sleeping tablets don't help. He is getting really desperate for some peace of mind. One day he meets a friend who says, 'I know what will help you. You need to meditate.' By this stage the man is ready to try anything, so he asks where he can learn to meditate and goes along to a class. His only concern is to get rid of the problem and get some sleep. But at the meditation classes he starts to hear about something new: Buddhism.

At first he is not particularly interested, but after a few months – rather to his surprise – he finds himself not just trying to get peace of mind but trying to follow the spiritual path. After a while he even starts thinking in terms of Enlightenment. So when did he take the first step in that direction? It was when, driven by his need for peace of mind, he joined the meditation class. In the same way the poor man, driven by his basic needs, made his way to his father's door without knowing it. This is the first stage of the return journey.

When the poor man eventually arrives at his father's door, his father is sitting outside surrounded by gold, jewels, and flowers. The poetic description of the rich man – who represents the higher self – is highly significant. He is a glorious archetypal figure, a god, even a Buddha, so he is described with light and colour, jewels and brilliance. But how does the poor man react? He is so terrified at the sight that he wants to run away. He thinks that he has come upon a king or nobleman, not recognizing in this glorious figure his own father. This goes to show that the alienation between the lower self and the higher self is quite severe. Even when the two confront each other, the lower self does not recognize the higher self as its own higher self, but thinks it is something strange and foreign. Such a confrontation occurs when we come face to face with an embodiment of the spiritual ideal. Whenever we read a description or see an image of the Buddha – or some god or saint – we think, or our lower self thinks, 'This has nothing to do with me. I'm down here, poor and humble. I'm not like that. I don't have those qualities.' The theistic systems which believe in a personal creator god, and indeed all dualistic systems, encourage this attitude.

We could call this the stage of religious projection. We project outwards all the qualities which are buried deep down in the depths of our own nature, not realizing that they are our own. As we see it, these glorious external figures are endowed with all the qualities which we lack. We are poor and they are rich. This religious projection is a step in the right direction; indeed, it is the next stage of the journey. It is a positive thing because it enables us to see spiritual qualities in a concrete way. But the projection must be resolved. These qualities belong to us – not to our ego, but to the deepest and truest depths of our being – and we must claim them as our own.

As yet, however, the son does not recognize his father, although his father immediately recognizes him and sends messengers to bring him back. But the poor man is terrified, thinks he is going to be arrested, and faints away. This reminds me of the account of the death experience given in the *Tibetan Book of the Dead*. At the time of death, so the text says, the Clear Light, a white light of absolutely unbearable brilliance, like a million suns, suddenly bursts on the vision of the dying person.[222] This light is the light of Reality, the light of Truth, the light of the Void. If we recognize that this is no light bursting upon us from without, but the light of our own intrinsic mind, our own true self, unfolding from deep within, if we can realize our oneness with that light, then we gain Enlightenment on the spot. But what happens? The light comes – blinding, terrible, overpowering – and most dying people shrink back in fear. 'Human kind cannot bear very much reality.'[223] This is true not only at the moment of death, but at all those moments when we encounter a truth that seems more than we can possibly bear.

The poor man, you notice, is not just terrified. His imagination is working overtime. He thinks that he is being arrested: already in his mind's eye he can see the block and the executioner's axe. His first thoughts are of imprisonment, slavery, violent death. Only too often when we come in contact with the Truth, it seems not liberating but an imprisonment, a limitation, or at least a nuisance. We do not want to change our ideas, or to change ourselves, and in that diseased state the liberating truth seems to us confining and narrow. Not only that, like the poor man in the parable we are afraid of dying. When the lower self – the I, the ego – comes in contact with Reality, it thinks, as it were, 'I'm for the chop. I'm finished; this is the end of me,' and so it shrinks back.

So the rich man lets his son slope off, but of course he has not given up hope, and by some clever planning he manages to get his son clearing away the heap of dirt at the back of his mansion. Now according to the interpretation of the parable which the four elders give, the son's clearing away dirt represents the narrow, selfish type of religious life which is aimed at individual development to the exclusion of any concern for others. The four elders identify this sort of approach with the lesser teaching which until so recently had been all they had known, but a better – or at least more contemporary – interpretation would suggest that the clearing away of the dirt represents the process of psychoanalysis, the heap of dirt representing all the repressions which the alienated person uncovers during analysis. The *sūtra* mentions that it takes twenty years to clear away the dirt, which seems rather a long time, but resolving repressions, negative emotions, complexes, and all the rest of it is rather time-consuming, so analysis does sometimes take as long as that.

Eventually, while the process of removing the dirt continues, the father manages to speak to his son, and confidence springs up between them. As this trust develops, the poor man begins to enter the rich man's mansion without hesitation, but he continues to live in his own hovel. So what does this mean? On one level it refers to the scholar, the academic specialist in comparative religion. He knows the texts, sometimes in the original languages, and he knows the teachings, even the higher teachings. Sometimes he even claims to know the esoteric teachings. In other words, he goes in and out of the mansion without hesitation, knowing exactly what is there – but he does not live there himself. He still lives in the straw hovel which represents all the things he is really interested in as an academic: promotion within his department; his annual increment; prestige within his profession; controversy and brisk exchange of articles and opinions with other scholars.

On a higher level, the poor man's going in and out of the mansion without hesitation refers to the average follower of religion. Such people are undoubtedly sincere and have perhaps had genuine religious experience – they go in and out of the mansion, as it were – but their home is elsewhere. Even though they have some spiritual experience, maybe during the weekly meditation class, they are preoccupied most of the time with mundane things. In one of his books William James, the great psychologist and author of *The Varieties of Religious Experience*, discusses the question, 'What is a religious person?' He says that a religious person is not one who has religious experiences – anybody can have those – but one who makes religious experiences the centre of their existence. It is not important where we visit; what is important is where we permanently live, or at least where we live most of the time – in other words, where our real centre of interest lies. As the Gospel says, 'Where your treasure is, there will your heart be also.'[224]

When the rich man falls sick, he hands the management of his affairs over to the poor man, who thus becomes familiar with riches but still continues to live in the hovel. This element of the parable represents the theist, or the theistically inclined mystic, and the dualistic approach in general. Such a person may have great, overwhelming, uplifting spiritual experiences, but they all seem to come from outside, not from within. The mystic says, 'These experiences are not mine; they are the gifts of God.'

Once you reach this stage of the journey, only time is required. The rich man sees that his son is becoming used to riches and ashamed of his poverty, that he aspires to be rich himself. In other words, the alienation of lower self from higher self is becoming less and less. When the rich man is at the point of death, the alienation is practically over, with just a thin thread remaining; the lower self and the higher self are almost one. And when at last the rich man acknowledges the poor man as his son, he dies, and there are no longer two – father and son, rich man and poor man – but only one, a rich man who was once a poor man. In other words, unity between the lower self and the higher self has been completely restored. The return journey has been accomplished.

Our journey also is nearly accomplished. The four elders who have told the parable compare themselves to the son – and the Buddha, of course, is the father. Formerly, they say, they had not dared to think in terms of becoming like the Buddha, thinking only of following his verbal teaching, which had seemed to indicate a lesser goal, the goal of individual emancipation, the goal of the destruction of negative emotions. But they now realize, they say, that that is not enough, for there are all sorts of positive qualities to be developed. It is not enough to have Wisdom; you need Compassion too. It is not enough to be an *arhant*; you can become like the Buddha himself. You can follow the bodhisattva path; you can aspire to supreme Enlightenment.

In other words, the four elders wake up to the truth of the Higher Evolution of humanity. They realize that the Buddha is not something unique and unrepeatable, but a forerunner, an example of what others can also become if only they make the effort. They realize that the religious life is not just a personal affair in a negative limited sense, but part of a cosmic adventure – and this is what we too have to try to realize. Religion, when properly understood, is not something remote from life, not just a dull, churchy little backwater, but life become conscious of its own upward tendency, its own tendency to grow and develop. And whether we know it or not, we are all involved, directly or indirectly, in this upward tendency of life. Each one of us is the poor man in the parable, the son who has run away; but each one of us also, if we only knew it, is the rich man, the father. And each one of us is making, even at this very moment, the return journey.

from *The Drama of Cosmic Enlightenment*

PART IV
BUDDHISM AND THE HEART

I

BUDDHISM AND EMOTIONAL LIFE

1. INVOLVING THE EMOTIONS IN SPIRITUAL LIFE

For most of us the central problem of the spiritual life is to find emotional equivalents for our intellectual understanding.

It appears that in ancient times Indian monks used to go from India to China in large numbers to preach the Doctrine, and that at one period of Chinese history there was a very pious Chinese emperor who was always eager to welcome great sages and teachers from India. Now one day it so happened that one of the greatest of the Indian teachers turned up in the Chinese capital, and the emperor, as soon as he heard the news, was very pleased indeed. He thought he would have a wonderful philosophical discussion with this newly-arrived teacher. So the teacher was invited to the palace, where he was received with due pomp and ceremony. When all the formalities were over and the teacher and the emperor had taken their seats, the emperor put his first question. 'Tell me,' he said, 'what is the fundamental principle of Buddhism?' and sat back, waiting to get the answer straight from the horse's mouth, as it were. The teacher replied, 'Ceasing to do evil; learning to be good; purifying the heart – this is the fundamental principle of Buddhism.'[225] The emperor was rather taken aback. He had heard all that before. (We have usually heard it all before!) So he said, 'Is that all? Is *that* the fundamental principle of Buddhism?' 'Yes,' replied the sage, 'That's all. Cease to do evil; learn to be good; purify the heart. That is indeed the fundamental principle of Buddhism.' 'But this is so simple that even a child of three can understand it,' protested the emperor. 'Yes, your majesty,' said the teacher, 'that is quite true. It is so simple that even a child of three can understand it, but so difficult that even an old man of eighty cannot put it into practice.'[226]

This story illustrates the great difference that exists between understanding and practice. We find it easy simply to *understand*. We can understand the Abhidharma; we can understand the Madhyamaka; we can understand the Yogācāra; we can understand Plato; we can understand Aristotle; we can understand the four Gospels; we can understand everything. But to put into practice even a little of all this knowledge and make it operative in our lives, this we find very difficult indeed. In the famous words of St Paul, 'The good that I would I do not: but the evil which I would not, that I do.'[227] He knows what he ought to do but is unable to do it; and that which he knows he should not do, that he cannot help doing. Again we see this tremendous, this terrible disparity between understanding and practice.

This state of affairs is not exceptional. It is not just a question of the Chinese emperor or St Paul. All religious people find themselves at some time or other, sometimes for years together, in this quite terrible and tragic predicament. They know the truth rationally, they know it from A to Z and from Z back to A. They can talk about it, write about it, give lectures about it. But they are unable to put it into practice. For those who are sincere this can be a source of great suffering. They may feel, 'I know this very well, and see it so clearly; but I am unable to put it into practice, unable to carry it out.' It is as though there were some blind spot in themselves, some 'x-factor' which was obstructing their efforts all the time. No sooner do they lift themselves up a few inches than they slip back what sometimes feels like a mile.

Why does this happen? Why is there this terrible gulf, this terrible chasm, between our theory and our practice, our understanding and our action? Why are most of us most of the time unable to act in accordance with what we *know* is true, what we *know* is right? Why do we fail so miserably again and yet again?

The answer to this question is to be sought in the very depths of human nature. We may say that we 'know' something, but we know it only with the conscious mind, with the rational part of ourselves. We know it theoretically, intellectually, abstractly. But we must recollect that we are not just our conscious minds. We are not all reason – though we may like to think we are. There is another part of us, a much larger part than we care to admit, which is no less important than our reason. This part is made up of instinct, of emotion, of volition, and is more unconscious than conscious. This wider, deeper, and no less important part of ourselves is not touched at all by our rational or intellectual knowledge. It goes its own way, as it were, dragging the mental part, still protesting, along with it.

Thus we see that we cannot go against the emotions. The emotions are stronger than reason. If we want to put into practice what we know to be right, what we know to be true, we have to enlist, in one way or another, the cooperation of the emotions. We have to be able to tap those deeper sources within ourselves and harness them, also, to our spiritual life, so that we may *implement* what we know to be right and true. *For most of us the central problem of the spiritual life is to find emotional equivalents for our intellectual understanding.* Until we have done this no further spiritual progress is possible. This is why Perfect Emotion comes as the second stage, or second aspect, of the Noble Eightfold Path, immediately after Perfect Vision.

from *The Buddha's Noble Eightfold Path*

2. BEING MOVED BY THE DHARMA

It is as though the Dharma touches some spring in you, opens something up that was hitherto blocked, melts something that was congealed, frees up energy that was imprisoned.

> Thereupon the impact of Dharma moved the Venerable Subhūti to tears. Having wiped away his tears, he thus spoke to the Lord: It is wonderful, O Lord, it is exceedingly wonderful, O Well-Gone, how well the Tathāgata has taught this discourse on Dharma. Through it cognition has been produced in me. Never have I before heard such a discourse on Dharma. Most wonderfully blest will be those who, when this Sūtra is being taught, will produce a true perception.

The teaching put forth in the *Diamond Sūtra* may seem quite abstract in form, but for Subhūti it is not abstract at all. His emotional response demonstrates a distinctive emphasis of the Mahāyāna. It is well known that when the Buddha died, the *arhants* that were there – and Subhūti is, according to this text, an *arhant* – exhibited no particular emotion. Only those who were relatively unenlightened felt any separation or loss at the removal of the Buddha's physical body.[228] Thus arose the view of *arhants* as cool, impassive figures. The Mahāyāna, however, recognized that there were appropriate objects for the expression of powerful emotion – even, and indeed all the more so, at the highest levels of spiritual development. In the *Aṣṭasāhasrikā Sūtra*, the *Perfection of Wisdom in Eight Thousand Lines*, for example, there is a bodhisattva called Sadāprarudita – *sada* meaning 'always', and *prarudita*, 'weeping' – and he is always weeping because he is constantly moved by the Dharma.[229]

Subhūti is of course only an *arhant*, so he just sheds a few tears – but the important thing is that he is deeply moved by the Dharma. It is essential that we feel strongly and deeply about the Three Jewels, and also about the particular context within which we practise, our Buddhist order, and indeed about the local spiritual community within which we live or work. It comes down to fidelity, staying true to your friends and keeping faith with the Dharma. It is quite significant that in Tibet the bodhisattva Tārā is known as 'faithful Tārā'.

In the modern West, our social mobility gives us a kind of freedom, but at the same time it tends to limit our ability to develop close, deep, and strong relationships. The ease with which we can move on to pastures new tends to blunt our appreciation of our experience. We can always go off and make new friends when a situation or a relationship begins to make deeper demands upon our emotions, and this means that we seldom expose ourselves to any experience deeply and lastingly enough for it to move us. But to be strong and healthy, emotions need to be rooted in loyalty and commitment. When people are moving from one place to another, from one relationship to another, from one religion to another, and when the idea of not being tied down, of not limiting our options, of not identifying with a particular set of values, is understood as freedom – when it no longer seems clear at what to weep and at what to rejoice – then a situation develops in which there is no longer any outlet for the natural expression of strong emotion.

Of course, this has not always been the case in our society. We have only to go back to the nineteenth century to find the whole country, even hard-boiled politicians, awash with tears over the death of Little Nell or Paul Dombey.[230] Dickens himself apparently used to laugh and cry and behave rather like a madman when he was writing, quite carried away by the events his imagination was conjuring up. Even fifty years ago, my mother and her friend would come back from the cinema on a Thursday night saying how much they'd enjoyed it – 'We had a really good cry.' Perhaps these days we are afraid of seeming sentimental. We are increasingly uneasy about responding naturally to what may seem to our social consciences rather less than worthy demands upon our emotions. Also, perhaps, the emotions gradually become constrained within a social context of increasing control and security.

But Subhūti does weep. He weeps because the Dharma has touched something in him that has not been touched before. Weeping when you hear the Dharma is a sign that something has got through to you. It is as though the Dharma touches some spring in you, opens something up that was hitherto blocked, melts something that was congealed, frees up energy that was imprisoned. And you are touched, you are moved, you are stirred. There is a powerful expression for this sort of state in Pāli: *saṃvega* – to be shaken by the Dharma. There is even quite a powerful word in English which gives some idea of the sort of emotional response we need to discover in ourselves before we can claim to have taken in even a little of this teaching – and that is the adjective 'sublime'. We begin to understand the *Diamond Sūtra* not when we imagine that we have worked out what it means, but when, as we contemplate it, we are moved – even to tears – by a sense of the sublime.

What the sublime represents is something vast and grand and overwhelmingly powerful which gives us a terrifying sense of our own smallness, but which at the same time – and this is what moves us, even exhilarates us – allows us the realization that on another level it is no greater than us, that there is that within us which resonates with that grandeur. The sublime moves us in a way that the simply beautiful cannot. It is there in the works of Michelangelo and Beethoven; among the *rāgas* of traditional Indian music it is expressed in the *bhairava*, the 'terrible' mode; and in the *Tibetan Book of the Dead* it is embodied in the wrathful deities, who are not beautiful like the peaceful forms, but sublime and awesome.

Subhūti is shaken by a revelation of something even more sublime than the Nirvāṇa that he has, presumably, so far attained. It is as though he was standing on a mountain peak imagining that it was the highest peak of all, and then, the mist clearing, he looked up, and there was another peak still, towering above him. As the Buddha carefully removes the Dharma beyond the reckoning of the most extravagant scale of values, it is the sublimity of the perspective revealed to him that moves Subhūti to tears.

from *Wisdom Beyond Words*

3. THE DIFFERENCE BETWEEN FEELINGS AND EMOTIONS

Being able to identify feelings is what makes it possible for us to follow the Buddhist path.

Judging from what one reads about them, one gets the impression that the people of previous times experienced their feelings in a much more full-blooded way than we do in the urbanized, modern world. What stands out in the accounts of ancient and traditional societies is their sheer emotional energy. Take the ancient Greeks, for example. In the days of Plato and Socrates, it seems that people took their friendships very seriously indeed. If they loved you, they would love you without reservation and do anything for you. But they hated unreservedly too, and made fearsome, even ruthless, adversaries. Life today might be more comfortable, but in comparison with the people of earlier times, we seem to live it in a very flat, lifeless emotional state. Going to work on the bus, or packed into a crowded train, our emotions are for the most part disengaged as we simply try to get through the day. One might well say that in this tepid, unresponsive state, we are 'out of touch with our feelings'.

Why is this? One obvious fact of life these days is that it is very complicated. The traditional society, in which one was born, lived, and died in the same place among the same people, is a thing of the past. Many people move every few years, and have to build up a new social network time after time. In these circumstances they have little chance to build up strong friendships outside the nuclear family, and the weakness of their connections with others makes it difficult for them to respond emotionally to the people around them.

However, as Western psychology tells us, those strong feelings do not go away, but remain repressed on a subconscious level. One of the aims of psychotherapy is to bring them to the surface and restore a full awareness of oneself as a whole personality. When Buddhist psychology refers to developing mindfulness of feelings, however, something rather different is meant from the 'getting in touch with one's feelings' with which psychotherapy is concerned – something less complex, though perhaps more useful. Indeed, being able to identify feelings (in the sense of *vedanā* as defined by Buddhist tradition and explained below) is what makes it possible for us to follow the Buddhist path.

The Pāli and Sanskrit term *vedanā* refers to feeling not in the sense of the emotions, but in terms of sensation. *Vedanā* is whatever pleasantness or unpleasantness we might experience in our contact with any physical or mental stimulus. To understand what we would call emotion, Buddhism looks at the way in which that pleasant or painful feeling is interwoven with our reactions and responses to it. In Buddhist psychology, *vedanā* is said to combine with *saṃskāra*, a volitional quality involving a tendency towards action. It is this combination of sensation with volition that approaches what we would recognize as fully developed emotion.

Feeling – whether pleasure or pain – is passive: that is, it arises as a result of all sorts of conditions. We can change feelings that arise in various ways by changing the conditions that give rise to them – opening the window when we're hot, to take the simplest of examples. But there is a certain kind of painful feeling against which we can do nothing to protect ourselves: the feelings that arise as a result of our past unskilful karma. These must simply be borne, although of course we can protect ourselves from future pain by making the effort to create fresh positive karma, even while we are experiencing pain.

It is very important that we learn to do this. Feelings of pleasure and pain are not themselves productive of fresh karma, but when we allow ourselves to react to them in the form of some emotion, and when that emotional reaction is negative, negative karmic consequences will follow. The practice of recollecting feelings is intended to help us be aware of our feelings before an emotional reaction to them sets in. If we can distinguish between the feelings we receive as impressions and what we then make of them, we will be able to take more responsibility for our emotions, while not suppressing our feelings. We need to know what we feel if we are to direct the flow of our emotional life in a positive way.

This is quite difficult because most of the time our feelings get lost in our emotional reactions to them. If you are meditating, for example, and you feel an itch or hear an ugly sound, the simple experience of feeling tends swiftly to be overlaid with an emotional reaction – in this case, of aversion. Our natural tendency is to want to get away from a feeling if it is painful and to want more of it if it is pleasant. Before we know where we are, we have thus shifted from the simple experience of pleasure or pain into some form of craving or hatred. The practice, therefore, is to keep returning to the bare feeling, allowing no space for these habitual reactions to establish themselves.

from *Living with Awareness*

4. CULTIVATING POSITIVE EMOTIONS

If spiritual practice is to transform your life, you need to think of it as something you can enjoy, not just a hard grind, and this means making sure that there is not too much of a contradiction between 'spiritual' activities and the activities of daily life – and looking for enjoyment in both.

Modern living seems almost designed to drain away energy and dissipate positivity. Continual contact with the day-to-day stress of ordinary life tends to damp down one's responses: walking through the city, you pass many people in quite negative mental states, and you can feel your energy being drained away just through warding off those influences and keeping all the noise at bay. City life seems to draw out energy and waste it senselessly, not just through noise and worry, but also through the mechanical and electronic devices that dictate the pace of life. Our senses are bombarded by all manner of powerful messages, both crude and subtle, and all demanding our attention. Another feature of modern life is the extraordinary range of superficial enjoyments available to us. Although many of these little outlets of energy are not harmful or unethical in themselves, if our attention is spread thinly across all of them, we will be unable to have any single experience of real depth.

If we are to make any progress spiritually we therefore need to intervene positively in the way we feel and the way we experience the world. In our own interests, we need to shield ourselves from negative influences. Feelings do not arise of their own accord; they come about in dependence on conditions and disappear when those conditions are removed. By being aware of how we are liable to be influenced by our environment and activities, we can manage the feelings that are likely to arise and cultivate a reserve of positive energy upon which to draw in the pursuit of stronger, brighter states of awareness.

This is all common sense, and easily verifiable in our own experience. If you are feeling depressed, for example, you might decide to spend a day in the country to put you in a more positive mood. If you feel uninspired, making contact with someone who shares your ideals and aspirations will give life a much more positive aspect. By taking a more active role in handling our sense impressions we can bring our feelings more effectively under our control. One might say that this is the purpose of going on retreat. A retreat centre is an environment dedicated to concentrating one's energies and directing them towards the attainment of higher states of awareness and more positive and refined emotion. It might take a little time to adjust to the absence of distractions to which you are accustomed in everyday life, but as you get used to it, your state of mind becomes much more contented, even blissful, just through simplifying your sensory impressions and cutting down on the activities through which your energy is usually frittered away. Sometimes on retreat one is asked to observe regular periods of silence, and people are often amazed to find that as a result they have much more energy than usual, with, strange to say, no diminution of their level of communication with others – a good basis from which to tap deeper sources of inspiration through meditation. One invariably comes back from retreat charged with energy. (Incidentally, this is also one reason for observing celibacy. Even athletes are said to conserve their energy in this way and some would say that it is essential if one intends to explore the deeper levels of meditative experience.) The stillness and simplicity of a retreat provides the ideal basis for a heightened and consistent emotional positivity. When you are not on retreat, one of the most effective ways of banking up your energies and preventing them from leaking away is a regular lifestyle which keeps energy flowing continuously through the same channels. Regular sleep, diet, working hours, and meditation all help to clarify and concentrate one's energies, harmonizing them in the service of one's higher aspirations.

But external conditions are not everything. Even if you went on solitary retreat and placed yourself in ideal conditions, free from any external factors that might dissipate your energies, even if you had plenty of time in which to meditate and reflect, you might still lack the inspiration to do it. Obviously you couldn't blame your surroundings; the reason would have to be subjective. You might look for a clue by investigating what does seem to stimulate an emotional response. You might discover that while higher thoughts and aspirations leave you cold, when your mind wanders towards visions of a succulent meal or some beautiful sexual partner, you are much more interested. Food and sex, after all, are likely to arouse almost everyone's interest, and the energy to pursue them is more or less ever-present.

So it is inaccurate to talk about having or not having energy in absolute terms. Emotional energy can't be measured in terms of a fixed quantity like water or heat or even the capacity to perform physical work. It is all about one's level of inspiration. The question is not how much energy you can muster, but how refined that energy is. Energy arises in connection with objects of pleasure and interest, and your relationship to those objects says a great deal about the kind of person you are. One way of thinking of the spiritual life is that it is about shifting the focus of your emotional energy from, say, food or sex, or watching football or boxing, to the more refined pleasures of art, music, friendship, and meditation.

Sometimes it is only when we are on retreat and our everyday supports and pleasures are removed that we find out what is really keeping us going from day to day. We may have an idea or even a conviction that higher pleasures are the most fulfilling, but our ability to enjoy them is unlikely to be as fully developed as our intellectual understanding that they are a good thing. In other words, our spiritual ideals may not have filtered very far into our deeper emotions and volitions, so that we continue to seek pleasure in the same old places. This is the usual pattern of spiritual life: our intellectual understanding will always be some way ahead of our emotional involvement. It is quite usual to find oneself oscillating between relatively crude pleasures and a rigid determination to engage with spiritual practice which has little of the warmth and ease characteristic of truly positive emotion.

But in the end this is not sustainable. If spiritual practice is to transform your life, you need to think of it as something you can enjoy, not just a hard grind, and this means making sure that there is not too much of a contradiction between 'spiritual' activities and the activities of daily life – and looking for enjoyment in both. If there is at least an element of enjoyment in our daily lives, we will be able to bring that positive attitude to puja, our study of the Dharma, and our meditation. The alternative – a dreary day followed by a meditation that is nothing short of a struggle – is hardly an inspiring prospect.

from *Living with Awareness*

5. DEALING WITH DESIRE

It cannot give you real satisfaction – but it's difficult to give up hoping that it might be able to, and trying just once more.

Often we feel desires for all sorts of things we think we want, but even if we get what we thought we wanted, our desires remain unsatisfied. We experience this, of course, because we are so busy going after things we don't really want. Only too often, when we have had it and enjoyed it – if it was enjoyable – we realize that we didn't really want it after all. We are not really satisfied; we have just been distracted or amused for a while, no more than that. When we think about it, we realize that we could easily have done without it – even have been better off without it.

But when you are in the grip of desire, it's hard to remember all this. When you think you want something, well, you think you want it. You can go through the same procedure time and time again, maybe hundreds of times, before you learn your lesson and accept that you're not going to get what you really want from that thing. It cannot give you real satisfaction – but it's difficult to give up hoping that it might be able to, and trying just once more. 'I'll give it another chance before trying Nirvāṇa!' You really have to wallow in it before you know it's muck.

Even if people tell you that the object of your desire will be a disappointment, and on a rational level you can see that they are right, this still won't help if, deep down, you remain unconvinced. However rational and reasonable the arguments against doing it are, you may well feel compelled to do whatever it is anyway, just to see for yourself.

But, of course, there is really no need to try out everything personally. If somebody tells you that if you put your finger in the fire it will burn, you don't have to test it to see. You might put your finger near enough to get warm, and a bit nearer to get warmer, but that will be enough to convince you. It's a delusion to think that we have to experience personally everything that the Buddha has warned us does not lead in the direction of Nirvāṇa. We just have to take the Buddha's word for it in at least certain areas, and not insist on a personal confirmation of the unsatisfactoriness of every vice.

It isn't even really necessary to experience something of every kind or category of vice. You can group them into one big group called 'worldly pleasures'; if you have had even a taste of one of them, that should be enough to disillusion you about them all. They all come under the same heading; they're all conditioned things, so they don't really differ in any essential respect from one another.

On the other hand, it could be quite dangerous to deprive yourself of all comforts on the basis of a purely rational understanding of the truth, before you have started to get any real satisfaction from practising Buddhism. If you did that, you could well feel so bored and frustrated, and find life so blank and meaningless, that you would be tempted to go to the opposite extreme. You must begin to enjoy being a Buddhist before you give up too much, otherwise you will associate being a Buddhist with a dull, dry, painful, difficult, joyless sort of existence.

This should not, of course, be used as a rationalization for not giving up anything at all. In fact, if you haven't got any enjoyment at all from the Dharma, it might be best to give up a few things and make things really uncomfortable for yourself. That might force the issue. Otherwise you could remain stuck indefinitely, just being mentally occupied with the Dharma, getting no real pleasure from it, and not being willing to give up even small things because you haven't yet started to enjoy the spiritual life. You could stay like that all your life. You might have to do something drastic, take a risk, make yourself really uncomfortable, get thoroughly bored and frustrated. Then you would have to get pleasure from the Dharma because you weren't getting it from anywhere else.

It is tempting to think that the golden light of the Dharma might be somehow reflected in the more refined worldly pleasures, but this is not so. It is true that in the case of aesthetic experiences at their very highest, like the music of Bach at its most sublime, you get distant reflections – or perhaps we should say echoes – of the golden light. But it's not enough just to have a glimpse in the distance in an indirect, remote way. We have to make the experience our own, and this involves a regular, disciplined way of life directed to that end.

In modern times we have got into the habit of sampling experience with no corresponding commitment to what the experience is meant to represent. To take the example of music, we don't usually think of it very seriously. It doesn't involve us in any responsibility towards it; it's just available for us to use and enjoy. We go along to concerts because it's a pleasant sensation. But we could go along and experience them as a revelation which would make a real difference to our lives. It is the nature of the aesthetic experience that you are lifted out of yourself a bit – that's part of its value – but most of us are then dropped right back into ourselves, virtually the same as we were before. Probably only a musician could listen to music with commitment. The rest of us are more like the so-called religious person who sits at home in the evening with a box of chocolates leafing through the life of Milarepa or the *Parinibbāna Sutta*. It's just an experience in a very superficial, untransforming sense.

We might have a taste of what Bach was trying to convey, but most of us can't become a musician like Bach. In the case of spiritual experience, however, it's different. Something is pointed out to us, or we experience something fleetingly, and then within the spiritual tradition we can make an effort, reproduce that experience within ourselves, and experience it fully. You might never become a Bach, but you can become a Buddha.

from *Transforming Self and World*

6. DESIRE FOR THE ETERNAL

All unillumined desire is really a groping in the dark for Enlightenment, a looking for Buddhahood in the wrong direction.

Desire for the transitory is doomed, sooner or later, to disappointment. Even if it is possible to strive after and obtain such an object of desire, it is not possible to grasp hold of it for ever. Only in the desire for the Eternal resides the possibility of permanent satisfaction and everlasting joy, for the Eternal gives itself freely to those who freely give themselves to it. All unillumined desire is really a groping in the dark for Enlightenment, a looking for Buddhahood in the wrong direction, as it were, so that even when we succeed in gaining the object of an unillumined desire we do not feel satisfied, because we were really not looking for that at all, but for something else. For this reason, also, when the Desire for the Eternal is satisfied, all other desires are satisfied simultaneously, since they were nothing but deformations of it. This is the meaning of the saying that if we seek first the Kingdom of Heaven, all things will be added unto us; although we should, of course, seek the Kingdom of Heaven for its own sake, and not for the sake of what, it is promised, will be added unto us if we do so. Otherwise we shall succeed in gaining neither the Kingdom of Heaven nor anything else. In the modern West we must once again recognize ourselves as essentially spiritual beings, and acknowledge the attainment of Enlightenment as the Supreme End of human life, otherwise we will continue to whirl round and round in the vortex of existence, ignorant, frustrated, and miserable.

from *Crossing the Stream*

7. RENUNCIATION: NOT GIVING UP BUT GROWING UP

If we really have some degree of vision of the true nature of existence, and have really to some extent seen the inadequacy of material things, then our hold on them will be relaxed, and we will be quite willing and happy to let at least some of them go.

There is no single uniform pattern of renunciation. No one has the right to say that because someone has not given up this or that particular thing they therefore have no Perfect Vision and are not practising Buddhists. Different people will give up different things first, but the net result must be the same: to make life simpler and less cluttered. Most of us have so many things we do not really need. If here and now you were to take a piece of paper and write down all the unnecessary things you possess it would probably be a very long list, but you would probably think a long time before actually giving any of them away.

Sometimes people think of giving things up in terms of sacrifice: that with a great painful wrench you give something up, but it should not be like that. In Buddhism there is really no such thing as 'giving up' in this way. From the Buddhist point of view what is required is not so much *giving* up as *growing* up. It is no sacrifice to the adolescent to give up the toys of childhood. In the same way it should not be a sacrifice for the spiritually mature person, or for a person who is at least verging on spiritual maturity, to give up the toys with which people usually amuse themselves. This is not to suggest that we do this in a dramatic or violent fashion; not like the gentleman I heard about who climbed up the Eiffel Tower and threw his television from the viewing platform. (He was protesting against the quality of French television programmes, but at least his action indicated a certain degree of detachment from his television!) The point to be made is that if we really have some degree of vision of the true nature of existence, and have really to some extent seen the inadequacy of material, worldly things, then our hold on them will be relaxed, and we will be quite willing and happy to let at least some of them go – to have just *one* car perhaps!

from *The Buddha's Noble Eightfold Path*

8. REMEMBERING THE RETREAT

> At the wood's edge, a solitary hut;
> Sharing my quiet room, a single friend.
> Here on the table, two or three books of verse;
> There on the shelf, half a dozen frost-blackened violets.
> Hour after hour, we exchange only a few words;
> Day after day, I polish a single poem.
> Who would have thought it? A whole world of content
> Found in these things!

from *Complete Poems*

9. THE PRACTICE OF FORBEARANCE

It is possible to learn to respond differently.

Kṣānti – to be distinguished from *śānti*, which means peace – is one of the most beautiful words in the whole vocabulary of Buddhism. It links a number of associated meanings, so there is no one English word which can do it full justice. It literally means patience or forbearance, and it is the antidote to anger (as *dāna* is to craving). As well as the absence of anger, and the absence of the desire for revenge, *kṣānti* has overtones of love, compassion, tolerance, acceptance, and receptivity.

It also includes gentleness and docility, and there is even a suggestion in it of humility – though not in any artificial self-conscious sense. When Mahatma Gandhi founded one of his ashrams in India he apparently drew up a list of virtues to be practised by the ashramites. It was a long list, and at the top he put 'humility'. But someone pointed out that if you practise humility deliberately, self-consciously, it becomes not humility but hypocrisy. So the Mahatma crossed out 'humility' and wrote at the bottom of the list, 'All the virtues are to be practised in a spirit of humility' – a rather different thing.

Kṣānti as forbearance is illustrated by a story from the life of the Buddha himself, a story found in the *Sūtra of Forty-two Sections* – which, incidentally, was the first Buddhist text to be translated into Chinese. The original version – we don't know whether it was in Pāli or Sanskrit – no longer exists, but historically the *sūtra* is of considerable importance. Anyway, apparently the Buddha was walking along one day when he happened to encounter somebody – probably a Brahmin, but we don't know – who for some reason wasn't very pleased with the Buddha and immediately started to call him all sorts of names. This sort of thing often happens in the Pāli scriptures; the Buddha was by no means universally popular in his own day. Some people resented the fact that he seemed to be enticing people away from their families and encouraging them to think of Nirvāṇa instead of thinking about making money.

So the man stood there for a while, abusing the Buddha with all the offensive words in his vocabulary. But the Buddha didn't say anything. He just waited for the man to stop speaking. And eventually the man did dry up – perhaps he ran out of breath. The Buddha quietly said, 'Is that all?' Rather taken aback, the man said, 'Yes, that's all.' The Buddha then said, 'Let me ask you a question. Suppose one day a friend brings you a present, but you don't want to accept it. If you don't accept it, to whom does it belong?' The man said, 'Well, if I won't accept it, it belongs to the person who is trying to give it to me.' So the Buddha said, 'Well, you have tried to make me a present of your abuse, but I decline to accept it. Take it; it belongs to you.'[231]

Of course, few of us would be capable of such a measured response. If someone verbally abuses us, we tend to come up with a stinging retort, or keep the insult burning in our mind and find a way of getting our own back later on. But it is possible to learn to respond differently. How? The great teacher Śāntideva gives some hints. He says, for example, suppose someone comes along and beats you with a stick. That's a painful experience, but it doesn't justify your flying into a rage. Instead, you need to try to understand what has happened. If you analyse it, he says, it is simply that two things have come together: the stick and your body. And who is responsible for this coming together? The other person has admittedly taken the stick to you, so he is partly responsible. But you have provided the body – and where did that body come from? It came from your previous *saṃskāras*: your ignorance and the things you did based on your ignorance in your previous lives. Why should you get angry with your enemy for bringing his stick, and not with yourself for bringing your body?[232] In his *Bodhicaryāvatāra* Śāntideva produces a number of reflections of this kind designed to help us practise forbearance.

Of course, it isn't just a question of practising forbearance towards people who assail us with harsh words or sticks. In Buddhist literature the contexts in which forbearance is to be practised are classified into three groups.[233] First of all, there is nature: the material universe which surrounds us, especially in the form of the weather. It is generally either too hot or too cold, or there's too much wind or too much rain or not enough sunshine. All these climatic changes demand a certain degree of forbearance. Then there are what are known in law as acts of God – natural disasters beyond human control, like fire and flood, earthquake and lightning. Occasionally we may need to practise forbearance in the face of such events as these.

Secondly, we need to be forbearing towards our own body, especially when it is sick or suffering. We shouldn't get angry with the body and all its aches and pains; we shouldn't start beating 'brother ass', as Saint Francis would say. After all, we have brought the body here; it is our responsibility. While we should always try to alleviate suffering, whether our own or that of other people, as best we can, we need to realize that there is a residue which cannot be relieved and must simply be borne with patience.

Even if we stay well, sooner or later old age and death will come. In the modern West many people refuse to grow old gracefully, with sometimes quite tragic consequences. In the East, and perhaps in traditional societies generally, by contrast, people often look forward to old age, and indeed tend to see it as the happiest time of life. All the passions and emotional turbulence of youth have subsided. One has gained experience, and with experience perhaps just a little wisdom. And having handed everything over to the younger generation, one has fewer responsibilities and plenty of time for reflection, even meditation. Death is another matter, though; for most people everywhere it is a sobering consideration. But whether we like it or not, death will come, and we are well-advised to practise forbearance towards the idea.

Thirdly, one should practise forbearance towards other people. This is, of course, far more difficult than being forbearing towards the weather, or even one's own aches and pains. Other people can be very difficult indeed. As a character in Jean-Paul Sartre's play *Huis Clos* famously puts it, 'Hell is other people.' One might add that heaven is other people too, but that's another story.

from *The Bodhisattva Ideal*

10. THE IMPORTANCE OF FEELING ALIVE

When you come in contact with the truth, with the Buddha's teaching, do you feel as though you are being refreshed by a great shower of rain?

The Buddha says that wherever you go in the great ocean, you can scoop a handful of water and it will have the same taste: the taste of salt.[234] Likewise, whatsoever part of his teaching you take up, it will have one taste: the taste of freedom. In other words, whatever aspect of the Buddha's teaching you practise, it has one essence, one purpose, one effect – to help you to get free from your conditioning. There are many different presentations of the Buddha's teaching. There are the lists: the Eightfold Path, the five spiritual faculties, the three Refuges. There are the teachings about suffering, impermanence, and no-self. And there are all sorts of methods of practice: the mindfulness of breathing, the *mettā bhāvanā*, the contemplation of the impurities, the *brahma vihāras*. But all these many teachings, traditions, and practices have just one aim: to help individual human beings to become free from their conditioning.

From this the important corollary follows that the Buddha's teaching is not to be identified with any one formulation. It is not possible to say that the Buddha's teaching is the Noble Eightfold Path and just that, or the contents of the Pāli canon and just that. The Buddha's teaching is not just Zen, or just Theravāda, or just what Professor so-and-so says it is. Buddhism cannot be identified with any one individual formulation, much less with any one individual school or sect. The Buddha's teaching or message can only be identified with that spirit of liberation, of freedom from conditionedness, that pervades all these formulations, just as the taste of salt pervades all the waters of the ocean. Whether it is the teaching of the Eightfold Path or the teaching of the bodhisattva ideal, whether it is this meditation practice or that, if it helps us to become free from our conditioning, it is part and parcel of the Buddha's teaching.

When we read about Buddhism, it is very important not only to remember this but to try really to feel it; otherwise all our studies and knowledge will be in vain. When we read the scriptures or hear about the Buddha's teaching, it is not enough just to pay attention to the words, the ideas and concepts. What really matters is to feel, through the concepts, through the images and symbolism, that which informs and gives life to them all – the experience of emancipation from all conditions whatsoever. In other words, we are trying to feel, at least to some degree, the absolute consciousness of the Buddha, the Enlightened consciousness from which all the teachings originally came.

To translate this into more simple terms, we must be nourished through both emotion and reason. Usually presentations of Buddhism in the West emphasize the rational aspect, or even give the impression that Buddhism is exclusively rational. We are told about Buddhist thought and philosophy, Buddhist metaphysics, psychology, and logic;

and sometimes it all seems very dry and academic. The other side, however, the side represented by myth, symbol, and the imagination, the emotions and vision, is no less important, and for many people perhaps even more important. This is why we need to absorb texts which appeal to our emotions, like the parables, myths, and symbols of the Mahāyāna in the *White Lotus Sūtra*.

It is not enough to understand the Buddha's teaching intellectually. Anybody who has the ability to read – and a moderate intelligence – can do that. We have to ask ourselves again and again not just 'Do I know? Do I understand?' but 'Do I feel? Do I vibrate with this?' We might even ask ourselves 'Do I really feel like a plant at the end of the hot season? Is this how I feel after a day's work or after I've been immersed in the ordinary daily round? Do I feel all dry and withered? Do I feel in need of nourishment? Do I really feel ready to take something in?' When you come in contact with the truth, with the Buddha's teaching, do you actually feel as though you are being refreshed by a great shower of rain? Do you really feel that you are going to drink something in after having been dry and thirsty for a long time?

Again, when you come in contact with the Dharma, do you really feel that the sun has come out? During the months of winter it is not unusual to feel dull and tired, and even miserable, because the sky is grey with fog and mist, and you are cold. You look forward to the spring sunshine, to your summer holiday, to the first beautiful, warm, bright weekend when you feel that spring is really on the way. When you see the buds begin to open and the flowers blooming in the parks and gardens, you can hardly help but feel a lifting of the heart. You feel as though a new spirit were rising within you.

But do you feel like this when you come into contact with the Buddha's teaching? Do you feel as though you are drinking in spiritual sunshine? If you do not respond in this way, your approach is still just intellectual. It is important that we should actually feel ourselves living, feel ourselves growing just like the plant when the rain falls and the sun shines.

from *The Drama of Cosmic Enlightenment*

2
MEDITATION

1. MEDITATION

    Here perpetual incense burns;
    The heart to meditation turns,
    And all delights and passions spurns.

    A thousand brilliant hues arise,
    More lovely than the evening skies,
    And pictures paint before our eyes.

    All the spirit's storm and stress
    Is stilled into a nothingness,
    And healing powers descend and bless.

    Refreshed, we rise and turn again
    To mingle with this world of pain,
    As on roses falls the rain.

from *Complete Poems*

2. RAINY SEASON RETREAT

Above all, I loved the way in which the rain insulated one from the rest of the world, weaving around one a silver-grey cocoon of silence within which one could sit, hour after hour, and quietly muse.

In June the rainy season began. The grey clouds came rolling up from the plains, first of all infiltrating the valley of the Teesta in loose, detached masses, then moving in across the hills in a solid wall of rain that at times blotted out the entire landscape. For days on end Mount Kanchenjunga could not be seen. Instead, even when the sky cleared, there was only thick white cloud piled up against the horizon. Though the rain fell heavily enough at times, the rainy season was much less severe in the hills than in the plains. In between the downpours the sun was hot and bright, and the sky intensely blue, though the thick white cloud hardly ever moved – hardly ever moved aside to reveal the snows of Mount Kanchenjunga sparkling through the rain-washed air. It was my fourth year in India. Already I had learned to love the rainy season. I loved the heavy drumming sound of the rain on the roof. I loved the sense of green things thirstily drinking up the rain and growing as they did so. Above all, I loved the way in which the rain insulated one from the rest of the world, weaving around one a silver-grey cocoon of silence within which one could sit, hour after hour, and quietly muse.[235] No wonder the Buddha had advised his monks not to wander about during the rainy season but to remain in one place, whether in a mountain cave, a woodland shrine, or a shed at the bottom of somebody's garden![236] No wonder the rainy season had come to be regarded, in the course of centuries, as a time of spiritual retreat – a time of more intensive study of the scriptures and more intensive practice of meditation!

from *Facing Mount Kanchenjunga*

3. THE FIVE BASIC METHODS OF MEDITATION

Meditation is not so much a science as an art, and in this art, as in all others, it is the inner experience rather than the technique that is all-important.

Here I want to focus on five methods of meditation which correspond to the five 'mental poisons' that stand between us and our own innate Buddhahood.[237] Enlightenment is within us all, but it is shrouded in spiritual ignorance or *avidyā* – as the vast azure vault of the sky may be obscured from horizon to horizon by dark clouds. This obscuring factor of *avidyā*, when it is analysed, is found to consist of the aforesaid five mental poisons.

The first poison is distractedness, inability to control wandering thoughts, mental confusion; and the meditation practice that acts as its antidote is the mindfulness of breathing. Then the second poison is anger, aversion, or hatred; and its antidote is the meditation practice called in Pāli the *mettā bhāvanā*, the cultivation of loving-kindness. The third poison is craving or lust, and it is countered by the 'contemplation of decay'. Ignorance, in the sense of ignorance of our own conditionality, is the fourth poison; and it can be tackled by the contemplation of the twelve links of conditioned co-production. Finally, the fifth poison is conceit, pride, or ego-sense, whose antidote is the analysis of the six elements.

The mindfulness of breathing

The mindfulness of breathing is the antidote to the mental poison of distractedness because it eliminates wandering thoughts. This is one of the reasons why it is generally the first meditation practice to be taught to beginners; no other method can be practised successfully until some degree of concentration has been mastered.

The mindfulness of breathing is not about concentration in the sense of a narrow, willed application of the attention to an object. It involves gradually unifying the attention around one's natural breathing process, integrating all one's mental, emotional, and physical faculties by means of gently but persistently bringing the attention back to the experience of the breath, again and again. The point is not to *think* about the breath, or do anything about it at all, but simply to be aware of it. There are four stages to the practice. For beginners, five minutes to each stage is about right.

Sitting still and relaxed, with the eyes closed, we begin by bringing our attention to the breathing. Then we start mentally to count off each breath to ourselves, after the out-breath, one to ten, over and over again. There is no particular significance to the counting. It is just to keep the attention occupied with the breathing during the early stages of the practice while the mind is still fairly scattered. The object of our developing concentration is still the breath (rather than the numbers).

In the second stage we continue to mark the breaths by counting them, but instead of counting after the out-breath we now count before the in-breath. Ostensibly there may not seem to be any great difference between these first two stages, but the idea of the second is that we are attentive right from the start of each breath, so that there is a quiet sharpening of the concentration taking place. There is a sense of anticipation; we are being aware before anything has happened, rather than being aware only afterwards.

In the third stage we drop the support of the counting and move to a general and continuous (at least, as continuous as we can manage) awareness of the whole process of the breathing, and all the sensations associated with it. Again, we are not investigating or analysing or doing anything special with the breath, but just gently nudging the attention to a closer engagement with it. As our concentration deepens, it becomes easier to maintain that engagement, and the whole experience of the breath becomes more and more pleasurable.

In the fourth and final stage we bring the attention to a sharper focus by applying it to a single point in our experience of the breath. The point we focus on is the subtle play of sensation where we feel the breath entering and leaving the body, somewhere round about the nostrils. The attention here needs to be refined and quiet, very smoothly and intensely concentrated in order to keep continuous contact with the ever-changing sensation of the breath at this point. The practice is brought to an end by broadening our awareness again to include the experience of the whole of the breath, and then the whole of the body. Then, slowly, we bring the meditation to a close and open our eyes.[238]

The *mettā bhāvanā*

The cultivation of universal love, or *mettā bhāvanā*, is the antidote to anger or hatred. *Mettā*, *maitrī* in Sanskrit, is a response of care and warmth and kindness and love to all that lives, a totally undiscriminating well-wishing that arises whenever and wherever we come into contact with, or even think about, another living being. The practice is divided into five stages.

In the first stage we develop love towards ourselves, something that many people find very difficult indeed. But if one can't love oneself one will find it very difficult to love other people; one will only project onto them one's dissatisfaction with – or even hatred of – oneself. So we try to appreciate or enjoy what we can about ourselves. We think of a time when we were happy and content, or we imagine being in a situation where we would feel quite deeply happy being ourselves, and then we try to tune in to that feeling. We look for and bring awareness to elements in our experience of ourselves that are positive and enjoyable.

Then, in the second stage, we develop *mettā* or love towards a near and dear friend. This should be someone of the same sex, to reduce the possibility of emotional projections – and it should be someone towards whom we have no erotic feelings, because the point of the practice is gradually to develop a focus on a very specific positive emotion that is closer to friendship than to erotic love. For the same sorts of reasons, this person should be still living and approximately the same age as oneself. So we visualize, or at least we get a sense of, this person, and we tune into the feeling they evoke in us, looking for the same response of benevolence that we have been developing towards ourselves. Usually this second stage is the easiest, for obvious reasons.

In the third stage, whilst maintaining the sense of an inner warmth, a sort of glow that we have generated towards ourselves and our good friend, we bring to mind in their stead a 'neutral' person. This is someone whose face we know well, whom we see quite often, but whom we neither particularly like nor dislike. It may well be someone who plays a more or less functional role in our life, like a postman, a shopkeeper, or a bank-clerk, or it may be someone we see regularly on the bus. We apply to this neutral person the same benevolence and care that we naturally feel for our friend. It must be emphasized that what we are trying to develop in this type of practice is not a thought – not an *idea* – about developing a feeling, but the actual feeling itself. Some people may find this quite difficult to achieve – they feel dry and numb when they try to be aware of their emotions. It is as if their emotional life is so unconscious that it is simply unavailable to them to begin with. However, with time and practice it all starts to flow more easily.

In the fourth stage, we think of someone we dislike, even someone we hate – an enemy – someone who has perhaps done us harm or an injury – though to begin with it may be best to think of someone with whom we just don't get on. In the meditation we deliberately allow our heart to stay open to them. We resist the urge to indulge in feelings of hatred or animosity or resentment. It is not that we necessarily condone their behaviour; we may well need to criticize and even condemn it; but we stay in touch with a fundamental care for their welfare. In this way, by continuing to experience our friendly attitude even in relation to an enemy, our emotion starts to develop from simple friendliness into real *mettā*.

These first four stages are introductory. At the beginning of the fifth and last stage, we bring together in our mind all these four persons – self, friend, neutral person, enemy – and we cultivate the same love equally towards them all. Then we go a little further, we spread our vision a little wider, to direct this *mettā* towards all beings everywhere, starting with those close to us, either emotionally or geographically, and then expanding outwards to include more and more people, and excluding no one at all. We think of all men, all women, all ages, nationalities, races, religions; even animals, even beings, maybe, who are higher than human beings – angels and gods – and even beings higher than that: bodhisattvas and spiritual teachers, whether Buddhist or non-Buddhist; whoever is eminent in good qualities. We may also expand out beyond our own planet, sending *mettā* to whatever beings may live in other parts of the universe, or in other universes. We develop the same love towards all living beings.[239]

In this way we feel as though we are being carried out of ourselves in ever expanding circles; we forget ourselves, sometimes quite literally, becoming enfolded in an ever-expanding circle of love. This can be a very tangible experience for those who practise the *mettā bhāvanā*, even after a comparatively short time. Not for everyone, of course: it is very much a matter of temperament. Some people take to it like ducks to water and enjoy it immensely within a matter of minutes. For others it is a struggle to get a fitful spark of *mettā* going, and the idea of radiating it seems a joke – they don't see how they are ever going to do it. But they can, and they do. In the end, with a bit of practice, a bit of perseverance, it happens, it arises. If the potential for Buddhahood is within all of us, then the potential for *mettā* certainly is.

The contemplation of decay

The contemplation of decay or impurity, which counteracts lust or craving or attachment, is not a practice that many people care to take up, though it is popular in some quarters in the East. There are three different forms of it. The first, and the most radical, is to go to a cremation ground and sit there among the corpses and charred remains. It may sound a drastic course of action, but it has to be so in order to counteract the fierce power of craving. You look closely at what death does to the human body and you think, 'This is what will happen to me one day.'[240]

There is no special teaching here, nothing esoteric or difficult to understand. There is no big secret in this practice. You simply recognize that one day your own body will be swollen and stinking with putrefaction like this one, your own head will be hanging off, and your own arm lying there on its own, like that one, or that you too will be a heap of ashes in somebody's urn (cherished somewhere, we hope).

These are all clear models of our own end, so why not admit it? Why not face the fact? And why not change the direction of our life to take account of this fact? It is in order to bring out such a vein of self-questioning that monks in the East make their way – often quite light-heartedly – to the cremation ground and sit looking at one corpse after another: this one quite fresh, recently alive; that one a bit swollen; and that one over there – well, rather a mess. They go on until they get to a skeleton, and then a heap of bones, and finally a handful of dust. And all the time a single thought is being turned over in the mind: 'One day, I too shall be like this.' It is a very salutary practice which certainly succeeds in cutting down attachment to the body, to the objects of the senses, the pleasures of the flesh.

If this practice seems too drastic, or even just rather impractical, there is another way of doing it. Rather than literally going to the cremation ground, you can go there in your imagination and simply visualize the various stages of the decomposition of a corpse. Or even more simply, you can just reflect on the fact that one day you must die. One day your consciousness must be separated from this physical organism. One day you will no longer see, you will no longer hear, you will no longer taste, or feel. Your senses will not function because your body will not be there. You will be a consciousness on its own

– you don't know where – spinning, perhaps bewildered, in a sort of void; you just don't know.

If even this sort of train of reflection seems a bit too harsh and raw, a bit too close to the bone, we can reflect on impermanence in general. Every season that passes carries its own intimations of impermanence. The sweetness of spring is all the more intense, all the more poignant, for its brevity, for no sooner are the blossoms on the trees in full bloom than they start to fade. And of course in autumn we can contemplate the decay and end of all things as we see the leaves turning yellow and falling, and our gardens dying back into the earth. This kind of gentle, melancholic contemplation, so often evoked in English poetry, particularly the odes of John Keats, and in the poetic tradition of Japan, can also have a positive effect in freeing us to some extent from our unrealistic perception of the solidity and permanence of things.

But there is no need to approach even the most drastic of these practices in a mournful or depressed spirit, because they are all about freeing ourselves from a delusion that just brings suffering in its wake. It should be exhilarating – if you take up this practice at the right time – to remind yourself that one day you will be free of the body.

I did the cremation ground practice myself once when I was a young monk in India. I went along to a cremation ground at night and sat there on the banks of the Ganges. There was a great stretch of silver sand, and at intervals funeral pyres had been lit and bodies had been burned, and there was a skull here and a bone there and a heap of ashes somewhere else…. But it was very beautiful, all silvered over by a tropical moon, with the Ganges flowing gently by. The mood the whole scene evoked was not only one of serious contemplation, but also one of freedom and even exhilaration.

This sort of mood probably reflects the fact that the practice overcomes fear. It is said that the Buddha himself used it for this purpose. If you can stay alone in a graveyard full of corpses at night, you are unlikely ever to be afraid of anything again, because all fear, basically, is fear of losing the body, losing the self. If you can look death – your own death – in the eye, if you can absorb the full reality of it and go beyond it, then you'll never be afraid of anything again.

However, the more challenging forms of this practice are not for beginners. Even in the Buddha's day, we are told, some monks who practised it without proper preparation and supervision became so depressed through contemplating the impurity and decay of the human body that they committed suicide.[241] Normally one is advised to practise the mindfulness of breathing first, then the *mettā bhāvanā*, and go on to contemplate corpses only on the basis of a strong experience of *mettā*. But all of us can at least recall the impermanence of all things around us, and remember that one day we too will grow old and sicken, that we too must die, even as the flowers fade from the field and the birds of the air perish, to rot and return to the ground.

The *nidāna* chain

The contemplation of the twelve links of conditioned co-production is the antidote to ignorance. In this meditation practice one consciously reflects on it, by means of the images that depict it in the outermost circle of the Tibetan wheel of life, as follows:

(1) Ignorance, *avidyā*: represented by a blind man with a stick; (2) volitions or karma formations, *saṃskāras*: a potter with a wheel and pots; (3) consciousness, *vijñāna*: a monkey climbing a flowering tree (we climb up into the branches of this world and reach out for its flowers and fruit); (4) mind and body, *nāma-rūpa* (i.e. name and form): a boat with four passengers, one of whom, representing consciousness, is steering; (5) the six sense-organs, *ṣaḍāyatana*: a house with five windows and a door; (6) sense-contact, *sparśa*: a man and woman embracing; (7) feeling, *vedāna*: a man with an arrow in his eye; (8) craving, *tṛṣṇā*: a woman offering a drink to a seated man; (9) grasping, *upādāna*: a man or woman gathering fruit from a tree; (10) becoming or coming-to-be, development, *bhava*: a man and a woman copulating; (11) birth, *jāti*: a woman giving birth; (12) old age and death, *jarā-maraṇa*: a corpse being carried to the cremation ground.

Here is the whole process of birth, life, death, and rebirth according to the principle of conditioned co-production. As a result of our ignorance, and of the volitions based upon our ignorance in previous lives, we are precipitated again into this world with a consciousness endowed with a psychophysical organism, and thus six senses, which come into contact with the external universe and give rise to feelings – pleasant, painful, and neutral. We develop craving for the pleasant feelings, and thus condition ourselves in such a way that inevitably we have to be born again and die again.

These twelve links are distributed over three lives, but at the same time they are also all contained in one life – even in one moment. They illustrate – whether spread over three lives or a day or an hour or a minute – the whole way in which we condition ourselves; how we make ourselves what we are by our own reactions to what we experience.

When we look at the wheel of life we are looking in a mirror. In all its circles and all its details, we find ourselves. When I contemplate anger, it is not anger in general I am concerned with. When I contemplate greed, I am not considering the universal psychological phenomenon of greed. When I contemplate ignorance, I am not studying some category of Buddhist thought. It is me there, just me: the anger, the greed, and the ignorance – they're all mine.

Seeing, next, a circle of people either going from a lower to a higher state or slipping from a higher to a lower state, I recognize myself in them. I am never standing apart from that wheel: at any one time I am going either one way or the other, up or down. Looking beyond these figures I may imagine that at last I am examining a representation of six different and separate realms of existence – which in a sense they are. The human realm is clearly my own, where people are communicating, learning, creating. But when I look at the realm of the gods I find there my own moments and dreams of bliss and joy, and in the realm of the titans, my own ambition and competitiveness. Grazing and snuffling with the animals is my own lack of vision, my own consumerism, my own dullness. In the realm of the hungry ghosts is my own desolate yearning for some solid satisfaction from the objects of my craving. And in hell are my own nightmares, my own moments of burning anger and cool malice, my own brief seasons of hatred and revenge.

Finally, in contemplating the twelve *nidānas* of the outermost circle we get a picture of how the whole process goes on, the mechanism of the whole thing. We see ourselves as a piece of clockwork, as indeed we are most of the time. Much of the time we are really no more free, no more spontaneous, no more alive, than a well-programmed computer. Because we are unaware, we are conditioned and therefore fettered. So in this practice we become aware of our conditionality, the mechanical, programmed nature of our lives, our tendency to react, our self-imprisonment, our lack of spontaneity or creativity – our own death, our spiritual death in a negative sense, our death-in-life. Almost everything we do is just tightening our bonds, chaining us more securely to the wheel of life. The contemplation of the twelve *nidānas* provides a traditional support for this kind of awareness.[242]

The six element practice

The analysis of the six elements is the antidote to conceit or pride or ego-sense: i.e. the antidote to the feeling that I am I, this is me, this is mine. In this practice we try to realize that nothing really belongs to us, that we are, in fact, spiritually (though not empirically) just nothing. We attempt to see for ourselves that what we think of as 'I' is ultimately (though not relatively) an illusion; it doesn't exist in absolute reality (even though clearly it does exist at its own level).

Before starting, we develop a degree of meditative concentration, and establish a healthy emotional basis for the practice to follow with perhaps a preliminary session of the *mettā bhāvanā*. Then we contemplate the six elements in an ascending order of subtlety: earth, water, fire, air, ether or space, and consciousness.

So first of all, earth – the earth upon which we're standing or sitting, and the earth in the form of trees and houses and flowers and people, and our own physical body. In the first stage of the practice we consider this element of earth: 'My own physical body is made up of certain solid elements – bone, flesh, and so on – but where did these elements come from? Yes, they came from food – but where did the food come from? Basically, the food from which my body is substantially made came in the first place from the earth. I have incorporated a portion of the earth into my physical body. It doesn't belong to me. I have just borrowed it – or rather, it is temporarily appearing in this form of myself. To claim that it is mine is, in a sense, theft, because it does not belong to me at all. One day I will have to give it back. This piece of earth that is my body is not me, not mine. All the time it is returning to the earth.' When we see this clearly enough we relinquish hold on the solid element in our physical body. In this way the sense of 'I' starts to lose its firm outlines.

Then we take the element of water, and we consider: 'So much of this world is water: great oceans and rivers, streams and lakes and rain. So much of my body, too, is water: blood, bile, spittle, and so on. This liquid element in me – where have I got it from? What I assume to be mine I have only taken on loan from the world's store of water. I will have to give it back one day. This too is not me, not mine.' In this way the 'I' dissolves further.

Now we come to a still subtler element: fire. In this stage we consider the one single source of light and heat for the whole solar system – the sun. We reflect that whatever warmth there is in our own physical body, whatever degree of temperature we can feel within us, all of it derives ultimately from the sun. When we die, when the body lies cold and still and rigid, all the warmth that we think of as our own will have gone from it. All the heat will have been given back, not to the sun of course, but to the universe. And as we do this the passion of being 'I' cools a little more.

Then, air: we reflect on the breath of life, on the fact that our life is dependent upon air. But when we breathe in, that breath in our lungs is not ours; it belongs to the atmosphere around us. It will sustain us for a while, but eventually the air we make use of so freely will no longer be available to us. When the last breath passes from the body we will give up our claim on the oxygen in the air, but in fact it was never ours to begin with. So we cease to identify ourselves with the air we are, even now, taking in; we cease to think, even tacitly: 'This is *my* breath.' And thus the 'I' gradually begins to evaporate.

The next element is called in Sanskrit *ākāśa*, a term translated either as 'space' or as 'ether'. It isn't space in the scientific sense, but rather the 'living space' within which everything lives and moves and has its being. We reflect that our physical body – made up of earth, water, fire, and air – occupies a certain space, and that when those constituent elements have gone their separate ways again, that space will be empty of the body that formerly occupied it. This empty space will merge back into universal space. In the end we see that there is literally no room for the sense of 'I'.

At this point we should, at least in principle, be dissociated altogether from the physical body. So sixthly and lastly we come to the element of consciousness. As we are at present, our consciousness is associated with the physical body through the five gross physical senses and through the mind. But when we die we are no longer conscious of the body; consciousness is no longer bound up with the material elements, or with physical existence at all. Then consciousness dissolves, or *re*solves itself, into a higher and a wider consciousness, a consciousness that is not identified with the physical body.

This higher and wider consciousness may be realized at many different levels. The individual consciousness, free from the body, may be expanded to a more universal, even collective, consciousness; from that to the *ālaya-vijñāna*, the repository or store-consciousness;[243] and from that we may even break through to the fringes of Absolute Mind. In this way our own petty individual mind is dissolved or resolved into the ocean of universal consciousness, so that we go completely beyond the sense of 'I', and become completely free from the sense of 'mine'.[244]

The five basic methods of meditation fall quite naturally into two important groupings (though there is some overlap between them). The mindfulness of breathing and the *mettā bhāvanā* are primarily concerned with developing *śamatha*, that is, tranquillity, calm, and expansion of mind or consciousness. Any technique of concentration on a simple object or developing a fundamental basis of positive emotion will fall into this category. And it should be said that some effective acquaintance with such techniques is essential before one attempts any more complex or advanced ones.

The other three basic practices are *vipaśyanā* practices – that is, they are concerned primarily with the development of insight, a deep, supra-rational understanding of reality. Any visualization or devotional practice or mantra recitation will also be concerned fundamentally with this goal.

The sheer wealth of different meditation techniques available may seem bewildering – or enticing. But in a way one needs to be wary of the very idea of a meditation 'technique'. All the five basic methods of meditation involve following certain tried and trusted procedures, and we need to be thoroughly familiar with these if we are to make progress in meditation. But the practice of meditation does not consist simply in the application of particular techniques. Meditation is not so much a science as an art, and in this art, as in all others, it is the inner experience rather than the technique that is all-important. It is even possible to become very proficient at the techniques of meditative concentration and yet realize nothing of the real spirit of meditation. Far better to master the spirit – as well as the technique – of just one practice, than manage the empty manipulation of a dozen of them.

from *What is the Dharma?*

4. FINDING A PLACE TO MEDITATE

The Westerner learning to meditate is quite likely to do so alone, buying a book on the subject and beginning the practice in the comfort of his or her own home, but this is not to be recommended.

In the *Satipaṭṭhāna Sutta* of the Pāli canon, having laid down the four foundations of mindfulness (mindfulness of the body, of the feelings, of thoughts, and of reality), the Buddha goes on to recommend a particularly accessible method of developing mindfulness: the mindfulness of breathing. The fact that it is *accessible* is very important. The plain truth is – and we had better face this squarely – that awareness of any kind is not easy to develop. The Buddha's method is therefore to start by encouraging us to develop awareness of the aspect of our experience that is closest to us: the body. Even this is not as easy as one might think. The first of the four foundations may be 'mindfulness of the body', but it is hard to focus on 'the body' as a whole; it is such a complex thing, within which all sorts of processes are going on at the same time. To lead your awareness towards a broader experience of the body, it is therefore best to begin by focusing on the breath. Breathing is a simple bodily activity, providing a relatively stable object of attention that is both calming and capable of sustaining one's interest. On this basis, you can go on to become aware of your bodily sensations and even of your feelings and thoughts, which are still more subtle and difficult to follow.

The breath is available to us at every moment of our lives, and becoming aware of it has a calming effect at stressful times, as we know from the received wisdom of our own culture: 'Take a deep breath.' But it is possible to cultivate a more systematic awareness of the breathing through a meditation which is widely practised throughout the Buddhist world: the mindfulness of breathing (*ānāpānasati* in Pāli), which some say was the meditation the Buddha was practising when he gained Enlightenment.[245] In the *Satipaṭṭhāna Sutta* the Buddha launches straight into a description of how the *bhikkhu* should go about this practice. He is directed to go into the depths of the forest, or to the foot of a tree, or just to an empty place. Then, sitting down with his legs crossed, he is to keep his body erect and his mindfulness alert or 'established in front of him', and start to become aware of his breathing.[246] Thus we learn straightaway that the right place, the right time, and the right posture are all important for successful meditation.

The right place, we gather, is a place of solitude. In the Buddha's time, of course, there was plenty of space in the depths of the forest for meditators to sit there for long periods without being disturbed, but I think the Buddha's instruction here means something more. We need to imagine what it would be like to take up this practice if you had always lived in the traditional Indian family, which was the core of Brahminical society in the Buddha's day. An Indian village, with all its noise and bustle, was hardly conducive to the development of mental calm, and the psychological and moral pull of the family group would have been just as inimical to spiritual practice. Even today in India, if you live in a traditional extended family it can be very difficult to steer your life in a direction not dictated by your family. For anyone seeking an awakening to truth, simply going forth to the undisturbed solitude of the forest, abandoning anything to do with home and family life, at least for a while, was – and continues to be – a major step.

Finding solitude is just as much of a challenge for us in the West today, although for us 'solitude' might mean getting a respite from the world and worldly concerns rather than literally getting away from other people. Indeed, the companionship of other people following the same spiritual tradition as yourself can be a great source of encouragement, especially when you are just starting out. To meditate in isolation, you need to know what you are doing and be very determined. It is all too easy for discouraging doubts to arise about whether you are doing the practice properly, and in the absence of an experienced guide you might lose interest in meditation altogether. While the Buddha's instruction to seek out the foot of a tree certainly suggests finding a place where you are likely to be undisturbed for a while, it does not necessarily mean going off into the depths of the forest or isolating yourself from other meditators.

People didn't always meditate alone even in the Buddha's day. The Pāli *sutta*s contain striking descriptions of the Buddha and his disciples sitting and meditating together, sometimes in very large numbers. We come upon such a scene at the beginning of the *Sāmaññaphala Sutta*. On a full-moon night, King Ajātasattu decides to have his elephants saddled up (500 of them) and ride with his entourage deep into the forest in search of the Buddha. It is quite a long way, and the king (who has a guilty conscience) is beset by all sorts of fears as they journey through the darkness. But at last they come upon the Buddha, seated in meditation with 1,250 monks, all of them perfectly concentrated and spread out before him like a vast, clear lake. The silence, says the *Sutta*, fills the guilty king – he has murdered his own father to gain the throne – with a nameless dread, making the hairs on his body stand on end. But he is sufficiently moved to ask to become a lay disciple of the Buddha on the spot.[247]

Since those early times, Buddhists throughout the tradition – especially in the Zen schools, which place a particular emphasis on meditation – have well understood the benefits of collective practice. The Westerner learning to meditate is quite likely to do so alone, buying a book on the subject and beginning the practice in the comfort of his or her own home, but this is not to be recommended. It is hard to tell from the printed page how much experience the author has, and in any case no book can cover every contingency. There is also the danger that you will end up just reading about Buddhist meditation and never getting round to doing any. It is certainly possible to learn the basic techniques from a book, but if you can, it is worth seeking out a meditation teacher and other meditators with whom to practise.

As for the Buddha's instruction that the *bhikkhu* should sit cross-legged,[248] this posture is recommended because it spreads the weight of the body more broadly and evenly than any other sitting position, and thus gives stability and enables you to sit comfortably for a long time. However, while it would have come naturally to the people of the Buddha's time and culture to sit cross-legged on the floor, we might find it more difficult. If so, any posture can be adopted, whether on the floor or on a chair, as long as it is stable and comfortable. Incidentally, this is another reason to go along to a meditation class – to get some help with working out a suitable meditation posture.

from *Living with Awareness*

5. HAPPINESS AND CONCENTRATION

Meditation is not about pushing parts of yourself away in order to force yourself into a superficially positive mental state.

A lot of Buddhist practice can seem very self-absorbed and in a way it is, especially at the stage of the path called *samādhi*, which means 'one-pointed concentration'. But there is no healthy alternative if one is to be effective in the world. Buddhist meditation is a clearing of the decks for action, a transforming of unskilful and unexamined mental states into integrated and refined energy, for a purpose beyond self-absorption.

As the Buddha states elsewhere in the Pāli canon, concentration is the natural outcome of spiritual bliss.[249] It increases with pleasure, and as pleasure turns into rapture and then bliss, this process of deepening and refining pleasure has the effect of deepening one's concentration even more. *Samādhi* is thus inseparable from *sukha* just as *sukha* was inseparable from *passaddhi* in the stage before. *Samādhi* is what arises naturally when you are perfectly happy; when you are not, you go looking for something to make you happy. In other words, to the extent you are happy, to that extent you are concentrated. This is a very important characteristic of *samādhi*, and should be clearly distinguished from the forcible fixing of attention that is often understood by the term 'meditation'.

It is a question of motivation. If you are looking for an experience of pleasure or excitement or bliss in meditation, the result is going to be as superficial as the motive. It is rather like the difference motivation makes to sexual relationships. There is a famous passage in Malory's medieval romance *Morte d'Arthur* in which the author bewails how times have changed: once upon a time, he says, a lover and his beloved would be faithful to each other for seven years with no 'likerous lust' between them, whereas now all a lover wants is to whisk his beloved into bed. Clearly not much has changed on that front since the fourteenth century. And something quite similar can happen in the case of meditation: people grab at the end result they want without working through the whole process – and so, of course, never get the desired result at all.

Probably this was what the Buddha realized when, recollecting his childhood experience of spontaneously entering the first *dhyāna*, he came to understand that this was the key to Enlightenment. This is a turning point in the story of his quest for Enlightenment. Having tried all kinds of methods and practices, having meditated and fasted and performed austerities, the Buddha-to-be remembered an experience he had as a boy. He had been sitting under a rose-apple tree out in the fields when he had spontaneously entered a state of meditative concentration. He sat there all day, absorbed and happy. And it was the recollection of this when he was on the very threshold of Enlightenment that gave him the clue he needed.[250] One might wonder what such an elementary spiritual attainment might signify to one who had advanced in meditation even as far as the formless *dhyānas* under the guidance of his teachers. But he knew that he had still not attained the goal to which he aspired, and now he understood why. What he realized was that his previous mastery of meditation had been forced, however subtly; this was why it was in the end useless. Progress had been made but only part of him had been involved in that progress, because it had been produced through sheer will-power. It was not so much the first *dhyāna* itself that was the answer, but the natural manner in which he had entered into that state. The answer was to allow a natural unfolding of the whole being to take place, through the steady application of mindfulness.

We too can make use of this important insight. The states of mind we have produced through our actions during the day and during the course of our life in general, whatever they are, will be the states of mind we have to address in our meditation. Meditation is not about pushing parts of yourself away in order to force yourself into a superficially positive mental state. If you are distracted, unreflective, self-indulgent, and reactive in your everyday life, you might as a novice meditator force yourself in the opposite direction to some short-term effect, but in the long run meditation is about transforming mental states, not suppressing or ignoring them.

from *Living with Awareness*

6. WHY ARE WE SO EASILY DISTRACTED?

Why is it that we are so easily distracted? How does it happen?

Suppose that you are writing a letter, an urgent letter that it is imperative should go off by the next post. But, as so often happens today, the telephone rings, and it is some friend of yours wanting a little chat. Before you know where you are you are involved in quite a lengthy conversation. You go on chatting maybe for half an hour, and eventually, the conversation completed, you put down the phone. You have talked about so many things with your friend that you have quite forgotten about the letter, and you have talked for such a long while that you suddenly feel quite thirsty. So you wander into the kitchen and put the kettle on for a cup of tea. Waiting for the kettle to boil you hear a pleasant sound coming through the wall from next door, and realizing it is the radio you think you might as well listen to it. You therefore nip into the next room, switch on the radio, and start listening to the tune. After that tune is finished there comes another, and you listen to that too. In this way more time passes, and of course you've forgotten all about your boiling kettle. Whilst you are in the midst of this daze, or trance-like state, there is a knock at the door. A friend has called to see you. Since you are glad to see him you make him welcome. The two of you sit down together for a chat, and in due course you offer him a cup of tea. You go into the kitchen and find it full of steam.[251] Then you remember that you had put the kettle on some time ago, and that makes you remember your letter. But now it is too late. You have missed the post.

This is an example of unmindfulness in everyday life. Indeed everyday life consists, for the most part, of this sort of unmindfulness. We can all no doubt recognize ourselves in the portrait. We can recognize that this is the chaotic, unmindful fashion in which, for the most part, we live our lives. Now let us analyse the situation, to give ourselves a better understanding of the nature of unmindfulness. First of all in our example we see the plain and simple fact of forgetfulness, which is a very important element in unmindfulness. We forget about the letter which we are writing when we are talking on the phone, and we forget the kettle which is boiling for tea when we are listening to the radio.

Why do we forget so easily in this fashion? Why is it that we lose sight of something we ought to be bearing in mind? The reason is that we are very easily distracted. Our mind is very easily turned away or turned aside. It often happens, for instance, that I am giving a lecture or talk of some kind. Everybody is paying close attention, and there is a pin-drop silence. But then the door opens, and someone comes in. What happens? Half the heads swivel round as though they had all been pulled by the same string. People are as easily distracted as that. Sometimes it is a bluebottle buzzing against the window pane, or the dropping of a sheet of my notes that distracts people. Such things show how easily we are distracted, which is why we tend to forget in the affairs of everyday life.

Why is it that we are so easily distracted? How does it come about? We are easily distracted because our concentration is weak. If for instance you were really listening to me, and really concentrating on what I was saying, an elephant could come in at the door and you would not notice it. Because we are not concentrated in this way distraction occurs very easily. We do not concentrate wholeheartedly on what we are doing. Usually we attend to what we are doing or saying or thinking only in a half-hearted way.

Why is our concentration so weak? Why does it happen? Our concentration is weak because we have no continuity of purpose. There is no one overriding purpose that remains unchanged in the midst of all the different things that we do. We switch from one thing to another, one wish to another, all the time, like the character in Dryden's famous satire who

> Was everything by starts, and nothing long;
> But, in the course of one revolving moon,
> Was chemist, fiddler, statesman, and buffoon.[252]

Because there is no continuity of purpose, because we are not bent on one main thing all the time, we have no real individuality. We are a succession of different people, all of them rather abortive or embryonic. There is no regular growth, no real development, no true evolution.

Some of the main characteristics of unmindfulness should now be clear. Unmindfulness is a state of forgetfulness, of distraction, of poor concentration, of an absence of continuity of purpose, of drift, and of no real individuality. Mindfulness of course has just the opposite characteristics: it is a state of recollection, of undistractedness, of concentration, of continuity and steadfastness of purpose, and of continually developing individuality.

from *The Buddha's Noble Eightfold Path*

7. THE JAPANESE TEA CEREMONY

If the Japanese tea ceremony represents a certain level of awareness in everyday life and a certain type of spiritual culture – that of Far Eastern Buddhism, especially Zen – what analogous ceremony or institution is there that represents the attitude of the West today?

On the face of it the Japanese tea ceremony revolves around a very ordinary act, which we do every day: the making and drinking of a cup of tea. This is something we have all done hundreds and thousands of times. But how do they do it in Japan? How is it done in the Japanese tea ceremony? There it is done in a quite different way, because it is done with awareness. With awareness the kettle is filled with water. With awareness it is put on the charcoal fire. With awareness one sits and waits for the kettle to boil, listening to the humming and bubbling of the water and watching the flickering of the flames. Finally, with awareness one pours the boiling water into the teapot, with awareness one pours out the tea, offers it, and drinks it, all the time observing complete silence. The whole act is an exercise in awareness. It represents the application of awareness to the affairs of everyday life.

This attitude should be brought into all our activities. All should be conducted on the same principle as the Japanese tea ceremony, everything being done with mindfulness and awareness, and therefore with stillness, quietness, and beauty, as well as with dignity, harmony, and peace.

But if the Japanese tea ceremony represents a certain level of awareness in everyday life, and a certain type of spiritual culture – that of Far Eastern Buddhism, especially Zen – what analogous ceremony or institution is there that represents the attitude of the West today? What do we have that breathes the whole spirit of our commercial culture? Perhaps it is the business lunch. In the business lunch you are trying to do two things at the same time: trying to have a good meal, and trying to pull off a good deal. This sort of behaviour, where one is trying to do two contradictory things at once, is quite incompatible with any true, real, or deep awareness. It is also very bad for the digestion.

Awareness of the body and its movements will, if practised continually, have the effect of slowing these movements down. The pace of life will become more even and more rhythmical. Everything will be done more slowly and deliberately. But that does not mean that we will do less work. That is a fallacy. If you do everything slowly because you are doing it with awareness and deliberation you may well accomplish more than someone who looks very busy, always dashing around and whose desk is piled high with papers and files on his desk, but who is in fact not busy but just confused. If you are really busy you go about things quietly and methodically, and because you don't waste time in trivialities and fuss, and because you are aware, in the long run you actually get more done.

from *The Buddha's Noble Eightfold Path*

8. MINDFULNESS AND SPONTANEITY

There's a certain energy in spontaneity which is refined and made more aware as you become more mindful.

You learn to draw the line between joy and intoxication when you are able to realize that you are losing your mindfulness. On the other hand, if you become stiff and self-conscious, that's not real mindfulness either. Your awareness has become 'alienated'.[253] Most people tend to begin practising Buddhism by being 'over-mindful' (or rather, falsely mindful), because they usually start off by being completely unmindful. It's as though you have to go to the other extreme for a while and learn to be mindful, and then – not exactly forget about mindfulness, but let go and loosen up a bit. Of course, if you're not careful, you go to extremes again, and need to introduce more mindfulness and awareness. You just have to see which extreme you're tending towards at the moment, and correct the imbalance. The aim is to reach the middle ground where you've got lots of spontaneous, happy energy, but you're mindful at the same time.

Although mindfulness is certainly a key factor in the development of individuality, so is spontaneity. Even 'animal' spontaneity can be turned into a more truly human or even spiritual spontaneity. It's as if there's a certain energy in spontaneity which is refined and made more aware as you become more mindful. Clearly some people need to check their exuberance and high spirits, but others need to get their energies flowing and express themselves more freely. It may be that they need to forget all about mindfulness for a while and let their hair down.

It isn't, of course, that you have spontaneity and mindfulness going on side by side; they are completely blended. It's like the deep absorption of creative activity. When you are painting a picture, for instance, your energy is freely flowing, but at the same time you are aware. You know just what you are doing, but you are not stiff – everything is flowing freely. This is the kind of state I'm talking about, but raised to a much higher pitch of intensity. Sometimes it happens in an emergency. When you've got to do something quickly, all your energy is mobilized, but at the same time you are very aware and alert – you know exactly what you are doing. In a dangerous situation you can act quickly and spontaneously, but very effectively, with full awareness of the total situation.

from *Transforming Self and World*

9. HOW TO SUCCEED AT MEDITATION

It is sometimes said in India that if people devoted the same energy and interest to the spiritual life that they devote to material things, success would be assured.

Meditation is like any other aspect of life: to succeed, one must want to succeed. Otherwise, one won't get far. A lot of people like the idea of making a lot of money, but they don't *really want* to make it; they are not prepared to go all out to make a million dollars by the time they're thirty. People who make money do it by sacrificing absolutely everything else. They think of nothing, day and night, except making that money; all their energies are bent in that direction. It's the same with someone who really wants to be a great writer or a great musician: they throw themselves into it, and in this way find out for sure whether they have it in them or not.

The only difference with meditation is that success is guaranteed. One can spend ten years producing an epic poem, and it may be a second *Paradise Lost* or a complete failure. But if you spend ten years meditating and you get into *dhyāna* states, there is no question of those *dhyāna* states not being the right ones. It is impossible to fail. It is sometimes said in India that if people devoted the same energy and interest to the spiritual life that they devote to material things, success would be assured, and one does see plenty of evidence that this is true. It is very noticeable how someone's energy seems to start flowing again if something they are really interested in doing comes up. Someone who professes to be too tired to go to a Dharma study class will suddenly perk up at the prospect of going to a film they have been wanting to see. If we are interested in something, we will find the energy to do it; and unless we really want to do it, we might just as well not bother.

But how does one transform a purely intellectual recognition of the rightness of something into an ardent desire to achieve it? The only way is to find some emotional connection; one has to want to want – which brings one straight back to the same problem. The only solution is to find out what one truly wants. Then one can try to link one's desire for that with whatever activity or interest or goal it is that as yet one only intellectually recognizes as being of value.

For example, one might be passionately interested in sculpture. At the same time, intellectually one knows that Buddhism makes sense. How is one going to bring head and heart together? To bridge the gap, one could perhaps make a special study of Buddhist sculpture: Gandhāran sculpture, Chinese and Japanese wooden sculpture, and so on. That interest could act as a bridge between what one has a strong feeling for and what one feels one ought to be doing. To put aside one's interest in sculpture and try to study Buddhist philosophy instead would be very difficult. Some people can force themselves for a while to study things they are not interested in, or do things they don't want to do, but no one can do that for very long. At some point there will be a strong reaction from the part of oneself that hasn't been involved and doesn't want to be involved.

So first of all, one has to ask oneself, 'What do I really want to do? Do I really want to meditate? Do I really want to study the Dharma? If not, what *do* I want to do? If I had a completely free choice, what would I do?' The answer may come quite readily to mind; or one may find oneself quite thrown by the question. Sometimes one has to stop, not do anything, and allow one's real desires, skilful or unskilful, to surface. Perhaps one has been so busy, so much swept along by the whirlwind of life, that one hasn't even asked oneself what one really wants to do.

Simply asking the question does not have to lead inexorably to indulging dark, unspoken desires. One tends to suspect that if one were to allow one's desires to surface, something dreadful would be sure to come up. Perhaps it will – maybe one will be shocked by what emerges – but why make that assumption? It is much more likely that what will surface will be some harmless, innocent yearning which one has never been able to fulfil. And even if one's desires turn out to be unskilful, one may be able to establish some connection between them and something more healthy, skilful, or Dharmic. One might, for instance, discover that one dislikes people, to the extent that one feels quite destructive towards them. Clearly that is unskilful, but it might be possible to transfer that animosity to certain ideas. One could think in terms of annihilating one's own wrong views, fishing around for *micchā-diṭṭhis* lodged deep in one's psyche towards which one could direct one's anger and hatred. Few desires are so irredeemably and utterly negative that they cannot possibly be connected with some aspect of the spiritual life.

from *The Bodhisattva Ideal*

10. MEDITATION ISN'T THE ONLY WAY

It does seem as if, for most people, a positive change of environment leads quite naturally to a raising of their level of consciousness – even without any further effort.

Some people appear to think that meditation is the only way there is to raise the level of consciousness, as if to say that consciousness must be raised directly by working on the mind itself or not at all. Such people therefore identify meditation with the spiritual life, and the spiritual life exclusively with meditation. They therefore claim that if you are not meditating you cannot possibly be leading a spiritual life. Sometimes they even identify the spiritual life with a particular kind of meditation, or a particular concentration technique. But this is far too narrow a view. It makes us forget what the spiritual life really is – which is to say that it consists in the raising of the level of consciousness – and it makes us forget, sometimes, what meditation itself really is. It is true, of course, that the raising of the level of consciousness by direct methods is at least as important as raising it by indirect methods; we might even say that it is perhaps more important. But we should not forget that other methods do exist; if we did forget this our approach would be too one-sided; and if we acted upon this, we would tend to make the spiritual life itself one-sided and even to exclude certain kinds of people – people of certain temperaments, for example – who were not, perhaps, particularly interested in meditation. So let us very briefly look at some of these indirect, non-meditative methods of raising the level of consciousness.

First of all, there is change of environment. This is quite consciously employed as an indirect means of changing, and hopefully raising, our level of consciousness when we go away on retreat – perhaps into the country, to a retreat centre. There we spend a few days, or even a few weeks, simply in more pleasant, more congenial surroundings, perhaps not even doing anything in particular. This is often more helpful than people realize, and it suggests that the environment in which we normally have to live and work is not particularly good for us – does not help in the raising of the level of awareness. It really does seem as if, for most people, a positive change of environment leads quite naturally to a raising of their level of consciousness – even without any further effort.

Another quite practical and simple indirect method of raising the level of consciousness is what we call, in Buddhism, right livelihood. Practically everybody has to work for a living. Quite a lot of us do the same kind of work every day, five days a week, fifty weeks of the year. We may do it for five, ten, fifteen, twenty, twenty-five, or thirty years, until we come to the age of retirement. All this has a continuous effect on our state of mind. If our work is unhealthy in the mental, moral, and spiritual sense, the effect on our minds will also be unhealthy. So therefore, in Buddhism, in the Buddha's teaching, we are advised very strongly to look at our means of livelihood and to practise right livelihood, which means earning our living in a way that does not lower our state of consciousness, that does not prevent us raising it, even, and that does no harm to other living beings. In Buddhist tradition there is a list of occupations that are seen not to be very helpful: the work of a butcher, of a trader in arms, of a dealer in liquor, and so on. By changing our means of livelihood (assuming that at present it is not quite right), then just that change of work, change of place, change of environment – that change in the sort of people we work with, the sort of thing that we have to do every day – will have a positive and helpful effect on our level of consciousness.

Then again, to become more specific and concrete, there is the leading of a regular and disciplined life: something which apparently is becoming less and less popular. This may consist in the observance and practice of certain moral precepts and principles, in having regular hours for meals, for work, for recreation, and for study, or in observing moderation in such things as eating, sleeping, and talking – perhaps even in fasting occasionally, or observing silence for a few days or weeks. In its fully developed form this more regular, disciplined life is what we call the monastic life. Among those who are leading such a regular, disciplined life, even without any meditation, over a period of years, one can see quite clearly a change taking place in their state, their level, of consciousness.

There are other indirect methods, such as yoga and t'ai chi ch'uan, which affect not only the body, but the mind as well. They affect the mind *through* the body, and even people who meditate regularly sometimes find them very helpful. Sometimes even the experienced meditator may be a bit too tired at the end of a day's work, or a bit too worried, to meditate properly. At such times he may practise a few yoga poses until his mind becomes calmer and more concentrated. Thus he loses his tiredness and becomes more refreshed, almost as though he had meditated.

Then again there are the various Japanese *tao* or 'ways' – like *ikebana*, flower arrangement. It might seem a very simple and ordinary thing just to arrange a few flowers in a vase in a traditional way, but people who have engaged in this over a period of years are definitely changed in their minds, changed in their consciousness. One can also think of things like t'ai chi ch'uan and so on. These all have an effect upon the mind. They are all indirect ways of raising the level of consciousness. Likewise, the enjoyment of great works of art – of great poetry, music, and painting – often helps to raise the level of consciousness, especially if the works of art issue from a higher state of consciousness in the artist.

On a more practical level, there is simply helping other people. You might devote yourself to helping the sick, the destitute, and the mentally disturbed, as well as to visiting those in prison. You might do these things very willingly and cheerfully, disregarding your own comfort and convenience – might do them without any personal, selfish motive. This is what in the Hindu tradition is called *Niṣkamakarma Yoga*, or the yoga of disinterested action. This too is an indirect means of raising one's state of consciousness.

Then there is association with spiritually-minded people, especially those who are more spiritually advanced than ourselves – if we are able to find them. Such association is regarded in some traditions, or by some teachers, as the most important of all the indirect methods. It is what is referred to again and again in Indian religious and spiritual literature as *satsaṅgh*. *Sat* means true, real, authentic, genuine, spiritual – even transcendental – while *saṅgh* means association, or communion, or fellowship. *Satsaṅgh* is simply a getting together – often in a very happy, carefree spirit – with people who are on the spiritual path and whose predominant interest is in spiritual things. This rubs off on oneself, almost without any effort on one's own part. Thus *satsaṅgh* too is an indirect means of raising the level of consciousness. It is what in Buddhism we call *kalyāṇa mitratā*: spiritual friendship.

Then again, there is chanting and ritual worship. Ritual is very much looked down upon today, especially by the more intelligent, or perhaps I should say 'intellectual'. But it is a time-honoured method of raising the level of consciousness. Even if we simply offer a few flowers, or light a candle and place it in front of an image or picture, all this has an effect upon the mind, and sometimes we are surprised to find how much effect it does have. We might read lots of books about the spiritual life, we might even have tried to meditate – might even have succeeded in meditating – but sometimes we find that the performance of a simple, but meaningful, symbolic ritual action helps us far more.

from *Human Enlightenment*

11. TANTRIC MEDITATION: THE *YIDAM*

For you, your yidam *is the whole Dharma, the whole teaching, distilled into a single figure with which you become spiritually intimate.*

Yidam is a Tibetan word which literally means 'oath-bound'. It is sometimes translated as 'guarantor', that is, one who guarantees that the disciple will eventually gain Enlightenment, and it is equivalent to, though not an actual translation of, the Sanskrit term *iṣṭa devatā*, which means 'chosen or selected divinity'. The *yidam* is thus that special aspect of the Dharma, that special aspect of reality, through which the disciple approaches the Enlightenment experience. The *yidam* is not an abstract concept or an idea but a figure – a figure of a Buddha or bodhisattva, embodying a particular aspect or attribute of Enlightenment. Your *yidam* could be Amitābha, the red Buddha of infinite light and eternal life; or Mañjughoṣa, the golden Bodhisattva of Wisdom with the flaming sword; or Tārā, the saviouress, usually white or green in colour, carrying lotus flowers; or Vajrasattva, the embodiment of the innate purity of one's own mind. Whichever figure it is, as a disciple of the Tantra, the whole of the Dharma is contained, embodied, in your *yidam*, and you direct all your attention to that. You don't bother too much about scriptures, studies, teachings, doctrines. The centre of your attention, spiritually speaking, is occupied by the figure of the *yidam*, and you devote yourself to becoming familiar with that figure.

You first make the acquaintance of the *yidam* in the course of Tantric initiation. In effect, in giving you the initiation of, say, Tārā, the guru is introducing you to her, saying to her, 'Tārā, this is So-and-so,' and to you, 'This is Tārā. Now I've introduced you to her, you know each other and there is a connection between you.' Once you have made the acquaintance of a *yidam* in this way, your practice is to keep the *yidam* at the centre of your attention. One way of doing this is to visualize the figure in meditation. With your inner eye you see the *yidam* before you, and you contemplate and become absorbed in that figure, and chant the *yidam*'s mantra. Becoming absorbed in the *yidam*, you thereby absorb the spiritual qualities and principles and experiences which the *yidam* represents, which the *yidam* is. Eventually, you are absorbed into the *yidam*, or the *yidam* is absorbed into you, so that the two of you become one. If you have been focusing on Mañjughoṣa, for example, you absorb the wisdom that Mañjughoṣa represents, while if your *yidam* is Tārā you develop the purity, the tenderness, the compassion, which is Tārā, and if you have Vajrapāṇi as your *yidam*, you acquire the energy, strength, courage, even spiritual ferocity he stands for. For you, your *yidam* is the whole Dharma, the whole teaching, distilled into a single figure with which you become spiritually intimate, and into whom, or into which, you are incorporated.

To give an idea of what this involves, I will say a little more about some of these figures. Avalokiteśvara is among the most prominent of all these figures. His name (at least according to one etymology) means 'the Lord who looks down', and he is so called because he looks down on the world in compassion; he represents the compassion aspect of Enlightenment. Imagine a vast blue sky, a sky which is completely empty, nothing but blueness stretching to infinity. Then in that blue sky you see – not even a face, just the barely visible lineaments of a compassionate smile. This is the compassion aspect of reality; this is Avalokiteśvara – though of course, where there is compassion, there must be wisdom: it is Avalokiteśvara who appears in the *Heart Sūtra*, the heart of the Perfection of Wisdom.

Iconographically he is pure white in colour and carries lotus flowers, symbolizing spiritual rebirth. His face is alive with a sweet, compassionate smile. In some depictions of him, one foot is tucked up in the posture of meditation, showing that he is deep in *dhyāna*, while the other foot hangs loose, showing his readiness to step down at any moment into the turmoil of the world to help living beings. For the bodhisattva inner tranquillity and external activity are not contradictory, but different aspects of the same thing.

Altogether there are 108 forms of Avalokiteśvara. One of the most famous is the eleven-headed, thousand-armed form. To us this is perhaps going to seem grotesque, but the symbolism is very interesting. It is said that once Avalokiteśvara was contemplating the sorrows of the world, the miseries of sentient beings, their suffering by fire, flood, famine, bereavement, separation, war, shipwreck, and so on. He was overwhelmed by such compassion that he wept, and went on weeping so violently, we are told, that his head shivered into eleven fragments, each of which became a face. There are eleven of them because there are eleven directions of space (north, south, east, west, the four intermediate points, up, down, and the centre), and compassion looks in all directions simultaneously. Not only that; he has a thousand arms – at least iconographically he is supposed to have a thousand arms. In truth the Bodhisattva of Compassion has millions of arms, each of which is stretched out to help living beings in one way or another. It wouldn't be possible for any one person in any historical situation to do everything that is needed, but each individual can imbibe the spirit of the bodhisattva and express that in their own way within their own life. One can aspire to be one of the thousand arms of Avalokiteśvara.

Another of the bodhisattvas is Mañjughoṣa, who represents the wisdom aspect of Enlightenment. He is a beautiful golden, orange, or tawny colour – his is the golden wisdom of Enlightenment that dispels ignorance, as the sun dispels the darkness – and he carries a sword and a book. The flaming sword in his right hand symbolizes his wisdom; he whirls it above his head, cutting asunder the bonds of ignorance and of karma, all the knotty tangles that keep tripping us up. And the book he holds in his other hand is the Perfection of Wisdom, which he holds close to his heart. His legs are crossed in the meditation posture, because wisdom springs, as the *Dhammapada* teaches us, from meditation.[254] Mañjughoṣa is the patron deity of all the arts and sciences. If you want to write a book, paint a picture, or compose a piece of music, you traditionally invoke Mañjughoṣa, and his mantra is repeated for retentive memory, understanding of the Dharma, eloquence, power of speech, and so on.

Then there is Vajrapāṇi, who represents the power aspect of Enlightenment – not power in the political sense, or in the sense of power over other people, but spiritual power. Although he has a peaceful form too, Vajrapāṇi is usually depicted in wrathful form, an image of furious energy to crush the forces of ignorance. The wrathful Vajrapāṇi is dark blue in colour, and he is not slim, slender, or graceful, but has a stout body, protuberant belly, and thick, short limbs. His countenance expresses extreme anger and he has long white teeth or tusks. He is more or less naked apart from ornaments of human bone and a tiger skin, and he carries in one hand a *vajra*, a thunderbolt, with which he destroys the forces of ignorance. This terrifying figure is crowned with five skulls, representing the five wisdoms. One foot is uplifted, to crush and trample all the forces of conditioned existence that separate us from the light of truth, and he is surrounded by a great halo of flames. This is the bodhisattva Vajrapāṇi, destroying and breaking up conditioned existence, rending the veil of ignorance, and scattering all the forces of darkness through the power of his spiritual energy.

Then, by way of contrast, there is Tārā, who appears in female form. Tārā is the spiritual daughter of Avalokiteśvara. She is usually either white or green in colour, and according to another beautiful legend she was born from the tears of Avalokiteśvara as he wept over the sorrows of existence. In the midst of a great pool of his tears there appeared a white lotus. The lotus opened, and there was Tārā, the very essence, indeed the quintessence, of compassion.

Often she bears a blue or white lotus flower, and in her white form she has seven eyes – two ordinary eyes, plus a third in the forehead, two in the palms of her hands, and two in the soles of her feet. All these eyes symbolize Tārā's awareness. There is nothing blind, sentimental, or foolish about compassion – it is informed by awareness, mindfulness, and knowledge. Sometimes what passes for compassion is really no more than pity, and it just makes things worse.

If there is one more archetypal bodhisattva to be mentioned along with the key figures so far described, it is Vajrasattva. He represents purity: not physical purity, moral purity, or even spiritual purity; not any purity that can be attained. Vajrasattva represents primeval purity, the original spotless purity of the mind, unsoiled and untouched from beginningless ages. We cannot purify the mind through spiritual practice. We may purify the lower mind, because the lower mind can become soiled, but we never purify the ultimate mind, because the ultimate mind never becomes impure. We purify ourselves truly by waking up to the fact that we have never been impure, that we were pure all the time. This ultimately inherent purity of the mind, above and beyond time, above and beyond the possibility of impurity, is represented by Vajrasattva.

Vajrasattva is pure, dazzling white, like sunlight reflecting from snow. He is sometimes depicted completely naked and sometimes as wearing the silks and jewels of a bodhisattva. His mantra, which has one hundred syllables, is recited and meditated upon to purify one's faults, or rather, to purify oneself of the impurity of thinking that one is not intrinsically pure.

from *Creative Symbols of Tantric Buddhism* and *The Bodhisattva Ideal*

12. WHITE TĀRĀ

Appearing from the depth of heaven,
The white-robed goddess, calm and bright,
Sheds moon-like on this lower world
The blessing of her silver light.

Seven eyes she has, all open wide,
In face and forehead, hands and feet,
For she of Pure Awareness is
Embodiment and paraclete.

One hand, in teaching gesture raised,
Imparts a wisdom thrice-profound;
The other, open on her knee,
For endless giving is renowned.

A lotus at her shoulder grows,
Complete with flower, and bud, and fruit;
Her form is straight and still, for she
Is grounded on the Absolute.

'Awake! Arise!' she seems to say,
'Leave dreams, leave sloth, leave passions vile!'
Oh may we, seeing her, go forth
Encouraged by her perfect smile.

from *Complete Poems*

3
FAITH, DEVOTION, AND RITUAL

1. VISITING GHOOM MONASTERY WITH LAMA GOVINDA

It was not that on taking up a new practice one discarded the old practice and put it behind one, so to speak. What one did was add the new practice to the old and incorporate both in a higher unity.

As we lifted the heavy felt curtain that screened the entrance I saw a colossal figure seated there in the semi-darkness, a golden face glimmering beneath the great jewelled tiara. Smaller figures gleamed from behind the glass doors of showcases and glowed with a subdued richness from the frescoed walls like reflections seen in deep water. Rosary in hand, Lama Govinda and Li Gotami moved clockwise round the chamber, pausing for a moment in front of each image or thangka and reciting the appropriate mantra, and I followed in their wake. Some of the mantras were new to me, and of these two in particular – the mantra of Śākyamuni and the mantra of Padmasambhava – not only sounded strangely familiar but also set up reverberations that made themselves felt in the remotest corners of my being. The whole experience affected me deeply. There was the rectangular chamber itself, dimly lit from above by the light that filtered in at a kind of skylight; there was the brooding presence of the images, with the colossal Maitreya silently dominating the rest; and there was the sound of the mantras as the two dark figures in *chubas* made their way with bowed heads round the chamber. What affected me most deeply, however, was the evident devotion with which Lama Govinda and Li Gotami recited the mantras and the way in which they seemed to feel, behind each image, the living spiritual presence of which the image was the representation or, indeed, even the veritable embodiment.

It was therefore only natural, perhaps, that of all the discussions Lama Govinda and I had in Kalimpong and Ghoom the only one to leave a distinct and separate impression on my mind should have taken place after our visit to the Ghoom Monastery and should have related to meditation and, in particular, to meditation on the different Buddhas and bodhisattvas. While I listened enthralled, Lama Govinda explained how one took up first one kind of spiritual practice, then another, in accordance with the various needs of one's developing spiritual life. It was not, however, that on taking up a new practice one discarded the old practice and put it behind one, so to speak. What one did was add the new practice to the old and incorporate both in a higher unity. In this way one's meditation or spiritual practice would, over the years, gradually become an ever richer and more complex thing. As Lama Govinda spoke, I had a vision of petal being added to petal, or facet to facet, until one had a thousand-petalled rose or a thousand-faceted crystal ball complete in all its glory. What Lama Govinda was doing, of course, was speaking of meditation or spiritual practice – indeed, of the spiritual life itself – in terms of the gradual building up of a mandala. In other words, he was speaking of it not only in terms of time but in terms of space. Hitherto I had thought of it as a progression from stage to stage, or level to level. Now I also saw it as an unfolding from an ever more truly central point into an ever increasing number of different aspects and dimensions.

from *Facing Mount Kanchenjunga*

2. THE NATURE OF BUDDHIST FAITH

If you leave out devotion you are closing the door on any emotional engagement with your spiritual ideal.

I have known people who have been surprised to find that there is any such thing as faith in Buddhism. They have come into contact with

Buddhism under the initial impression that it is essentially rational, that emotion is not really involved at all. This confusion arises out of two mistaken ideas: that emotion is essentially irrational, and that faith is the same thing as belief.

Belief – in the sense of accepting as true on authority something that one can never verify, or something that is even inherently absurd – is not faith, at least not in Buddhism. In Buddhism, as we have already seen in connection with the spiral path, *śraddhā* or faith covers the entire devotional or feeling aspect of spiritual life. Faith in Buddhism could never be said to be contrary to reason – or even beyond reason. Faith is the emotional counterpart of reason. What you understand with your intelligence you must feel also with your emotions. The two go together, and cannot be separated.

Śraddhā in Buddhism is faith in the Three Jewels: the Buddha, the Dharma, and the Sangha. But it is especially faith directed towards the Buddha himself, because – at least from our point of view – the Buddha comes first. Even though the Dharma represents immemorial Truth, we would know nothing of it without the Buddha, and there would certainly be no Sangha without him. In Buddhism faith is essentially faith in the founder of Buddhism himself.

However, it's not just belief; it's not even just feeling. Faith in the Buddha is the sort of emotional response that you have when you are confronted by the embodiment of Enlightenment. This confrontation can take place in various ways. You can of course be confronted personally by some living human being who is the embodiment of Enlightenment. Alternatively, you can be confronted through literature, by reading about someone who was such an embodiment – if not the life of the Buddha himself, then perhaps the biography of the great Tibetan yogi, Milarepa, or that of Huineng, the sixth patriarch of Chan or Zen Buddhism. With any of the great masters or teachers, there is the possibility of an immediate emotional response to accounts of their lives – whether historical or legendary – a response that is not just sentimental, but engaged, challenging, personal, real.

Then again, you can be confronted by an image, an artistic representation – a painting or a statue – of someone who was Enlightened. Here I am reminded of a French Buddhist nun whom I knew in Kalimpong in the 1950s.[255] She told me that in her student days in Paris she used to like visiting museums and art galleries, which is how she found herself eventually in the Musée Guimet of oriental art. She was a rather militant, aggressive woman; she told me that she used to go around with a pair of ice-skates with which to defend herself if she was attacked. 'Well, I thought if I carried these skates with me, if anyone tried to attack me I'd slash the blades across his face.'

But as she strode along the galleries of the Guimet – having left the skates in the cloakroom – looking to left and right rather fiercely as she usually did, suddenly she encountered an image of the Buddha. From her description I gather that it was an image from ancient Cambodia. She just turned a corner and there was the celebrated smile – faint and delicate and rather withdrawn – so characteristic of this Khmer style of sculpture. The whole expression of the face is intensely peaceful.

The face of this image just stopped her in her tracks. She told me that she stood looking at it without moving, almost without blinking, for forty-five minutes. She couldn't take her eyes off it. The impression of peace, tranquillity, and wisdom that emanated, that streamed as it were, from those features, was so strong that she couldn't pull herself away. She hadn't yet studied anything about Buddhism, but as soon as she saw this image, she felt compelled to ask herself, 'What is it that gives its expression to this image? What is it trying to tell me? What depths of experience does it come from? What could the sculptor have experienced, to be able to express something like this?'

Confronted by this embodiment of Enlightenment, she could not move away unchanged. In fact, it determined the whole subsequent course of her life. This is the kind of emotional response we can have to an embodiment of Enlightenment simply rendered in stone, let alone one in the form of a living person. And it is a response that amounts to faith.

What it is in fact is the response of our potential Enlightenment – our own deeply hidden capacity for Enlightenment – to the actual Enlightenment with which we find ourselves confronted. There's something deep down within us that has a sort of affinity with what is fully realized, fully expressed, fully achieved, in that embodiment of Enlightenment. There's a sort of kinship. It's as though you have two stringed instruments side by side: if you sound the strings of one, the other starts softly vibrating too.

And what this response gives rise to is devotion. There are all sorts of different ways of expressing devotion, but traditionally it is done by means of prostration or worship, the offering of flowers, the lighting of candles and incense, and so on. Some people in the West are a little shy of Buddhist devotional practices. They would like to think that Buddhism had nothing to do with the kind of apparently superstitious activities that they were trying to get away from when they abandoned Christianity. They feel, perhaps, that these are practices for children, and that it is time to be grown-up and stop bowing and scraping and offering candles and the like.

However, if you leave out devotion you are closing the door on any emotional engagement with your spiritual ideal. A healthy spiritual life, just as much as a healthy psychological life, must include the expression of emotion.[256] Having said that, there is a balance to be maintained. Faith and devotion can go to extremes, and when they do so they become superstition, fanaticism, or intolerance. It is for this reason that, according to this teaching of the five spiritual faculties, faith – the whole emotional and devotional side of the spiritual life – should be balanced by wisdom.

from *What is the Dharma?*

3. THE NECESSITY OF DEPENDENCE

To attain Enlightenment is not such a light undertaking that we can afford to make it more difficult for ourselves than it already is.

There are people to whom the idea of dependence of any kind is extremely distasteful, and who maintain with great vehemence that a true Buddhist should be independent of all external aids. It must be observed of them that they have failed to understand the Dharma. One of the most important teachings of the Tathāgata is that nothing arises without at least two causes, a teaching which is no less true of the mental than of the material world. We have already seen that each stage of the path arises not only as a result of direct individual volition but also in dependence upon the whole complex of conditions which constitute the stage preceding it. If we rely for the achievement of Nirvāṇa solely upon our own unaided efforts we shall be like the man who tried to lift himself from the ground by means of his own boot-straps. Whether we choose to recognize the fact or not, it is the presence of certain objective conditions which enable us to lead the holy life. To begin with, if the Dharma was not a law inherent in the very nature of things, if the universe was not so constituted that different causes produce different effects, a certain action an equivalent and equal reaction, and if everything depended instead upon chance, which is say upon nothing, then it would no more be possible for a human being to progress spiritually than it would be for a bird to fly in a vacuum, or for a man to walk without the existence of gravity.

Again, if the sequence of conditions upon which the attainment of Enlightenment depends had not been revealed to the world by the Buddha it is extremely doubtful whether any of us would have ever succeeded in discovering them for ourselves. The independent spirit of those who wish to be entirely free from all external assistance is certainly to be admired, but if they wish to be consistent they cannot be Buddhists, since a Buddhist is one who takes refuge in the Buddha, the Dharma, and the Sangha, and such refuge cannot be taken without surrendering at least a little of one's independence. Moreover, the leading of the holy life depends upon numerous other conditions which the spiritual individualist either overlooks or ignores. It depends, for example, upon the possession of a human body, upon the enjoyment of moderately good health, upon the vicissitudes of climate and weather, on social and political environment, upon whether one meets a 'good friend' or not. All such aids must be relinquished if one intends to achieve Nirvāṇa by the pure unaided exercise of personal volition, in which case the desired achievement should take place instantaneously.

There is no doubt at all that if the thrust of our volition were sufficiently powerful Nirvāṇa could indeed be won within the twinkling of an eye. But it is weak, and instead of piercing the dense cloud of ignorance by which the sun of supernal wisdom is obscured, it beats feebly upon it, like a moth fluttering against the window pane. We therefore are compelled to bethink ourselves of how to remove ignorance; but this task also we find beyond our powers, and we are forced to enquire how to bring the oscillations of the mind to a point of perfect balance. In this way we are brought step by step down to dependence upon the simplest supports of the normative life, to dependence upon ethical observances, rites and ceremonies, recitation of prayers, telling of beads, and many other humble and homely religious observances upon which the spiritual individualist looks down with a smile of contempt, but which are nevertheless humanity's first faltering steps upon the Path that leads to Peace.

Some spiritual individualists do not, indeed, regard external supports to the religious life as being entirely without use, and admit that for some types of people they may be helpful, even necessary; but the admission is generally made in a patronizing and condescending spirit, with the ungracious reservation that supports of this kind are concessions to the deplorable infirmity of people too weak, childish, and spiritually undeveloped to be able to manage without them. Forgetting that it is impossible to tread the Path to Nirvāṇa without some kind of external assistance, some strange perversity of thought constrains them to assert that the spiritual individualist alone is the true Buddhist, although the words of the Buddha himself afford no warrant whatever for the adoption of such an attitude. Whether one depends for the time being upon meditation, or whether one depends upon the turning of a prayer wheel, the fact of dependence is there, and since both practices are means to an end, which is Enlightenment, neither can be regarded as intrinsically 'better' or 'worse' than any other. It is simply a question of suitability, of the fitness of a particular means for a person of a particular temperament at a certain stage of his or her spiritual development.

Similarly, no method is intrinsically 'harder' or 'easier' than any other. Those who believe that they follow the path of self-reliance merely because it is more difficult than the alternative path simply delude themselves. In the spiritual life, as in any other, one naturally takes the line of least resistance. To attain Enlightenment is not such a light undertaking that we can afford to make it more difficult for ourselves than it already is, and if one path was in truth less arduous only pride of Luciferian dimensions could induce us to reject it in favour of another more arduous. Some people, it seems, would rather preserve their independence and remain in *saṃsāra* than renounce it even for one moment and thereby win the bliss and peace of *nirvāṇa*. In the spiritual life we have to depend not only upon our own will, our own strength, but also upon a greater or lesser number of external supports most, if not all, of which fall into one or other of the three 'stages' into which the Path has been divided: *śīla*, *samādhi*, and *prajñā*. There is neither absolute dependence nor absolute independence, but a Middle Way which passes between these extremes by escaping into a third dimension wherein the opposition does not exist. For this reason the Buddha has advised us to take refuge in the Dharma, as well as in ourselves, and to regard the Dharma as our light (or island), and not simply to rely, with prideful independence, upon 'our own unaided efforts'.[257]

from *Crossing the Stream*

4. WHAT IS RITUAL TRYING TO ACHIEVE?

It is unfortunate that in the West we like to think we have gone beyond ritual altogether.

There has been in recent times a considerable reaction against anything that smacks of faith and devotion. This has been in part caused by the fact that popular faith has been divorced from what I have termed the 'higher thinking faculty'[258] and so become unacceptable to the intellect, bringing the whole notion of faith and devotion into disrepute, and along with it the practice of ritual. But unfortunately it has to be said that the rejection of faith, devotion, and ritual is for most people not the result of their own earnest and searching intellectual endeavour. More often than not it is just a received view, a part of their conditioning which has no more intellectual legitimacy than the 'blind faith' that they look down upon.

Before we reject ritual we should really think about what is meant by it. What does ritual really signify? What is it really trying to achieve? It tends to be taken for granted that ritual is a sort of outgrowth upon religion. Some people have a very simplified picture of the history of religion, imagining a pristine, simple, purely spiritual teaching at the outset which in the course of a few centuries has degenerated and become loaded down with a lot of unnecessary ritual and dogma, so that periodically it must be purified of these things. People who think in this way see ritual not as really belonging to the essence of religion, but as something added on afterwards, something that they can very well do without – even something harmful.

Other people again regard ritual as a kind of socio-cultural habit surviving from primitive times. Vaguely imagining tribal communities dancing around a bonfire at night, perhaps waving their spears, they think that something of this kind represents the basic, primal form of ritual, and that remnants of this sort of thing survive even in modern life and in the higher religions. According to this view, dancing around the maypole and taking part in a mass are the same sort of thing.

These rather dismissive views of ritual are beginning to shift in some radical circles, but they remain prevalent even among Buddhists, especially in the West. Some Western Buddhists have even been under the strange impression that there is no ritual in Buddhism. Indeed this is one reason why some of them are attracted to Buddhism, or at least to what they think is Buddhism.

It is true that there are elevated states of consciousness in which the need for ritual is transcended, in which our spiritual aspiration is so intrinsic to our being and so refined that it expresses itself purely spiritually and mentally, leaving the physical plane behind. If those who avoid taking part in ritual have attained to such states, that is fine. But we must not confuse that sort of highly positive development with the far more common case of someone who is inhibited about ritual expression because of all sorts of fears and misunderstandings.

The traditional Eastern Buddhist approach starts with devotion. Buddhists who are unable even to observe the precepts, let alone meditate or reflect on the Dharma, are at least able to attend a puja and offer flowers to the Buddha. However, in the West we tend to have to work our way towards devotional practices through meditation and study. The Protestant religion in particular has involved, from its beginnings, a devaluation of ritual, and in its more extreme forms, like Quakerism, has allowed people to profess the Christian faith without any expression of devotion whatsoever. It is of course necessary to resist easy emotional tricks. It may even be necessary sometimes to withdraw from devotional ritual for a while if one has problems with it. But it is unfortunate that in the West we like to think we have gone beyond ritual altogether.

Ritual is an integral part of Buddhism, as it is of all other religions, and an integral part of every school of Buddhism, whether Tibetan, Zen, or Theravāda. Some people like to contrast Theravādin Buddhism with, say, Tibetan Buddhism in this respect, implying that there is no ritual in Theravāda whereas Tibetan Buddhism is full of it (with the assumption that ritual represents a degeneration). But this view is quite wrong. The Theravāda, like any other form of Buddhism, is highly ritualistic. I remember, for instance, that when I visited the Tooth Relic Temple at

Kandy in Sri Lanka many years ago, there were elaborate rituals going on all morning in front of what is believed to be the Buddha's tooth. Zen, in China and Japan, is also highly ritualistic. In a Zen monastery they don't spend all their time meditating. There are all sorts of rituals to engage in: recitation of *sūtras*, chanting of mantras, and a good deal of bowing down. This might come as rather a shock to some Western Zen enthusiasts.

This is not of course to say that there are no differences between the schools as regards the significance accorded to ritual. I would say that, in Tibetan Buddhism especially, the ritual is much more symbolically and spiritually significant. In Theravādin countries it tends to be more of the nature of ceremony than ritual proper; it is not so well integrated into the doctrinal tradition.

My main point is that we cannot get away from ritual in Buddhism, nor should we try to do so. Instead we should try to understand ritual and see what it really is. Erich Fromm, who first introduced the psychoanalytical distinction between rational and irrational ritual, gives an excellent definition of rational ritual as 'shared action, expressive of common strivings, rooted in common values'.[259] Every word of this definition is of import, and worth discussing in some detail.

First of all, ritual is 'shared action'. The fact that ritual is a kind of action is indicated by the traditional Buddhist word for ritual, *kriyā*, which in fact means 'action' – being etymologically connected with the word *karma*, which means action in a more ethical and psychological sense. So *kriyā* or ritual is something done, it is an action, and this fact should, if nothing else, remind us that religion, the spiritual life, is not just a matter of thought and feeling, but also of action: both moral action and ritual action. According to Buddhist tradition, human nature is threefold: body, speech, and mind together make up our total personality. Religion, which is concerned with our total personality, must cater for all three – and in order to involve the body, it must entail action.

Only too often in the West our approach to Buddhism is too one-sided. We pick and choose what we feel suits us, and the result is that part of us is simply never engaged in our practice. We may meditate and study, but if we miss out devotion and ritual, part of us is not involved. We need a Buddhist tradition in the West which provides not only for the head, not only for the heart, but even for the body and speech.

Ritual is not only action, but action that is shared, done together with other people. Here we come to an important difference between irrational, obsessive-compulsive ritual, and rational ritual. Neurotic ritual tends to isolate people. Like washing your hands every ten minutes, it is something done alone which does not bring the person doing it closer to others – quite the reverse. Rational ritual, however, tends to bring people together, and not just physically so. The sense of togetherness can also be, indeed should also be, spiritual. The performance of ritual action in company with others should celebrate a common spiritual attitude. For this reason a feeling of fellowship is essential, which means that ritual implies a spirit of *mettā* (loving-kindness) and solidarity. If this is present, a very powerful spiritual atmosphere can be created.

Fromm's definition goes on to say that rational ritual is 'expressive of common strivings'. Ritual expresses a striving. It is something we make the effort – certainly in Buddhism – to do ourselves. It is not something which is done for us, say by a priest. We don't just sit back and watch someone else conduct it for us. Ritual of that kind is a degeneration. Meaningful ritual is a matter of striving and exertion. It is part of the Buddhist practitioner's *sādhana*, or spiritual practice, or spiritual *exertion*. Ritual is not for the lazy person. Anyone who believes that ritual is a comfortable substitute for the more demanding methods of spiritual practice has not experienced it as it should be performed.

To be a really good ritualist is at least as difficult as, say, giving a lecture, or meditating, if not more so. A good ritualist has to be very mindful. You have to say each phrase and do each action in the correct order, in the correct manner, and with the right emphasis, often doing several things at the same time. You need to have your wits about you.

Ritual also requires attention to detail – you need to see that there is water in the offering bowls, that there are incense sticks, that the candles are alight, that the flowers are properly arranged. For a complex ritual, an expert may be required. Once when I lived in Kalimpong, I invited Dhardo Rimpoche, my friend and teacher, to perform a rather complex ritual and, as the custom is, all the offerings were to be placed ready on the shrine before his arrival. Usually my own Tibetan students and disciples made the preparations themselves, but on this occasion they were not satisfied with that. They did set up the elaborate offerings – lots of little lamps, torma,[260] and so on – on lots of little tables, but they then called in a lama to check it all before the Rimpoche arrived. The lama came and cast his eye over the arrangements. 'No. This should be there, that should be over here, these should be the other way round….' In about five minutes he had made the necessary adjustments and satisfied himself that everything was in order. This is the kind of attention to detail required of a good ritualist.

Good ritual must not only be correctly done, it must also be beautiful. If it is not beautiful, it is not inspiring. So an aesthetic sense is essential. Hindus don't generally mind any amount of disorder and dirt in their temples, even while rituals are being conducted. I have seen temples littered with old bits of newspaper (used for wrapping offerings), remnants of coconuts (coconuts being a common offering), and heaps of long-deceased flowers trodden into the floor. But in a Buddhist temple or shrine-room everything is beautifully arranged, clean, and bright. This is true in Tibet, in Sri Lanka, indeed in all Buddhist countries, and Hindus themselves are the first to be impressed by it.

Perhaps most importantly, a good ritualist must understand the meaning of it all. It is no use being able to do the ritual mechanically, to go through all the right actions, without understanding what is really going on. That would be empty ritual.

Finally, I would say a good ritualist needs plenty of physical stamina. You may have to sit chanting for long periods, from time to time performing various ritual actions, and always maintaining graceful composure and appropriate hand gestures or *mudrās*. This takes considerable physical vigour.

Sometimes we in the West like to think that ritual is a sort of kindergarten stage of religion, something for beginners, but the Tibetans do not think like that. Tibetan tradition permits only the spiritually advanced to do lengthy and complex rituals. Certainly every Tibetan Buddhist has a form of ritual which he or she does. But it is only the Rimpoches and the more highly developed people in general who are sanctioned to enact very long and complicated rituals, because ordinary folk do not have the necessary mindfulness, understanding, and stamina.

Dhardo Rimpoche, who was well versed in Buddhist philosophy, an excellent organizer, and highly knowledgeable about Buddhist yoga, was also a very good ritualist. I often watched him for hours on end going through certain rituals, and I sometimes wondered how he was able to correlate it all. He would be chanting maybe for half an hour or an hour, ringing his bell and making offerings. Sometimes as he was chanting and got towards the end of his text, he would start folding the silken cover in which the book was wrapped in a very elaborate way, to make a particular pattern. And I noticed that as the last tinkle of the bell died away, and the last word of the ritual was recited, the last flower thrown – at that very moment, the last fold of the cloth would be put in place. It was all synchronized, effortlessly, so it seemed. It was harmonized like a piece of music and all the elements ended together, just at the right moment, like a closing cadence. His gestures or *mudrās*, like those of many lamas, were very beautiful to watch. He had been trained in these skills for many years and was a perfect master of them.

Most of us will not develop our capacity for ritual to that degree, but nonetheless the ritual we perform at our own level should be something which we work at, and make as harmonious and expressive as we possibly can. It should involve striving – and not only our own striving, but a common striving. The implication of this important point is that the practice of ritual is possible only within a spiritual community. If you are just doing it on your own, it will not be ritual in the full sense. It may be a striving, but it will not be a common striving.

Ritual in the full sense does not just presuppose a common striving; it also *expresses* that common striving. This is the most important point of all: that ritual is an expression. To quote a further definition of Fromm's, ritual is 'a symbolic expression of thoughts and feelings by action'.[261] So what exactly is meant by 'expression'? Essentially expression means bringing something out from within, even from the depths within. It is in order to express our depths that symbolic expression is necessary. Conceptual expression isn't enough. Conceptual expression brings something out only from the conscious level of our minds – and we have got to do more than that. We have got to plumb the depths beneath the conscious level, to contact the parts of our being to which myth and symbol speak. We could say, in fact, that ritual is like an acting out of symbol or myth. By expressing what is deep within our being, we externalize it, see it, make it something we can know. We can then begin to understand it and incorporate it into our conscious attitude. In this way our whole being will be enriched and integrated. Tension between the conscious and the unconscious will be reduced. We will become more whole.

Through ritual expression, not only do we externalize and make conscious our deep spiritual feelings; we also strengthen and intensify them. This touches on another reason why quite a lot of people feel hesitant about expressing themselves through ritual speech and action. They are simply not sure about the feelings themselves. Perhaps in the case of many of us our devotional feelings are still quite underdeveloped. It is a big step to put our trust in these feelings, to give them space to grow and to exert their influence on our conscious lives.

All of this is a matter of experience. By participating in ritual to any degree, we come to know it. It happens even within very simple devotional meetings when we recite the Sevenfold Puja – as long as we do it properly, with concentration. (The Sevenfold Puja is an expression of seven different devotional moods or aspirations, each of which is evoked by a few lines of a Mahāyāna text called the *Bodhicaryāvatāra*.) In ritual we create a very specific atmosphere. Just as meditation has its own atmosphere, which is very beautiful, just as a talk on the Dharma has its own very positive and happy ambience, so the Sevenfold Puja also has a distinctive atmosphere of its own which derives from what is brought up from the depths, externalized, and made conscious.

This atmosphere can have a distinct and noticeable effect. At a Buddhist Society summer school which I attended shortly after my return to England in 1964, I remember being rather surprised that, although there were many lectures on the programme – and also a little meditation – there was no provision for any sort of puja. So one day I suggested that we might try out a little ritual in the evening. At first this suggestion was not very well received. I was told that English Buddhists had no interest in ritual; they preferred the rational approach. So I said, 'Well, never mind. Even if only five or six people want to do it, let's try it.' It was announced, therefore, that there would be a short and simple puja conducted by myself at nine o'clock that evening. In the event, instead of having five or six people, we had practically the whole summer school, about 140 people. It was difficult to get them all into the room. They continued to come every night after that and seemed thoroughly to enjoy it. Many people remarked that a special atmosphere was created. Something special manifested, they knew not how, they knew not why. But it came from the depths and it created an altogether more meaningful and harmonious atmosphere.[262]

Sometimes people are starved of this sort of thing. They get just the intellectual, conceptual approach: books, talks, ideas, philosophy, theory. It is an imbalance which is even encouraged in some places in the East. I've known Theravādin *bhikkhus* apologize for pujas and say that they were only for lay people, unintellectual people. Intellectuals – and of course Westerners were supposed to be honorary intellectuals – didn't need them at all. What was important was the intellectual understanding of the Dharma. I've even heard Buddhist *bhikkhus* say, 'Well, we *bhikkhus* don't do pujas ourselves.' But although the intellectual approach is no less necessary than the devotional or the imaginal approaches, sooner or later we must begin to engage the depths, the vast resources of energy which lie in the unconscious mind. We must begin to speak the language of myth, symbol, and image, and in this way integrate the unconscious with the conscious. And this is what ritual, among other things, helps us to do.

Lastly, in terms of Fromm's definition, ritual is 'rooted in common values'. Ritual is never just ritual. It is not self-contained. It issues from a whole religious philosophy, a system of beliefs and values. And broadly speaking, the more highly developed the religion is, the richer its ritual expression. The two most highly developed religions of the world are probably Buddhism and Christianity, and these two are, at least in their dominant forms, highly ritualistic. In Christianity, the main forms, the Eastern Orthodox Church and the Roman Catholic Church, are both very ritualistic. And in the case of Buddhism the Tibetan schools, Chan, Zen, and even the Theravāda all give an important place to ritual.

Having studied Fromm's definition of ritual, let us apply it to a simple example drawn from Buddhism: the ritual of Going for Refuge, which is very basic but also very important. First of all, it is an action. We say, '*Buddhaṃ saraṇaṃ gacchāmi*', *gacchāmi* meaning 'I go'. In the Pāli and the Sanskrit, the verb comes out very powerfully because it comes at the end. It is often translated as 'I go for refuge to the Buddha', but a far more powerful translation is 'To the Buddha for refuge I go'. This stresses the fact that Going for Refuge is an action, an action of the whole being. We go for Refuge with body, speech, and mind. In the Tantric tradition it is not felt to be enough to go for Refuge mentally and verbally. You also go for Refuge physically, literally prostrating in front of the image. It is a threefold practice which involves the whole being.

Not only is it an action; it is a shared action, because we repeat the verses of Refuge together, in unison. In traditional Buddhist countries, the *bhikkhu*, or monk, recites first and the others recite after him. What emerges is almost a dialogue; an almost dramatic element is introduced. This emphasizes the fact that we are not just doing something in the same way as other individuals who happen to be there. We do it *with* them, with heart and mind and body.

Next, the Going for Refuge expresses a common striving, which is that we aspire to realize the common goal of Nirvāṇa or Enlightenment. We all want to become like the Buddha. We all want to follow the path of the Dharma. We all want to help, and to receive help from, other members of the Sangha.

Finally, our strivings are rooted in common values, the values which permeate the whole body of the Buddha's teaching. The Going for Refuge is not something isolated in itself. It grows out of the whole teaching and tradition. If one were to expound the meaning of the Three Jewels to which we go for Refuge in full detail, such an exposition would incorporate the whole of Buddhism.

So Fromm's definition of ritual is readily applicable to the fundamental Buddhist practice of Going for Refuge, and it helps to give us some understanding of the psychology of ritual and some appreciation of its value. But the real way to appreciate the value of ritual is to practise it.

from *Ritual and Devotion in Buddhism*

5. A VISION OF AMITĀBHA

How long the experience lasted I do not know, for I seemed to be out of time as well as out of the body, but I saw the Buddha as clearly as I had ever seen anything under the ordinary circumstances of my life, indeed far more clearly and vividly.

One night I found myself as it were out of the body and in the presence of Amitābha, the Buddha of Infinite Light, who presides over the western quarter of the universe. The colour of the Buddha was a deep, rich, luminous red, like that of rubies, though at the same time soft and glowing, like the light of the setting sun. While his left hand rested on his lap, the fingers of his right hand held up by the stalk a single red lotus in full bloom and he sat, in the usual cross-legged posture, on an enormous red lotus that floated on the surface of the sea. To the left, immediately beneath the raised right arm of the Buddha, was the red hemisphere of the setting sun, its reflection glittering golden across the waters. How long the experience lasted I do not know, for I seemed to be out of time as well as out of the body, but I saw the Buddha as clearly as I had ever seen anything under the ordinary circumstances of my life, indeed far more clearly and vividly. The rich red colour of Amitābha himself, as well as of the two lotuses and the setting sun, made a particularly deep impression on me. It was more wonderful, more appealing, than any earthly red: it was like red light, but so soft and, at the same time, so vivid, as to be altogether without parallel. In the course of the next few days I composed a series of stanzas describing the vision. Contrary to my usual practice, I failed to write them down afterwards, with the result that they gradually faded from my mind. But the experience itself never faded. Nearly a quarter of a century later, the figure of the red Buddha is as clear to me, in recollection, as it was the next morning in the Virupaksha Guha.

from *The Rainbow Road from Tooting Broadway to Kalimpong*

6. SECRET WINGS

We cry that we are weak although
We will not stir our secret wings;
The world is dark – because we are
Blind to the starriness of things.

We pluck our rainbow-tinted plumes
And with their heaven-born beauty try
To fledge nocturnal shafts, and then
Complain 'Alas! we cannot fly!'

We mutter 'All is dust' or else
With mocking words accost the wise:
'Show us the Sun which shines beyond
The Veil' – and then we close our eyes.

To powers above and powers beneath
In quest of Truth men sue for aid,
Who stand athwart the Light and fear
The shadow that themselves have made.

Oh cry no more that you are weak
But stir and spread your secret wings,
And say 'The world is bright, because
We glimpse the starriness of things.'

Soar with your rainbow plumes and reach
That near-far land where all are one,
Where Beauty's face is aye unveiled
And every star shall be a sun.

from *Complete Poems*

7. THE IMPORTANCE OF SPIRITUAL RECEPTIVITY

As a Buddhist one need not be too scared of the idea of prayer.

Spiritual receptivity is of the utmost importance; without it, spiritual progress simply cannot be maintained. We need to hold ourselves open to the truth as the flower holds itself open to the sun. This is what spiritual receptivity means: holding ourselves open to the higher spiritual influences that are streaming through the universe, but with which we are not usually in contact, because we usually shut ourselves off from them. We should be ready if necessary to give up whatever we've learned so far, which isn't easy by any means, and to give up whatever we have *become* so far, which is still more difficult.

How does one become spiritually receptive in this way? For a start, one can pray. As a Buddhist one need not be too scared of the idea of prayer. It doesn't necessarily have theistic connotations. When a Tibetan Buddhist engages in an activity he calls 'prayer', he is not praying to God in the sense of the creator of heaven and earth, because such a conception is not part of the Tibetan Buddhist system of belief. He is praying to the Buddha, the bodhisattvas, or the *ḍākinīs*.[263]

Prayer in its proper sense, anyway, is not for material things, but for blessings, higher understanding, wisdom, compassion. One's prayers simply express the fact that one doesn't have those qualities and would like to have them. If you want something in an ordinary sense, you just say to someone, 'Please pass me the toast,' 'Please give me some money,' or whatever it may be. In the case of the Buddhas and bodhisattvas, they have got wisdom and compassion, which you haven't got but would like to have, so your aspiration to develop wisdom and compassion takes the form of a request to the Buddhas and bodhisattvas to *give* you those qualities. As an informed Buddhist, you know very well that wisdom and compassion cannot be handed over like a slice of toast. But nonetheless you continue to use the language of petition. Why?

The reason is that the nature of language almost compels us to think of wisdom and compassion as qualities that can be acquired or received. If we use the language of prayer, we do so because it has a certain emotive value, and expresses an openness and receptivity. It certainly doesn't reflect a literal belief that one can be given those qualities by Buddhas and bodhisattvas. In any case, one understands that those Buddhas and bodhisattvas are not really separate from oneself. They can be regarded as symbolizing unrealized states of one's own being that one is trying to activate through prayer.

Prayer, understood in this way, is not out of place in Buddhism. It is very different from meditation. And it isn't that one is thinking, 'I'll make a pretence of asking, but I know I've really got to do it myself.' When one is praying, one really *feels* that one hasn't got what one desires, and that one must therefore ask for it. One may have an intellectual understanding that it is all within oneself, but that is not one's experience when one is praying. If one experiences the desire to pray, there is no need to stop oneself on the strength of a purely rational understanding that the Buddhas and bodhisattvas are not really 'out there'.

Quite a few people over the years have told me that sometimes they feel like praying to the Buddha or to bodhisattvas but that they tend consciously to inhibit the impulse, thinking that it is a weakness, and not a very Buddhistic one, to imagine that the Buddhas and bodhisattvas can give one anything. Surely, they say, any truly spiritual goal can be achieved only by one's own efforts. My reply is always that if one feels like praying, one should go ahead and do it, and work out the 'theology' later. If it is a genuine feeling, don't suppress it. At the very least, prayer is a means of concentrating one's emotional energies. And in any case, it is as true to say that the Buddhas and bodhisattvas are outside oneself as that they are within. Either way, one is still operating within the subject–object duality. It is no more valid to think of them as existing in the depths of one's own being than to think of them as existing beyond anything one can experience or conceive of. Both are equally real – or equally unreal. Whether one thinks of that reality (which is neither subject nor object) as a sort of super-object outside oneself or a super-subject within oneself doesn't make any difference.

The experience of many poets is rather like this. Poetic inspiration can be experienced as welling up from within or as coming in from outside. Some poets genuinely experience being visited by the Muses, so to speak. But whether poetic inspiration is called up from within or called down from above amounts to the same thing. Language has severe limitations here. One is trying to introduce into one's experience within the subject–object duality something which is beyond it, and which can be thought of either as emerging from within the depths of one's own being or as something transcendentally aloof towards which one must direct one's prayers and aspirations.

from *The Bodhisattva Ideal*

8. 'IN THE WOODS ARE MANY MORE'

Selling wild orchids at my door one day
A man said, 'In the woods are many more ...
Deep in the gloom, high on the thickset trees,
Wild orchids hang like clouds of butterflies,
Golden and white, spotted with red and black,
As huge as birds, or tiny as a bee,
Wild orchids which no eye has ever seen
Save ours, who wander in these rich green glooms
All day throughout the year.' I bought his sprays,
Paid him, and bore them in; and as I went

My eyes by chance fell on a shelf of books, –
The Buddha's Teachings, – and thereafter glanced
Up to the Buddha's image as He smiled
Above them from the alcove. Strange it was
That, as my eyes from book to image passed,
Dwelling an instant on that calm, pure Face,
There, with the frail cold blossoms in my hands,
The words that man spoke at my door should ring
Through my stilled heart again and yet again
Like music – 'In the woods are many more ...'

from *Complete Poems*

9. EVERYTHING THAT LIVES IS HOLY

Religion is not confined to particular places, but saturates and sanctifies the whole of nature.

Society has, unfortunately, acquired the habit of regarding certain actions, such as attending a temple, church, or mosque, or visiting a place of pilgrimage, as religious in themselves, without reference to the background of consciousness which stands behind them. Similarly, certain occupations or avocations, such as those of the monk or priest, are regarded as possessing, in some almost magical fashion, a certain virtue or sanctity. Particular places, buildings, costumes, books, languages, countries, colours, and so on are, in exactly the same way, set apart as sacred from the mass of profane objects of the same class by which they are surrounded, and from which they are so sharply distinguished. The result of this dichotomization of things into sacred and profane is an unhealthy division of the collective or social consciousness analogous to the split produced in the individual consciousness by its arbitrary classification of actions as 'good' and 'bad'. This is not to deny the power which is certainly possessed by certain external places and objects of inducing corresponding states of consciousness internally. This is because we have, either by deliberate individual choice or by passive acceptance of the cultural or religious tradition into which we are born, come to regard some material thing as the symbol of a spiritual value. But the sacredness or profaneness of that thing nevertheless continues to depend upon the state of mind which it is capable of inspiring. If a 'holy' object no longer inspires holy thoughts then it ceases to be a symbol and becomes a superstition. For the very essence of superstition consists in regarding things – whether particular persons, places, or practices – as holy in themselves, without reference to the state of mind which accompanies them. That thought, word, or deed alone is holy concerning which the idea that 'I am the doer' does not arise.

The most unfortunate practical consequence of regarding things as in themselves sacred or profane is that the vast mass of people consider themselves to be totally excluded from participation in the practice of religion. Religion, they think, belongs to the temple or church, not to the home; to the priest, not to the layman. It can be found within the covers of some musty book, but not among the flowers that bloom so freshly in the fields, or in consort with 'all the airs and madrigals that whisper softness in chambers'. Priests and ecclesiastical bodies of every religious denomination have not only deliberately encouraged, but even sedulously inculcated, this wrong attitude of mind, in order to strengthen their positions and swell their revenues. But the truth of the matter is that you cannot see anything as holy until you see everything as holy. Distinctions are useful, even necessary, at the beginning of one's spiritual career; but they should not be clung to. A flower is sacred, a tree holy, if you look at it with an illumined mind, just as a religious observance is profane if you do it with a greedy, malicious, or deluded consciousness. It is better to sweep a floor egolessly than to meditate with the prideful sense that 'I am meditating.'

Swinging thus the emphasis from the external to the internal, from the act to the thought, from the symbol to the thing symbolized, we can see that religion is not confined to particular places, but that it saturates and sanctifies the whole of nature; that it is, properly understood, not for the few only, but inevitably and inescapably for all; and that there is, to the Eye of Enlightenment, no division between sacred and profane but that, in the words of a great poet-seer, 'Everything that lives is holy.'

from *Crossing the Stream*

10. DEVOTION AT LUMBINI

'Here the Blessed One was born'

The Aśoka Pillar stood beneath the open sky behind a low iron railing. On its highly polished surface the ancient Brahmi letters were cut deep and clear, and we could still spell out the announcement 'Here the Blessed One was born'. For some reason or other, I felt even more deeply moved here than I had done either at Sarnath or Kusinārā. The truncated stone shaft stood so calmly and so simply beneath the cloudless blue sky; it seemed so unpretentious, and yet to mean so much. Lingering behind when Buddharakshita and the others had moved on in the direction of the mounds, I gathered some small white flowers and with a full heart scattered them over the railing at the foot of the column. As I did so I heard Buddharakshita's voice. 'What are you messing about with those flowers for?' he shouted roughly. 'Come on, we can't wait for you all day!'

from *The Rainbow Road from Tooting Broadway to Kalimpong*

11. TIBETAN PILGRIMS

True it is, indeed, that faith without knowledge breeds the rank and luxuriant growth of superstition, even as it is equally true that knowledge without faith conjures up the dismal spectres of doubt and scepticism. Yet it is perhaps less difficult for faith to give birth to knowledge than it is for knowledge to generate faith. Therefore we may well envy these simple people the possession of a faith which has enabled them to scale mountains and cross deserts, to suffer patiently and cheerfully for many months hardships which we could scarcely brook even for a single day.

From the dazzling white wastes of the Tibetan plateau, down through the steep and dangerous mountain passes, along the hot and dusty roads of what was once the Middle Kingdom, with sticks in their hands and sturdy backs bowed beneath the weight of heavy loads carried in wicker cradles suspended from their shoulders, with the sacred mantra *oṃ maṇi padme hūṃ* ever on their lips, in rough red homespun garments, knowing no other language than their own native Tibetan, by day and by night, year after year, impelled by their simple but profound faith, come these strange pilgrims from the far-off Land of Snows. *We* have come here with all the comforts and conveniences of a second-class railway carriage; but *they* have walked every single mile of the long road which stretches from their own country almost halfway across India here to Bodh Gaya. *We* admire the architecture of the Temple, speculate upon the probable date of its construction, and lament its present neglected and ruinous condition; but *their* simple faith pierces the diaphanous veil of such archaeological irrelevancies and is lost in the contemplation of the naked fact of the Lord's Enlightenment. Probably they are quite ignorant of the precise number of centuries which have passed by since he attained the sublime consummation of his noble quest, and perhaps, were they questioned about it, they would scratch their tousled heads in surprise at the question and smilingly reply that they had never given thought to the matter; but from the evident earnestness with which they perform their devotions, from the unsophisticated sincerity of their demeanour, it seems as though that great event was as vivid and tangible to them as if the Lord had sat but yesterday upon the Diamond Throne and listened to the leaves of the bodhi tree whispering jubilantly above his head.

Some of the pilgrims are old, some young. Mostly they come in parties of four or five; but sometimes they arrive in pairs or singly. Some are dressed in garments of coarse red homespun cloth, with wide swinging skirts and full bosoms, and have ornaments of silver and turquoise around their necks and suspended from holes pierced in their ears; while others are clad in filthy black tatters that flutter and dance in the breeze, and wear strings of plain wooden beads. Some are shod with scarlet or yellow Chinese boots with upturned toes, while others – the poorer sort – go barefoot. Some are heavy laden with blankets, bags of rice, cooking utensils, and even little yellow-faced, rose-cheeked babies, suspended in wicker frames from their sturdy shoulders; and some carry miniature shrines of chased silver, through the tiny glass window of which is visible the gilded image of their tutelary Buddha or bodhisattva within. A few of them carry long knives in ornamental silver scabbards slung at their side, and most of them have prayer-wheels, either tucked away idle in the capacious bosom of their dress, or twirling busily in their hand as they trudge along. But all of them, men, women, and children alike, are strongly and sturdily built, with round, smiling, rose-cheeked faces, cheerful salutations uttered in unfamiliar speech but with unmistakable friendliness, and hearts undaunted by the difficulties and dangers of their long and toilsome journey. They have walked perhaps a thousand miles, enduring with equal fortitude icy snow and burning sun; they have plodded on through wind and rain and dust, beholding now the dazzling white peaks of their native Himalayan ranges, now the swift-rushing streams and dense green foliage of the foothills, now the emerald rice-fields, barren burning plains, and dried-up river beds of India; and now at last they have reached their destination, and with broad smiles of greeting come stumbling through the gates of the rest house. They have endured great hardships and many tribulations, experiencing not only the inclemency of nature but the cruelty and heartlessness of man; for some, taking advantage of the innocence and helplessness of these travellers in a strange land, have robbed and cheated them upon the way. Yet they do not complain; nor, now that they have at last arrived, do they look for compensating comforts, but spread their blankets on the cold stone floor of the veranda, or even bivouac out in the open air.

The clear blue winter sky and hard bright sunshine are perhaps even pleasant to them in comparison with the whirling snowstorms and icy cutting winds of their native land. Before an hour has passed they have kindled a fire and cooked thereon a frugal meal of rice-gruel flavoured with bits of chopped radish, onion, and chilli. Then they sit in democratic circle round their improvised kitchen and fill and refill their bowls with the steaming pottage that bubbles over the fire. They are easily satisfied, these simple pilgrim folk. They do not care for succulent dishes or rich clothes, nor yet for any of the luxuries which have become necessities to the pampered and perverted sons and daughters of modern city-bred civilization. Their food and clothing are simple but serviceable, even as their physical bodies are strong and sturdy, and their faith plain and unsophisticated. A casual glance might dismiss them with mingled contempt and disgust as simply ignorant and dirty. And it is indeed true that their clothes are black with grime, that their hair is as uncombed and thickly matted as the mane of a wild horse, and that they would perhaps have difficulty in remembering the date on which their skins last felt the contact of water. Neither are they educated in the sense in which we pride ourselves we are. Yet they carry in the bosom of their ragged, dirty garments a precious jewel which we, the doubt-torn, world-weary children of the twentieth century, would give much to possess – the precious jewel of faith.

True it is, indeed, that faith without knowledge breeds the rank and luxuriant growth of superstition, even as it is equally true that knowledge without faith conjures up the dismal spectres of doubt and scepticism. Yet it is perhaps less difficult for faith to give birth to knowledge than it is for knowledge to generate faith. Therefore we may well envy these simple people the possession of a faith which has enabled them to scale mountains and cross deserts, to suffer patiently and cheerfully for many months hardships which we could scarcely brook even for a single day. *Our* knowledge is a listless and anaemic thing: it does not inspire to great deeds of heroism and selfless love. But *their* faith is full of nerve and vigour: it kindles a warm and life-giving flame in their hearts, and with its beams illuminates their steps – even when they walk in a strange land. Therefore we may well wish that our complicated modern knowledge could be wedded to the simple faith of these Tibetan pilgrims – *prajñā* (wisdom) united to *karuṇā* (compassion) – that from their mystic union in our hearts might spring forth the glorious bodhisattva of Buddha-ward aspiration.

Some of us might even wish that we could exchange our indigent and sterile knowledge for their rich and fruitful faith. But that may never be. We are the offspring of the twentieth century, they of the Ages of Faith – yet of a faith, surely, that is not blind, but founded on a deeper, truer knowledge belonging to the race, to the civilization, ultimately to the religion they profess itself, rather than to the individual believer. But we, for all our vaunted 'knowledge', grope and stumble in the dark; while they, for all their 'ignorance', walk along the road of life with humbly bowed but unwearied bodies, and slow but steady steps – walk as though the path beneath their feet and the destination at which they would one day arrive were both plainly visible before their eyes.

O, let us doff the glittering brocade of superficial modern intelligence, and don the coarse red homespun garment of simple faith! With the burden of long-suffering on our backs, and with the staff of endurance in our hands, let us join these humble pilgrims from the mysterious Land of Snows and trudge with them along the long and dusty road that leads to Bodh Gaya. With the sacred words on our lips, with the golden flame of faith and love burning in the transparent alabaster chalice of wisdom within our hearts, and with the Blessed One himself for our guide, let us set forth as pilgrims upon the Middle Way that will lead us, one day, even to the heart's Enlightenment.

from *Crossing the Stream*

12. CALL FORTH AS MUCH AS YOU CAN

The love, the respect, and the faith are all there, latent within us: they are natural human endowments.

> Call forth as much as you can of love, of respect and of faith!
> Remove the obstructing defilements, and clear away all your taints!
> Listen to the Perfect Wisdom of the gentle Buddhas,
> Taught for the weal of the world, for heroic spirits intended![264]

So here we are given a cautionary word of advice. Reflect on the emotional attitude you are bringing to this *sūtra*. If the Buddha's first aim is to awaken a joyous emotional response, then we need to think again about our whole approach to the Perfection of Wisdom. It is not good enough, if we do not understand it, to assume that we are just not up to it intellectually. The first thing the Buddha asks is not 'I hope you have your wits about you,' or 'Do you have a degree in philosophy?' but 'Are you emotionally positive? Are you receptive to the Dharma? And are you allowing this positivity and receptivity to develop without limitation?'

The expression 'call forth', after all, suggests that we are to bring out something that is already there. The love, the respect, and the faith are all there, latent within us: they are natural human endowments. It is as though the Buddha is saying, 'Let them express themselves, let them manifest themselves. They are there, and they are the appropriate emotions to bring to the Perfection of Wisdom. So don't place any limitation on them by imagining that you have to start laboriously manufacturing them. You are better than you think you are.'

This idea, fundamental to Buddhism, is one that goes against the grain for those of us who imagine that our socialized selves are sitting on a lot of unattractive, basic animal urges, and that if we become less inhibited, all sorts of unpleasant negative emotions are going to come pouring out. But that is a one-sided view of things; there is a lot that is good and positive that also gets repressed. In a largely secular society this is perhaps especially true of devotional feelings. If you no longer believe in the Blessed Virgin Mary, for example, you cannot offer even so much as a candle in a church, and in this way your love and reverence and faith remain unused and stifled. You may even come to the conclusion that you simply have no devotional feelings. I have known a lot of apparently quite intellectual people who, while they used to find the devotional demands of Christianity quite suffocating, nevertheless discovered, when they eventually took up Buddhist devotional practices, that they enjoyed being devotional. They found – rather to their surprise – that they really rather enjoyed offering flowers and lighting candles; that it was, in fact, quite a relief to feel able to do so at last. So 'Call forth as much as you can of love, of respect, and of faith!'

from *Wisdom Beyond Words*

4
BUDDHISM AND THE NATURAL WORLD

I. ANIMISM AND SPIRITUAL LIFE

The universe we know and love in the form of our native land and folklore puts heart into our highest ideals, making them personal, something we can love.

> Hence, all ye spirits, hear attentively.
> Look lovingly upon the race of men,
> And, since they bring thee offerings day and night,
> Keep watch and ward about them heedfully.[265]

This verse clearly reflects an animistic attitude to nature. It is perhaps not easy for us, with our Christian conditioning, to imagine having such a strong feeling for nature and for the things of nature. The people of India are much closer to their pagan roots: if you give them half a chance to worship anything, village people especially will happily take it. This at least was the view of my teacher Bhikkhu Jagdish Kashyap, who told me once of a curious example of it that he observed as a boy in a village in a remote part of the Indian state of Bihar. A new road was being built and marked out with milestones, and one morning he saw a woman making her way from the village to the nearest milestone, carrying a tray upon which she had placed some vermilion, some flowers, and a few sticks of incense. On reaching the milestone she anointed it with the vermilion, scattered the flowers, and stuck the sticks of incense in the ground in front of it. She then bowed to the milestone with folded hands. She evidently thought it was a new kind of god.

The attitude behind such undiscriminating devotion is essentially animistic, and for all its primitiveness and simplicity, it is a healthy basis for spiritual life. You feel that everything is alive; you feel a rapport with the forces of nature, and you want to propitiate them, be on friendly terms with them. Mechanistic materialism suggests that everything is just dead matter, but it is surely much better to think that all things – trees, stones, streams, clouds – are alive, even if you personify them in a rather childish way.

Some western scholars are disturbed to find that in some traditional Buddhist cultures, the pure philosophical and ethical teachings of Buddhism have been corrupted, as they see it, by being mixed up with a lot of animism and spirit worship. I myself do not share their unease. At a certain level we *are* a part of nature, we are surrounded by all sorts of natural forces and energies that are also present within us, and we cannot help feeling and experiencing them, even in the form of spirits and gods of the earth and sky. And if you do experience them in that way, you naturally want to keep up a positive relationship with them: you give them offerings and in return they protect you.

In this verse from the *Ratana Sutta* the compiler of the *sutta* is taking up this archaic, pagan, animistic way of looking at things and giving it wider significance. He is saying, 'Be on friendly terms with the universe. If you feel friendly towards the universe, the universe will feel friendly towards you.' It's as though the universe (in the form of the gods) is prepared to strike a bargain with us. We agree to worship the gods and provide them with oblations, and in return they agree to protect us. Today it is considered more realistic to regard the universe as implacably hostile and threatening, but really this view is just more paranoid, the natural result of living in a universe conceived of as impersonal.

It is difficult to feel good will and love towards something you think of as impersonal. Before you can feel positive emotion towards it, you have to invest it with personal qualities, and you can see this in the way some people love their car or motorbike almost as though it were human. Making a living connection with something whose workings are ultimately perhaps a bit of a mystery involves personalizing it, calling it 'he' or 'she'. You may end up saying things like 'She's not going very well today. I don't think she's very happy. Maybe she doesn't like the change in the weather.' Similarly, to the extent that you feel positive towards life as a whole, you will start personalizing things, so that they are not just things but 'spirits' – spirits at least in a poetic sense. If you want to enter into relationship with the universe, if you want to love it, you have to see it as personal.

Throughout the Buddhist tradition one finds this same sense of the importance of propitiating local spirits. For example, in one of his songs Milarepa sings:

> Ye local demons, ghosts, and gods,
> All friends of Milarepa,
> Drink the nectar of kindness and compassion,
> Then return to your abodes.[266]

These gods and goddesses and spirits can also be seen as representing aspects of oneself. The basic energies that find their expression in nature through the folklore of our indigenous culture also exist in us, and we cannot afford to ignore them or cut ourselves off from them. Instead, we can take notice of them, absorb, assimilate, and direct them, as Padmasambhava is said to have harnessed the demons of Tibet. And just as we must harness our inner drives, so we must harness the same forces as they express themselves through the indigenous culture. For example, rather than building an exact replica of a Tibetan or Japanese Buddhist temple in England, which might seem somewhat alien, one could build it in an English style. You would still want to centre it upon a Buddha image, but you could introduce motifs or symbols with indigenous significance. Instead of *bodhi* leaves, for example, you could decorate the shrine with carvings of oak leaves, which have deep associations for the English. Druids worshipped the oak tree, and the mistletoe that grows upon it, and in more modern times the oak has developed associations of strength and stability – 'hearts of oak' – based on the extraordinary success of the English ships that were built from it. All the energy bound up with these old associations would contribute to whatever was done in the temple.

In India, when Buddha images were first made, the principal gods of the indigenous tradition, Indra and Brahmā, were not banished completely. You find for example, in images of the Buddha descending from the *devaloka*, that he comes escorted by these two deities. They are smaller than the Buddha – very much attendants – but they have not been excluded, they have been given their place. The ethnic, one might say, has been integrated with the universal, the lower ideal with the higher. The universe we know and love in the form of our native land and folklore puts heart into our highest ideals, making them personal, something we can love.

from *Creative Symbols of Tantric Buddhism*

2. FEELING THAT THE UNIVERSE IS ALIVE

Concepts are vital – but they do not exhaust the whole of life's mystery.

In our modern techno-scientific culture we are able to do all kinds of things with and to the natural world, but as a result we have lost our affinity with it. Alienated from nature, no longer experiencing it as a living presence, we sorely need to recapture the sense that to be human is to be part of nature.

This feeling, of course, came naturally to people in the early days of Buddhism. The Buddha and his disciples lived in the midst of nature, wandering on foot for eight or nine months of the year from one village to another through the jungles of northern India. Their days and nights were spent in forests, in parks, on mountains, or by rivers; out in the elements, sleeping under the stars. Theirs was a world populated not only by human beings and animals, but by gods and spirits of the hills and streams, trees and flowers. The sense of the physical environment experienced as a living presence is a significant theme in all the oldest texts of the Buddhist tradition. For all its factual content, the Pāli canon also reminds us that the supernatural world was a reality for the early Buddhists; and one might say that it was the continuous presence of nature that made it so.

All the episodes of major significance in the Buddha's life history unfolded in close contact with a natural world which actively responded to his presence. He was born in the open air, we are told, while his mother supported herself by holding a bough laden with flowers. He gained Enlightenment beneath the bodhi tree, seated on a carpet of fresh grass. And in the end he passed away between twin *sāl* trees which sprinkled his body in homage with blossoms out of season. This sense of nature as a vibrant and animated presence is often the part of the Pāli canon that is edited out of selected translations into English; the editors tend to leave intact the outline of the Buddha's teaching but include little of the world in which it is set. If some mythic strands are left, the modern reader is likely to skip over the accounts of *nāgas*, *yakṣas*, and other supernatural beings to concentrate on the 'real' stuff, the doctrine. But the gods and goddesses, and all the various kinds of non-human beings, are not there simply as ornamentation. Their presence is itself part of the teaching. They provide glimpses of an ancient mode of human consciousness fully integrated into a universe of value, meaning, and purpose. To miss them is to miss the poetry, and the heart of the Buddha's message.

If we are really to understand the traditional Buddhist practice of the contemplation of the elements – earth, water, fire, air, and sometimes additionally space and consciousness – as taught by the Buddha and recorded in texts like the *Satipaṭṭhāna Sutta*, therefore, we need to find ways of deepening our understanding of what this elemental imagery meant to the early Buddhists, how they knew those mythic figures and lived in relation to them. To help us do this, we can return to the term *mahābhūta*, whose meaning hints at the living, inherently ungraspable quality of the elements. *Mahābhūta*, 'great ghost', means something that has somehow arisen, or has been conjured up – a mysterious, other-worldly apparition. To think of the four elements as 'great ghosts' suggests that we are dealing not with concepts or inanimate matter, but with living forces. The universe is alive, magically so, and the haunting appearance within it of the four great elements makes that experience inherently mysterious and inaccessible to definitive knowledge. Rather than trying to pin down reality with technical and scientific thinking, the Buddhist conception of the four elements helps to bring about a fusion of objective and subjective knowledge, enabling us, like Shakespeare's King Lear, to 'take upon 's the mystery of things'.[267]

This does not mean that the Buddhist conception of the elements is vague or imprecise, nor that the rational faculty is no longer necessary. Concepts are vital – but they do not exhaust the whole of life's mystery. To understand the four elements as psychophysical states rather than as material substances or states of matter undermines the conventional idea of what the body is. It reminds us that the division between inner and outer worlds is a product of dualistic thinking. Rather than any division between a thing called matter and a thing called mind, or a thing called body and a thing called consciousness, there is a continuity running all the way through, a continuity of our awareness patterned in different ways. If we can really understand this, those inner and outer worlds become interfused in a deeper, more meaningful vision of what it is to be alive.

All this runs counter to the way we in the West have been conditioned to experience the body and the world of which it is a part. But it must surely be better – or at the very least more fun – to be an animist and feel that the whole world is animated by spirits, rather than gazing out at a world of non-living matter which occasionally and haphazardly comes to life, and in which even our own life is ultimately reducible to inanimate matter. All the same, it is not easy for us to develop a genuine feeling that the material elements are really living entities. Conversely, it is all too easy to generate a false and sentimental notion that 'the hills are alive' by projecting all kinds of imaginary properties on to the world. We cannot generate a belief in, say, naiads and dryads by force of will; nor can we deny what we know scientifically about the way the universe operates. We have somehow to hunt for a real feeling for the life of things, even from our sophisticated viewpoint. It starts with intuitive knowledge, not a set of beliefs.

There is a hierarchy: rocks are not as alive as plants, and plants are not as alive as human beings. We have to draw the line somewhere – it would be hard to regard, say, stainless steel as a living substance; each of us will have a point at which we stop acknowledging and respecting the life of another being or 'thing' and start simply using it for our own convenience. For some unfortunate people this line is drawn even at certain other human beings – of course this is also unfortunate for the people with whom they come into contact. At the other end of the spectrum, the Tibetans used to refuse to engage in mining for minerals: they would pan for gold but not, as the Chinese are now doing in Tibet, disturb the earth and the dragons that they believe guard the gold it conceals.

I would go so far as to say that a universe conceived of as dead cannot be a universe in which one stands any chance of attaining Enlightenment.

(Whether you stand any chance in a living universe is of course up to you.) It may be difficult for us to get back to the view of the world that came naturally to our ancestors, but poets have persisted in seeing the universe as alive: surely no poet could have a totally Newtonian outlook, the kind of attitude that Blake termed 'single vision' and 'Newton's sleep'.[268] Milton, for example, traces the origin of mining to Hell itself: in *Paradise Lost* the devils start excavating minerals in order to manufacture artillery to use against heaven.[269] One could even interpret the whole Romantic movement as expressing a great protest against the Newtonian picture of nature and a reassertion of essentially pagan values.

from *Living with Awareness*

3. THE TRADITIONAL SOCIETY

For modern men and women there is in the common things of life no hint of anything beyond.

In a traditional civilization every branch of knowledge, and every kind of activity, is integrated with conceptions of a metaphysical order. Every aspect of life, even the lowest and most mundane, is given a transcendental orientation that enables it to function, in a general way, as a support, if not for the actual living of the spiritual life, then at least for a more or less constant awareness of the existence of spiritual values. In such a civilization, religion (to use the narrow modern term) is not something from which you can escape, even if you want to; it encounters you at every step, with the familiar objects of home and the accustomed routine of daily life. Nurtured in such an environment, in which the whole of existence appears to be a great Smaragdine Tablet, constantly reminding us that 'the things below are copies' and that the originals are above, sensitive hearts and minds become more subtle and sensitive still.[270] To them 'rocks, and stones, and trees', and other natural objects, are not simply lumps of matter of various shapes and sizes, but 'huge cloudy symbols of a high romance' traced, not by the 'magic hand of chance', but by the irresistible finger of omnipresent spiritual law.[271] Nature is not dead, but alive with many voices, and to an eye accustomed to see and to hear things that point beyond themselves even

> An old pine tree is preaching wisdom,
> And a wild bird crying out truth.²⁷²

Through the non-traditional civilization of the modern West, however, the sledge-hammer blows of science have driven a wedge that threatens to split asunder the whole fabric. 'Religious' and 'secular', 'sacred' and 'profane' interests and activities are sharply distinguished and ruthlessly divided the one from the other. The sphere of 'religion' has progressively shrunk, so that it now has little or no connection with, or influence over, the vast majority of the activities in which men at present engage. It may no longer be compared with the ocean bed which supports (*Dharma* is derived from a root meaning 'to support') the mighty mass of waters rolling above, but to a small volcanic island reeling and shuddering beneath the relentless impact of the hostile element by which it is surrounded and well-nigh overwhelmed. For the modern men and women there is in the common things of life no hint of aught beyond; for them there falls, like moonlight upon shifting leaves, no steady radiance of the Eternal upon the flickerings of their days. They are the true descendants of Peter Bell, in whom Wordsworth, writing when the smoke of the Industrial Revolution had already begun to darken the skies of England, described a type of humanity now fast becoming universal:

> A primrose by a river's brim
> A yellow primrose was to him
> And it was nothing more.²⁷³

Religion, banished from the affairs of men, sits dark and solitary in the temple. Life goes on, or seems to go on, as before; but that which was 'the life of life' is no longer there, and it is problematical how long the ghastly simulacrum will be able to continue its antics.

Such a displacement of civilization from its age-old foundations in spiritual values, and the consequent opening of a breach between the 'religious' and 'secular' aspects of life, will inevitably find a counterpart not only in the student's life but in his approach to the study of Buddhism. Brought up in a non-traditional environment, wherein few objects and activities have any significance beyond themselves, he will be naturally prone to think that the study of Buddhism is one activity among many to be pursued without the necessity of considering either what influence it may have on other activities or what effect they may have upon it. In a traditional society such negligence would not have very serious consequences; for, as already stated, in such a society everything receives, ultimately, a transcendental orientation, and few activities other than those which violate the moral law could be positively deleterious in their effect upon the study of Buddhism. The 'spiritual' life and 'religious' studies point in the same direction as the 'worldly' life and its duties; but one points directly, the other indirectly.

In a non-traditional society, however, there is a constant tug of war between those departments of life which have been dissociated from their transcendental principles, on the one hand, and the isolated remnants of tradition on the other. Even the sincerest student cannot entirely withdraw himself from activities which, being no longer traditional, are in principle, or rather because of their very lack of principle, at variance with the proper method of studying the Dharma. If you are in this situation, your life, lacking a common guiding principle for all its activities, will be to some extent disintegrated. You will be like a man who, clinging desperately to a rock in midstream, feels against his body the mighty rush of waters which seeks to tear him from his refuge and whirl him to destruction. In order to integrate your life and strengthen your hold upon the unshakeable rock of the Dharma, you will have to withdraw yourself from as many profane activities as possible, and to reinforce the traditional supports not only of your own life but, as far as you can, of society as well. You should take part, and encourage others to take part, in traditional observances of all kinds; taking care, first, to understand the meaning and value of each observance. Worship of the image of the Buddha with the traditional offerings of flowers, lights, and incense; paying homage to spiritual teachers, to sacred objects and buildings, and to elders and members of the Holy Order, in the manner traditionally prescribed; the wearing of the traditional costume (in societies that still have one); participating in celebrations such as those held in honour of the Buddha's Enlightenment – in these and many other similar ways, by multiplying opportunities for contact with Tradition and consequent recollection of the Dharma, it is possible to effect at least a partial integration not only of your own life but also, albeit to a lesser extent, of the lives of your associates.

Abstention from participation in untraditional activities of all kinds, particularly from forms of entertainment which are calculated to excite the senses and stimulate the lower mind, is no less essential to the successful study of the Dharma. If your aim is to be a Dharma student, but you think that if you devote an hour a day or two or three hours a week to the study of the Dharma it will be sufficient, and that when not so engaged you can spend your time playing games, reading a trashy novel, or under the hypnotic influence of the latest popular film, with no effect on your state of mind, you are making a big mistake. It is no accident of language that the words 'whole' and 'holy' are etymologically connected, or that one of the definitions of 'holy' should be 'spiritually whole'. The quest for holiness, which the study of the Dharma subserves, is a quest for spiritual wholeness, for complete integration of the 'personality' not with any subjective principle merely, but with Reality. The more faithfully the study of Buddhism is pursued, the more difficult will it be to allow even activities of minor importance to remain outside the circle of its influence. Only from the intellectual or dogmatic scientific point of view is it possible to regard Buddhism as being merely one among hundreds of other possible subjects for scholarly research and doctoral dissertation. To one who studies it with some attempt at approximation to the fully traditional method we have endeavoured to describe, it can appear as nothing less than what it actually is, the dominating and controlling influence of the whole of life.

from *A Survey of Buddhism*

5
FRIENDS AND TEACHERS

1. WHY SHOULD A BUDDHA NEED A FRIEND?

In spiritual friendship we take delight in the spiritual beauty of our friend.

Although the Buddha had had some difficulty in finding a satisfactory personal attendant, Ānanda was by no means in a hurry to take on the task. It is as though he realized that it would be no easy matter to be the constant companion of an Enlightened one. Ānanda had made steady progress in the spiritual life. He was certainly a Stream Entrant: he was irreversible from full Enlightenment. But he was not a Buddha. And even for someone like Ānanda, even for a Stream Entrant, even for someone who had grown up with the Buddha, it was a rather awe-inspiring prospect to be the Buddha's constant companion, to be with him, by day and by night, in rain and in sun, year in and year out. Ānanda therefore thought the matter over very carefully. He had seen some previous attendants come somewhat to grief, and was reluctant to give the Buddha any further trouble.

In the end, however, Ānanda decided to accept the challenge, but laid down certain conditions, of which a couple are relevant here. One of these was that he should not be given any share in the various offerings and invitations that were given to the Buddha. He argued that, if people saw him benefiting from the offerings that were made to the Buddha – all the new robes and so on, then they might think he was acting as the Buddha's companion just for the sake of what he could get out of it. He also realized that there would be times when he might have to be away from the Buddha, running errands, taking messages, and so on. While he was away, someone might come to see the Buddha and ask for a teaching. In consequence, the Buddha might give a discourse, might even give an important teaching, in his absence. So another condition he laid down was that the Buddha should repeat whatever teaching he had given during his absence.

The Buddha accepted these conditions,[274] and Ānanda became his constant companion for twenty years. How successful this arrangement was can be seen from an incident that occurred shortly before the Buddha's *parinirvāṇa*, his final passing away. Ānanda was very deeply upset by the prospect of losing the Buddha. Apparently he stood leaning against the door, weeping. As he wept, he said, 'Alas, I am still a pupil with much to be done, and my Master will be passing utterly away, *he who was so kind to me.*'[275] This was Ānanda's impression of the Buddha after twenty years of constant, day to day, companionship. He did not say that the Buddha was *wise*, or *energetic*, but that the Buddha was *kind*.

Fortunately, we also know about the Buddha's impression of Ānanda, for when he was told that Ānanda was weeping outside, he sent for him and spoke the following words of encouragement:

> For many a long day, Ānanda, the Tathāgata has been waited on by you with kindly body-service, that is profitable, ease-giving, undivided, and unstinted; waited on with kindly service of speech, that is profitable, ease-giving, undivided, and unstinted; with kindly service of thought, that is profitable, ease-giving, undivided, and unstinted.[276]

Thus the Buddha's predominant impression of Ānanda was that he too was kind, that Ānanda had served him with kindness of body, speech, and mind, that he had kept nothing back, that he had given himself totally. The relation between the Buddha and Ānanda was essentially one of mutual kindness, even though the Buddha was spiritually by far the more developed of the two.

This may seem like a very small thing, but if we reflect we shall realize that it is actually a very big thing. Their kindness had never failed, had never been found wanting even for a moment on either side. When two people are constant companions, and when the relation between them is of unfailing mutual kindness, you can only say of them that they are *friends*. Indeed, you can only say that they are *spiritual friends*, because such unfailing mutual kindness over such a long period of time is possible only on a deeply spiritual basis.

To some, it may seem a little strange that the Buddha and Ānanda were friends. It may seem strange, perhaps, that the Buddha should have had a friend. One may wonder whether a Buddha *needs* a friend. But this depends on one's conception of Enlightenment. In response, I can give only a hint.

The Enlightenment experience is not self-contained in a one-sided way. The Enlightenment experience contains an element of 'communication', and contains, therefore, an element of spiritual friendship, even 'transcendental friendship', or friendship of the highest conceivable level. This, perhaps, is the significance of the Buddha's having a constant companion. There is surely no question of the Buddha keeping up the 'dignity' of a Buddha. Ānanda is not a sort of spiritual valet-cum-private-secretary. The fact that he is 'in attendance', as the translator has it, represents the fact that there exists within the Enlightenment experience, within the heart of Reality, an element of communication, an element of spiritual friendship, something that found expression in the later history of Buddhist thought as that rather mysterious concept of *sambhogakāya*.[277]

We can see how the Buddha and Ānanda worked together as friends in a story that is told of how they once came upon a monk who was sick. We will join them as they make their way around the lodgings of a group of monks.

> The Exalted One was going his rounds of the lodgings, with the Venerable Ānanda in attendance, and came to the lodging of that brother.

A point to notice here is that the Exalted One was going his rounds of the *lodgings*. In the original, the word for 'lodging' is *vihāra*, and that is all that *vihāra* really means. We must not imagine the Buddha going his rounds of a large, palatial, well-furnished monastery. The lodgings in question were probably just clusters of thatched huts scattered over an area of parkland just a few miles outside the city gates.

The Buddha was making his *rounds* of these lodgings. In other words, he was taking a personal interest in the monks. How were they getting on? What were they doing? How were they passing their time? There was of course no question of them sitting outside their thatched huts reading newspapers, or listening to the radio, or watching television. But they might possibly have been up to other things that they should not have been up to. They might have needed some encouragement, some teaching, or even a little ticking-off. The Buddha was seeing things for himself. In this way, he and Ānanda came to the lodging of that brother.

> Now the Exalted One saw that brother lying where he had fallen in his own excrements, and seeing him He went towards him, came to him, and said: 'Brother, what ails you?'
>
> 'I have dysentery, Lord.'
>
> 'But is there anyone taking care of you, brother?'
>
> 'No, Lord.'
>
> 'Why is it, brother, that the brethren do not take care of you?'
>
> 'I am useless to the brethren, Lord: therefore the brethren do not care for me.'[278]

There are a number of points to be noted here. The Buddha goes towards the sick monk, asks him what is wrong with him, and gets very quickly to the heart of the matter, especially in the sick monk's last reply: 'I am useless to the brethren, Lord: therefore the brethren do not care for me.'

This is a very significant statement indeed. It is a shocking, terrible statement. Of course, we have only the bare words of the printed page to go by. We do not know how those words were spoken – and this can of course make a difference. Did the Buddha say, 'Why is it, brother, that the brethren do not take care of you?' indignantly, or with concern, or sadly? And did the sick monk reply with dignity, with resignation, with weariness, or with bitterness and anger? We do not know. All we have is the bleak, shocking, statement itself, 'I am useless to the brethren, Lord: therefore the brethren do not care for me.'

However the words were spoken, they must imply, sadly, that people are interested in you only so long as you are useful to them, only so long as they can get something out of you. It implies that they see you not as a person but as a thing. To treat a person as a thing is to treat them unethically. And this, apparently, is how the other monks were treating the sick monk. He was not useful to them, also they were not interested in him. He was left lying in his own excrement. No one took care of him. There was no kindness between the sick monk and the other monks as there was between the Buddha and Ānanda. There was no ordinary human friendship – not to speak of spiritual friendship; neither was there any sympathy or sensitivity or awareness. There could not be, because these are qualities that you can experience only in relation to a person whom you actually see as a person. The other monks did not see the sick monk as a person. To them he was like an old worn-out broom or a broken pot. He was useless to them so they did not care for him.

Only too often we ourselves can behave like this. We often consider people primarily in terms of their usefulness. We do this even within the spiritual community. Sometimes we are more interested in someone's talents and capacities – as a bricklayer, accountant, or lecturer – than in what they are in themselves. If you are treated in this way, then, when you are no longer able or willing to employ your talents, you may have the disappointing and disillusioning experience of finding that nobody wants to know you, nobody wants to be friends with you any more. We must therefore learn to see persons as persons. There must be kindness between us, there must be spiritual friendship, as there was between the Buddha and Ānanda. There must be sympathy, sensitivity, and awareness.

There are two principal aspects to persons treating each other as persons. These are communication and taking delight. These two are of the essence of friendship. Even in the case of ordinary friendship there is the great benefit and blessing of being able to share our thoughts and feelings with another human being. It has been said that self-disclosure, the making of oneself known to another human being – being known by them and knowing that you are known by them – is essential to human health and happiness. If you are shut up in yourself, without any possibility of communication with another person, you don't stay healthy or happy for long. In the case of spiritual friendship, we share our experience of the Dharma itself. We share our enthusiasm, our inspiration, and our understanding. We even share our mistakes. Here, communication takes the form of confession.

The aspect of 'taking delight' means that we not only see a person as a person, but also *like* what we see, enjoy and take delight in what we see, just as we do with a beautiful painting or poem – except that here the painting or poem is alive: the painting can speak to you, and the beautiful poem can answer back! This makes it very exciting and stimulating indeed. Here we see, we like, we love and appreciate a person entirely for their own sake, and not for the sake of anything useful that we can get out of them. This also happens in ordinary friendship to some extent, but it happens to a far greater extent in spiritual friendship – *kalyāṇa mitratā*. The primary meaning of *kalyāṇa* is 'beautiful'. In spiritual friendship we take delight in the *spiritual* beauty of our friend: we rejoice in his or her merits.

from *The Buddha's Victory*

2. THE NETWORK OF RELATIONSHIPS

However calm, kind, and wise we may feel in the privacy of our own hearts or shrine-rooms, the true test of how fully we have developed these qualities comes when we are faced with the realities of life as represented by the challenges offered by 'other people'.

Some verses I once composed for the dedication of a Buddhist shrine-room include the aspiration: 'May our communication with one another be sangha.'[279] This reflects the very great importance that has always been given in Buddhism to the quality of communication both between members of the sangha and in the context of all the relationships an individual Buddhist has with other people. The Buddha had a great deal to say about communication – about the importance of truthful, kindly, meaningful, and harmonious speech, and about the necessity to pay attention to one's relationships in general, making sure that one is relating in ways that accord with one's Buddhist principles.

The reasons for this are quite obvious. To be human is to be related to other human beings. We cannot live our lives in isolation; whatever efforts we make to develop as individuals are continually tested in the fires of our relationships with other people. However calm, kind, and wise we may feel in the privacy of our own hearts or shrine-rooms, the true test of how fully we have developed these qualities comes when we are faced with the realities of life as represented by the challenges 'other people' represent.

The first human being to whom we are related is of course our mother. That relationship is very intimate, and it affects us for the whole of our lives. After that, our father comes into view, and perhaps brothers and sisters as well, together with grandparents, if we are fortunate. A little later we may also become aware of aunts, uncles, and cousins. This is usually the extent of our family circle. But then there are neighbours, and from the age of 4 or 5 there are teachers, schoolfellows, and friends. Later, there may be a husband or wife, and perhaps children. On top of these relationships we will probably have connections with employers and workmates, perhaps even employees. And we will also, sooner or later, have to have relationships of a kind with government officials, bureaucrats, even rulers, whether in our own country or abroad. By the time we reach maturity, we will find ourselves in the midst of a whole network of relationships with scores, perhaps hundreds, of people, and connected indirectly or distantly to very many more.

This network of relationships is the subject matter of a Buddhist text known as the *Sigālaka Sutta*, which is to be found in the *Dīgha Nikāya*, the 'Collection of Long Discourses', in the Pāli canon.[280] It is a comparatively early text, the substance of which, we can be reasonably certain, goes back to the Buddha himself. It is called the *Sigālaka Sutta* because it is a discourse given by the Buddha to a young man called Sigālaka. One translator describes the *sutta* as 'Advice to Lay People'. In it the Buddha lays down a pattern for different kinds of relationships, explaining how each should be conducted. All this is set forth with such clarity and succinctness that it remains of considerable interest today.

Sigālaka is a young Brahmin, which means that he belongs to the priestly caste, the highest and most influential caste of Indian society. The introduction to the *sutta* reports that the Buddha happens to meet Sigālaka early one morning. Sigālaka's clothes and hair are still dripping wet from his purificatory ritual bath. (This is something you can still see today – Brahmins standing in the holy Ganges at Varanasi, dipping into the water and reciting mantras.) Having taken his bath, Sigālaka is engaged in worshipping the six directions: north, south, east, west, the zenith, and the nadir.

He is doing this, so he informs the Buddha, in obedience to his father's dying injunction, in order to protect himself from any harm that might come from any of the six directions. The Buddha thereupon tells Sigālaka that although worshipping the six directions is right and proper he is not going about it in the right way, if he wants such worship to protect him effectively. He then proceeds to explain what the six directions really represent.

The east, he says, means mother and father (in Indian languages mother comes before father) because one originates from them just as the sun – or at least the day – originates in the east. So the first relationship the Buddha refers to is that between parent and child. As for the other directions, they refer to the other key relationships in life: the south to the relationship between pupil and teacher; the west to that between husband and wife; the north to friends and companions; the nadir to the relationship between 'master and servant' (employer and employee, in modern terms); and the zenith to the relationship between lay people and 'ascetics and Brahmins'.

True worship of the six directions, the Buddha explains, consists in carrying out one's duties with regard to these six kinds of relationship. Such ethical activity is naturally productive of happiness, and it is in this sense that one protects oneself through this kind of 'worship'. Here the Buddha envisages the individual as being at the centre of a network of relationships, out of which he enumerates just six. The Buddha seems to give equal emphasis to these six primary relationships, which represent a fairly wide spread of human interaction, and in this respect he is characteristic of his culture, that of north-east India in the sixth century BCE.

But most other cultures emphasize one kind of human relationship rather more than the others. For example, a similar list to the one the Buddha gave Sigālaka can be found in Confucianism, according to which there are five standard relationships: between ruler and subject (sometimes described as prince and minister), between parent and child, between husband and wife, between brother and brother, and between friend and friend. But in ancient China particular emphasis was always placed on the relationship between parents and children, and especially on the duties of children towards parents. According to some Confucian writers, filial piety is the greatest of all virtues, and in classical times sons and daughters who were conspicuous examples of it were officially honoured by the government with a title, or a grant of a large piece of land, or a monument erected in their honour. The whole idea can only seem rather strange to us now, living as we do in very different times, when independence from one's parents is the goal as far as most people are concerned.

Turning to the ancient Greeks, we find no particular list of significant relationships. However, if we take Plato's account of the teachings of Socrates as representative of the highest Greek ideals, it is clear that for them the relationship between friend and friend was the most significant. The moving description of Socrates' death puts this emphasis into stark perspective. Some time before his death we find him bidding a rather formal farewell to his wife and children, who are nevertheless described as sobbing bitterly. He then dismisses them, and devotes his last hours to philosophical discussion with his friends.[281]

In medieval Europe, on the other hand, the emphasis was placed on the relationship between master and servant, particularly that between the feudal lord and the vassal. Such was the centrality of this relationship that a whole social system was built around it. In the feudal system the great virtue was loyalty, especially to the person directly above you in the social pecking order. If you were a great lord it would be the king; if you were a small landowner it would be the local lord; if you were an ordinary servant or serf it would be your knight. And you would be prepared and willing to die for your feudal superior.

In the modern West, of course, we find the main emphasis placed upon the sexual or romantic relationship. One may move from one such relationship to another, but through all these ups and downs, their current sexual relationship nevertheless remains the central relationship for most people, giving meaning and colour to their lives. The romantic relationship is the principal subject matter of films, novels, plays, and poems, and as an ideal it is all-consuming – lovers commonly declare that they cannot live without each other, even that they are prepared to die for each other. Thus for most people in our culture, the sexual/romantic relationship is the central and most important one – an idea which people of the ancient civilizations would probably have found ridiculous. This is not to say that they would necessarily have been right, but we can at least remind ourselves that people have not always felt as we feel today.

In the modern West other relationships often tend to be superficial because they are simply not given the same weight. We tend to neglect our relationships with our parents and with our friends, rarely taking these relationships as seriously as we do our romantic liaisons. That, we think, is the way things are meant to be. We tend to think that the tremendous value we give to this particular relationship compared with the lesser value we accord to others is perfectly normal; indeed, we are apt to assume that it has always been like that everywhere in the world. But that, as we have seen, is not really the case. On the contrary, our position is a distinctly abnormal one. I am not aware of another society that has raised the sexual relationship so high above all others.

Quite apart from the neglect of other relationships, our attitude has the unfortunate result of overloading the romantic relationship. We come to expect from our sexual partner far more than he or she is able to give. If we are not careful we expect him or her to be everything for us: sexual partner, friend, companion, mother, father, adviser, counsellor, source of security – everything. We expect this relationship to give us love, security, happiness, fulfilment, and the rest. We expect it to give meaning to our lives, and in this way it becomes like an electrical cable carrying a current that is too much for it. The result is that the poor, unfortunate sexual relationship very often blows a fuse – it breaks down under the strain. The obvious solution is to work at the development of a greater spread of relationships, all of which are important to us, and to all of which we give great care and attention.

But one can see it the other way round too. As well as contributing to the decline of other relationships, the present-day centrality of the sexual or marital relationship also reflects the fact that other relationships have become more difficult or have tended to fall into abeyance. Teacher–pupil, employer–employee, and ruler–subject relationships have all been seriously depersonalized – indeed, often they are not seen as relations that should involve a personal element at all. But this was not the case in older societies. Centuries ago – as little as 150 years ago, in some areas of Europe – if you were a servant or an apprentice, you would probably have lived with your master under the same roof. You would have shared in his day-to-day existence, eating the same food at the same table, just as though you were a member of the family, albeit one who knew his or her place. Under the traditional apprenticeship system, a very close personal relationship could grow up between master and apprentice or servant, or in modern terms, between employer and employee.

The novels of Dickens, which date from the 1840s, by which time the industrial age was well under way, could still portray the relation between master and servant in distinctly feudal terms, because those terms were still a reality for many people. When in *The Pickwick Papers* Sam Weller, Mr Pickwick's faithful servant, wants to get married, Mr Pickwick naturally offers to release Sam from his service. Sam declares his intention to stay with Mr Pickwick, who says, 'My good fellow, you are bound to consider the young woman also.' But Sam says that she will be happy to wait for him. 'If she don't, she's not the young woman I take her for, and I give her up with readiness.' His duty, he says, is to serve Mr Pickwick.[282]

In this way he was harking back to the situation where you served a feudal chief who led you in battle, who was more powerful than you, who protected you, and to whom you were unconditionally loyal. This commitment made it a truly personal relationship, and very often the most important relationship in a man's life, even emotionally, and one for which other relationships would be sacrificed if necessary.

This attitude was still around to some extent in the East when I was there in the 1950s. In Kalimpong I sometimes had to engage Tibetan or Nepalese cooks, handymen, or gardeners, and it was noticeable that they quickly became very loyal. They weren't interested in just getting the money at the end of the month. Some of them didn't even want to work for money at all. They were much more concerned to have a decent relationship with a good master.

Nowadays, for better or worse, all this is on the way out, with the steady incursion of Western values. The very word 'master' makes people today feel slightly uneasy. The result is that you cannot generally have any truly personal relationship with your employer. You work not for a master but for a department in a company, and your work is overseen by people who have more power than you have, but no loyalty or commitment to you. Only in truly archaic situations, like an army regiment, in which loyalty and devotion to duty is the key to success, do you still find anything like this sort of relationship. Likewise, we have a very remote, impersonal relationship with those who are meant to protect our interests, and we certainly don't think in terms of serving them. You may get round to shaking hands with your local Member of Parliament or Congressman, but usually that's about as close to them as you are likely to get.

One might think that the relation between teacher and pupil would be a naturally personal one; it certainly can be so in the tutorial system of some universities. However, in general, teaching these days is a businesslike process of passing pupils from one teacher to another in the hope that a balanced ingestion of facts will result. Under the usual classroom system, one teacher sometimes has to address as many as forty pupils, and then moves on to teach another large group of pupils. A relationship is necessarily an individual thing, and it is virtually impossible to develop such relationships with every pupil in your care in such circumstances. Nor can you have favourites, as this will lead to resentment.

Anyway, most of us come in contact with teachers only when we are comparatively young, so that any relationship we might have with a teacher never gets a chance to mature. We don't generally think in terms of learning anything beyond the point at which we stop accumulating qualifications; that is the end of the teacher–pupil relationship for us, although certain relationships later on may involve an unofficial mentoring element which can have a profound effect on our development.

In modern life, relationships between friends are not, in the case of men anyway, meant to go deep enough to produce problems. We tend to keep such relationships at an easygoing, undemanding level, probably because in many people's minds there is a fear of homosexuality. Any strong emotional relationship between two people of the same sex, especially between two men, tends in our times to be rather suspect.

We can also say that relationships among brothers and sisters are much less important than formerly. One obvious reason for this is that some of us don't have brothers and sisters. It is all too common to find oneself an only child – very different from the large families of earlier times, when (especially before the advent of the Welfare State) members of the family would be expected to care for one another.

The fact that these various kinds of relationship have become more superficial means that we are left with only two effective personal relationships in our lives nowadays. The ancient Indians had six, the ancient Chinese had five, but we, for all practical purposes, have two: the parent–child relationship, and the husband–wife or boyfriend–girlfriend relationship. And of these two, it is the second that is for many people by far the more important.

Of course, there are various complicating factors in sexual relationships, the most obvious one being sex itself. Under the conditions of modern life, sexual needs are not only biological but also psychological. For example, a man will tend nowadays to associate the expression of his manhood less with his activity in the world than with his sexual activity, particularly if his work is fairly meaningless and undemanding.

Another complicating factor is that, as in most civilizations, the man–woman relationship is institutionalized – whether as marriage or as cohabitation. Apart from the parent–child relationship (which is on a rather different basis), marriage is the only one of our relationships that we legalize and institutionalize in this way. It is not just a personal understanding between two people; it involves a legal obligation, which under certain circumstances is even enforceable in a court of law. It is not always easy to make changes in such a relationship, and this can lead to difficulties.

When a conflict arises between our need to develop as an individual on the one hand and our sexual relationship on the other, the psychological pressure can build up to create intense distress. Indeed, any personal relationship has the potential to get in the way of our attempts to grow spiritually. There is something of a paradox here. On the one hand, personal relationships are absolutely necessary for human development. On the other hand, if we are committed to spiritual development, it is much easier to sustain a personal relationship with another person who is also trying to lead a spiritual life. Problems are likely to arise – especially in the context of a sexual relationship – when one of the two people wishes to engage in spiritual practice and the other does not, and such problems are difficult to resolve because we are unlikely to be completely wholehearted in our commitment to the spiritual life anyway. Part of us, so to speak, is likely to side with the other person against our spiritual aspiration, so that we may find ourselves agreeing that setting aside time to meditate, for example, is simply selfish.

Some people find that as they get involved with spiritual practice, the importance to them of their old personal relationships diminishes, at least for a time. This can be very difficult to accept. It sounds unbearably harsh to say that as you grow, you just have to leave family and friends behind in some sense. But in a way this is only to be expected. Spiritual life does involve an element of going forth, as we have already seen. And if you are interested in things that your friends and family have little or no knowledge of or interest in, you can't help losing contact with them to some extent.

However, many people find that as they mature in their spiritual practice, their increased positivity, sensitivity, and sense of gratitude brings them into much deeper and closer relationship, especially with their families, and this is very much to be welcomed, and indeed consciously worked on. After all, as the Buddha reminded Sigālaka, our parents gave us this life, which we increasingly feel to be very meaningful and precious; great love and respect is due to them for that, whatever has happened since. At the same time, as we move more deeply into spiritual practice, we will be forming new personal relationships with other people who are trying to live a spiritual life – in other words, we are likely to join or help form a spiritual community.

from *What is the Sangha?*

3. THE IMPORTANCE OF SPIRITUAL FRIENDSHIP

The real significance of the deep individual-to-individual contact that Going for Refuge to the Sangha involves lies in a simple psychological fact: we get to know ourselves best in relation to other people.

It has been said that the history of Buddhist philosophy can be summed up as the struggle between Buddhism and the abstract noun. So to guard against the ubiquitous enemy, abstraction, we should be clear that when we speak of the spiritual community, we are not referring to some ethereal entity apart from the people who comprise it. Membership of a community means relationship with people within that community. We can now put our question another way: how is it that entering into relationship with other people who hold a common ideal and follow a common path should help us in our spiritual life?

In a sense, it comes down to the simple saying: 'Birds of a feather flock together.' That is how they survive. There was an occasion when the Buddha addressed the Vajjians, a tribe from the Vaiśālī area who had come under some threat. Among other things, he told them that they would prosper as long as they continued to meet regularly, in full and frequent assemblies, conducting their business in harmony and dispersing in harmony. Afterwards he went on to apply the same criteria to the spiritual survival of the sangha.[283]

The heart of the sangha is *kalyāṇa mitratā*, a very beautiful phrase. It is less a philosophical term than a poetic one. *Kalyāṇa* means beautiful, charming, auspicious, helpful, morally good. Thus the connotations are aesthetic, moral, and religious. The term covers much the same ground as the Greek expression *kalos kai agathos*, which means 'good and beautiful'. *Mitratā* means simply friendship or companionship. *Kalyāṇa mitratā* therefore means something like 'beautiful friendship', or 'morally good companionship', or simply 'spiritual friendship'. There is an exchange between the Buddha and his disciple Ānanda which spells out its importance in the Buddha's eyes. Ānanda was the Buddha's cousin and became his attendant for the last twenty years of the Buddha's life. He accompanied the Buddha wherever he went, and they had an understanding that if by any chance Ānanda was not present when the Buddha delivered a discourse, or discussed the Dharma with anyone, when they were alone together the Buddha would repeat to Ānanda everything he had said.[284] Ānanda had an astonishingly retentive memory. Indeed, it is said that we owe our knowledge of the Buddha's teachings to him. Because he made a point of listening to everything the Buddha said, storing it away in his memory so that he could repeat it later on for the benefit of others, his testimony was used to authenticate the teachings that were preserved after the Buddha's death.

On this particular occasion the Buddha and Ānanda were on their own when Ānanda suddenly came out with something to which he had obviously given a bit of thought. He said, 'Lord, I think that *kalyāṇa mitratā* is half the spiritual life.' And then one presumes that he sat back and waited for some kind of appreciative affirmation from the Buddha. It seemed to Ānanda that what he had said was incontrovertible: having like-minded people around you who are also trying to grow and develop must be half the battle won. But the Buddha said, 'Ānanda, you're wrong. *Kalyāṇa mitratā* is not half the spiritual life; it's the whole of it.'[285]

Why is this? Of course we learn from those we associate with, especially those who are more mature than we are, and learning will clearly be important if we are to make progress in the spiritual life. But in what does 'progress in the spiritual life' really consist? What are we *really* learning? The knowledge we need, in the end, is self-knowledge. And the real significance of the deep individual-to-individual contact that Going for Refuge to the Sangha involves lies in the simple fact that we get to know ourselves best in relation to other people. If you spent your whole life alone on a desert island, in a sense you would never really know yourself. As it is, though, we have all had the experience of clarifying our ideas through discussion – and even of discovering that we knew more than we thought we did – simply through trying to communicate with another person. It is as though trying to communicate activates an understanding that is already there but has never manifested until now, and even brings forth new aspects of oneself – aspects which one only ever discovers as a result of contact with another person. Through meeting the challenge of real communication, one comes to know oneself better.

It is not only a matter of activating one's understanding. Meeting certain people can disturb aspects of ourselves that had been rather deeply buried. We say that a particular kind of person 'brings out the worst in us'. Perhaps nothing is said, but they somehow touch a raw nerve. It can be a shock to realize what that individual has evoked in us, to find ourselves behaving in a way that we like to think is uncharacteristic of us, even expressing hatred or contempt towards the person who has triggered this behaviour. Of course, that unpleasant side of us was always there, but it needed that person to bring it to the surface. In this apparently negative but highly spiritually beneficial way too, other people can introduce us to ourselves. We cannot transform ourselves unless we have a full sense of what lies within us.

Conversely, certain people seem to 'bring out the best in us'. Again, nothing necessarily needs to be said, but just being with them makes us feel lighter, more cheerful, more energetic, more positive. Other people can also sometimes activate resources of kindness and decency that we didn't know we had in us. And in a specifically Buddhist context, there will be certain people who activate a quality of faith in us simply through contact with their own faith. Something that was not active before is stirred up.

The sangha is necessary, in short, because personal relationships are necessary for human development. This applies at all levels – cultural, psychological, and spiritual. The vast majority of people undoubtedly develop most rapidly, and even most easily, in the company of others – or at least in contact with others. Not that it is impossible to develop entirely on one's own; indeed, there is a Buddhist term for those who do so: *pratyekabuddhas*, private or solitary Buddhas.[286] However, although there are a number of canonical references to them, it is significant that all these solitary Buddhas are located in the remote and legendary past. There appear to be no historical examples.

We generally need the stimulation, reassurance, and enthusiasm of others who are going in the same direction as we are. We are naturally stimulated by someone who shares our special interest in something. Even though we still have to put in the effort ourselves, at least we see the point of it more clearly – we are less undermined by doubts. Membership of the sangha also gives us the opportunity to serve others, to express our generosity and helpfulness. Even in such a simple activity as providing tea and biscuits at a Buddhist festival, we can discover in ourselves the capacity for generosity, altruism, and general positivity.

Thus the sangha is there to help us know ourselves and express ourselves better. It is able to do this because everyone who participates in it is committed to the Buddha as the ideal of self-knowledge in the highest and deepest sense, and to the Dharma, the various principles and practices by which that self-knowledge may be achieved. A common allegiance to the first two Refuges constitutes the bond of unity between the members of the spiritual community. We are all following – albeit at different stages – the same path to the same ultimate goal.

By the same token, if one is not really aiming for Enlightenment, and not really trying to practise the Dharma, then one may say that one is committed to these ideals, but whatever one may say, one is no more a member of the sangha than a donkey following a herd of cows can be a member of that herd. This is the image used by the Buddha in the *Aṅguttara Nikāya*: as he puts it, 'The donkey may say, "I am a cow too, I am a cow too" … but neither in his horns nor in his hoofs is he anything like a cow, whatever he may say.' Likewise, simply reciting the Refuges does not make one a member of the sangha. The bond is inner and spiritual.[287]

At a certain point in our development, however much we may meditate and read books about spiritual practice, we have to recognize that these are not enough. There is no doubt that we can learn a lot on our own, but if we are to grow spiritually in a fully rounded way, we eventually have to experience the vital part that communication has to play in our spiritual life. The following verse comes from the *Dhammapada*, a very early collection of the Buddha's teachings, here quoted in the original Pāli:

Sukho buddhānamuppādo,
sukhā saddhammadesanā.
Sukhā saṅghassa sāmaggī,
samaggānaṃ tapo sukho.[288]

The first line means 'Happy – or blissful, or blessed (*sukho*) – is the arising of the Buddhas.' When someone becomes a Buddha, this is a happy thing for all humanity. The second line may be translated 'Happy is the preaching of the true doctrine.' The teaching of the Dharma is a blessing for the whole world. The third line is 'Happy is the spiritual community in following a common path.' In the fourth line *tapo* means 'heat' and refers to spiritual practices which are like a fire burning up all impurities. The line therefore runs, 'The blaze of spiritual practice of those on the same path is happy or blessed.'

So it is not enough to have a distant idea of Enlightenment, the theory of the Buddha's teaching, or a Buddhist organization. There is no future for Buddhism without a truly united and committed spiritual community, dedicated to practising together. And when Buddhists do come together in the true spirit of the sangha, there is then the possibility of inhabiting, for a while at least, the *dharmadhātu*, the realm of the Dharma. In this realm, all we do is practise the Dharma, all we talk about is the Dharma, and when we are still and silent, we enjoy the Dharma in stillness and silence together. The clouds of stress and anxiety that so often hang over mundane life are dispersed, and the fountains of inspiration within our hearts are renewed.

from *What is the Sangha?*

4. FRIENDSHIP: THE WHOLE OF THE SPIRITUAL LIFE?

No one else can practise the Dharma for us; we have to practise it ourselves. But we do not have to practise it by ourselves.

In the modern world, friendship is arguably the most neglected of all the primary human relationships. But according to the Buddha himself friendship has a direct connection with the spiritual life. Speaking to Sigālaka on the subject, he says that friends and companions are to be served and looked after in five ways.[289] In other words, we have five duties towards our friends, and if we perform these, our friendships will flourish.

First of all, it is our duty to be generous. We should share with our friends whatever we have. This should ideally be taken quite literally. Some Buddhist residential communities live on the basis of a common purse, pooling all their resources. This isn't easy to do, of course – some people find it difficult even to share a book – but it reflects the ideal relationship between friends. Ideally, your friend should not even have to *ask* you for money. If you take the principle of sharing seriously, you share everything: time, money, resources, interest, energy – everything. You keep nothing back for yourself.

The second duty is never to speak harshly or bitterly or sarcastically to our friends, but always kindly and compassionately. Speech is taken very seriously in Buddhism. The five basic Buddhist precepts include just one speech precept – to refrain from false speech – but it is not enough just to speak truthfully, and this is reflected in the ten precepts taken by some Buddhists. These include no less than four speech precepts, because it is so easy to fall into harmful, destructive speech, to speak in an indifferent, careless, or even callous way.[290]

Our third duty to our friends is to look after their welfare, especially their spiritual welfare. As well as seeing that they are all right in terms of their health and economic well-being, and helping them with any difficulties they have, we should help them in whatever way we can to grow and develop as human beings.

Fourthly, we should treat our friends in the same way we treat our own self. This is a very big thing indeed, because it means breaking down the barrier between oneself and others. One of the most important Mahāyāna texts, the *Bodhicaryāvatāra* of Śāntideva, deals with this topic in great depth and considerable detail.[291]

And fifthly, we should keep the promises we make to our friends. We should keep our word. If we say we will do something for a friend, we just do it, come what may. If we are careless about fulfilling our promises, it is usually because we make them carelessly. We therefore have a duty to make our promises so mindfully that we treat them as serious obligations. Once we have given our word, that should be that.

Just as we have these five duties towards our friends, they have the same duties towards us; it's a two-way thing. Our friends and companions minister to us, serve us, reciprocate our friendship. Having listed our duties towards our friends, the *Sigālaka Sutta* therefore gives a list of five ways in which our good friends look after us. Firstly, according to the *sutta*, they take care of us when we are sick. Secondly, they watch over our property when we are neglectful; in other words they take more care of our possessions than we do ourselves – that is a sure sign of friendship. Thirdly, they are our refuge in time of fear: they can allay our anxiety, and if we have genuine cause for fear they help us deal with the situation. Fourthly, they do not forsake us when we are in trouble; as the proverb says, 'A friend in need is a friend indeed.' And lastly, they show concern for our dependants. If we have children, our friends are just as concerned for their welfare as we are ourselves, and the same goes for the welfare of our disciples, if we happen to have disciples.[292]

These, in brief, are the duties of a friend. Clearly they represent a very high ideal of friendship, and they repay careful reflection. Here I will just point out one or two salient features. It is interesting, for example, that the first four duties are identical with another well-known list that occupies an important place in Mahāyāna Buddhism: the four *saṃgrahavastus*, usually translated as the four elements of conversion.[293] These form part of the seventh *pāramitā*, the seventh of the ten perfections to be practised by the bodhisattva: *upāyapāramitā*, the perfection of *upāya* or skilful means. The four *saṃgrahavastus* are thus an aspect of the bodhisattva's skilful means.

The fact that these elements of conversion are the same as the first four duties of a friend says something deeply significant about how the sangha operates at its best. It suggests that the best way of converting people is simply by being friends with them. Some people try to convert others to their point of view or their religion almost forcibly, but this is not the Buddhist way. Buddhists should convert people – if that is really the right word – simply by being friendly. We make friends and that's an end of it. There is no need to preach to people, to knock on their doors and say, 'Have you heard the word of the Buddha?'

As a Buddhist one should not be thinking about 'converting' someone, or in any way manoeuvring them onto the path that one follows oneself. One's business is just to be a friend, to be generous, to share whatever one has, to speak kindly and affectionately, to show concern for one's friend's welfare, especially their spiritual welfare, to treat them in the same way that one treats oneself, and to keep one's word to them.

However, the fact that these four things are elements of conversion means that in themselves they constitute a communication of the Dharma. You communicate the Dharma itself by practising friendship in this way. One could even go so far as to say that friendship *is* the Dharma. William Blake, the great English poet, artist, and mystic, said, 'Religion is politics,' but he went on to say, 'Politics is brotherhood.'[294] Religion, therefore, is brotherhood. We can say, following him, that the Dharma is friendship. If you are practising friendliness you are not only practising the Dharma, but communicating it.

One further issue raised by the duties of friendship has particularly important implications. It concerns the fourth duty: treating our friends and companions like our own self. The Sanskrit term here is *samānārthatā* – *samān* meaning equal. A friend is one whom you treat equally. But what does this mean? A clue is to be found in the etymology of the word 'friend', which is apparently cognate with the word 'free'. Friendship is a relationship that can exist only between two or more free people – that is to say, people who are equals. Understanding this, the Ancient Greeks maintained that there could be no friendship between a free man and a slave.

We can take this metaphorically as well as literally. Friendship, we can conclude, can never involve any kind of power relationship. The relation between master and slave is based upon power, and where one person has any kind of power over another, there can be no friendship, because friendship is based upon love – to use the word love in the sense of the Pāli term *mettā* rather than in the sharply differentiated sense of the term *pema*, which is love as sticky attachment or possessiveness. *Pema* is fundamentally selfish, and it can easily turn into hatred; sexual love, of course, is often of this kind. But *mettā* is unselfish or non-attached, concerned only with the happiness and well-being of others.

The Pāli word for friend, *mitta* (Sanskrit *mitra*), is closely related to the term *mettā* (Sanskrit *maitrī*). With the help of the *mettā bhāvanā* meditation practice we can develop a friendly attitude. In other words, we shift from operating in the power mode to operating in the love mode. There are many ways of operating in the power mode – that is, focusing on getting what we want in a situation that involves other people. Usually, if we are clever enough, we don't have to use force. Subtly and indirectly we manipulate other people into doing what we want them to do, not for their good but for our own purposes. Some people are very good at this. They are so subtle, they seem so unselfish and so frank, that you hardly know that you are being manipulated, and it's so indirect that they may not even realize they're doing it. But in one way or another we deceive people, and ourselves, as to our real motives. We cheat, we lie, we commit emotional blackmail. But in *mettā*, in friendship, there is none of this, but only mutual concern for each other's happiness and well-being.[295]

Thus, friendship has a definitely spiritual dimension, and the Buddha has other things to say on the subject in other places. In chapter 4 of the *Udāna*, which may be an even earlier text than the *Sigālaka Sutta*, we find the Buddha staying at a place called Cālikā, accompanied by his attendant, who is at this time a monk called Meghiya. The two of them are alone together one day when Meghiya, who seems to be quite a young monk, happens to see a lovely grove of mango trees. In India you often get these on the outskirts of a village; the trees are very beautiful, with an abundance of dark green leaves, and they grow close together, so that as well as producing mangoes, they provide cool shade in the hot Indian summer.

Meghiya thinks to himself, 'What a beautiful grove of mango trees! And what a very fine place in which to sit and meditate – so cool and refreshing!' He therefore asks the Buddha if he may go and spend some time there. The Buddha, however, asks him to wait a while until some other monk arrives, because, for one reason or another, the Buddha needs someone to be with him. But Meghiya is not concerned with what the Buddha needs. Instead, he comes up with a clever and apparently unanswerable argument. He says, 'It's all very well for you – you've reached the goal of Enlightenment – but I have a long way to go in my practice. It's such a beautiful mango grove, I really want to go there and meditate.' In the end the Buddha has to agree, and off Meghiya goes, leaving the Buddha on his own. However, although Meghiya has got what he wanted, and the mango grove turns out to be just the peaceful place he thought it was going to be, he finds that he can't settle into his meditation at all. Despite his enthusiasm and energy, as soon as he sits down his mind is overwhelmed with greed, jealousy, anger, lust, false views – the lot. He just doesn't know what to do.

In the end he trudges back to the Buddha and reports on his abject failure. The Buddha doesn't scold him, but he gives him a teaching. He says, 'Meghiya, when you are spiritually immature there are five things that conduce to spiritual maturity. And the first of these is spiritual friendship. The second thing is the practice of ethics; and the third is serious discussion of the Dharma. Fourthly, you need to direct energy towards eliminating negative mental states and developing positive ones. And fifthly, you must cultivate insight in the sense of a deep understanding of universal impermanence.'[296]

The Buddha marked out these five things as necessary for the spiritually undeveloped, and of course he was implying that Meghiya should put spiritual friendship first. If you have a spiritual friend, whether the Buddha or someone much less eminent, they cannot be disregarded in the careless way that Meghiya has brushed off the Buddha. But like Meghiya, we are often unaware of the extent to which we are dependent spiritually on having personal contact with our spiritual friends, particularly those who are more developed than we are. It is very difficult to make any spiritual progress without them. The Buddha himself is no longer around, but most of us, like Meghiya, would not be ready for such a friend anyway. We would probably act rather as Meghiya did.

We may not have the Buddha, but we do have one another. We can help one another, encourage one another in our practice of the Dharma. We can confess our faults and weaknesses to one another. We can share our understanding with one another. We can rejoice in one another's merits. In these ways we can make a practice of spiritual friendship.

No one else can practise the Dharma for us; we have to practise it ourselves. But we do not have to practise it *by* ourselves. We can practise it in the company of like-minded people who are trying to do the same, and this is the best way – in fact, the only effective way – to practise.

As the Buddha was to say to his disciple and cousin Ānanda, some years later at a place called Sakkara, 'Spiritual friendship is the whole of the spiritual life.'[297] But how are we to take this? We can understand that friendship is important, but the idea that friendship, even spiritual friendship, should be the whole of the spiritual life, does seem hard to swallow. But let us look a little more closely at what is being said here.

The Pāli word I have translated as 'spiritual life' is *brahmacariya*, which sometimes means celibacy or chastity – that is to say abstention from sexual activity – but in this context it has a much wider meaning. It consists of two parts. *Brahma* means high, noble, best, sublime, and real; it also means divine, not in the theistic sense but in the sense of the embodiment of the best and noblest qualities and virtues. And *cariya* means walking, faring, practising, experiencing, even living. Hence *brahmacariya* means something like 'practising the best' or 'experiencing the ideal'; we could even render it 'the divine life', or just 'spiritual life', as I have done.[298]

There is a further aspect to the term *brahmacariya* that brings us to a deeper understanding of what it means in this context. In early Buddhism there is a whole series of terms beginning with *brahma*, and one of these is *brahmaloka*, which means the sublime realm, the divine world, or simply the spiritual world in the highest sense. So the *brahmacariya* or spiritual life is that way of life that leads to the *brahmaloka* or spiritual world. But how is it able to do this? For the answer, we must turn to yet another early Buddhist text: the *Mahāgovinda Sutta*. Without going into the background to this *sutta* – it's a long story – we find in it this very question being asked: 'How does a mortal reach the immortal *brahma* world?' In other words, how can one pass from the transient to the eternal? And the answer given is short and simple. 'One reaches the *brahma* world by giving up all possessive thoughts, all thoughts of me and mine.' In other words, one reaches the *brahmaloka* by giving up egoism and selfishness, by giving up all sense of 'I'.[299]

Thus the intimate connection between spiritual friendship and spiritual life starts to come into focus. Spiritual friendship is a training in unselfishness, in egolessness. You share everything with your friend or friends. You speak to them kindly and affectionately, and show concern for their welfare, especially their spiritual welfare. You treat them in the same way you treat yourself – that is, you treat them as being equal with yourself. You relate to them with an attitude of *mettā*, not according to where the power between you lies. Of course this is very difficult; it goes against the grain, because we are naturally selfish. The development of spiritual friendship is very difficult. Leading the spiritual life is very difficult. Being a Buddhist – a real Buddhist – is very difficult. We need help.

And we get that help not only from our teachers but also from one another. We can't be with our spiritual teacher all the time, but we can be with our spiritual friends all the time, or at least much of the time. We can see them regularly, perhaps live with them, perhaps even work with them. If we spend time with spiritual friends in this way, we will get to know them better, and they will get to know us better. We will learn to be more open and honest, we will be brought up against our weaknesses, and in particular we will be brought up against our natural tendency to operate in accordance with the power mode. If we have spiritual friends, they will try not to relate to us in this way and they will expect us to operate in the love mode as well, to relate to them with *mettā*. Learning to relate to our friends in this way, we will gradually learn to respond to the whole world with *mettā*, with unselfishness. It is in this way that spiritual friendship is indeed the whole of the spiritual life.

from *What is the Sangha?*

5. IS A GURU NECESSARY?

One could say that there are many misconceptions about the guru, but only one true conception.

Is a guru necessary? This is not a question that is likely ever to have occurred to anyone at the time of the Buddha; then, the first question anyone would have asked you would have been 'Who is your teacher?' not 'Do you think a teacher is necessary?' But this question will inevitably arise sooner or later for any modern Westerner who genuinely tries to develop as an individual, to be authentically himself or herself. In particular, it is likely to arise if one attempts quite specifically and consciously to follow what we usually refer to as the spiritual path, and it will demand an answer all the more imperatively when one tries to follow that spiritual path in one or another of its oriental forms.

However, before we address the question itself, we must banish the haze of imaginative associations that gather around the magic word 'guru'. We must, unfortunately, dispel the vision of brilliant blue skies, beautiful white snow peaks, and, just above the snow line, the snug little caves which are in the popular imagination the natural habitat of that rare creature, the guru. We must come down to earth from those inaccessible valleys of Shangri-la in which benign and wise old men with long white beards and starry eyes pass on the secret of the very highest teaching to a very few devoted disciples. We must ruthlessly dismiss any notion of those lucky disciples effortlessly floating up to Nirvāṇa on the strength of having secured the most advanced techniques from the most esoteric lineage holder.

We need to consider the whole question of the guru in as sober and matter-of-fact a fashion as possible, and try to understand what a guru is, and what a guru is not. On that basis, it should become clear to what extent and in what way a guru is necessary, if at all. We can also consider the attitudes it may be appropriate to adopt in relation to the guru.

Let us begin by seeing what a guru is not. First of all, a guru is not the head of a religious group. By a religious group I do not, of course, mean a spiritual community, but rather a number of non-individuals organized into a power structure around the forms or conventions of some kind of religious practice. Religious groups are of many kinds – sects, churches, monasteries, and so on – and they each have someone at their head. Such heads are regarded with great veneration by other members of the group, but there is likely to be something unfocused or off-key about this devotion. They are venerated not for what they are in themselves, as individuals, but for what they represent, what they stand for, even what they symbolize.

It might seem obvious that they should stand for or symbolize something spiritual, and in a superficial sense they do. But in fact they represent the group itself. That they are the head of a group is their principal significance. It is easy to see when this is the case; you just have to wait for the head of a group to be criticized or even vilified, as in course of time will inevitably happen. Members of groups usually feel that an attack on the head of their group is an attack on them. Any disrespect shown to the head of the group by those outside the group is interpreted by group members as lack of respect for the group itself.

The Buddha refused to countenance any such attitude among his followers. The *Brahmajāla Sutta* of the *Dīgha Nikāya* tells the story of how the Buddha and a great crowd of his followers were once travelling on foot between Rājagṛha and Nālandā, and found themselves in company with a wanderer called Suppiya and a follower of his, a young man called Brahmadatta. These two, in the hearing of the Buddha and his followers, began to argue, and kept arguing as they walked. And the subject of their argument, one can imagine, must have upset some of the Buddha's disciples considerably, for Suppiya, the text tells us, was finding fault in all sorts of ways with the Buddha, the Dharma, and the Sangha – though Brahmadatta was praising them just as strongly. All the travellers found themselves staying in the same place overnight, and still Suppiya and Brahmadatta kept on arguing.

Not surprisingly, when dawn came, the Buddha's followers gathered together and started talking among themselves about this disconcerting behaviour on the part of their fellow travellers. Coming to join them, the Buddha asked them what they had just been talking about, and they told him. Reading between the lines, we can gather that they were somewhat upset, even angry, at what had happened. But the Buddha said, 'Monks, if anyone should speak in disparagement of me, of the Dharma or of the Sangha, you should not be angry or displeased at such disparagement; that would only be a hindrance to you.'

Nor did the Buddha let the matter rest there. He said, 'If others disparage me, the Dharma or the Sangha, and you are angry or displeased, can you recognize whether what they say is right or not?' And the monks had to admit that, in those circumstances, they would be in no state to think about things objectively. So the Buddha said, 'If others disparage me, the Dharma or the Sangha, then you must explain what is incorrect as being incorrect, saying, "That is incorrect, that is false, that is not our way, that is not found among us."'[300]

If one reflects on this episode, one realizes that the Buddha is pointing out to his disciples a tendency that is all too human. If they had become angry, they might have thought their anger had arisen because the Buddha was being criticized, but in fact it was much more likely that anger had arisen because the group to which they belonged was being criticized, and so, in effect, *they* were being criticized. A disciple in that position might well feel that his wisdom in being a member of that group, and a follower of the person being criticized, was being called into question.

Examples of such sensitivity are not confined to the Pāli canon. I have come across Buddhists who would hunt through books on comparative religion, dictionaries of religion and philosophy, and the like, to see if they could find unfavourable references to Buddhism. When they found them, they would write off to the publishers, call public meetings, and organize protests and demonstrations. The most interesting aspect of the whole business was that the Buddhists who thus spluttered and seethed with rage were invariably convinced that they were thereby demonstrating their devotion to the Dharma. What they were exhibiting, however, was their group spirit – a thing that has nothing to do with the spiritual life or the Buddha's teaching.

Hence a guru is not the head of a religious group. Nor is he an ecclesiastical superior, someone higher up in the power structure of a religious group. When prominent religious personalities come from the East, they are sometimes heralded by advance publicity in which one is told that this particular personality is in charge of an important group of monasteries, or that he is second-in-command of an ancient and historic temple. Sometimes in India one is told simply that he is very wealthy. I was once in Calcutta at a time when preparations were being made for the arrival of a monk from a famous temple in Sri Lanka, and I was told by the head monk of the temple where I was staying that I ought to go and see him, as he was very important and influential. Naturally I asked, 'In what way is he important?' The head monk replied, 'He's the richest monk in Sri Lanka.' It was on that basis that I was expected to go and pay my respects to him.

This is an extreme example, but it is representative of a general expectation that one should be impressed by people who are higher up in the ecclesiastical structure, and regard them as gurus. But a guru is not this sort of figure at all. Someone who is organizationally important or influential is not thereby a guru.

A guru is not a teacher either – a statement that may come as something of a surprise. It is comparatively easy to understand that a guru is not the head of a religious group, but it is quite usual to think that a spiritual teacher is just what a guru is supposed to be. But what is meant by a teacher? A teacher is one who communicates information. A geography teacher teaches facts and figures about the Earth; a psychology teacher teaches facts and figures about the human mind. In the same way, a teacher of religion may teach the general history of all the different religions of the world, or the theology or doctrinal system of a particular tradition. But a guru, as such, doesn't teach religion. In fact, he or she doesn't necessarily teach anything at all.

People may ask questions, and he may answer those questions – whether or not he does so is up to him. But he has no vested interest in teaching. If nobody asked him any questions, he probably wouldn't bother to say anything. The Buddha himself made this perfectly clear. In several places in the Pāli scriptures he is reported as saying that he has no *diṭṭhi* – no view, no philosophy, no system of thought. 'There are lots of other teachers,' he says, 'who have this system of thought to expound, or that philosophy to teach; but I have none. I have no "view" to communicate. The Tathāgata (Buddha) is free from views, liberated from doctrines, emancipated from philosophy.'[301]

Outside the Pāli canon the Buddha is further reported as saying that he has no Dharma to impart. The great *Diamond Sūtra* describes innumerable bodhisattvas and disciples sitting and waiting for the Buddha to teach them the Dharma. But the Buddha tells them, 'I have nothing to teach.'[302] In another celebrated Mahāyāna text, the *Laṅkāvatāra Sūtra*, the Buddha goes so far as to say that he has never taught anything. 'Whether you have heard me speaking or not, the truth is that from the night of my Enlightenment, all through the forty-five years until the night of my *parinirvāṇa*, the night of my passing from the world, I have not uttered a single word.'[303] So the Buddha, the ultimate Buddhist guru, has no view, no teaching to impart. He is not a teacher.

Something else that the guru is not relates to one of the most striking facts about the human race as a whole, which is that the majority of its members do not grow up. People develop physically, of course, and they also develop intellectually in the sense that they learn how to organize their knowledge more and more coherently. But they don't grow up spiritually, or even emotionally. Many people remain emotionally immature, even infantile. They want to depend on someone stronger than themselves, someone who is prepared to love and protect them absolutely and unconditionally. They don't really want to be responsible for themselves. They want some authority or system to make their decisions for them.

When one is young, one depends on one's parents, but as one grows older, one is usually obliged to find substitutes for them. Many people find such a substitute in a romantic relationship, which is one of the reasons marriage is so popular, and also, often, so difficult. Others find their parent-surrogate in a concept of a personal God. One might even follow Freud in saying that God is a father-substitute on a cosmic scale. The believer expects from God the kind of love and protection that a child expects from his or her parents. It is highly significant that in Christianity, God is addressed as 'our Father'.

The role of father-substitute is often played by a guru – or rather a pseudo-guru. Mahatma Gandhi, for instance, was a great Indian politician, thinker, activist, even revolutionary, but it is rather significant that as a religious figure for much of his life he was addressed by his disciples as Bapu, 'Father'. Nor was this sort of title at all unusual in India. When I lived there I was in contact with quite a number of religious groups and their gurus, many of whom liked to be addressed as Dadaji, or 'Grandfather'. Their disciples, it seemed, were only too happy to fall in with their wishes in this respect.

This rather amused me, and when I was in Kalimpong and had some pupils of my own – most of them Nepalese rather than Indian – I asked them out of curiosity how they regarded me. At that time I was about thirty, and they were in their late teens and early twenties, so when they clasped their hands together and said with great fervour, 'Oh sir, you are just like our grandfather,' I was taken rather by surprise.

In India I also met a number of female gurus, and they were invariably addressed as Mataji, 'Mother', or even Ma, which means 'Mummy'. One of these gurus, who was well into middle-age when I first got to know her, was surrounded by young male followers, most of whom, as I discovered later, had lost their mothers. In the evenings they would gather in the meeting-hall to sit gazing up at 'Mummy' and singing in chorus the word 'Ma' – nothing else, just that word, 'Ma' – to the accompaniment of drums and cymbals. They would keep it up for two or three hours at a time: 'Ma, Ma, Ma, Ma, Ma'.[304] They believed that what they called 'Ma-ism' was a radical new development in religious history, and that the worship of Mother – this particular mother, anyway – would be the future religion of humanity. I was not at all surprised to find that there was intense competitiveness and jealousy among her disciples, as if they were all vying with one another to be the favourite, if not the only, son. It was also noticeable that they tended to disparage other groups. In the same way that children will say, 'My daddy is much stronger/richer than your daddy,' or 'Our house is bigger than your house,' they would maintain that in comparison with their own guru, other gurus were insignificant.

Fortunately, I have known gurus who knew how to manage their followers in a much more healthy manner – particularly certain Tibetan gurus. A story about three great lamas I knew personally in Kalimpong will illustrate this. All three were eminent lamas of deep and genuine spiritual experience, and they all had many disciples. Though they all belonged to the predominantly 'Red Hat' tradition, their characters were very different. One wore a sheepskin robe, dyed red, and was always on the move, so that it was difficult to catch him. Another lived with his wife and son, and gave initiation to thousands of people – initiations that were said to be particularly powerful. The third was the scholarly head of an important monastery.

The story I was told by one of their disciples – and they had a number of disciples in common – was that a discussion had once arisen among the disciples as to which of the three gurus was the greatest. In the end, one of the bolder spirits plucked up courage and approached one of the gurus. He said, 'Look, there's been a lot of discussion as to how the three of you would place yourselves with respect to each other. We all have immense veneration for all three of you, but we would appreciate it if you could clear up this point: Which of you is the greatest? Who has gone furthest? Who is nearest to Nirvāṇa?' So the guru smiled and said, 'All right, I'll tell you. It is true that among us three there is one who is much more highly developed than the other two. But none of you will ever know which one that is.'[305]

A real guru does not fall into the role of a father figure. This is not to say that people do not need father-substitutes, at least for a while. Such a projection may be necessary for their psychological development. One must also allow that the function of the guru is analogous to that of the true father: the guru fulfils the same function on a spiritual level that the true father fulfils on the ordinary human level. But the guru is not a substitute for a father where the father has been lacking, or where he is still required.

Neither should a guru be taken for a problem-solver. This brings us to a distinction that I find it helpful to draw between a problem and a difficulty. The difference is that a difficulty can be overcome or resolved with effort, whereas a problem cannot. If you put a lot of effort into what I call a problem, you only make it more problematic. It's like finding a knot in a piece of string and pulling on the two ends in order to untie it. You can pull as hard as you like, but you'll only succeed in tightening the knot. The genuine guru may help people overcome their difficulties, but he will not attempt to grapple with their problems.

There are fundamentally two kinds of problem: doctrinal problems and personal, usually psychological, problems. The problems of Westerners tend to be of the second type, whereas in the East people's problems are often doctrinal – they want to resolve technical questions to do with Nirvāṇa, the *skandhas*, the *saṃskāras*, and so on. However, even such doctrinal problems are very often psychologically motivated, or at least psychologically oriented. One asks even the most abstract theoretical question ultimately for personal psychological reasons, though usually one is not conscious of this.

If you have a problem, it embodies a self-contradictory situation; it cannot be solved on its own terms. But if you bring it to your guru, you are in effect asking him or her to solve the problem on its own terms. For instance, a woman comes along in great distress, so upset that she can hardly speak. Eventually she tells her guru that she just can't live with her husband any longer. She's had enough. If she has to put up with any more, she'll go stark staring mad. She's just got to leave him. But her problem is that if she leaves her husband, she will have to leave her children too – because the children cannot be taken away from their father – and leaving her children is no less impossible than continuing to live with her husband. She will go mad if she has to stay with her husband, but she will also go mad if she has to leave her children. 'What am I to do?' she asks her guru expectantly.

Then somebody else comes along and complains of lack of energy: 'I'm always tired,' he says. 'I feel exhausted all the time. I can't do a thing. I don't seem able to work up any interest in anything; I just lie around all day like a limp, wet rag. I can watch a bit of television or listen to the radio, but that's it. I feel utterly drained all the time. There's just one thing that I know will help: meditation. I can get energy through meditation – I'm convinced of that.' So the guru says, 'Well, why don't you meditate?' And the unfortunate disciple replies wearily, 'I just don't have the energy.'

But if the guru has to send this person away with his problem still unresolved, there are still more problems waiting in the wings. To take yet another example, someone comes along and says that he just wants to be happy. That's all he asks from life. And he feels that he could be perfectly happy if only someone would give him a satisfactory reason for being happy. He has examined all the reasons offered by religions, philosophies, and friends, but none of them has proved truly convincing.

Can the guru do better? If anyone has the answer, surely the guru will. Surely a guru is there to provide the answers to the big problems. Of course, the guru knows quite well that every reason he can produce will be rejected as unsatisfactory. But still the man demands a reason.

If you asked any of these people what they are really looking for, all of them would say that they want to find a solution to their problem. That is why they have come to the guru. They firmly believe he can solve their problems if he chooses to do so. But, in fact, this is not the situation at all. What these people really want to do is defeat the guru. They present their problem in such a way that the guru cannot solve it without their consent or cooperation – which they have no intention of giving.

Such people are sometimes very cunning. Especially in the East they will very often approach the guru with a great show of devotion and humility, bearing presents, making offerings, bowing, and declaring their unshakeable faith in the guru. They say, 'I've taken this problem of mine to lots of other gurus, to all the most famous teachers and masters, and not one of them could solve it. But I've heard so much about you, and I'm sure that you are the one person who can.'

Only a guru who lacks experience, or isn't a true guru, will be taken in by all this. The true guru will see what is going on at once, and will refuse to play the role of problem-solver, even if, as is very likely, the person with the problem goes away disgruntled, and starts saying that the guru cannot be a true guru because he hasn't got the down-to-earth compassion to deal with his disciples' problems. Some gurus are rewarded with quite damaged reputations for refusing to play this sort of game.

So a guru is not the head of a religious group, or a teacher, or a father-substitute, or a problem-solver. This does not mean that he or she may not, from time to time, function in these ways, and in many others. A guru can function, for instance, as a physician, a psychotherapist, an artist, a poet, a musician, or even just a friend. But he or she will not identify with any of these roles.

The guru may be the head of a religious group, although this rarely happens, because the qualities that make a guru are not those that assist promotion within an ecclesiastical system. Much more often, particularly within the Buddhist sangha, the guru may be a teacher – that is, he or she may function outwardly as a teacher. But it remains important to distinguish the teacher from the guru as such. Some gurus may be teachers, but by no means all teachers are gurus. A guru may even function as a provisional father-substitute or problem-solver, but the emphasis is on 'provisional'. As soon as possible, he or she will discard this role and function as a guru.

But if the guru is none of these things, what is a guru? Aristotle said that there are many different ways of being wicked, but only one way of being good (which in the eyes of some people makes goodness seem rather dull).[306] One could also say that there are many misconceptions about the guru, but only one true conception. There is therefore much that can be said about what a guru is not, but comparatively little to be said about what he or she positively is. Of course, this doesn't mean that it is any less important. Indeed, from a spiritual point of view, the more important a thing is, the less there is to be said about it.

Perhaps, above all, the guru is one who stands on a higher level of being and consciousness than ourselves, who is more evolved, more developed, more – in a word – aware. Also, a guru is someone with whom we are in regular contact. This contact may take place at different levels. It may take place on a higher spiritual plane – that is, telepathically – as the direct contact of mind with mind. There may be contact between the guru and the disciple in dreams or during meditation. But for the ordinary disciple, it generally takes place on the physical plane – that is, on the ordinary social plane, in the ordinary way. The relatively undeveloped disciple will need regular and frequent physical contact with the guru. According to Eastern tradition, ideally he or she would be in day-to-day contact with the guru, even living under the same roof.

Contact between the guru and the disciple should be 'existential' – that is, there should be real communication between them – not just the sharing of thoughts or ideas or feelings or experiences, even spiritual experiences, but communication of being, or, if you like, action and interaction of being. The guru and the disciple need to be themselves as fully as possible in relation to each other. The guru's business is not to teach the disciple anything, but simply to be himself in relation to the disciple. Nor, as the disciple, is it your business to learn. You simply have to expose yourself to the being – and to the effect of the being – of the guru, and at the same time, be yourself in relation to him.

Spiritual communication, like integration, can be thought of as being of two kinds: 'horizontal' and 'vertical'. Horizontal communication takes place between two people who are on more or less the same level of being and consciousness. Because their states of mind fluctuate from day to day, sometimes one of them will be in a better state of mind than the other, but the next day it may be the other way round. Vertical communication, on the other hand, takes place between people one of whom is on a consistently higher level than the other, quite apart from any ups and downs. It is such vertical communication that takes place between guru and disciple.

In all communication, whether horizontal or vertical, there is mutual modification of being. In the case of horizontal communication, in the course of communication anything one-sided or unbalanced in one's nature is corrected. People who really communicate gradually develop a similarity of outlook, responding to things in the same spirit; they have progressively more in common. At the same time, paradoxical as it may seem, they become more truly themselves.

Suppose, for example, a very rational person were to engage in true communication with a very emotional person. If they sustained this communication long enough, the emotional person would become more rational, and the rational person more emotional – each rubbing off on the other. At the same time, if you are the rational person (to take that example) you do not just have emotionality added to you from without. Through communicating with the emotional person, you are enabled to develop your own undeveloped emotionality which has been there all the time (as it were) beneath the surface. A quality emerges that was there but not active. The communication has simply enabled you to become more yourself, more whole, more complete. And it's the same, obviously, if you are, at least to begin with, the emotional one of the two.

Vertical communication is different. The disciple grows in the direction of the guru's higher level of being and consciousness, but the guru does not become correspondingly more like the disciple. The principle of mutual modification of being does not mean that the guru slips back in his development as a result of his communication with someone less developed. He does not meet the disciple halfway, as it were. In the intensity of his or her communication with the guru, the disciple is in a sense compelled to evolve. He or she has no choice, unless they break off the relationship altogether, and a real disciple cannot even do that. It is said that the true disciple is like a bulldog puppy. When offered a towel, the puppy will snap at it and not let go, even if the towel was lifted off the ground with his jaws still attached to it. The true disciple has that sort of tenacity.

As a result of his vertical communication with the disciple, the guru also grows spiritually. The only guru who doesn't do this is a Buddha, a fully and perfectly Enlightened one, and even among gurus a Buddha is extremely rare. It is sometimes said in Tantric circles that disciples are necessary to a guru's further development, that nothing helps a guru so much as having a really good disciple – not an obedient, docile disciple, but one who really engages in communication, one who is really trying to grow. A good disciple may give the guru quite a lot of trouble, sometimes more trouble than all the other disciples put together. It also occasionally happens that the disciple overtakes the guru, and a reversal of roles takes place. This situation is less problematic than it might seem from the outside, because the relationship is not one of authority or power, but of love and friendship.

So is a guru necessary? Well, to grow spiritually without any contact with a guru is extremely difficult. Generalizing, one might say that for most people spiritual growth does not take place without at least two factors being present: the experience of suffering, and contact with a more highly developed person or persons. Why? Because personal relationships and real communication are necessary to human development. Not only that – we need real communication that includes a vertical element. Through communication with our friends, we develop horizontally – we become more whole, more ourselves. But most people seem to need communication with a guru to enable them to rise to a higher level of being and consciousness. Just as a child develops into an adult mainly through contact with his or her parents, regular contact with at least one person who is more highly developed than we are is necessary for our spiritual development. Not that it is absolutely impossible to make progress without being in contact with such a person, but that kind of contact certainly speeds up and intensifies the whole process.

But if a guru is necessary, how do you go about choosing one? How do you know whether someone is more highly evolved than you are? Obviously, it is important not to make any mistake in this matter. The problem is that it is very difficult indeed to know if someone is really more advanced – perhaps impossible, without prolonged contact. Some gurus in the East say not only that it is impossible for the disciple to choose the guru, but that it is quite presumptuous for the disciple to think that he can do so, or that he can know whether someone is more developed than himself. What actually happens, they say, is that the guru chooses the disciple. You may think that you are choosing a guru, but in fact the only choice you are capable of making is of a religious group (with the guru as its head), or a religious teacher, or a father-substitute or problem-solver. You are not choosing a guru as such, because you are not equipped to see who is of greater spiritual attainment.

As a would-be disciple, what are you to do? All you can do is make as much progress as possible by yourself so that you can recognize and make contact with a spiritual community (as distinct from a religious group). Then you must hope that some member of that community will take you on as a friend, or refer you to somebody else who can. In any case, you should always be ready and receptive for the advent of the guru.

In a way, the guru cannot be overvalued. Nothing can be more valuable than the person who helps you to develop spiritually. All the same, it is true to say that in the East the guru often tends in a sense to be overvalued, while in the West he is usually undervalued. What can happen in the East is that a false and inflated value is attached to the guru. People in India sometimes say that the guru is God. This is asserted not just as a figure of speech, but quite literally. If you are sitting in front of the guru, you are not just looking at a human being, seated on a cushion on the floor. You're sitting in front of God – in fact, all the gods rolled into one, the all-powerful, the all-knowing himself. He may look just like an ordinary human being, but he knows everything that is going on in the whole universe, including everything going on in your mind. He can read your thoughts like an open book. If you've got a problem, you don't have to tell him – he knows already. He can do anything he likes. He can bless you, give you riches, promotion, fame, children, all with just a word of blessing. He can give you Enlightenment if he wants to. It is all in his hands – it's all the 'grace of the guru', as they say.

All the disciple has to offer is faith in the guru, faith that the guru is God. If the disciple only has enough of this kind of faith, the guru can work miracles on his behalf. Such faith is therefore regarded as of the very greatest importance. There are, of course, little difficulties. It sometimes happens that the guru appears not to know something, or to forget something you have told him, and you may get a bit upset by this. But the true disciple isn't bothered at all because he knows that these apparently human limitations and failings are tests of faith. The guru is only pretending to have slips of the mind to see if your faith is still firm and sound, just as a potter taps a pot after it's been baked, to see whether or not there's a crack in it.

It is no wonder that over the years the disciple comes to inhabit a fantasy world in which whatever happens is seen to do so on account of the guru's 'grace' and the guru's will. If the guru isn't careful, he may come to inhabit this fantasy world too, especially if he isn't a real guru. After all, it isn't easy to escape such a fantasy world if you yourself are at the centre of it. If someone comes and tells you that their child was sick and has now recovered due to your blessing, you may not be inclined to dispute that interpretation, even if you hadn't given the child a moment's thought.

The problem from the guru's point of view is that sooner or later it will dawn on certain of his more perceptive disciples that he isn't really God. While he may have a deep level of insight and spiritual experience, he also has some quite human limitations. Perceiving this, they are likely to conclude that he isn't a true guru, and go off to look for someone who is a true guru, someone who *is* God. If they do that, the same thing will inevitably happen all over again. They will start noticing little discrepancies, get disillusioned, and see that this guru too is 'only' a human being after all. And so the merry-go-round continues.

This happens among Buddhists as well to some extent. A Tibetan friend of mine, a lama and guru living in Kalimpong, recalled that when he first arrived there, the local Nepalese Buddhists used to flock to see him, bringing him wonderful offerings and eager to take initiations from him. But after a few years they got a bit tired of him. They continued to come to pay their respects, but he was amused to observe that they didn't bring quite such big offerings as before. Then a new lama arrived on the scene (he was a friend of the first one) and everybody abandoned my friend to get their new initiations from the new lama – to the amusement of both lamas. Eventually, as the Chinese communists seized power in Tibet, more and more gurus started to arrive in town, which was very bewildering for the local community. No sooner had they identified a supremely powerful guru and rushed to make him offerings, than another one arrived, who – according to some people – was even more eminent and accomplished. In the end they must have run through perhaps twenty gurus, looking for the 'real' one.

Clearly, the guru is overvalued in this manner in the East because he is regarded as an idealized parent figure: all-knowing, all-powerful, infinitely loving and tolerant. The disciple in such cases wants to adopt an attitude of infantile dependence. Gurus are usually very popular in India, but there is one thing demanded of them, regardless of almost anything else: they must always be kind and affectionate, soft-spoken and gentle. What they teach and how they live are side-issues by comparison.

In the West we have traditionally gone to the opposite extreme. Here, far from overvaluing the guru, we have hardly any concept of the guru at all. This is no doubt largely due to the influence of Christianity. On the one hand you have belief in God with all his various attributes, and on the other you have submission to the head of the particular religious group to which you belong, your ecclesiastical superior, but there seems to be no room for the guru in the true sense.

The gurus who do appear – who may eventually be identified as saints – are usually subject to the rule of the ecclesiastical authorities. In medieval times, even a great saint sometimes had to submit to a bad pope. Perhaps that didn't do the saint much harm, but it was bad for the pope, and for the Church as a whole. However, we must not imagine that the Christian tradition is the only spiritual tradition the West has ever known. Nor should we accept the assumption that the concept of the guru in the Eastern sense is alien to the Western mentality. There were certainly gurus in ancient Greece and Rome – for example Plato, who maintained a sort of school or academy, Pythagoras, who founded spiritual communities, Apollonius of Tyana, and above all perhaps, Plotinus. From Porphyry's life of Plotinus, especially the description of his later life in Rome, one gets the definite impression of a sort of spiritual community, set up more along the lines of an Indian ashram than in a manner typical of the kind of institution one might think of as characteristic of the later Roman Empire.[307]

Such great figures of classical times were gurus in the true sense of the term. And in modern post-Christian times there are signs that the importance of the guru is again beginning to be appreciated in the West, despite our democratic and egalitarian prejudices, our modern belief that no one should be seen as better than anybody else. Even in modern cultures so apparently hostile to the possibility of spiritual development, there are signs that people are beginning to appreciate the significance of those who are more highly developed than the average person.

As Buddhists, we have to follow a middle way. We have to recognize above all that we are capable of evolving from our present state of being and consciousness to a more fully developed degree of self-consciousness and even to a realization of transcendental consciousness, leading to what, without really being able to understand it, we can only call absolute consciousness. In order to do this, we have also to recognize that different human beings are at different stages of this great process of spiritual development. Some are lower down than we are, while others are higher up, even a great deal higher up. We have to recognize that those who are higher up in the scale of the evolution of humanity are in a position to help us, and that we will develop through communication with them. It is gurus in this sense whom we need to recognize as being superior. The kind of guru we don't need is one to whom we give an unrealistically inflated value, and onto whom we project our desire for an idealized father-figure. It is a great mistake to expect from a guru what we can only get, ultimately, from ourselves.

The Buddha did not ask anybody to regard him as a god or as God. He never asked anybody to have faith – much less to have absolute faith – in him. In fact, this is a very important aspect of Buddhism. The Buddha never said, 'You must believe in me, and believe what I say, if you want to be saved, or if you want to realize your own true nature.' Again and again in the Buddhist scriptures he is presented as saying, 'Let any reasonable man come to me, one who is willing to learn; I will teach him the Dharma.'[308] All he asks is that we should be rational and open-minded. All he requires is reasonable and receptive human contact. He seems to have been quite convinced that he could introduce anyone to the spiritual life without making any appeal for absolute faith and devotion, but purely by rational and empirical means. On this basis alone he could awaken anyone to the truth that the path to Enlightenment is the most worthwhile thing to which as human beings we can possibly devote ourselves.

from *What is the Sangha?*

6. SPIRITUAL HIERARCHY

It is this kind of spontaneous emotion that creates the spiritual hierarchy: a spontaneous feeling of devotion when one encounters something higher; a spontaneous overflowing of compassion when one is confronted by other people's distress or difficulty; and a spontaneous welling up of love and sympathy when one is among one's peers.

According to the Pāli canon, just after the Buddha became Enlightened – or rather, while he was still exploring the different facets of that experience which we usually refer to as though it were a single undifferentiated occurrence – he became aware of a very powerful aspiration. He knew that he had to find somebody or something that he could revere and respect. His fundamental impulse, it seems, so soon after his experience of Enlightenment, was to reverence: to look up, not down. After some reflection he realized that, having attained Enlightenment, there was now no person he could look up to, because no one else had attained what he had attained. But he saw that he could look up to the Dharma, the great spiritual law by virtue of which he had attained Enlightenment. He therefore decided to devote himself to reverencing the Dharma.[309]

This episode cannot be called to mind too often, especially because it is so contrary to the modern spirit of not wanting to honour or be indebted to anybody or anything. We are sometimes only too willing to look down on others, but we are unwilling to look up, and even feel resentful if others appear to be superior to us in any way. We are generally happy enough to admire and even venerate the superior physical strength, quickness of eye, and will to win of the athlete, but very often we are unwilling to respect or reverence qualities that are superior from a spiritual point of view.

Someone once made the point that in any culture where a particular principle is of such fundamental importance that it is taken for granted, no word for that principle exists in the local language. One quite interesting reflection of this is to be found in the fact that in Buddhism there is no traditional term that corresponds to 'tolerance'. It's as though in order to appreciate the tolerance of Buddhism you have to be able to look at it from the standpoint of a tradition or culture that is *not* tolerant. Buddhism traditionally does not think of itself as tolerant.

It doesn't promote that concept, doesn't recommend itself as being a tolerant religion; it has never attained that sort of self-consciousness with regard to its own nature.

It is the same with hierarchy. Buddhism is traditionally saturated in it, to the extent that Buddhists are almost unable to step aside and see Buddhism as hierarchical. The very fact that the spiritual path consists of a series of steps or stages shows how deeply the hierarchical principle is embedded within Buddhism. In fact, the spiritual life itself is inseparable from the hierarchical principle. There is a hierarchy of wisdoms: the wisdom you hear or read about (*śruta-mayī-prajñā*), the wisdom you cultivate through reflection (*cintā-mayī-prajñā*), and, as the highest form, the wisdom cultivated in meditation (*bhāvanā-mayī-prajñā*).[310] There is a hierarchy of the different levels of the cosmos, from the *kāmaloka* up to the *rūpaloka* and the *arūpaloka*.[311] And of course there is a hierarchy of persons: both the *ariya-puggalas* of the Theravāda and the bodhisattvas of the Mahāyāna are organized into hierarchies.[312] It would seem that the concept of hierarchy is absolutely fundamental to Buddhism; without it, Buddhism as we know it can hardly exist. And for that very reason, perhaps, there is no traditional word or concept for hierarchy. There are certain words that express the idea of a sequence of increasing value within a particular context, but there is no overall, generalized term covering all the different, more specific hierarchies.

But when as Westerners we approach Buddhism from the outside, as it were, its hierarchical nature certainly strikes us, and some people have to struggle with this in a way that Eastern Buddhists, with different cultural and psychological conditioning, do not. After many years as a Buddhist myself, however, my own difficulty lies in trying to sympathize with the non- or anti-hierarchical concept of equality, which seems very limited and restricting. It would seem to me that inequality is one of the most obvious things about life.

Of course, there are true hierarchies and false ones. In Europe in the eighteenth century, especially in France, the social and ecclesiastical hierarchy was completely false; it did not correspond to any facts or realities. For example, court favourites with barely the faintest pretence to piety were appointed to bishoprics. When the name of a certain courtier was proposed to Louis xv for Archbishop of Paris, he demurred: 'No, no, the Archbishop of Paris should at least believe in God!' – which shows how far things had gone. In the case of poor

Louis XVI, who was guillotined, his real interest was in making locks, and that is what he spent most of his time doing. He had no idea about government; in other words, he wasn't really a king in the true sense of the word.

Eventually there was the great upheaval of the French Revolution and the false hierarchy was overthrown in both church and state. But in negating the false hierarchy people asserted not true hierarchy but no hierarchy, or anti-hierarchy: hence the famous slogan 'Liberty, Equality, Fraternity'. We have inherited a great deal from that period, politically, socially, intellectually, and spiritually. In particular, we have inherited an anti-hierarchical tendency – opposition not just to false hierarchies but to hierarchies as such. That is unfortunate. One can understand people in revolutionary France being unable or unwilling to distinguish between genuine hierarchy and false hierarchy. They didn't want to give a false hierarchy any reason for existing at all. But in calmer times we shouldn't have to reject the very idea of hierarchy in that way.

It is sometimes said that everybody is as good as everybody else 'as a person'. But this assumption is questionable. It is not as though the terms 'person' and 'individual' refer to something static; they suggest a degree of development. And some people are more developed than others; that is to say, some are better as persons or individuals than others.

The point of such an assertion of hierarchy is not to put people in their place. Quite the opposite is true, because this hierarchy is not fixed. All that matters is that everybody should be encouraged to grow, and that none of us should accept some fixed idea of our value as individuals. Our value consists in the effort we make at the level we are at rather than in some fixed position we hold in the hierarchy. If we have done our best, there can be no criticism of us.

It does seem that competition helps people to give of their best, achieve their best, *be* their best. In one of his discourses, the Buddha spoke of each of his more intimate disciples in turn, declaring who was best at what. And, it seems, each of them could indeed be found to be the best at something or other. One was the best at giving talks, another was the best meditator, another was the best at going for alms. Everybody excelled at something.[313]

Still, the word hierarchy is very unpopular these days, and the dictionary definition – 'a body of ecclesiastical rulers' – does nothing to make the term more appealing. But in its original sense, hierarchy meant something like an embodiment, in a number of different people, of different degrees of manifestation of reality. So one can speak, for instance, of a hierarchy of living forms – some lower, expressing or manifesting less reality, others higher, expressing or manifesting more reality. There is a continuous hierarchy of living forms from amoebas right up to human beings – the higher the level, the greater the degree of reality.

And there is another hierarchy of living forms: the hierarchy from the unenlightened human being right up to the Enlightened Buddha. This corresponds to what in other contexts I have described as the Higher Evolution. Just as the unenlightened human being embodies or manifests more reality, more truth, than the amoeba, in the same way the Enlightened human being embodies or manifests more reality in his or her life and work, and even speech, than does the unenlightened person. The Enlightened person is like a clear window through which the light of reality shines, through which that light can be seen almost as it is. Or one can say that he or she is like a crystal or diamond concentrating and reflecting that light.

Between the unenlightened human being and the Enlightened one, the Buddha, there are a number of intermediate degrees, embodied in different people at different stages of spiritual development. Most people are still short of Enlightenment, to a greater or lesser extent, but at the same time they are not wholly unenlightened. They stand somewhere between the unenlightened state and the state of full Enlightenment, and thus make up the spiritual hierarchy, the higher reaches of which can be referred to as the bodhisattva hierarchy. We may have an appreciation of the intensity of a bodhisattva's aspiration and commitment to the spiritual life, but even among bodhisattvas there are degrees of spiritual attainment.

The principle of spiritual hierarchy is very important. As human beings we are related to ultimate reality both directly and indirectly. We are related to reality directly in the sense that in the very depths of our being is something which all the time connects us with reality, a kind of golden thread which, though it may be gossamer thin, is always there. In some people that thread has become a little thicker, a little stronger, in others it has strengthened almost into a rope, while in those who are Enlightened there is no need for a connecting thread at all, because there is no difference between the depth of their being and the depth of reality itself. So we are directly connected in the depth of our being with reality, although most of us don't realize it. Though we don't see that thin golden thread shining in the midst of the darkness within us, nevertheless, it is there.

We are related *in*directly to reality in two ways. In the first place, we are related to those things that represent a lower degree of manifestation of reality than ourselves. We are related to nature: rocks, water, fire, the different forms of vegetable life, and the forms of animal life that are lower in the scale of evolution than ourselves. This relationship may be compared with seeing a light through a thick veil; sometimes the veil seems to be so thick – especially in the case of material forms – that we are unable to see the light at all.

We are indirectly related to reality also through those forms that represent a higher degree of manifestation of reality than ourselves. This is like seeing a light through a *thin* veil – a veil that seems at times as fine as gossamer, and even, just occasionally, parts and falls away to allow the light of reality to be seen directly, as it is, without any mediation at all. We could say that this thin veil, through which we see the light of reality, is the spiritual hierarchy, especially the bodhisattva hierarchy.

It is of the utmost importance for us to be in contact with people who are at least a little more spiritually advanced than we are ourselves, through whom the light of reality shines a little more clearly than it shines through us. Such people are known traditionally in Buddhism as our spiritual friends, our *kalyāṇa mitras*, and they are more important to us than even a Buddha would be. If we happened to have the opportunity to meet a Buddha, we probably wouldn't be able to make much of the encounter, or even realize the nature of the person in front of us. We are likely to benefit much more from contact with those who are just a little more spiritually developed than we are.

In this connection there is a beautiful passage in that great Tibetan spiritual classic, the *Jewel Ornament of Liberation* of Gampopa. Speaking of spiritual friends, Gampopa says:

> Since at the beginning of our career it is impossible to be in touch with the Buddhas or with bodhisattvas living on a high level of spirituality, we have to meet with ordinary human beings as spiritual friends. As soon as the darkness caused by our deeds has

lightened, we can find bodhisattvas on a high level of spirituality. Then when we have risen above the Great Preparatory Path we can find the *nirmāṇakāya* of the Buddha. Finally, as soon as we live on a high spiritual level we can meet with the *sambhogakāya* as a spiritual friend.

Should you ask, who among these four is our greatest benefactor, the reply is that in the beginning of our career when we are still living imprisoned by our deeds and emotions, we will not even see so much as the face of a superior spiritual friend. Instead we will have to seek an ordinary human being who can illumine the path we have to follow with the light of his counsel, whereafter we shall meet superior ones. Therefore the greatest benefactor is a spiritual friend in the form of an ordinary human being.[314]

We can't get far on our own. If week after week, year after year, we had no meditation classes to go to, if we never met another person who was interested in Buddhism, if we couldn't even get any books – because reading books of the right kind is also a sort of *satsaṅgh* – if we were entirely on our own, we wouldn't get far, however great our initial enthusiasm and sincerity. We get encouragement, inspiration, and moral support from associating with others who have similar ideals and who are following a similar way of life. This is especially the case when we associate with those who are a bit more spiritually advanced than we are, or, to put it more simply, who are just a bit more human than most people are – a bit more aware, a bit kinder, a bit more faithful, and so on.

In practice, this means that we should try to be open and receptive towards those whom we can recognize to be above us in the spiritual hierarchy, those who clearly have greater insight, understanding, sympathy, compassion, and so on. We should be ready to receive from them, just as a flower opens its petals to receive the light and warmth of the sun. As for those who are, as far as we can tell (and bearing in mind we might be mistaken), below us in the spiritual hierarchy, our attitude should be one of generosity, kindliness, and helpfulness – giving them encouragement, making them feel welcome, and so on. And with regard to those who seem to be roughly on the same level as ourselves, our attitude should be one of mutuality, sharing, reciprocity.

These three attitudes correspond to the three great positive emotions of the Buddhist spiritual life. First of all, there is *śraddhā*. This is often translated as 'faith' or 'belief', but it really means a sort of devotion, a receptivity to the light streaming down – as it were – from above. Secondly, there is compassion, which is a giving out of what we have received from above to those who are lower in the spiritual hierarchy. And thirdly, there is love or *mettā*, which we share with all those who are on the same level as ourselves.

In *The Jewel Ornament of Liberation*, Gampopa goes on to say: 'The Enlightenment of a Buddha is obtained by serving spiritual friends' – a strong statement, to say the least, and possibly not a palatable one.[315] The whole idea of service is rather alien to us. We are familiar with the idea of devoting ourselves to caring for our children, perhaps, or looking after our parents when they are old, but it is not always easy for us to transpose that feeling to other situations. This is very much connected with the collapse of the idea of spiritual hierarchy, or any kind of hierarchy. If we are all equal, why should you do something for someone else? Why shouldn't he or she do it for you? Or why can't you do it on an exchange basis? 'I'll do it for you today, if you'll do it for me tomorrow.'

To put oneself in the position of serving someone is to acknowledge that the person one is serving is better than oneself in some respects. It is this that many people are unwilling to do. But unless one can make that acknowledgement, one cannot grow spiritually. In 'serving spiritual friends' one grows to become more like them – and then one finds that there are other spiritual friends to be served. Even when one becomes an advanced bodhisattva, one finds that the universe is full of Buddhas to whom one can give devoted service. There is always someone whom one can serve.

Gampopa also says that one should 'think of a spiritual friend as the Buddha'. The idea of this is not to burden one's friend – as an ordinary human being – with the idea that he or she is a Buddha, or to try to convince oneself that they are a Buddha when one's reason tells one that they are not. One need not regard everything they do or say as the action of a Buddha. What is important is that, while one's spiritual friend may be very far from being a Buddha, he or she is at least a little more spiritually developed than one is oneself. It's as though behind one's friend stands his or her own teacher, and behind that teacher another one, back and back until, behind them all, stands the Buddha. So the Buddha is shining, as it were, through all these people, who are of varying degrees of translucency.

At least, this is one way of interpreting the advice to 'think of a spiritual friend as the Buddha'. However, Gampopa, who belonged primarily to the Tantric tradition, being a guru of the Kagyu school of Tibet, as well as one of Milarepa's main disciples, might well have intended this statement to be taken quite literally. Fundamental to the Vajrayāna is the idea that each of the Three Jewels has its esoteric aspect. And esoteric as it is, this notion is a profoundly practical one. The Vajrayānists said, in effect, that the Buddha's Enlightenment, his teaching of the truth he had discovered, and the growth of the circle of his Enlightened followers – these Three Jewels which have been revered down the ages of Buddhist tradition – all happened a very long time ago. We ourselves can have no direct contact with them, and cannot benefit from their direct influence. We have to find, in effect, our own Three Jewels. The question is where to find them. The answer the Vajrayāna came up with was that one should regard one's Dharma teacher, one's guru, as the Buddha, the exemplar of Enlightenment as far as one is personally concerned. Similarly, one should see one's *yidam*, the Buddha or bodhisattva upon whom one meditates, as the embodiment of the truth itself. And the esoteric Sangha refuge is the company of *ḍākinīs*, with whom, according to Vajrayāna tradition, one can be in living contact. In one's own particular context the guru or teacher stands for the Buddha, and even – in the Tantric context – *is* the Buddha.

Another way of approaching Gampopa's maxim is to reflect on the teaching that every human being is potentially a Buddha. According to some Buddhist schools, if one could only look hard enough, one would see that every human being *is* in fact a Buddha, whether they realize it or not. In the case of a spiritual friend, since he or she has become at least a little Buddha-like, it is easier to see in him or her the fundamental Buddha-nature that we all possess.

Gampopa goes on to recommend not just that we should serve our spiritual friends, but that we should please them. That is, we should give them cause to rejoice in the qualities they perceive developing in us. If you please a spiritual friend and they please you, both of you will be in this state of sympathetic joy (*muditā*), and communication will be established and will flow. They will be able to teach, and you to learn.

In an interesting passage in the Great Chapter of the *Sutta-Nipāta*, a certain Brahmin is not sure whether the Buddha is in fact the Buddha, the Enlightened One, or whether he is just a great man, a 'superman' or *mahāpurisa*. But it seems that this Brahmin has heard of a way to find out. He has heard that the Buddhas reveal their true self, their true nature, if they are praised.[316] Praising is related to pleasing – a sort of pleasing in words. If you praise a Buddha, he cannot but show his true nature. And conversely, even a Buddha cannot show his true nature unless the situation is positive enough to allow him to do so.

It is much the same, on another level, with a spiritual friend. To please him or her is to make communication more effective, whereas to displease him or her is to set up a barrier to communication. 'Pleasing' here doesn't mean gratifying someone's ego, but relating to them in an open, free, sincere, genuine, and warm way, showing *mettā*, *muditā* or 'sympathetic joy' – that is, joy in the virtues of others – and equanimity. If you please a spiritual friend, it makes it easier for them to communicate with you, for their true nature to emerge. And you are the one who benefits from that; it is you who gains in the long run.

Although I have referred to those who are 'higher up' and those who are 'lower down', there is no question of any official grading. If we start even thinking in terms of being higher or lower than other people, we have failed to grasp the nature of spiritual hierarchy. Everything should be natural and spontaneous; the appropriate emotion, whether of devotion, compassion, or love, should flow forth unselfconsciously and spontaneously in response to whomsoever we meet.

I used to go with Tibetan friends, both lamas and lay people, to visit monasteries and temples, and it was interesting to see their responses when they entered such places. When we in the West go to a place of worship, a great cathedral or something like that, we may not know quite what to do, how to respond, what to feel. But when I used to visit temples with my Tibetan friends, there was none of that sort of confusion or inner conflict. As soon as they saw an image of the Buddha, one could almost see the feelings of devotion and faith and reverence welling up within them. They put their hands to their foreheads and often prostrated themselves flat on the ground three times. They did this completely unselfconsciously; it was natural to them because of the context in which they had grown up (a context which has now, of course, largely been shattered).

It is this kind of spontaneous emotion that creates the spiritual hierarchy: a spontaneous feeling of devotion when one encounters something higher; a spontaneous overflowing of compassion when one is confronted by other people's distress or difficulty; and a spontaneous welling up of love and sympathy when one is among one's peers. These are the emotions that should influence the whole Buddhist community. People in such a community are like roses in different stages of growth all blooming on a single bush, or like a spiritual family of which the Buddha is the head and the great bodhisattvas the elder brothers and sisters. In such a family, everybody gets what they need; the younger people are cared for by the older ones, everybody gives what they can, and the whole family is pervaded by a spirit of joy, freedom, warmth, and light.

The bodhisattva hierarchy concentrates all this into a single focal point of dazzling intensity. It has its own degrees, its own radiant figures, at higher and ever higher stages of spiritual development, right up to Buddhahood itself.

from *The Bodhisattva Ideal*

7. GRATITUDE

The newly Enlightened Buddha was a grateful Buddha, an idea which is perhaps unfamiliar to us.

Usually, influenced by books or even Buddhist scriptures, we think of the Buddha's Enlightenment as having taken place at a particular time, roughly 2,500 years ago – which, of course, in a sense, it did. We also tend to think of it as having taken place on a particular day, at a particular hour, even at a particular minute, at the instant when the Buddha broke through from the conditioned to the Unconditioned.

But a little reflection, and a little further study of the scriptures, will show us that it didn't happen quite like that. Here we can consider the distinction between the Path of Vision and the Path of Transformation – a distinction usually made in connection with the Noble Eightfold Path. On the Path of Vision one has an experience of the transcendental, a profound insight into the true nature of reality that goes far beyond any merely intellectual understanding. This insight comes gradually to pervade and transform every aspect of one's being – one's body, speech, and mind, to use the traditional Buddhist classification. It transforms all our activities. It transforms one, in fact, into a very different kind of person – a wiser and more compassionate person. This process is known as the Path of Transformation.[317]

Something like this takes place in the spiritual life of each and every one of us. And we see the same sort of thing happening, on a much more exalted plane, in the case of the Buddha. The Buddha's vision is unlimited, absolute, and all-embracing, and his transformation of body, speech, and mind can therefore be described as total, even infinite. But all the same, it did take a little time for this final transformation to take place. Buddhist tradition speaks of the Buddha as spending seven – or nine – weeks (accounts vary) in the vicinity of the bodhi tree, the tree beneath which he attained Enlightenment. In the course of each of those weeks something of importance happened. We could say that the Buddha's experience of Enlightenment started percolating through his being, until by the end of the last week (whether the seventh or the ninth) the process of transformation was at last complete.

One week a great storm arose, and the Buddha was sheltered from the rain, so the story goes, by the serpent king Mucalinda, who spread his sevenfold hood over the Buddha's head as he meditated. Another week, Brahmā Sahāmpati, the ruler of a thousand worlds, requested the Buddha to teach the Dharma, saying that at least some of the beings in the world would be capable of understanding it, their eyes being covered with only a little dust.[318] And the Buddha, out of compassion, agreed to teach.

But here I want to focus on another episode, one that occurred quite early in the period after the Buddha's attainment of Enlightenment – during the second week, according to one source. According to this tradition, the Buddha stood at a distance to the north-east of the bodhi tree and remained for one week gazing at the tree with unblinking eyes.[319]

Centuries later, a stupa was erected on that very spot, to mark the place where the Buddha had gazed at the bodhi tree. It was known as 'the stupa of unblinking eyes', and Xuanzang, the great Chinese pilgrim, saw it when he visited India in the seventh century CE. In the memoirs he dictated to his disciples in his old age back in China, he described it thus:

On the left side of the road, to the north of the place where the Buddha walked, is a large stone on the top of which, as it stands in a great vihara, is a figure of the Buddha with his eyes raised and looking up. Here in former times the Buddha sat for seven days contemplating the bodhi tree.[320]

He says 'sat' but the source text says 'stood'. Perhaps the Buddha didn't literally stand or sit there for a whole week, but we may take it that he gazed at the bodhi tree for a very long time. And the source text makes it clear why. He did it because he was grateful to the tree for having sheltered him at the time of his attainment of Enlightenment. According to the scriptures, the Buddha demonstrated gratitude in other ways too. After Brahmā Sahāmpati had made his request that the Buddha should teach the Dharma, and the Buddha had decided to do so, he then wondered to whom he should teach it. He thought first of his two old teachers, from whom he had learned to meditate not long after he left home. Finding their teaching insufficient, he had left them, but they had been helpful to him at a particular stage of his career, and after his Enlightenment he remembered that. It's as though he had a spiritual debt to them that he wanted to repay. But he quickly realized that his old teachers were dead.

He then thought of his five former companions. They too were people he knew from an earlier period of his spiritual quest, from the time of his experiments in asceticism. After leaving his first two teachers, he started practising extreme self-mortification, in the company of five friends who became disciples of his and admired him greatly because he had gone further in his self-mortification than anybody else at that time. But eventually the Buddha-to-be saw the futility of asceticism, realized that this was not the way to Enlightenment, and gave it up. When he started taking solid food again, just a few handfuls of rice to sustain himself, the five ascetics left him in disgust, saying, 'The śramaṇa Gautama has returned to luxurious living.' But this parting was not what remained in the Buddha's mind. Having realized that his two old teachers were dead, he reflected, 'The five ascetics were of great help to me when I was practising the penances. I would like to preach the Dharma to them.'[321] So this is what he did. He went to them, he taught them, and eventually they too realized the Truth that he had realized. And he did this out of gratitude.

So the newly Enlightened Buddha was a *grateful* Buddha, an idea which is perhaps unfamiliar to us. We think of the all-wise Buddha, the compassionate Buddha, the resourceful Buddha, but we don't usually think of the grateful Buddha. But one of the very first things the Buddha did after his attainment of Enlightenment was show his gratitude to those who had helped him. He was even grateful to a tree.

This incident gives us food for thought. The Buddhist scriptures contain a number of references that show that the Buddha and his disciples regarded trees and stones not as inanimate dead matter, but as living things. They would even have a relationship with them; they would talk to a tree or a flower, or rather to the spirit – the *devatā*, as they called it – inhabiting it. It is surely much better to have this attitude, to be an animist, than to think that trees and flowers and rocks and stones are just dead matter. The Buddha certainly didn't think in that way, and it was therefore possible for him to be grateful even to a tree.

It is not surprising, given that this was the Buddha's attitude, that gratitude finds a place in his ethical and spiritual teaching. It is found, for example, in the *Maṅgala Sutta*, the 'Sutta of Blessings or Auspicious Signs'. This short *sutta*, found in the Pāli canon, is often regarded as summarizing the whole duty, as we may call it, of the serious-minded Buddhist, and it enumerates gratitude as one of the auspicious signs. According to the *Maṅgala Sutta*, it is a sign that you are making spiritual progress.[322]

But what is gratitude? To find this out, we can turn to the dictionaries – and, of course, we should be very grateful to the makers of dictionaries. I am personally very grateful to Samuel Johnson. His historic dictionary is always at my elbow in my study, and when I am writing I sometimes consult it several times a day. Johnson defines gratitude as 'duty to benefactors' and as 'desire to return benefits'. Coming to more modern dictionaries, the *Concise Oxford* says, 'being thankful; readiness to show appreciation for and to return kindness', and *Collins* has 'a feeling of thankfulness or appreciation, as for gifts or favours'.

These definitions of the English word give us some understanding of what gratitude is, but from a Buddhist point of view we need to go further, and look at the Pāli word being translated as gratitude: *kataññutā*. *Kata* means that which has been done, especially that which has been done to oneself; and *aññutā* means knowing or recognizing; so *kataññutā* means knowing and recognizing what has been done to one for one's benefit. These definitions indicate that the connotation of the Pāli word is rather different from that of its English translation. The connotation of the English word gratitude is emotional – we speak of *feeling* grateful. But the connotation of *kataññutā* is rather more intellectual. It makes it clear that what we call gratitude involves an element of *knowledge*: knowledge of what has been done to us or for us for our benefit. If we do not know that something has benefited us, we will not feel grateful.

The Buddha knew that the bodhi tree had sheltered him, and he knew that his five former companions had been helpful to him, so he felt gratitude towards them. Not only that: he gave expression to that feeling. He acted upon it by spending a whole week simply gazing at the bodhi tree, and then by going in search of his five former companions so that he could communicate to them the truth that he had discovered. The important implication is that it is a perfectly natural thing to feel grateful for benefits we have received.

But the benefit has to be recognized as a benefit. If we don't feel that someone or something actually has benefited us, we won't feel grateful to them or to it. This suggests that we have to understand what is truly beneficial, what has really helped us to grow and develop as human beings. We also have to know who or what has benefited us, and remember that they have done so – otherwise no feeling of gratitude is possible.

In Buddhism there are traditionally three principal objects of gratitude: our parents, our teachers, and our spiritual friends. We have already considered some aspects of each of these relationships. Here I want to reflect a little on gratitude in relation to each of them.

I came back to England after spending twenty years uninterruptedly in the East studying, practising, and teaching the Dharma. When I came back, I found that much had changed. Quite a few things struck me as unusual – I hadn't encountered them in India, or at least not to the same extent – and one thing that definitely surprised me was finding out how many people, at least among those I knew, were on bad terms with their parents. Perhaps I noticed this especially because I was in contact with people who were concerned about their spiritual development, and wanted to straighten themselves out psychologically and emotionally.

If one is on bad terms with one's parents, something is quite seriously wrong. Perhaps it wouldn't even be an exaggeration to say that one's whole emotional life is likely to be affected, indirectly at least, by this state of affairs. I therefore used to encourage people to get back into positive contact with their parents, if it happened that they were estranged from them for any reason. I encouraged people to be more open with their parents and to develop positive feelings towards them. This was especially necessary in connection with the practice of the *mettā bhāvanā*, the development of loving-kindness. People had to learn to develop *mettā* even towards their parents, and for those who had had difficult childhoods, or had even suffered at the hands of their parents in some way, this was not easy. But even so, it was necessary in the interests of their own emotional, psychological, and spiritual development to get over whatever feelings of bitterness or resentment they were harbouring.

Some people, I discovered, blamed their parents in all sorts of ways for all sorts of things – an attitude that is reflected in a well-known little poem by Philip Larkin called 'This Be The Verse'. In this poem, Larkin gives expression in rather crude language to what he thinks your mum and dad have done to you, and he draws a rather depressing conclusion from that. The last verse of the poem reads:

> Man hands on misery to man,
> It deepens like a coastal shelf;
> Get out as early as you can,
> And don't have any kids yourself.

What a grim, nasty little poem! In 1995, however, it was voted one of Britain's favourite poems, coming in between Thomas Hood's 'I Remember, I Remember' and D. H. Lawrence's 'The Snake'. The fact that Larkin's poem should be so popular among intelligent poetry readers gives food for thought, suggesting as it does that negative attitudes towards parents are fairly widespread in our society.

The Buddha himself had quite a lot to say about our relation to our parents. In the *Sigālaka Sutta* he is represented as saying that there are five ways in which a son or daughter should minister to his or her mother and father as the eastern direction. He or she should think, 'Having been supported by them, I will support them, I will perform their duties for them. I will keep up the family tradition. I will be worthy of my heritage. After my parents' deaths I will distribute gifts on their behalf.'[323] There is a lot that could be said about the five ways in which one should minister to one's parents. Here, though, I want to touch on something even more fundamental – so fundamental that in this *sutta* the Buddha seems to take it for granted. It is hinted at, however, in the imagery of the *sutta*. The Buddha explains to Sigāla that one pays homage to the east by ministering to one's parents in five ways. But why the east?

The reason is perhaps obvious. The sun rises in the east, it has its origin in the east, so to speak, and similarly we owe our origin to our parents – leaving aside questions of karma, of which perhaps parents are only instruments. If it were not for our parents, we would not be here now. They have given us life, they have given us a human body, and in Buddhism the human body is regarded as a very precious thing. It is precious because it is only in a human body that one is able to attain Enlightenment. In giving us a human body, our parents are therefore giving us the possibility of attaining Enlightenment and we should be intensely grateful to them for that, especially if we are actually practising the Dharma.

Not only do our parents give us a human body; despite Larkin, they bring us up as best they can. They enable us to survive, they educate us. They may not always be able to send us to university and all that, but they teach us to speak, and this is the basis of most of the things we subsequently learn. Usually it's our mother who teaches us our first words, and this gives us the expression 'mother tongue'. It is through our mother tongue that we have access to all the literature that has been written in the language we learn in our earliest days, and we can enjoy that literature fully because it is in our mother tongue, rather than in a language we learn in later life.

Of course, not everybody cares to acknowledge their debt to their parents. We will consider the question of why people are so ungrateful later on. First, though, let us turn to the second of the principal objects of gratitude in Buddhism: our teachers. By teachers here I mean not Dharma teachers, but all those from whom we derive our secular education and culture. Here our school teachers obviously have an important place. From them we derive the rudiments of such learning as we have, and we therefore have to be grateful to them. The fact is that we have found out very little of what we know, or what we think we know, as a result of our own efforts. Practically everything we know has been taught to us in one way or another. If we think of our knowledge of science or history, for example, few of us have even performed a single scientific experiment – or discovered a single historical fact – that no one else had performed, or discovered, before. All our work in this field has been done for us by others. We have benefited from their efforts, and our knowledge is little more than the echo of theirs.

As well as learning from living teachers, we also learn from people who have been dead for hundreds of years, from the writings they have left and the records of the words they spoke. It is not just a question of learning from them in a purely intellectual sense, acquiring information. Among those books are great works of the imagination – poems, novels, dramas – and these works are a source of infinite enrichment, without which we would be immeasurably poorer. They help us deepen and enlarge our vision. We should therefore be grateful to the great men and women who have produced them. We should be grateful to Homer and Virgil, Dante and Milton, Aeschylus and Kālidāsa, Shakespeare and Goethe. We should be grateful to Murasaki Shikibu, Cervantes, Jane Austen, Dickens, Dostoyevsky, and hundreds of others, who have influenced us more than we can possibly realize. The American critic Harold Bloom has gone so far as to claim that Shakespeare is the creator of human nature as we know it, which is a very big claim indeed (though he gives his reasons for it).[324]

Of course, our experience is also deepened, and our vision enlarged, by the visual arts and by music. The great painters, sculptors, and composers are also among our teachers. They too have enriched our lives, and to them too we should be grateful. I won't mention any names in this connection because there are simply too many to choose from – both ancient and modern, Eastern and Western – certainly not because I think that the great artists and composers are any less important than the great poets, novelists, and dramatists.

Thus by 'teachers' I mean all those who between them have created our collective cultural heritage, without which we would not be fully human. Remembering what we owe them, and feeling grateful to the great artists, poets, and composers, we should not only enjoy their work but also celebrate their memory and share our enthusiasm for them with our friends.

Before we go on to consider the third principal object of gratitude, our spiritual friends, I want to make the general point that we need not think of these three objects of gratitude as being completely separate and distinct from one another. There's a certain amount of overlap between the first and second, and between the second and third. Our parents are also our teachers to an extent. In Buddhist tradition parents are called *porāṇacariyas*, which means 'former (or ancient) teachers'. They are called this because they are the first teachers we ever had, even if they only taught us to speak a few words. We can be grateful to our parents not only for giving us life but also for giving us at least the rudiments of knowledge, and initiating us into the beginnings of our cultural heritage.

Similarly there is some overlap between teachers and spiritual friends. The very greatest poets, artists, and composers can inspire us with spiritual values, help us rise to spiritual heights. In the course of the last few hundred years, great changes have taken place, at least in the West. Previously, Christianity as represented by the Church was the great, even the sole, bearer of spiritual values. But now, having lost faith in Christianity, many people look elsewhere to find meaning and values, and they find them in great works of art: in the plays of Shakespeare, the poetry of Wordsworth, Baudelaire, and Rilke, the music of Bach, Beethoven, and Mozart, the great painters and sculptors of the Italian Renaissance. These great masters become, as it were, our spiritual friends, especially if we remain in contact with them and with their work over many years. Learning to admire and love them, we feel intensely grateful to them for what they have given us. They are among our spiritual friends in the broadest sense.

But now let us come to our spiritual friends 'proper'. Here, as with the word gratitude, we have to go back to the Sanskrit words behind the English equivalent. As we have already seen, the Sanskrit phrase translated as 'spiritual friend' is *kalyāṇa mitra*. *Mitra* comes from the word *maitrī* (Pāli *mettā*), and *maitrī* is strong, unselfish, active love, sharply distinguished in Buddhist tradition from *prema* (Pāli *pema*), in the sense of sexual love or attachment. A *mitra* or friend is therefore one who feels a strong unselfish active love towards one. And *kalyāṇa* means firstly 'beautiful, charming', and secondly 'auspicious, helpful, morally good'. Thus *kalyāṇa mitra* has a much richer connotation than the English phrase 'spiritual friend'.

Our spiritual friends are all those who are spiritually more experienced than we are. The Buddhas are our spiritual friends. The *arhants* and the bodhisattvas are our spiritual friends. The great Buddhist teachers of India and China, Tibet and Japan, are our spiritual friends. Those who teach us meditation are our spiritual friends. Those with whom we study the scriptures are our spiritual friends. Those who ordain us are our spiritual friends. And all these spiritual friends should be the objects of our intense, heartfelt gratitude. We should be even more grateful to them than we are to our teachers.

Why? Because from our spiritual friends we receive the Dharma. We have not discovered or invented the Dharma. We have received it as a free gift from our spiritual friends, from the Buddha downwards. In the *Dhammapada* the Buddha says, 'The gift of the Dhamma surpasses all gifts.'[325] The greater the gift, the greater the gratitude we should feel. We should not only feel that gratitude in our hearts; we should give expression to it in words and deeds. We can do this in three ways: by singing the praises of our spiritual friends, by practising the Dharma they have given us, and by passing on that Dharma to others to the best of our ability.

The greatest of our spiritual friends is the Buddha Śākyamuni, who discovered – or *re*discovered – the path that we as Buddhists follow today. It is to him that we go for Refuge, it is the Dharma he taught that we try to practise, and it is with the support of the sangha he founded that we are able to practise the Dharma. We therefore have reason to be intensely grateful to him – more grateful, in principle, than we are to anyone else. Our parents have indeed given us life, but what is life without the gift of the Dharma? Our teachers have given us knowledge, education, and culture, but what value do even these things have without the Dharma? It is because they are so intensely grateful to the Buddha that Buddhists perform pujas in devotion to him, and celebrate his life in the context of the various Buddhist festivals.

But people don't always find it easy to be grateful to their parents, or their teachers, or even their spiritual friends. Why is this? It is important to understand the nature of the difficulty. After all, gratitude is an important spiritual quality, a virtue exemplified and taught by the Buddha and many others. Cicero, the great Roman orator and philosopher, said that gratitude is not just the greatest virtue, but the mother of all the rest.[326] Ingratitude therefore represents a very serious defect. On one occasion the Buddha said that ingratitude was one of the four qualities that bring about *niraya* in the sense of rebirth in a state of suffering – a very serious and weighty statement.[327]

But why are we ungrateful to our parents, our teachers, our spiritual friends? One would have thought that as Buddhists we would be simply bubbling over with gratitude to all these people. A clue is to be found in the Pāli word that we translate as gratitude, *kataññutā*. As we have seen, it means knowing or recognizing what has been done for one's benefit. Similarly, *akataññutā* (*a* being the negative prefix), ingratitude, means not knowing or recognizing what has been done for one's benefit.

There are a number of reasons for ingratitude. Firstly, one may fail to recognize a benefit as a benefit. There are some people who do not regard life itself as a benefit, and hence do not feel grateful to their parents for giving them life. Sometimes people say things like, 'Well I didn't ask to be brought into this world.' If you believe in karma and rebirth, of course, this isn't quite true – but anyway, it is what some people say. In a few cases, they may not regard life as a benefit because they experience it as painful, even predominantly painful, and therefore don't appreciate its value, don't realize the immense potential of human life. In Buddhist terms, they don't realize that it is possible for a human being, and only for a human being, to attain Enlightenment, or at least to make some progress in that direction.

Similarly, there are people who don't regard knowledge or education or culture as benefits. They feel no gratitude towards their teachers, or towards those who at least try to teach them something. They may even feel resentment. They may feel that education or culture is being imposed upon them. Such people are unlikely to come into contact with spiritual values, with the Dharma, or with spiritual friends, and even if they do, such contact will be external and superficial. They will not be able to recognize it for what it is. They may even see those who try to be their spiritual friends as enemies, and therefore the question of gratitude will not arise.

This was true of some people's responses to the Buddha himself. Not all those who heard him speak or teach felt grateful to him, by any means. There were many people in his day who saw him as a rather eccentric, unorthodox teacher. They certainly didn't feel any gratitude towards him for the gift of the Dharma. Sometimes people slandered him, and some people even tried to kill him.[328]

On the other hand, we may recognize benefits as benefits, and even recognize that they have been given to us by other people, but we may take those benefits for granted. Not realizing that they are a free gift, we may think that they are owed to us, that we have a right to them, and that therefore in a sense they belong to us already, so that we have no need to be grateful for them.

This attitude is widespread in society today. People tend to think that everything is due to them, that they have a right to everything. Parents, teachers, or the state have a duty to provide them with whatever they want. Even spiritual friends, they may think, have a duty to provide them with what they want. If they don't get what they want from one spiritual friend, or teacher, or guru, and get it quickly, in the way they want it, off they will go to try to get it from someone else. Once again, the question of gratitude doesn't arise. Of course, parents, teachers, and friends have a duty to bestow benefits to the best of their ability. But it should be recognized that those benefits have been *given*, and that the response to them should therefore be one of gratitude.

Another reason for ingratitude is egoism. Egoism takes many forms, and has many aspects. Here I mean by it an attitude of chronic individualism: the belief that one is separate from others, not dependent on others in any way, and that one therefore does not owe anything to others. One feels that one is not obliged to them, because one can do everything oneself. Examples of this sort of attitude abound in literature: Mr Bounderby in Dickens' *Hard Times*, Satan in Milton's *Paradise Lost*, and 'Black Salvation' in *The Life and Liberation of Padmasambhava*. The person who is egoistical in this sense is incapable of feeling gratitude, and cannot admit that they have been benefited by others. They may not actually say so in the way Mr Bounderby does, but this is their underlying attitude.

This attitude sometimes finds expression in the sphere of the arts. Some writers and artists don't like to think that they owe anything to their predecessors. Wanting to be original, to strike out on a completely new path, they don't like to think that there is such a thing as cultural heritage, or a literary canon. In some circles this attitude has taken an extreme, even a virulent form, and has resulted in an attempt to repudiate the greater part of our literary and artistic heritage on ideological grounds. This is an extremely unfortunate, even potentially disastrous development, and it is to be resisted wherever possible. Egoism in the sense in which I am using the word also finds expression in the sphere of religion. It happens when we don't acknowledge the sources of our inspiration, or when we try to pass off as our own a teaching or practice that we have in fact learned from our spiritual friends.

The fourth and last reason for ingratitude that I want to mention here is forgetfulness. There are two main reasons for forgetfulness of benefits received. First, there is simply the passage of time. Perhaps the benefits were given to us a long time ago – so long ago that we have no distinct recollection of them, and no longer feel grateful to whoever bestowed them upon us, even if we did originally feel grateful. This is perhaps the principal reason for our not feeling actively grateful towards our parents. Over the years so much has happened in our life: early memories have been overlaid by later ones, other relationships have assumed importance, and perhaps we have moved away from our parents, geographically, socially, or culturally. And the result is that – practically speaking – we forget them. We forget the numerous ways in which they benefited us when we were young, and we cease therefore to feel grateful. The other possible reason for our 'forgetting' to be grateful is that we did not feel the positive effects of the benefits very strongly in the first place, and therefore did not feel much gratitude. In such circumstances, it is easy for the gratitude to fade away and be forgotten altogether.

These, then, are the four most important general reasons for ingratitude: failure to recognize a benefit as a benefit, taking benefits for granted, egoism, and forgetfulness. Ingratitude is, unfortunately, liable to crop up in various ways in the context of the life of a practising Buddhist. Of course, beyond a certain point of spiritual progress, it is simply impossible to feel ungrateful. A Stream Entrant is incapable of it, and in fact will be overflowing with gratitude to parents, teachers, and spiritual friends. But until we have reached that point, we are in danger of forgetting to be grateful.

Over the years – more than thirty, at the time of writing – since I myself founded a Buddhist movement, I have received many, many letters, perhaps thousands, from people who have recently discovered the Dharma through one of the centres of the movement I founded, or through contact with individual members of the Order. Every year I receive more and more of these letters. They come from young people and old people, from people in many different walks of life, from many different cultural backgrounds and nationalities. And all these letters say, among other things, one and the same thing. They say how glad the writers are to have discovered the Dharma. Not only that, the writers of the letters want to express their gratitude to the Three Jewels and to this Buddhist movement, and to me personally for having founded it. Some people express their feeling of gratitude very strongly indeed. They say that the Dharma has changed their lives, given their lives meaning, saved them from despair, even saved them from suicide.

Such letters of gratitude reach me nearly every week, and they make me think that I have not altogether wasted my time all these years. But over the years I've also noticed that while some people, perhaps the majority, stay grateful, and even become more and more grateful, in the cases of a few people, unfortunately, the feeling of gratitude weakens. They start forgetting the benefits they have received, and even start questioning whether they really were benefits at all. No longer knowing or recognizing what has been done for them, they become ungrateful. Feeling ungrateful to their spiritual friends, they may even start finding fault with them. This is a very sad state of affairs indeed, and in recent years I have given some thought to it and have come to certain conclusions about how it happens.

It seems to me that people forget the benefits they have received because they no longer actually feel them. And they no longer feel them because for one reason or another they have put themselves in a position where they cannot receive them. Let me give a concrete example. Suppose you have started attending a meditation class. You learn to meditate, and you achieve some success. You start practising at home. But one day, for one reason or another, you stop attending the class and then you gradually stop practising at home. You cease to meditate. Eventually you forget what meditative experience was like. You forget the peace and the joy you felt. You forget the benefits of meditation. So you cease to feel grateful to those who introduced you to the practice. The same thing can happen with regard to retreats, Dharma study, spending time with spiritual friends, taking part in pujas, and attending Buddhist celebrations. People can get out of touch. They can forget how much they did, once upon a time, benefit from those activities, and therefore they can cease to feel grateful to those who made the activities possible.

Sometimes people reconnect after a while; they start attending the meditation class again, or go on retreat again, perhaps after many years. I have known people who have re-established contact after anything up to twenty-two years – rather a long time in anybody's life. When this happens, they nearly always say the same thing: 'I had forgotten how good it was.' And therefore they feel renewed gratitude.

This is entirely appropriate. It is appropriate that we should be grateful, that we should recognize the benefits we have received. It is appropriate that we should be grateful to our parents, with all their admitted imperfections – parents are not perfect any more than children are. It is appropriate that we should be grateful to our teachers, to our spiritual friends, and to the Buddhist tradition. Above all, it is appropriate that we should be grateful to the Buddha, who, as we have seen, was himself utterly and instinctively full of gratitude.

from *What is the Sangha?*

PART V
BUDDHISM AND THE WORLD

I
COMPASSIONATE ACTIVITY

1. THE BODHISATTVA'S REPLY

What will you say to those
Whose lives spring up between
Custom and circumstance
As weeds between wet stones,
Whose lives corruptly flower
Warped from the beautiful,
Refuse and sediment
Their means of sustenance –
What will you say to them?

That woman, night after night,
Must sell her body for bread;
This boy with the well-oiled hair
And the innocence dead in his face
Must lubricate the obscene
Bodies of gross old men;
And both must be merry all day,
For thinking would make them mad –
What will you say to them?

Those dull-eyed men must tend
Machines till they become
Machines, or till they are
Cogs in the giant wheel
Of industry, producing
The clothes that they cannot wear
And the cellophaned luxury goods
They can never hope to buy –
What will you say to them?

Or these dim shadows which
Through the pale gold tropic dawn
From the outcaste village flit
Balancing on their heads
Baskets to bear away
Garbage and excrement,
Hugging the wall for fear
Of the scorn of their fellow-men –
What will you say to them?

And wasted lives that litter
The streets of modern cities,
Souls like butt-ends trampled on,
Human refuse dumped
At the crossroads where civilization
And civilization meet
To breed the unbeautiful –
What will you say to them?

'I shall say nothing, but only
Fold in Compassion's arms
Their frailty till it becomes
Strong with my strength, their limbs
Bright with my beauty, their souls
With my wisdom luminous, or
Till I have become like them
A seed between wet stones
Of custom and circumstance.'

from *Complete Poems*

2. THE ATTRACTION OF THE BODHISATTVA IDEAL

Since the arising of the bodhicitta – *and becoming a bodhisattva – was in fact the altruistic dimension of Going for Refuge, this in turn had the effect of making me think of myself simply as a monk who went for Refuge, or even as a human being who went for Refuge and who happened to live in monastic or semi-monastic fashion. Commitment was primary, lifestyle secondary.*

The bodhisattva ideal has attracted me from quite an early period of my Buddhist life. Indeed, it had attracted me from the time when, shortly after reading the *Diamond Sūtra* and the *Sūtra of Wei Lang* (which were the first Buddhist texts I ever read), I came across a copy of *The Two Buddhist Books in Mahāyāna*. The second of these books, which had been translated and compiled by Upasika Chihmann (Miss P. C. Lee of China), Bodhisattva in Precepts, was 'The Vows of the Bodhisattva Samantabhadra', which formed part of the *Avataṃsaka* or 'Flower Ornament' *Sūtra*. I read this work repeatedly, and its picture of the infinitely wise and boundlessly compassionate bodhisattva must have made a deep impression on me for the words 'Thought succeeding thought without interruption, and in bodily, oral and mental deeds without weariness' kept going through my head for days together.[329] It was as though they embodied Samantabhadra's – or any other bodhisattva's – constant, unflagging fulfilment of his great vows through infinite time and infinite space. Seven or eight years later, shortly after my arrival in Kalimpong, I came across Śāntideva's *Śikṣā-samuccaya* or 'Compendium of Instruction (for Novice Bodhisattvas)' and as a result was more strongly attracted to the bodhisattva ideal than ever – so strongly, in fact, that attraction is far too weak a word for what I then felt.[330] The truth was that I was thrilled, exhilarated, uplifted, and inspired by the bodhisattva ideal, and my feeling for it found expression in some of the poems and articles I wrote during this period, as well as in chapter 4 of *A Survey of Buddhism*. There were two reasons for my being so strongly affected. In the first place, there was the sheer unrivalled sublimity of the bodhisattva ideal – the ideal of dedicating oneself, for innumerable lifetimes, to the attainment of Supreme Enlightenment for the benefit of all living beings. In the second, there was the fact that, as enjoined by my teacher Kashyapji, I was 'working for the good of Buddhism',[331] and that I could not do this without strong spiritual support, the more especially since I received very little real help or cooperation from those who were supposedly working with me. This spiritual support I found in the bodhisattva ideal, which provided me with an example, on the grandest possible scale, of what I was myself trying to do within my own infinitely smaller sphere and on an infinitely lower level.

It was therefore not surprising that on 12 October 1962 – nine days before receiving the Padmasambhava initiation – I should have received the bodhisattva ordination. By that time I had been a Buddhist for more than twenty years, and a monk for thirteen, and I had been working for the good of Buddhism for twelve years. For the last five years I had, indeed, been working for it not only in Kalimpong and the neighbouring hill towns, as originally enjoined, but among the ex-Untouchable Buddhists of central and western India. I therefore felt ready to take the bodhisattva ordination and, in this way, give formal expression to my acceptance of the bodhisattva ideal.[332] Moreover, I had found a preceptor from whom I could take the ordination. This was Dhardo Rimpoche, the Greatly Precious One of Dhartsendo, whom I had known since 1953 and whom I had come to revere as being himself a living bodhisattva. On the occasion of my *śrāmaṇera* ordination U Chandramani had been concerned that I should pronounce the words of the Refuge-going formula correctly, but he had said nothing about the meaning of those words or about the significance of the act of Going for Refuge itself. Similarly, at my *bhikṣu* ordination my Burmese preceptor had explained to me only the four reliances of the monk. Dhardo Rimpoche, however, not only gave me the bodhisattva ordination but subsequently explained the sixty-four bodhisattva precepts to me in considerable detail, so that I was able to translate them from Tibetan into English.[333] What was no less important, whereas I had had no further contact with my two previous preceptors after receiving ordination at their hands, in the case of Dhardo Rimpoche I was able to remain in regular personal contact with him for the rest of my stay in India.

But what effect did the taking of the bodhisattva ordination have on me? At the time it gave me a definite sense of spiritual progression, for I still thought of the Hīnayāna, Mahāyāna, and Vajrayāna as representing successive phases or stages of development and still, therefore, thought of the bodhisattva ordination as being 'superior' to the *bhikṣu* ordination, just as the *bhikṣu* ordination was 'superior' to the *upāsaka* ordination. In the long run, however, the taking of the bodhisattva ordination had the effect of making me think of myself not as a monk who happened to accept the bodhisattva ideal but rather as a (*triyāna*) Buddhist who happened to be a monk. Since the arising of the *bodhicitta* – and becoming a bodhisattva – was in fact the altruistic dimension of Going for Refuge, this in turn had the effect of making me think of myself simply as a monk who went for Refuge, or even as a human being who went for Refuge and who happened to live in monastic or semi-monastic fashion. Commitment was primary, lifestyle secondary.

from *The History of My Going for Refuge*

3. COMPASSION: THE MOST IMPORTANT VIRTUE

Since you have learned compassion – you'll do!

In the Mahāyāna form of Buddhism, that is to say in the teaching of the 'Great Way', the highest possible importance is attached to compassion. In one of the Mahāyāna *sūtras*, in fact, the Buddha is represented as saying that the bodhisattva – the one who aspires to be a Buddha – should not be taught too many things. If he is taught only compassion, learns only compassion, that is quite enough. No need for him to know about conditioned co-production, or about the Madhyamaka, or the Yogācāra, or the Abhidharma – or even the Eightfold Path. If the bodhisattva knows only compassion, has a heart filled with nothing but compassion, that is enough. In other texts the Buddha says that if one has only compassion for the sufferings of other living beings, then in due course all other virtues, all other spiritual qualities and attainments, even Enlightenment itself, will follow.[334]

This is illustrated by a very moving story from Japan. We are told there was a young man who was a great wastrel. After running through all his money, and having a good time, he became thoroughly disgusted with everything, including himself. In this mood he decided that there was only one thing he could do, and that was to enter the Zen monastery and become a monk. This was his last resort. He didn't really *want* to become a monk, but there was nothing else left for him. So along to the Zen monastery he went. Maybe he knelt outside in the snow for three days, in the way we are told applicants have to kneel. In any event, the abbot agreed to see him. The abbot was a grim old soul. He listened to what the young man had to say, himself not saying very much, but when the young man had told him everything, he said, 'Hmm, well … is there *anything* you are good at?' The young man thought, and finally said, 'Yes, I'm not so bad at chess.' So the abbot called his attendant and told him to fetch a certain monk.

The monk came. He was an old man, and had been a monk for many years. Then the abbot said to the attendant, 'Bring my sword.' So the sword was brought and placed before the abbot. The abbot then said to the young man and the old monk, 'You two will now play a game of chess. Whoever loses, I will cut off his head with this sword!' They looked at him, and they saw that he meant it. So the young man made his first move. The old monk, who was not a bad player, made his. The young man made his next move. The old monk made his. After a little while the young man felt the perspiration pouring down his back and trickling over his heels. So he concentrated: he put everything he had into that game, and managed to beat back the old monk's attack. Then he drew a great breath of relief, 'Ah, the game isn't going too badly!' But just then, when he was sure he would win, he looked up, and he saw the face of that old monk. As I have said, he was an old man, and had been a monk many years – maybe twenty or thirty, or even forty years. He had undergone much suffering, had performed many austerities, and had meditated for many, many hours. His face was thin and worn and solemn.

The young man suddenly thought, 'I have been an absolute wastrel! My life is no use to anybody. This monk has led such a good life, and now he is going to have to die.' So a great wave of compassion came over him. He felt intensely sorry for the old monk, just sitting there and playing this game in obedience to the abbot's command, and now being beaten and soon to have to die. A tremendous compassion welled up in the young man's heart, and he thought, 'I can't allow this.' So he deliberately made a false move. The monk made a move. The young man deliberately made another false move, and it was clear that he was losing, and was unable to retrieve his position. But suddenly the abbot upset the board, saying, 'No one has won, and no one has lost.' Then to the young man he said, 'You have learned two things today: concentration and compassion. Since you have learned compassion – you'll do!'³³⁵

from *The Buddha's Noble Eightfold Path*

4. RESPONDING TO THE NEEDS OF OTHERS

Caring for others on the basis of a spiritual motivation is much more difficult than caring for them out of a sexual or family interest.

It is not often that we see people just as themselves rather than as instruments of our own needs, and very rare indeed for us to put ourselves out for other people in a completely disinterested way. We might do it for our own mother or father, friend, lover, or child, but mostly we look after number one. For monks or nuns there is a particular danger in this regard, inasmuch as they have left behind the natural and biological attachments that will draw the ordinary lay-person out of complete selfishness. The danger of the monastic life is well illustrated in the *Mahāvagga* section of the Vinaya, which recounts how the Buddha finds a monk suffering from dysentery and who is neglected by the other monks. When the Buddha asks why the poor fellow is not being looked after, the monks reply, 'Lord, he is not useful to us': a dreadful admission. They are duly reprimanded, and even though in the Pāli canon there is no sort of mention of the bodhisattva ideal as such, something like it, or the seeds of it, are clearly implied. 'You have no father and mother to look after you', the Buddha says. As a member of a spiritual community you do not belong to any natural group to the members of which you may look for help simply on account of the ties of blood. The help you give one another can only be motivated by a purely spiritual impulse, a feeling of common membership of a purely spiritual body.³³⁶

Caring for others on the basis of a spiritual motivation is much more difficult than caring for them out of a sexual or family interest. If your son needs a new pair of shoes, you may well be willing to put off getting yourself a new shirt – and this sort of thing has a maturing effect. So the danger of falling into selfishness and self-preoccupation is much greater for the monastic community than it is for lay people with all their kith and kin to care for. The advantage of being a monk or nun is of course that you are able to avoid the often unconscious mutual exploitation that so often disguises itself as the caring and meaningful sexual relationship.

There is in fact only one need of one's own that has to be fulfilled before one can preoccupy oneself effectively with the needs of others, and it is not a physical or material need, but simply a matter of emotional positivity and security. We need to appreciate our own worth and feel that it is appreciated by others, to love ourselves and feel that we are loved by others. On this basis we can begin to develop the sensitivity and awareness to appreciate the real needs of others – not only their material needs, or even their educational needs, but their need for an ideal to which they can devote themselves, a spiritual path they can follow. At the same time, the group of others to whom our concern extends can grow to include not only our own family and friends, but people beyond our own kind, race, gender, and even views. It can even include quite different classes of beings.

from *Wisdom Beyond Words*

5. WITHDRAWAL AND INVOLVEMENT

There is a conflict, if you are big enough and rich enough in your nature to embrace the possibilities of such a conflict.

The will to Enlightenment is said to arise as a result of the coalescence of two trends of experience which are generally considered to be contradictory, since in ordinary experience they cannot both be pursued simultaneously. We might call these the trend of withdrawal from the world and the trend of involvement in the world.

The first of these trends represents renunciation in the extreme sense, a withdrawal from worldly activities, worldly thoughts, and secular associations. This withdrawal is aided by a particular practice, that of reflection on the faults or imperfections of conditioned existence. You reflect that life in this world, whirling round and round in the wheel of life, is profoundly unsatisfactory, involving as it does all sorts of disagreeable experiences. You experience physical pain and discomfort, you don't get what you want, you're separated from people you like, you have to do things you don't want to do. There's the whole wretched business of having to earn a living, doing your daily chores, taking care of your body – feeding it, clothing it, housing it, looking after it when it gets sick – not to mention taking responsibility for looking after your dependants. It all seems too much. All you want to do is get away from it all, away from the fluctuations, vicissitudes, and distractions of mundane life into the peace of the perfection of the Unconditioned, the unchanging rest of Nirvāṇa.

The second trend in our experience – involvement – represents concern for living beings. You reflect, 'Well, it would be all right for me to opt out and withdraw from it all – I'd like that – but what about other people? What will happen to *them*? There are people who have a much harder time in this world than I do, who can stand it even less than I can. How will they ever get free if I abandon them?' This trend of involvement is aided by the practice of reflection on the sufferings of sentient beings. In the trend of withdrawal, you reflect on the sufferings and imperfections of conditioned existence only in so far as they affect you, but here you reflect on them as they affect other living beings. You just look around at all the people you know, your friends and acquaintances, all the people you meet, and you reflect on all their troubles and difficulties. Perhaps one or two have lost their jobs, another's marriage has broken up, yet another may have had a nervous breakdown, and there may well be someone who has recently been bereaved. If you think it over, there is not a single person you know who is not suffering in some way. Even if they seem comparatively happy in the ordinary sense, there are still things that they have to bear: separation or illness, the weakness and tiredness of old age, and finally death, which they almost certainly don't want.

Then, when you cast your gaze further afield, there is so much suffering in so many parts of the world: wars, catastrophes of various kinds, floods and famines, people dying in horrible ways. You can even think of animals and how they suffer, not only at the teeth and claws of other animals but at the hands of human beings. The whole world of living beings is involved in suffering. And when you reflect on this, you ask yourself, 'How can I possibly think simply in terms of getting out of it all on my own? How can I possibly think of getting away by myself to some private Nirvāṇa, some private spiritual experience, which may be very satisfactory to me but is of no help to others?'

So there is a conflict, if you are big enough and rich enough in your nature to embrace the possibilities of such a conflict. On the one hand you want to get out; on the other you want to stay here. Of course, the easy solution is simply to choose between them. There are some people who withdraw into spiritual individualism, private spiritual experience, while others remain in the world without much of a spiritual outlook at all. But although these trends are contradictory, both of them must be developed in the course of the spiritual life. The trend of withdrawal may be said to embody the wisdom aspect of the spiritual life, while the trend of involvement embodies the compassion aspect.

These two practices – reflecting on the faults of conditioned existence and reflecting on the sufferings of sentient beings – form part of a traditional method of creating the conditions in dependence upon which the *bodhicitta* can arise. This is the method taught by a great Indian master of the Mahāyāna, Vasubandhu, who lived, so the Mahāyāna tradition says, in the latter half of the fifth century CE. Vasubandhu enumerated four practices which would provide a basis for the arising of the *bodhicitta*; they are known as Vasubandhu's four factors.[337] We have already identified two of these factors. The other two are 'the recollection of the Buddhas' and 'the contemplation of the virtues of the Tathāgatas' (Tathāgata being another word for Buddha).

In recollecting the Buddhas, one brings to mind the historical Buddha Śākyamuni, who lived in India about 2,500 years ago, and the lineage of his great predecessors of which the Buddhist tradition speaks. In particular, one reflects that these Buddhas started their spiritual careers as human beings, with their weaknesses and limitations, just as we do. Just as they managed to transcend all limitations to become Enlightened, so can we, if only we make the effort.

There are several ways of approaching the fourth practice: the contemplation of the virtues of the Tathāgatas. One can dwell on the life of an Enlightened One – the spiritual biography of the Buddha or Milarepa, for example. One can perform pujas in front of a shrine, or perhaps just sit and look at a Buddha image, really trying to get a feeling for what the image represents. Then again, one can do a visualization practice in which – to be very brief indeed – one conjures up a vivid mental picture of a particular Buddha or bodhisattva, an embodiment of an aspect of Enlightenment such as wisdom, compassion, energy, or purity.

We can think of these four factors as forming a kind of sequence. First, through recollecting the Buddhas, we become convinced that

Enlightenment is possible for us. Then, on seeing the faults of conditioned existence, we become detached from it, and the trend of our being is set in the direction of the Unconditioned. Thirdly, through observing the suffering of sentient beings – whether in imagination or close at hand – compassion arises, and we want to rescue not only ourselves but other beings from suffering. Then, as we contemplate the virtues of the Tathāgatas, we gradually become assimilated to them, and approach Enlightenment itself.

However, although we can think of the four factors sequentially in this way, the *bodhicitta* in fact arises in dependence on all four simultaneously. This means – returning to the tension between withdrawal and involvement – that we must not allow the tension between these two trends to relax. If we do that, we are lost. Even though they are contradictory, we have to follow both trends simultaneously, seeing the faults of conditioned existence and at the same time feeling the sufferings of sentient beings, developing both wisdom and compassion. As we develop and pursue both of these, the tension – and this tension is not psychological but spiritual – builds up and up until we simply can't go any further.

At that point, something happens. It is very difficult to describe exactly what does happen, but we can think of it provisionally as an explosion. The tension which has been generated through following simultaneously these two contradictory trends results in a breakthrough into a higher dimension of spiritual consciousness. Withdrawal and involvement are no longer two separate trends, not because they have been artificially amalgamated into one, but because the plane or level on which their duality existed, or on which it was possible for them to be two things, has been transcended. When that explosion occurs, one has the experience of being simultaneously withdrawn and involved, simultaneously out of the world and in the world. Wisdom and compassion become non-dual, not separate, not-two – without, at the same time, being simply numerically one. When this breakthrough occurs, when for the first time one is both withdrawn and involved, when wisdom and compassion are not two things side by side but one thing, then the *bodhicitta* has arisen. There has occurred a conversion from spiritual individualism to a life of complete selflessness – or at least such a life has been initiated.

from *The Meaning of Conversion in Buddhism*

6. GIVING: THE BASIC BUDDHIST VIRTUE

According to Buddhist teaching we should be giving in some way or other, on some level or other, all the time.

In a sense *dāna* or giving is the basic Buddhist virtue, without which you can hardly call yourself a Buddhist. *Dāna* consists not so much in the act of giving as in the feeling of wanting to give, of wanting to share what you have with other people. This feeling of wanting to give or share is often the first manifestation of the spiritual life – the first sign that craving and attachment have decreased to some extent. *Dāna* is discussed at great length in Buddhist literature, and many different forms are enumerated.[338]

First, there is *the giving of material things*, or sharing what you have of the good things of life: food, clothing, and so on. Some people in the East make it a practice to try to give something of a material nature every day, be it food to a beggar, a small sum of money, or just a cup of tea, so that every day something is given, or something shared, on the material plane.

Secondly, there is *the giving of time, energy, and thought*. Time is a very precious thing, and if we give some of it to help other people this is also a form of *dāna*, giving, or generosity.

There is also *the giving of knowledge*, in the sense of the giving of culture and education. This has always ranked very highly in Buddhist countries. Intellectual acquisitions should not be kept to oneself, but should be shared with all. All should be able to benefit from them. This was particularly emphasized in Buddhist India, because the Brahmin caste, the priestly caste of Hinduism, invariably sought to monopolize knowledge and keep other castes in a state of ignorance and subservience. Buddhism has always stressed that knowledge, even secular knowledge and secular culture, should not be a monopoly of any particular caste or class of people, but should be disseminated amongst the whole community.

Another important kind of giving mentioned in Buddhist literature is *the giving of fearlessness*. This might seem a rather strange kind of 'gift'. You cannot hand anyone fearlessness on a plate, or wrapped up in a little parcel tied with ribbon. But you can share your own confidence with other people. You can create among people a feeling of fearlessness or security by your very presence, your very attitude. Buddhism attaches great importance to this ability to reassure people by your mere presence. According to Buddhism this form of *dāna* is an important contribution to the life of the community.

Yet another form of *dāna* which is mentioned in Buddhist literature is *the giving of life and limb*. For the sake of other people, or for the sake of the Dharma, the Teaching, one should be prepared to sacrifice one's own limbs, even one's own life. *Dāna*, giving or generosity, can go as far as this.[339]

Finally, surpassing even the giving of one's own life, there is what is called in Buddhism *the giving of the gift of the Dharma*: the gift of truth itself; the gift of the knowledge, or understanding, of the way to Enlightenment, Emancipation, Buddhahood, or Nirvāṇa. The gift of this sort of knowledge surpasses all other gifts whatever.[340]

These are just some of the things which one can give, and looking at them we begin to see how vast and comprehensive the practice of giving can be. According to Buddhist teaching we should be giving in some way or other, on some level or other, all the time.[341] In the Buddhist East *dāna* or giving penetrates and permeates all aspects of social and religious life. If you are going to a temple, for instance, you don't go empty handed: you take flowers, candles, and incense, and offer them there. In the same way if you go to see a friend, even if the visit is only a casual one, you always take a present. Among Tibetans, for example, this is absolutely *de rigueur*. A friend would not think of appearing on your doorstep without a tin of biscuits or some other gift under his arm. In this way the spirit of giving permeates all aspects of life in many Buddhist countries. No doubt all this does sometimes become just a custom, and often there might not be much feeling attached to it. But nonetheless when you are giving all the time in one form or another it does have some influence upon the mind – even if you are doing it only because you are expected to. You get into the habit of giving and sharing, and of thinking a little bit about others, instead of all the time about yourself.

from *The Buddha's Noble Eightfold Path*

7. THE ALTRUISTIC DIMENSION OF GOING FOR REFUGE

If you are even a little bit open-handed, then whatever else you may be, there is some hope for you, from a spiritual point of view.

Dāna – literally giving or generosity – is the practical, altruistic aspect of the bodhisattva's life and activity, and the first of the six *pāramitās*, the six perfections or transcendental virtues. *Dāna* is right at the top of the list of perfections for a very good reason, which is that our natural tendency is not to give, but to take. If any new proposition comes up, whether in connection with work or home, professional activity, sport, or entertainment, our usual reaction, at least half-consciously, is 'What's in it for me?' There is always this self-referential tendency, this grasping. The fact that it is put right at the hub of the wheel of life is a recognition of the fact that craving – not just ordinary healthy desire, but craving – occupies a very important place in our life and activity. In fact it dominates our life, at least unconsciously. We are all in the grip of craving, swept along, impelled, by this thirst. Everything we do, everything we are interested in, has an element of self-reference.

If we are to get anywhere near Enlightenment, we have to reverse this tendency. Giving is the first *pāramitā* because giving is the direct opposite of grasping. It's as if the teaching is saying, 'You may not be morally scrupulous. You may not be able to meditate even for five minutes at a time. You may not dip into the scriptures from one year to the next. But if you aspire to lead any sort of higher life, then at the very least you will give.' If you find it difficult to part with things, difficult to look to the needs of others, you aren't going to get very far, spiritually speaking. On the other hand, if you are even a little bit open-handed, then whatever else you may be, there is some hope for you, from a spiritual point of view. This is the message of the Mahāyāna.

It isn't just a question of handing over one's possessions. Generosity is above all an attitude of heart and mind, indeed, of one's whole being. Walt Whitman says, 'When I give, I give myself,'[342] and this is very much the bodhisattva's attitude. To forget about traditional definitions for a moment, perhaps we could simply define a bodhisattva as someone who gives themself all the time, to everybody.

The bodhisattva may, upon occasions, need to give his or her very life. This form of giving is the subject of many a *Jātaka* story (the *Jātakas* being stories about the Buddha's previous lives). Some of these stories may seem lurid, melodramatic, or simply weird. The story of Prince Vessantara, for example, describes the Bodhisattva ('Bodhisattva' in this context referring to the Buddha-to-be) giving away his wife and children.³⁴³ We may be inclined, perhaps thinking of incidents from our own society, to feel upset or even outraged at the very idea. Were his wife and children the property of the Bodhisattva that he should give them away like so many goods and chattels? And, of course, in our society men – and sometimes women – have been known to give up their families not for any noble or altruistic reason, but simply in pursuit of their own happiness.

But the story of Prince Vessantara (which is after all from a cultural context very different from our own) is intended to illustrate how bodhisattvas may need to give up even those who are naturally nearest and dearest to them. For some, this will seem an even harder sacrifice than that of one's own life – a sacrifice which the Bodhisattva hero of many *Jātakas* also makes, on one occasion, for example, sacrificing his body to a starving tigress so that she could feed her cubs.³⁴⁴

We are unlikely ever to find ourselves in a situation anything like that, but we should never forget that if we take Buddhism seriously, we may be required under certain circumstances to make great sacrifices for our ideals. In the West at present, if we want to practise Buddhism, nobody can stop us. We can study texts, we can meditate, we can practise *dāna*, we can perform devotional ceremonies, we can do whatever we like, and we are fortunate that this should be so. But it isn't the case in all parts of the world, even now. We need to recognize how fortunate we are to have religious freedom.

We might even have to be prepared to sacrifice our lives for the sake of our principles. In present circumstances it may be easy enough to go along to a meditation class; but suppose one had to make one's way to it under cover of darkness, watching out for the police or the informer? If one meditated in peril of one's life, or read a book on Buddhism in peril of one's life, or stood up and spoke about the Dharma in peril of one's life – as is the case in some countries in the world today – would one do it? Or would one think, 'Well, I'll be a Buddhist in my next life; it's too difficult in this one'? One just doesn't know. All this is not to suggest that there is any virtue in throwing away one's life in a reckless or showy manner; but we must ask ourselves whether, if the sacrifice were necessary, we would be prepared to make it.

from *The Bodhisattva Ideal*

8. IS THE BODHISATTVA IDEAL REALISTIC?

How can we take this as a workable aspiration for a real live human being? We find it difficult enough to help with washing the dishes sometimes.

As ordinary individuals we can perhaps allow ourselves to think in terms of rebirth – even in terms of a series of rebirths extending over quite a long period of time. We can perhaps imagine ourselves as continuing our spiritual life through a succession of lives. But can we think in terms of a bodhisattva career literally extending over three *kalpas*? A *kalpa* is a very long time. The traditional description of a *kalpa* asks us to imagine a rock a mile high, a mile wide, and a mile long. Then we imagine that once every hundred years someone comes and strokes a piece of Benares silk, just once, along the top of the rock. A *kalpa* is the amount of time it would take to wear down the whole rock, at that rate.[345] It is a truly immense period of time.

Gampopa, the great Tibetan Kagyu teacher, who lived at about the time of the Norman Conquest in Britain, quotes the *Bodhisattvabhūmi* in his *Jewel Ornament of Liberation*:

> I shall rejoice at staying in hell for thousands of aeons if only to save one single being from misery, to say nothing of still longer periods and of still greater miseries. Such is a bodhisattva's armour of strenuousness.[346]

So apparently the bodhisattva volunteers for sojourns of millions of years in various hells for the sake of helping just one living being. But can we really imagine ourselves doing that? Surely it would be impossible for any human being to say that and sincerely believe it. If we try to imagine what the pains of hell would be like, we realize we wouldn't be able to stand even a hundredth part of that sort of pain. How can we take this as a workable aspiration for a real live human being? We find it difficult enough to help with washing the dishes sometimes. When the texts speak of the bodhisattva in this way, it makes most sense to think that they are referring to a sort of cosmic trend, or recognizing the existence of a potentiality for Enlightenment even under the most unfavourable circumstances.

We find a similarly formidable prospect in *The Precious Garland*, in which Nāgārjuna says:

(A bodhisattva) stays for a limitless time [in the world],
For limitless embodied beings he seeks
The limitless (qualities of) enlightenment
And performs virtuous actions without limit.[347]

So here again we find a Mahāyāna text describing the bodhisattva, the embodiment of the ideal we are exhorted to fulfil, but it doesn't seem at all practicable for us. Indeed, to judge from this description, the bodhisattva hardly seems like a person at all. The impression one gets is that the bodhisattva is beyond individuality as we usually understand it, a disembodied impersonal spiritual energy.

This being the case, we can gather that the Mahāyāna isn't expecting us to behave in literally the manner described. We don't have to imagine ourselves performing infinite good deeds, establishing Buddhafields, liberating infinite numbers of beings.... It is more practical to take the bodhisattva as representing a universal, even omnipresent, spiritual energy at work in the universe – an energy we get a sense of every now and then. We can't literally think of being a bodhisattva, but we can be open to the ideal, aspiring to be a channel for that energy within our own particular sphere. That is the most realistic, even the most honest way to see it. We have to stick very close to our actual situation; otherwise we can get lost in unrealistic aspirations. It can all become a bit theatrical; and this does sometimes happen in the Mahāyāna countries of the Buddhist East. The Theravāda is much more sober, much closer to the facts of the situation.

But the Mahāyāna conveys very well the spirit of the whole process: the fact that this process takes place within a much wider, even a cosmic context. In *The Precious Garland* Nāgārjuna says:

Through faith in the Mahāyāna
And through the practices explained therein
The highest enlightenment is attained
And along the way all pleasures.[348]

Why should there be 'all pleasures' along the way on the Mahāyāna – as distinct from the 'Hīnayāna' – path? The difference, one can say simply, is the bodhisattva ideal. The 'Hīnayāna' speaks more in terms of giving things up, disciplining oneself, getting rid of craving, and so on. If the goal is mentioned at all, it is usually referred to in terms of the cessation of suffering or the cessation of craving – not, for most people, a very inspiring prospect, not in the early stages of their spiritual life anyway. The Mahāyāna's ideal of the bodhisattva is quite simply more inspiring.

During the Buddha's lifetime, when the ideal was visibly present in the form of the Buddha himself, there was presumably no need to talk about it very much. But when the Buddha was no longer around, the ideal he represented had to be formulated somehow. Something had to be created to take the place of the actual presence of the Buddha. With the emergence of the bodhisattva ideal, the bodhisattva came to represent the sort of person you had to become if you wanted to be like the Buddha.

It's all about vision. If one is to be inspired to build a Buddhist centre, to take that example, one will need to be given a vision of what one is creating. If one has a picture in one's mind of beautiful Buddha images, spacious, peaceful rooms, and a wonderful community of people, even if what one is doing is plastering a ceiling or knocking down a wall, one will be inspired to do it. If someone just came along and said, 'Knock down that wall,' that would feel entirely different. If one is doing what one is doing for the sake of a positive goal, one can work much more happily. Indeed, it becomes pleasure all the way.

So we need to find a balance between vision and pragmatism. Perhaps the best solution is to take the two together: take the smaller view for here and now, for daily practice, and the cosmic view as a guide to the ideal as it exists outside space and time, independent of one's own small efforts.

All one really needs is a faith in the conservation of spiritual values beyond death. If one has that, one can be sure that if one practises the Dharma here and now, the future – how and where one will be reborn, whether or not one will become a Buddha in some distant world system, and so on – will look after itself. Perhaps one can't realistically make one's future Buddhahood the object of an aspiration. We need not take the Mahāyāna *sūtras* literally; they can be regarded as giving an inspiring glimpse of an archetypal world, but not as providing a pattern for Buddhist living in a detailed sense. One gets a much stronger sense of such a pattern from the Pāli canon.

from *The Bodhisattva Ideal*

9. WAYS OF HELPING

There is so much that can be done if we have the will and the heart to do it.

One can't do anything with or for other people without at least a touch of the bodhisattva ideal to keep one going, otherwise there will be a reaction sooner or later. Resentment will set in the moment one feels taken for granted. One can even start hating the people one is trying to help; at the very least it will feel a strain. But the bodhisattva feels no tension or strain because he or she is acting on the basis of the arisen *bodhicitta*.

The *Bodhicittavivaraṇa* says,

> One who understands the nature of the *bodhicitta* sees everything with a loving heart, for love is the essence of the Bodhicitta.... All bodhisattvas find their *raison d'être* ... in this great loving heart.[349]

It's the *bodhicitta* that makes the bodhisattva. However altruistic one is, or tries to be, one is not a bodhisattva if that transcendental dimension hasn't entered one's being. It could even be said that only when the *bodhicitta* has arisen is one really on the spiritual path; until then one is just preparing the ground.

But whether or not the *bodhicitta* has arisen, there are certainly a great many people in need of help, and we should not delay in helping where we can. There are certain groups of people who are perhaps especially in need of whatever help we can give them. First of all, old people are often in need of help. Many of them have to live alone, and they often, not unnaturally, feel lonely and neglected. If one can offer a few old people in one's neighbourhood a bit of warm human contact on a regular basis, it may make a great deal of difference to their lives.

Then there are the sick: not just those who are down with flu for a couple of days – though they need help too – but especially those who are confined to the hospital, sometimes with serious, painful diseases, for long periods of time. It sometimes happens that after a while even their closest relations begin to neglect them, thinking, 'Ah well, I can go next week or the week after. After all, old so-and-so's there all the time; they don't go away.' In the end they may stop visiting altogether. Many hospital patients, especially those who have been there a long time and those who are old, have no relations or friends to visit them. So this is something very practical we can do.

Then what about those confined to prison for one reason or another? We may not be able to visit them, but we could write. A lot of prisoners get a great deal of support from people writing to them and helping them to keep in touch with what is happening outside, helping them to feel that they still belong to the world to which one day they will have to return.

Also, those who are suffering mentally in one way or another need help and support. Many people whose psychological balance is disturbed need expert help – we certainly shouldn't try to do more than we are qualified to do – but it may be that simple friendliness will help someone a great deal. Much mental distress is due to a lack of communication with other people, a lack of any opportunity to disclose oneself. In such cases befriending someone and making it possible for them to talk about what's on their mind can be very helpful.

I once read about a catatonic patient in a mental hospital who didn't respond at all, ever, to anybody or anything. But there was a young nurse in the ward who became convinced that he could be brought to respond. So every day she simply took his hand and held it for half an hour. She did this for six months without any response at all, but then one day the patient squeezed her hand in return, and that was the turning point. Over a period of a few months she was able to open up some sort of communication with him, and in the end he came out of his catatonic state. Such things are possible. In psychotherapy, one of the main factors that contributes to helping the patient is that the analyst is listening to them. Ordinary doctors are sometimes put in this position – the person who comes ostensibly as a patient is just desperate for somebody to talk to. We shouldn't underestimate the value of simple communication.

And sometimes expert help doesn't help. Psychotherapy can help people in many ways, but in cases where there are symptoms of some deeper existential disturbance, psychotherapy in the ordinary medical sense may not help much. The effectiveness of a system of psychotherapy depends very much on the ideas it is based on, especially its idea of what it is to be a human being. If you have a limited view of human beings, you cannot help having a limited view of mental illness, and therefore a limited view of psychotherapy. There is a great difference between somebody who sees a human being as a potential Buddha and somebody who sees a human being merely as a rational animal, or even an irrational one.

Today, schools of psychotherapy are increasingly aware of the need to help people to confront existential problems. We are ultimately spiritual beings, and if our need for spiritual life is frustrated, that may result in mental distress. There will always be people whose psychological problems call for therapy rather than meditation, but ultimately there is no such thing as a psychological solution. In the long run the key to mental health is not psychological but spiritual. In any case, communication is always the key factor, and whenever our friendship may help someone in psychological difficulties, we should not hesitate to offer it.

There are, of course, many other kinds of people to whom we can offer help: refugees, the homeless, the starving, the under-privileged all over the world. It is difficult to help directly – not everybody can just go off to Africa or India – but we may be able to help indirectly through a charity. There is so much that can be done if we have the will and the heart to do it. And this is the first thing that the bodhisattva sets out to do: to help living beings – human beings and animals – out of their immediate, practical, material difficulties. At this stage one doesn't presume to think of leading anybody to Enlightenment. To begin with it's enough to give them a helping hand in the affairs of everyday life according to one's capacities.

However, whether or not we are qualified to give spiritual help and guidance, this is what many people in the modern West do need more than anything else. If we ourselves are not in a position to give that sort of help directly, we can give it indirectly, by helping those who *can* give it, perhaps by freeing them from other responsibilities or providing facilities of some kind. For example, a good writer, or a good meditation or Dharma teacher, will very often need financial support if they are to put their valuable gifts to best use.

One should be careful to avoid the feeling that the way one has found is the only way. Years ago, when I was working among the most socially deprived Buddhists in India, often treated as untouchables, I met a man on a train who, in no uncertain terms, expressed the opinion that I was wasting my time. According to him the people who needed help were the lepers, and I ought to be devoting my time to them. I could see his point, but he couldn't see mine. I certainly didn't feel that it was wrong for him to be working among the lepers, or that he should be working among the neo-Buddhists instead. But he could not see that working for the neo-Buddhists might be just as valid as working for the lepers. Indeed, the only way we can extend the relief of suffering in the world is by taking an interest where others have not yet done so.

from *The Bodhisattva Ideal*

2
BUDDHIST ETHICS

1. BEFORE DAWN

Cut off from what I really think and feel,
The substance of my life becomes ideal.

A whited sepulchre, a plaster saint,
Is not much use, however bright its paint.

Dreaming, awake, I must do all I can
To join the inward and the outward man.

Death stares me in the face: I watch and pray.
So near the goal, and yet so far away!

from *Complete Poems*

2. THE BASIS OF BUDDHIST ETHICS

We can perhaps summarize the position of traditional ethics today by saying that it consists in not doing what we want to do, and doing what we do not want to do, because – for reasons we do not understand – we have been told to by someone in whose existence we no longer believe. No wonder we are confused.

Churchmen and others are fond of lamenting what they call the decline of morals. In the course of the last few decades everybody is supposed to have become progressively more immoral, and it has been suggested that we are now in a pretty bad state. The decline of morals is usually linked very firmly with the decline of religion, especially orthodox religion. Having turned our back on the Church, we are told, we have at once plunged into the pit, the mire, of immorality. Indeed we may argue that traditional ethics have, to a very great extent, collapsed. Many people are no longer convinced that there are any fixed standards of right and wrong. In the seventeenth century one of the Cambridge Platonists, Ralph Cudworth, wrote a book which he called *A Treatise on Eternal and Immutable Morality*.[350] If anyone, even the Archbishop of Canterbury or the Pope, were to write a book with this title nowadays it would seem quite ridiculous. Even the great humanists and freethinkers of the nineteenth century, widely as they might range in their intellectual questioning, continued to conform to Christian ethics. Apart from one or two slips, when it came to their 'home life', as the Victorians called it, people like Darwin, Huxley, or even Marx, were models of morality.[351] But that is all changed now. Some people say, 'If you do something and it makes you feel good, then that thing is right, at least for you.' This is a very widely held view. It may not always be expressed very explicitly and openly, but it is, in fact, what many people think.

This development is not necessarily a bad thing. In the long run it might even be a good thing that morals should be thrown – temporarily we hope – into the melting-pot, and that we should have to re-think and re-feel, even re-imagine, our morality. It is good that, ultimately, as we hope, a new ethic should emerge from the ruins of the old.

Judaeo-Christian ethics

The Western ethical tradition is a composite thing. There are elements deriving from the classical Greek and Roman tradition, there are Judaeo-Christian elements, and, especially in some of the northern European countries, there are elements of Germanic paganism. But though our Western ethical tradition is made up of many interwoven strands, it is the Judaeo-Christian element which predominates. This is the 'official' ethic to which, at least in the past, everybody paid lip-service, whatever their private practice or preference may have been.

In this Judaeo-Christian ethic morality is traditionally conceived very much in terms of Law. A moral obligation or moral rule is something laid upon man by God. This is well illustrated by the biblical account of the origin of the Ten Commandments. Moses goes up Mount Sinai and there, amidst thunder and lightning, he receives the Ten Commandments from God. On coming down from Mount Sinai with – according to Christian art – the two stone tablets on which they were inscribed, Moses in turn gives the Ten Commandments to the Children of Israel.[352] This illustrates the idea of ethics as something imposed on man, almost against his will, by a power or authority external to himself. According to the Old Testament, God has created man, has formed him out of the dust of the earth and breathed life into his nostrils.[353] So man is God's creature, almost God's slave, and his duty is to obey. To disobey is a sin.

This attitude is again illustrated by the story of the Fall. Adam and Eve were punished, as we all know, for disobeying an apparently arbitrary order. God said, 'of the tree of the knowledge of good and evil, thou shalt not eat'.[354] But he did not give them any reason for the prohibition. Nowadays we know that stories of this sort are mythical, but though few people any longer believe them to be literally true the attitudes they represent still persist. The word *commandment* itself is significant. It is significant that a moral law or rule should be a *commandment* – something you are commanded to do, obliged to do, almost coerced into doing, by some power or authority external to yourself.

These two illustrations are both from the Old Testament, and Christianity certainly goes beyond this conception of ethics; but it does not go very far beyond it, and even then only in a rather imperfect manner. The sources of specifically Christian ethics are, of course, to be found in Jesus's teaching as contained in the four Gospels; but according to Christian tradition Jesus is God, so when God himself tells you to do something the order obviously comes with a tremendous weight of authority behind it. Thus one does something not so much because it is good to do it but because one is asked to do it, even commanded to do it, by one in whom reposes all power and all authority in heaven and upon earth. Even within the context of Christian ethics, therefore, there is, generally speaking, this same idea of ethics as something obligatory, as something imposed upon one from without to which one must conform. This is our traditional heritage. This is the mode of thought by which, consciously or unconsciously, we are all influenced when we think in terms of ethics.

Nowadays the majority of people in Britain, for example, are not Christian in any meaningful sense, but nevertheless they still tend to think of morality, of ethics, in this way: as an obligation laid upon them from without, a command which they are obliged to obey. We can perhaps summarize the position of traditional ethics today by saying that it consists in not doing what we want to do, and doing what we do not want to do, because – for reasons we do not understand – we have been told to by someone in whose existence we no longer believe. So no wonder we are confused. No wonder we have no ethical signposts, and therefore have to try to muddle through somehow or other. But though we try to make some sort of sense of our lives, try to discover some sort of pattern in events, where ethics is concerned the picture is mostly one of chaos.

The Buddhist criterion

Now without wanting to exaggerate, or to make the contrast seem too abrupt or dramatic, as between black and white, the traditional Buddhist attitude to ethics is quite different from the one just described. In fact this is true of the whole Eastern, especially Far Eastern, tradition. According to the Buddha's teaching, as preserved in the traditions of whatsoever sect or school, actions are right or wrong, perfect or imperfect, according to the state of mind with which they are performed.[355] In other words the criterion of ethics is not theological but psychological. It is true that in the West we are not unacquainted with this idea, even within the context of Christianity; but so far as Buddhist ethics is concerned – indeed so far as Far Eastern ethics is concerned, whether Buddhist, Taoist, or Confucian – this criterion is the only one. It is a criterion which is universally applied and rigorously carried through to the very end.

According to Buddhist tradition there are two kinds of action, skilful and unskilful. This is significant, because the terms skilful and unskilful, unlike the terms good and bad, suggest that morality is very much a matter of intelligence. You cannot be skilful unless you can understand things, unless you can see possibilities and explore them. Hence morality, according to Buddhism, is as much a matter of intelligence and insight as one of good intentions and good feelings. After all, we have been told that the path to hell is paved with good intentions; but you could hardly say that the path to hell is paved with skilfulness.

Unskilful actions are defined as those which are rooted in craving or selfish desire; in hatred or aversion; and in mental confusion, bewilderment, spiritual obfuscation, or ignorance. Skilful actions are those which are free from craving, free from hatred, free from mental confusion; positively speaking they are motivated instead by generosity, or the impulse to share and to give, by love and compassion, and by understanding. This very simple distinction at once places the whole question of morality in a very different light. The moral life becomes a question of acting from what is best within us: acting from our deepest understanding and insight, our widest and most comprehensive love and compassion.

from *The Buddha's Noble Eightfold Path*

3. THE FIVE PRECEPTS

One must be quite honest with oneself, and not pretend that one is mindful when one is merely merry.

The best known pattern of ethical behaviour is that of the five *śīlas*, generally known as the five precepts.[356] The five precepts, as usually transmitted, are negative in form. They tell us what *not* to do. In the case of each precept, however, there is a positive counterpart. It is very significant that in modern Buddhist teaching the positive counterpart is far less widely known than the negative formulation. Many people will have heard of the five precepts who have not heard of the five *dharmas*, as the five positive counterparts are called. In this context, the five *dharmas* may be translated as the five ethical principles. We shall briefly consider both the five precepts and the five *dharmas*, one by one, examining first the negative and then the positive formulation. This will give us a balanced picture of this particular pattern of Buddhist ethics.

The first of the five precepts is *abstention from harming living beings*. This is the literal translation. Although sometimes rendered as 'not to kill', it is really abstention not only from killing but from harming in any way. It conveys the meaning of abstention from all forms of violence, all forms of oppression, all forms of injury. Violence is wrong because ultimately it is based, directly or indirectly, on an unskilful mental state – on the state of hatred or aversion – and if we indulge in violence this unskilful mental state, of which violence is the natural expression, will become stronger and more powerful than it is already.

The positive counterpart of abstention from violence is the practice of *maitrī* (Pāli *mettā*): love or friendliness. Here *maitrī* is not just an emotion or a feeling, but is embodied in deeds and put into practice. It is not enough simply to *feel* goodwill towards others. This feeling must be expressed in action. Otherwise, if we simply gloat over it in our own mind, thinking how much we love everybody and how kind we are, it becomes a sort of emotional self-indulgence – not to say something worse. So we should watch ourselves in this respect. We often consider we love other people. At least, we consider we love *some* other people. But if we examine ourselves, we find that we seldom express our love: we take it for granted that it is understood.

A familiar example is that of the couple who have been married for twenty or thirty years, and the husband never bothers to give his wife as much as a bunch of flowers or a box of chocolates. If someone were to ask him, 'Don't you love your wife? You never give her as much as a bunch of flowers or a box of chocolates,' the average husband would reply, 'What's the need? Of course I love her, but she should know that after all these years!' This is very bad psychology. People should not have to take it for granted, or just imagine, that we do have feelings towards them. It should be quite obvious from our words and actions. Indeed we should actually take steps to keep alive the spirit of love and friendship. That is why in all social life, and in Buddhist social life especially, such things as exchanging gifts and extending invitations are very much emphasized. It is not enough to sit in your own room, or even in your own cell, radiating thoughts of love. Good and wonderful though that may be, it must come down to some concrete expression. Only then will such thoughts be reciprocated in a tangible way by other people.

The second of the five precepts is *abstention from taking the not-given*. This, again, is a literal translation. It is not just abstention from theft. That would be too easy to evade or to circumvent. The second precept involves abstention from any kind of dishonesty, any kind of misappropriation or exploitation, because all these are expressions of craving, or selfish desire. The positive counterpart of abstention from taking the not-given is *dāna*, or generosity. Here again it is not simply the generous feeling, the will to give, that is meant, but the generous act itself. There is no need for me to elaborate. *Dāna* is something which all those who have contact with living Buddhism for any length of time very quickly come to understand.

The third precept is *abstention from sexual misconduct*. In the *sūtras* the Buddha makes it clear that in the context of the five precepts sexual misconduct comprises rape, abduction, and adultery.[357] All three are unskilful because they are expressions, simultaneously, of both craving and violence. In the case of rape and abduction, which in the comparatively unorganized society of the Buddha's day seem to have been fairly common, violence is committed against the woman herself, and also, if she happens to be a minor, against her parents or guardians. In the case of adultery, the violence is committed against the person's usual sexual partner, inasmuch as their domestic life is deliberately disrupted. It should be noted at this point that in Buddhism marriage is a purely civil contract, not a sacrament. Moreover, divorce is permitted, and from a religious point of view monogamy is not compulsory. In some parts of the Buddhist world there are communities which practise polygamy, and this is not considered sexual misconduct.[358]

The positive counterpart of abstention from sexual misconduct is *saṃtuṣṭi* (Pāli *santuṭṭhi*), or contentment. In the case of the unmarried, contentment means contentment with the single state. In the case of the married it means contentment with one's recognized, socially accepted sexual partner(s). Here contentment is not just passive acceptance of the status quo. In modern psychological terms, it means a positive state of freedom from using sex to satisfy neurotic needs in general and, in particular, using it to satisfy the neurotic need for change.

The fourth precept is *abstention from false speech*. False speech is speech which is rooted in craving, hatred, or fear. If you tell a lie, it is either because you want something, or because you wish to harm or hurt someone, or because for one reason or another you are afraid of telling the truth. Untruthfulness, therefore, is rooted in unskilful mental states. This requires no demonstration. The positive counterpart of abstention from false speech is *satya* (Pāli *sacca*), or truthfulness.

The fifth precept is *abstention from drink and drugs the taking of which results in loss of awareness*. There is a certain amount of disagreement about the interpretation of this precept. In some Buddhist countries it is interpreted as requiring strict teetotalism, that is, total abstinence; in other Buddhist countries it is interpreted as requiring moderation in the use of anything which, taken in excess, is likely to result in intoxication. So one is free to take one's choice between these two interpretations. The positive counterpart of the precept is *smṛti* (Pāli *sati*): mindfulness or awareness. This is the real criterion. If you can drink without impairing your mindfulness (it might be said), then drink; but if you can't, then don't. However, one must be quite honest with oneself, and not pretend that one is mindful when one is merely merry. Thus, even if the fifth precept is interpreted as requiring simply moderation, in the light of its positive counterpart total abstinence will still be required in the vast majority of cases.

from *The Buddha's Noble Eightfold Path*

4. NATURAL MORALITY AND CONVENTIONAL MORALITY

It is quite important to be sure within oneself whether one is really leading a moral life or just respecting the prejudices of the group within which one happens to be.

Natural morality refers to behaviour that is directly related to mental states, while conventional moral behaviour is a matter of custom and tradition, and has no basis in psychology, not being related to a specific mental state. For instance, that one should try not to do things based on a mental state of craving, especially in its more neurotic forms, is a matter of natural morality; but whether one has one spouse or two, or four, is a matter of conventional morality.

Conventional morality also includes matters of etiquette and behaviour such as whether you take off your hat in a holy place or keep it on. There isn't necessarily any connection between whether you are wearing your hat or not and the degree of reverence you feel; it is simply customary in one society or culture to show reverence by keeping one's hat on, while in another culture one shows reverence by taking one's hat off. The feeling of reverence is a matter of natural morality, but how it is shown is a matter of conventional morality in most cases, although it could be said that there is a psychological connection between certain mental states and certain bodily attitudes.

Within Buddhist tradition there are some precepts, especially precepts to be practised by monks, which have nothing to do with natural morality. That a monk wears yellow robes, shaves his head, and so on is simply a matter of convention. This is clearly recognized in Theravāda tradition, in theory, though often in practice, and certainly as far as public opinion is concerned, very great importance is attached to matters of conventional morality – as much as to even the most important precepts of natural morality – and this is rather unfortunate.

Unfortunately also, sometimes people feel very guilty about not observing matters of conventional morality, especially if the society to which they belong attaches great importance to those matters, virtually as though they were matters of natural morality. For instance, in some societies it is regarded as moral to work, and therefore immoral not to work; so people who don't work in the sense of being gainfully employed are looked down upon, regarded as slightly immoral, even made to feel guilty. Indeed, they themselves may feel guilty, as though they have done something wrong, when they have not offended against natural morality, but only gone against custom and convention. In a sense this is the difference between virtue and respectability. Sometimes the two coincide, but often they don't. One may be both virtuous and respectable, but it is also possible to be very respectable and not at all virtuous, or highly virtuous and not at all respectable.

Only matters of natural morality have any direct connection with the question of karma. One should not entangle a matter of real, substantial virtue, a matter of natural morality, with one's prejudices about what is right and wrong, which may be based merely on local custom, and have nothing to do with skilful or unskilful mental states.

It is quite important to be sure within oneself whether one is really leading a moral life or just respecting the prejudices of the group within which one happens to be. Moral life is essentially a matter of skilful mental states expressed in skilful behaviour and skilful speech. The precepts of natural morality are those precepts which prevent one from committing unskilful actions – that is to say, actions based upon craving, aversion, and ignorance – and help one to perform actions based on skilful states of mind such as generosity, love, and wisdom.

And this is the nature of the traditional precepts of Buddhism, which guide the application of ethical principles to all aspects of life. There is a set of five precepts: one 'undertakes the training principles', as the traditional wording has it, not to take life, not to take what is not given, not to engage in sexual misconduct, not to lie, and not to take intoxicants. A set of ten precepts – an elaboration of the five – involves a threefold purification of body, speech, and mind. And there are sixty-four special precepts for bodhisattvas. There is much that could be said about the practice of these precepts, but here I want to concentrate on Buddhist ethics as applied to three basic spheres of human life: food, work, and marriage.

The most basic of these is, of course, food. You had some not long ago, and so did I; eating is just part of everyday life. Some people in some places can only afford to eat once a day, or even every other day, but most of us eat several times a day; food occupies a very important place in our lives, and takes many hours of our lifetime. An activity to which we devote so much time, energy, and money, and for which we require special provision in our houses in the form of kitchens and dining rooms and utensils, very definitely needs to be brought within the influence of our Buddhist principles.

The most important principle here is non-violence, reverence for life. This means, among many other things, vegetarianism. Some of the Mahāyāna *sūtras* say that the bodhisattva can no more think of eating the flesh of living beings than a mother can think of eating the flesh of her child. If one is to practise the first precept, therefore, one needs to make a definite move in the direction of vegetarianism. Sometimes circumstances at home may be difficult – it may be impossible to be strictly vegetarian – but at least one can move towards it, perhaps by giving up meat and fish on certain days of the week, or on certain occasions. No one is perfectly non-violent; it is always a matter of degree, but we should reverence life as much as possible. Vegetarianism, practised to any degree, is a direct application of the principle that guides the life of the bodhisattva: the principle of compassion.

It should be said that the Buddha himself did not insist on vegetarianism. He considered it more important for mendicants to practise not picking and choosing what they ate, but accepting what they were given (provided they were sure that any meat they were offered had not been killed especially for their benefit). However, it seems surprising that so few Buddhists in the East have subsequently made any attempt to encourage, where they could, this most basic application of a basic Buddhist principle. In the harsh climate of Tibet vegetarian foodstuffs are certainly scarce, but many Tibetan Buddhists living in India continue to eat meat although they no longer need to do so. It isn't just the Tibetans; Thai and Burmese Buddhists are, if anything, even greater meat-eaters, and the majority of Sinhalese monks and laymen are non-vegetarian too. But perhaps non-vegetarianism is especially strange among Mahāyāna Buddhists like the Tibetans, given the Mahāyāna's special emphasis on compassion. The *Laṅkāvatāra Sūtra* contains a whole chapter about the unskilfulness of eating meat, but people don't seem to take that very seriously.[359]

In this connection Tantric teachings, misunderstood, play a part. Tibetan lamas sometimes say that when an animal is slaughtered, if certain mantras are recited over it, its consciousness is at once released and goes to a sort of heaven. Some even go so far as to say that the fact that the flesh of an animal passes through their system ensures the salvation of that animal. It isn't possible to prove or disprove such a statement, of course, but it has all the hallmarks of a rationalization.

The Thai *bhikkhus* I knew in India used to say that the lay people gave them meat and therefore they couldn't refuse it – it was just dropped into their bowls. But the lay people were Buddhists and had been so for hundreds of years, and the *bhikkhus* had taught them to do all sorts of things, for example devising elaborate ways for women to make offerings without coming into physical contact with the *bhikkhus*. If they could teach the lay people things like that, why couldn't they teach them not to offer them meat? After all, they were able to explain that certain kinds of meat were prohibited and should not be offered according to the Theravāda Vinaya: human flesh, tiger flesh, and so on.[360] Could they not ask them to refrain from offering any flesh at all?

When I stayed with some of my Thai *bhikkhu* friends – in the place of the Buddha's Enlightenment, Bodh Gaya, of all places – every single dish they ate was mixed with meat. Sometimes when I had a meal with them, all I could eat was rice. They weren't very sympathetic, though; they clearly felt that I was just being awkward and that they were under no obligation to help me out of the difficulty I had created for myself.

The Sinhalese were much more sympathetic. Some Sinhalese *bhikkhus* are vegetarians, and Sinhalese lay Buddhists are very cooperative about that. Tibetans, when challenged about it, will often say, 'Yes, we know we should be vegetarian, but it's difficult in Tibet.' They do make an exception when they are engaged in any kind of puja or spiritual practice connected with the bodhisattvas Tārā and Avalokiteśvara. Then they do observe vegetarianism, even if the pujas last for as long as ten days, because Avalokiteśvara and Tārā are especially associated with compassion.

As well as being vegetarian, one should practise loving-kindness towards oneself by eating pure and wholesome food. ('Pure' here does not mean refined to such an extent that there is no goodness left in it.) At the same time, one should eat only as much as is necessary for maintaining good health. Sometimes we forget that the purpose of eating is just to keep the body going. If one is down to a subsistence level diet, as people are in so many parts of the world, one knows this very well, but it isn't so obvious in the West, where we have an optimum diet, to say the least.

Also, one shouldn't eat neurotically; one shouldn't use food in an attempt to satisfy some other need. And one should eat quietly and peacefully. These days many people have business lunches, during which they try to do business and eat at the same time. This is grossly uncivilized conduct. Eating should be quiet, peaceful, even meditative. To eat in a public restaurant or coffee bar, where there is a lot of noise and clatter, and loud conversations going on, is not good for any sensitive, mindful person. The principle here is that one should eat mindfully, with full awareness of what one is doing. One shouldn't eat while reading a newspaper at breakfast time, or having a family argument, or even discussing some practical matter.

For an example of mindfulness in this respect, there is nothing more beautiful than the Japanese tea ceremony. A small group of people gather together in some quiet corner, a little rustic hut in the garden perhaps, and they sit around a charcoal stove and listen to the kettle simmering away. Then, with slow, graceful, delicate, mindful movements, the tea is poured out and handed round to the guests. And people sip it, just sitting peacefully together, engaging in the ordinary, everyday activity of drinking tea.

The Japanese tea ceremony shows to what a pitch of perfection even everyday activities can be raised if we apply mindfulness. Indeed, although this statement could easily be misunderstood, one might almost say that it is better to eat steak and onions mindfully than to eat vegeburgers unmindfully. The main point is that even eating, this ordinary activity, can be made into a sort of art, a way – a *dō*, to use the

Japanese word. Someone who ate and drank mindfully every day, year after year, might even gain as much spiritually as they would gain from a sustained practice of meditation. To encourage oneself to be mindful in this way, one could perhaps bring to mind a little verse or saying, reflecting, perhaps, on the source of the food one is eating.

Another area of ethics that is particularly important in the West has to do with work. We tend to think that everybody should work – that is, for money; we think it is wrong, sinful even, not to be gainfully employed. This is undoubtedly a legacy from Protestantism. Some people can't take a few days off, or even spend a few extra hours in bed in the morning, without feeling horribly guilty about it. We usually feel that we ought to be doing something. Sometimes if we see someone else just sitting around not doing anything, we feel all fidgety and uncomfortable and want to get them moving, as though the very fact of their sitting there quietly while we are so busy is a threat to us.

This is not a new thing. It is to be found, for example, in the Gospels, in the story of Martha and Mary – Martha bustling around getting everything ready, while Mary just sat at the feet of Jesus listening, when there was food to be prepared and served, and washing-up to be done. Martha was most indignant. Jesus, however, said that Mary had chosen the better part.[361] In the West we tend to be Marthas rather than Marys; this feeling that we ought to be doing something is a sort of disease.

The Buddha never worked for his living, as far as we know. He was born into a wealthy, aristocratic family. He had lots of servants. According to all the accounts he spent most of his time in palaces with singing girls, dancing girls, and musicians. Then, after he left home as a mendicant, other people gave him food and clothing. He never did anything to earn his keep. Of course he taught the Dharma, but he would have done that anyway; it was his nature, just as the nature of the sun is to shine. He never worked for money; he never did a day's work in his life.

I have so far been referring to work in the sense of employment; but there is such a thing as creative work. Indeed, creative work is a psychological necessity. It may be in the form of bringing up and educating children. It may be in the form of writing or painting or cooking, or engaging in some constructive social venture. To produce, to create, is a human need, but it need not be linked with employment. In an ideal society, no one would have to work for wages. One would give to the community whatever one could, and the community would give to each person whatever they needed.

However, such an ideal state of affairs is no doubt a long way off, and in the meantime we do have to be gainfully employed in the ordinary sense – and so we have to apply the principle of right livelihood. In brief, this is that our means of livelihood should involve no exploitation of others and no degradation of oneself. And however one is employed, there should always be time for study, meditation, contact with friends, and other positive and creative activities.

Another aspect of life that affects practically everybody in one way or another, formally or informally, is marriage. The Buddhist conception of marriage is very different from the traditional Western one. In the first place, in Buddhism marriage is regarded neither as a religious sacrament nor as a legally binding contract. According to Buddhist tradition, marriage is simply a human relationship which is recognized by society in the form of one's family and friends.

Even in the West the white dress, the orange blossom, the church bells ringing, and all that sort of thing are not *de rigueur* in the way they used to be, but in the Buddhist East there has never been any marriage ceremony of that kind. If anything at all is done to mark the event, the couple concerned will give a feast for their friends and relations, and just make an announcement that they are living together. A Sikkimese friend of mine and his wife didn't give their feast until they had been together for twenty years and their children had grown up. But they were not regarded as 'living in sin' in the interval. If a man and woman are living together, they *are* married. This is the Buddhist view. Marriage consists in living together, not in a legal contract, a social convention, or even an official announcement. The marriage is primarily the relationship itself. After the feast held to initiate it or celebrate it, the couple may go along to the temple or monastery and ask for a blessing, but this isn't a wedding ceremony. The monks may bless the relationship, but they don't create it – they just recognize it and give their blessing that the couple concerned may live together happily in accordance with the spirit of the Dharma, helping each other to practise the Buddha's teaching.

With that background, it is not surprising that in all Buddhist countries, from ancient times, there has never been any difficulty about dissolving a marriage, if the people concerned wish it. Also, after marriage the woman retains her own name. This practice is now increasingly common in the West, but here it is quite a new thing, whereas in the East it has never been any other way. In the Buddhist countries of the East there is no one pattern of marriage relationship; nowhere does Buddhism say that monogamy is the only possible form of marriage. Monogamy, polygamy, and even polyandry are all to be found in Buddhist countries, and are recognized as perfectly respectable. Buddhists direct their attention entirely upon the quality of the human relationships involved.

from *The Bodhisattva Ideal*

5. BEYOND 'BUDDHIST RESPECTABILITY'

It is easy to forget that the Buddhist message is a subversive one, that its values run counter to mundane or worldly norms, and that your commitment to its ethical principles may lead you on occasion to offend conventional notions of morality.

I remember that when I was a small child, most children were not allowed to run about and play when they were dressed in their Sunday best. They were made to sit at home so that they would stay neat and tidy. This had nothing to do with religion; it was all about social niceties. Even during my youth, if a man didn't wear a tie or a hat, he was considered not to be fully dressed, while wearing a coloured shirt was an act of flagrant recklessness. Those particular signs of respectability have changed, but the concern to display the appropriate marks of submission to group norms is still very apparent. In an age of consumerism, respectability is less a matter of a rigid dress code and more about a carefully maintained range of purchases and recreational activities that will ensure peer acceptance. You need to have the right sort of job and live in the right part of town, go on holiday to the right ski resort, drive the right kind of car, and even follow the right religion.

The perception of things as all-important when they are nothing of the kind is reinforced by vulnerability to group disapproval, and also by lack of imagination, an inability to contemplate stepping outside the range of possibilities that society thinks acceptable. Unfortunately,

Buddhists have all too often succumbed to this kind of failure of nerve and vision. When you get a narrow and rigid monasticism, when the monastic rules and even the way you dress and shave your head have turned into a kind of Buddhist respectability, or when it becomes all-important to spend the right number of years studying Buddhist philosophy in the right monastic universities, then what is really all-important is to re-emphasize what is really all-important. It was for this reason that some Tantric yogis originally set out to flout convention, to challenge what other people considered important, even within the Buddhist world.

When I first came back to England in the early 1960s, after some twenty years in Asia, it was impressed upon me as all-important that Buddhism should be respectable. I soon realized that what the people who were trying to influence me meant by this was that Buddhism should be made as acceptable as possible to the values of the English middle classes. But if Buddhists agree to such a thing, Buddhism ceases to be Buddhism. The same may be said for the versions of Buddhism that are peddled to the consumer society these days, and the way that Buddhism is profiled to appeal to different niche markets, to fit in with whatever that society considers to be all important. It may well find acceptance in this way, but it ceases to be Buddhism.

Of course, if you want to communicate the Dharma to a lot of people, you cannot afford to alienate them by causing offence, especially by breaking their taboos. At the same time, you need to be careful not to lose sight of what you are trying to communicate. It is easy to forget that the Buddhist message is a subversive one, that its values run counter to mundane or worldly norms, and that your commitment to its ethical principles may lead you on occasion to offend conventional notions of morality. If the Buddha 'discreetly follows worldly customs', he does so only in so far as these did not compromise the ideals of the Dharma and the integrity of the lifestyle he had chosen through which to express those ideals.

It is normal to be ashamed of anything that excludes one from the group, and social inclusion is fundamentally predicated on the respect given to taboos, whether one observes them or breaks them. Milarepa, a Tibetan yogi of the eleventh century CE, speaks from a position that is not in opposition to social convention, but simply beyond it. That is to say, it is not a position at all. He avoids any fixed position, whether of conformity or individualism. He is not a conformist or an individualist, but an individual. He does not define himself in relation to the group, whether by joining it or by setting himself apart from it.

A true individual is someone who has developed self-awareness, through one discipline or another, and on that basis a confidence and self-respect that does not depend upon convention or fashion. If you are a true individual, your sense of identity and purpose in life does not rely on your social identity – whether you are a citizen, family member, worker, rebel, or iconoclast. As a mature human being, your self-awareness transcends human social groups of all kinds. Your defining relationship is an inner relationship with the deeper reality of things, the truth behind appearances. One might even say that the true individual is one through whom that deeper reality of things functions and is present in the world. If you are a true individual you can stand on your own two feet and at the same time maintain a harmony with the way things really are.

Milarepa is an individual in the true sense because he is free of the power of social conventions. He doesn't need to conform to other people's expectations of how a spiritual practitioner should look; it doesn't matter to him how he is seen. We tend to be most ashamed of matters over which we have no control, like our social background or what we look like. Milarepa, by contrast, is ashamed only of 'sinful, evil, and meaningless deeds'. The things that preoccupy the vast majority of people are quite simply of no concern to him at all; and conversely, he sees how important it is to feel real shame about deeds and activities about which most people would feel no compunction.

from *The Yogi's Joy*

6. THE ETHICS OF SPEECH

Speaking the truth really means being ourselves. Not in the conventional, social sense, as when we are said to 'be ourselves' at a party, which usually means not being ourselves at all, but in the sense of giving expression in terms of speech to what we really and truly are and know we are.

If we reflect we shall see that a great part of our culture depends, directly or indirectly, on speech. Through speech the parent and the teacher educate the child. Through books, which are, as it were, frozen, crystallized speech, we get information, we get knowledge; we may even get Enlightenment. All our culture, all knowledge, even our spiritual insight, is to a great extent derived directly or indirectly from the *word* – from speech, from utterance. It is therefore natural, even inevitable, that in the moral and spiritual life we should give as much consideration to speech as we do to thought and action.

In Buddhist texts Perfect Speech is usually described as speech which is truthful, which is affectionate, which is helpful, and which promotes concord, harmony, and unity. Similarly wrong or imperfect speech is described in precisely opposite terms, as speech which is untruthful, harsh, harmful, and which promotes discord, disharmony, and disunity.[362]

1. The level of truthfulness

First of all, Perfect Speech, or ideal communication, is truthful. We all think we know exactly what is meant when it is said that all speech should be truthful. We have been told since we were 2 years old not to tell a lie, like George Washington.[363] But do we really know what is meant by speaking the truth? Have we considered all the implications? Speaking the truth does not mean just adhering to factual accuracy, saying that this cloth is yellow and that *that* is a microphone. The concept of truthfulness is not exhausted in this way. Factual accuracy is of course important. It is one of the elements of truthfulness, and we cannot dismiss it. But it is not the whole.

Anyone who knows Boswell's classic biography of Samuel Johnson, will remember Johnson's famous remark about factual truthfulness. He remarks that if your children say that something happened at one window, when in fact it happened at another, then they should be instantly checked, because once it begins you do not know where deviation from the truth will end.[364] Thus factual truthfulness is important. It is the basis or foundation of Perfect Speech. Recognizing this, we should accustom ourselves to what Johnson calls 'accuracy of narration', which is a sort of training ground for us in the higher, more refined kinds of truthfulness. Usually we are shaky and shoddy even on this level. Few people really practise accuracy of narration. We usually like to make things a little bit different. We like to pad out, we like to exaggerate, or to minimize, or to embroider. It may just be a poetic streak in us which makes us do this, but we do it even in the best of circles, even at the best of times.

We all tend to twist, or distort, or at least slightly bend facts, in the direction in which we would like them to go, so we have to be extremely careful here. If we say for instance that it was a lovely day, it must have been a lovely day. We must neither exaggerate nor minimize. If we say that there were ten people at the meeting, let us be sure that there were ten. If there were a thousand, let us say that there were a thousand. But if there were only fifty, let us not make it one-hundred-and-fifty. Or in the case of somebody else's meeting, if there were a thousand, let us not make it one-hundred-and-fifty! Thus we must pay strict attention to factual accuracy, though it must again be emphasized that truthfulness in the real sense, in the deepest, the fullest, the most spiritual sense, is something very much more than mere factual accuracy, important as this is.

Truthfulness is also psychological, also spiritual. Besides factual accuracy speaking the truth also involves an attitude of honesty and sincerity. It involves saying what we *really* think. You are not speaking the truth unless you speak the whole truth and say what is really in your heart and mind – say what you really think, even what you really feel. If you do not do that you are not being truthful, you are not really communicating.

But then another question arises: do we really even know what we think? Do we really know what we feel? Most of us live or exist in a state of chronic mental confusion, bewilderment, chaos, disorder. We may repeat, as the occasion arises, what we have heard, what we have read. We may regurgitate it when we are required to do so, whether at the time of examinations in the case of students, or on social occasions in the case of other people. But we do all this without really knowing what we say. How can we, therefore, really speak the truth? Since we do not really know what we think, how can we be truthful?

If we want to speak the truth in the full sense, or at least in a fuller sense than is usually understood, we must clarify our ideas. We must introduce some sort of order into this intellectual chaos of ours. We must know quite clearly, quite definitely, what we think, what we do not think, what we feel, what we do not feel. And we must be intensely aware. We must know what is within us, what are our motivations, what are our drives and our ideals. This means that we have to be completely honest with ourselves. It means that we have to know ourselves. If we do not know ourselves, in the depths as well as on the heights, if we cannot penetrate into the depths of our own being and be really transparent to ourselves, if there is not any clarity or illumination within – then we cannot speak the truth.

This is something we all have to realize. If we do realize it we shall see that speaking the truth is no easy matter. We might even go so far as to say – and I do not think this is an exaggeration – that most of us, most of the time, do not speak the truth. If we wanted to put it forcefully, not to say paradoxically, we might even say that most of us, nearly all the time, speak what is in fact a lie, and that our communication is in fact most of the time a lie, because we are not capable of speaking anything else. We are incapable of speaking the truth in the fullest sense. If we reflect we might have to admit that most of us go through life, year after year, from childhood or at least adolescence into old age, without perhaps being able even once to speak the truth in the fullest and clearest sense of that much abused term.

We do know that if ever we are in a position to speak the truth, then it is a great relief to be able to do so. Often we do not realize how many lies we have been telling until we have an opportunity, once in a while perhaps, of speaking the truth. We all know that if something has been weighing on our mind or on our heart, something about which we were very worried or concerned, if we can only speak out – or tell somebody the truth of the matter, without holding back – then it is a great relief. Unfortunately for most people this is something that happens very rarely in their lives, if indeed at all.

Speaking the truth really means being ourselves. Not in the conventional, social sense, as when we are said to 'be ourselves' at a party, which usually means not being ourselves at all, but in the sense of giving expression in terms of speech to what we really and truly are and know we are. Speaking the truth, however, even in this more rarefied, fuller, deeper, and more spiritual sense, is not done in a vacuum. You do not just go to the top of the highest building and speak the truth to the stars. The truth is always spoken to someone – another person, another human being. This brings us to the second level of Perfect Speech, or the second stage of communication.

2. The level of affectionateness

Perfect Speech is not only truthful, even in the fullest sense; it is also affectionate and loving. It is the truth spoken in or with love. This does not mean just using terms of endearment, or anything of that sort. Speaking with affection or love in this context means speaking the truth in its fullness, with complete awareness of the person to whom you are speaking. How many of us can do this? If we think about it we will realize that when we speak to people we do not usually look at them. Have you ever noticed this? It is probably true in your case, and in the case of people who speak to you. When they speak to you, or when you speak to them, you do not look at them. You look over their shoulder, you look at their forehead, up at the ceiling, down at the ground – anywhere, almost, except at the person to whom you are speaking. If you do not look at them, you cannot be aware of them.

We can say that love, in the sense in which I am using the term at present, means awareness of the being of another person. But if you do not *know* the other person, how can you speak affectionately to them? It just is not possible. We like to think, of course, that we have love for people, that we are affectionate, but this is very rarely so. We usually see other people in terms of our own emotional reactions to them. We react emotionally to them in a certain way, and then we attribute that emotional reaction *to* them as a quality *of* them. If, for instance, people do what we would like them to do, then we say that they are good, kind, helpful, and so on. Thus we are not really communicating with that particular person. What really happens, most of the time, is that we are communicating, or trying to communicate, or pretending to communicate, with our own mental projections.

This is especially so in the case of those who are – allegedly – near and dear to us. Parents and children, brothers and sisters, husbands and wives, very rarely know one another. They might have lived together for twenty, or thirty, or forty years, but they do not know one another. They know their own reactions to one another, and those reactions they attribute to the other person. They think, therefore, that they know them; but they do not really know them at all. They know only their own projected mental and emotional states.

This is a sobering thought. There used to be a saying, 'It is a wise father that knows his own child.' Well, it is a wise child that knows his own father; it is a wise wife that knows her own husband; it is a very wise husband that knows his own wife: because the more you live with people, especially those to whom you are related by blood or by strong emotional ties, the less, in the real spiritual sense, you know them. After all, to the baby, what is mother? Mother is just a wonderful sensation of warmth and comfort, security and well-being: *that* is what mother is. The child does not know mother as a person. The same is true with other relations. And it usually remains like that for most of our lives, with a bit of refinement and rationalization here and there. This is true for most of us, most of the time.

This is why there is so much misunderstanding between people, so much failure to communicate, so many disappointments, especially in the more intimate relationships of life. People are at cross purposes because one person does not know another and therefore cannot love another. There is just pseudo-communication between projections, and nothing more. This may sound drastic and perhaps rather horrifying, but it is true, and it is best and most salutary if we face up to the truth about ourselves and other people as quickly as possible, and realize that, in most cases, our so-called relationships are just a maze of such mutual projections, with no mutual knowledge and understanding at all – not to speak of mutual love.

But if there *is* such a thing as mutual awareness and mutual love, and if we *are* able to speak the truth to another person, being aware of that other person – which means, of course, loving that other person, love being awareness of their being – we shall also know what they need. If we really know the other person we shall know what they need – as distinct from what we think they ought to have because it would be good for us if they had it, which is what most people mean by 'knowing what is good for others'. Knowing what people need means knowing what is good for them quite objectively, without reference to ourselves. We will then know what has to be provided, what given, how they have to be helped, and so on. This brings us to the third level of Perfect Speech, or the third stage of communication.

3. The level of helpfulness

According to the Buddha we should speak that which is useful, in the sense of speaking in such a way as to promote the growth, especially the spiritual growth, of the person to whom we are speaking.[365] This need not involve anything as formal as specifically religious instruction, although this too is very useful. Broadly speaking this aspect of Perfect Speech – speaking that which is useful – consists in speaking in such a way that the person or persons to whom we are speaking are raised in the scale of being and consciousness, and not lowered. At least we can be positive and appreciative. Most people are so negative. You tell them about something good, something happy, and they either pull a long face, or depreciate it, or try to undermine you. In the end you may feel quite guilty about having enjoyed that particular thing, or having liked and appreciated it. So we must at least be positive and appreciative, realizing that when we have this kind of attitude the other person is helped to grow – not when we are negative, critical, or destructive. Constructive criticism, based on emotional positivity and genuine concern for the other person, is not of course excluded. Such criticism – which may be mutual – promotes spiritual growth. It is therefore useful in the best sense of the term, and to be included under Perfect Speech.

There is a time of course for criticism, even destructive criticism: that is a legitimate activity. But most of us take to it far too readily and easily, to the neglect of the more positive side. Even if we are not in a position to give specifically spiritual instruction, or to enlighten people – and very few of us can do that in any way, or to any extent – we can at least be helpful. We can at least be positive, and appreciative of whatever good we see growing in, or emerging from, that other person. In any case even if we do on occasion give some sort of instruction, this will only be effective if given in a helpful, positive, and constructive spirit.

If we communicate in the way we have described: if we speak the truth, the whole truth, and nothing but the truth; if we speak with love, that is with awareness of the other person's being; if we speak in such a way as to promote the other's growth, to have a healthy, positive effect on them; if we are more concerned about their needs than about our own; if we are not projecting our own emotional states, or using or exploiting them; then the result will be that in speaking to, or communicating with, another person we will forget all about ourselves. This brings us to the fourth and highest level of Perfect Speech, or the fourth and final stage of communication.

4. The level of promoting concord, harmony, and unity

As well as all the qualities we have already described, Perfect Speech is speech that promotes concord, harmony, and unity. This does not just mean verbal agreement. It does not mean saying yes all the time. It does not even mean sharing the same ideas – it is not a matter of 'You believe in Buddhism, I believe in Buddhism.' That is not what is meant here. 'Speech that promotes concord, harmony, and unity' really means mutual helpfulness, based on truthfulness and awareness of each other's being and each other's needs, leading to mutual self-transcendence. This mutual self-transcendence is Perfect Speech *par excellence*. It is not only Perfect Speech, but also the perfection of communication. When this sort of concord, harmony, and unity, this sort of understanding, is complete, is perfect, nothing more need be said. Even on the ordinary level, when you get to know someone for the first time, for a while you do a lot of talking, exchange ideas, get to know each other, but the more you get to know each other, in a sense the less there is to say. When Perfect Speech culminates in harmony, oneness, and mutual self-transcendence, it also culminates in silence.

We should not think that silence is mere absence of sound. When all sound dies away – when the sound of the traffic in the street or the creaking of the chairs in the room, the sound of our own breath, and even the 'sound' of our thoughts, is utterly stilled – what is left is not just something negative or dead, not just a vacuum. What is left is a living silence.

In this connection, I remember the great example of the Indian sages and teacher, Ramana Maharshi, who died in 1950.[366] I had the good fortune to be with him for some time, about a year before he died, and he perfectly exemplified this attitude. He just sat there on a dais in the hall of the ashram, on a kind of settee with a tiger skin spread on it, and most of the time he said nothing at all. He had sat there for forty years, more or less, and though the hall was usually full of people, when one entered there was a strangely vibrant quality to that silence. It quite literally seemed as though the silence flowed from him. One could almost see waves of silence flowing from him, flowing over all those people, flowing into their hearts and minds and calming them down. As you sat down yourself you quite literally felt the silence flowing over you, calming and quieting you, washing away all your thoughts. This is not to speak poetically or imaginatively – you felt it quite literally. You felt it as a sort of positive wave-like power flowing over you all the time. *This* was the silence – the real silence, the true silence – that Ramana Maharshi so beautifully exemplified.[367]

Silence of this quality is very rare. Even ordinary silence, the lowest form of silence, is only too rare in modern life. Certainly in most of our lives there is far too much noise, and usually far too much talking. 'Talking', here, does not mean real communication through speech, but mere verbalization, the multiplication of words without too much meaning. One cannot help thinking that speech, which is so precious and so wonderful, so expressive and such a treasure, should be something exceptional. At least it should be something, like eating, that you do occasionally, after thought and preparation; but all too often speech precedes thought, while talking is the rule, and silence the exception.

But perhaps there is hope for us all, as there was for the young Macaulay, about whom the great wit Sydney Smith remarked, 'Macaulay is improving. He has flashes of silence.'[368] Most of us are in this position. Maybe we *are* improving. Maybe we *do* have, occasionally, even quite brilliant flashes of silence. We should therefore perhaps try to make more time for silence in our lives: make more time just to be quiet, just to be alone, by ourselves. Unless we do this from time to time, say at least for an hour or two every day, we shall find the practice of meditation rather difficult.

from *The Buddha's Noble Eightfold Path*

7. RIGHTS AND DUTIES

Peace springs naturally and spontaneously from duties quietly and unobtrusively done, just as from the rose tree comes the rose, or as the lotus rises from the lotus lake.

Duties consist in what is due from us to others, and are based upon giving, whereas rights consist in what is due from others to us, and are based (from the subjective point of view) upon grasping and getting. The performance of one's duty does not mean merely the grudging recognition and half-hearted rendering of what is legally or even morally due to one's family and friends, social or national group, political party, or religious organization, but in the unobstructed outward flow of one's love and compassion over the whole world. Duty is not, as the poet calls her, the 'Stern daughter of the Voice of God',[369] but the sweet child of the realization of emptiness – *śūnyatā* – within the depths of our own heart. The conscientious performance of one's duties to mother and father, child and wife, friends and acquaintances, masters and disciples, and to the complementary halves of all the other human relationships in which we are inevitably involved, results in the gradual loosening of the bonds of selfishness and egotism. The word for duty and the word for religion (which consists at bottom in the eradication of the ego-sense) are, in the language of India, one word: Dharma. But the clamorous insistence upon our rights, upon what is legally, morally, or even spiritually due from others to us, only strengthens greed, strengthens desire, strengthens selfishness, strengthens egotism.

The performance of one's duties results in the establishment of love and peace, the attempted extortion of one's rights in the outbreak of hatred and violence. Duties unite, rights divide. Duties are cooperative, rights competitive. The former depend upon our own selves, and are therefore swift and easy of accomplishment; the latter depend on others, and are therefore tardy and difficult, if not impossible, of achievement. Rights are wrested forcibly from other human beings outside, but duties are softly and sweetly laid upon us by the voice of the Divine – of our own potential Buddhahood – reverberating within.

Buddhism, being based upon the realization of emptiness, upon egolessness, upon unselfishness, teaches the doctrine of the mutual interpenetration of all things, inculcates the practice of love and compassion, exhorts men and women to perform their duties in every walk of life, and therefore tends naturally towards the ultimate establishment of peace, both in the hearts and minds of men and in the world of events outside us. Western political systems, on the contrary, however different or even antagonistic they may outwardly seem, are all based upon the concept, ultimately of dogmatic Christian origin, of the existence of separate, mutually exclusive ego-entities which are socially, politically, and even spiritually valuable and significant in themselves. All such systems therefore justify hatred and excuse violence, all insist on the intrinsic reasonableness of clamorous agitation for rights, and all therefore, without exception – despite emphatic protestations to the contrary – result in the eventual outbreak of war, both in the individual psyche and in the life of societies and nations. Emptiness, egolessness, the performance of duties, and internal and external peace and harmony, are members of the same nirvāṇic series, just as egotism, individualism, the claiming of rights, and external violence and warfare are the indissoluble links of the same saṃsāric chain.

The world today truly needs peace, but does not sincerely desire it. For peace is sought not in the dynamic equilibrium of selfless mutual performance of duties, but in the mechanical manipulation of merely superficial and therefore unstable adjustments between a host of conflicting egotistic claims. There can be peace in the world between men and between nations only when the hidden roots of disharmony – the concept of a separate soul, self, or ego – are ruthlessly dug up and cast into the blazing fire of selflessness. There can be peace in the world only when doing one's duty is stressed more emphatically than getting one's rights, when it is considered more intrinsically valuable to confer a benefit upon one's fellow human beings than to receive one from them. It is no more possible to get peace by means of the egotistic assertion of rights than it is possible to gather grapes of thistles or figs of thorns. But peace springs naturally and spontaneously from duties quietly and unobtrusively done, just as from the rose tree comes the rose, or as the lotus rises from the lotus lake.

'But', some will protest, 'if we simply perform our duties, without demanding our rights in return, we shall be taken advantage of and exploited by unscrupulous politicians and crooked capitalists; we shall be abused and trampled upon by people on every side.' This objection would be valid only if the performance of duty were envisaged as something which applied not to all sections of society, but to some only. But since the two ends of a human relationship are as inseparable as the two ends of a stick, and since our rights become duties when looked at from the other end, and since no one will consider himself to be without rights, the performance of duties is an obligation which rests equally upon the shoulders of all of us and from which none can escape. The remedy for any injustice or inequality in human relationships, whether domestic, social, civic, political, cultural, racial, or religious, is not an insistence upon the rights of one party, but on the duties of the other. The reminder of their duties appeals to all that is best and noblest in people and nations, to their innate selflessness and love; whereas the reminder of their rights appeals to all that is basest and worst in us, to our innate selfishness and greed, hatred, and violence. The appeal to the performance of duties is constructive and positive, and results in cooperation, harmony, and peace. The appeal to the claiming of rights is destructive and negative, and issues eventually in competition, discord, and open war. The former is based upon the Wisdom and Compassion of all the Buddhas, the latter upon the sophistry and mutual antagonism of the founders of the various schools of Western political thought. One is profound, the other superficial; one transcendental, the other mundane.

from *Crossing the Stream*

8. MINDFULNESS OF PURPOSE

If we are to act skilfully, we need to focus our attention on the objective situation rather than on ourselves and how we feel about what we are doing.

If we do not stay continually aware of our purpose and aim in life – which for a Buddhist is ultimately the attainment of Enlightenment – we will succumb to *asamprajanya*, which could be described as a sort of neurotic introspection with no clear purpose or point. We can be aware in some degree of what is going on in our mind, we can even have a measure of faith in the possibility of attaining to higher states of being, but if we aren't fully mindful – that is, if we aren't watchful with regard to our mental states, our speech, and our actions – we will 'fall from one's level of being' to a lower level of existence through the process of karma and rebirth.

If we do not bring our activities of body, speech, and mind into line with our discriminating awareness and our faith – that is, if our approach is purely psychological – we will come to grief. If we are careless or cavalier with regard to ethics, no amount of discriminating awareness will save us. The point is that it is possible to examine and analyse our mental states without actually being mindful or watchful with regard to them any more than to our speech and physical actions. If we are preoccupied with our mental states in this unhealthy, even neurotic way to such an extent that we don't heed the ethical implications of those mental states in terms of our actions of body, speech, and mind, there is bound to be an overall deterioration in our level of being.

This is because our level of being is determined by our volitional actions, by whether they are skilful or unskilful, not by whether or not we feel good while performing those actions. Unfortunately, there is a tendency in the West to be far more concerned about the complexities of our inner psychological states than about the much simpler questions of how to live an ethical life. We may perhaps fear, for example, that giving up some unskilful activity may disrupt the free flow of our energies: it may well do this, but we should then be able to redirect that energy into a more skilful activity.

It is true that Buddhist ethics are ethics of intention, but this does not mean that they are simply about how we feel; rather, they are about our intentions with regard to objective situations. If we are to act skilfully, we need to focus our attention on the objective situation rather than on ourselves and how we feel about what we are doing. It may be reasonable to expect to get something out of what we do, at least occasionally, but the paradox is that we are only going to get something out of it to the extent that our focus is not on getting anything out of it at all.

from *Know Your Mind*

9. WHY WE CONCEAL THINGS

What prevents many of us from confessing and from being more open generally is the feeling that if other people knew us as we were, then they would no longer accept us.

We often conceal things not just from other people, but even from ourselves. We don't like to admit that we have done something wrong, that we have made a mistake. It's a form of humiliation to feel that we have not lived up to our image of ourself. Someone once said that when you sit down to write your autobiography, the first thing you become aware of is what you are going to leave out. Almost inevitably you don't tell the whole story. 'Oh no, I'm not going to say that. I'll say everything else, but not that.' To be happy for others to see you exactly as you are, warts and all, is very difficult. Usually there is some little nook or cranny of your character or your life or your past that you don't want anybody to know about. You don't even think about it yourself very much; you hide it even from yourself. Nietzsche said, 'Memory says I did such and such, pride says I couldn't possibly have done it, and pride wins.'[370]

Ideally, of course, it should be possible to lead such a life that you can be open with everybody – one's life should ideally be an open book – but most people have at least a few pages, not to say the odd chapter or two, which they would prefer other people not to look at.

It's a strain relating to others with only a part of yourself, keeping back another part that they are never allowed to see. If you never relate to them as a complete, whole person, they don't know who you are, or at least they don't know the whole of you. This doesn't mean that if you have committed a crime you should tell it to everybody – that might be unwise – but certainly there should be a few people with whom you can be completely frank. Assuming you share with them a common spiritual ideal, they will be for you the spiritual community in the full sense. If you don't have friends whom you can trust totally, you are in quite a difficult position.

What prevents many of us from confessing and from being more open generally is the feeling that if other people knew us as we were, then they would no longer accept us. 'If people knew what I was really like, they wouldn't want to have any more to do with me.' But within the context of the spiritual community you are still accepted, even though people may strongly disapprove of what you have done. You may find it difficult to make that distinction – and it may be difficult for your friends in practice – but in principle they will try to retain the same *mettā* for you even though they may be very grieved at what you have done. To be open, you have got to have this kind of confidence in other people's genuine, basic goodwill towards you, which you are convinced will remain unchanged under all circumstances. Even if they tell you off, it will be with basic good will.

Of course, trust – the confidence that people will deal with you from a basis of love rather than from a basis of power – cannot be forced, even in the spiritual community. True confession cannot be the kind of mechanical procedure which goes under the name of confession in so many parts of the Buddhist world. You need to be in close, trustful communication with the person to whom you confess, and you can only trust people if you feel they are not going to hurt you, not going to take advantage of your openness. In a way you need to feel that their attitude towards you is basically like that of the Buddha. Whatever you have done, they are going to forgive you. Their basic attitude towards you is not going to change; they will have the same *mettā* for you even after you have confessed, when they know the worst about you.

from *Transforming Self and World*

10. BUDDHIST CONFESSION

Ideally we should be open with our friends all the time, and anything obstructing communication should be cleared up at once, so confession should be an everyday practice.

You may discover that there is something in your life which is incompatible with one's spiritual commitment, but which you are unwilling to give up. It becomes a sore and sensitive area that one is not prepared to discuss with anybody, especially not with one's spiritual friends. Yes, you feel guilty; you know that what you are doing is unskilful. But you are determined to hang on to this pet weakness. You don't come clean and confess it because you would then be openly confronting the fact that you were doing something unskilful – and you would also be urged by your friends to give it up, so as to clear the path to more positive states.

In concealing your fault from others you are also in a sense concealing it from yourself, in that you are not really facing up to its implications, which are that it is obstructing the realization of the positive. You are sort of hoping to muddle through somehow. Thus it is not unconnected with *vicikitsā*, doubt and indecision. You may even start to rationalize your unskilful behaviour, find all sorts of arguments to justify it. Because you are avoiding clarity, one's state of mind becomes duller and duller. Your friends may be aware that there is something wrong, that you are not making progress for some reason, and they may try to get you to bring your difficulty out into the open. But you stubbornly pretend that there's nothing the matter.

As long as there is this sacred area of your life that is off-limits as far as your friends are concerned, you are effectively closing yourself off from them. You become increasingly out of touch – not because of your unskilful activity (otherwise we should all be out of touch with each other most of the time) but because you insist on holding back from communicating, to those who are supposed to be your friends, something that is evidently a very pressing problem. The longer you put off coming clean with your friends, the more difficult it becomes to do it, and the stronger becomes your commitment to your pet weakness. So this *upakleśa* of slyness-concealment, once it becomes entrenched, is one of the most problematic to deal with.

The danger is that you will eventually break off contact with your spiritual friends altogether in favour of people who are less demanding. At this point, the most important thing is to feel that your spiritual friends are on your side, that they are not against you. If they really are your friends, they will do their best to maintain contact even though you may be getting quite defensive and isolated as a result of your secrecy and feelings of guilt.

The principal antidote to slyness-concealment is confession of faults. Ideally we should be open with our friends all the time, and anything obstructing communication should be cleared up at once, so confession should be an everyday practice. But what is confession? It is not just admission or acknowledgement of what we have done. It is true that in a legal context admission and confession are more or less interchangeable expressions; they are interchangeable, however, only if they are both taken to have only a psychological significance. But confession in a spiritual context is primarily not a psychological but an ethical act. If we confess to a spiritually unskilful action there is obviously a psychological element there, inasmuch as we are referring to a mental attitude, something pertaining to our own psyche. But there is more to it than this. Indeed, the psychology of the Abhidharma as a whole is not just about psychology. Although it does involve becoming a healthy human being, it is also about developing beyond that level.

When we confess to an unskilful action we are confessing to a failure to live up to our own ideals. We are invoking a norm, a set of ethical and spiritual ideals that we have accepted for ourselves, and that we share with other members of the spiritual community. These ideals are not imposed upon us. There is no veiled threat behind them that if we don't try to live by them we'll be in big trouble. It is this, in fact, that makes them truly ethical and spiritual ideals. And it is this also that makes a refusal to confess one's ethical failures so damaging towards one's integrity as an individual.

A general confession – 'I'm afraid I sometimes behave rather badly' – is not enough. To be effective, confession should be very specific, and it should be addressed to someone who understands the seriousness of what we are confessing. If we have any doubt about whether or not to confess something, we need to make a particular point of confessing it, because that doubt is quite likely to be the first stirrings of slyness-concealment. As its name suggests, it is a slippery customer that has to be watched out for carefully.

We should ideally confess to the person we have offended, but if they don't share our ideals, all we can really do is make an *admission* to them. To make our confession in the spiritual sense, we will need to talk to someone else who understands the Buddhist distinction between skilful and unskilful. In this case it is more important to make the confession than to make the admission.

Confession has been an aspect of the relationship between teacher and disciple in the Buddhist tradition from the earliest times. It is customary in any well-ordered monastic situation for the pupil to go to the teacher every morning and evening and confess any unskilful actions they are aware of having committed during those twelve hours, and ask for forgiveness for any they are not aware of. One says, 'Whatever faults I have committed of body, speech, and mind, please forgive me.' And the teacher says '*Khamāmi, khamāmi*,' 'I forgive, I forgive.'

This practice differs from Catholic confession and absolution in that the teacher doesn't forgive on behalf of God; in fact, he doesn't forgive offences committed against anyone apart from himself. It is a purely personal exchange. One is asking forgiveness for any offences committed against him personally. If, for example, one had committed an offence against the rules of the order, then that would be dealt with by the order as a whole. However, in respect of offences that don't concern him personally, the teacher can, if not forgive, certainly listen to one's confession and advise one what to do, or what practice to take up, to help one avoid repeating that particular fault.

If – as is usual among modern Western Buddhists – one is not in a traditional teacher–disciple situation but part of a spiritual community, confession can still be very much part of one's spiritual life. Spiritual friends (*kalyāṇa mitras*) can help one another a great deal through mutual confession and exploration of how to act more skilfully in future.

There is a Tibetan practice, originally deriving from the Sarvāstivāda school, of confessing to the thirty-five Buddhas of confession, who each preside over a different set of the monastic rules. That is, one confesses to whichever Buddha presides over the set of rules that includes the rule that one has transgressed. It is important, though, not to misunderstand this idea of confessing to the Buddhas. When Buddhist texts speak of asking forgiveness of the Buddhas and Bodhisattvas, this is not to say that the Buddhas might not forgive one if one didn't placate them.

After all, what is forgiveness? It is to let someone off the consequences of their action in terms of one's own personal reaction to it. It is to say that in effect the matter is now closed, the slate is wiped clean. No vicious circle of action and reaction, offence and retaliation, has been initiated. But as far as the Buddhas are concerned, one's breaking a precept is no offence to them. It is essentially an offence against oneself – because one will be reaping the *vipāka* of one's karma in the future. In that sense one is going to have to forgive oneself. Of course, as already discussed, one should be careful not to be too self-referential; as well as harming oneself through one's action one will in most cases have caused harm to someone else. One cannot forgive oneself on their behalf, so to speak. Nor can one effectively confess to oneself, though it may be a start.

from *Know Your Mind*

11. 'THE OPPRESSION OF EXISTENCE'

It's as though there is some force at work in the world almost compelling us to do unskilful things against our better judgement and our own wishes.

> In the oppression of existence (or) through foolish thought, whatever severe evil I have done, in the presence of the Buddha, I confess all this evil. And I confess that evil which has been heaped up by me in the oppression of birth, by the various oppressions of activity due to passion, in the oppression of existence, in the oppression of the world, in the oppression of the fleeting mind,

in the oppression of impurities caused by the foolish and stupid thoughts, and in the oppression of the arrival of evil friends, in the oppression of fear, in the oppression of passion, in the oppression of hatred and in the oppression of folly and darkness, in the oppression of the opportunity, in the oppression of time, in the oppression of gaining merits, standing in (my) oppression before the Buddha, I confess all this evil.[371]

The word translated as 'oppression' is the Sanskrit *saṃkaṭa*, for which the dictionary gives the following definitions: 'brought together, contracted, closed, narrow, strait, crowded together, dense, impervious, impassable, crowded with, full of; a strait, difficulty, critical condition, danger to or from'. That gives one quite a good idea of what *saṃkaṭa* means, and makes it clear that this term 'oppression', though not bad, is not a fully adequate translation by any means.

The *saṃkaṭas* are those factors by which one is surrounded, which crowd in upon one, which oppress one, which squeeze and limit one. This suggests that there are all sorts of unskilful acts that one performs, as it were, under duress. Our unskilful acts are not those of a free, untrammelled will. If only conditions had been a bit more favourable, we might not have done them at all. There are so many factors in existence which oppress us, making it more likely that we will do something unskilful, and more difficult for us to act skilfully. Circumstances are so often against us. Our surroundings tend almost to compel us to do what is unskilful. Not that that is really any excuse, ultimately, because it is due to our weakness that we feel the oppression *as* oppression. But once again we come back to the point that people are not deliberately wicked; it's more that they are weak and give in to pressure.

The list of oppressions is a long one: existence, birth, bodily activity, the world, the fleeting mind, impurities caused by the foolish thought, the arrival of evil friends, fear, passion, hatred, folly and darkness, the opportunity, time, gaining merits. The *sūtra* confesses evil committed under the oppression of all these things. So clearly they are not factors that we occasionally encounter and have to resist; they are things that surround us and almost crush us all the time. It's not as though they are just there but don't bother us; they are all around us, hemming us in, breaking in upon us, weighing upon us, and restricting our movements. They are a constant chronic danger, and if we are not conscious of the fact it is because we go along with them to such an extent that there is nothing in us to be oppressed.

The list begins with 'the oppression of existence'. This implies that conditioned existence itself – just being a human being – is pressurizing us to perform unskilful actions. All you have to do is go out for a little walk and you see all sorts of things that cannot but give rise to unskilful thoughts, even unskilful activities, on your part. To be more specific, city life, we could say, is an oppression. In the city, we have to put so much energy into keeping the world at bay – keeping the world from encroaching upon what we have gained already in the way of mindfulness and positivity – that we don't have much left over with which to make real progress. Still, we have to admit that this only happens because something within us has an affinity with these oppressions of the world.

The sense in which 'foolish thought' might become an oppression is fairly obvious. Thoughts are running through our minds involuntarily all the time. We don't deliberately set out to think an unskilful thought; it just pops into our head. We didn't ask it to come, we didn't want it to be there; it just came. This is our experience. We call it 'our' thought, but sometimes it seems as though it is coming from outside, invading us. When we sit to meditate, we try to concentrate our minds, keep them clear and pure, and all these unskilful foolish thoughts keep rushing in and undoing all our best efforts. This is how we feel. And yet we cannot escape the fact that these thoughts are our own; they belong to us.

Then, 'the oppression of birth'. According to some psychologists, birth itself is a traumatic experience. There you are in the womb before birth: warm, relatively quiet, quite comfortable. Then suddenly you are violently squeezed through a narrow aperture, and come out at the other end into a terrible bright light to be seized and plunged into water. This must surely be a very traumatic experience. You are slapped to make you breathe, rubbed with a rough towel, then dressed, tied up, and then you start feeling hungry. This might well be described as the oppression of birth.

But next, in what way might bodily activity be an oppression, or even 'various oppressions'? Well, think about it. You wake up in the morning, you've got to get up and dress yourself, go to the lavatory, brush your teeth, and then you've got to eat. All these are bodily activities which are needed to keep you going. Sometimes there seem to be so many of them that you forget what you are living *for*. As you get older, physical existence becomes more and more of a burden. In the end you can hardly walk, or even get up from a chair without help. You can't get on to a bus without a helping hand. Maybe you can't dress yourself or go to the toilet without help. This is when this oppression really strikes home – although when you are young, you sometimes get a foretaste of it when you are ill. You can't think of very much at all beyond your physical state, your aches and pains, your medicine, and so on.

As for 'the oppression of the world', this could be taken in a narrower sense than the oppression of existence, to mean the whole of social life. Indeed, whatever the specific oppression may be, it is all-pervasive. Take, for instance, 'the arrival of evil friends'. It is not that we occasionally meet an evil friend, someone who is going to try to induce us to perform unskilful actions; we are surrounded by them. Go for a ride on a bus; there they all are. Go to watch a football match; there they all are. We are surrounded by people who are in a sense 'evil friends', in that their influence on us is not a positive, skilful one.

Then there is 'the oppression of the instant', having to act or make a decision when one may be off guard, and 'the oppression of time', or as we would say 'pressure of time', which is what so often seems to keep us from skilful action. Certainly under the conditions of modern life we often feel that we don't have enough time to do things properly, or think about what the skilful way to act would be. We act hastily, and the chances are that we act unskilfully.

Even gaining merits, according to the *sūtra*, is an oppression – odd as it may sound. What the *sūtra* is of course pointing to is the danger of getting too attached to our merit. If we think of the spiritual life in terms of acquiring merits too much then it becomes quite oppressive so far as our real spiritual life is concerned. The text doesn't explicitly say so, but I take it that the merits referred to here are of the lower kind, the kind which guarantee you a place in a higher heavenly world after death. I don't see how merits which are dedicated to Enlightenment could be an oppression. Oppression, after all, only arises when you are trying to do something skilful and external factors are getting in the way. Life itself can get in the way, time can get in the way, but merits that are dedicated to Enlightenment surely can't get in the way.

This list draws attention to the fact that there are all sorts of unskilful factors in existence which are always pressing in on us, and from which it is very difficult for us to escape, because we are experiencing them all the time. They never let up. It's as though there is some force at work in the world almost compelling us to do unskilful things against our better judgement and our own wishes. If we are surrounded by these things, sooner or later they are going to have some definite effect. It is not that they give rise to unskilfulness in some mysterious, indirect way. If we are constantly surrounded by evil friends, sooner or later they will have some influence on us. The list is of course selective; all unskilful or unhelpful factors are of this nature.

This is not to suggest that the individual is absolved from responsibility for his behaviour. In confessing the evil you have committed, you accept responsibility for it. It may be understandable when you fail to stand up to the oppressions, but it is your responsibility to stand up to them. If something is not your fault, why should you confess it? There would be no point. The fact that you confess means that you accept responsibility, even though you were strongly tempted. To make a technical distinction, one could say that these oppressions are the occasion of unskilful actions, but not their cause. You are their cause, and therefore the responsibility is yours. Perhaps you are very strongly tempted, but you still have the capacity to resist.

from *Transforming Self and World*

3
THE NATURE OF SPIRITUAL EFFORT

1. LIVING WITH PURPOSE

The question is always the same: what effect is this going to have on my development as a human being?

Whatever situation confronts us, whatever experience befalls us, whatever opportunity presents itself to us, we always have to ask ourselves: 'What bearing does this have – directly or indirectly – on the higher purpose I have set myself?' We have to raise this question in relation to our work, our personal relationships, our social, cultural, and sporting activities, our interests – the books we read, the music we listen to, the films we watch. The question is always the same: what effect is this going to have on my development as a human being?

Making the living of a religious or even spiritual life in a conventional sense our main consideration will not necessarily have any kind of positive impact on our development. But if we make the development of consciousness the primary motivation in everything we do, we will make sure progress. And if we don't – well, we won't.

from *What is the Sangha?*

2. THE SPIRAL PATH

No doubt it is good to have the concept of Enlightenment before us, but it needs to be brought down to earth.

According to Buddhist tradition, our mundane experience naturally consists in action and reaction between opposite factors: pleasure and pain, love and hatred, and so on. Upon taking up the spiritual life – which in this context means becoming a novice bodhisattva – you get the same process of interaction between factors, but one factor augments rather than opposes the other. One traditional description of this process is in terms of the sequence of positive *nidānas* or links: awareness of the inherently unsatisfactory nature of existence, in dependence upon which arises faith, then joy, rapture, bliss, calm, meditative concentration, and 'knowledge and vision of things as they really are'.[372] However, although this sequence is progressive or spiral rather than cyclical, it is reversible; you can revert back through the sequence until you are back where you started. It's a bit like playing snakes and ladders.

So the crucial point of the spiritual life is the point at which one passes from this skilful but reversible state to a state that is irreversible. This is the point of insight, the point at which one enters the Stream, the point at which – in terms of the sequence outlined above – one gains knowledge and vision of things as they really are. This is the real object of the spiritual life. There is no need to think in terms of Enlightenment or Buddhahood; that is simply the inevitable culmination of the irreversible sequence of skilful mental states that ensues from insight. Once you have entered the Stream, you are irreversibly bound for Enlightenment, one could say; you have sufficient spiritual momentum to take you all the way. You may still have a long way to go, but you are now safe from any danger of losing what you have gained.

It is therefore said of the Buddha's 'victory', his attainment of Enlightenment, that it is irreversible. It cannot be undone. There is no outside power that can make a Buddha no longer a Buddha. This applies not only to the Buddha, but also to the *arhant*, the once-returner, and the Stream Entrant – and of course the irreversible bodhisattva.

But until we have passed through that gate of irreversibility we are in a precarious position. This is why we need to make a constant effort in our spiritual life and also make sure that we are living and working in conditions that support our spiritual efforts. Until we have reached that point of no return, we need the most positive situation, the most helpful environment, we can possibly get.

This is what the Buddha was getting at in his last words, '*appamādena sampādetha*', which can be translated 'with mindfulness, strive'.[373] To reach the point of irreversibility one has to go on making an effort – including the effort to be mindful and aware enough to ensure that the conditions one lives in are conducive to one's making the best effort one possibly can. One can make a great deal of effort, but if it does not include an effort to create more favourable conditions, one is almost wasting one's energy. On the other hand, one can be in the most favourable conditions imaginable, but if one is not making an effort, what use are those conditions? Both are necessary.

Many people become aware of the effect of positive conditions when they go on retreat for the first time. The degree to which one can change in the course of just a few days is remarkable. Just leaving the city and staying in the country, being undisturbed by the pull of trivial distractions, and doing a bit more meditation and Dharma study than you usually have time for, can transform you into quite a different person – much happier, much more positive. So it isn't enough to try to change one's mental state through meditation; one needs the cooperation of one's environment. Without this it is very difficult, even impossible, to develop spiritually up to the point of irreversibility.

This fundamental concept of irreversibility – the point at which one's commitment to the spiritual path is so strong that no conditions can sway it – has been lost sight of to some extent, both in the Theravāda and in the Mahāyāna. This is a pity. No doubt it is good to have the concept of Enlightenment before us, but it needs to be brought down to earth; and thinking in terms of Stream Entry – in the broad sense, not in the narrow sense which opposes it to the bodhisattva ideal – helps us to do that, reminds us that we cannot afford to slacken off our spiritual effort until we have reached the point of irreversibility.

from *The Bodhisattva Ideal*

3. THE FOUR EXERTIONS

Most of us have our own private dream-picture of ourselves. Closing our eyes we see ourselves as though in a mirror and think 'How beautiful! How noble!'

Perfect Effort, the sixth stage of the Noble Eightfold Path, consists of a set of exercises that are to be practised at this stage. These exercises are known as the four exertions. The four perfect exertions – as they are also called – consist in preventing, eradicating, developing, and maintaining their common object, which is good and bad thoughts, or as we say in Buddhism, skilful and unskilful mental states.[374] The effort which consists in preventing means the effort to prevent the arising in our minds of those unskilful thoughts or mental states which have not yet arisen. Similarly, eradicating means eradicating from our minds those unskilful states which are already present therein. Developing means developing within our minds those skilful states which are not there already, while maintaining means maintaining within our minds those skilful states which already exist there. Thus Perfect Effort is primarily psychological. It consists in unremitting work on oneself and upon one's own mind by means of preventing, eradicating, developing, and maintaining.

This classification is given as an incentive and a reminder, because it is so easy to slacken off. People start with lots of enthusiasm: they are all for Buddhism, all for meditation, all for the spiritual life; but very often it quickly wears off. Enthusiasm wanes, and after a while it is almost as though it had never been at all. This is because the forces of inertia within ourselves, the forces holding us back and keeping us down, are very strong indeed – even in simple matters like getting up early in the morning to meditate. You might make a resolution to get up half an hour earlier, and you might succeed once or twice, or even three times; but by the fourth morning temptation will almost certainly have set in, and it will be a matter of quite serious mental struggle and conflict whether you get up or whether you stay a few minutes longer in that warm, cosy bed. You are nearly always the loser, of course, because the forces of inertia are so strong. It is so easy for enthusiasm to wane, dwindle, and vanish.

Before we discuss these four exertions in detail there is one very important observation to be made. We cannot even begin to prevent, eradicate, develop, or maintain unless, to begin with, we know ourselves. That is to say, unless we know which way our minds are going, or know what the contents of our minds are. And to know ourselves requires great honesty – at least, great honesty with ourselves. It is not expected that we should be completely honest with other people, but at least so far as the four exertions are concerned we should be honest with ourselves.

If we want to practise the four exertions we must at least try to see ourselves as we truly are, so that we know what needs to be prevented, or eradicated, or developed, or maintained. Most of us have our own private dream-picture of ourselves. Closing our eyes we see ourselves as though in a mirror and think, 'How beautiful! How noble!' This is the highly idealized picture which most of the time we have of ourselves. Not endowed, perhaps, with all the virtues, not quite perfect, but a really warm, lovable, sympathetic, intelligent, kind, well-intentioned, honest, industrious human being – that is what we usually see. What we have to try to develop, what we have to demand and almost to pray for is, in the words of the poet, the grace 'to see ourselves as others see us';[375] and to see ourselves as others see us is not easy. We have to undertake a mental stocktaking of our own skilful and unskilful mental states – our own 'vices' and 'virtues'. Though no moral absolutes are involved here, we at least have to understand our own minds, or our own mental states and mental qualities, very seriously and honestly before we can even think of applying the four exertions. Otherwise we shall not know how to proceed, and no real improvement – no real development – will be possible.

from *The Buddha's Noble Eightfold Path*

4. WHAT COUNTS AS LAZINESS?

Being lazy really means being busy doing something that is not conducive to skilful mental states.

We tend to think of laziness as being about lack of exertion, but the Buddhist idea of laziness is quite different – and quite revealing. For Gampopa, for example, the most extreme form of laziness is devoting oneself day and night to defeating enemies and making money.[376]

Being lazy really means being busy doing something that is not conducive to skilful mental states: one's busyness actually prevents one from being aware of what one might otherwise be engaging in. In fact the fourteenth-century Tibetan teacher, Tsongkhapa, goes further than that: laziness, he is saying, is taking delight in the fact that one is not occupying oneself with something of higher value. It involves a sort of complacency and satisfaction in the fact that one is occupying oneself with lower things. To overcome laziness we need to be able to distinguish that which is worthwhile from that which is less so. This means that we need to think deeply about the implications of attaining concentrated mental states (*dhyāna*): what it will mean to attain *dhyāna* and what it will mean *not* to attain it. Eagerness (*chanda*) is based on this, and it is established to counteract laziness.

Tsongkhapa's remarks on laziness are especially important for those who are tempted to immerse themselves so deeply in various discussions and arguments about the teachings of Buddhism that they miss the whole point of them. However conscientiously one occupies oneself with the teachings, if one doesn't put them into practice, such occupation is no more than a form of laziness. This is not at all to say that Dharma study and Dharma practice are necessarily two different things. Study can be a method of practice just as meditation is. Study is, after all, an aspect of the first of the three wisdoms (listening, reflecting, and meditating).[377] Laziness sets in when one does not go on to reflect and meditate on the teachings one has studied.

from *Know Your Mind*

5. DISCIPLINE

Following a system of discipline doesn't necessarily have any spiritual value at all.

It is a good thing to have a definite framework of behaviour, definite guidelines, especially when one is young, and it is even a good thing to be quite strict in observing those guidelines. An old Brahmin lawyer I used to know in India, a very rigid, orthodox old man, was fond of saying, 'A disciplined life gives strength,' and this is true. In the case of this old man, he derived his strength from following the Brahminical rules, with some of which I would violently disagree because they involved the strict observance of the caste system. But they did make him into a very strong character, because he believed that he was following a divinely inspired way of life.

But following a system of discipline doesn't necessarily have any spiritual value at all. You develop a kind of strength in the army, in which you are governed by a certain ethos and have to observe certain rules. And even the 'rules' of Buddhism, the guidelines which you find in the traditional Vinaya Piṭaka, are not necessarily helpful to us now. The principle behind all of them is probably still valid, but it may require a different application, a different expression. It might be a useful exercise to go through all the Vinaya rules systematically, examining each rule to see what principle is involved, how it was applied or formulated in the Buddha's day, whether that formulation still applies, and, if not, what fresh formulation of that principle might be helpful.

Some would argue that one should continue to observe the rules out of faith in the Buddha. This sort of attitude cannot be disregarded altogether, but one could argue that it could not be the result of faith, because the Buddha encouraged his followers to think for themselves. The value of observing rules is not to be underestimated, but one has to give careful thought to what rules one does observe and why; one should not be inflexible about it.

It is no good trying to defend the Vinaya rules by saying, 'If it was good enough for the Buddha, it's good enough for me.' We shouldn't just accept the tradition unthinkingly. It's a question of finding a middle way. You can't go it alone, relying in a one-sided, individualistic way on your own judgement, your own opinion; you need to consult with those who are wiser and more experienced than yourself. On the other hand, you don't want to submit unquestioningly to authority. It is not easy to follow this middle path, but we have to try. There has to be a place for faith and there has to be a place for healthy scepticism. It is very easy to go from one extreme to the other, rather than searching for the middle way. But if we are going to accept some authority unquestioningly, why bother with Buddhism? Why not just go and join the Catholic Church, which is so much closer to us in culture? Why give ourselves the trouble of going to the East and setting up an infallible authority there? And on the other hand, if you're going to be a thoroughgoing sceptic, why bother with Buddhism at all? Go and be a humanist, go and be an agnostic. The way to advance in the Dharma is a middle way between the extreme of authoritarianism and the extreme of individualistic thinking for oneself.

from *The Inconceivable Emancipation*

6. A REGULAR ROUTINE

It is strange that people are often reluctant to adopt regular habits, because these do in fact make life easier.

In the *Satipaṭṭhāna Sutta* the Buddha exhorts the monk to apply clear comprehension in all the activities of daily life. Bending and stretching, wearing robes, carrying the begging-bowl, eating, drinking, chewing, savouring, attending to the calls of nature, speaking and keeping silent, are all carried out with awareness of what you are doing and why, so that that aspiration is allowed to permeate everything you do. Any activity, however small or apparently insignificant, can be done with a sense of purpose. You can even fall asleep mindfully, with a sense of when and why your period of rest is necessary. If you have to be up in the morning at 6.30 for meditation, your clear comprehension might take the form of making sure that you get to bed in good time so that you have enough sleep and won't just feel like a lie-in when the time comes to meditate.

If you are serious and passionate about reaching your spiritual goal, it is absolutely necessary to take a regular, disciplined approach to what you do. Success, as in any other enterprise – sport or art or business – depends on establishing a disciplined and committed lifestyle. It is strange that people are often reluctant to adopt regular habits, because these do in fact make life easier. If you live haphazardly, just doing what you feel like when you feel like it, you can end up not finding the time or inclination for things you know will benefit you. But with a regular routine you will still, for example, sit to meditate even when you don't feel like it, because you are aware of the benefits of doing so. You can take the likely outcomes of particular courses of action for granted – you don't have to reassess them every time you think about doing them.

It is equally important, however, not to get too rigid about this. The 'path' is not a set of rules that you can stick to mechanically and be sure of getting the results you want. At dinner time you might be able to get away with shovelling food into your mouth in the knowledge that your stomach will take care of the rest of the process, but it isn't like that with meditation, puja, or Dharma study. These practices are designed to be liberating, but if you lose touch with why you are doing them, they become so many obstacles to your progress. Mindfulness is an intelligent, responsive awareness to ever-changing conditions. If the urgent need to develop insight gets lost in the lacklustre business of keeping everything ticking over, it is time to look again at the balance of your life.

from *Living with Awareness*

7. CERTAINTY OF SUCCESS

Our tendency is perhaps to think of spiritual life as difficult and worldly life as easy, but there is no objective reason for this view.

In his *Bodhicaryāvatāra* Śāntideva says that the effect of giving, of puja – in short, of committing yourself to the spiritual life – is that you become 'without fear of being or becoming'.[378] The would-be bodhisattva has no more worries. You just give yourself to the spiritual life. You aren't bothered whether you are going to live or die, be rich or poor, be praised or blamed, or anything like that. You are just on the spiritual path and that's that. So long as you are still wondering what to do with your life – perhaps weighing up how much time to give to spiritual things and how much to worldly things – you remain unsure, unclear, and therefore unconfident. But once you have made up your mind and committed yourself, in a sense everything is looked after and there's nothing to worry about.

Our tendency is perhaps to think of spiritual life as difficult and worldly life as easy, but there is no objective reason for this view. Sometimes it is less trouble just to lead a spiritual life than to try to put things right in the world or even to try to have a successful and happy worldly career. In a way, it takes less effort to gain Enlightenment.

It's very difficult to be successful in the world – there are all sorts of factors that might upset one's plans – but if one follows the spiritual path one knows that, if one makes the effort, sooner or later success will come.

from *The Bodhisattva Ideal*

8. ENCOUNTERING THE *ḌĀKINĪ*

Sometimes it is said that the ḍākinī throws herself into the spiritual life just as a passionate woman flings herself into the arms of her lover.

Ḍākinīs are mysterious female figures who appear in the Tantric tradition. The word *ḍākinī* is derived from a Sanskrit root meaning direction, space, sky; and when Tantric texts were translated into Tibetan, *ḍākinī* was rendered as *khadroma*, which is usually translated 'sky-walker' or 'traveller in space'. Empty space represents absence of obstruction and therefore freedom of movement. This is not, of course, literal movement within space. Space or sky also represents mind in its absolute aspect; so the *ḍākinīs* represent the free-moving energies of the mind itself – they are the thrills or tremors of emotional energy that pass quivering through the mind, bubbling up from its very depths.

In developed Tantric Buddhism, especially in its Tibetan form, there are said to be three kinds of *ḍākinī*, representing three levels on which the *ḍākinī* principle, as we may call it, is experienced. First, there is the *ḍākinī* as female Buddha form. In early Buddhism, the Enlightenment principle, Buddhahood, was usually represented in the form of a perfect human body sitting cross-legged as though in meditation – and the body was usually male. But there is no reason why it should be male rather than female, and in the case of the *ḍākinī* as female Buddha, it happens to be female. Secondly, the *ḍākinī* is the embodiment of one's own upsurging energies. And thirdly, the *ḍākinī* can be seen as a spiritual companion and as representing the esoteric Tantric form of the third refuge – the refuge in the Sangha. The *ḍākinī* in this sense, as encountered in, for example, *The Life and Liberation of Padmasambhava*, is a highly advanced female spiritual practitioner in association with whom a male practitioner practises the Dharma and whose company is spiritually inspiring. She has a highly developed moral awareness, though not in a conventional sense. *Ḍākinīs* are usually described as being youthful and extremely beautiful, as well as having intense faith and devotion, and being pure-minded and given to meditation. As such, they are not at all common.

To get a real feeling for the *ḍākinī*, we can do no better than encounter one. I propose, therefore, simply to give a description of a particular *ḍākinī* figure, one who occupies an important place in the Tantra as practised in Tibet. We have already encountered her in the context of the *guru yoga*. She is known as Vajrayoginī, and in Tibetan Narokhachö, and she is also described as Sarvabuddhaḍākinī. *Sarva* means 'all', and *Buddha* of course means 'Enlightened one', so Sarvabuddhaḍākinī is the *ḍākinī* of all the Buddhas, the embodiment of all the energies that have carried all the Buddhas, past, present, and future, to Enlightenment. She is thus a very powerful figure indeed, as her appearance dramatically demonstrates. She is also, in a way, a Buddha figure in her own right.

She is not depicted sitting down meditating. She stands with her legs wide apart, her right leg straight and her left knee bent. She is moving towards the right, with her breasts, which are very full, thrust out, and her head tilted back. Her right arm hangs a little away from her side, while her left arm is raised above her head and bent back, the hand almost touching the head. The whole figure is brilliant red in colour, and completely naked. She wears only a few ornaments – which are of human bone – and an enormous garland of human skulls that hangs down below her knees. She has long dishevelled hair which falls straight down her back to her waist. In her right hand she holds a chopper with a *vajra* handle, while with her left hand she lifts a skull-cup filled with blood to her mouth and drinks it with evident enjoyment. She has what is called a wrathful smile, and three eyes, the extra one being in the middle of her forehead. She wears a crown of five human skulls, and on her left shoulder, lying horizontal and passing behind her upturned head, is a long staff, from the top of which there hangs down a type of small drum, called a *ḍamaru*, and a bell, with streamers. The head of the staff is formed by the vase of initiation, which is surmounted by crossed *vajras*, and, above them, three human heads, one on top of the other: a freshly severed head, a head that was severed some time ago and has begun to dry out and go yellow, and – at the top – a skull, on top of which a *vajra* stands upright. She tramples underfoot two figures, one red, the other black. Each has four arms. Usually the red figure holds a skull-cup filled with blood and a staff like the *ḍākinī*'s, while the black figure holds a small drum and a curved sword. Each has one pair of hands raised in supplication. And surrounding the naked red figure of the *ḍākinī* is a halo of flames.

I am not going to say what the *ḍākinī* 'means' – the figure makes its own impact. I will just elaborate a little on some aspects of the symbolism, and suggest a few associations. First of all, the *ḍākinī* is red in colour. In Tantric Buddhism, red is the colour of love, passion, and emotional arousal – which, in the case of any *ḍākinī*, is total. Blood suffuses not only her face; her whole body blushes crimson. So the *ḍākinī* represents the state of total emotional involvement in the spiritual life. This is also why her hair is dishevelled. She doesn't care about decorum, about keeping tidy, about what people may think or say. She just abandons herself. Sometimes it is said that the *ḍākinī* throws herself into the spiritual life just as a passionate woman flings herself into the arms of her lover. She represents that spiritual ideal of self-abandonment to the Three Jewels.

Usually people find it very difficult to give themselves in this way, not just to the spiritual life, but to anything. They find it difficult to plunge in, commit themselves, get totally involved, put all their emotions into what they are doing. As a result they don't achieve much in any direction, certainly not in a spiritual one. In many cases people can't give themselves in this way because they are emotionally blocked. They have to learn to loosen up, get their emotions flowing more freely – flowing, ultimately, in the direction of Enlightenment. This is what the red colour of the *ḍākinī* suggests – that in the spiritual life one should not be afraid to feel.

And the *ḍākinī* is naked. She is concerned only with direct experience, reality, truth. She has nothing to hide. She is completely open, completely honest. Nakedness is a prominent feature of Tantric symbolism, to underline the importance in the Tantra of being direct, unveiled, radical. In Tantric art, yogis, *ḍākas* (the *ḍākinī's* male counterpart), and *ḍākinīs*, even Buddhas, are often depicted naked, which is entirely scandalous from the point of view of Theravāda Buddhism, or even Zen. The nakedness is, of course, spiritual nakedness, nakedness of one's emotions, of one's being. However, it is not in the spirit of the Tantra to hide behind the idea of symbolism, and sometimes even literal nakedness is not without its significance, and even value.

from *Creative Symbols of Tantric Buddhism*

4
GREAT BUDDHISTS OF THE TWENTIETH CENTURY

Buddhism began with lives; it didn't begin with books.

Hero-worship is not in fashion at this time in history, at the end of the twentieth century – except, perhaps, in a perverted, degenerate or trivial form. History is nowadays presented – even to children – in terms of the small doings of ordinary people rather than the momentous actions of great individuals. It would appear that children are offered facts and figures – and of course pocket calculators – rather than the inspirational examples of heroes like Nelson and Florence Nightingale. And this does seem to me a very unfortunate development. We need people we can look up to, people on whom we can model ourselves, and from whom we can derive inspiration. We need, in short, heroes in the true, positive sense.

Above all, we need spiritual heroes; and not only heroes – even legendary heroes – from the dim and distant past, but also heroic exemplars from our own time. Nor is there any dearth of contemporary or near-contemporary ones. I have to say that I started turning over in my mind this subject of great Buddhists of the twentieth century with the assumption that there would be no more than a handful of individuals to consider. But it did not take me long to realize that I had a problem. There seemed to have been dozens upon dozens of them.

Unless one is going to attempt an exhaustive guide to the great Buddhists of the twentieth century one has to select. And unless one is going to do this according to mere whim, then one has to look around for some meaningful principles by which to make one's selection. On what basis could I focus on certain individuals and not others?

In the end I allowed two principles to direct my choice. First, I decided not to touch upon any great Buddhists who were still alive. After all, there is always the faint possibility of great Buddhists ceasing to be so, either by changing their religion or by losing their greatness of character – and then where would that leave us? Such things happen from time to time, unfortunately. We should heed Sophocles' warning: 'Call no man happy until he is dead,' and be wary of calling someone a great Buddhist too definitively before he or she is safely dead.

As for my second principle of selection, this was to consider no one with whom I had not had some kind of personal contact. I did, however, make an exception for Anagārika Dharmapala, the first of my five great Buddhists, who died in India in 1933 when I was still a small boy living in Tooting, London. I feel justified in making this exception because I do have the sense that I lived with him for several weeks while composing my biography of him in 1952, having spent this time among the many volumes of his diaries.

Just one preliminary question remains to be cleared up, but it is quite an important one. How do we define a great Buddhist? Well, in the first place, great Buddhists have to be Buddhists. That is, they have to go for Refuge to the Three Jewels, to the Buddha, the Dharma, and the Sangha. It is not enough in itself to be a great scholar of Buddhism, to be learned in Sanskrit and Pāli, to make outstanding and original contributions to Buddhist studies.

It's not enough, either, to occupy a prominent position in a Buddhist organization. During my time in the East it was a recurring puzzle to me, when I came into contact with various Buddhist organizations, and met their presidents and secretaries, to discover that these dignitaries weren't actually Buddhists. So it is not enough to have a position of influence in the Buddhist world. Nor of course is it enough to have been born into a position of influence in the Buddhist world – to have been born into a Buddhist royal family, say.

Moreover, a great Buddhist is not just a great individual with Buddhist leanings. To be a great Buddhist, one would have to possess at least some of the characteristically Buddhist qualities to an eminent degree. Great Buddhists possess not just a little bit of *mettā*, not just an occasional burst of *vīrya*, not just the beginnings of *prajñā*. They have, we may say, at least some of these qualities 'in spades'.

Naturally, it goes without saying that they have, too, the basic human virtues – straightforward kindness and awareness of the needs of others, an integrated personality, self-knowledge, and so on – and these also to an eminent degree. One can't be a great – or even a good – Buddhist without being a great or good human being.

Besides having at least some of these virtues, they should deploy them in their life and work in such a way as to influence many other people, especially many other Buddhists. Thus a great Buddhist contributes to the making of Buddhist history. Furthermore, a great Buddhist is a paradigmatic figure, providing a model or an example for other Buddhists, both when alive and after death. That is, he or she functions as a source of permanent inspiration and guidance for other Buddhists.

Not all the five people mentioned here could be said to be equally great – though it is difficult to compare them very accurately in that way as they were great in very different ways. And I must also say that I personally don't necessarily agree with everything that each of them said or did or wrote. But they were all undoubtedly great in the sense that I have defined.

Finally, in our definition of terms, we come to 'twentieth century'. Strictly speaking, from a Buddhist point of view we should perhaps be talking about the 'twenty-fifth century' (after the Buddha's Enlightenment) – which concluded in 1956–7 CE – rather than the twentieth century after the birth of Christ. But never mind. 'Twentieth century' can be taken simply as convenient shorthand for 'more or less within living memory'. The first four of our great Buddhists were, in fact, all born in the nineteenth century, though they did most, if not all, their significant work for Buddhism in the twentieth.

My concern in these biographical sketches is not so much with the everyday biographical details – what they used to have for breakfast, say. It is rather with the significance of their lives for us, living as we do in the fresh wake of their achievements and in something of the same world as they did.

Anagārika Dharmapala

Dharmapala, the future 'Lion of Lanka' as he came to be called, was born in 1864 in Colombo, Sri Lanka – except that here we must call this island 'Ceylon', because that is the name it had in those days. His father was the proprietor of a furniture manufacturing business, so he had a solid, middle-class background; and his parents were good, pious Buddhists, so one might have thought that he would have had a solid Buddhist background as well.

However, he was christened 'David' – his name was David Hewavitarne, and from the time he was 5 until the time he was 8, and again from ten to eighteen, he attended a series of Christian schools, both Catholic and Protestant. So this calls for some explanation. Why did his pious Buddhist parents send him to Christian schools?

The reason is simply that they had no choice. Ceylon had been a British colony since 1802, and before that, between 1505 and 1796, large parts of the island had been ruled first by the Portuguese and then by the Dutch. The result was that Buddhism and Buddhist culture at the time of Dharmapala's birth were at a very low ebb in Ceylon. In fact, it was not possible to be a Buddhist at all – at least, not officially. Children of Buddhist parents had to be taken for registration of their birth to a church – either Catholic or Protestant – and there given a Christian name. Otherwise, according to a law that was not repealed until 1884, the child would be illegitimate and unable to inherit property. And all education beyond primary level was in the hands of the missionaries.

So by the time he was in his early teens, Dharmapala knew by heart four complete books of the Old Testament, all four Gospels, and the Acts of the Apostles. However, he never lost faith in the Dharma. Dharmapala picked up a basic understanding of Buddhism at home, and being unusually argumentative, even for an adolescent boy, he used to get into trouble with his teachers for the persistence with which he picked away at inconsistencies in Christian doctrine. A much more serious offence, however, was his insistence on celebrating Wesak, the festival in honour of the Buddha's attainment of Enlightenment. At that time, of course, it wasn't a public holiday. Christmas was a public holiday, Easter was a public holiday, but Wesak wasn't.

But when Dharmapala was in his early teens he realized that as a Buddhist he ought to celebrate Wesak, and in order to do this he would have to be given the day off school. So he went to the headmaster and asked to have the day off in order to celebrate the most important festival in the Buddhist calendar. Unsurprisingly, the headmaster said no. Equally unsurprisingly, Dharmapala took his umbrella, walked out of the school, and simply didn't turn up for school the next day. He celebrated Wesak, and the following day he was soundly thrashed. This little drama was enacted between Dharmapala and his headmaster once a year for three consecutive years. This was how obstinate and determined he was, even as a boy.

We know a lot of details about Dharmapala's life, even before he became well known, because he kept a diary more or less from the time he left school until his death in 1933. He also wrote some memoirs later on in life, and in these we find described another incident from his schooldays that shows a deeper side to his character.

It so happened that one of his schoolfellows died, and the corpse was laid out in the school. The teachers apparently invited the students to gather round the dead body of the boy and offer up prayers, and Dharmapala joined them. But as he looked around, a question came into his mind. He asked himself, 'Why are they praying?' And as he continued to look at the faces of his schoolfellows, at the faces of the teachers, the answer came to him quite clearly that they were afraid; they were afraid of death. This was why they were praying. He saw that prayer – petitionary prayer – was born of fear. And from that day onward he had no temptation to pray in that sort of way.

This uppish, confrontational teenager, however, was also a rather dreamy lover of poetry, reading widely in English literature, especially the Romantics, and particularly Shelley. He read Keats and Shelley constantly. And this poetic streak went in counterpoint with marked mystical and ascetic tendencies.

Fortunately for this idealistic youth, things were changing, even in colonial Ceylon, and the tide was beginning to turn in Buddhism's favour. In 1875 in New York, Madame Blavatsky and Colonel Olcott had founded the Theosophical Society. They were both very sympathetic to what they understood of Buddhism, and in 1880 they arrived in Ceylon, declared themselves to be Buddhists, and publicly took the Refuges and Precepts from a prominent Sinhalese *bhikkhu*. This created a tremendous sensation from one end of the island to the other, because they were the first Europeans to publicly embrace Buddhism.

The Christian missionaries were understandably very upset, and they continued to be upset because Colonel Olcott took rather a liking to Ceylon. He stayed on and devoted himself to the cause of Buddhist education, eventually setting up more than three hundred Buddhist schools, some of which are still in existence. Sri Lankans still celebrate his work on 'Olcott Day'.

As for the still very young Dharmapala, he helped Colonel Olcott in his work, particularly by acting as his translator. Dharmapala also became quite close to Madame Blavatsky. In his late teens he had wanted to study occultism, as so many Theosophists did, but Madame Blavatsky advised him to follow a very different course. She advised him to study Pāli and to work for the good of humanity – which is what he did. And it was at this time that he changed his name from David to Dharmapala (meaning 'Guardian of the Dharma').

In 1891 he paid his first visit to the holy places of northern India and found them in a shockingly neglected condition. Some of them were no more than ruins. This should not really have been any cause for surprise because Buddhism had disappeared from India several centuries before. Whatever was left of Buddhism that had not been absorbed by Hinduism had been destroyed by Muslim invaders.

The ancient Maha Bodhi temple at Bodh Gaya, the most sacred of all the Buddhist holy places, had been restored by Sir Alexander Cunningham. However, there was no one to look after the place, and when Dharmapala arrived there he was profoundly saddened by its desolate aspect. He sought out the *vajrāsana*, or 'diamond throne', the carved black marble slab that marks the spot where the Buddha, according to tradition, actually sat when he attained supreme Enlightenment, and bowing down before it he touched the edge with his forehead. As he did so he was seized with a sudden inspiration. He would stay and look after the place until Buddhist monks could arrive and take over. At the age of 29 he had found his life's work.

It was not going to be as straightforward as he had thought it would be. Legally, the temple belonged to a Hindu monk, who was not pleased to have Dharmapala there, and at one point even had him thrown out and beaten up. Out of this ensued a long legal battle, which Dharmapala finally lost in 1906. Meanwhile, however, Dharmapala founded the Maha Bodhi Society to help him in his work. Initially, this work comprised the task of restoring Bodh Gaya to something of its former splendour; but the scope of the society's activities soon expanded to involve the promotion of Buddhism in India and eventually the development of Buddhism throughout the world. A natural extension of this work was to set up, in 1892, the *Maha Bodhi* journal.

In 1893 Dharmapala was invited to attend the Parliament of World Religions in Chicago as representative of 'Southern Buddhism' – which was the term applied at that time to the Theravāda. He was a great success. In fact some journalists paid him what to them was the ultimate compliment, and compared him to Jesus. By his early thirties he was already a global figure, and he continued to travel and give lectures and establish viharas around the world during the next forty years. At the same time he concentrated on establishing schools and hospitals in Ceylon and building temples and viharas in India. Among the most important of the temples he built was one at Sarnath, where the Buddha first taught the Dharma. Here, in 1933, when he was already a very sick man in a wheelchair, he was ordained as a *bhikkhu*, and he died there in December of the same year, aged 69.

Dharmapala was a leading figure in initiating two outstanding features of Buddhism in the twentieth century. He was a great pioneer in the revival of Buddhism in India after it had been virtually extinct there for several centuries, and he was the first Buddhist in modern times to preach the Dharma in three continents, in Asia, in America, and in Europe.

Clearly, Dharmapala led a very active life. However, he invariably started his day, often before dawn, with two hours of meditation. In his younger days in Ceylon he had failed to find a meditation teacher; for various reasons, the practice of meditation there had simply died out. But in his twenties he met a Burmese lay yogi who was able to give him some instruction. And the practice that we may say fuelled his life and work was the *mettā bhāvanā*, the cultivation of universal loving-kindness. This is a vitally important aspect of his life. He wasn't simply a Buddhist activist, flitting from one Buddhist conference to another. His work for Buddhism sprang out of a deep experience of Buddhism – an experience that is enormously difficult to achieve without regular meditation.

One other significant aspect of his life was that he was the first *anagārika* – that is, a celibate, full-time worker for Buddhism – in modern times. He wasn't, until his last months, a *bhikkhu* – but he wasn't a layman in the ordinary sense either. It seems that he took a vow of celibacy or *brahmacarya* at the age of 8 and remained faithful to it all his life. He also wore a yellow robe, however, it wasn't of the traditional *bhikkhu* pattern, and he didn't shave his head. He felt, it would appear, that the observance of all the Vinaya rules would have got in the way of his work, especially as he flew around the world.

Ultimately, the key to Dharmapala's life and work is before one's eyes wherever one opens his voluminous diaries. At the top of every alternate page he wrote: 'The only Refuge for him who aspires to true perfection is the Buddha alone.' This is what he reminded himself, every day of the year, year after year. Going for Refuge is the fundamental, decisive, definitive act of the Buddhist life. It is what makes us Buddhists, and it is what unites us all as Buddhists.

Alexandra David-Néel

Born in Paris in 1868, at the time of the Napoleon III, Alexandra David-Néel died in southern France in 1969, when Pompidou was president of France. She would have worn crinolines as a young woman, and she survived to see young women in miniskirts. So this gives us some idea of the historical parameters of her very long life.

Her father was a wealthy middle-class Protestant, socialist, and an ardent republican, whereas her mother was a Belgian Catholic and an ardent supporter of the Belgian monarchy. Alexandra David – as she was originally called – seems to have been very much closer to her father. Her mother had wanted a son who would become a Catholic bishop, and a daughter was a bitter disappointment to her. So Alexandra grew up in these circumstances something of a tomboy. She was educated in various Catholic convent schools, but she remained a tomboy, and from the age of 16 she started running away from home. She would come back again, but before long she was bicycling – this was in the 1880s – all the way to Spain. She also visited Holland, England, Italy, again all on her own, while still a teenager.

On her second visit to England she came in contact with Theosophists. In the library of the British Museum she started reading up the more alternative mystical traditions – Gnosticism, Catharism, and so on. On her return to France she settled in Paris with a group of French Theosophists. She started to study Sanskrit, and in doing so came across the *Lalitavistara*, an imaginative and poetic, not to say legendary, life of the Buddha. However, this was not her first contact with Buddhism. At the age of 13 she had apparently come across one of the most ancient and beautiful Buddhist legends, the *Jātaka* tale of how the Buddha, in one of his previous incarnations, had given his body to a starving tigress and her cubs. She had thought, at 13, that this was the most beautiful story she had ever heard.

Living in Paris she was also in contact with Buddhist art, because the Musée Guimet in Paris housed one of the most famous collections of oriental art in the world. There, one day, she stood before a magnificent Japanese Buddha image, joined her hands together, and bowed in salutation before it. She continued to study other religions, especially Hinduism, but she already regarded herself as a Buddhist.

At the age of 21 she came of age and inherited some money, which she spent on a trip to India, on her own, where she met maharajahs and swamis. She returned to Europe virtually penniless. She made a little money out of the occasional bit of journalism, but it wasn't enough, so she trained as a singer, and supported herself in this way for seven years. She had quite a successful and rather colourful career as a singer, and in the course of it learned a lot about human nature, but her voice was evidently not very well trained because it started to deteriorate, so she decided, regretfully, that she would have to get married.

In 1904, at the age of 36, Alexandra David married Philippe Néel, an aristocratic French engineer, then aged 40. They lived in French North Africa for a number of years, during which her beloved father died and she published her first book on Buddhism, called *Buddhist Modernism and the Buddhism of the Buddha*.

Alexandra David-Néel left for the East again in 1911, and she did not return for fourteen years. She travelled in Ceylon, India, Sikkim, Nepal, Japan, China, and Tibet, and continued her study of Buddhism. Not only that: she was putting what she studied into practice, which was unusual at that time. Not only was it unusual for a student of Buddhism to practise it; what she was doing was also unusual in another way. She met the thirteenth Dalai Lama – in exile in Kalimpong after an invasion by the Chinese – and he was astonished, on asking how she had become a Buddhist, to be told that it had been by reading books. He had never heard of such a thing.

In Sikkim she met the Gomchen of Lhachen, who was famous as a meditator and yogi (Gomchen meaning 'great meditator'). She became his disciple and spent two years there, practising meditation and studying Tibetan. She also adopted a Sikkimese boy – Lama Yongden as he afterwards became – and he remained with her for the rest of his life.

David-Néel's husband seems to have taken her extended absence very well. She wrote to him every day, so clearly she was fond of him, though equally clearly she could be fond of him only from a distance. In return he sent her money regularly – and she evidently needed plenty of it, to be frank. She usually travelled in some style, with a number of servants and a good deal of equipment.

There was one journey she took in rather less than grand style, and that was her famous journey to Lhasa. At that time foreigners were prohibited from entering Tibet, so she travelled in disguise. Her only companion was Yongden, who took the part of a travelling lama, with herself as his old mother. They spent four months travelling on foot. They travelled through China to approach Lhasa from the north-east, crossing vast deserts, scaling lofty mountains, and braving bandits, starvation, and landslides to reach their destination. They spent two months in Lhasa and David-Néel subsequently wrote *The Journey of a Parisienne to Lhasa*.

In 1925 she returned to France with Yongden and settled in the Alps of Provence, at Digne. By now she was a rather famous elderly lady, giving lectures and writing books. She took a journey east just once more, in 1939, but this proved to be ill-timed. The Second World War broke out and she and Yongden were stranded in a small town in south-east Tibet called Darsendo (or Dhartsendo) for six years. Her husband was dead by the time they returned and Yongden died in 1955. She continued to write. It was during this last period of her life that I had some contact with her. We exchanged letters and she contributed to magazines I was editing; and I noticed that her handwriting, despite her years, remained firm and clear.

Her life was noteworthy in three particular respects. First of all, she was one of the first Westerners to take Buddhism seriously – that is, to take it as a way of life, not just as a subject for scholarly study. Secondly, there was her readiness to defy convention, especially when convention stood in the way of the realization of her cherished ideals. Nowadays, when defying convention is often a meaningless convention in itself, it is difficult for us to realize how strong, how rigid, certain conventions were during her lifetime. For her, being unconventional took real courage. Thirdly and lastly, she showed what a really determined woman is capable of. Her life is thus an inspiration to all Buddhists, but perhaps to Buddhist women in particular.

B. R. Ambedkar

So far we have looked at individuals from wealthy, middle-class families. By contrast, Bhimrao Ramji Ambedkar came from the very bottom of the social heap. He was born in 1891 at Mhow in central India into an Untouchable Hindu family, and this background to his life is very much what his career was about. To have any idea of what Ambedkar achieved one has to be clear about what this term 'Untouchable' really means.

Hindu society is divided into castes, with the Brahmins, the priestly caste, at the top, and the Shudras, or labouring caste, at the bottom, and others, with all sorts of subdivisions, in between. Having been born into a particular caste you can't get out of it – it is regarded as very wrong even to try. As for 'Untouchables', they are even lower than Shudras, and in a sense they are outside the caste system altogether. They are called 'Untouchables' because any contact with them pollutes so-called 'caste Hindus'. Even their shadow pollutes.

Traditionally, Untouchables lived in ghettoes of their own, outside the main community. They could engage only in very menial occupations such as removing night-soil, and they would serve the caste Hindu villagers in this way in return for a few scraps of food. They weren't allowed to enter Hindu temples or attend Hindu schools. They had no economic or political rights – they could not even own property. They were not allowed to better themselves in any way. Once an Untouchable, always an Untouchable – at least, so far as this life was concerned.

This system had been rigidly in force for a thousand years (and to all intents and purposes it still is in many areas). But when Ambedkar was born there were already faint signs that it was beginning to weaken. The rule of the British over India was no doubt unfortunate in many ways, but for the Untouchables it did have its advantages, because the British army accepted Untouchables into its ranks. In fact it had Untouchable regiments, and Ambedkar's father belonged to one of these. Members of these regiments were given a certain amount of education, and some, including Ambedkar's father, even became army schoolmasters.

With help and encouragement from his father, Ambedkar became a brilliant student, and at the age of 17 was the first Untouchable to matriculate. He was given a scholarship by a liberal Indian prince, and eventually graduated in politics and economics. He studied further at Columbia University and then at the London School of Economics, and also qualified as a barrister. He returned to India in 1923, aged 32, and took his place as one of the most highly gifted and qualified men in Indian public life.

However, he had not equipped himself so comprehensively for a political career out of self-interest. He never forgot that he himself was an Untouchable – nor was he allowed to. Many Indians continued to treat him as an Untouchable, and this was a source of great disappointment and bitterness to him; but it only hardened his resolve to devote his life to the uplift of his people. He founded newspapers, he started schools and colleges, he entered politics, he fought legal battles, and we may say that from 1923 until his death in 1956, the story of his life is inseparable from the history of modern India.

In 1927 Dr Ambedkar focused attention on the problems faced by his people by provoking the 'Chowdar Tank case'. In the town of Mahad in what is now Maharashtra state, Untouchables were not allowed to take water from this tank until 1927, when it was opened to them by the local municipality. Whether or not the Chowdar Tank actually belonged to the municipality would be later contested, but meanwhile Ambedkar held a conference of 3,000 Untouchables at Mahad, and at its conclusion led them to the edge of the tank to drink from it.

This may all seem a very tame business to us – a local dispute over who is allowed to use a water tank, and 3,000 people gathering together in order to dare to make use of what has been made available to them. But in India in those days it was a terrific, extraordinary, revolutionary thing to do. There was a furious reaction from the caste Hindus, and some of Ambedkar's followers were assaulted in one way or another for their impious – in the eyes of the caste Hindus – temerity. The Untouchables had, by drawing water from the tank, polluted it.

The question now was how to purify the tank again. Brahmins were called together, and they took 108 earthenware pots of water from the tank and mixed the water with curds, milk, cow-dung, and cow's urine. Then the pots, with the water and the aforementioned 'purifying' elements, were put back in the tank and Vedic mantras were recited. In this way the tank was purified.

Naturally, a response to this insulting procedure was called for on the part of the Untouchables under Ambedkar, and it had to be an appropriate response, one that would get to the heart of the issue. In the same year, 1927, they burned the *Manusmṛti*, or the 'Laws of Manu'. The significance of this book as a symbol resided in the fact that it is the source of all the laws regarding caste. It lays down who can eat with whom, who can marry whom, who can touch whom; and it also lays down how those who infringe those laws should be punished. Thus, for example, it is decreed that any Shudra who presumes to teach Brahmins their duty should have boiling oil poured into his mouth and into his ears. The burning of the *Manusmṛti* had the desired effect. It shocked orthodox Hindus all over India, and it symbolized the repudiation by the Untouchables of the authority of the Hindu scriptures.

The man generally lauded nowadays as the great hero of this period in India, during the drive towards independence, is of course Mahatma Gandhi. But the Untouchables cannot see him in quite this idealized light. Gandhi was himself a caste Hindu who claimed to represent the Untouchables as well as caste Hindus, but the Untouchables did not recognize him in this role. They believed that only an Untouchable could safeguard their interests.

Gandhi had already agreed that Muslims, Christians, and Sikhs should have separate electorates, and Ambedkar argued that in a democratic India there should be separate electorates for Untouchables as well. This was because Untouchables did not want to be governed by caste Hindus. However, in 1932 Gandhi resisted Ambedkar's demands by going on one of his 'fasts to death', and during the period of the fast Ambedkar described himself as the most hated man in India. Gandhi did indeed come close to death, and in the end Ambedkar was forced to compromise. If Gandhi had fasted to death Ambedkar would have faced the prospect of the wholesale murder of Untouchables by caste Hindus.

In 1935 Ambedkar's wife died. He had married her very young, when he was 16 and she just 9; only one of their five children had survived. By this time his political position was hardening. He no longer believed in the possibility of reform within Hinduism. He was convinced that the caste Hindus were not going to change their ways; they weren't going to treat the Untouchables as human beings, and in 1935 he made his famous declaration that though he had been born a Hindu, he would not die one.

In 1947 Ambedkar became Law Minister in the first government of the independent state of India, but he resigned from the Cabinet four years later because of fierce opposition from caste Hindus – even in the Cabinet – to his attempts to reform Hindu law. It was at about this time that I myself had some correspondence and then a series of meetings with him.

At the end of 1954 Ambedkar announced that he would devote the remainder of his life to the propagation of Buddhism in India. This was not a sudden decision. He had been a student of Buddhism for some time, and had known something about it ever since he was 16, when he had been given a copy of the Marathi translation of Edwin Arnold's *The Light of Asia*, a life of the Buddha in English verse (which had also been an early discovery and favourite of Dharmapala's).

Over the years Ambedkar had gradually become convinced that Buddhism was the best religion for himself and for the Untouchable community as a whole. There were various reasons for his choice, but the main ones were, firstly, that Buddhism did not conflict with the dictates of reason; secondly, that it did not condone man's inhumanity to man, and it certainly did not condone the caste system; and thirdly, that it was of Indian origin, it was not the product of a foreign culture.

So in 1956, in a ceremony at Nagpur in central India, Dr Ambedkar became a Buddhist – along with 380,000 of his followers. The conversions in Nagpur sparked off others all over India. It was the greatest event for Buddhism in India for many hundreds of years. Though these were 'mass conversions' the effect on the individuals who took part, who became Buddhists at that time, was profound. I used to ask people, months or even years afterwards, 'What difference has becoming a Buddhist meant for you?' Nine times out of ten they would reply, 'Now that I'm a Buddhist I feel free.' That seems to have been the most important aspect of the experience: a sense of freedom. They felt socially, psychologically, spiritually free.

Six weeks later, Ambedkar was dead, at the age of 64. I was in Nagpur at the time and I well remember the reaction of shock and grief that swept through the ex-Untouchable community. There were fears that the conversion movement would simply collapse. But happily it didn't collapse, and it continues to this day.

The significance of Dr Ambedkar's life and work is exceptionally profound and far-reaching. The problem he faced was how to lift up his people, socially, economically, educationally – in every respect. And he felt that the only overall solution to this problem was a change in religion. It wasn't enough just to reject Hinduism, just to leave the religion that generally condoned the caste system. Ambedkar himself was a deeply religious man; he believed that religion was essential to human life, that we cannot really live without it. So for him there was no question of pursuing, for instance, the communist option. He believed that a real social and economic revolution was possible only on the basis of a *spiritual* revolution.

It was for this reason that he inaugurated what we now call the 'Dhamma revolution'. This is not just a nominal change of religion, but a transformation of one's whole life in every aspect. It is not just individual transformation, but even collective transformation as well. This is the movement that Ambedkar set in motion. He showed that a change in religion, even in the midst of the twentieth century, could bring about a change for the better in the lives of millions of people.

The conversion movement in India is also of profound significance for Buddhism itself. Ambedkar was well aware that Buddhism had already disappeared once from India, and having revived it he didn't want it to disappear again. So he looked at why it had disappeared. He saw that one of the principal factors leading to its decline was the separation that had developed between the monks and the laity.

The monks lived together in monasteries, and in the course of centuries these monasteries became bigger and bigger, each in the end housing thousands of monks leading self-contained lives apart from the laity. So without much contact with the monks and without any lay ordination, the lay people began to feel less and less like they themselves were Buddhists at all, and they came more and more under the influence of the Hindu Brahmins. This process was accelerated after the great monasteries were destroyed by Muslim invaders in the tenth, eleventh, and twelfth centuries. Thus, eventually, the lay Buddhists were simply absorbed into the Hindu community. Buddhism disappeared from India, and only ruins marked what it once had been.

On the basis of this analysis of the decline and fall of Indian Buddhism, Ambedkar decided that there had to be ordination for laypeople corresponding to monastic ordination for monks. He called this lay ordination '*dhamma diksha*', and it consisted of two parts: first, taking the traditional three Refuges and five Precepts; and secondly – and this was quite new – taking twenty-two vows.

These twenty-two vows were devised by Ambedkar himself, and their purpose was to clearly and completely separate the new Buddhists from their old Hindu religion. They constituted an explicit renunciation of every vestige of Hinduism, of every Hindu practice, like, for example, offering animal sacrifices to gods and goddesses. These vows made it clear what it was to be a Hindu and what it was to be a Buddhist, and that it was not possible to be both. They helped to root out a very commonly held belief in India at this time that if you were a Buddhist you were necessarily also a Hindu, that Buddhism was an accretion on the main body of Hinduism. I myself remember a Hindu swami asking me after my ordination why I had not done the job properly and become a Hindu monk. 'Hinduism is like the great ocean,' he said, 'Buddhism is just a little stream.' In fact, any idea that Buddhism might be combined with another faith, whether Hinduism or Christianity, represents a serious confusion of thought. Dr Ambedkar thought that this principle was so important that it needed to be embodied in vows taken as part of the ordination ceremony.

The way it was done at Nagpur on 14 October 1956 was as follows: Dr Ambedkar took the three Refuges and five Precepts from U Chandramani, a very senior *bhikkhu*. After this, Ambedkar publicly recited his twenty-two vows. He then proceeded to administer the Refuges and Precepts and the twenty-two vows himself to the 380,000 of his followers who were assembled there at Nagpur. In this way he established a very significant principle.

Ambedkar was initiated into Buddhism by a monk, but his followers were initiated into Buddhism by a layman. Thus the monk and the layman were placed, in a sense, on an equal footing. Dr Ambedkar was asserting the fact that it is Going for Refuge to the Three Jewels – the Buddha, the Dharma, and the Sangha – which makes one a Buddhist, not one's lifestyle. Going for Refuge is the primary act of a Buddhist; lifestyle – whether one is monk or lay – is secondary.

Lama Govinda

Lama Govinda was rather a mysterious figure – particularly when he was Ernst Lothar Hoffmann – which is the name with which he began life. We know very little about his early years. He was born in 1898 in Germany, into a middle-class family of partly Spanish descent, but his mother died when he was 3, and he was brought up by her sister. He originally wanted to be a mining engineer, but developed an increasing interest in philosophy, especially the work of Schopenhauer. He went on to study comparative religion, and Buddhism in particular, until, toward the end of the First World War, he was called up to spend two years in the German army.

After the war he took up residence in Capri, where began a very important period in his life. He studied Pāli, he took up art and a bit of archaeological research, and he met an elderly German lady who became, for much of the rest of his life, a sort of foster-mother. He started practising meditation, and he started as well to make pastel drawings of the meditative states he experienced. So he was evidently already making the connection between meditation and art which would later be the subject of much of his thinking.

In 1928, aged 30, Govinda moved to Ceylon – with his foster-mother as well, of course. For a couple of years he studied Pāli and Abhidhamma with the famous German *bhikkhu* Nyanatiloka, during which period he took the name of Govinda and became an *anagārika* (*anagārika* literally means 'homeless one'; becoming an *anagārika* usually implies celibacy). He also visited Burma and researched cases of alleged recollection of previous lives, a subject he was always interested in.

His next move was to India, and at a Buddhist conference in Darjeeling he came into contact for the first time with Tibetan Buddhism, which thereafter exercised a compelling influence on his life and work. There are not many firm dates in what we know of Govinda's life, but around 1930 he settled – again with his foster-mother – in Ghoom near Darjeeling, where he met his Tibetan guru, the famous Tomo Geshe Rimpoche. During the next few years he was based partly in Ghoom and partly in Shantiniketan, the forest university established by Rabindranath Tagore a hundred miles north of Calcutta.

Govinda lectured, he wrote, he travelled – until in 1942 he was interned by the British because of his German descent. Conditions in the camp near Dehradun were very mild: he studied Chinese, he studied the

I Ching, and he enjoyed the companionship of Nyanaponika, another German disciple of Nyanatiloka. After the war he returned to Ghoom and to Shantiniketan, and in 1947 he married a former student of his at Shantiniketan, Rati Petit, who became known as Li Gotami.

In 1948 they made their celebrated journey to Tsaparang in western Tibet, and they made it just in time, because within a year or two the Chinese had occupied the whole of Tibet. The two of them spent several months working in conditions of great hardship, sketching and photographing ruined Buddhist temples and monasteries, and copying ancient frescoes. They were greatly impressed, not so much by the religious life they found there as by the vastness of the open spaces, by the views, by the brilliant colours, by the light, and of course by the ancient art that they discovered.

In 1952 Govinda announced the formation of the Arya Maitreya Mandala, an organization through which he hoped to spread Buddhism, especially Tibetan Buddhism, in the West. Shortly afterwards, he and Li Gotami moved to Almora in the foothills of the western Himalayas, where they remained for the next twenty-five years, and where Govinda had the most creative phase of his career, producing at least two Buddhist literary classics: the semi-autobiographical *Way of the White Clouds*, documenting the journey to western Tibet; and *Foundations of Tibetan Mysticism*. In the 1960s and 1970s they made several trips to Europe and America, where there was a growing interest in Buddhism, and they spent their last years in San Francisco, where Govinda died in 1985, aged 87. Li Gotami died in India about three years later.

I got to know Lama Govinda quite well. We discovered that we had a good deal in common, especially in our approach to Buddhism. In a letter he wrote to me four days before he died he made a couple of points that seem to indicate what the overall direction of his life and work had been. Firstly: 'I'm a great admirer of Italian art and, like you, I always uphold the importance of European culture. Without knowing the roots of our own culture how can we absorb the essence of Buddhist culture?' Secondly: 'Now it is up to the next generation to take Buddhism out of the merely academic atmosphere and make it a living experience.'[379]

Lama Anagarika Govinda always emphasized that intellectual understanding and the observance of rules wasn't enough, but that Buddhism could be made a living experience by means of meditation, together with ritual and particularly colour – colour in the full, literal sense – in the spiritual life. He also stressed the importance of what he called 'creative imagination' and thus the importance of art. As a meditator and an artist himself, he did not see these two activities as completely different. In fact, he saw a sort of parallelism between them. The way he put it was that in meditation we pass from the world of outward expression to the world of inner experience; and in art we pass from the world of inner experience to the world of outward expression.

Edward Conze

Eberhart Julius Dietrich Conze was born in London in 1904 of mixed German, French, and Dutch ancestry. His father belonged to the German landed aristocracy, and his mother to what he himself would have called the 'plutocracy'. His background was Protestant, though his mother became a Roman Catholic in later life. He seems to have had a rather bad relationship with his mother.

He was born in England simply because his father happened to be posted there as German Vice-Consul, but this meant that he had British nationality, should he ever need it (which he would). He was educated at various German universities and with a flair for languages picked up a command of fourteen of them, including Sanskrit, by the age of 24. Like many other Europeans, he came into contact with Theosophy quite early on, but he also took up astrology. He took it seriously, remaining a keen astrologer all his life. While still a young man, he wrote a very substantial book called *The Principle of Contradiction*. Apparently his mother said that she was not surprised he'd written such a book since he himself was a bundle of contradictions.

During the rise to power of Hitler, Conze found himself so strongly opposed to the Nazi ideology that he joined the Communist Party and even made a serious study of Marxist thought. It seems that for a while he was the leader of the communist movement in Bonn, and his life was consequently in some danger.

In 1933 he came to England, having earlier taken the precaution of renewing his British nationality, and he arrived at the age of 29, virtually without money or possessions. He supported himself by teaching German and taking evening classes, and he became a member of the

Labour Party. He met a lot of prominent figures and intellectuals in the Labour movement and was not impressed. He had, after all, been to a whole series of German universities. He met trades union leaders and he met Pandit Nehru and Krishna Menon of the India League, and he was not impressed by any of them either. He was not easily impressed.

He became very active in the socialist movement in Britain, lecturing and writing books and pamphlets, until eventually he became disillusioned with politics. At the age of 35 he found himself in a state of intellectual turmoil and collapse. Even his marriage had failed. Indeed, in his memoirs he admits, 'I am one of those unfortunate people who can neither live with women nor without them.'[380]

At this point he discovered – or rather rediscovered – Buddhism. At the age of 13 he had read *Gleanings in Buddha Fields* by Lafcadio Hearn (and at the beginning of each chapter he would have read quotations from the *Diamond Sūtra*, as if presaging his future life's work). However, Conze's first significant contact with Buddhism was at this mid-point in his life, at the beginning of the Second World War, and it was through the writings of D. T. Suzuki. They were literally his salvation.

After this there was no turning back. Conze devoted the rest of his life to Buddhism and in particular to translating the Prajñāpāramitā or Perfection of Wisdom *sūtras*, which are the fundamental scriptures of the Mahāyāna. But he wasn't just a scholar in the academic sense. During the war he lived on his own in a trailer in the New Forest, and he practised meditation, following very seriously the instructions given by Buddhaghosa in the *Visuddhimagga*, and achieving some degree of meditative experience.

After the war he moved to Oxford and re-married. In 1951 he brought out *Buddhism: Its Essence and Development*, a very successful book which is still in print. However, his real achievement over the following twenty years was to translate altogether more than thirty texts comprising the Prajñāpāramitā *sūtras*, including of course two of the most well known of all Buddhist texts, the *Diamond Sūtra* and the *Heart Sūtra*.

It was in connection with these translations that I myself came into contact with him. I started publishing his *Selected Sayings from the Perfection of Wisdom* in a magazine I was editing called *Stepping-Stones* in about 1951. We corresponded, and when I came to England in 1964 we met a number of times and found that we agreed on quite a lot of issues.

In the 1960s and 1970s he lectured at several universities in the United States, and he went down well with the students. However, he was very outspoken, and gained the disapproval of the university authorities and some of his colleagues. With the combination of his communist past and his candid criticism of the American involvement in Vietnam, he was eventually obliged to take his talents elsewhere. He died in 1979.

Dr Conze was a complex figure, and it is not easy to assess his overall significance. He was of course a Middle European intellectual refugee, fleeing from Germany before the War like so many others. But he wasn't at all representative of this dominant strain in twentieth-century intellectual life, because he was very critical of many trends in modern thought. He was a self-confessed élitist, which is usually something people are ashamed of nowadays, but he wasn't ashamed of it at all. Indeed, he entitled his autobiography *The Memoirs of a Modern Gnostic*, believing as he did that Gnosticism was essentially élitist. Nor did he approve of either democracy or feminism, which makes him a veritable ogre of 'political incorrectness'.

He is certainly representative of a whole pre-war generation in the West which became disillusioned with Marxism, especially with Marxism in its Soviet form. Where he differed from others was in the fact that he did not really lose his sense of faith. He did not simply become disillusioned while carrying on within the milieu he was familiar with. He transferred his uncompromising idealism from politics to Buddhism.

Dr Conze was one of the great Buddhist translators, comparable with the indefatigable Chinese translators Kumārajīva and Xuanzang of the fifth and seventh centuries respectively. It is especially significant, I think, that as a scholar of Buddhism he also tried to practise it, especially through meditation. This was very unusual at the time he started his work, and he was regarded then – in the 1940s and 1950s – as being something of an eccentric. Scholars were not supposed to have any personal involvement in their subject. They were supposed to be 'objective'. So he was a forerunner of a whole new breed of Western scholars in Buddhism who are actually practising Buddhists.

This overview of some great Buddhist lives does not in any way provide a comprehensive view of the achievements of the great Buddhists of the twentieth century. For that, we would have to introduce many others.

The thirteenth Dalai Lama, the Zen scholar and translator D. T. Suzuki, Dr G. P. Malalasekera of Sri Lanka, Bhikkhu Buddhadasa of Thailand, the great Chinese Chan meditation master the Venerable Xuyun, and the great Chinese abbot Taixu are just some of them.

However, I hope I have been able to suggest what we may gain, as Buddhists, from reading, studying, reflecting, and meditating on the lives, the biographies, and memoirs of Buddhists who have lived, in one way or another, truly inspiring lives. They enable us to see Buddhism being actually lived. Purely doctrinal studies – good and necessary though they may be – sometimes give us the impression that Buddhism is rather remote from our own lives. Biographies help to redress this balance. After all, Buddhism began with lives; it didn't begin with books. Buddhism began with the lives of the Buddha and his Enlightened disciples.

While preparing these sketches of great Buddhists I noticed two things. I noticed first of all that the five were all very different. They had very different characters and they grew up in very different circumstances. In many ways they did very different things. But they were all great Buddhists. This is very important. It reminds us that though we are all Buddhists, though we all go for Refuge, we don't all have to be the same; we don't have to live in the same way; we don't have to do the same things. This is because what unites us is more important than what divides us.

The second thing I noticed was that there were certain qualities which, despite their differences, all five seemed to possess. To begin with, they were all very single-minded. Once they had discovered their purpose in life, they never wavered. Then, they were all characterized by fearlessness. They were also all unconventional. And they were self-motivated. They were autonomous individuals, they 'did their own thing', they went their own way, sometimes in the face of tremendous opposition. They were all true individuals.

In short, they were all heroes, in the best sense of the term. We need to cherish our heroes and heroines. We need to admire them, we need to cherish their memory, we need to rejoice in their merits. We need to appreciate that our great Buddhists, whether of the twentieth or any other century, are among our greatest and most precious possessions.

from *Great Buddhists of the Twentieth Century*

5
LIVING IN THE WORLD

1. THE IDEAL SOCIETY

Even in political affairs ethical and spiritual considerations and values should be paramount.

Though most daydreaming is what may be described as unproductive fantasy, daydreams are occasionally blueprints for the future. Today's dream may be, in some cases, tomorrow's reality. Looking at the history of the world, at the history of culture, of religions, of the arts, of philosophy, we find that the greatest men and women of the past have sometimes been the greatest daydreamers. If we go back to the days of ancient Greece, to Plato – surely one of the greatest men who ever lived – we find that Plato too dreamed his dreams. The most famous of his dreams is *The Republic*, the great dialogue in twelve books in which Plato dreams his dream of an ideal society, the society based upon justice. Moving to other times and cultures – and other dreams – we have in the *Book of Revelation*, the last book of the Bible, the marvellous vision of the new Jerusalem with its walls of jasper and gates of pearl – a vision of great archetypal and mythic significance. Coming nearer to our own times there is More's *Utopia*, Bacon's *New Atlantis*, Campanella's *City of the Sun*, and so on, down to H. G. Wells's *Men Like Gods*.[381] These are all daydreams of an ideal society, daydreams of a world transfigured and transformed.

Buddhism too has its daydreams. One Buddhist daydream of the ideal society is found in the conception – or vision – of Sukhāvatī, the 'Pure Land' of Amitābha, the Buddha of Infinite Light, as described in some of the great Mahāyāna *sūtras*.[382] Especially as taught by the Shin schools of Japanese Buddhism, a Pure Land of the type represented by Sukhāvatī – the 'Happy Land' – is a place, a world, a plane of existence, where there is no pain, no suffering, no misery, no separation, no bereavement, no loss of any kind. It is a place where there is no old age, no sickness, and no death. It is a place of perfect peace in which there is no conflict, no war, no battle, nor even any misunderstanding – it is as perfect and happy as that! These great Mahāyāna *sūtras* also tell us that the Pure Land or Happy Land is a place where there is no distinction of male and female, where no one ever has to do any work. Food and clothing appear of their own accord whenever they are needed. In the Pure Land no one has anything to do except sit on their golden or purple or blue lotus at the feet of the Buddha and listen to his exposition of the Dharma. To crown it all, especially from our English point of view, we are told that in the Pure Land the weather is always perfect. This is a Buddhist daydream, a vision of an ideal society and an ideal world.

This may all seem rather remote, rather archetypal and mythical, and not of much direct concern to us; but Buddhism, although it can dream, and dream very beautifully, is not content to leave it at that. The whole approach of the Buddha's teaching to these questions is very sane, very practical, and very realistic. Buddhism is not content to dream about some ideal society of the future, or some ideal world on another plane; it tries to create the ideal society, the ideal community, here and now on this earth. It tries, therefore, to transform, to transfigure, this society and this world into the image of the future, into the image of the Ideal; and it tries to do this in a number of different ways. One of these ways is the teaching of Perfect Livelihood, the fifth step of the Buddha's Noble Eightfold Path.

The preceding stages of the Noble Eightfold Path are concerned with our initial spiritual experience of insight into the nature of existence, including ourselves, and the transformation by that experience of our emotional life, our communication with one another, and our ordinary everyday behaviour. In other words up to this point the Eightfold Path has been concerned with the transformation of our separate, individual selves. With this step, Perfect Livelihood, we are concerned with the transformation of the collective life, the life of the community, the life of society. This is an aspect of Buddhism which is not very much emphasized, in fact it is sometimes rather played down; but the idea that we should transform not only our individual lives but also society at large is very definitely a part of the total teaching.[383]

Buddhism stands for the creation of an ideal society as well as for the creation of an ideal individual. After all, we are all members of society, all parts one of another, and it is very difficult for us to change ourselves while society remains unchanged. The Indians have a proverb, 'You can't work in the kitchen without getting a bit of soot on you.' (Cooking in India is apt to be a rather messy affair.) In the same way you cannot live and work in a corrupt, basically unethical society without to some extent being besmirched by it. So even in the interests of one's own individual moral and spiritual life one has to make some effort to transform the society in which one lives. It is all very well to talk about the lotus blooming in the midst of the mire, but it is very difficult to be a lotus when the mire is particularly nasty and all-pervasive.

Our collective existence has three principal aspects – the strictly social aspect, the political aspect, and the economic aspect – and Buddhism has teachings which cover all three.

Buddhism has various social teachings, especially in the context of ancient Indian life. For example we find that the Buddha was not at all in favour of the caste system, which was a dominant feature of social life in India at his time, and still exists today.[384] According to this system your position in society was dependent on your birth. If you were the son of a Brahmin you were a Brahmin, if you were the son of a trader you were a trader, and there was nothing you could do to change your status. Even now this system is very strong and all-pervasive in India, especially in the villages, and it has a stultifying effect upon human initiative generally. For this reason the Buddha said clearly and emphatically that the criterion which determines a person's position in society should not be birth, but worth. This is just one example of his social teaching.

In the same way we find that in the political sphere Buddhism upholds – or rather upheld in ancient times – the ideal of what is called Dharmarāja, a number of *sūtras* being devoted to this topic.[385] *Dharma* means truth, righteousness, reality. *Rāja* means king, or even government. Thus the ideal of the Dharmarāja represents the ideal of government by righteousness: the ideal that even in political affairs ethical and spiritual considerations and values should be paramount. It represents the idea that politics should not just be a cockpit of rival interests and factions, not just a question of manipulation and string-pulling, but that one should try to see the ethical and spiritual principles involved, and apply these to this aspect of one's collective existence.

In India the greatest example of this political ideal was the Emperor Aśoka. He was a great ruler of the Maurya dynasty, and lived about 200 years after the Buddha.[386] He inherited from his father the kingdom of Magadha, which he proceeded to expand, promptly swallowing up nearly all the other states of the subcontinent. A series of mopping-up operations increased the dimensions of Magadha even beyond those of present day India and Pakistan. The last state left for Aśoka to subdue, in the days before he became a Buddhist, was the state of Kalinga on the east coast, roughly corresponding to the modern state of Orissa. As Aśoka himself recorded in one of his Rock Edicts, 'One-hundred-and-fifty thousand persons were carried away captive, one hundred thousand were slain, and many times that number died.'[387]

Seeing the havoc that had been wrought, Aśoka realized the misery brought about by war and by his own conquests. In his own words he felt profound sorrow and regret because the conquest of a people previously unconquered involved slaughter, death, and deportation ... even those who escaped calamity themselves are deeply afflicted by the misfortunes suffered by those friends, acquaintances, companions, and relatives for whom they feel an undiminished affection.[388]

So he gave up this career of conquest – possibly the only example in history of a great conqueror who stopped in mid-career because he realized the moral wickedness of his actions. He stopped and he completely reversed. Instead of being known as Caṇḍāśoka or Aśoka the Fierce, as he was before his 'conversion', he became known as Dharmāśoka or Aśoka the Righteous, and from that day onward seems to have considered himself the father of his people.

Aśoka did not give up his political path, but he quite explicitly proclaimed as his ideal the service of those he was supposed to be governing, and he upheld their welfare as the main object of his administration. He also gave great support to Buddhism, dispatching missionaries not only to different parts of India and Sri Lanka but also to Alexandria, Palestine, and Greece. Unfortunately so-called Buddhist rulers have not always followed in the footsteps of Aśoka. He is perhaps the only real example in Indian history of someone trying to apply Buddhist teaching directly to political life, and for that he deserves much credit. H. G. Wells wrote movingly about Aśoka in *The Outline of History*. 'Amidst the tens of thousands of names of monarchs that crowd the pages of history,' he said, 'their majesties and graciousnesses and serenities and royal highnesses and the like, the name of Aśoka shines, and shines almost alone, a star.'[389]

The third aspect of our collective existence is the economic aspect. In this sphere Buddhism teaches Perfect Livelihood, that is to say it teaches the complete transformation, in the light of Perfect Vision, of the whole economic aspect of our collective life.

Now at this point a question arises. We have seen that our collective existence has three principal aspects, the social, the political, and the economic; but Perfect Livelihood represents only one of these, the economic. So why is this? Assuming that the fifth stage of the Noble Eightfold Path deals with our collective existence, why does it deal only with the economic aspect? Why are the political and social aspects not included in the Path? Why only Perfect Livelihood and not Perfect Citizenship or Perfect Administration?

The answer to this question is partly to be found in the conditions obtaining in India in the Buddha's day. The social system was comparatively simple and unorganized – luckily – and apart from the caste system there was not much in this area which needed revision. In the political sphere, the Buddha taught and propagated the Dharma mainly in areas where monarchy was the only existing form of government, which means that ordinary people had little if any share in political life and activity. So in those days there was not much point in asking people in general to practise Perfect Government or Perfect Administration, or even Perfect Citizenship, when they had very little say in these matters. Everyone, however, had to work. They may not have had a vote or known what the king was up to, but they all had to earn a living, so the question of Perfect Livelihood was one which concerned everybody, even in the Buddha's day; and for this reason, no doubt, Perfect Livelihood was included in the Noble Eightfold Path. We might even hazard a speculation here and suggest that the Buddha himself felt that the economic aspect of our collective existence was more basic than either the social or the political aspect, and that for this reason too he included Perfect Livelihood, as representing that aspect, in the Noble Eightfold Path.

from *The Buddha's Noble Eightfold Path*

2. THE BASIS OF ETHICAL WORK

The economic relationship is one of the commonest fields of exploitation in the whole range of human life.

The principle of non-exploitation should ideally hold good in all the relationships of life. It should be possible for us to take what we need, whether food, clothing, education, or anything else, and give whatever we can. There is no need for there to be any connection between what we give and what we receive. Unfortunately, however, the way things usually work is that each person involved in any transaction, whether as the giver or as the receiver, thinks only of himself or herself, giving as little as possible in exchange for as much as possible. This is how ordinary life generally works: we negotiate transactions in which what we give is determined by what we can get for it, not by any regard for the consequences of the transaction for other people.

Beyond a certain point, any commercial profit made is necessarily at the expense of someone else; but the plight of the losers in the game does not generally bother the winners. A particularly brazen form of this universal phenomenon is to be found in poor places like India, where hugely wealthy dealers in grain, especially rice, hoard their stocks, refusing to admit that they have anything to sell, in order to force prices up. This may go on for weeks at a time, especially in remote parts of the country, to the point where people are actually starving, yet the merchants will hold onto those stocks as long as they possibly can, before slowly releasing them at extortionate prices on the black market. The poor have then to scrape together every penny in order to buy enough food to live on. Such exploitation happens – albeit usually in more subtle ways – in all walks of life, in all parts of the world.

The idea of non-exploitation is clearly related to the second of the five precepts (the precepts which form the basis for the ethical life of all Buddhists). The second precept asks that one should not take what is not given. This is more than simply a roundabout way of saying 'not to steal'. Not stealing isn't enough. It leaves too many loopholes. Someone may be a perfectly honest person according to the letter of the law, but they may still build up their business in all sorts of irregular, dubious, or downright shady ways. Thus a great deal of wealth is amassed through highly unethical means without the breaking of any conventional ethical codes.

But the Buddhist precept is an undertaking not to take something unless those who are its present owners, whether individuals or the community as a whole, are willing and ready to give it to you. If it has not been given to you, you do not take it. I mentioned that there should be no connection between what we give and what we take. However, what we take must at the same time be given – in this respect giving and taking are two aspects of the same action. In some Buddhist countries monks are supposed to be so strict in the observance of this precept that when food is given to them on formal occasions, they are not allowed to eat it unless the plate containing the food is lifted up and actually placed in their hands.

The same principle finds application in the fifth stage of the Buddha's Noble Eightfold Path: right or perfect livelihood.[390] The very fact that right livelihood is included in the list suggests the importance given within Buddhism to the way one earns one's living. People may talk of getting the perfect job, but we can guess that this is not what is meant by 'perfect livelihood'. But how does something so apparently mundane as employment find a place in this august collection of ideals?

We all have to earn a living – those who are not monks, anyway – but however we do it, no harm should come either to others or to ourselves through the work we do. The early scriptures even offer a rough and ready guide to right livelihood in the form of a list of occupations that are prohibited for those following the spiritual path.[391] The first of these concerns any commercial activity that involves trading in living beings, whether humans or animals. Slavery is and always has been condemned and prohibited in Buddhist countries – Buddhists did not have to wait until the eighteenth or nineteenth century for a clear line on this issue. Of course, trading in human beings still goes on in the world today, but even more widespread is trading in animals for slaughter, also prohibited in Buddhist societies: you will never find a Buddhist butcher or slaughterman. This form of livelihood is harmful not only to the animals being slaughtered, but also to those doing the slaughtering. To spend eight hours a day killing pigs, cows, sheep, or chickens will necessarily bring about some degree of mental or emotional damage to the slaughterman, as a result of stifling his natural feelings of compassion for other living beings.

Another early Buddhist prohibition was placed upon trade in poisons – not of course medicinal poisons, but poisons used to take life. Before the days of autopsies, this was an almost foolproof way to dispose of someone; a dealer in poisons would give you a phial of the requisite potion – whether fast or slow working, painful or painless – and you would then dose that inconvenient person's curry with it. Like slavers, dealers in poisons are, in a sense, found less frequently today than they used to be. But, of course, the modern equivalent – the widespread dealing in what are called class A drugs (like heroin and cocaine) – is just as harmful. Also, many people are involved in the manufacture and sale of cigarettes and other indisputably harmful drugs, including advertising them and dealing in shares in them.

The third prohibition was against making or trading in weapons. For the early Buddhists this meant bows and arrows, spears and swords. From these primitive beginnings of the arms trade, however, our more advanced cultures have made considerable progress – so they would say – in the development of wonderfully safe and refined methods of ensuring victory over the enemies of civilized values. But any involvement in making these means of destruction, however 'intelligent' they may be, is to be condemned as wrong livelihood. There is no question of justifying any war, any idea that weapons are a deterrent, any bombs, however 'smart'.

These prohibitions are of course directed at the laity, but there are also certain ways of earning a living which are forbidden specifically to monks. For example, various forms of fortune-telling, of which there were very many in the Buddha's day, are enumerated and roundly condemned in the scriptures.[392] However, all over the Buddhist world monks to this day are relied on by the laity to foretell the future, and unfortunately many monks take advantage of this trust in their powers of prognostication.

Monks are also prohibited from earning a living through the display of psychic powers, or by promising psychic powers to others. The reason for this is obvious, really. People are naturally very interested in psychic phenomena, supernormal powers, and so on. Such things are generally taken more seriously on an everyday level in the East, but in certain circles in the West there is also an intense and unhealthy fascination with the idea of acquiring mysterious and occult powers that other people don't possess. If you dangle psychic powers in front of someone's nose, you can, if they are easily led, lead them almost anywhere.

I was once presented with the opportunity of doing this myself. When I lived in Kalimpong in the 1950s, an Englishman arrived on my doorstep one evening in the midst of the rainy season. I was quite accustomed to unexpected visitors, so I invited him in and he introduced himself. He was a medical man who had trained in Dublin. Quite soon I got round to asking him what had brought him to Kalimpong. He said straight out, 'I want to develop psychic powers.' This was not the first time someone had expressed to me this kind of interest, so I just said, 'What sort of psychic powers do you want to develop?' He said, 'I want to be able to read other people's thoughts, and to see the future.' He was not at all coy about it; he was quite open about what he wanted. I then asked him, 'Why do you want to develop these powers?' He simply said, 'It will help me in my work.' What that work turned out to be is not germane to this specific issue; I will mention only that he had been a disciple of Lobsang Rampa, who wrote a lot of books about the more fabulous and fanciful aspects of Tibetan Buddhism. Inspired by one of the most successful of these books, *The Third Eye*, my visitor was searching for a Tibetan lama who could perform an operation to open his third eye. It involved, he believed, drilling a little hole in the middle of his forehead and thereby endowing him with the clairvoyant vision he wanted.

One can see the temptation that this kind of person puts in the way of monks and lamas. He could have been milked by any unscrupulous teacher who was ready to pander to his desire for developing psychic powers. What he said to me made this very clear: 'If anyone can teach me these things I'm quite prepared to place at their disposal a very large sum of money.' He came to an untimely end, unfortunately, but before he did so, several people got quite a lot of money out of him in one way or another.[393]

So much for general prohibitions as regards earning a living. However, the Buddha did not leave it at that, for, as we know, the economic relationship is one of the commonest fields of exploitation in the whole range of human life. Employers exploit employees if they can, and employees exploit their employers whenever they get the chance. We tend to think that problems of suspicion and exploitation between management and workforce, capital and labour, boardroom and factory floor, are peculiarly modern, but the Buddha gave considerable attention to this issue in his advice to Sigālaka as recorded in the *Sigālaka Sutta*. In the section of the discourse devoted to the employer–employee relationship the Buddha enumerates five duties of the employer towards the employee, and five duties of the employee towards the employer.[394] Together, these amount to a general guide to capital and labour relationships, and a business code of economic ethics for Buddhists.

Taking the duties of the employer first, the Buddha says that the employer must give the employee work according to his bodily and mental strength – that is, work he or she can do without injury. Unfortunately, 2,500 years later, this principle is still not being observed – certainly not in India. In India today, thousands of men and women earn their living as coolies, that is, as unskilled labourers. They are treated as beasts of burden, carrying heavy loads on their backs, or more usually on their heads. Coolies are at the very bottom of the economic ladder, and they have virtually no hope of rising above that level, even though they may have to support a growing family as well as themselves.

The problem from the point of view of the merchant hiring a number of coolies to carry, say, sacks of rice is that some coolies cannot carry as much as others, and they do not move as fast, particularly if they are old or unwell. It is shocking to say that the solution for a great many well-to-do merchants is to make sure they get their money's-worth out of all their coolies equally. This is a pitiable sight indeed – some old man, old before his time, staggering along, his veins standing out, muscles stretched like whipcord, and the perspiration streaming down, under loads which he has no business to be carrying at all. It's the same with the rickshaw pullers that you used to find all over Asia (though not any more, I am glad to say). Their life expectancy was no more than a few years. They used to start pulling rickshaws when they were 15 or 16; by the time they were 25 they usually had tuberculosis, and that would be the end of them within a few months. Their inadequate diet and the huge physical stress of their work quite literally killed them.

But for a very long time it was not an issue that bothered anyone. I remember vividly the first time I was in Sri Lanka, taking a ride in a rickshaw – rather against my will. As we moved smartly through the streets I kept telling the coolie to go slower, but he didn't understand me – he thought I was telling him, as most of his fares must have done, to go faster. The more I expostulated with him, the faster he went, until I had to tell him to stop altogether. Thereafter I used a rickshaw only in an emergency; and even then I would pick someone who was fairly strong and sturdy, and insist that he went at a reasonably leisurely pace. In retrospect, I should not, probably, have used them at all, but at the time it seemed there was no other work for them to do. However, the Buddha was quite clear that no human being should be hired to work beyond his natural capacity.

Secondly, the Buddha said that the employer should give the employee sufficient food and pay. This is still the custom in certain parts of India. If you employ someone you give them food and clothes, plus some cash, rather than a salary. But the operative principle is to give enough food and wages to enable the employee to live a full and decent human existence, not simply sufficient in relation to the work done. There shouldn't be any correlation between the amount of work done and the amount of pay received. Even if the employee is strong and healthy, and his output is prodigious, he should not get paid more than his weaker or even lazier fellows; he should just get what he needs by way of remuneration. We have become accustomed to thinking in terms of rewarding hard work and penalizing those who underperform: so much work done, so much pay received. But while this is an effective incentive to invention and enterprise, a Buddhist should ideally find that incentive somewhere else. If the incentive is greed, you are feeding that mental poison.

The employee is enjoined by the Buddha to work as faithfully as he can, and the employer is enjoined to provide for the employee's needs. These needs constitute not just a bare subsistence, but the means to live a richly human existence. We no longer have a society that divides quite so rigidly into employer and employee as the society of the Buddha's day, but the Buddha was not of course recommending the particular social structure of his day, he was simply pointing out the essential principle by which the people in his society could make an economic relationship an essentially human one.

We have to try to do the same within our own society. One radical plan that used to get an airing from time to time, and did seem to express the principle of non-exploitation very effectively, is the idea that on the attainment of their majority everyone should be given by the government a basic stipend to cover the cost of food, clothing, and shelter, regardless of whether they work or not. If they want more than this – if they want to travel, buy expensive electronic equipment, go out to cinemas and restaurants, have the luxury lifestyle that most people see as a virtual necessity – they will have to work. But in a luxury culture people should work because they want to – because they want to make a creative contribution to their society, or because they want a few extras, or both – not simply in order to live. In this way the state would support the spiritual community, enabling individuals who wanted to devote themselves to creative but financially unremunerative activity – to meditation, study, even the arts – to do so, if they were prepared to live a very simple, even monastic life.

Thirdly, the Buddha says that the employer should provide the employee with medical treatment and support after retirement. This we do have nowadays, with pensions, insurance, and so on, but it has taken two millennia for us to get round to this scheme of the Buddha's. Fourthly, the Buddha says that the employer should share with the employee any extra profit he makes. That is, you don't take the profits for your own purposes while telling your employees that they must make do with a basic level of support. Once again, we have caught up with this idea rather late in the day, in the form of bonus schemes. Fifthly and lastly, it is the duty of the employer, according to the Buddha, to grant the employee holidays and special allowances – and this, too, has something of a modern ring to it. However, we should not lose sight of the essential principle expressed in the Buddha's advice – that of establishing the human dimension of the economic relationship – which is not always what bonus schemes, holiday allowances, and pension schemes are about.

So these are the five points made by the Buddha for the guidance of the employer in relationship to the employee. The employee also has certain duties. The first of these is that he or she should be punctual. The Buddha's principle here is not just about clocking in on time, but of not needing to clock in at all. Indeed, the Buddha suggests that you try to be already working before your employer arrives: you are not coming to work simply to be seen to be working.

Secondly, the employee should finish work after the employer. You should try to become free of the whole clock-watching mentality. You don't fling down your tools as soon as the clock strikes. Thirdly, the employee should be sincere and trustworthy. This is quite obvious, as is the fourth point, which is that the employee should perform his or her duties to the satisfaction of the employer. Fifthly, the employee should speak in praise of his employer. The Buddha must have been aware of how readily workers abuse the boss behind his or her back, and it's the same now. Employees may be dutiful and respectful during working hours, but what you hear outside the company gates can tell a different story.

The Buddha is reminding us that, as with any relationship, the economic relationship should not be one of antagonism, in which all you feel you can express is impotent frustration. Ideally, it is a happy, harmonious relationship, in which there is no exploitation on either side. Each takes from the other what he or she needs, without causing harm, and gives what he or she can. If you are an employer, you make use of the labour and skills of your workers, and also take responsibility for seeing that their needs are met. And if you are an employee, you work to the best of your ability and take what you need from that work situation. There is then no need for a grim, protracted bargaining between employers and unions, as though they were in opposite camps, arranging a truce between opposing armies.

from *What is the Sangha?*

3. RIGHT LIVELIHOOD BUSINESSES

We have to be prepared to live in a capitalist world without partaking in capitalist values, practices, and objectives.

There is work which is not in accordance with the principles of right livelihood, and there is work which is. Most people are only too familiar with the first kind: work which is concerned with the production of harmful or frivolous things, work which is boring, repetitive, and non-creative, work which is done under conditions that are unfavourable to personal development, and in the company of people who are indifferent or even hostile to spiritual life. But there is an alternative: work done for the sake of the Dharma, not for the sake of a wage or one's own creature comforts. It is done so that the wealth produced or acquired can be given to the Dharma, and it is ideally done with others similarly committed to the spiritual life.

Of course, efforts are being made in the direction of more ethical work practices even within the capitalist system. There is now some ethical stockbroking: companies that advertise themselves as guaranteeing that any money you invest won't go into arms dealing, tobacco, or any other unethical enterprise. This would suggest that some non-capitalist ideology must have got a toehold; usually capitalists want to make money at any price, regardless of ethical considerations. So ethical investment is at least a step in the right direction, even though it is a modification of the system rather than a replacement of it by something more ethical and idealistic.

But I am doubtful as to whether there is an alternative economic system that can supply us with consumer goods in the way and to the extent that the capitalist system does. People tend to assume that we could change from the capitalist system to some other ethically more desirable one and still have the consumer goodies coming in just as before. I personally rather doubt that. I don't even know that one could come up with a viable alternative, but if there *were* an alternative, I think it would be at the expense of at least some of the consumer goodies. It would therefore be an alternative that most people would not be prepared to contemplate – at least, not without a great deal of education, perhaps over a period of centuries.

To give a crude example, suppose everybody did go back to the land and grow their own food. To do that they would probably have to give up their cars and televisions, and most people simply wouldn't be prepared to do that. There is a price to be paid if you want to introduce a more ethical system, and I doubt whether most people would be prepared to pay that price. So we have to be prepared to live in a capitalist world without partaking in capitalist values, practices, and objectives.

I regard the cooperative structure as being opposed to the capitalist one, and that is one reason I favour it. But it is not at all easy to apply. In a team-based right livelihood situation, as distinct from a business of the ordinary capitalist type, there is an equal sharing of responsibility – or rather, everybody has responsibility to the measure of their understanding and experience of the business. This principle gives rise to a lot of difficulty, because for various reasons people don't find it easy to cooperate with each other in the way that is essential if the business is to work. Some people *want* to be bosses, although the co-op structure doesn't really allow for that, and others *want* to be told what to do rather than taking a share of the responsibility. These opposite tendencies both detract from the application of the cooperative principle. It is important, therefore, to be realistic about what setting up a right livelihood business involves. People sometimes get starry-eyed about how easy and lovely it will be just because you are all working together, but it isn't really as simple as that. However, it is well worth making the effort and having faith in the cooperative principles – that you take what you need and give what you can.

A Buddhist team-based right livelihood project has three aims. First, it aims to provide its workers with a means of support – that is, it aims to provide for their needs: not just their need for food, clothing, and shelter, but also their need to go on retreat, buy Dharma books, and so on. Secondly, it aims to provide a working situation that is conducive to spiritual progress. This means that it functions, within that particular economic context, as a sort of spiritual community, inasmuch as its workers are friends with one another and share the ideals of the project. In short, it should provide the people working within it with an experience of *kalyāṇa mitratā*, spiritual friendship. The third aim is to help finance Buddhist activities: Buddhist centres, publications, and so on. To be considered fully successful, the right livelihood business needs to fulfil all these three objectives.

from *Transforming Self and World*

4. BEING EASY TO SUPPORT

We do not necessarily have to accept the traditions as they have come down to us, especially when these are influenced by the Indian social and cultural conditions of some 2,500 years ago.

Among the desirable qualities of a meditator, according to the *Karaṇīyamettā Sutta*, is that he or she should be *subharo* – 'easy to support'.[395] In the context of the *sutta*, this refers to the economic situation of the monk. The suggestion seems to be that we renounce work and commit ourselves to a life of contemplation, relying on the support of others to give us the necessities of life. The quality we have just been discussing, contentment, clearly also supports this. If they are not contented within themselves, the monk or nun will not be able to sustain their chosen lifestyle.

The fact is that in the Buddha's time, the monks were completely dependent upon lay people, who provided them with food, clothing, and even sometimes with shelter. With the basic necessities of life taken care of, the monks and nuns were free to devote their energies to meditation, study, and devotional practice. This being the case, it was the responsibility of the monks to be easy to support, and not to make life difficult for those who were considerate enough to provide them with their material needs.

The tradition of the homeless wanderer being supported by society at large was not instituted by the Buddha; he inherited it, it existed in Indian society already. In the Buddha's day, the renunciation of social identity was a common and accepted practice all over northern India, and the homeless wanderer or *paribbājaka* (Sanskrit *parivrājaka*) was thus an accepted outsider. When the Buddha started out on his journey to Enlightenment, he too left the home life to become a *paribbājaka*, and after the Enlightenment many of his disciples came from that same casteless social category, or rather non-category, and continued to go on foot from village to village with their alms bowls, accepting whatever food they were given. In the early days of the Buddhist community, the sangha, the priority was to establish a spiritual community on principles that transcended the worldly concerns of the wider society. As the figure of the itinerant spiritual practitioner was already a feature of Indian society and the support of such individuals by the wider community an accepted tradition, the Buddhist sangha adopted this model quite naturally.

The withdrawal of the monk or nun from the world of work went with an attitude to work, particularly manual labour, which still persists in Indian society today: the view that it is inherently unspiritual. The ancient Indians had a similar view to that of the ancient Greeks, except that whereas the Athenian state relied on a class of slaves to carry out any manual labour that might be necessary, Indian society depended on a number of lower castes. The Greeks have of course given up slavery, but to a large extent India continues to run on the basis that physical work is inherently degrading, and that no respectable person would do such work if he or she could possibly avoid it.

Thus in the India of the Buddha's day the possibility of taking up the spiritual life and continuing to do physical work simply did not arise. You could not be a full-time spiritual practitioner and continue to support yourself. But by virtue of the same attitude, you could rely on the lay people to support you. Indeed, the religious renunciant was almost compelled to depend for alms on the lay community if he was to form any kind of socially acceptable relationship with them. Nor did the Buddha think it worth challenging this convention. It is not after all such a bad thing in principle for the more spiritually committed to be supported by the less committed, and he accepted the customary division between monks or wanderers and lay communities as a reasonable way to make this happen, and a way of propagating the Dharma in the process. But as Buddhism developed and spread, the range of activities that the full-timers were able to take up expanded. In the beginning, they were expected to devote all their energies to meditation, study, and teaching. For the first 500 years the teaching was passed on entirely through oral transmission, so a good deal of the time would have been spent learning the *sutta*s by heart and chanting them communally to impress the doctrine on the memory of every monk. Then, when the *sutta*s began to be written down, a great deal of literary activity ensued. Later still, with the building of the great monasteries, monks would have been involved in the sculpting and gilding of images, as well as in the design and decoration of the monasteries and temples themselves.

Later, when Buddhism, especially in its Mahāyāna form, travelled to China and Tibet, whose cultures had a more practical inclination than that of India, monks began to take up everyday physical tasks. Tibet, for example, has no cultural prejudice against manual labour, and in a Tibetan Buddhist monastery you will find monks energetically engaged in all manner of necessary activities according to their various abilities. In the Chan and Zen schools, work is considered to be an integral part of a fully committed spiritual training. As in Tibetan monasteries, monks are expected to throw themselves wholeheartedly into every task that needs to be done, from cooking, cleaning, chopping wood, and drawing water, to the printing of Buddhist *sūtras*.

So we have to be careful not to be trapped by our respect for ancient texts such as the *Karaṇīyamettā Sutta* into thinking of practical, physical, and even economic activity as being necessarily worldly or unspiritual. A human being is not only a mind, but also a body inhabiting a sensory, physical universe. We need productive activity for our physical and psychological well-being. If our mind is the only part of us that gets any real exercise, whether through study or teaching, or at an office desk or computer, there will be an imbalance in our being as a whole, and we will be in need of physical work and exercise to bring it back into balance.

I know from my own contact with Buddhist monks in South-east Asia (admittedly as far back as the 1950s) that they can get into quite an unhealthy state – not just physically or psychologically, but also spiritually – from lack of exercise. Their dependence upon the laity, who in most cases looked after them extremely well, was such that even though the monks would have liked to have done more for themselves, the lay people would not let them. As I remember it, the lay people felt embarrassed, or even affronted, if the monks tried to do things for themselves. It is after all through service to the monks that lay people traditionally express their devotion to the ideal of Enlightenment.

On the face of it, the dependence of the full-time spiritual practitioners on the laity ought to contribute to the simplicity of their lifestyle, enabling them to concentrate more of their energy on purely spiritual matters. But in reality it can hinder them from engaging their energies at all. Perhaps in the early days of Buddhism this unequal distribution of labour between monks and laity was necessary. The dawn-to-dusk burden of physical labour was no doubt so heavy that a degree of freedom from such duties was essential if one was to have the time and energy for reflection and other higher pursuits. It is understandable that a conflict emerged between the demands of farm and field on the one hand and those of spiritual pursuits on the other, and an outright separation of the two was probably the most straightforward solution. However, the cost was a certain alienation: from worldly affairs on the part of the monks, and from any real spiritual life on the part of the laity.

It would seem then that this concept of *subharo*, 'easy to support', owes its appearance in the *Sutta* to the social conventions prevalent in India at the time of the Buddha. In view of this it would be a mistake to interpret the term as suggesting that someone committed to leading the spiritual life must be materially supported by others, and should not get involved in practical or economic activity. In the market economies of the modern world, we are very fortunate in being able to be full-time

Buddhists while at the same time involving ourselves unashamedly in straightforward, practical tasks. We should take that opportunity. In our practice of the Dharma there is invariably a healthy tension between the need to be involved in the sphere of worldly human activity, and thus practise the other-regarding aspect of the Dharma, and the need to withdraw from worldly activity for the purposes of meditation and reflection. As modern Buddhists we have a unique opportunity to decide for ourselves how this balance may be struck in our lives. In doing so, we need to return to the basic principles of Buddhism, and specifically to the principle of right livelihood, that is, ethical work.

To practise right livelihood, we may have to question our overall attitude to work. Like ancient cultures, industrialized societies have their own conventional attitudes to work, these attitudes being based in the case of the latter on the strict division between paid work and leisure. For many of us, work is an activity we don't *want* to do but *have* to do in order to support ourselves, and leisure time is 'our own time', in which we are free to pursue our personal interests. This unhappy distinction seems to affect much that we do. Jobs, tasks, physical activities with some practical purpose or end in view, like cleaning or cooking, are considered a burden, a chore, and resented as such; and we imagine that when we are not working we should be continuously diverted. We certainly don't want to have to do 'chores'.

However, all human beings, even spiritual full-timers, need work, in the sense of some productive, useful activity, whether paid or unpaid, that is beneficial to themselves and to others; and simple, practical physical work may be better than intellectual work from the point of view of fulfilling this human and spiritual need. If you are able to devote all your time and energy to meditation, study, teaching, and writing, all well and good. But not everyone is able to meditate or study the Dharma day in, day out. Many people, including many monks, are quite unsuited to teaching or writing. So, for them, an injunction to refrain from working and physical activity would be quite unhelpful. Of course, this means that we have to be able to carry out such work without resentment, without considering it demeaning or a burdensome imposition.

Today we have the opportunity to reappraise the whole question of work and financial support. We do not necessarily have to accept the traditions as they have come down to us, especially when these are influenced by Indian social and cultural conditions of some 2,500 years ago. In modern post-traditional societies, you can renounce family life and worldly occupation without having to rely for your livelihood on those who have chosen to engage with them. You can choose to work with other Buddhists – that is, others who share your aspirations – in such a way as to support one another's spiritual development and at the same time provide for the material needs of each one of you. The necessity to support oneself financially can become an opportunity to deepen communication, share skills, and learn new ways of cooperation and mutual support. Working in such a situation you can take full account of individual temperaments and attitudes to allow each person to work in a way that is appropriate to their spiritual needs. Some people might find it suited them best to do mainly manual work, while others would benefit from gradually taking on more managerial responsibility. Of course, everyone would need to have time for meditation and Dharma study.

In today's world, it is up to the individual to choose their own way, to make their own decisions, according to whatever principles they wish to live by. There can no longer be blanket rules for spiritual life and practice. What is appropriate at one time and in one place may not work in another. We need a new kind of Buddhist culture in which economic relations can be constantly recreated to meet a constantly changing world. This is probably as close to the Mahāyāna ideal of the Pure Land – the perfect environment for spiritual practice – as we can hope for.

Taking the *Sutta* at face value, therefore, we can interpret the term *subharo*, 'easy to support', as referring to how a monk should behave in terms of his economically dependent role with respect to the laity. But there is a deeper and less historically specific principle at work in this part of the *Sutta*. Whether we are monk or lay, or neither one nor the other, we are supported by society at large, and dependent on the labour of innumerable other people for the necessities of life. We do not grow all our own food or draw our own water; we do not build and furnish our own houses or weave and sew all our own clothes.

If we reflect on how it is that we can enjoy so many consumer products for so little outlay – if we think of the hours of cheap labour that go into what we are able to buy for next to nothing – we will find that we are not at all easily supported. There are also environmental and ecological considerations to take into account. The natural and human resources available to our society should not be expended heedlessly or needlessly. The fact that we have the financial resources to help ourselves to what we fancy does not justify our consuming the wealth of the world without consideration for the claims of others – both in the present and in the future – on those same resources. We owe it to the society that supports us to give what we can to support others. There are very few people who would benefit spiritually from being entirely supported by others in the way the traditional monastic sangha was.

The principle behind this term *subharo* therefore comes down to taking from the world and from society no more than you need, and freely contributing whatever you can. You are entitled to rely on others for the help and support that one human being can be reasonably expected to give another, but you also need to be prepared to stand on your own two feet, as far as you can. You cannot expect to be propped up by others as a right.

This principle operates on all levels of exchange, not only on the material and economic level. We need the emotional support of others, for example, but we should not expect from our friends what we are capable of providing for ourselves with a little effort. Once they have helped us back on our feet, we shouldn't expect them to prop us up indefinitely. If you are emotionally needy, you are clearly not yet 'capable', and as such you are not 'easy to support'. You are therefore unlikely to make much progress in meditation. Of course, if you are such a person it is quite possible that you will not understand that you are making undue emotional demands on others, and that their time and energy might be better spent in other ways. In that case it is up to your friends to help you to see the truth of your situation, and perhaps direct you towards getting some therapeutic help, rather than offering 'support' that will just perpetuate the problem.

If you are aiming to be easy to support, the way to do it is to keep your wants and needs to a manageable level, however you manage to do so. This is the ideal to which the term *sallahukavutti* refers: a livelihood, *vutti*, that is *lahuka*, literally 'trifling' or 'lightweight'. It suggests a basic simplicity in one's attitude to life, a determination not to be weighed down by a multiplicity of wants and desires or onerous material commitments. Clearly a taste for hard work, and a relish for the challenge of practical tasks and problems to be overcome, is a virtue, but it is possible to like these things too much for one's own good, especially if they become distractions from more spiritually pressing challenges. So the *Sutta* goes on to say that one should be *appakicco*, 'with little work' or 'with few duties'.

The fact is that one can become too busy even with religious or spiritual activities. Again with reference to the monastic context of early Indian Buddhism, the *Sutta* warns against giving yourself too many things to do. The monk shouldn't be too occupied with performing ceremonies for the laity or running errands for his teachers or preceptors, or even with teaching his own pupils. He should allow himself enough time for study, meditation, reflection, and just spending time quietly by himself – all the things that the lay people in fact support him to do.

Work, in the sense of pleasurable, productive activity, is a necessary part of life for most people. But there is a difference between this and a kind of neurotic, compulsive activity that masquerades as work but is really a way of keeping the deeper emotions at bay. Work can be an unhealthy means by which to escape from being alone with oneself and one's feelings. We should beware of feeling that we have to keep busy, that we can never be without something to do. So yes, by all means work, but don't let busyness be an escape from your true self. Be occupied only with those activities that are really necessary.

The division of labour between monk and lay person has other disadvantages. Relying completely on other people for your support puts you in a passive relationship with regard to them. There is a suggestion of this danger in the *Sutta*, in which the Buddha now enjoins the monk to be *apagabbho kulesu ananugiddho*. Like *subharo*, the term *apagabbho* clearly has to do with the relationship between wandering monks and the lay people upon whom they depend. It is the negative form of *pagabbho*, which means 'impudent', 'over bold', 'tending to push oneself forward', and Saddhatissa translates it quite neatly as 'modesty'. Together with the term that follows, *kulesu ananugiddho*, 'not greedily attached to families' it would seem to refer to the danger of monks insinuating themselves into special relationships with particular families. It could happen that a family would end up adopting a particular monk and in a way 'domesticating' him. To avoid this, the *Sutta* directs the monk to avoid making strong connections with anyone or soliciting special favours from them when on his almsround, as this is against the whole spirit of renunciation for which he stands.

Reading between the lines of the *Sutta*, we can see that even the homeless wanderer of the Buddha's day was not necessarily free from attachment to the things that came his way, few as these must have been. He might well be tempted to secure creature comforts and a certain sense of belonging by getting to know certain families, out of a yearning for the approval and acceptance of ordinary people. To guard against this, he is counselled to cultivate a sense of identity based on inner stability and contentment.

But how should we ourselves interpret this exhortation? After all, we don't knock on doors for alms. For us, perhaps, the danger is of depending for our sense of identity upon the acceptance or approbation of others, being afraid of exclusion. The possible result of such dependence is that one is unable to make decisions, hold opinions, dress, eat, or do all manner of other things without reference to the norms of the group whose approval one seeks. To protect ourselves from this, we should avoid making ourselves too much at home in any one human grouping, or identifying with a group too rigidly. We should avoid becoming too comfortable with the feeling that we 'belong' in the course of our involvement with groups, systems, and ideologies. If you are skilled in working for your own good and wish to attain Nirvāṇa, you cannot afford to be too attached to the approval of any group, whether it is your biological family, your cultural or ethnic group, your caste or nationality. A mature individual has an existence, as it were, in his or her own right, without needing to have recourse to the affirmation of any group, be it a family, a community, or even a religious movement. Such a person is capable of finding a sense of fulfilment within the experience of his or her own being, independent of external circumstances.

from *Living with Kindness*

5. BEGGING IN INDIA

We were followed to the mango grove by a crowd of about a hundred people who, with the dull curiosity of sheep or cows, stood staring at us from among the trees as though they intended to do so for the rest of the day. Feeling a little uncomfortable under all those eyes and wishing to be left in peace, we asked them to go away until we had finished our meal. This they eventually did, though not without much urging on the part of our Muslim friend and many backward glances at us over their shoulders.

Our main preoccupation next morning was to find a place where we could start putting our begging-bowls to the use for which they were intended and go for alms. Now that we were *śrāmaṇeras* we were resolved to do this in strictly traditional fashion. We would beg from door to door until we had obtained enough cooked food for our one meal of the day, not skipping so much as a single house. We would not accept people's invitations, nor would we even sit down inside a house in order to eat the food that we had collected. After walking from 5.30 until 10.30, with only a little *chatua* to sustain us on the way, we were feeling rather hungry. But at the first township to which we came we found the atmosphere so forbiddingly commercial that our courage failed us and tired as we were we decided not to stop there. Luckily there was a village only a mile further on. Before reaching the village proper, which was called Barspar, we halted at a well and asked a woman who was drawing water there to pour some into our lotas or brass pots. Respectfully she refused. She belonged to the Chamar or leather-worker caste, she explained, and for high-caste holy men like ourselves contact with anything that she had touched would mean pollution. Buddharakshita and I could hardly believe our ears. The woman at the well was saying exactly the same thing as the Mātaṅgī woman had said to Ānanda, cousin and personal attendant of the Buddha, 2,500 years ago, and saying it in exactly the same circumstances. History was repeating itself. Making exactly the same reply as Ānanda had done, we told the woman that what we wanted was water, not caste, whereupon she gladly filled our lotas. India had not changed much since the days of the Buddha, it seemed.

Having quenched our thirst, we made our way to the woman's hut, which was situated nearby, on the outskirts of the village, and stood silently in front of the door with our bowls in our hands. Before very long a man came out and after looking at us in a rather puzzled manner asked us what we wanted. When begging at orthodox Buddhist doors, of course, a monk never spoke, but here there seemed to be no alternative, and we therefore told the man that we had come for alms. On hearing this he went inside and quickly returned with a small quantity of paddy or unmilled rice. This we refused, saying that we accepted only cooked things. He thereupon offered us money; but this too we refused. Either there was no cooked food in the hut or, what was more likely, he was afraid to give it on account of his caste. Not wishing to cause him further embarrassment, we quietly departed.

On entering the village we took our stand at the entrance to what was probably either a Brahmin or a Kshatriya house, where a number of people had assembled on the veranda. After gazing at us for some time with undisguised astonishment they asked us what we wanted, to which we again replied that we had come for alms. Like the man in the hut, they at first wanted to give us some paddy, but on being told that we accepted only cooked food they eventually dropped into our bowls a handful of puffed rice, which, having been parched, was not in orthodox Hindu eyes cooked food in the technical sense that boiled rice was. From the buzz of comment that rose from the veranda it was clear that astonished as they were by the unfamiliar cut and colour of our robes, and by the fact that we stood holding our bowls in silence instead of shouting out 'Give alms!' as the Hindu ascetics and holy men did, the villagers were still more astonished by our insistence on accepting only cooked food. In their experience, holy men were strict observers of the caste system, and avoided the risk of pollution by accepting as alms only uncooked food. Since from our complexion, dress, and deportment we were, so far as they could see, high-caste holy men, they were completely mystified by our disregard of the conventional code. For our part, we could now see that by obliging his homeless disciples to beg from door to door without regard to caste, and to accept only cooked food, the Buddha had initiated a social revolution – a revolution that had been checked, in the end, by the forces of brahminical reaction.

Our next stop was at a Muslim house. On learning what we wanted, the sarong-clad occupant told us to go round to the back door. If the Hindus saw him giving us alms, he said, he would be in danger of a beating. Who was it that had really divided India, we wondered.[396] Besides giving us alms himself, this friendly son of the Prophet accompanied us to all the other houses we visited and his explanations saved us a lot of trouble. Indeed, thanks to his exertions we were able to complete the remainder of our alms-round in silence. Some of the people at whose doors we stood were sympathetic, others sarcastic. One well-to-do Brahmin asked us to come in and sit down, saying that since he had just finished eating and there was nothing left he would prepare a meal specially for us. This kind offer we refused, as we already had something in our bowls, and our refusal impressed him more than ever. Another Brahmin, who had also just eaten, poured into each of our bowls a pint of milk, in which the puffed rice, boiled rice, curried vegetables, fruits, curds, pickles, and all the other things we had been given were soon afloat. Before long we had more than enough for our requirements, and we therefore made our way to a mango grove on the outskirts of the village. Since this was the first time we had gone out begging in the traditional Buddhist manner, the occasion was one of unprecedented importance in both our lives, and it was with a sense of elation that we sat down in the deep, cool shade of the handsome trees. Apparently it was something of an event in the life of the village too, for we were followed to the mango grove by a crowd of about a hundred people who, with the dull curiosity of sheep or cows, stood staring at us from among the trees as though they intended to do so for the rest of the day. Feeling a little uncomfortable under all those eyes and wishing to be left in peace, we asked them to go away until we had finished our meal. This they eventually did, though not without much urging on the part of our Muslim friend and many backward glances at us over their shoulders.

As soon as they had gone we put our hands into our bowls, kneaded the contents into a uniform if rather sticky mess, and started on our meal. While we were eating someone came running up with an enormous tray piled high with rice, curries, and lentil soup. Although we already had all that we really wanted, we accepted a small quantity, and asked that the rest should be distributed as *prasad*. According to the scriptures, the first time the future Buddha had tried to eat almsfood he had nearly vomited with disgust. Either we had been brought up less delicately than he had, or we were more fortunate in what we had collected. Far from feeling any disgust, as soon as we got used to the idea of eating everything mixed up together we thoroughly enjoyed our meal. What was left over we scattered at the foot of a tree for the birds. When the villagers saw that we had finished they started drifting back to the mango grove, whereupon, having collected them together and made them sit down on the ground, Buddharakshita addressed them on the necessity of leading a moral life and the importance of observing the five precepts of ethical behaviour. Though this was probably drier spiritual fare than that to which they were accustomed, they listened attentively, and we had the satisfaction of repaying them for their hospitality by preaching the Dharma in the traditional manner.

from *The Rainbow Road from Tooting Broadway to Kalimpong*

6. THE GROUP AND THE INDIVIDUAL

Where there are no individuals, there will be no spiritual community, call it by whatever name you please.

Wanting to belong to a group is in our bones, in our blood. We have a long history of gathering together in groups. If we include our primate ancestors, we have about twenty million years of group conditioning, as ape-man, man-ape, and human. To begin with we used to live in something like an extended family group or small tribe of perhaps fifty individuals, with just occasional encounters with other small tribes. With the development of language we have been able to accommodate a somewhat larger tribal grouping than this. But almost all our relationships would have been within this home group, and in some ways this is the size of group that we would all naturally like to get back to.

It is only within the last few thousand years (which is really no time at all by comparison) that we have developed all sorts of much more complicated social groupings. Today we find ourselves struggling to get what we need from ever more distorted, even aberrant social institutions. It is more and more difficult to find groups of the right scale. On the one hand we have the isolated nuclear family, which can be so cramping as to be a breeding ground for neurosis; and on the other, we belong to a group – the nation state – which is so big as to be meaningless on a personal level. Between these two institutions we establish, in a partial and intermittent fashion, membership of or loyalty to all sorts of other groups, but none of these seem to satisfy our ancient need to belong to a small tribe of between thirty and sixty people, a group in which we can live and work, in genuine and continuous personal relationship with all its members.

We have all been born into groups, and we are all therefore subject to the conditioning arising from those affiliations. Our ideas, our views, our feelings, the way we react to people and situations, our convictions – all these will tend to be determined by group conditioning of one kind or another, except in so far as we become conscious of such conditioning and distance ourselves from its influence. The groups themselves often overlap or even cohere. And all these overlapping groups together make up 'the world'.

Groups fear individuality and all its manifestations, and always tend to discourage it. The group requires conformity. This is because it is based on power, which whether physical, intellectual, or economic is always the power of the strong over the weak, the power of those who have the resources, the cunning, or the knowledge to be able to impose their will on others, deploying brute force or subtle manipulation in order to exploit others for their own, usually selfish, purposes. The group consists of those who wield that power and those who give it to them. Such power is exercised within any group, whether political, cultural, tribal, familial, or even religious.

The spiritual community

The purposes of a community of individuals, a spiritual community, are utterly different from those of the group. They are twofold: firstly, its members help one another to develop spiritually; secondly, in whatever way they can, they help others outside the community to develop their individuality. In essence, a spiritual community is a free association of individuals. To form one, therefore, the first requirement is a number of individuals. You can no more have a spiritual community without individuals than you can have an omelette without eggs. A spiritual community is not created by acquiring a building, an exotic form of dress, and a long list of rules. You don't need a building, you don't need an 'authentic tradition', you don't even need a religion. You need individuals: that is the basic ingredient. In other words, you need a number of people who are relatively emancipated from the group, relatively integrated and aware, and have an inner direction and positive purpose to their lives. Where there are no individuals, there will be no spiritual community, call it by whatever name you please.

from *What is the Sangha?*

7. THE INTEGRATION OF BUDDHISM INTO WESTERN SOCIETY

We cannot isolate ourselves from society or ignore the conditions in which we and others live.

The integration of Buddhism into Western society involves changing Western society. Inasmuch as our level of consciousness is affected by external conditions, it is not enough for us to work directly on the mind itself through meditation. We cannot isolate ourselves from society or ignore the conditions in which we and others live. We must make it easier for anyone within that society who wants to live a life dedicated to the Dharma to do so. To the extent that Western society has not been changed by Buddhism, to that extent Buddhism has not been integrated into Western society. In order to change Western society it is necessary to create Western Buddhist institutions and Western Buddhist lifestyles.

In general, Buddhist movements try to create conditions that are conducive to human development. They do this in three main ways corresponding to three central aspects of ordinary human life which on balance are not conducive to spiritual development – the conventional nuclear family, work, and leisure activities. The idea is to open up and revolutionize these keystones of modern life, and where appropriate offer a more positive alternative to them.

Firstly, residential communities are meant to offer an alternative to stagnant relationships, particularly those of the tightly-knit family unit – or rather, the claustrophobic and neurotic closed system of a couple who no longer communicate with each other, orbited by one or two children, two cars, three televisions, a dog, a cat, and a budgerigar. Secondly, team-based right-livelihood projects are meant to offer an alternative to earning money in ways which are harmful to one's own development and which exploit others. And thirdly, the various activities provided and promoted by the spiritual community, both those that are directly Dharmic and those that are more indirectly helpful to spiritual growth, give us something positive to do with our free time. They give us an alternative to activities which merely enable us to pass the time, to forget about the stresses of work or family life, and all too often to forget about our own selves. These three things between them constitute the nucleus of the new society; they represent the transformation of conditions that tend to be unconducive to spiritual development into conditions that are conducive.

How each project goes about this work is up to the individuals concerned. Every one of these institutions is meant to function autonomously. Those who run it have to make their own decisions and take responsibility for them. At the same time, as an aspect of the development of this sangha, people with similar responsibilities for similar institutions make sure that they meet regularly to swap notes, and support and advise each other.

It is also important to communicate the fundamental concepts of Buddhism in a way that is both intelligible to a Western audience and faithful to the Buddhist tradition. This is yet another point of interaction with Western society: the introduction of Buddhist ideas into Western intellectual discourse. By Buddhist ideas I do not mean doctrinal refinements or philosophical subtleties. I mean ideas so fundamental that Buddhists themselves often take them for granted, and fail to realize their full significance. Such, for example, is the idea that religion does not necessarily involve belief in the existence of God, of a creator and ruler of the universe. Another, related, idea is that it is possible for us to lead an ethical life, to raise the level of our consciousness, and to realize a transcendent reality, without invoking the aid of any outside supernatural power. If Buddhism is to be integrated into Western society, ideas of this fundamental kind will have to become familiar to all educated Westerners.

However, the most important kind of integration – without which the other kinds cannot exist – is the integration of the individual Buddhist into Western society. It is, after all, the individual Buddhist who meditates – meditation does not exist in the abstract. Likewise, it is the individual Buddhist who goes on retreat, who works in a right-livelihood business, who communicates the fundamental ideas of Buddhism. Without the individual Buddhist there can be no integration of Buddhism into Western society.

The individual Buddhist is someone who goes for Refuge to the Three Jewels. He or she does so not in isolation but in the company of other individuals who are also Going for Refuge. That is, he or she belongs to the sangha or spiritual community in the widest sense. It is this sangha rather than the individual Buddhist which will raise the level of consciousness of people living in Western society, which will change that society by creating Buddhist social and economic institutions, and which will introduce fundamental Buddhist ideas into Western intellectual discourse. It is this wider spiritual community that will effect the psychological, social, economic, and intellectual integration of Buddhism into Western society. This is what the sangha is really for; this is what the sangha really is.

from *What is the Sangha?*

8. GETTING COMFORTABLE IN THE PURE LAND?

The bodhisdattva cannot keep people in the Buddha-land against their will.

According to the Mahāyāna, an advanced bodhisattva is quite capable of purifying or building the Buddha-land single-handed, just as a magician is capable of creating a magical elephant through his own power. But what would be the use? Yes, you can create a Buddha-land and give people a glimpse of it. You may even be able to keep them in it for a little while. But you cannot keep them there indefinitely – not even if you are a bodhisattva. This is because they are not going to cooperate, they are not going to want to stay there indefinitely, or even for very long, because they will not feel at home there. They are not ready for it.

There's a little Indian story that illustrates this point, and it will perhaps bring us down to earth somewhat, but never mind. The story is about a woman who sold fish. She lived in a small village on the banks of a big Indian river, and every week she took her fish to the market in a big basket. Now, one week, for some reason or other, it took her rather a long time to sell all her fish. She decided that rather than make her way back to the village so late at night, she had better stay in town. Fortunately she found a flower shop still open, and the flower-seller was sympathetic to her plight and said she could spend the night in his shop. Indian flower shops don't sell cut flowers in bunches as Western ones do; they sell sweet-smelling garlands, and little bunches of sweet-scented flowers for the ladies to put in their hair. The fish seller lay down to sleep among all those sweet-smelling flowers, but she tossed and turned, and couldn't get to sleep. She couldn't bear the scent of the flowers – they were so sweet, so beautiful. In the end, she got her old fish basket, which of course smelled strongly of fish, and put it right next to her, right by her nose. And after that, she slept quite soundly.

We might laugh at the fish-seller's plight, but we ourselves are in much the same position. She felt uncomfortable in the flower shop among all those sweet-smelling flowers; but we would feel no less uncomfortable in the Pure Land. We could manage a short visit, perhaps a weekend, but eventually we would want to introduce some equivalent of her smelly old fish basket into the Pure Land. We would want to bring along some physical or mental distraction – perhaps our television, our motorbike, our record collection, our lover, or our office files. Then we would feel more comfortable, more at home. But then, of course, the Pure Land would no longer be the Pure Land.

So the bodhisattva cannot keep people in the Buddha-land against their will. In any case, that would be a contradiction in terms, because the spiritual life is essentially the autonomous life, the free life, the emancipated life. So what is the bodhisattva to do? He cannot create a Buddha-land by magical power and then hold people in it – at least, not for very long. They will soon start getting uncomfortable, and then – no more Buddha-land.

The answer is that the Buddha-land has to be a joint creation. It has to be built by a number of people – bodhisattvas and would-be bodhisattvas – working together. One of them may be more advanced than the others, may have more vision, may even be the first to attain Enlightenment and then help the others to take that final step. But all must be inspired by the same ideal, the ideal of supreme perfect Enlightenment for the benefit of all beings. They all therefore follow the bodhisattva path, follow it for thousands of lives – and all follow it together. This is a truly wonderful conception: the whole spiritual community being reborn together as a spiritual community, living and working together, helping one another, life after life, until the Buddha-land is established.

from *The Inconceivable Emancipation*

6
BUDDHISM AND THE FUTURE OF THE WORLD

1. BUDDHISM AND WORLD PEACE

The failure of communication which is so striking a feature of our times is based, ultimately, on a breakdown of the notion of objective truth, that is to say, on a breakdown of the notion that truth is truth regardless of our subjective feelings about it and regardless of the way in which it affects our personal interests.

Gautama the Buddha gained Enlightenment at about the same time that Cyrus the Great captured the city of Babylon and founded the Persian Empire. Five years later the Buddha paid a visit to his home town, Kapilavastu, just inside the modern state boundary of Nepal. It was fortunate that he did so. A dispute had arisen between the Śākyans of Kapilavastu and their neighbours the Koliyans of Devadaha, to whom the Buddha was related through his mother, and as a result of this, war was about to break out between the two peoples. The original cause of the dispute was comparatively trivial. Both the Śākyans and the Koliyans were accustomed to irrigate their fields with water from the River Rohiṇī, which flowed between their respective territories, but that year it was obvious that there would not be enough water for them both. The Koliyans proposed that they should have the water, on the grounds that their crops would ripen with a single watering, but the Śākyans flatly rejected this proposal, saying that they would have no mind to beg food from the Koliyans later on in the year and that in any case their crops too would ripen with a single watering. Neither side would give way, the dispute became very bitter, and eventually blows were exchanged. To make matters worse, the Koliyans started casting aspersions on the origins of the leading Śākya families, saying that they had cohabited with their own sisters like dogs and jackals, while the Śākyans cast aspersions on the leading Koliya families, saying that they were destitute outcastes who lived in the hollows of trees like animals. Reports of these aspersions soon reached the ears of the leading families themselves, who immediately came forth armed for battle, the Śākya warriors shouting, 'We will show the strength of those who have cohabited with their sisters!' and the Koliya warriors shouting, 'We will show the strength of those who live in the hollows of trees!'

Thus it was that, one fine morning, the Buddha came to know that war was about to break out between his paternal and maternal relations. Realizing that unless he intervened they would destroy each other, he at once went to the place where the two armies were gathered. As soon as they saw him his kinsmen on both sides threw away their weapons and respectfully saluted him. When the Buddha asked them what the quarrel was all about, however, they were unable to tell him. Eventually, after cross-examining various people, the Buddha succeeded in establishing that the cause of the quarrel was water. Having established this, he asked, 'How much is water worth?' 'Very little, Reverend Sir.' 'How much are warriors worth?' 'Warriors are beyond price, Reverend Sir.' 'Then,' said the Buddha, 'it is not fitting that because of a little water you should destroy warriors who are beyond price.' And they were silent.[397]

Some features of this incident are only too sickeningly familiar to us today. They are in fact characteristic of disputes and wars from the Stone Age down to modern times. There is the same clash of vital interests between different groups of people, the same unwillingness to compromise, the same dreadful escalation from harsh words to isolated acts of violence, and from isolated acts of violence to preparations for full-scale war. There is the same fatal spirit of belligerence, the same readiness on the part of large numbers of people to fight without really knowing what they are fighting for. There is even, we note, the same irrelevant mutual vilification, suggestive of antipathies that have long lurked beneath the surface and now have an opportunity of breaking out. But there is also – and this is more encouraging – the same solitary voice of sanity and compassion that, if only we listen carefully enough, we can hear even today. There is the same appeal to reason, the same reminder of what is truly most valuable, that has been heard if not from the Stone Age then at least from the Axial Age, and heard, perhaps, with increasing frequency, regardless of whether people listened or not.

But although there are similarities between the Rohiṇī incident and the situation in which we find ourselves today, there are differences too. The quarrel between the Śākyans and the Koliyans involved the inhabitants of two small city states living side by side at the foot of the Himalayas, whereas the quarrel between the superpowers of the twentieth century involves hundreds of millions of people occupying continents separated by vast oceans and affects the whole world, directly or indirectly. Like the heroes of Ancient Greece, the Śākyans and the Koliyans were armed with swords and spears and bows and arrows, and they fought either on foot or from horse-drawn chariots. The superpowers are armed with a variety of nuclear weapons, capable of destroying life on a scale unprecedented in history and unimaginable before the present century. The Śākyans and Koliyans could actually see each other across the waters of the River Rohiṇī. They spoke the same language and worshipped the same gods, and it was possible for one man to make himself heard by the warriors on both sides. Today it is possible for hundreds of millions of people to quarrel without actually seeing one another, and even to prepare to destroy one another without knowing, humanly speaking, who it is they are preparing to destroy. They speak the same language neither literally nor metaphorically, they certainly do not worship the same gods, and despite our marvellously improved facilities of communication it is not really possible for one man to make himself heard by them all. Indeed, these marvellously improved facilities of communication are used only too often either for the exchange of insults or for the reiteration of positions known to be unacceptable to the other side. Thus facilities of communication are used for purposes of non-communication.

Peace has become a seamless garment, and the world has to wear the whole garment or go naked to destruction. There can no longer be any question of a scrap of peace covering one part of the world's nakedness and not another. This makes it impossible for us to think in merely geopolitical terms. We have also to think in geo-ethical, geo-humanitarian, and geo-philanthropic terms. Since peace is indivisible, the stark choice before us is either world peace or no peace, one world or no world. We shall be able to achieve peace only if we realize that humanity too is indivisible, and if we consistently act on that realization. In other words, we shall be able to achieve peace only by regarding ourselves as citizens of the world, and learning to think not in terms of what is good for this or that nation state, this or that political system, this or that ideology, but simply and solely in terms of what is good for the world, or for humanity, as a whole. There can be no world peace so long as the governments of sovereign nation states insist on regarding their separate, sometimes mutually exclusive, interests as paramount and to be pursued at all costs.

Nationalism is the curse of modern history. It is nationalism that was responsible for the rise of sovereign nation states, and it is sovereign nation states that produced nuclear weapons in the first place, that produce and possess them now, and that have the power to unleash their destructive capacity upon mankind. Peace and nationalism are therefore incompatible. Nationalism is not, of course, the same thing as patriotism. Nationalism is an exaggerated, passionate, and fanatical devotion to one's national community at the expense of all other national communities and all other interests and loyalties. It is a pseudo-religion, an idolatrous cult that demands bloody sacrifices. Patriotism, on the other hand, is simply love of one's country, in the sense of an attachment to, and a desire to care for and protect, the place where one was born and grew up, and it does not exclude smaller or larger interests and loyalties, or honest pride in such things as one's own history and culture. Thus patriotism, unlike nationalism, is not incompatible with peace, even though peace goes beyond patriotism, which, in the famous words of Edith Cavell, is 'not enough'.[398] This does not mean that in order to achieve peace we have to stop loving our own village or city, our own province, our own country, or our own continent, but rather that we have to love them because they are all part of the world and because we love the world. It means that we have to identify ourselves with humanity, rather than with any particular section of it, and love humanity as ourselves. We have to feel for the different national communities, and the different ethnic and linguistic groups, the same kind of love that we feel for the different limbs of our own bodies.

Of this kind of love the Buddha, as he stands between the opposing Śākya and Koliya forces, is the supreme exemplar. The Buddha identified himself with both the Śākyans and the Koliyans, so he could love them both. After all, even apart from the fact that he had attained Enlightenment and thus identified himself with all living things not in any abstract, metaphysical sense, but in the sense of experiencing the joys and sorrows of others as his own, he was related by blood to both parties in the dispute. Through his father he was related to the Śākyans, and through his mother to the Koliyans. Among the warriors on both sides he had uncles, cousins, and nephews, besides old friends and childhood companions. Thus the Buddha's position was similar to our own. We too stand between opposing forces, though the forces with which we have to deal are as much superior to those of the Śākyans and Koliyans as the Buddha's sanity and compassion are superior to ours. Moreover, in our case we do not stand unambiguously between these forces but only too often identify ourselves with one or the other of them and are perceived so to identify ourselves. If peace is to be achieved, however, we have to identify ourselves with both parties, just as the Buddha identified himself with both the Śākyans and the Koliyans. Though we may not be related to them by blood in the way that the Buddha was related to his embattled paternal and maternal relatives, nevertheless we are related to them, inasmuch as we all belong to the same organic species, *Homo sapiens*, and it should not be necessary for us to attain Enlightenment in order to realize this fact. If we identify ourselves with both parties and with humanity in this manner, then we shall be able to stand cleanly and unambiguously between the 'fell incensèd points of mighty opposites' of our day.[399] We shall be able to speak as the Buddha spoke, because we shall love as the Buddha loved. We shall be a voice of sanity and compassion in the world. We shall be able to appeal to reason. We shall be able to remind humanity, in its own name, what things are of greater value and what of less. We may even be able to remind it what is the most valuable thing of all.

When the Buddha asked the Śākya and Koliya warriors to tell him what the quarrel was all about, they could understand the meaning of his question, and were eventually able to give him a reply. He in turn could understand their reply, and when he went on to ask them how much water was worth and how much warriors were worth they knew exactly what he was talking about and could reply accordingly. Similarly, they knew exactly what he was talking about when he told them it was not fitting that because of a little water they should destroy warriors who were beyond price. There was no problem of communication, as we call it nowadays. The Śākyans and the Koliyans, and the Buddha himself, all spoke the same language, both literally and metaphorically. When the Buddha wanted to know what the quarrel was about, neither the Śākya nor the Koliya warriors denied that they were quarrelling. Neither protested that *they* had simply staged a peaceful demonstration on which the warriors on the other side had proceeded to launch a vicious and entirely unprovoked attack. In the same way, neither the Śākya nor the Koliya warriors attempted to argue that 'water' could mean 'earth' or that in the case of the warriors on the other side 'beyond price' really meant 'worthless', or that there was in any case no question of destroying warriors but only of *eliminating* them.

The failure of communication which is so striking a feature of our times is ultimately based on a breakdown of the notion of objective truth, that is to say, on a breakdown of the notion that truth is truth regardless of our subjective feelings about it and the way in which it affects our personal interests. That people do not in practice exhibit total loyalty to the notion of objective truth, even though they may uphold it in theory, is of course well known and widely accepted. Indeed, in the ordinary transactions of life due allowance is generally made for this fact. We no more expect the used car dealer or the estate agent to dwell on the less favourable features of the car or the house he is trying to sell us than we expect him to tell us a deliberate, downright lie. But even if people do not in practice exhibit total loyalty to the notion of objective truth, it is important that such loyalty as they do display to it is not allowed to fall below a certain point, since otherwise the transactions of ordinary life will become impossible. Unfortunately, it often does fall below that point. Loyalty to the notion of objective truth becomes *selective*. Actual lies may not be told, but those facts that are not in accordance with the feelings and interests of this or that individual or group are increasingly ignored, misrepresented, distorted, and suppressed. In extreme cases such facts are not acknowledged ever to have existed at all.

From the stage where loyalty to the notion of objective truth becomes selective – that is to say, becomes that which is in accordance with certain personal or sectional interests – it is not a very big step to the stage where that which is in accordance with those interests becomes the truth. At this stage, there is a breakdown of the notion of objective truth. 'Truth' is whatever happens to be in accordance with the interests of a particular class, sovereign nation state, or ideology. Since there are many classes, sovereign nation states, and ideologies, and therefore many different, even conflicting, interests, there will be not one truth but many truths. Thus there is not only a breakdown of the notion of objective truth but also a substitution of the notion of objective truth by the notion of subjective truth. Subjective truth in effect becomes, for a particular group, objective truth, and since there can be only one objective truth the objective truth of all other groups – including what might be termed objectively objective truth – necessarily becomes untruth. Under these circumstances, communication is impossible. Words no longer have the same meaning for everybody, and what one group regards as facts another regards as non-facts. There is a failure of communication. Indeed, those whose views and attitudes are not in accordance with the interests of a particular group are treated as non-individuals in the same way that facts that are not in accordance with these same interests are regarded as non-facts. Such an individual is not so much wrong as, in theory, non-existent, and since he is non-existent in theory it is only natural that he should very quickly become non-existent in practice too. Thus we arrive at a state of affairs such as is characteristic of the nightmare totalitarian world of George Orwell's *Nineteen Eighty-Four*, where the three slogans of the Party are 'War is Peace', 'Freedom is Slavery', and 'Ignorance is Strength', where Newspeak is fast replacing Oldspeak, where history is being continually rewritten, and where a word from Big Brother can turn a person into an unperson overnight.[400]

Fortunately, the 1984 which has come to pass is not wholly that of Orwell's grim foreboding. The nightmare has not yet come true to more than a limited extent. Nevertheless, the situation in which we find ourselves today is sufficiently alarming, and one of its most dangerous features is that we are faced by a failure of communication between large and important sections of the human race, particularly between the superpowers. As I have tried to show, this failure is based, ultimately, on a breakdown of the notion of objective truth, so that if communication is to be restored, and if the superpowers are to learn to speak the same 'language', the notion of objective truth will have to be reinstated to its former central position in human affairs. Only then will we be able to speak to the opposing forces of our day as the Buddha spoke to the

Śākyans and Koliyans, because only then will it be possible for us really to communicate with them. Only then will it be possible to ascertain the facts of the situation. Only then will it be possible for the voice of sanity and compassion to make itself heard at last. Only then will it be possible to appeal to reason.

Ever since the dawn of history – perhaps from the very beginning of the present cosmic cycle – two great principles have been at work in the world: the principle of violence and the principle of non-violence or, as we may also call it, the principle of love – though love in the sense of *agape* rather than in the sense of *eros*. The principle of violence finds expression in force and fraud, as well as in such things as oppression, exploitation, intimidation, and blackmail. The principle of non-violence finds expression in friendliness and openness, as well as in such things as gentleness and helpfulness, and the giving of encouragement, sympathy, and appreciation. The principle of violence is reactive, and ultimately destructive; the principle of non-violence is creative. The principle of violence is a principle of Darkness, the principle of non-violence a principle of Light. Whereas to live in accordance with the principle of violence is to be either an animal or a devil or a combination of the two, to live in accordance with the principle of non-violence is to be a human being in the full sense of the term, or even an angel. So far, of course, human beings have lived in accordance with the principle of violence rather than in accordance with the principle of non-violence. We could do this because it was possible for us to live in accordance with the principle of violence without destroying ourselves completely. But this is no longer the case. Owing to the emergence of superpowers armed with nuclear weapons it is now virtually impossible for us to live in accordance with the principle of violence without sooner or later annihilating ourselves. We are faced with the necessity of either learning to live in accordance with the principle of non-violence or not living at all. The possibility of nuclear holocaust has enabled us to realize the true nature of violence by showing us what the consequences of violence on the biggest conceivable scale would be, and it has also given us a much deeper appreciation of the real value of non-violence.

It is because of this deeper appreciation of the real value of non-violence that we are able to realize what peace in the full sense of the term would really mean, as well as how the problem of its achievement is to be solved. World peace is something we can hardly imagine today.

We can hardly imagine a state of affairs in which disputes between groups and between individuals are settled entirely by non-violent means because all of us are committed to the principle of non-violence and live in accordance with its precepts. A world in which the principle of Light had overcome the principle of Darkness to so great an extent would be a world that surpassed More's *Utopia*, Bacon's *New Atlantis*, Campanella's *City of the Sun*, and Morris's *Nowhere* as much as these dreams of an ideal world surpassed the real worlds of their respective days.[401] Such a world would be a heaven on earth. It would be a world of the gods.

But even the gods have their problems. Even if we achieved world peace in the full sense of the term we still would not have solved all our problems by any means. One problem that the gods have to face is the problem of leisure, the problem of what to do with their time, and although we have less leisure than the gods this is the kind of problem that faces us too. Indeed, it faces us in the still more acute form of what we are to do with our lives. It would be a thousand pities if, having achieved world peace in the full sense of the term, we were to make no better use of our time, or of our lives, than many of us do at present. In Tennyson's 'The Lotos-Eaters' the gods of Homeric Greece are imagined as lying beside their nectar and looking over lands wasted by plague, famine, earthquake, and war, and on a human race subject to the painful necessity of wringing a laborious subsistence from the cultivation of the soil.[402] It would be a thousand pities if when we had solved the problem of world peace, the gods were to look down on a world that in many respects resembled theirs only to see us playing bingo or watching third-rate television programmes. Idealists or cynics might even be tempted to wonder whether it was really worthwhile delivering humanity from the horrors of nuclear war only that it might fall victim to trivial interests and worthless pursuits. Even if we succeed in solving the problem of peace in the full sense of the term we shall still be faced – as we are now faced – with the even greater problem of what to do with our lives.

But even if that problem too had been solved and we were living in a manner that was truly worthy of a human being, there would still be one problem that we had not solved. It would not be strange that we had not solved it, for it is a problem that the gods themselves, despite their nectar, are unable to solve. Indeed, it is a problem that no form of sentient conditioned existence is able to solve so long as it remains merely conditioned. As we know from Tibetan Buddhist scroll-paintings of the wheel of life, there are six main forms of conditioned existence, or six main classes of sentient beings: gods, anti-gods, men, animals, hungry ghosts, and beings in states of torment. These six classes occupy the six 'worlds' or 'spheres' depicted as occupying the six segments into which the third and widest circle of the wheel of life is divided. The innermost circle is depicted as being occupied by a cock, a snake, and a pig, symbolizing greed, aversion, and delusion, the three unskilful mental states that keep the wheel of life turning. The second circle is divided into two segments, one representing the path of light, the other the path of darkness, and the outermost circle is divided into twelve segments representing the twelve 'links' that make up the entire process in accordance with which one passes from one form of sentient conditioned existence to another. All four circles, and thus the wheel of life in its entirety, are supported from behind by a dreadful monster, whose four sets of claws are seen curving round the edge of the wheel, while his scaly reptilian tail protrudes below and his bared fangs project over the top of the wheel beneath fiercely glaring eyeballs and locks crowned with skulls. This dreadful monster is the demon of Impermanence, the demon of Death, who holds in his inexorable grasp not only the six worlds but the whole of conditioned existence, from the electron spinning about its nucleus to the extragalactic nebulae receding from us at an unimaginable rate. He holds in his grasp the highest as well as the lowest heavens, the least evolved as well as the most highly evolved forms of earthly life, from the amoeba to *Homo sapiens*. Even if we succeed in abolishing nuclear weapons, even if we achieve world peace in the full sense of the term, even if we live in a way that is meaningful and purposeful, we shall still have to face the problem of death. Whether we live in a hell or in a heaven on earth, we shall still see the demon of Impermanence, the demon of Death, glaring down at us over the edge of the wheel.

More than that. The demon of Death glares at us not only individually but collectively. He glares not only at you and at me but at the whole world, the whole earth. Whether or not nuclear war is averted, we shall still have to die, each one of us. The human race will still have to go the way of the dinosaurs. Civilization will still have to collapse. The earth itself will still have to come to an end, even if after thousands of millions of years. Indeed, the very solar system to which the earth belongs will come to an end, as will the galaxy of which that solar system forms part. All conditioned things are impermanent. Whatever comes into existence must one day cease to exist. Thus the solution of the problem of world peace and nuclear war does not really solve anything at all. We still have to face the problem of death. Even though the Buddha was able to prevent the Śākyans and Koliyans from destroying each other on that morning twenty-five centuries ago, he could not save them from death itself. In the case of the Śākyans, he could not even save them from an untimely death at the hands of their enemies. So thoroughly had his paternal relations been converted to the principle of non-violence that when, some years later, they were attacked by the King of Kosala, they decided to offer no resistance and were massacred to a man – thus giving us, for the first time in history, an example of personal – as distinct from political – pacifism.[403] It was not fitting, they declared, that the relations of the Enlightened One should commit the sin of taking life.

Not only could the Buddha not save the Śākyans and Koliyans from death, he could not save himself from death. Truth to tell, he did not wish to do so, or even to prolong his earthly existence to the extent that, according to tradition, he could have prolonged it had he been requested to do so. Forty years after the Rohiṇī incident, therefore, when the Śākyans themselves were dead and when the ashes of his two chief disciples, Śāriputra and Maudgalyāyana, lay beneath their memorial mounds, the Buddha came to the little wattle-and-daub township of Kusinārā and lay down between the two *sāl* trees in the *sāl* grove of the Mallas to die or, in traditional Buddhist phrase, to enter into *parinirvāṇa*, a state as much beyond non-existence as it is beyond what we call existence. And having lain down between the twin *sāl* trees, with his head to the north and his feet to the south, he did, at the age of 80, die. No miracle intervened to save him. Having traversed all eight *dhyānas* or meditations his consciousness came down to the first *dhyāna*; having come down to the first *dhyāna* it traversed the first four *dhyānas* a second time and then, as it passed from the fourth *dhyāna* and entered *parinirvāṇa*, the Buddha died. His body was cremated, and the ashes placed beneath a memorial mound. The Buddha had to die, as we all have to die, and there was no resurrection, whether on the third day or any other day. In connection with the sublime scene in the *sāl* grove the notion of a bodily resurrection indeed appears, if I may say so, a little cheap, as indicating an inability to accept the fact of death, or a clumsy attempt to negate the fact of death on its own level instead of transcending it. The Buddha had to die, as we all have to die, because he had been born, and because even for him there could be no exception to the rule that, birth having taken place, death must inevitably follow. Even his Enlightenment could not save him, any more than our knowledge, or virtue, or riches, or friends and relations, can save us. When the messengers of death come, willing or unwilling, ready or unready, Enlightened or unenlightened, we have to go.

Only too often we try to ignore this fact. We refuse to face the problem of death, as though we hoped that if we don't look at the monster with the fiercely glaring eyeballs he won't look at us. We may even try to convince ourselves and others that it is morbid to think about death. But the truth of the matter is that it is morbid *not* to think about death. Not only do we know that we must die, but it is the one thing about ourselves that we really do know. However unsure we may be about other things, we can at least be quite sure of this. Not to think about death is therefore to deprive ourselves of the most certain knowledge that it is possible for us to have, the one thing on which we can rely absolutely. Not to think about death is to deprive ourselves of the possibility of knowing what we really and truly are. It is to deprive ourselves of our very humanity. All conditioned things are impermanent. All sentient beings are subject to death. We are the only beings (in the sense of the only form of terrestrial life) who are not only subject to death but also aware that we are subject to death. We are the only beings for whom death is a problem. Indeed, a human being may be defined as one for whom death is a problem. For us to ignore the fact of death, or to refuse to face the problem of death, is therefore to be untrue to our nature. It is not to be a human being in the real sense of the term.

The Buddha certainly did not refuse to face the problem of death. He faced it, in fact, quite early in life. According to what became the standard traditional account, he faced it when, as a young Śākya warrior of the ruling class, he drove out from the luxurious mansion in which he lived with his wife and infant son and saw, for the first time in his life, an old man, a sick man, and a corpse. On seeing them he realized that although young, healthy, and very much alive, he too was subject to old age, disease, and death. He also realized that being himself subject to birth, old age, disease and death, sorrow and corruption, he sought what was subject to birth, old age, disease, death, sorrow, and corruption, and thus lived an unethical and unspiritual life. In other words the Buddha, or Buddha-to-be, became aware of the fact of death. He faced the problem of death. But there was another sight that he saw for the first time, and that was a yellow-robed wandering 'monk' who had gone forth from home into the homeless life. On seeing him the Buddha-to-be realized something else about himself. He realized that although he was subject to birth, old age, disease, death, and corruption, and sought what was of like nature, he could change; he could seek, instead, what was *not* subject to birth, old age, disease, death, and corruption, and thus lead an ethical and spiritual life. He could seek Nirvāṇa. He could seek the Unconditioned. In other words, he became aware of the possibility of there being a solution to the problem of death and that the finding of that solution was somehow connected with the homeless life. Accordingly he left home, sat at the feet of various teachers, none of whom could satisfy him for long, practised extreme self-mortification and realized the futility of that, adopted a middle way, refused a half share of a kingdom, and eventually, at the age of 35, sat down under a peepul tree at what afterwards became known as Bodh Gaya. While meditating he realized that death arises in dependence on birth, and that birth, i.e. rebirth, arises in dependence on craving, i.e. craving for continued existence on this or that plane of conditioned being. He realized that when craving ceases birth ceases, and that when birth ceases death ceases. With the cessation of craving one attains Nirvāṇa, or the Unconditioned. One attains a state of irreversible spiritual creativity in which there is no birth and no death because in passing beyond the cyclical and entering upon the spiral order of existence one has transcended all such pairs of opposites. Paradoxically, though the Buddha had solved the problem of death, he still had to die beneath the twin *sāl* trees forty-five years later. But it did not really matter that he had to die. Because he had eradicated craving and the other unskilful mental states that make for rebirth, he had solved the problem of birth, and because he had solved the problem of birth he had solved the problem of death in the sense that he would not have to die again.

The Buddha faced the problem of death when he saw his first corpse, and because he could face it – because he could look at the monster with its fiercely glaring eyeballs without shrinking – he could also find the solution to the problem of death. In our case it usually takes much more than the sight of a single corpse to make us realize that we too are subject to death and to convince us that death is a problem. We are usually able to ignore any number of corpses, especially if we only read about them in the newspapers or see them on television. Even if we do become vaguely aware of the problem of death we usually hope, no less vaguely, that we can somehow solve it without having to solve the problem of birth, just as we usually hope, with the same vagueness, that we can somehow achieve peace without having to give up violence. In other words, we usually become aware of the problem of death only to the extent of hoping – or perhaps praying – for the impossible. So far as the problem of death, at least, is concerned, it is a true saying that 'What men usually ask of God when they pray is that two and two should not make four.'[404]

But now all that has changed. We have begun to realize that we cannot have peace without abolishing war. We have begun to realize that we cannot have birth without also having death. We have, in short, woken up to the problem of death. In fact, we have woken up to it to a greater extent than ever before in history. The reason for this is not far to seek. The reason is that we, the human race, are now faced by the possibility of full-scale nuclear war. We are faced by the fact that each one of us may at any time meet with a premature, painful, and horrible death, and that the whole human race may be destroyed. It is the realization of this frightful fact that has had, upon some of us at least, the same kind of effect that the sight of his first corpse had upon the Buddha. It has made us aware of the problem of death. It has made us aware that the fundamental problem is not the abolition of nuclear weapons, or even the achievement of world peace in the full sense of the term. The fundamental problem is not living in a way that is worthy of a human being. For a human being worthy of the name, the fundamental problem is the problem of death, and the real significance of the possibility of nuclear holocaust that now confronts us is that it sharpens our awareness of this problem to a greater extent than has ever before been the case. The possibility of nuclear holocaust thus represents not only the greatest threat that humanity has ever faced but also the greatest opportunity. Formerly, it was possible for some people to dwell in peace while others were at war, for some people to live in accordance with the principle of non-violence while others lived in accordance with the principle of violence, for some people to face the problem of death while others ignored it. This is no longer the case. The possibility of nuclear holocaust means that we must all dwell in peace, learn to live in accordance with the principle of non-violence, and become more aware of the fundamental problem of death. We must all rise to our full stature as human beings, or perish.

What, then, are we to do? Once again we look at the figure of the Buddha, not only as he stands between the Śākyans and the Koliyans but as he stands beside – and above – the wheel of life. In some Tibetan Buddhist scroll-paintings the Buddha is depicted in the top right-hand corner, well outside the wheel, with one arm raised and pointing in an upward direction. He is pointing the way – the way to Nirvāṇa, the state where there is no death because there is no birth. What we have to do is to realize not only the significance of the Rohiṇī incident, and the meaning of the Buddha's exchange with the Śākyans and Koliyans, but also the significance of that solitary wordless gesture. We have to solve both the problem of world peace and nuclear war *and* the problem of death. The very enormity of the problem of world peace and nuclear war indeed serves to make us – if we have any imagination at all – more aware than ever of the problem of death, and unless we can solve the problem of death even the solving of the problem of world peace and nuclear war would, despite the unexampled magnitude of such an achievement, be only the most magnificent of our failures. We must therefore not only abolish nuclear weapons, achieve peace in the full sense of the term, and learn to live in accordance with the principle of non-violence, as well as deepen our realization of the indivisibility of humanity and restore communication by the reinstatement of the notion of the objectivity of truth, but we must also eradicate craving, transcend both birth and death, and attain Nirvāṇa, or the Unconditioned.

The situation in which we find ourselves today is dangerous in the extreme, perhaps more dangerous for humanity than at any other period in history, and time is running out. Whether we shall be able to achieve world peace and avert nuclear war we do not know. We can only do our best in a situation which, to a great extent, is not of our own personal making. But whether we succeed in achieving world peace and averting nuclear war or not we shall still have to die. If we can solve the problem of death it will not, in the most fundamental sense, matter whether we solve the problem of world peace and nuclear war or not – though, paradoxically, if we do succeed in solving the problem of death then we shall, in all probability, succeed in solving the problem of world peace and nuclear war too. In any case, if we solve the problem of death, the problem of birth, the problem of craving, then we shall be able to live in the world as the Buddha and his disciples lived. We shall be able to join them in chanting those celebrated verses of the *Dhammapada*, the first three of which the Buddha, according to tradition, recited to the Śākyans and Koliyans by way of admonition immediately after he had prevented them from destroying each other:

> Happy indeed we live, friendly amid the haters. Among men who hate we dwell free from hate.
> Happy indeed we live, healthy amid the sick. Among men who are sick we dwell free from sickness.
> Happy indeed we live, content amid the greedy. Among men who are greedy we dwell free from greed.
> Happy indeed we live, we for whom there are no possessions. Feeders on rapture shall we be, like the gods of Brilliant Light.
> Victory begets hatred, (for) the defeated one experiences suffering.
> The tranquil one experiences happiness, giving up (both) victory and defeat.[405]

from *Buddhism, World Peace, and Nuclear War*

2. A BUDDHIST APPROACH TO WORLD PROBLEMS

The central problem for all of us is how do we ourselves, individually, react to whatever we perceive to be the world's problems?

In 1943 I was posted to India as a signals operator, and after the war I stayed on to spend the next twenty years in the East, seventeen of them as a Buddhist monk. During this time I attended a large number of public meetings of the kind that are very popular in India – open air meetings held late at night, under the glare of arc-lights, which tend to go on and on. In fact, the bigger they are, and the longer they go on, the better. I thus used to hear a lot of speeches, and some of the topics – and even their treatment – became very familiar to me indeed. A favourite topic was Buddhism and world peace, and whoever was giving the talk, it was practically always the same.

First of all, you would be treated to a graphic description of the terrible plight of mankind in the modern world. You would be reminded of the prevalence of flood, fire, pestilence, and war; then you would be led through the various incontrovertible signs of a universal and unprecedented breakdown of moral and spiritual values, focusing in particular on the behaviour and attitudes of young people today. Then, when you were judged to be fully reconciled to an altogether bleak prospect culminating in nuclear holocaust and no solution in sight, Buddhism would be brought in to save the day. Buddhism, you would be told, teaches non-violence; it teaches peace, love, and compassion. If everybody in the world followed the teachings of the Buddha we would have world peace, and all our problems would be solved. And that would be it – end of talk. Spontaneous applause would break out, the speaker would sit down, beaming with satisfaction, and the audience would clap away, happy in the knowledge that there was hope for the world after all. And, of course, the world would go on just as before.

The problem with this sort of analysis of our situation is not that it isn't true. If everybody in the world meditated every day and tried to develop kindness and love and compassion and joy, and worked at the precepts and followed the Noble Eightfold Path, then – well, we wouldn't just have peace, we'd have heaven on earth. No, the problem with this line of argument is that it's an over-simplification of both problem and solution. In the abstract, it's beautiful, but that is where it remains: in the abstract.

Another difficulty with talking about Buddhism and world peace is that Buddhists are not the only people with values that support world peace. If everyone in the world followed the teachings of Jainism, or Taoism, or certain forms of Hinduism, you would still get world peace, without any need to mention Buddhism. There's no need, in fact, to bring in any religion at all – religions don't have a monopoly on peaceful values. If everybody followed the teachings of Plato, or even Bertrand Russell, you would have world peace on the spot.

So if one is not simply going to present Buddhism as a universal panacea for the world's ills, what *does* Buddhism offer? One cannot talk about *the* Buddhist view of world problems because there isn't an official Buddhist party line on these or any other issues. All one is left with is *a* Buddhist view of world problems. One can talk about world problems only from one's individual standpoint. And as a Buddhist standpoint, its validity can only be measured by how deeply one has been influenced by Buddhist teachings.

There is still, however, the question of what an individual Buddhist can have to say that is truly relevant to world problems. All I can say for myself is that the work I have engaged in as a Buddhist has arisen, to some considerable extent, out of the view I take of current world problems. This topic is not of academic or peripheral interest to me. In approaching it I am in some sense trying to make clear the *raison d'être* of my own existence as a practical working Buddhist; that is, as a Buddhist not just inwardly, in faith and conviction, but also as far as outward activities are concerned. My view of current world problems constitutes a sort of philosophical autobiography, even a confession of faith. It will, I hope, show where I stand and perhaps, to some extent, why I stand there.

We can probably all make our own list of world problems, and we hardly need reminding of them: most of them have been with us since the dawn of history, and the news industry keeps us abreast of those that are of more recent provenance. What is new about the problems of today is the very fact that we hear about them. They are global in character, world-scale problems. It really is as though we live in a global village, and although this is a matter of common knowledge, even a truism, it perhaps does not sink as decisively and deeply into our awareness as it should.

The result of globalization is that all world problems affect all of us in some way, either directly or indirectly, either potentially or in actuality. Not very long ago, the vast majority of people knew absolutely nothing about the problems of people who lived just a few valleys away, let alone people on the other side of the world. Catastrophic events hardly impinged at all on the lives of those who were not directly and immediately involved. Even in a country ravaged by years of terrible warfare there would be peasants within its borders going about their everyday lives knowing nothing whatsoever about it.

But not any more. We have the world's problems at our fingertips. The real problem for us is how to respond to them personally. How do we ensure that every individual citizen in the world grows up healthy and sound in body and mind? What can be done about the apparently increasing incidence of mental illness in the West? What is the role of women – and what is the role of men – in modern society? How do people with jobs avoid making themselves ill through overwork? How do people without work make the best use of their enforced leisure? How do we ensure that people are not discriminated against or abused on account of their racial origin? How do we reconcile the claims of law and order with those of individual freedom? How do we reconcile the conflicting interests of sovereign nation states? How can we all get along with one another?

Fresh outbreaks of hostilities between rival factions in some former European colony, food shortages and unrest in some ex-communist state, inner-city deprivation and crime, drug dependency and alcoholism, child labour, racial violence, industrial pollution, nuclear accidents, disease, drought, famine, starvation, 'ethnic cleansing' – these are just a few of the problems and crises that confront us, or at least pluck at our sleeves every now and then, and are recorded for us on the television and analysed for us in the newspapers. No doubt there are many others, equally pressing, that I have failed to mention. We all have our own pet world problems that seem more crucial than others. But the central problem for all of us is: how do we ourselves, individually, react to whatever we perceive to be the world's problems?

Sometimes our initial reaction will be very strong. For a while we may get quite carried away by our indignation: we are outraged; this should never be allowed to happen; something must be done; those responsible – if particular perpetrators can be identified – should be brought to justice; and so on. And we may be anxious on our own account, if the problem seems likely to affect us directly at some point. In the end, however, when that initial reaction has exhausted itself, we are overtaken – overpowered – by a different kind of reaction: helplessness. The problem is too big, too involved, for us to do anything about it. So we try to forget about it and get on with our own lives, and deal with our own personal problems. We are very sorry that others suffer, but at least we can try to enjoy our own lives.

This is, I suspect, how many people react to world problems. However, my own view is that such a withdrawal from public concerns into purely personal ones is not worthy of a human being – not worthy, at least, of someone who is trying to be a human being in the full sense of the term. It represents an abdication of responsibility. So, given that one is helpless to effect any kind of solution to these large issues, and given too that one can't turn aside and ignore them either, what is one to do?

World problems, by their very nature, are essentially group problems, as they always have been. What is new today is the size of the groups involved and the destructive power available to them. But whatever their size, the problems arising from these groups cannot be solved on the group level. All that can be achieved on the level of the group is a precarious balance of power between conflicting interests. And that balance, as we know only too well, can be disturbed at any moment.

The only hope for humanity is therefore necessarily a long-term solution, involving more people becoming clearer about how they need to develop as individuals and cooperating in the context of spiritual communities in order to make, in their various ways, a significant impact on the world, or on 'the group'. The alternatives before us are, in my opinion, evolution – that is, the Higher Evolution of the individual – or extinction. That would be my overall diagnosis of the situation facing us. As for practical ways to effect a remedy, I would prescribe four courses of action for the individual to undertake.

1. Self-development

This means essentially the development of the mind, the raising of consciousness to ever higher levels of awareness. Human development essentially consists in this, and for most people the route to achieving it is through meditation. The practice of meditation essentially involves three things. Firstly, it involves concentration, the integration of all our energies, conscious and unconscious. Secondly, it involves the raising of consciousness to supra-personal states, leaving the ego-realm for higher, wider, even cosmic dimensions. And thirdly, it involves contemplation: the direct insight of the uncluttered mind – the mind in a state of higher consciousness – into the ultimate depths of existence, the seeing of reality face to face. Meditation is concerned with achieving all this. There are many different methods; you just need to find a teacher who will introduce you to one or two of them. After that, you stick with the methods and practise them regularly. That's all there is to it, really.

The more demanding aspect of self-development consists in what one does with the rest of one's life in order to support one's meditation practice. One will look after one's health. One will simplify one's life as far as possible, dropping all those activities, interests, and social contacts which one knows to be a waste of time. One will try to base one's life, and in particular one's livelihood, on ethical principles. One will make time – perhaps by working part-time – for study; for study of the Dharma, of course, but also for study of other subjects of general human interest: philosophy, history, science, comparative religion. Finally, one will find opportunities to refine and develop one's emotions, especially through the fine arts.

Self-development always comes first. However active you might be in all sorts of external areas – political, social, educational, or whatever – if you are not trying to develop yourself, you are not going to be able to make any truly positive contribution to anything or anyone.

2. Join a spiritual community

This does not necessarily mean joining some kind of organized body or living under the same roof as other aspiring individuals. It simply means being in personal, regular, and substantial contact with others who are trying to develop as individuals. It means being able to enjoy, and seeking out, not just the psychological warmth of the herd, but the challenge of real communication, genuine spiritual exchange.

3. Withdraw support from all groups or agencies that discourage, directly or indirectly, the development of the individual

Groups derive their strength from their members, so it is a basic first step to weaken the power of the group by removing yourself from among its contributing members. Otherwise you are pulling in two directions at once: on the one hand trying to be an individual, and on the other lending your support to the very forces that hinder this process. If you wanted to take this principle to its ultimate conclusion you would withdraw support from the state, as the ultimate group of groups, though this would clearly be extremely difficult, however desirable from one point of view; and in practice we need also to bear in mind our responsibilities as citizens.

4. Encourage the development of individuality within all the groups to which one unavoidably belongs

It may be that one cannot help having a circle of friends or acquaintances, whether at home or at work, who are not interested in any kind of self-development. One may have to remain very nominally a member of a group. Still, one can stand up for what one believes in, and speak up whenever it is appropriate to do so. It is always possible to act in accordance with one's ideals even when others cannot – or do not appear to – understand what one is doing. The way to disrupt a group is simply to encourage people within it to think for themselves, develop minds of their own. So in the context of the group one can still work to undermine it. Even in the enemy camp, so to speak, one need not surrender one's individuality.

These, then, are the four strategies to get under way in order to begin to make a meaningful impact on world problems. A network of spiritual communities of all kinds, many of whose members would be in contact with one another, could exert a significant degree of influence, such as might – just possibly – shift the centre of gravity in world affairs. Spiritual communities have had a crucial impact in the past, and they may, with sufficient vitality, do so again.

It doesn't matter how humble a level we are operating at, or how undramatic our work may be. The true individual is not so much the king of the jungle as the indefatigable earthworm. If enough earthworms burrow away under the foundations of even the most substantial building, the soil begins to loosen, it starts to crumble away, the foundations subside, and the whole building is liable to crack and collapse. Likewise, however powerful the existing order may seem, it is not invulnerable to the undermining influence of enough individuals working – whether directly or indirectly – in cooperation.

A spiritual community is necessarily small, so the best we can hope for is a multiplicity of spiritual communities, forming a sort of network through personal contact between their members. A silent, unseen influence is exerted in this way, which we must hope will be able, at some point, to shift the centre of gravity in world affairs from the conflict of groups to the cooperation of communities. If this were achieved, if the influence of the spiritual community were to outweigh that of the group, then humanity as a whole would have passed into a new, higher stage of development, a kind of Higher Evolution as I like to call it – into what we might even describe as a new period of human history.

Such a shift in the governing values of the world is probably all that can save us from extinction as a species in the not very distant future. There are certainly signs of hope, but there is also perhaps little time left. In this situation it becomes the duty of every thinking human being to take stock of his or her position, and the responsibilities that it implies. We have to appreciate that it is, without exception, the most important issue we shall ever face, either individually or collectively. It is certainly more important than any merely religious question, anything that concerns Buddhism in the sense of a formal or established religion. It concerns both the purpose and the very survival of human life.

from *What is the Sangha?*

3. THE MIRACLE OF SPIRITUAL DEVELOPMENT

Dissatisfaction – if it is not just disgruntlement but a genuine and creative mood of inner revolt – is a positive and powerful impulse.

What one brings to the Buddhist centre, at least initially, is a sense of dissatisfaction. This might seem an unlikely attitude for Buddhists to encourage – we are all surely familiar enough with dissatisfaction. Anyone who has ever ordered some product by mail or online will know this feeling, despite the manufacturer's guarantee of full and complete satisfaction. When the thing finally arrives and you unwrap it, somehow it seems less glamorous, less luxurious, flimsier, smaller, than in the photograph. Sometimes it is even the wrong colour, or there's a part missing. Our disappointment may be such that we have no hesitation in sending the offending article, unsatisfactory as it is, back for a refund, perhaps accompanied by a strongly-worded note.

But we have all taken delivery of one article which, when we compare it with the design specifications, is clearly incomplete or botched, and yet we seem more than satisfied with it. That article is, of course, ourselves. We want everything else in our lives to be properly made, polished and shiny, but we cherish ourselves in our imperfect state. So how can we become dissatisfied? We need to compare ourselves as we are here and now with how we could be in the future. We become dissatisfied when we get a glimpse of a potential which is without any limit and see that by comparison we are at present distinctly unsatisfactory and limited. When we espouse that vision we are in a sense taking the first steps towards sending ourselves back in disgust and demanding a properly functioning human individuality.

Dissatisfaction – if it is not just disgruntlement but a genuine and creative mood of inner revolt – is a positive and powerful impulse. Indeed, such a mood is the starting point. You are dissatisfied, perhaps, with the quality of your relationships, with your work, with your leisure activities – and perhaps, more often than not, you are pretty fed up with yourself as well. You start looking around for a new direction, and you hear, perhaps, about Buddhism, and then about the Buddhist centre, about meditation classes, and you start going along to those classes, and to listen to talks. You may even go on a weekend retreat. As a result of all this, you start to change.

Such change is quite noticeable. I have seen it taking place many times. One sees people visibly changing almost before one's eyes – and this, one might say, is a miracle: that people can change, not just piecemeal, but from top to bottom. Indeed, the Buddha himself referred to this as the greatest of all miracles. In general he condemned the display of so-called miracles or supernormal powers. The ancient Indians were very interested in these things, and even now people tend to perk up and take notice as soon as the subject comes up. The Buddha was often asked to demonstrate miraculous powers, and sometimes he did, if he saw good reason to do so. But for him they were entirely insignificant, and if he thought that they were being taken too seriously, he refused to have anything to do with them. He even went so far as to say, 'I condemn and abhor them, I look down upon them.' 'These,' he went on to say, 'are not real miracles. The real miracle is when someone who was following the dark path changes and starts following the bright path, the path of skilful activities, the path of the spiritual life.'[406]

It is a miracle that continues to occur – often, it seems, against all the odds. People come along quite literally off the street, looking hopeless and dejected, as if they carried all the cares of the world on their shoulders. They start meditating, they become more aware, and in the course of a few weeks, sometimes in the course of a weekend retreat away in the country, you see them beginning to look bright and cheerful. They begin to see something of the Buddha's vision of existence, and they change. One might think that when someone has travelled along the same old rut for decades, it is too late. But that is a great mistake. If you find the right sort of encouragement and the right sort of conditions, you can change at any time of your life.

from *What is the Sangha?*

4. 'COMING HOME' TO BUDDHISM

The system of spiritual teaching and training that we call Buddhism is, in reality, neither Eastern nor Western, any more than we ourselves, in the depths of our being, are either Eastern or Western.

On the occasion of their first contact with Buddhism, whether that contact takes the form of reading a Buddhist book, seeing an image of the Buddha, or paying a visit to a Buddhist spiritual community, many people experience a paradoxical feeling of absolute newness and, at the same time, complete familiarity. They feel not just that they have gained something infinitely precious but that they have *re*gained it. They feel that, after many wanderings, they have not only arrived at last at the gates of a glorious palace but also that, incredible as it seems, they have 'come home'. Some of them seek to account for this feeling of complete familiarity by saying that to them Buddhism represents what they have, in fact, always believed, though without fully realizing it. Others seek to account for it by saying, with varying degrees of conviction, that they must have been Buddhist in a previous existence. However they may account for the feeling, or even if they choose not to account for it at all, such Western Buddhists are naturally astonished when somebody tells them, as somebody occasionally does, even today, that he or she is unable to understand how it is possible for one born and brought up in the West, as a member of Western society and in the midst of Western culture, to accept an Eastern religion like Buddhism or, in other words, to accept a religion that is foreign and exotic. But such a thing is possible, as is daily becoming more evident, and the reason why it is possible is that the system of spiritual teaching and training that we call

Buddhism is, in reality, neither Eastern nor Western, any more than we ourselves, in the depths of our being, are neither Eastern or Western. When we accept the so-called Eastern religion of Buddhism we accept it, even as we encounter it, on a level where the terms Eastern and Western no longer have any meaning.

If a few words of personal confession may be permitted, this was very much my own experience many years ago when, at the age of 16, I had my first real contact with Buddhism. That contact took place when I read two short but exceptionally profound Buddhist scriptures of great historical and spiritual significance. These were the *Diamond Sūtra*, a work belonging to the 'Perfection of Wisdom' corpus, and the *Sūtra of Wei Lang*, a collection of discourses by the first Chinese patriarch of the Chan or Zen school, who is better known as Huineng. Reading these two works, I realized that although in one sense the truth they taught, or the reality they disclosed, was new to me, in another sense it was not new at all but strangely familiar. I certainly did not feel that I was accepting an Eastern religion, or a religion that was foreign and exotic. Rather I felt that contact with Buddhism was, at the same time, contact with the depths of my own being: that in knowing Buddhism I was knowing myself, and that in knowing myself I was knowing Buddhism.

from *The Priceless Jewel*

SOURCES

Page numbers refer to the Complete Works (CW) volumes in which source texts are to be found and book titles to the books in which they were originally published (as noted at the end of each extract in this volume). Titles of the relevant sections in this volume are presented in alphabetical order.

Aspects of Buddhist Psychology (Lecture Series)(CW12)
Archetypal symbolism in the biography of the Buddha (180–93)

Beating the Drum (CW8)
Learning to stand still (290–1)

A Bird's-Eye View of Indian Buddhism (CW7)
What do all the schools of Buddhism have in common? (488–90)

The Bodhisattva Ideal (CW4)
The altruistic dimension of Going for Refuge (93–101); The Buddhist attitude to death (75–7); Buddhists should state their views clearly (124–7); Certainty of success (48–9); How to succeed at meditation (150–2); The importance of spiritual receptivity (129–31); Inspiration from the Buddha's life (10–18); Is the bodhisattva ideal realistic? (60–3); More and more of less and less (144–8); Natural morality and conventional morality (109–15); The practice of forbearance (118–21);

A revival of paganism? (104–9); Should Buddhists have a sense of humour? (136–8); The spiral path (182–4); Spiritual growth: developmental or immanent? (200–3); Spiritual hierarchy (168–77); Tantric meditation: the *yidam* (190–3); Ways of helping (70–2); What is myth? (36–8)

The Bodhisattva Principle (CW4)
Formulations of the Buddhist path (644–8)

Buddha Mind (CW11)
Mind reactive, mind creative (19–26)

The Buddha's Noble Eightfold Path (CW1)
The arising of vision (479–82); The basis of Buddhist ethics (527–30); Compassion: the most important virtue (504–5); The ethics of speech (514–24); The five precepts (532–5); The four exertions (554–5); Giving: the basic Buddhist virtue (500–2); The ideal society (539–43); Involving the emotions in spiritual life (492–4); The Japanese tea ceremony (572–3); Learning to see (570–2); Renunciation: not giving up but growing up (497); Why are we so easily distracted? (567–9)

The Buddha's Victory (CW11)
The Buddha's victory (396–409); Why should a Buddha need a friend? (435–40)

Buddhism for Today and Tomorrow (CW11)
Misunderstandings about Buddhism (142–3); Wrong views, right views, and Perfect Vision (158–61)

Buddhism, World Peace, and Nuclear War (CW12)
Buddhism and World Peace (338–62)

Complete Poems (CW25)
'Above me broods…' (175); After Rilke (359); Bamboos (217); Before Dawn (348); The Bodhisattva's Reply (260–1); 'In the woods are many more' (241); Life is King (324); Meditation (41); Remembering the Retreat (311); Secret Wings (185); Sonnet (278); White Tārā (417)

Creative Symbols of Tantric Buddhism (CW13)
Animism and spiritual life (271–4); The emergence of myth in Buddhism (302–5); Encountering the *ḍākinī* (236–42); Going for Refuge and the concept of escape (191–5); How to reflect (227–9); The nature of Tantric Buddhism (117–8); The shattering nature of reality (171); Tantric meditation: the *yidam* (200–1); The Tibetan wheel of life (124–41)

Crossing the Stream (CW7)
Desire for the eternal (307–8); Everything that lives is holy (283–4); The necessity of dependence (258–61); Pauses and empty spaces (322–3); Religion as revelation or discovery (365–7); Rights and duties (277–9); The sea of Buddhist literature (332–3); The simple life (319–21); Tibetan pilgrims (415–8); The voice within (266–9)

Dharma Life article (CW11)
Entering a spiritual dimension through writing (673–7)

The Drama of Cosmic Enlightenment (CW16)
The importance of feeling alive (125–30); The myth of the return journey (85–99); The parable of the burning house (68–80)

The Essence of Zen (CW13)
What do we really know? (344–8)

The Eternal Legacy (CW14)
Buddhist stories (61–6)

Facing Mount Kanchenjunga (CW21)
Art as an integral part of spiritual life (249–51); The Dharma in Western poetry (434); Rainy season retreat (40); The snows of the Himalayas (436–7); Visiting Ghoom Monastery with Lama Govinda (258–9)

The Glory of the Literary World (CW14)
The Bible designed to be read as literature (298–304)

A Guide to the Buddhist Path (2011)
The Buddha's Journey to Enlightenment (27–30)

The History of My Going for Refuge (CW2)
The attraction of the bodhisattva ideal (454–6); My own Going for Refuge and Going Forth (407–16)

Human Enlightenment (CW11)
Meditation isn't the only way (116–9)

The Inconceivable Emancipation (CW16)
A creative relationship with the world (474–5); Discipline (552–3); Getting comfortable in the Pure Land? (470–1); How to read Buddhist texts (443–4); Pāli scriptures and Mahāyāna *sūtras* (531–4); Taking myths literally (528); The transcendental critique of religion (499–516)

In the Realm of the Lotus (CW26)
Beauty as a characteristic of life (241–3)

Know Your Mind (CW17)
The *anātman* doctrine (624–6); Buddhist confession (647–51); Getting a clear idea of Buddhism (615–7); Is it necessary for a Buddhist to believe in rebirth? (468–73); Mindfulness of purpose (679–80); No 'ready-made' Buddhist answers (627–8); The path as a symbol (433–5); What counts as laziness? (534–5)

Living with Awareness (CW15)
Cultivating positive emotions (152–5); The difference between feelings and emotions (149–51); *Dukkha* as an example of conditionality (227–8); Feeling that the universe is alive (136–9); Finding a place to meditate (101–4); Happiness and concentration (221–3); Learning to think (191–3); Reflections on impermanence (147–8); A regular routine (97–8)

Living with Kindness (CW15)
Being easy to support (277–85)

The Meaning of Conversion in Buddhism (CW2)
Withdrawal and involvement (271–4)

Moving Against the Stream (CW23)
Going to Covent Garden (173–4)

New Currents in Western Buddhism (CW11)
The forms of Eastern Buddhism (371–6); The individual and the group (352–62); What Going for Refuge is (383–6); 'What is your Dharma?' (364–7, 369–70)

The Priceless Jewel (CW16)
'Coming home' to Buddhism (217–8)

The Rainbow Road from Tooting Broadway to Kalimpong (CW20)
Begging in India (414–7); Devotion at Lumbini (421); 'The impossibility of retracting an opinion I believe to be true' (379); Music and mystical experience (68–74); The rainbow road (225–6, 401, 408–10); Realizing I was not a Christian (63–4); Sangharakshita I and Sangharakshita II (451–2); The temple bell (340–1); A vision of Amitābha (345)

The Religion of Art (CW26)
The connection between philosophy and practice (102–4); Stretching the mind through art (188–9); The transformative power of art (115–8)

Ritual and Devotion in Buddhism (CW11)
What is ritual trying to achieve? (205–15

A Survey of Buddhism (CW1)
The Buddha's attitude toward the teachings of his time (60–3); The ideal student of Buddhism (19–21); The traditional society (27–31); Variety and unity in the Buddhist tradition (192–202)

The Taste of Freedom (CW11)
Breaking the fetters (47–50); The path of regular steps and the path of irregular steps (54–67)

The Three Jewels (CW2)
The essence of the Dharma (53–7); The ideal approach to Buddhism (49–52)

Through Buddhist Eyes (CW24)
Early experiences of beauty (546–7)

Transforming Self and World (CW16)
Buddhism and Western culture (374–5); Dealing with desire (283–6); Mindfulness and spontaneity (301–2); 'The oppression of existence' (319–23); The origin of the Buddhist scriptures (233–4); Right livelihood businesses (411–3); The value of the dream state (251–3); Why we conceal things (314–5)

Travel Letters (CW24)
The arising of the poetic state (167–9)

What is the Dharma? (CW3)
The characteristics of existence (207–18); The five basic methods of meditation (340–51); The nature of Buddhist faith (299–301); What is Nirvāṇa? (222–9)

What is the Sangha? (CW3)
The basis of ethical work (581–8); A Buddhist approach to world problems (613–9); Friendship: the whole of the spiritual life? (573–80); Gratitude (595–609); The group and the individual (437–9); The importance of spiritual friendship (398–402); The integration of Buddhism into Western society (621–4); Is a guru necessary? (545–62); Living with purpose (485); The miracle of spiritual development (462–4); The network of relationships (521–9); The religion of art (515–6); What Going for Refuge is (397–8)

Who is the Buddha? (CW3)
The Buddha's journey to Enlightenment (21–31); The Buddha's victory (44–8); Buddhism and evolution (9–17); Karma and rebirth (92–101); The symbolic meaning of the four sights (34–6)

Wisdom Beyond Words (CW14)
Being moved by the Dharma (470–2); Call forth as much as you can (533–4); The greater mandala of aesthetic appreciation (516–9); The Perfection of Wisdom – the flavour of irrelevance (480–2); The playful arts (521–4); Responding to the needs of others (414–5)

The Yogi's Joy (CW18)
Beyond 'Buddhist respectability' (134–6)

NOTES AND REFERENCES

1 Ñāṇamoli, *The Life of the Buddha*, first published by the Buddhist Publication Society, Kandy, in 1972.
2 Vishvapani Blomfield, *Gautama Buddha: the Life and Teachings of the Awakened One*, Quercus, 2011.
3 *Dhammapada* 54–6.
4 This was published as *Living Wisely*; see *Complete Works*, vol. 17, pp. 319–418.
5 These are *sekhiyas* 49–53 of the *prātimokṣa* at Vinaya Piṭaka iv.197–8. See I. B. Horner (trans.), *The Book of the Discipline*, part 3, Pali Text Society, Oxford 1997, pp. 137–8.
6 The story of Queen Māyā is told in many of the legendary accounts of the Buddha's life. See, for example, the *Nidāna-kathā*, published as T. W. Rhys Davids (trans.), *Buddhist Birth-stories (Jātaka Tales): The Commentarial Introduction entitled Nidāna-kathā, the Story of the Lineage*, Routledge, London n.d., pp. 152–5. See also J. J. Jones (trans.), *Mahāvastu*, vol. i, Pali Text Society, London 1987, pp. 115–9; and the *Acchariya-abbhūta Sutta*, *Majjhima Nikāya* 123; see Bhikkhu Ñāṇamoli and Bhikkhu Bodhi (trans.), *The Middle Length Discourses of the Buddha*, Wisdom Publications, Boston 1995, pp. 979–84; or I. B. Horner (trans.), *Middle Length Sayings*, vol. iii, Pali Text Society, Oxford 1993, pp. 163–9. Also Aśvaghoṣa, *Buddhacarita*, book 1, verses 15–26.
7 The Buddha is represented as telling a simple account of his realization under the rose-apple tree in the *Mahāsaccaka Sutta*, *Majjhima Nikāya* 36

(i.246); see Bhikkhu Ñāṇamoli and Bhikkhu Bodhi (trans.), *The Middle Length Discourses of the Buddha*, Wisdom Publications, Boston 1995, p. 340; or I. B. Horner (trans.), *Middle Length Sayings*, vol. i, Pali Text Society, London 1976, p. 301. An embellished version of the story is found in later texts like the *Mahāvastu* and the *Nidāna-kathā*, and it is these that add the detail of how the shadow of the rose-apple tree did not move. See, for example, the *Nidāna-kathā*, published as T. W. Rhys Davids (trans.), *Buddhist Birth-stories (Jātaka Tales)*, Routledge, London n.d., pp. 164–5.

8   Discrimination against lower castes is illegal in India under article 15 of its Constitution. However, societal stratification, and the inequality that comes with it, still exists. Government policies aim at reducing this inequality by reservation quotas for backward classes, but paradoxically have thus also created an incentive to keep this stratification alive. It was this caste discrimination that motivated Dr Ambedkar and his followers to become Buddhist and leave the Hindu caste system entirely; see *Complete Works*, vol. 9.

9   The story of Asita's encounter with the infant Buddha is told in many places in the traditional literature, for example in the *Nālaka Sutta* of the *Sutta-Nipāta* (3.11); but it is the more legendary accounts that include the two possibilities: that Siddhārtha may become either a great ruler or a great sage. See *Lalitavistara Sūtra* in Gwendolyn Bays (trans.), *The Voice of the Buddha*, vol. i, Dharma Publishing, Berkeley 1983, pp. 150–63; or Aśvaghoṣa, *Buddhacarita*, trans. E. H. Johnston, Motilal Banarsidass, Delhi 1984, book 1, verses 54–85, pp. 12–18.

10 See the *Sukhamāla Sutta*, *Aṅguttara Nikāya* i.144, in Bhikkhu Bodhi (trans.), *The Numerical Discourses of the Buddha*, Wisdom Publications, Boston 2012, pp. 239–40; or F. L. Woodward (trans.), *The Book of the Gradual Sayings*, vol. i, Pali Text Society, Oxford 2000, p. 128; see also Aśvaghoṣa, *Buddhacarita*, trans. E. H. Johnston, Motilal Banarsidass, Delhi 1984, book 2, verses 29–32, pp. 25–6.

11 The story of the birth of the Buddha's son and his being named Rāhula is told in T. W. Rhys Davids (trans.), *Buddhist Birth-stories (Jātaka Tales)*, Routledge, London n.d., p. 169.

12 It is Aśvaghoṣa's *Buddhacarita* that describes the effect of the sights on Siddhārtha as being 'like a bull on hearing the crash of a thunderbolt nearby'; see E. H. Johnston (trans.), *Buddhacarita* (iii.34), Motilal Banarsidass, Delhi 1984, part 2, p. 38.

13 The four sights are not mentioned in the Pāli canon as concrete encounters of the historical Buddha. They are presented as 'the thought occurred to me ...': see note 10 above; see also the *Ariyapariyesanā Sutta*, *Majjhima Nikāya* 26 (i.163); Bhikkhu Ñāṇamoli and Bhikkhu Bodhi (trans.), *The Middle Length Discourses of the Buddha*, Wisdom Publications, Boston 1995, p. 256; or I. B. Horner (trans.), *Middle Length Sayings*, vol. i, Pali Text Society, London 1976, p. 207. In early Pāli sources the legendary account of the four sights is only described in connection with the Buddha Vipassi; see the *Mahāpādana Sutta*, *Dīgha Nikāya* 14 (ii.22–8); M. Walshe (trans.), *The Long Discourses of the Buddha*, Wisdom Publications, Boston 1995, pp. 207–210; or T. W. Rhys Davids (trans.), *Dialogues of the Buddha*, part 2, Pali Text Society, London 1971, pp. 18–22. In later texts, for example the *Nidānakathā*, *Buddhavamsa*, and *Lalitavistara*, the story is applied to the Buddha. The *Mahāvastu* gives a particularly graphic account of the four sights; see J. J. Jones (trans.), *Mahāvastu*, vol. i, Pali Text Society, London 1987, pp. 145–53. See also Aśvaghoṣa, *Buddhacarita*, book 3, verses 26–62.

14 See, for example, T. W. Rhys Davids (trans.), *Buddhist Birth-stories (Jātaka Tales)*, Routledge, London n.d., p. 173.

15 A stirring account of Siddhārtha's leaving the palace is given in the *Mahāvastu*; see J. J. Jones (trans.), *Mahāvastu*, vol. i, Pali Text Society, London 1987, pp. 155–6. See also Aśvaghoṣa, *Buddhacarita*, book 5. But the detail of how the charioteer held on to the horse's tail is given in T. W. Rhys Davids (trans.), *Buddhist Birth-stories (Jātaka Tales)*, Routledge, London n.d., p. 174:

> The Future Buddha rode on the mighty back of the mighty steed, made Channa hold on by the tail, and so arrived at midnight at the great gate of the city.

16 In most legendary accounts Siddhārtha gives his clothes to his charioteer, Channa, though in Aśvaghoṣa's version, the clothes are swapped with those of a hunter. See E. H. Johnston (trans.), *Buddhacarita* (iii.34), Motilal Banarsidass, Delhi 1984, pp. 89–90.

17 This description comes from L. Adams Beck, *The Life of the Buddha*, Collins, London 1959, p. 114. The Buddha described the great lengths he went to in practising austerities in the *Mahāsaccaka Sutta*, *Majjhima Nikāya* 36 (i.242–6): see Bhikkhu

Ñāṇamoli and Bhikkhu Bodhi (trans.), *The Middle Length Discourses of the Buddha*, Wisdom Publications, Boston 1995, pp. 337–40, or I. B. Horner (trans.), *Middle Length Sayings*, vol. i, Pali Text Society, London 1976, pp. 297–301. An account of the austerities is also given in the *Mahāvastu*; see J. J. Jones (trans.), *Mahāvastu*, vol. ii, Pali Text Society, London 1987, pp. 120–6.

18   One version of the story of how Siddhārtha fell into a river is told in the *Fo-Sho-Hing-Tsan-King (A Life of Buddha)*, by Aśvaghoṣa, published as vol. 19 of the *Sacred Books of the East* series, trans. Samuel Beal, Motilal Banarsidass, Delhi 1998. p. 144.

19   The story of how the Buddha-to-be settled down to meditate by the river comes from a number of sources. See, for example, J. J. Jones (trans.), *Mahāvastu*, vol. ii, Pali Text Society, London 1987, pp. 126–7. See also the *Lalitavistara Sūtra*, in Gwendolyn Bays (trans.), *The Voice of the Buddha*, vol. ii, Dharma Publishing, Berkeley 1983, pp. 433–7.

20   This story is found in the *Doṇa Sutta, Aṅguttara Nikāya* ii.38: see Bhikkhu Bodhi (trans.), *The Numerical Discourses of the Buddha*, Wisdom Publications 2012, pp. 425–6; or F. L. Woodward (trans.), *The Book of the Gradual Sayings*, vol. ii, Pali Text Society, Oxford 1995, pp. 43–4. It resembles a story told in the *Ariyapariyesanā Sutta, Majjhima Nikāya* 26 (i.170–1) about a meeting between the Buddha and the first person who met him after his Enlightenment, a man by the name of Upaka, but the details of the story make it clear that in this case the meeting with Doṇa is meant. Bhikkhu Ñāṇamoli and Bhikkhu Bodhi (trans.), *The Middle Length Discourses of the Buddha*, Wisdom Publications, Boston 1995, pp. 263–4; or I. B. Horner (trans.), *Middle Length Sayings*, vol. i, Pali Text Society, London 1976, pp. 214–5.

21   The parable is addressed to Śāriputra. See Bunnō Katō et al. (trans.), *The Threefold Lotus Sūtra*, Kosei Publishing, Tokyo 1975, ch. 3, pp. 85–7; also *The Drama of Cosmic Enlightenment* in *Complete Works*, vol. 16, pp. 68–9. See also pp. 340–52 below.

22   *Ariyapariyesanā Sutta, Majjhima Nikāya* 26 (i.163); see Bhikkhu Ñāṇamoli and Bhikkhu Bodhi (trans.), *The Middle Length Discourses of the Buddha*, Wisdom Publications, Boston 1995, p. 256; or I. B. Horner (trans.), *Middle Length Sayings*, vol. i, Pali Text Society, London 1976, p. 207.

23   *Mahāgovinda Sutta, Dīgha Nikāya* 19 (ii.241); see M.

24. Walshe (trans.), *The Long Discourses of the Buddha*, Wisdom Publications, Boston 1995, p. 308; or T. W. Rhys Davids (trans.), *Dialogues of the Buddha*, part 2, Pali Text Society, London 1971, pp. 273–4.

24. The three *lakṣaṇas* are enumerated in many places in the Pāli canon; see, for example, *Saṃyutta Nikāya* xxxv.1; xxii.46; *Udāna* iii.10; *Aṅguttara Nikāya* iii.47; *Dhammapada* 277–9.

25. Of the many canonical references, see especially the *Mahāsatipaṭṭhāna Sutta*, *Dīgha Nikāya* 22 (ii.305–7): M. Walshe (trans.), *The Long Discourses of the Buddha*, Wisdom Publications, Boston 1995, pp. 344–6; or T. W. Rhys Davids (trans.), *Dialogues of the Buddha*, part 2, Pali Text Society, London 1971, pp. 337–45.

26. Shakespeare, *Measure for Measure*, III.i.128–31.

27. For example, the *Alagaddūpama Sutta*, *Majjhima Nikāya* 22 (i.140); see Bhikkhu Ñāṇamoli and Bhikkhu Bodhi (trans.), *The Middle Length Discourses of the Buddha*, Wisdom Publications, Boston 1995, p. 234; or I. B. Horner (trans.), *Middle Length Sayings*, vol. i, Pali Text Society, London 1976, p. 180.

28. See, for example, *Itivuttaka* 100: 'Bhikkhus, I am ... an unsurpassed physician and surgeon.' John Ireland (trans.), *The Udāna and the Itivuttaka*, Buddhist Publication Society, Kandy 1997, p. 226.

29. See Edward Conze, *Buddhism*, Cassirer, Oxford 1957, pp. 46–8.

30. For the story of the hawk with the piece of meat, see H. T. Francis and R. A. Neil (trans.), *The Jātaka: or Stories of the Buddha's Former Births*, vol. iii, book 4: Catukanipāta no. 330, *Sīlavīmaṃsa-Jātaka*, Pali Text Society, London 1973, pp. 66–8.

31. For more on this theme, see Sangharakshita's essay 'Desire for the Eternal' in *Complete Works*, vol. 7, pp. 306–8.

32. *Saṃyutta Nikāya* ii.94; see Bhikkhu Bodhi (trans.), *The Connected Discourses of the Buddha*, Wisdom Publications, Boston 2000, p. 595; or C. A. F. Rhys Davids, *Book of the Kindred Sayings*, part 2, Pali Text Society, Oxford 1997, pp. 65–6.

33. Of the many texts which bear the name Upanishad, there are thirteen principal ones. They originated in the eighth to fourth centuries BCE, and form the basis of the school of Hindu philosophy known as the Vedānta. The *ātman* is one of their main themes.

34. *Dhammapada* 103, trans. Sangharakshita.

35. In Vajrayāna Buddhism Trailokya Vijaya became a wrathful deity, sometimes a Buddha (a form of Vairocana),

sometimes a *deva*. Some Vajrayāna archetypal figures were also depicted making a *trailokya vijaya mudra* or gesture. In Japan, Vajrasattva is known as 'the Subduer of the Three Worlds'.

36 *Dhammapada* 122.
37 *Ariyapariyesanā Sutta, Majjhima Nikāya* 1 (i.163) in I. B. Horner (trans.), *The Collection of the Middle Length Sayings*, vol. i, Pali Text Society, London 1976, p. 207; or Bhikkhu Bodhi (trans.), *The Connected Discourses of the Buddha*, Wisdom Publications, Boston 2000 p. 256.
38 For a full exposition by Sangharakshita of the twelve positive *nidānas* see *The Three Jewels* in *Complete Works*, vol. 2, pp. 103–19. For a canonical source see the *Nidānavagga, Saṃyutta Nikāya* ii.29–32 in Bhikkhu Bodhi (trans.), *The Connected Discourses of the Buddha*, Wisdom Publications, Boston 2000, pp. 553–6; or C. A. F. Rhys Davids, *The Book of the Kindred Sayings*, part 2, Pali Text Society, Oxford 1997, pp. 25–27.
39 Mallinātha Sūri was a critic known for his clarifications of the five *mahākāvyas* (great classical epics) of Sanskrit and on śāstric works. Based on the evidence of various inscriptions, it is probable that he lived c. 1350–1450 CE.
40 *Ariyapariyesanā Sutta, Majjhima Nikāya* 26 (i.168).

See I. B. Horner (trans.), *The Collection of the Middle Length Sayings*, vol. i, Pali Text Society, London 1976, p. 212; or Bhikkhu Bodhi (trans.), *The Connected Discourses of the Buddha*, Wisdom Publications, Boston 2000, p. 261.

41 Quoted in Dr B. R. Ambedkar, *The Buddha and his Dhamma*, Siddharth Publications, Bombay 1991, p. 327, and Christmas Humphreys, *Zen Buddhism*, Unwin, London 1984, p. 27. In neither case, however, is a canonical source given.
42 *Sutta-Nipāta* 2.103–4, in F. L. Woodward (trans.), *Some Sayings of the Buddha*, Oxford University Press, London 1939, p. 36.
43 A famous quotation from the Smaragdine Tablet, an ancient alchemical document ascribed to Hermes Trismegistus states the 'Hermetic correspondence' between higher and lower levels of reality:

> That which is above is like that which is below and that which is below is like that which is above, to accomplish the miracle of one thing.

44 *Jātakas* (literally 'belonging to, or connected with, what has happened') and *Avadānas* (literally 'glorious or heroic deeds') are stories illustrating the workings of the law of karma, showing how the spiritual stature of

the Buddha and his disciples is consequent upon their skilful actions in former lives. The *Jātakas* are devoted mainly to the previous lives of the Buddha, in which the Bodhisattva practices the perfections. They incorporate much material from Indian folklore in the form of fables, fairy tales, and so on. In the canonical *Jātakas*, the Buddha is invariably a wise ruler or famous teacher; in the non-canonical stories, he is also depicted as an animal. The *Avadānas* deal mainly with the careers of the Buddha's disciples or other famous Buddhist figures.

45 Nāgārjuna, the author of *The Precious Garland*, lived in the second century CE in India. He is credited with establishing the doctrinal basis of the Mahāyāna and in particular is regarded as the founder of the Madhyamaka school. Legend has it that he descended to the depths of the ocean to receive the Perfection of Wisdom teaching from the king of the *nāgas*.

46 Padmasambhava was a great Indian teacher who was mainly responsible, in a short visit, for establishing Buddhism in Tibet in the eighth century CE. The highly symbolic but deeply stirring account of his life can be read in Yeshe Tsogyal's *The Life and Liberation of Padmasambhava*, Dharma Publishing, Emeryville 1978.

47 Milarepa was a Tibetan Buddhist master of the eleventh century CE from whom the various Kagyu lineages are descended. He is famous for his asceticism, living on nettles in a cave in the snow-mountains and wearing only a thin cotton garment. His songs and the stories of the circumstances in which they were sung provide some of the best loved literature of Buddhist Tibet.

48 *Vajra* (Sanskrit) literally means 'diamond' or 'thunderbolt'. In Indian mythology, it is wielded by Indra, the king of the gods; it is similar to the thunderbolt wielded by Zeus. The *vajra* is also like a diamond in that it can cut through anything but is itself indestructible. In Tantric Buddhism, known as 'Vajrayāna', the *vajra* became a symbol for the nature of Reality. The *vajra* is extensively used in Tantric ritual and various figures in Tantric iconography – the most famous being Vajrapāṇi and Vajrasattva – are depicted holding or wielding it.

49 It is the Mahāyāna accounts of the Buddha's life that recount the mythical attack of Māra's hordes. See, for example, Aśvaghoṣa's *Buddhacarita*, ch. 13; or the *Lalitavistara*, published as Gwendolyn Bays (trans.), *The Voice of the Buddha*, Dharma Publishing, Oakland 1983, vol. ii, p. 480.

50 See *The Voice of the Buddha*, ibid. pp. 481–2.

51 In early Buddhism, the perfections are the moral observances which the Buddha has practised and brought to perfection in the course of his thousands of lives as a bodhisattva; they are an essential ingredient in his preparation for Buddhahood. In the Mahāyāna, the practising of the six or ten perfections is a crucial aspect of the bodhisattva's spiritual career.

52 The Sanskrit word *mudrā* literally means 'gesture' or 'seal'. A *mudrā* is a symbolic gesture of the hands either performed in the course of a ritual or depicted iconographically in the statues and pictures of Buddhas, bodhisattvas, or other eminent Buddhist figures.

53 Vinaya Piṭaka i.5–7. See I. B. Horner (trans.), *The Book of the Discipline*, part 4, Pali Text Society, Oxford 1996, pp. 7–10.

54 Vinaya Piṭaka i.3; ibid. p. 4.

55 For the position, names, and significance of the psychic centres, see Lama Anagarika Govinda, *Foundations of Tibetan Mysticism*, Century, London 1987, pp. 138–46.

56 *Mahāparinibbāna Sutta*, Dīgha Nikāya 16 (ii.158); see M. Walshe (trans.), *The Long Discourses of the Buddha*, Wisdom Publications, Boston 1995, p. 272; or T. W. Rhys Davids (trans.), *Dialogues of the Buddha*, part 2, Pali Text Society, London 1971, p. 177.

57 The Abhidharma (the word simply means 'about Dharma', though its adherents came to think of it as 'the higher Dharma') began as a project to systematize the Buddha's teachings, including establishing the meaning of technical terms, collating references to the same topics, and so on. In the course of its history – which lasted several hundred years – it developed an exhaustive analysis of mind and mental events, a kind of 'Buddhist psychology'. See *The Eternal Legacy* in *Complete Works*, vol. 14, pp. 72–95, and *Know Your Mind* in *Complete Works*, vol. 17, pp. 439–54.

58 The story is told at Vinaya Piṭaka i.301–3 (*Mahāvagga* 8.26); see I. B. Horner (trans.), *The Book of the Discipline*, part 4, Pali Text Society, Oxford 1996, pp. 431–4. See also 'A Case of Dysentery' in *Complete Works*, vol. 11, pp. 432–44.

59 See C. A. F. Rhys Davids and K. R. Norman (trans.), *Poems of Early Buddhist Nuns* (*Therīgāthā*), Pali Text Society, Oxford 1997, pp. 88–91.

60 *Mahāparinibbāna Sutta*, Dīgha Nikāya 16 (ii.143); M. Walshe (trans.), *The Long Discourses of the Buddha*, Wisdom Publications, Boston 1995, p. 265; or T. W. Rhys Davids (trans.), *Dialogues of the Buddha*, part 2, Pali Text Society, London 1971, p. 158.

61 See *The Rainbow Road from Tooting Broadway to Kalimpong* in *Complete Works*, vol. 20, p. 85.

62 The Buddha's *udānas* are collected in the *Udāna*, see John D. Ireland (trans.), *The Udāna and the Itivuttaka*, Buddhist Publication Society, Kandy 2007. The lion is a traditional epithet for the Buddha. See *Aṅguttara Nikāya* v.33; Bhikkhu Bodhi (trans.), *The Numerical Discourses of the Buddha*, Wisdom Publications, Boston 2012, p. 1362; or F. L. Woodward (trans.), *The Book of the Gradual Sayings*, vol. v, Pali Text Society, Oxford 1996, pp. 23–4.

63 According to the Vinaya Piṭaka, the first two people to encounter the Buddha after his Enlightenment (two merchants called Tapussa and Bhalluka) declared: 'We go for refuge to the Blessed One, and to the Dhamma.' Vinaya Piṭaka i.4 (*Mahāvagga* 1.4); see I. B. Horner (trans.), *The Book of the Discipline*, part 4, Pali Text Society, Oxford 1996, pp. 5–6.

64 See *Mahā-assapura Sutta*, *Majjhima Nikāya* 39 (i.276–9); Bhikkhu Ñāṇamoli and Bhikkhu Bodhi (trans.), *The Middle Length Discourses of the Buddha*, Wisdom Publications, Boston 1995, pp. 366–7; or I. B. Horner (trans.), *The Collection of the Middle Length Sayings*, vol. i, Pali Text Society, London 1976, pp. 329–30.

65 *Dhammapada* 189–92, trans. Sangharakshita.

66 *The Rainbow Road from Tooting Broadway to Kalimpong* in *Complete Works*, vol. 20, p. 85.

67 Ibid., p. 102.

68 *Aṅguttara Nikāya* iv.280 (8.53). See E. M. Hare (trans.), *The Book of the Gradual Sayings*, vol. iv, Pali Text Society, Oxford 1995, pp. 186–7; or Bhikkhu Bodhi (trans.), *The Numerical Discourses of the Buddha*, Wisdom Publications, Boston 2012, p. 1193.

69 *Saṃyutta Nikāya* i.138; see Bhikkhu Bodhi (trans.), *The Connected Discourses of the Buddha*, Wisdom Publications, Boston 2000, p. 233; or C. A. F. Rhys Davids (trans.), *The Book of the Kindred Sayings*, part 1, Pali Text Society, London 1979, p. 174. Also Vinaya Piṭaka i.6; see I. B. Horner (trans.), *The Book of the Discipline*, part 4, Pali Text Society, Oxford 1996, p. 9. See also the *Ariyapariyesanā Sutta*, *Majjhima Nikāya* (i.169), Bhikkhu Ñāṇamoli and Bhikkhu Bodhi (trans.), *The Middle Length Discourses of the Buddha*, Wisdom Publications, Boston 1995, pp. 261–2.

70 See Bunnō Katō et al. (trans.), *The Threefold Lotus Sūtra*, Kōsei Publishing Company, Tokyo 1995, pp. 126–34.

71 *Saṅgīti Sutta, Dīgha Nikāya* 33 (iii.211); see M. Walshe (trans.), *The Long Discourses of the Buddha*, Wisdom Publications, Boston 1995, p. 480; or T. W. and C. A. F. Rhys Davids (trans.), *Dialogues of the Buddha*, part 3, Pali Text Society, London 1971, p. 203. In the text Mahāvīra is referred to as 'the Nigaṇṭha, Nātha's son'.

72 Pāli: *patimokkha*, the hundred-and-fifty rules observed by the monks, still observed in many cases.

73 Vasubandhu, *Abhidharmakośabhāṣya*, vol. iii, chapter 6, trans. L. de la Valleé Poussin, translated into English by L. M. Pruden, Asian Humanities Press, Berkeley 1991, p. 895.

74 Richard Maurice Bucke (1837–1902) was a Canadian psychiatrist. His *Cosmic Consciousness* was subtitled, 'a study in the evolution of the human mind'. The term 'cosmic consciousness' was probably coined by Bucke's English friend, the socialist and poet Edward Carpenter (1844–1929).

75 William Wordsworth (1770–1850), 'The World is Too Much With Us' (c.1802) is a sonnet which begins, 'The world is too much with us; late and soon, / Getting and spending, we lay waste our powers…'

76 *Tao-Teh-King* xxxv, in Lin Yutang (trans.), *The Wisdom of Laotse*, Random House, 1948.

77 See R. A. F. Thurman (trans.), *The Holy Teaching of Vimalakīrti*, Pennsylvania State University Press, University Park and London 1976, p. 77; and *The Inconceivable Emancipation* in *Complete Works*, vol. 16, p. 549.

78 e.g. Thomas Cleary (trans.), *The Flower Ornament Sūtra (Avataṃsaka Sūtra)*, Shambhala Publications, Boston and London 1993, p. 1136: 'They had spacelike knowledge, pervading all universes with a net of lights.'

79 The Buddha speaks of the sixty-two wrong views all of which emerge from 'the feeling of those who do not know and see, the worry and vacillation of those immersed in craving'. See *Brahmajāla Sutta, Dīgha Nikāya* 1 (i.40). M. Walshe (trans.), *The Long Discourses of the Buddha*, Wisdom Publications, Boston 1995, p. 87; or T. W. Rhys Davids (trans.), *Dialogues of the Buddha*, part 1, Pali Text Society, London 1973, p. 53.

80 These similes occur as a description of a mind free from all the hindrances, for example, the *Sāmaññaphala Sutta, Dīgha Nikāya* 2 (i.71–3). M. Walshe (trans.), *The Long Discourses of the Buddha*, Wisdom Publications, Boston 1995, pp. 101–2; or T. W. Rhys Davids (trans.), *Dialogues of the Buddha*, part 1, Pali

Text Society, London 1973, pp. 82–4.

81 Just as the great ocean has one taste, the taste of salt, so also this Dhamma and Discipline has one taste, the taste of liberation.

Uposatha Sutta, *Udāna* 5.5. J. D. Ireland (trans.), *The Udāna and the Itivuttaka*, Buddhist Publication Society, Kandy 1997, pp. 74; or Vinaya Piṭaka ii.239 (*Cullavagga* 9.1) in I. B. Horner (trans.) *The Book of the Discipline*, part 5, Pali Text Society, London 1975, p. 335.

82 Herbert V. Guenther and Leslie S. Kawamura (trans.), *Mind in Buddhist Psychology*: A Translation of Ye-shes rgyal-mtshan's 'The Necklace of Clear Understanding', Dharma, Berkeley 1975, p. xvi.

83 The term is *maggam bhavati*. Nyantiloka notes that many Pāli *suttas* offer similar descriptions of what he calls 'the gradual course of development in the progress of the disciple'. For more on this see Nyanatiloka, *Buddhist Dictionary*, Buddhist Publication Society, Kandy 1988, p.169, 'The Progress of the Disciple'.

84 This is referred to in case 46 of the Zen classic *Mumonkan, The Gateless Gate*. See Katsuki Sekida (trans.), *Two Zen Classics*, Weatherhill, New York 1996, pp. 128–31.

85 St Simeon Stylites (387–459 CE) lived for the last forty or so years of his life at Telanessa, near Antioch, on top of a pillar about twenty metres high from which he preached to visiting crowds. His name comes from the Greek *stulos*, meaning column or pillar.

86 For example, *Jambukhādakasaṃyutta, Saṃyutta Nikāya* iv.251; see Bhikkhu Bodhi (trans.), *The Connected Discourses of the Buddha*, Wisdom Publications, Boston 2000, p. 1294; or F. L. Woodward (trans.), *Book of the Kindred Sayings*, part 4, Pali Text Society, London 1980, p. 170.

87 *Dhammapada* 204: *nibbāṇaṃ paramaṃ sukhaṃ*: 'Nirvāṇa is the highest bliss.'

88 *Kleśa nirvāṇa* is synonymous with the attainment of arhantship; *skandha nirvāṇa* is synonymous with *parinirvāṇa* ('full' *nirvāṇa*), a term which is normally used to refer to the death of the Buddha but in fact applicable to the death of any *arhant*.

89 This is from Blake's poem 'London', in *Songs of Innocence and Experience*.

90 Ryosetsu Fujiwara et al (trans.), *The Tanni Shō*, Ryukoku University Translation Centre, Ryogkoku University, Kyoto 1990, chapter 3, p. 22.

91 These were members of the Order of Buddhist Contemplatives, whose English founder, Jiyu-Kennett Rōshi, had been ordained in Japan

and moved to the USA. Their British retreat centre, Throssel Hole Priory, was established in 1972.
92 *Udāna* 6.4. See John D. Ireland (trans.), *The Udāna and the Itivuttaka*, Buddhist Publication Society, Kandy 1997, pp. 86–9.
93 Edward Conze, *Buddhism: Its Essence and Development*, Windhorse Publications, Birmingham 2001, p. 16.
94 For example, in the periodical *Buddhist World* the 'pure, pristine Dhamma' was synonymous with Theravāda Buddhism. See *Facing Mount Kanchenjunga* in *Complete Works*, vol. 21, p. 246.
95 'The Truth is the whole.' G. Hegel (1770–1831), *The Phenomenology of Mind*, Preface, paras. 81–2 (*Phänomenologie des Geistes*, 1807).
96 E.g. *Vajracchedikā Prajñāpāramitā* 3.
97 Vinaya Piṭaka i.182. I. B. Horner (trans.), *The Book of the Discipline*, part 4, Pali Text Society, Oxford 1996, pp. 240–1.
98 *Saṃyutta Nikāya* v.200. See Bhikkhu Bodhi (trans.), *Connected Discourses of the Buddha*, Wisdom Publications, Boston 2000, p. 1674; or F. L. Woodward (trans.), *The Book of the Kindred Sayings*, part 5, Pali Text Society, London 1979, p. 176.
99 *Śikṣā-samuccaya* 316. See Śāntideva, *Śikṣā Samuccaya*, trans. Cecil Bendall and W. H. D. Rouse, Motilal Banarsidass, Delhi 1971, p. 283.
100 D. L. Snellgrove, *The Hevajra Tantra*, vol. ii, Oxford University Press, London 1959, ch. 8, section 8–9.
101 Alexander Pope (1688–1744), *Essays on Criticism*, part 2 (1711).
102 Edwin Arnold, *The Light of Asia*, Windhorse Publications, Birmingham 1999, p. 11.
103 See 'The Advice to the Three Fortunate Women before the Departure', canto 103, Yeshe Tsogyal, *The Life and Liberation of Padmasambhava*, Dharma Publishing, Emeryville 1978.
104 According to Heinrich Dumoulin in *Zen Buddhism: A History – India and China*, Macmillan, New York 1988, p. 8, the earliest version of this apocryphal story is told in a Rinzai school text, *The T'ien-sheng Record of the Widely Extending Lamp*. The story of the golden flower is also told in *The Gateless Gate*, case no. 6; see Mumonkan, *The Gateless Gate*, in K. Sekida (trans.), *Two Zen Classics*, Weatherhill, New York 1996, p. 129; or Paul Reps, *Zen Flesh, Zen Bones*, Penguin 1972, p. 100.
105 Zhiyi (538–597 CE), the fourth Tiantai patriarch, is regarded as the first major figure of Chinese Buddhism to make a significant discontinuity with the Indian tradition.

106 Mentioned at the beginning of the preface to *Dhyāna for Beginners*, in *A Buddhist Bible*, ed. Dwight Goddard, Beacon Press, Boston 1966, p. 437.

107 Samuel Taylor Coleridge, *Table Talk*, 15 May 1833, in *Table Talk and Omniana*, Humphrey Milford, Oxford 1917, p. 241.

108 Goethe, *Maxims and Reflections*, Macmillan, New York 1906, p. 200.

109 Phrases of this kind are usually associated with Socrates. For example, in Plato's *Apology* (21d), Socrates is quoted as saying (after a discussion with someone):

> I am wiser than this man, for neither of us appears to know anything great and good; but he fancies he knows something, although he knows nothing; whereas, as I do not know anything, I do not fancy I do. In this trifling particular, then, I appear to be wiser than he, because I do not fancy I know what I do not know.

110 See D. T. Suzuki (trans.), *The Laṅkāvatāra Sūtra*, George Routledge, London 1932, pp. 124–5.

111 This translation of the line from *The Awakening of Faith in the Mahāyāna* is taken from Dwight Goddard, *A Buddhist Bible*, Beacon Press, Boston 1966, p. 363.

112 From a verse that stands above the introductory plate to William Blake's *Jerusalem*, headed 'To the Christians'. See William Blake, *Jerusalem: The Emanation of the Giant Albion*, chapter 1, plate 77.

113 *Dhammapada* 1–2, trans. Sangharakshita.

114 This verse is attributed to Bodhidharma. See D. T. Suzuki, *Essays in Zen Buddhism* (First Series), Rider & Company, London 1949, pp. 20, 176. For Sangharakshita's commentary on the verse, see *The Essence of Zen* in *Complete Works*, vol. 13, pp. 335–64.

115 From 'The Clod and the Pebble' by William Blake.

116 Lewis Carroll (real name Charles Dodgson, 1832–1898) was the author of *Alice's Adventures in Wonderland* and *Alice Through the Looking Glass*, and other works, all of which contain 'nonsense verse' ('Jabberwocky' is a well-known example). Edward Lear (1812–1888) was also a master of the art of nonsense verse, writing many limericks and longer poems such as 'The Owl and the Pussycat' and 'The Pobble Who Has No Toes'. The reference to 'pure Zen' is an allusion to Christmas Humphreys' description of *Alice's Adventures in Wonderland*. See *Complete Works*, vol. 8, p. 594.

117 This is the *Diamond Sūtra*, one of the first two Buddhist texts that Sangharakshita

came across and which convinced him he was a Buddhist. (See *The Rainbow Road from Tooting Broadway to Kalimpong* in *Complete Works*, vol. 20, p. 85.) For Sangharakshita's commentary on the text see *Wisdom Beyond Words* in *Complete Works*, vol. 14, pp. 369–510.

118 See, for example, *Saṃyutta Nikāya* iv.396–7 (44.10), in Bhikkhu Bodhi (trans.), *The Connected Discourses of the Buddha*, Wisdom Publications, Somerville 2000, pp. 1393–4; or F. L. Woodward (trans.), *The Book of the Kindred Sayings*, part 4, Pali Text Society, London 1980, pp. 278–9.

119 From the poem 'The Scholar-Gipsy' by Matthew Arnold (1822–1888).

120 Cromwell was about to ravage the whole of Christendom; the royal family had been brought down, and his own would have been established forever but for a small grain of sand that formed in his bladder. Rome would have trembled beneath him, but once that little gravel was there, he died, his family fell from power, peace reigned, and the King was restored.

Blaise Pascal, *The Pensées*, trans. J. M. Cohen, Penguin, Harmondsworth 1961.

121 Rabindranath Tagore, *Gitanjali (Song Offerings)*, no. 95.

122 The Buddha is widely referred to by this title, which literally means 'Thus-come' or 'Thus-gone', so it means one who has 'gone beyond' conditioned existence, leaving no trace.

123 A *śramaṇa* is someone who has taken up a homeless religious life. *Śramaṇa* literally means 'one who is washed, purified,' and it shares this literal meaning with the words 'Sufi' and 'Cathar'.

124 This story is told at Vinaya Piṭaka i.39 (*Mahāvagga* 1.23); see I. B. Horner (trans.), *The Book of the Discipline*, part 4, Pali Text Society, Oxford 1996, pp. 52–4.

125 Thomas Gray, 'Elegy in a Country Churchyard', 1750.

126 *Mahāsaccaka Sutta, Majjhima Nikāya* 36 (i.248); see Bhikkhu Ñāṇamoli and Bhikkhu Bodhi (trans.), *The Middle Length Discourses of the Buddha*, Wisdom Publications, Boston 1995, p. 341; or I. B. Horner (trans.), *Middle Length Sayings*, vol. i, Pali Text Society, London 1976, p. 303.

127 The five *niyamas* are listed in the Abhidharma in, for example, the *Aṭṭhasālinī*, Buddhaghosa's commentary on the *Dhammasaṅgani*, published as Pe Maung Tin (trans.), *The Expositor*, Pali Text Society, London 1921, p. 360.

128 *Aṅguttara Nikāya* iii.415; see Bhikkhu Bodhi (trans.), *The Numerical Discourses of the*

	Buddha, Wisdom Publications 2012, p. 963; or E. M. Hare (trans.), *The Book of the Gradual Sayings*, vol. iii, Pali Text Society, Oxford 1995, p. 294.
129	According to Buddhist tradition a *kalpa* is the time taken for a world system to evolve and involve; a *kalpa* is divided into four *asamkheyya-kalpas* (Pāli *asankheyya-kappas*). See also p. 542 below.
130	See, for example, *Saṃyutta Nikāya* iv.229; F. L. Woodward (trans.), *The Book of the Kindred Sayings*, part 4, Pali Text Society, London 1980, pp. 155–6; or Bhikkhu Bodhi (trans.), *The Connected Discourses of the Buddha*, Wisdom Publications, Boston 2000, p. 1278–9.
131	*Dhammapada* 1–2.
132	See Rachel Theodosia Gribble Knight (trans.), *Stanisław Schayer: Mahāyāna Doctrines of Salvation*, Probsthain & Co., London 1923. See also *The Religions of the World*, vol. 1, Ramakrishna Mission Institute of Culture, 1938, p. 218.
133	*Kālāma Sutta*, *Aṅguttara Nikāya* i.189. F. L. Woodward (trans.), *The Book of the Gradual Sayings*, vol. i, Pali Text Society, Oxford 2000, pp. 171–2. See also Bhikkhu Bodhi (trans.), *The Numerical Discourses of the Buddha*, Wisdom Publications, Somerville 2012, p. 280.
134	*Vinaya Piṭaka* ii.258–9 (*Cullavagga* 10.5) and *Aṅguttara Nikāya* iv.280–1. I. B. Horner (trans.), *The Book of the Discipline*, part 5, Pali Text Society, London 1975, p. 359; or E. M. Hare (trans.), *The Book of the Gradual Sayings*, vol. iv, Pali Text Society, Oxford 1995, pp. 186–7; or Bhikkhu Bodhi (trans.), *The Numerical Discourses of the Buddha*, Wisdom Publications, Boston 2012, p. 1193.
135	John 8:32.
136	Blasphemy laws were abolished in England and Wales in 2008, and in Scotland in 2021, while Northern Ireland still maintains 'blasphemy' provisions.
137	See the *Alagaddūpama Sutta*, *Majjhima Nikāya* 22 (i.134–5); Bhikkhu Ñāṇamoli and Bhikkhu Bodhi (trans.), *The Middle Length Discourses of the Buddha*, Wisdom Publications, Boston 1995, pp. 228–9; or I. B. Horner (trans.), *Middle Length Sayings*, vol. i, Pali Text Society, London 1976, pp. 173–4.
138	The idea of an Axial Period, or Age, comes from the existentialist philosopher Karl Jaspers (1883–1969). Sangharakshita's account of the theory in relation to Buddhism appears in *What is the Sangha?* in *Complete Works*, vol. 3, pp. 424–8. See also Karl Jaspers, *The*

139 *Origin and Goal of History*, Routledge and Kegan Paul, London 1953.
140 *Gaṇakamoggallāna Sutta, Majjhima Nikāya* 107 (iii.6) in I. B. Horner (trans.), *The Collection of the Middle Length Sayings*, vol. iii, Pali Text Society, Oxford 1993, p. 56.
140 *Dhammapada* 275.
141 *Mahāparinibbāna Sutta, Dīgha Nikāya* 16 (ii.81); see M. Walshe (trans.), *The Long Discourses of the Buddha*, Wisdom, Boston 1995, p. 234; or T. W. Rhys Davids (trans.), *Dialogues of the Buddha*, part 2, Pali Text Society, London 1971, p. 86.
142 *Rathavinīta Sutta, Majjhima Nikāya* 24; see Bhikkhu Ñāṇamoli and Bhikkhu Bodhi (trans.), *The Middle Length Discourses of the Buddha*, Wisdom Publications, Boston 1995, pp. 240–5; or I. B. Horner (trans.), *The Collection of the Middle Length Sayings*, vol. i, Pali Text Society, London 1976, pp. 187–94. The seven stages are: purification of moral virtue; purification of the mind; purification of views; purification by overcoming doubt; purification by knowledge and vision of the path and the not-path; purification by knowledge and vision of the way; and purification of knowledge and vision. For Sangharakshita's account of the seven stages of purification, see *What is the Dharma?* in *Complete Works*, vol. 3, pp. 290–4.
143 The ten *bhūmis* are enumerated in many Mahāyāna texts. For a particularly elaborate and beautiful description, see book 26 of the *Avataṃsaka Sūtra*; Thomas Cleary (trans.), *The Flower Ornament Scripture*, Shambhala Publications, Boston and London 1993, pp. 695–811.
144 Another classification of the bodhisattva's career made by the *Bodhisattvabhūmi*, a Yogācāra elaboration, is the division into twelve or (including the Buddha stage) thirteen *vihāras*, 'abodes'. Edward J. Thomas, *The History of Buddhist Thought*, Kegan Paul, Trench, Trubner & Co., London 1933, p. 210.
145 H.P. Blavatsky, *The Voice of the Silence* (published 1898), section 58.
146 The *Gaṇḍavyūha Sūtra* is the final section, 'Entry into the Realm of Reality', of the *Avataṃsaka Sūtra*, published as Thomas Cleary (trans.), *The Flower Ornament Scripture*, Shambhala Publications, Boston and London 1993. Sudhana, 'an outstanding boy', first makes his appearance on p. 1173 of this edition and is 'greeted in a friendly manner by the Bodhisattva Mañjuśrī, no less; it is Mañjuśrī who explains to him how to set out upon the path to Enlightenment.

147 Edward Conze (trans.), *The Perfection of Wisdom in Eight Thousand Lines and its Verse Summary*, Four Seasons Foundation, San Francisco 1983, pp. 277–98.
148 For Sangharakshita's commentary, see *The Drama of Cosmic Enlightenment* in *Complete Works*, vol. 16, pp. 85–115. The 'Hymn of the Pearl' is outlined on pp. 90–1.
149 Xuanzang (Yuan Chwang or Hsüan-tsang) was a Chinese Buddhist monk and scholar who in 629 CE left China on pilgrimage to India and spent sixteen years on the journey, visiting all the Buddhist pilgrimage sites in India and bringing back to China many texts which he then spent the rest of his life translating. His book *Great Tang Records on the Western Regions* tells the story of his extraordinary journey. It was also fictionalized in *Journey to the West*, a novel published in China in the sixteenth century and attributed to Wu Cheng'en. It became known in the West through Arthur Waley's translation, *Monkey: a Folk-Tale of China*, published in 1942.

Narrow Road to the Deep North, written by the Chinese poet Bashō, is a travelogue describing the poet's five-month walk in 1689 in the remote regions of northern Japan.
150 *Cūlasakuludāyi Sutta*, *Majjhima Nikāya* 79 (ii.32).

I. B. Horner (trans.), *The Collection of the Middle Length Sayings*, vol. ii, Pali Text Society, Oxford 1994, p. 229; or Bhikkhu Ñāṇamoli and Bhikkhu Bodhi (trans.), *The Middle Length Discourses of the Buddha*, Wisdom Publications, Boston 1995, p. 655. Also *Nidānasaṃyutta*, *Saṃyutta Nikāya* ii.28, in C. A. F. Rhys Davids (trans.), *The Book of the Kindred Sayings*, part 2, Pali Text Society, Oxford 1997, p. 23; or Bhikkhu Bodhi (trans.), *The Connected Discourses of the Buddha*, Wisdom Publications, Boston 2000, p. 552. See also *A Survey of Buddhism* in *Complete Works*, vol. 1, p. 89ff.
151 See, for example, the *Bhayabherava Sutta*, *Majjhima Nikāya* 4 (i.22–3); Bhikkhu Ñāṇamoli and Bhikkhu Bodhi (trans.), *The Middle Length Discourses of the Buddha*, Wisdom Publications, Boston 1995, pp. 105–6; or I. B. Horner (trans.), *The Collection of the Middle Length Sayings*, vol. i, Pali Text Society, London 1976, pp. 28–9.
152 Pierre Teilhard de Chardin (1881–1955) was a Jesuit priest and also a palaeontologist and geologist who developed a theology of evolution of the form known as teleological orthogenesis, that is, the idea that evolution is directed by an inner force

towards a particular end. He called this culmination the Omega Point, a kind of supreme consciousness. He outlined this in, for example, *The Phenomenon of Man*, published in 1955.

153 The theory of the descent of species is fully developed in Immanuel Kant, *Critique of Judgement*, part 2, trans. J. C. Meredith, Oxford 1952. Nineteenth-century theories of evolution, especially Darwin's, added factual details to Kant's theory without changing anything in its basic framework. For more information, see *Complete Works*, vol. 3, pp. 625–6, notes 4 and 5.

154 The G. K. Chesterton epigram is given in various forms, one (said to derive from a combination of remarks in Chesterton's Father Brown stories) being 'The first effect of not believing in God is to believe in anything.' Although variants of this epigram are widely attributed to Chesterton, the specific origin of the phrase is evidently a mystery.

155 Thus the human life of a Buddha must be seen in an entirely different perspective: it becomes a mere fraction of a far bigger and more important development, in which the human element is essentially the vehicle for the rediscovery of the universal (and in this sense 'transcendental') character of mind or consciousness, which according to the *Prajñāpāramitā Sūtra* is 'inconceivable in its true nature'.

Lama Anagarika Govinda, 'The Buddha on the Ideal of the Perfect Man and the Embodiment of the Dharma', Maha Bodhi, Vaishakha number, April 1954.

156 See note 69.

157 *Gandhatthena Sutta*, *Saṃyutta Nikāya* i.204 (9.14); see Bhikkhu Bodhi (trans.), *The Connected Discourses of the Buddha*, Wisdom Publications, Boston 2000, p. 303; or C. A. F. Rhys Davids (trans.), *The Book of the Kindred Sayings*, part 1, Pali Text Society, London 1979, p. 260.

158 *Terza rima* is an Italian verse form in which the second line of one stanza provides the rhyme for the first and third lines of the next. Dante is said to have originated the form, but its difficulty, especially in languages lacking Italian's rich rhymes, has prevented widespread use. A rare example from English literature is Percy Bysshe Shelley's *Ode to the West Wind*.

159 W. H. Davies (1871–1940), opening lines of his poem 'Leisure' published in *Songs of Joy and Others* (1911).

160 See Richard Burnett Carter, *The Language of Zen*, Sterling Publishing, 2010, note 21. The celebrated artist may have been Muqi Fachang (c.1210–c.1270), painter and monk of the Chinese Chan tradition.

161 'The white lofty mountain appears as if it was accumulated out of the loud laughter of Shiva', C. R. Devadhar (ed.), *Works of Kalidasa*, vol. 2, p. xxxiv.

162 The *Skanda Purāṇa* is the largest of the eighteen *Mahāpurāṇas* of Hindu religious literature.

163 T. S. Eliot, 'The Dry Salvages' part V, in *Four Quartets*.

164 Rongzompa Chökyi Zangpo lived in the eleventh century CE. For this definition of his see, for example, Herbert V. Guenther, *Matrix of Mystery*, Shambhala Publications, Boulder 1984, p. 42.

165 *Aṅgulimāla Sutta*, *Majjhima Nikāya* 86 (ii.97–105). Bhikkhu Ñāṇamoli and Bhikkhu Bodhi (trans.), *The Middle Length Discourses of the Buddha*, Wisdom Publications, Boston 1995, pp. 710–17; or I. B. Horner (trans.), *The Collection of the Middle Length Sayings*, vol. ii, Pali Text Society, Oxford 1994, pp. 284–92.

166 *The Religion of Art* in *Complete Works*, vol. 26, pp. 89–196.

167 This was the French nun Thupten Chhokyi (Ani-la) whom Sangharakshita knew in Kalimpong, and of whom he writes extensively in his memoirs.

168 *Rhythmische Aphorismen*, Dresden 1926, and *Gedanken und Gesichte*, Dresden 1927. The titles translate as something like 'Rhythmic Aphorisms' and 'Thoughts and Visions'.

169 Presumably from Lama Anagarika Govinda, *Art and Meditation*, Allahabad Block Works, Allahabad 1936. What appears to be a revised version of this essay is included under the title 'Parallelism Between Art and Meditation' in Lama Anagarika Govinda, *Creative Meditation and Multi-Dimensional Consciousness*, Unwin, London 1977, pp. 151–6.

170 Irwin Edman, *Arts and the Man: A Short Introduction to Aesthetics*, Norton, New York 1939, p. 128.

171 For further reflections on the place music played in his life, see Sangharakshita's 'And On His Dulcimer He Played' in *Complete Works*, vol. 26, pp. 499–506.

172 Richard Wagner (1813–1883) was a German composer of opera. *Lohengrin*, first performed in 1850, and *Tannhäuser*, first performed in 1845, are Romantic operas set in medieval times. *Der Ring des Nibelungen* (*The Ring of the Nibelung*) consists of four operas based on the Norse sagas and a medieval German epic.

173 *Kūṭadanta Sutta*, *Dīgha Nikāya* 5 (i. 127–49). T. W. Rhys Davids (trans.), *Dialogues of the Buddha*, part 1, Pali Text Society, London

173   1973, pp. 173–85. See also M. Walshe (trans.), *The Long Discourses of the Buddha*, Wisdom Publications, Boston 1995, pp. 133–41.

174   *Complete Poems, Complete Works*, vol. 25, pp. 354–6.

175   *Aṅguttara Nikāya* i.259, in Bhikkhu Bodhi (trans.), *Numerical Discourses of the Buddha*, Wisdom Publications, Boston 2012, p. 342; or F. L. Woodward (trans.), *Gradual Sayings* vol. i, Pali Text Society, Oxford 2000, p. 239. Bhikkhu Bodhi's translation is: 'To laugh excessively, showing one's teeth, is childishness.'

176   See the *Abhidhammattha Saṅgaha of Ācariya Anuruddha*, chapter 1, section 10, in Bhikkhu Bodhi (ed.), *A Comprehensive Manual of Abhidhamma*, Buddhist Publication Society Pariyatta Editions, Onalaska WA 1999, p. 45:

> Smile-producing consciousness (hasituppādacitta): This is a citta peculiar to Arahants, including Buddhas and Paccekabuddhas who are also types of Arahants. Its function is to cause Arahants to smile about sense-sphere phenomena.

177   Sigmund Freud, *Jokes and their Relation to the Unconscious*, Penguin, Harmondsworth 1978, p. 199.

178   The expression 'dim religious light' comes from John Milton's poem *Il Penseroso* (line 160).

179   While this point is well made, in the *Daodejing* Laozi in fact makes quite a different point, stating (in chapter 76) that it is the tall, strong trees that are cut down.

180   For the story of the *saṅgīti*, see Vinaya Piṭaka ii.284–93; I. B. Horner (trans.), *The Book of the Discipline*, part 5, Pali Text Society, London 1975, pp. 393–406.

181   M. Winternitz, *A History of Indian Literature*, Munshiram Manoharlal, Calcutta 1933, vol. ii, p. 149.

182   See *The Rainbow Road from Tooting Broadway to Kalimpong* in *Complete Works*, vol. 20, pp. 54–64.

183   Thomas De Quincey, 'The Literature of Knowledge and the Literature of Power', first published in the *North British Review*, August 1848, as part of a critical essay on Alexander Pope.

184   Ibid.

185   For more information see note 363 in *Complete Works*, vol. 16, pp. 629–30.

186   See note 364 in ibid., p. 630.

187   Never did eye see sun unless it had first become sunlike, and never can the Soul have vision of the First Beauty unless itself be beautiful.

Plotinus, *The Enneads*, I.vi.9, trans. Stephen MacKenna, Penguin 1991, p. 55.

188 This famous verse is attributed to Pang Yun (also called Hōkoji), a lay disciple of the eighth century; see, for example, D. T. Suzuki, *Essays in Zen Buddhism*, Rider, London 1958, p. 319.

189 *Mahāparinibbāna Sutta*, *Dīgha Nikāya* 16 (ii.158); see M. Walshe (trans.), *The Long Discourses of the Buddha*, Wisdom Publications, Boston 1995, p. 266; or T. W. Rhys Davids (trans.), *Dialogues of the Buddha*, part 2, Pali Text Society, London 1971, p. 161.

190 The *Mahāsudassana Sutta*, *Dīgha Nikāya* 17 (ii.168–172); see M. Walshe (trans.), ibid., pp. 279–80; or T. W. Rhys Davids (trans.), ibid., pp. 199–202.

191 See the *Larger Sukhāvatī-vyūha Sūtra*, section 16, in *Buddhist Mahāyāna Texts*, ed. E. B. Cowell et al., Dover Publications, New York 1969, pp. 33–6. See also Ratnaguna and Śraddhāpa, *Great Faith, Great Wisdom*, Windhorse Publications, Cambridge 2016.

192 The nineteenth-century writer was Brian Houghton Hodgson (1800–1894), the British Resident in Kathmandu from 1833, who became deeply interested in Himalayan culture and proficient in Pāli and Sanskrit. He collected the first Sanskrit text of the *Lotus Sūtra* and acquired many Tibetan works; his collection of writings and drawings is now held by the Royal Asiatic Society in London.

The Theosophist Madame Blavatsky picked up on his coinage 'Dhyani-Buddha' in, for example, *The Secret Doctrine*, in which she wrote,

> Dhyani-Buddha is a Sanskrit compound term from *dhyāni* ('contemplative, one who meditates') and buddha (an 'awakened one' or 'the enlightened one'), which could be translated as 'Buddha of Contemplation'.

Helena Petrovna Blavatsky, *The Secret Doctrine*, vol. i, Theosophical Publishing House, Wheaton 1993, p. 109.

193 For an account of what is called the 'Great Miracle', see Eugene Watson Burlingame (ed.), *Buddhist Legends*, part 3, Luzac, London 1969, pp. 45–7.

194 What has become known as the Tibetan wheel of life is said to have originated among the followers of the Sarvastivāda school of Indian Buddhism, which formed around the third century BCE. For more information see note 43 in *Creative Symbols of Tantric Buddhism*, Complete Works, vol. 13, pp. 679–81.

195 *The Awakening of Faith in the Mahāyāna* is a fifth-century Chinese Yogācāra work, a systemization of the teachings of the *Laṅkāvatāra Sūtra* which was traditionally said

to have been translated from a Sanskrit original by the great Indian *ācārya* Aśvaghoṣa, but has more recently been shown to be the work of a Chinese author.

196 This essay appears in Edward Conze, *Thirty Years of Buddhist Studies*, Cassirer, London 1967, pp. 185–90.

197 As on the unwholesome plane hatred does not cling, does not stick to its object, so wisdom on the wholesome plane. As hate seeks for faults, even though they do not exist, so wisdom seeks for the faults that do exist. As hate leads to the rejection of beings, so wisdom to that of all conditioned things.

Buddhaghosa, *Visuddhimagga* 102, quoted in Edward Conze (trans.), *Buddhist Scriptures*, Penguin Books, London 1959, pp. 116–7; also Edward Conze, *Thirty Years of Buddhist Studies*, Cassirer, London 1967, pp. 186–7.

198 See the *Dhammacakkappavattana Sutta*, *Saṃyutta Nikāya* v.421; Bhikkhu Bodhi (trans.), *The Connected Discourses of the Buddha*, Wisdom Publications, Boston 2000, p. 1844; or F. L. Woodward (trans.), *Book of the Kindred Sayings*, part 5, Pali Text Society, London 1979, p. 357; also I. B. Horner (trans.), *The Book of the Discipline*, part 4, Pali Text Society, Oxford 1996, p. 15.

199 Gampopa, *The Jewel Ornament of Liberation*, trans. H. V. Guenther, Rider, London 1970, p. 41.

200 This is from William Blake's 'Auguries of Innocence', a 132-line poem probably composed in the early years of the nineteenth century and found in what is called the *Pickering Manuscript*; the poem was not published until 1863.

> Joy & Woe are woven fine
> A Clothing for the soul divine
> Under every grief & pine
> Runs a joy with silken twine.

201 *Dhammapada* 182.
202 See *Saṃyutta Nikāya* v.455–6 (56.47); Bhikkhu Bodhi (trans.), *Connected Discourses of the Buddha*, Wisdom Publications, Boston 2000, pp. 1871–2; or F. L. Woodward (trans.), *The Book of the Kindred Sayings*, part 5, Pali Text Society, London 1979, pp. 383–4. The Buddha uses the same metaphor in the *Bālapaṇḍita Sutta*, *Majjhima Nikāya* 129 (iii.170), though there it is to illustrate the amount of time it would take a 'fool' who had been born in a hell realm to regain the human state; see Bhikkhu Ñāṇamoli and Bhikkhu Bodhi (trans.), *The Middle Length Discourses of the Buddha*, Wisdom Publications, Boston 1995, pp. 1020–1; or I. B.

Horner (trans.), *The Collection of the Middle Length Sayings*, Oxford 1993, vol. iii, pp. 214–5.

203 The teaching of the twelve cyclical *nidānas* has its origin in the Pāli canon; for example, the *Mahātaṇhāsaṅkhaya Sutta*, *Majjhima Nikāya* 38 (i.261–4). See Bhikkhu Ñāṇamoli and Bhikkhu Bodhi (trans.), *The Middle Length Discourses of the Buddha*, Wisdom Publications, Boston 1995, pp. 353–7; or I. B. Horner (trans.), *The Collection of the Middle Length Sayings*, vol. i, Pali Text Society, London 1976, pp. 318–9. Alternatively, the *Mahānidāna Sutta*, *Dīgha Nikāya* 15 (ii.55–9); see M. Walshe (trans.), *The Long Discourses of the Buddha*, Wisdom Publications, Boston 1995, pp. 223–4; or T. W. Rhys Davids (trans.), *Dialogues of the Buddha*, part 2, Pali Text Society, London 1971, pp. 50–5. For Sangharakshita's commentary, see *What is the Dharma?* in *Complete Works*, vol. 3, pp. 192–204.

204 The distinction between the reactive and the creative process is considered in detail in Sangharakshita's lecture 'Mind – Reactive and Creative' in *Complete Works*, vol. 11, pp. 19–38.

205 See H. T. Francis and R. A. Neil (trans.), *The Jātaka*, vol. iii, Allen & Unwin, London 1973, no. 316, pp. 34–7.

206 For the parable within the *sūtra*, see Bunnō Katō and W. E. Soothill (trans.), *The Threefold Lotus Sutra*, Kosei Publishing, Tokyo, 1975, pp. 85–109.

207 *Vinaya Piṭaka* i.34; see I. B. Horner (trans.), *The Book of the Discipline*, part 4, Pali Text Society, Oxford 1996, p. 45; and *Saṃyutta Nikāya* iv.19–20; see F. L. Woodward (trans.), *The Book of the Kindred Sayings*, part 4, Pali Text Society, London 1980, p. 10, or Bhikkhu Bodhi (trans.), *The Connected Discourses of the Buddha*, Wisdom Publications, Boston 2000, p. 1143.

208 For an account of the Tibetan wheel of life, see p. 324ff. above.

209 The story of Krishna's flute is told in the *Srimad-Bhāgavata*. See Radhakamal Mukerjee, *The Lord of the Autumn Moons*, Asia Publishing House, Bombay 1957, pp. 97–102.

210 *The Voice of the Silence* is the title of a book of verses, many of which are of Mahāyāna Buddhist character, composed by H. P. Blavatsky on the basis of an original Tibetan text and published in 1889. See also Sangharakshita's essay, 'Paradox and Poetry in *The Voice of the Silence*' in *The Religion of Art*, *Complete Works*, vol. 26, pp. 197–212.

211 It was the Mahāyāna that placed special emphasis on this quality, as an aspect of the

Bodhisattva's practice. Indeed, when the list of six perfections (*pāramitās*) practised by the bodhisattva was extended to ten, *upāya kauśalya pāramitā* was counted as the seventh perfection, explained by Har Dayal in *The Bodhisattva Doctrine in Buddhist Sanskrit Literature* (Motilal, Kegan Paul, London 1932, p. 248) as 'skilfulness or wisdom in the choice or adoption of the means or expedients for converting others or helping them'. For more about this, see *A Survey of Buddhism* in *Complete Works*, vol. 1, pp. 445–454.

212 For a fuller account of these three *yānas*, see ibid., pp. 211–19.

213 'There is a book, who runs may read, / Which heavenly truth imparts': John Keble (1792–1866), *The Christian Year: Septuagesima*.

214 Here 'universalism' refers to the view that all religious teachings are equally true and lead equally to salvation. This sense of the term has nothing to do with the usage of the term Universalism within a specifically Christian context. Although Buddhism is not 'universalist', it is universal, in that its teachings are addressed and applicable not to one section of humanity only, but to all people whatsoever.

215 Arnold offered a definition of God as 'that stream of tendency by which all things seek to fulfil the law of their being'. The phrase 'stream of tendency' is apparently borrowed from William Wordsworth, who wrote in his long autobiographical poem *The Prelude* of

> the mighty stream of tendency
> Uttering, for elevation of our thought,
> A clear sonorous voice.

Prelude 9:88–90.

216 Sophocles, *Antigone*, 322.

217 For the parable within the *sūtra*, see Bunnō Katō and W. E. Soothill (trans.), *The Threefold Lotus Sutra*, Kosei Publishing, Tokyo, 1975, pp. 110–25.

218 Luke 15:11–32.

219 For a translation of the 'Hymn of the Pearl', see, for example, Hans Jonas, *The Gnostic Religion*, Beacon Press, Boston 1958, pp. 113–16.

220 The parable of the poisoned arrow is told in the *Cūlamālunkya Sutta, Majjhima Nikāya* 63 (i.427–32); see Bhikkhu Ñāṇamoli and Bhikkhu Bodhi (trans.), *The Middle Length Discourses of the Buddha*, Wisdom Publications, Boston 1995, pp. 533–6; or I. B. Horner (trans.), *Middle Length Sayings*, vol. ii, Pali Text Society, Oxford 1994, p. 99.

221 See Abraham Maslow, *Toward a Psychology of Being*, Van Nostrand Reinhold, New York 1968, pp. 21–60.

222 See Francesca Fremantle and Chogyam Trungpa (trans.), *The Tibetan Book of the Dead*, Shambhala Publications, Boston and London, p. 37.

223 T. S. Eliot, 'Burnt Norton', part 1, in *Four Quartets*.

224 Matthew 6:21.

225 *Dhammapada* 183.

226 This legendary conversation is variously ascribed, frequently being held to have taken place between Bodhidharma, regarded as the first patriarch of the Chinese Chan tradition who lived in the fifth–sixth centuries CE and Xiao Yan, Emperor Wu of Liang (reigned 502–549). The verse he quotes to the emperor is from the *Dhammapada* verse 183. According to Dōgen, the exchange took place between Haku Kyo-i, the governor of Hangzhou, and Zen master Choka Dorin. See Master Dōgen, *Shobogenzo*, book 1, trans. Gudo Nishijima and Chodo Cross, Windbell, Woking 1994, pp. 106–8. Also quoted in Thomas Cleary (trans.), *Rational Zen: The Mind of Dōgen Zenji*, Shambhala Publications, Boston 1995, pp. 91–4.

227 Romans 7:19.

228 See *Mahāparinibbāna Sutta*, *Dīgha Nikāya* 16 (ii.158); M. Walshe (trans.), *The Long Discourses of the Buddha*, Wisdom Publications, Boston 1995, p. 272; or T. W. Rhys Davids (trans.), *Dialogues of the Buddha*, part 2, Pali Text Society, London 1971, p. 177.

229 Sadāprarudita's story is told in Edward Conze (trans.), *The Perfection of Wisdom in Eight Thousand Lines and its Verse Summary*, Four Seasons Foundation, San Francisco 1995, chapters 30–2, pp. 277–300.

230 Little Nell (in *The Old Curiosity Shop*) and Paul Dombey (in *Dombey and Son*) are both child characters in Dickens' novels who die young. As the novels were published in instalments, readers were aware of the story so far while it was still being written. Dickens was often implored to give his characters happy endings, but (famously in the case of Little Nell), he did not relent.

231 See J. Blofield (Chu Ch'an) (trans.), *The Sūtra of Forty-two Sections and Two Other Scriptures of the Mahāyāna School*, Buddhist Society, London 1977, section 8, p. 13.

232 Śāntideva, *Bodhicaryāvatāra* vi.43.

233 See Har Dayal, *The Bodhisattva Doctrine in Buddhist Sanskrit Literature*, Motilal Banarsidass, Delhi 1978, pp. 209–13.

234 See note 81.

235 See Sangharakshita's poem 'Rain', written at this time, which begins:

> How sweet it is, how sweet again

> To hear and see and smell
> the rain!
>
> *Complete Poems, Complete Works*, vol. 25 p. 177.

236 The Buddha's teachings on how the *bhikkhus* should conduct themselves during the rains retreat is found at Vinaya Piṭaka, *Mahāvagga* 3 (i.137–56). See I. B. Horner (trans.), *The Book of the Discipline*, part 4, Pali Text Society, Oxford 1996, pp. 183–207.

237 The idea of five methods of meditation as antidotes to the five poisons or *kleśas* identified in the Mahāyāna tradition was suggested to Sangharakshita by his teacher C. M. Chen, whom he knew in Kalimpong. For Mr Chen's own account, see C. M. Chen, *Buddhist Meditation, Systematic and Practical*, published by Dr Yutang Lin, El Cerrito 1989, chapter 8, 'The Five Fundamental Meditations to Cure the Five Poisons', pp. 121–42. See also Sangharakshita, *The Purpose and Practice of Buddhist Meditation, Complete Works*, vol. 5, pp. 29–35.

238 The mindfulness of breathing is described in many places in the Pāli canon. See, for example, the *Ānāpānasati Sutta*, *Majjhima Nikāya* 118 (iii.82–5); Bhikkhu Ñāṇamoli and Bhikkhu Bodhi (trans.), *The Middle Length Discourses of the Buddha*, Wisdom Publications, Boston 1995, pp. 943–6; or I. B. Horner (trans.), *Middle Length Sayings*, vol. iii, Pali Text Society, Oxford 1993, pp. 124–6. Also the *Satipaṭṭhāna Sutta*, *Majjhima Nikāya* 10 (i.55–6); Bhikkhu Ñāṇamoli and Bhikkhu Bodhi (trans.), *The Middle Length Discourses of the Buddha*, Wisdom Publications, Boston 1995, pp. 145–6; or I. B. Horner (trans.), *Middle Length Sayings*, vol.i, Pali Text Society, London 1976, pp. 71–2. Also the *Mahāsatipaṭṭhāna Sutta*, *Dīgha Nikāya* 22 (ii.291), see M. Walshe (trans.), *The Long Discourses of the Buddha*, Wisdom Publications, Boston 1995, pp. 335–6, or T. W. Rhys Davids (trans.), *Dialogues of the Buddha*, part 2, Pali Text Society, London 1971, p. 328. Also the *Ānāpānasaṃyutta*, *Saṃyutta Nikāya* v.311, in Bhikkhu Bodhi (trans.), *The Connected Discourses of the Buddha*, Wisdom Publications, Somerville 2000, pp. 1765–6, also F. L. Woodward (trans.), *The Book of the Kindred Sayings*, part 5, Pali Text Society, London 1979, pp. 275–80.

239 This meditation is described by Buddhaghosa at *Visuddhimagga* 295–7; see Pe Maung Tin trans.), *The Path of Purity*, Pali Text Society, London 1975. pp. 342–3. See also *Living With Kindness*

in *Complete Works*, vol. 15 pp. 247–345.

240 This practice is described in, for example, the *Mahāsatipaṭṭhāna Sutta, Dīgha Nikāya* 22 (ii.295–7); see M. Walshe (trans.), *The Long Discourses of the Buddha*, Wisdom Publications, Boston 1995, p. 338–9; or T. W. and C. A. F. Rhys Davids (trans.), *Dialogues of the Buddha*, part 2, Pali Text Society, London 1971, p. 332.

241 This is related at Vinaya Piṭaka iii.68 (*Pārājika* 3.1); see I. B. Horner (trans.), *The Book of the Discipline*, part 1, Pali Text Society, Oxford 1996, p. 117.

242 This meditation practice is a recapitulation of the process the Buddha describes himself as having experienced just before his Enlightenment:

> I thought: What is there when ageing and death come to be? What is their necessary condition? Then with ordered attention I came to understand: Birth is there when ageing and death come to be; birth is a necessary condition for them.

In this way he traced back each of the links of conditioned co-production. The translation quoted here is part of a passage in Bhikkhu Ñāṇamoli, *The Life of the Buddha*, Buddhist Publication Society, Kandy 1972, pp. 25–7.

See also the *Nidānasaṃyutta, Saṃyutta Nikāya* ii.10; Bhikkhu Bodhi (trans.), *The Connected Discourses of the Buddha*, Wisdom Publications, Somerville 2000, pp. 537–40, also C. A. F. Rhys Davids (trans.), *The Book of the Kindred Sayings*, part 2, Pali Text Society, Oxford 1997, pp. 6–7.

243 For an explanation of the *ālaya-vijñāna*, see *The Meaning of Conversion in Buddhism* in *Complete Works*, vol. 2, pp. 279–82.

244 A canonical reference to the 'six element practice' is to be found in the *Mahārāhulovāda Sutta, Majjhima Nikāya* 62 (i.421–4); see Bhikkhu Ñāṇamoli and Bhikkhu Bodhi (trans.), *The Middle Length Discourses of the Buddha*, Wisdom Publications, Boston 1995, pp. 528–30; or I. B. Horner (trans.), *Middle Length Sayings*, vol. ii, Pali Text Society, Oxford 1994, pp. 92–5.

245 Bhikkhu Bodhi, *The Connected Discourses of the Buddha*, Wisdom Publications, Boston 2000, p. 1516. At *Visuddhimagga* 269, Buddhaghosa says that the mindfulness of breathing is 'foremost among the various meditation subjects of all Buddhas'. See Bhikkhu Ñāṇamoli (trans.), *The Path of Purification*, Buddhist Publication Society, Kandy 1991, p. 263; or Pe Maung Tin

246 (trans.), *The Path of Purity*, Pali Text Society, London 1975, pp. 308–9.

246 *Satipaṭṭhāna Sutta, Majjhima Nikāya* 10 (i.57). See Bhikkhu Ñāṇamoli and Bhikkhu Bodhi (trans.), *The Middle Length Discourses of the Buddha*, Wisdom Publications, Boston 1995, pp. 145–6; or I. B. Horner (trans.), *The Collection of the Middle Length Sayings*, vol. i, Pali Text Society, London 1976, pp. 71–2.

247 For the story of Ajātasattu's visit to see the Buddha, see the *Sāmaññaphala Sutta, Dīgha Nikāya* 2 (i.47–86); M. Walshe (trans.), *The Long Discourses of the Buddha*, Wisdom Publications, Boston 1995, pp. 91–109; or T. W. Rhys Davids (trans.), *Dialogues of the Buddha*, part 1, Pali Text Society, London 1973, pp. 65–94.

248 *Satipaṭṭhāna Sutta, Majjhima Nikāya* i.56 (Bhikkhu Ñāṇamoli and Bhikkhu Bodhi (trans.), *The Middle Length Discourses of the Buddha*, Wisdom Publications, Boston 1995, p. 145; or I. B. Horner (trans.), *The Collection of the Middle Length Sayings*, vol. i, Pali Text Society, London 1976, p. 71.)

249 See, for example, the *Vatthūpama Sutta, Majjhima Nikāya* 7 (i.37): Bhikkhu Ñāṇamoli and Bhikkhu Bodhi (trans.), *The Middle Length Discourses of the Buddha*, Wisdom Publications, Boston 1995, p. 119; or I. B. Horner (trans.), *The Collection of the Middle Length Sayings*, vol. i, Pali Text Society, London 1976, p. 47.

250 For this story see note 7, pp. 687–8 above.

251 Sangharakshita had in mind the kettle that one puts over a gas flame rather than a modern electric kettle that turns itself off.

252 John Dryden (1631–1700), from his satirical poem, 'Absalom and Achitophel' (1681). These lines describe the character of Zimri, who represents the Duke of Buckingham.

253 For an account of alienated awareness, see *What is the Sangha?* in *Complete Works* vol. 3, pp. 487–8.

254 See, for example, *Dhammapada* 23.

255 See note 167.

256 For a detailed look at the place of devotion in Buddhism, see Sangharakshita, *Ritual and Devotion in Buddhism* in *Complete Works*, vol. 11, pp. 191–294.

257 On the one hand we must never imagine that our own unaided efforts can be relied on to carry us even through the next twenty-four hours as 'decent' people. If He does not support us, not one of us is safe from some gross sin.

C. S. Lewis, *Mere Christianity*, Macmillan, New York 1986, p. 172.

258 The higher thinking faculty is
> a knowledge that is derived not from the senses and reason alone, but from a fusion of reason with emotion in a higher faculty of archetypal knowledge which we may call 'vision', 'insight' or 'imagination'.

Who is the Buddha? in *Complete Works*, vol. 3, p. 11.

259 Erich Fromm, *Psychoanalysis and Religion*, Yale University Press, New Haven 1950, p. 108.

260 *Torma* are small objects made of flour and butter used in rituals or as offerings in Tibetan Buddhism.

261 Erich Fromm, *Psychoanalysis and Religion*, Yale University Press, New Haven 1950, p. 109.

262 Sangharakshita's experiences at the summer school are described in *Moving Against the Stream* in *Complete Works*, vol. 23, pp. 32–8.

263 In the Tibetan tradition a *ḍākinī* ('sky-dancer') is a female figure representing the energies of Enlightenment. See *Creative Symbols of Tantric Buddhism* in *Complete Works*, vol. 13, pp. 221–47.

264 Edward Conze (trans.), *The Perfection of Wisdom in Eight Thousand Lines and its Verse Summary*, Four Seasons Foundation, San Francisco 1983, p. 9.

265 The *Ratana Sutta* is found at *Sutta-Nipāta* 2.1. This translation is by Sangharakshita, published in full in *Complete Works*, vol. 15, pp. 63–6.

266 This is from 'The Tale of Red Rock Jewel Valley' in Garma C. C. Chang (trans.), *The Hundred Thousand Songs of Milarepa*, Shambhala Publications, Boston and London 1999, p. 5. For Sangharakshita's commentary, see *Complete Works*, vol. 18, p. 26.

267 *King Lear*, Act V, Scene iii.

268 Now I a fourfold vision see
And a fourfold vision is given to me
Tis fourfold in my supreme delight
And threefold in soft Beulahs night
And twofold Always. May God us keep
From Single vision & Newtons sleep.

William Blake, letter to Thomas Butt, 22 November 1802, quoted in Geoffrey Keynes (ed.), *The Letters of William Blake* (1956). In Blake's thinking 'Single vision & Newton's sleep' equates to a kind of single-minded materialism, whereas the 'fourfold vision' combines reason and imagination, sense and emotion.

269 *Paradise Lost*, book 6, lines 509–20.

270 W. B. Yeats (1865–1939), 'Supernatural Songs', stanza 2, line 6.

271 'Rocks, and stones, and trees' comes from William Wordsworth (1770–1850), 'A Slumber Did My Spirit Seal'.

'Huge cloudy symbols of a high romance' is from the sonnet by John Keats (1795–1921), 'When I Have Fears That I May Cease To Be'.

272 Tōyō Eicho (1429–1504), *Zenrinkushū*, no. 217.

273 William Wordsworth (1770–1850), 'Peter Bell: A Tale', part 1, verse 12.

274 *Theragāthā* 17:3. See C. A. F. Rhys Davids (trans.), *Psalms of the Brethren*, Oxford University Press, Oxford 1913, pp. 350–1.

275 *Mahāparinibbāna Sutta*, *Dīgha Nikāya* 16 (ii.143); see M. Walshe (trans.), *The Long Discourses of the Buddha*, Wisdom Publications, Boston 1995, p. 265; or T. W. and C. A. F. Rhys Davids (trans.), *Dialogues of the Buddha*, part 2, Pali Text Society, London 1971, p. 158.

276 *Dīgha Nikāya* ii.144 in F. L. Woodward (trans.), *Some Sayings of the Buddha*, Oxford University Press, London 1939, p. 349.

277 *Sambhogakāya* is a term from the *trikāya* doctrine of the Mahāyāna, referring to archetypal Buddhas, as distinct from historical Buddhas. For an account of the Mahāyāna *trikāya* doctrine see, for example, *A Survey of Buddhism* in *Complete Works*, vol. 1, pp. 250–64.

278 *Vinaya Piṭaka* i.301–2. I. B. Horner (trans.), *The Book of the Discipline*, part 4, Pali Text Society, Oxford 1996, pp. 431–2.

279 See *Puja*, Windhorse Publications, Birmingham 1999, p. 37.

280 *Sigālaka Sutta*, *Dīgha Nikāya* 31; see M. Walshe (trans.), *The Long Discourses of the Buddha*, Wisdom Publications, Boston 1995, pp. 461–9; or T. W. Rhys Davids (trans.), *Dialogues of the Buddha*, part 3, Pali Text Society, London 1971, pp. 173–84.

281 See Plato, *The Last Days of Socrates*, trans. Christopher Rowe, Penguin, Harmondsworth 2010.

282 Charles Dickens, *The Pickwick Papers*, ch. 61.

283 *Mahāparinibbāna Sutta*, *Dīgha Nikāya* 16 (ii.73); see Maurice Walshe (trans.), *The Long Discourses of the Buddha*, Wisdom Publications, Boston 1995, p. 231; or T. W. Rhys Davids (trans.), *Dialogues of the Buddha*, part 2, Pali Text Society, London 1971, p. 79.

284 See note 274 above.

285 *Upaddha Sutta*, *Samyutta Nikāya* v.2; see Bhikkhu Bodhi (trans.), *The Connected Discourses of the Buddha*, Wisdom Publications, Boston 2000, pp. 1524–5; or F. L. Woodward (trans.), *The Book of the Kindred Sayings*, part 5, Pali Text Society, London 1979, p. 2.

286 For an account of the *pratyekabuddhas*, see Reginald Ray, *Buddhist Saints in India*, Oxford University Press, Oxford and New York 1994, ch. 7.

287 Suppose, monks, an ass follows close behind a herd of kine, thinking: I'm a cow too! I'm a cow too! But he is not like cows in colour, voice or hoof. He just follows close behind a herd of kine thinking: I'm a cow too! I'm a cow too! Just in the same way, monks, we have some monk who follows close behind the Order of Monks thinking: I'm a monk too! I'm a monk too! But he has not the desire to undertake the training in the higher morality which the other monks possess, nor that in the higher thought, nor that in the higher insight which other monks possess. He just follows close behind thinking: I'm a monk too! I'm a monk too!

Gadrabha Sutta, Aṅguttara Nikāya i.229; see Bhikkhu Bodhi (trans.), *The Numerical Discourses of the Buddha*, Wisdom Publications, Boston 2012, p. 315; or F. L. Woodward (trans.), *The Book of the Gradual Sayings*, vol. i, Pali Text Society, Oxford 2000, p. 209.

288 *Dhammapada* 194.

289 *Sigālaka Sutta, Dīgha Nikāya* 31 (iii.190); see M. Walshe (trans.), *The Long Discourses of the Buddha*, Wisdom Publications, Boston 1995, pp. 467–8; or T. W. Rhys Davids (trans.), *Dialogues of the Buddha*, part 3, Pali Text Society, London 1971, p. 182.

290 The four speech precepts are among the list of ten precepts first referred to in the *Kūṭadanta Sutta, Dīgha Nikāya* 5 (i.138–9); M. Walshe (trans.), *The Long Discourses of the Buddha*, Wisdom Publications, Boston 1995, p. 137; or T. W. Rhys Davids (trans.), *Dialogues of the Buddha*, part 1, Pali Text Society, London 1973, p. 179. They enjoin abstention from false, harsh, frivolous, and slanderous speech and encourage truthful, kindly, meaningful, and harmonious speech. Sangharakshita's comments on the four speech precepts can be found in *The Ten Pillars of Buddhism* in *Complete Works*, vol. 2, pp. 374–84.

291 Śāntideva, *Bodhicaryāvatāra*, ch. 8, verses 112 ff.

292 *Sigālaka Sutta, Dīgha Nikāya* 31 (iii.190); see M. Walshe (trans.), *The Long Discourses of the Buddha*, Wisdom Publications, Boston 1995, pp. 467–8; or T. W. Rhys Davids (trans.), *Dialogues of the Buddha*, part 3, Pali Text Society, London 1971, p. 182.

293 See *The Inconceivable Emancipation* in *Complete Works*, vol. 16, pp. 485–8.

294 Are not religion and politics the same thing? Brotherhood is religion.
O demonstrations of reason dividing families in cruelty and pride!'

William Blake, *Jerusalem*, plate 57, lines 10–11.

295 For more on the love mode and the power mode, see *The Ten Pillars of Buddhism* in *Complete Works*, vol. 2, pp. 357–63.

296 *Meghiya Sutta*, *Udāna* 4.1 in John D. Ireland (trans.), *The Udāna and the Itivuttaka*, Buddhist Publication Society, Kandy 1997, pp. 50–4.

297 *Upaddha Sutta*, *Saṃyutta Nikāya* v.2: see Bhikkhu Bodhi (trans.), *The Connected Discourses of the Buddha*, Wisdom Publications, Boston 2000, pp. 1524–5; also F. L. Woodward (trans.), *The Book of the Kindred Sayings*, part 5, Pali Text Society, London 1979, p. 2.

298 See *The Ten Pillars of Buddhism* in *Complete Works*, vol. 2, pp. 370–3.

299 *Mahāgovinda Sutta*, *Dīgha Nikāya* 19 (ii.241); see M. Walshe (trans.), *The Long Discourses of the Buddha*, Wisdom Publications, Boston 1995, p. 308; or T. W. Rhys Davids (trans.), *Dialogues of the Buddha*, part 2, Pali Text Society, London 1971, p. 273.

300 *Brahmajāla Sutta*, *Dīgha Nikāya* 1 (i.3); see Maurice Walshe (trans.), *The Long Discourses of the Buddha*, Wisdom Publications, Boston 1995, p. 68; or T. W. Rhys Davids (trans.), *Dialogues of the Buddha*, part 1, Pali Text Society, London 1973, p. 3.

301 See, for example, the *Aggivacchagotta Sutta*, *Majjhima Nikāya* 72 (i.486); Bhikkhu Ñāṇamoli and Bhikkhu Bodhi (trans.), *The Middle Length Discourses of the Buddha*, Wisdom Publications, Boston 1995, pp. 592; or I. B. Horner (trans.), *Middle Length Sayings*, vol. ii, Pali Text Society, Oxford 1994, p. 165.

302 Subhūti, what do you think? Has the Tathāgata attained the consummation of incomparable enlightenment? Has the Tathāgata a teaching to enunciate?

Subhūti answered: As I understand Buddha's meaning there is no formulation of truth called consummation of incomparable enlightenment. Moreover, the Tathāgata has no formulated teaching to enunciate. Wherefore? Because the Tathāgata has said that truth is uncontainable and inexpressible. It neither is nor is not.

A.F. Price (trans.), *The Diamond Sūtra*, Shambhala Publications, Boston 1990, p. 24.

303 See *The Laṅkāvatāra Scripture* in *A Buddhist Bible*, Beacon Press, Boston 1970, p. 348.

304 An account of Sangharakshita's meeting with Anandamayi, 'the blissful mother', is to be found in *The Rainbow Road from Tooting Broadway to Kalimpong* in *Complete Works*, vol. 20, pp. 183–92.

305 Sangharakshita also tells this story in *Precious Teachers* in *Complete Works*, vol. 22, p. 384.

306 Aristotle, *Nicomachean Ethics*, book 2, 1105.b9.

307 Porphyry, in *Plotinus*, trans. A. H. Armstrong, Heinemann, London 1966. vol. i, pp. 3ff.

308 *Udumbarika-Sīhanāda Sutta*, *Dīgha Nikāya* 25 (iii.55); see Maurice Walshe (trans.), *The Long Discourses of the Buddha*, Wisdom Publications, Boston 1995, p. 393; or T. W. Rhys Davids (trans.), *Dialogues of the Buddha*, part 3, Pali Text Society, London 1971, p. 50.

309 *Garava Sutta*: 'Reverence', *Saṃyutta Nikāya* i.139. See C. A. F. Rhys Davids (trans.), *The Book of the Kindred Sayings*, part 1, Pali Text Society, London 1979, pp. 175–6; or Bhikkhu Bodhi (trans.), *The Connected Discourses of the Buddha*, Wisdom Publications, Boston 2000, pp. 234–5. For further commentary, see *Who is the Buddha?* in *Complete Works*, vol. 3, pp. 57–71 and *What is the Sangha?*, ibid., pp. 595–8.

310 The three levels of wisdom are enumerated in, for example, the *Sangīti Sutta*, *Dīgha Nikāya* 33 (iii.219); see M. Walshe (trans.), *The Long Discourses of the Buddha*, Wisdom Publications, Boston 1995, p. 486; or T. W. Rhys Davids (trans.), *Dialogues of the Buddha*, part 3, Pali Text Society, London 1971, p. 212.

311 *Loka* means 'place', 'plane', or 'world', and Buddhist cosmology envisages an ascending hierarchy of these: hell realms at the bottom, then the abode of human beings (and various abodes of non-human beings), and then various heavenly realms. The *kāmaloka*, the plane of sense-desire, encompasses all non-heavenly realms, and some of the heavens also; the higher heavens belong to the *rūpaloka*, the plane of (archetypal) form, and – higher still – the *arūpaloka*, the formless plane. The fact that the *rūpaloka* and the *arūpaloka* are associated with various higher states of consciousness suggests that this 'cosmology' can be taken to refer to inner psychological and trans-psychological realities, as well as to the external world.

312 Early Buddhist tradition enumerates a hierarchy of eight *ariya-puggalas*, 'noble persons', often listed as 'four

pairs of persons': the Stream Entrant and the one who has won the fruits of Stream Entry; the once-returner (that is, the one who will live only one more human existence before Enlightenment) and the one who has realized the fruition of that stage; the non-returner (who will gain Enlightenment from a heavenly realm) and the one who has realized its fruition; and the *arhant*, who has attained Enlightenment, and the one who has realized the fruits of arhantship. The Buddha is recorded as making this fourfold classification on many occasions, for example, in the 'Mirror of Dhamma' he gave to Ānanda in the last days of his life; see *Mahāparinibbāna Sutta*, *Dīgha Nikāya* 16 (ii.93); Maurice Walshe (trans.), *The Long Discourses of the Buddha*, Wisdom Publications, Boston 1995, p. 241; or T. W. Rhys Davids (trans.), *Dialogues of the Buddha*, part 2, Pali Text Society, London 1971, pp. 99–100. The list of the eight individuals, the four pairs of persons, is also given in *Udāna* 5.5 (*Uposatha Sutta*); see John D. Ireland (trans.), *The Udāna and the Itivuttaka*, Buddhist Publication Society 2007, pp. 69–74.

313 *Aṅguttara Nikāya* i.23–6; see Bhikkhu Bodhi (trans.), *The Numerical Discourses of the Buddha*, Wisdom Publications, Boston 2012, pp. 109–111; or F. L. Woodward (trans.), *The Book of the Gradual Sayings*, vol. i, Pali Text Society, Oxford 2000, pp. 16–21.

314 See Gampopa, *The Jewel Ornament of Liberation*, trans. H. V. Guenther, Shambhala Publications, Boston 1986, pp. 32–3.

315 Ibid. p. 35.

316 This is from the *Sela Sutta*, *Sutta-Nipāta* 3.7. E. M. Hare, in *Woven Cadences of Early Buddhists*, Oxford, London 1947, p. 87, gives:

> 'I have heard it said by brahmans of old, venerable teachers of teachers, that those who have become men-of-worth, all-awakened, manifest the self when praise is uttered about them. What if I were to chant seemly verses in the presence of the recluse Gotama?'

317 For more on the Path of Vision and the Path of Transformation, see *The Buddha's Noble Eightfold Path* in *Complete Works*, vol. 1, pp. 477–91.

318 The story of Brahmā Sahāmpati's request is told in various places in the scriptures, for example in the *Ariyapariyesanā Sutta*, *Majjhima Nikāya* 26 (i.167–70); see Bhikkhu Ñāṇamoli and Bhikkhu Bodhi (trans.), *The Middle Length Discourses of the Buddha*, Wisdom Publications, Boston 1995, pp. 260–2; or

I. B. Horner (trans.), *Middle Length Sayings*, vol. i, Pali Text Society, London 1976, pp. 211–3. Another version is to be found at *Saṃyutta Nikāya* i.137; see Bhikkhu Bodhi (trans.), *The Connected Discourses of the Buddha*, Wisdom Publications, Boston 2000, pp. 232–3; or C. A. F. Rhys Davids (trans.), *The Book of the Kindred Sayings*, part 1, Pali Text Society, London 1979, p. 173.

319   See, for example, the *Lalitavistara Sūtra* in Gwendolyn Bays (trans.), *The Voice of the Buddha*, Dharma Publishing, Berkeley 1983, vol. ii, p. 570; or the *Abhiniṣkramaṇa Sūtra* in Samuel Beal (trans.), *The Romantic Legend of Śākya Buddha*, Motilal Banarsidass, Delhi 1985 (first published 1875), p. 237.

320   Xuanzang, *Buddhist Records of the Western World*, trans. Samuel Beal, Motilal Banarsidass, Delhi 1981 (first published 1884), part 2, p. 123.

321   See Vinaya Piṭaka i.7 (*Mahāvagga* 1.6), in I. B. Horner (trans.), *The Book of the Discipline*, part 4, Pali Text Society, Oxford 1996, p. 11.

322   'Reverence, humility, contentment, gratitude and timely hearing of the Dhamma; this is the most auspicious performance.' *Mahāmaṅgala Sutta* in *Sutta-Nipāta* verse 265. This translation by H. Saddhatissa, Curzon Press, London 1985, p. 29. See also *Auspicious Signs*, *Complete Works*, vol. 15, p. 62.

323   From the *Sigālaka Sutta* (also known as the *Sigālovāda Sutta*), *Dīgha Nikāya* 31 (iii.188). This translation is from M. Walshe (trans.), *The Long Discourses of the Buddha*, Wisdom Publications, Boston 1995, p. 467. For an alternative translation, see T. W. Rhys Davids (trans.), *Dialogues of the Buddha*, part 3, Pali Text Society, London 1971, p. 179.

324   Harold Bloom, *Shakespeare: The Invention of the Human*, Fourth Estate, London 1998.

325   *Dhammapada* 354, trans. Sangharakshita.

326   [Of] all the virtues, there is no quality I would sooner have, and be thought to have, than gratitude. For gratitude not merely stands alone at the head of all the virtues, but is even mother of all the rest.

'Pro Cnaeo Plancio', in N. H. Watts (trans.), *Cicero: The Speeches, with an English Translation*, Loeb Classical Library, Heinemann, London 1923, p. 513.

327   Ingratitude is listed as one of the four qualities that bring about rebirth in a state of suffering at *Aṅguttara Nikāya* ii.226; see Bhikkhu Bodhi (trans.), *The Numerical*

Discourses of the Buddha, Wisdom Publications, Boston 2012, p. 597; or F. L. Woodward (trans.), *The Book of the Gradual Sayings*, vol. ii, Pali Text Society, Oxford 1995, p. 234.

328 For example, according to tradition, the first person whom the Buddha met on the road after his Enlightenment – his name was Upaka – despite being impressed by the Buddha's appearance, having questioned him and been told that he was indeed Enlightened, simply said, 'May it be so, friend,' and walked away. See *Ariyapariyesanā Sutta, Majjhima Nikāya* 26 (i.172); also Bhikkhu Ñāṇamoli and Bhikkhu Bodhi (trans.), *The Middle Length Discourses of the Buddha*, Wisdom Publications, Boston 1995, pp. 263–4; or I. B. Horner (trans.), *Middle Length Sayings*, vol. i, Pali Text Society, London 1976, pp. 214–5.

The Buddha often gave his followers advice on how to handle abuse, and on one occasion demonstrated this himself when a Brahmin called Akkosaka Bhāradvāja 'insulted and cursed him with rude, harsh words'. The Buddha points out that, just as if the Brahmin offered him food and he declined to accept it, the food would remain the Brahmin's property, on this occasion he declines to accept the Brahmin's abuse. See *Akkosa Sutta, Saṃyutta Nikāya* i.161–3; Bhikkhu Bodhi (trans.), *The Connected Discourses of the Buddha*, Wisdom Publications, Boston 2000, pp. 255–7; or C. A. F. Rhys Davids (trans.), *The Book of the Kindred Sayings*, part 1, Pali Text Society, London 1979, pp. 200–3.

See also pp. 386–5 above. And the person who famously tried to kill the Buddha was his cousin Devadatta.

329 Upasika Chihmann (trans.), *The Two Buddhist Books in Mahāyāna*, H. K. Books, n.d., p. 7.

330 Śāntideva's *Śikṣā-samuccaya* is a compendium of quotations from Mahāyāna *sūtras*. Sangharakshita found this volume in a cupboard in the Dharmodaya Vihara where he first took up residence after arriving in Kalimpong in March 1950.

331 See *Facing Mount Kanchenjunga* in *Complete Works*, vol. 21, p. 7.

332 Sangharakshita describes his bodhisattva ordination in *Precious Teachers* in *Complete Works*, vol. 22, pp. 542–4.

333 The sixty-four bodhisattva precepts are listed in *Complete Works*, vol. 2, pp. 657–9.

334 As it is said in the holy Dharmasangiti Sutra: 'Then indeed the Bodhisattva Avalokitesvara, the Great Being, said to the Blessed One: The Bodhisattva,

Blessed One, should not be taught too many things. One virtue should be fully mastered and learnt by him, in which are included all the virtues of the Buddha. And what is that? It is great compassion.'

Quoted in C. Humphreys, *The Wisdom of Buddhism*, Michael Joseph, London 1960, p. 147.

335 The story is told in Trevor P. Leggett, *A First Zen Reader*, Charles E. Tuttle Company, Vermont 1960, pp. 235–6.

336 The story is told at Vinaya Piṭaka i.301–3 (*Mahāvagga* 8.26); see I. B. Horner (trans.), *The Book of the Discipline*, part 4, Pali Text Society, Oxford 1996, pp. 431–4. See also 'A Case of Dysentery' in *Complete Works*, vol. 11, pp. 432–44.

337 *The Treatise on Discourses about Giving Rise to the Bodhicitta: The Bodhicittotpādasūtra Śāstra of Vasubandhu*, trans. K. Crosby and A. Skilton, section 2, in *Western Buddhist Review*, vol. iv. See also *The Bodhisattva Ideal*, *Complete Works*, vol. 4, pp. 49–54.

338 At *Dhammapada* 223 the Buddha says: *jine kadariyaṃ dānena*, 'Overcome the miserly by giving'.

Elsewhere in the Pāli canon giving (*dāna*) or generosity (*cāga*) are often mentioned as virtues to be cultivated by the Buddhist laity, in particular the giving of alms to the *bhikkhus* who would in their turn give the Dharma, the greatest of all gifts. The practice of giving was said to lead to wealth and happiness in this and the next life. See e.g. *Dīghajāṇu Sutta*, *Aṅguttara Nikāya* iv.281–5 in Bhikkhu Bodhi (trans.), *Numerical Discourses of the Buddha*, Wisdom Publications, Boston 2012, pp. 1194–5 & p. 1196; or E. M. Hare, *The Book of the Gradual Sayings*, vol. iv, Pali Text Society, Oxford 1995, p. 180 & p. 190. For other examples, see note 383 in *Complete Works*, vol. 1, pp. 627–8.

339 This is illustrated by a story preserved in the Sanskrit *Jātaka* tradition. In this story the Buddha in a former life gives his body to feed a starving tigress and her cubs, see Āryaśūra, *Jātakamāla*, trans. J. S. Speyer, Motilal Banarsidass, Delhi 1971 and *The Sūtra of Golden Light*, R. E. Emmerick (trans.), Pali Text Society, London 1970, pp. 93–6. See also note 344 below.

340 *Dhammapada* 354: *sabbadānaṃ dhammadānaṃ jināti*.

341 'Give again and again, in order to fulfil wishes most perfectly' from Asaṅga, *Abhidharmasamuccaya*, quoted by Gampopa in *Gems of Dharma, Jewels of Freedom*, trans. Ken & Katia Holmes, Sherab Ling Institute

342 Walt Whitman, 'Song of Myself', part 40.
343 See E. B. Cowell (trans.), *The Jātaka Book* xii, *Jātaka Stories*, vols. v and vi, Pali Text Society, London 1973, no. 547, *Vessantara-jātaka*. See also Har Dayal, *The Bodhisattva Doctrine in Buddhist Sanskrit Literature*, Motilal Banarsidass, Delhi 1978, p. 185.
344 For *The Sūtra of Golden Light*'s version of the story of the starving tigress, see R. E. Emmerick (trans.), *The Sūtra of Golden Light*, Pali Text Society, Oxford 2001, pp. 93–6. The story is not preserved in the Pāli *Jātaka* tradition, but is the first story in Āryaśūra's Sanskrit *Jātakamālā* ('garland of birth stories'); for a translation, see for example Peter Khoroche (trans.), *Once the Buddha Was a Monkey: Ārya Śūra's Jātakamālā*, University of Chicago Press, Chicago 1989.
345 See *Saṃyutta Nikāya* ii.181; Bhikkhu Bodhi (trans.), *The Connected Discourses of the Buddha*, Wisdom Publications, Boston 2000, p. 654; or F. L. Woodward (trans.), *The Book of the Kindred Sayings*, part 2, Pali Text Society, Oxford 1997, pp. 121–2.
346 Gampopa, *The Jewel Ornament of Liberation*, trans. H. V. Guenther, Shambhala Publications, Boston 1986, p. 184.
347 Nāgārjuna, *The Precious Garland*, trans. Jeffrey Hopkins and Lati Rimpoche, Harper and Row, New York 1975, verse 219.
348 Ibid. verse 398.
349 See D. T. Suzuki, *Outlines of Mahāyāna Buddhism*, Schocken, New York 1970, pp. 297–8.
350 Ralph Cudworth (1617–1688), classicist, philosopher, and theologian. *A Treatise on Eternal and Immutable Morality* was published in 1731.
351 Charles Darwin (1809–1882), botanist and geologist who developed the theory of evolution by natural selection; Thomas Huxley (1825–1895, grandfather of Julian and Aldous Huxley), biologist who defended Darwin's writings; Karl Marx (1818–1883), German-born philosopher and materialist socialist who, with Friedrich Engels, published *The Communist Manifesto* (1848).
352 The tablets of stone are referred to in Exodus 31.18. The Ten Commandments are listed in Exodus 20.
353 Genesis 2:7.
354 Genesis 2:17.
355 See, for example, the *Kālāma Sutta*, *Aṅguttara Nikāya* i.189, where the Buddha, in dialogue with the Kālāmas, shows that states of mind of greed, hatred, and delusion give rise

to actions that cause harm and suffering, and that these things are unwholesome or unskilful; and that states of mind of non-greed, non-hatred, and non-delusion, i.e. skilful states of mind, lead to actions that bring about 'welfare and happiness for a long time'. See Bhikkhu Bodhi (trans.), *Numerical Discourses of the Buddha*, Wisdom Publications, Boston 2012, pp. 280–1; or F. L. Woodward (trans.), *The Book of the Gradual Sayings*, vol. i, Pali Text Society, Oxford 2000, p. 170ff.

356 The five precepts are enumerated many times in the Pāli canon, for example, *Aṅguttara Nikāya* iii.212: see Bhikkhu Bodhi (trans.), *Numerical Discourses of the Buddha*, Wisdom Publications, Boston 2012, p. 792; or E. M. Hare (trans.), *The Book of the Gradual Sayings*, vol. iii, Pali Text Society, Oxford 1995, chapter 18, 'The Lay Disciple', p. 155. See also *Aṅguttara Nikāya* iv.246–7 in Bhikkhu Bodhi, as above, p. 1174, and E. M. Hare, *The Book of the Gradual Sayings*, vol. iv, Pali Text Society, Oxford 1995. In this *sutta* the disciple's practice of the precepts is said to bring 'freedom from fear, enmity and affliction' not only to himself but to an 'immeasurable number of beings'.

357 See for example *Cunda Sutta*, *Aṅguttara Nikāya* v.263. F. L. Woodward (trans.), *The Book of the Gradual Sayings*, vol. v, Pali Text Society, Oxford 1996, pp. 176–7; and Bhikkhu Bodhi (trans.), *The Numerical Discourses of the Buddha*, Wisdom Publications, Boston 2012, p. 1519.

358 Although the laws of so-called Buddhist countries do not necessarily reflect Dharmic values, it is interesting to note that polygamy was legal in Thailand until 1935. King Mongkut (reigned 1851–1868) famously had thirty-two wives. Polyandry (one woman, several husbands) is still legal in Myanmar (though not widely practised). It has been accepted in Tibet, although it is now illegal under Chinese law.

359 D. T. Suzuki (trans.), *The Laṅkāvatāra Sūtra*, chapter 8, 'On Meat Eating', Motilal Banarsidass, Delhi 1999, pp. 211–21.

360 Vinaya Piṭaka i.219–20 (*Mahāvagga* 6.23); see I. B. Horner (trans.), *The Book of the Discipline*, part 4, Pali Text Society, Oxford 1996, pp. 298–300.

361 Luke 10:38–42.

362 See note 290 above.

Readers familiar with Sangharakshita's *The Buddha's Noble Eightfold Path* will note the reference here to the stages of the path as 'Perfect' rather than 'right'. The distinction is clarified in *Wisdom Within Words* in *Complete Works*, vol. 11, pp. 653–4.

363 This is a reference to a story about George Washington (1732–1799), first president of the United States. It appeared in his first biography, written soon after Washington's death by Mason Locke Weems. The story recounts how the six-year-old George admits to his father that it was he who cut his father's much-loved cherry tree with his hatchet. 'You know I can't tell a lie,' he tells his father.

364 James Boswell, *The Life of Samuel Johnson*, Jones & Co, London 1827, p. 361.

365 In the *Kathāvatthu Sutta, Aṅguttara Nikāya* v.128, the Buddha describes the ten wholesome topics of conversation. See F. L. Woodward (trans.), *The Book of the Gradual Sayings*, vol. v, Pali Text Society, Oxford 1996, p. 88; and Bhikkhu Bodhi (trans.), *Numerical Discourses of the Buddha*, Wisdom Publications, Boston 2012, p. 1424.

366 Ramana Maharshi (1879–1950) went to live at the Arunachala Hill at Tiruvannamalai in southern India after a spiritual experience when he was 16 years old. He remained there for the rest of his life and an ashram grew up around him. He was widely regarded as a holy or enlightened teacher, and was associated with the Hindu Advaita Vedanta tradition. He spent years meditating in the Virupaksha Cave where, much later, Sangharakshita meditated and there came to him a vision of Amitābha, see *The Rainbow Road from Tooting Broadway to Kalimpong*, in *Complete Works*, vol. 20, p. 345. Ramana Maharshi was one of three great spiritual teachers of the Hindu tradition whom Sangharakshita visited in 1949 during his time as a wandering ascetic. See ibid., pp. 319–63.

367 Ibid., pp. 342–3.

368 Sydney Smith (1771–1845), Church of England clergyman, known for his witticisms and writings on philosophy, quoted in Lady Holland, *A Memoir of the Reverend Sydney Smith By His Daughter With A Selection From His Letters*, Harper & Brothers, New York 1856, vol. i, p. 320. Lord Macaulay (1800–1859) was a member of the British Parliament holding office during Queen Victoria's reign.

369 William Wordsworth in 'Ode to Duty'.

370 'I have done that', says my memory. 'I cannot have done that' – says my pride, and remains adamant. At last – memory yields.

Friedrich Nietzsche, *Beyond Good and Evil*, trans. R. J. Hollingdale, Penguin, 2003, p. 91.

371 R. E. Emmerick (trans.), *The Sūtra of Golden Light*, Pali

372 Text Society, third edition, Oxford 2001, p. 13.

372 These are the first eight links of the twelvefold spiral path. For more, see *What is the Dharma?* in *Complete Works*, vol. 3, pp. 258–79.

373 *Mahāparinibbāna Sutta, Dīgha Nikāya* 16 (ii.156); see M. Walshe (trans.), *The Long Discourses of the Buddha*, Wisdom Publications, Boston 1995, p. 270; or T. W. Rhys Davids (trans.), *Dialogues of the Buddha*, part 2, Pali Text Society, London 1971, p. 173.

374 See for example: *Mahāsatipaṭṭhāna Sutta, Dīgha Nikāya* 22 (ii.311): T. W. & C. A. F. Rhys Davids, *Dialogues of the Buddha*, part 2, Pali Text Society, London 1971, p. 344; or M. Walshe (trans.), *The Long Discourses of the Buddha*, Wisdom Publications, Boston 1995, p. 348. See also *Aṅguttara Nikāya* ii.15. F. L. Woodward (trans.), *The Book of the Gradual Sayings*, vol. ii, Pali Text Society, Oxford 1995, p. 15; or Bhikkhu Bodhi (trans.), *The Numerical Discourses of the Buddha*, Wisdom Publications, Boston 2012, p. 401.

375 'O wad some Power the giftie gie us / To see oursels as ithers see us!', from the poem 'To a Louse: On Seeing One On A Lady's Bonnet, At Church' (1786) by Robert Burns (1759–1796).

376 See Gampopa, *The Jewel Ornament of Liberation*, trans. H. V. Guenther, Shambhala Publications, Boston 1986, p.183.

377 See note 310 above.

378 Śāntideva, *Bodhicaryāvatāra* ii.9.

379 This correspondence can be found in *Complete Works*, vol. 11, pp. 560–4.

380 Edward Conze, *The Memoirs of a Modern Gnostic*, Part 1, Samizdat Publ. Co, Sherborne 1979, p. 30.

381 Thomas More's *Utopia* was published in Latin in 1516, and in English in 1551. Francis Bacon's *New Atlantis* was published in Latin in 1624 and in English two years later. Tommasso Campanella's *City of the Sun* was published in Italian in 1602 under the Latin title of *Civitas Solis*. H. G. Wells' *Men Like Gods* was published in 1923.

382 See Ratnaguna and Śraddhāpa, *Great Faith, Great Wisdom*, Windhorse Publications, Cambridge 2016, which includes translations of Sanskrit versions of both *Larger* and *Shorter Sukhāvatī-vyūha sūtras* which describe Sukhāvatī in lavish detail. Translations by Luiz O. Gomez in *The Land of Bliss*, University of Hawaii, 1996, draw on both Sanskrit and Chinese versions, while Hisao Inagaki, *The Three Pure Land Sutras*, Nagata Bunshōdō,

Kyoto 1995 (second edition) is a translation from the Chinese.

383   See *Transforming Self and World*, Sangharakshita's commentary on the *Sūtra of Golden Light* (*Complete Works*, vol. 16, pp. 225ff). The great Indian statesman and reformer, Dr B. R. Ambedkar, perhaps more than anyone in modern times, saw the potential of the Dharma to transform societies. See *Complete Works*, vol. 9.

384   In the *Vasala Sutta, Sutta-Nipāta* 1.7, the Buddha makes it clear that one's status in life is not to be decided by the caste assigned to one at birth but by one's virtuous deeds. See H. Saddhatissa (trans.), *The Sutta-Nipāta*, Cursor Press, London 1995, pp. 13–15.

Elsewhere he affirms that he does not recognize himself as belonging to any caste: see *Pūralāsa Sutta, Sutta-Nipāta* 3.4, in Saddhatissa's translation, ibid. p. 51. The order of *bhikkhus* and the order of *bhikkhunīs* ('monks' and 'nuns') which the Buddha founded admitted people from all four castes, as well as those regarded as outcastes, all of whom he taught equally, and all of whom were considered able to progress on the path to Enlightenment.

385   See for example the *Mahāsudassana Sutta, Dīgha Nikāya* 17, and the *Cakkavattisīhanāda Sutta, Dīgha Nikāya* 26, in M. Walshe (trans.) *The Long Discourses of the Buddha*, Wisdom Publications, Boston 1995, p. 279ff. and p. 395ff; or T. W. & C. A. F. Rhys Davids (trans.), *Dialogues of the Buddha*, part 2, Pali Text Society, London 1971, pp. 192ff and pp. 53ff.

386   The dates of Aśoka's reign are 268/9–232 BCE. He was born c.304 BCE.

387   Aśoka's edicts were set up all over his kingdom. They were written on boulders, rocks, and pillars that he himself caused to be erected. This quotation is from Rock Edict XIII in Kandahar, Afghanistan, where it was written in both Aramaic and Greek.

388   Rock Edict XIII. See *The Edicts of Aśoka*, trans. N. A. Nikam and R. McKeon, Asia Publishing House, Calcutta 1959, pp. 25–6.

389   H. G. Wells, *The Outline of History*, revised edition, Cassell, London 1961, p. 402.

390   For more on right livelihood as a limb of the Noble Eightfold Path, see *The Buddha's Noble Eightfold Path* in *Complete Works*, vol. 1, pp. 538–51.

391   This list of prohibited occupations is to be found at *Aṅguttara Nikāya* iii.208; see Bhikkhu Bodhi (trans.), *The Numerical Discourses of the Buddha*, Wisdom Publications, Boston 2012, p. 790.

392   For example, *Brahmajāla Sutta, Dīgha Nikāya* 1; see

M. Walshe (trans.), *The Long Discourses of the Buddha*, Wisdom Publications, Boston 1995, pp. 71–2; or T. W. Rhys Davids (trans.), *Dialogues of the Buddha*, part 1, Pali Text Society, London 1973, pp. 16–9.

393 For more about Jivaka, as he was called, see *Precious Teachers* in *Complete Works*, vol. 22, pp. 434–45.

394 *Sigālaka Sutta*, *Dīgha Nikāya* 31 (iii.191); see M. Walshe (trans.), *The Long Discourses of the Buddha*, Wisdom Publications, Boston 1995, pp. 468; or T. W. Rhys Davids (trans.), *Dialogues of the Buddha*, part 3, Pali Text Society, London 1971, p. 182.

395 *Karaṇīyamettā Sutta*, *Sutta-Nipāta* 1.8. Sangharakshita's commentary on the sutta is published as *Living with Kindness* in *Complete Works*, vol. 15, pp. 245ff.

396 A reference to the controversial 1947 Partition of India, which resulted in the deaths of around a million people.

397 The story is told in the *Dhammapada* commentary, as the occasion on which the Buddha spoke *Dhammapada* verses 197–9. See Eugene Watson Burlingame (trans.), *Buddhist Legends, Translated from the Original Pali Text of the Dhammapada Commentary*, Harvard University Press 1921, part 3, xv.1, pp. 70–2.

398 Edith Cavell (1865–1915) was an English nurse and hospital matron who worked in Belgium during the First World War. She tended soldiers from both sides, and helped Allied soldiers to escape, for which she was executed by firing squad. She is remembered for her words: 'Patriotism is not enough. I must have no hatred or bitterness towards anyone.' Sangharakshita writes about her in *Adhisthana Writings* in *Complete Works*, vol. 26, pp. 589–90.

399 'Tis dangerous when the baser nature comes
Between the pass and fell incensèd points
Of mighty opposites.

Hamlet, Act V, Scene ii.

400 A reference to George Orwell's dystopian novel *Nineteen Eighty-Four*, first published in 1949.

401 These are all fictional Utopias, to use the title of the first. Sir Thomas More's *Utopia*, a satire about a fictional island of that name, was first published in 1516. Bacon's *New Atlantis* depicts the creation of a utopian land where 'generosity and enlightenment, dignity and splendour, piety and public spirit' are the commonly held qualities of the inhabitants of the mythical Bensalem. Though unfinished, it was published in 1626. *The City of the Sun* is a

philosophical work by the Italian philosopher Tommaso Campanella, written in 1602, shortly after his imprisonment for heresy and sedition. A Latin version was written in 1613–14 and published in Frankfurt in 1623. In *News From Nowhere* (1890), William Morris imagines a utopian future in which money, 'wage slavery', and marriage have been abolished.

402 'The Lotos-Eaters' was published by the English poet Alfred Lord Tennyson in a poetry collection published in 1832.

403 This was King Viḍūḍabha. The story is told in the *Dhammapada* commentary, and concludes with the Buddha's exhortation which became *Dhammapada* 49. See Eugene Watson Burlingame (trans.), *Buddhist Legends, Translated from the Original Pali Text of the Dhammapada Commentary*, Harvard University Press 1921, part 2, iv.3, pp. 44–5.

404 Hugo Grotius, *On the Law of War and Peace (De jure belli ac pacis)* (1625), Kitchener 2001, p. 10.

405 *Dhammapada* 197–200, trans. Sangharakshita.

406 This is what the Buddha calls 'the miracle of instruction'. See the *Kevaddha Sutta, Dīgha Nikāya* 11 (i.214); M. Walshe (trans.), *The Long Discourses of the Buddha*, Wisdom Publications, Boston 1995, pp. 176; or T. W. Rhys Davids (trans.), *Dialogues of the Buddha*, part 1, Pali Text Society, London 1973, p. 279.

INDEX

Abhidhammattha Saṅgaha of Ācariya Anuruddha 294, 706n
Abhidharma (Pāli Abhidhamma) 61, 134, 199, 250, 294, 309, 320, 580, 616, 694n, 700n
Abhidharmakośabhāṣya 90, 696n
Abhidharmasamuccaya 539, 723n
Abhiniṣkramana Sūtra 51, 721n
Acchariya-abbhūta Sutta 687n
Aeschylus 253–4, 516
aesthetic
  appreciation 259–61, 297 *see also* beauty
  impoverishment 267
  pleasure 267, 329, 331, 381
Aggivacchagotta Sutta 718n
Ajātasattu, King 403–4, 714n
Akkosa Sutta 722n
Akṣobhya xviii, xxiv, 332
Alagaddūpama Sutta 26, 218, 691n, 701n
alienation or alienated awareness 126, 259, 359, 361, 363, 366, 410, 639, 714n
alms 11, 105, 114, 300, 502, 637–8, 643–7, 723n *see also* begging-bowls; Sangharakshita on alms round
altruism xix, 91, 476, 540 *see also* other people, helping; service
Ambedkar, B. R. xv, 610–15, 688n, 728n
Ambedkar and Buddhism xxiii
Amitābha xviii, xix, xxiv, 120, 417, 437–8, 623, 726n
Amoghasiddhi xviii, xix, xxiv, 332
amṛta 327, 333–4
anagārikas 606–7, 616 *see also* celibacy
Ānanda 60–3, 88–9, 272, 300–1, 320, 460–3, 464, 474, 645

Anandamayi 489, 719n
Ānāpānasaṃyutta 712n
ānāpānasati see mindfulness of breathing
Ānāpānasati Sutta 712n
anātman (Pāli *anattā*) 23, 31–2, 157, 181–4, 245–6 *see also* self, emptiness of; selflessness
anger *see also* hatred 54, 108–9, 250, 291, 294, 332, 343, 391, 398, 413, 482, 486
  mettā as antidote 391, 392
  patience and 304, 384
Aṅgulimāla Sutta 263, 705n
Aṅguttara Nikāya xxv, 7, 15–16, 87, 200, 213, 294, 476, 502, 552, 570–1, 688n, 690n, 691n, 695n, 700n, 701n, 706n, 717n, 720n, 721n, 723n, 724n, 725n, 726n, 727n, 728n
Ani-la (Thupten Chhokyi) 274, 424–5, 705n
anima/animus 58, 59, 60
animals
  Buddha as in previous lives 693n *see also Jātakas*
  realm of *see* worlds, of animals
  slaughter of 628–9 *see also* vegetarianism
  three, in wheel of life 325, 328, 663
animism 450–7, 512 *see also* paganism
anxiety and worry *see also* restlessness 28–9, 38, 264, 376, 477, 479, 568, 595, 696n
archetypal
  forms or figures xviii, 50, 58, 692n, 716n *see also* Buddhas and Bodhisattvas
  knowledge 244, 715n
  reality (*sambhogakāya*) 311–14

archetypal (*cont.*)
    realms or worlds *see under* worlds
    significance worked out on historical plane 319
archetypes 48, 50, 57–60, 253–4, 287 *see also* myths; patterns; symbolism
arhant ideal 146, 347
arhants (Sanskrit *arahants*) 73, 134, 156, 366, 372, 517, 588, 697n, 720n
    smile of 294, 706n
arhantship 697n, 720n
Aristotle 243, 493, 719n
ariyapariyesanā 22
Ariyapariyesanā Sutta 21, 37, 46, 87, 689n, 690n, 692n, 695n, 720n, 722n
Arnold, E. 51, 144, 613, 698n
Arnold, M. 186, 250, 350, 700n, 710n
art
    Buddhist 17, 34–5, 39, 45, 54–6, 58, 273, 608 *see also* thangkas
    Far Eastern 255–6, 267, 273
    and expansion/raising of consciousness 273–5, 281–2, 415, 516
    four categories of 273
    Lama Govinda and 276–7, 616, 617–18
    and meditation 277–8
    of ordinary activity (*dō* or *tao*) 415, 560–1 *see also* Japanese tea ceremony
    spiritual life as 267 *see also* aesthetic, appreciation
    and the sublime *see* the sublime
    world as poem or work of 259–60, 286–7
arts xviii, xxiv, 172, 192, 268–9, 273–8, 331, 520 *see also* music; poetry
    Mañjughoṣa and 334, 419
    playfulness of 295
    and refining emotions 674
    Sangharakshita and the 249–50, 253–4, 270–1, 277, 280, 283–4, 286–7, 705n
    and vision/breaking through 20, 91
arūpaloka see worlds, three, formless
āryas 178–9 *see also* hierarchy, spiritual, of persons
Āryaśūra 539, 541, 723n, 724n
Asaṅga 723n
asceticism 12, 136, 215, 511, 604, 693n
ascetics, the five 13, 14, 39, 193, 342, 511, 513

Asita's prediction 6, 688n
Aśoka 625–6, 728n
    pillars of 444, 728n
asuras see worlds, of the *asuras*
Aśvaghoṣa 51, 167, 331, 687n, 688n, 689n, 690n, 693n, 708n
Aśvajit 193–4
atakkāvacara 156 *see also* intellectual understanding, truths beyond
ātman 31, 233, 691n *see also anātman*; self
attachment 29, 37, 86–7, 291, 337, 395, 644
    to religious observances 183 *see also* superficiality
Aṭṭhasalinī 700n
authority 181, 212, 305–6, 424, 488, 551, 593 *see also* power
    projection *see under* projections
Avadānas 51, 303, 692–3n
Avalokiteśvara 192, 330, 418–19, 560, 722n
Avataṃsaka Sūtra 97, 239, 529, 696n, 702n
aversion 41, 43, 54, 376 *see also* hatred
    craving and delusion *see* mental states, unskilful; poisons
The Awakening of Faith in the Mahāyāna 167, 331, 699n, 707–8n
awareness *see also* consciousness; mindfulness 9, 108–11, 160, 179, 216, 225, 263–4, 402, 409–11, 455, 534
    alienated *see* alienation
    ethics and 576–7
    higher self and 362
    love as 569
    mutual 172, 570
    self- *see* consciousness, reflexive
    transcendental 168, 239
Axial Age or Period 222–3, 656, 701n

Bach, J. S. 269, 270, 271, 381, 517
Bacon, F. 312, 622, 662, 727n, 729n
Bālapaṇḍita Sutta 338, 708n
bamboos 255–7
Bashō 240, 703n
Baudelaire, C. 271, 517
beauty 94, 152, 190, 251, 274, 275, 282, 433 *see also* aesthetic appreciation; *kalyāṇa*; purity
Buddha of xviii, 322
    in friendship 465, 474
    Sangharakshita and 253–4, 257

truth and goodness 94, 254, 267, 277, 285, 474
becoming (*bhava*) 397
Beethoven, L. van 270, 271, 373, 517
begging-bowls 11, 14, 59, 83, 105, 114, 327, 334, 594, 645
Beowulf 196, 353
Bhayabherava Sutta 241, 703n
bhikkhus see monks
bhūmis 239, 702n
Bible 196–7, 299
  Ecclesiastes 196–7
  Exodus 551, 724n
  Genesis 551, 724n
  Gospels 233, 321, 365, 370, 551, 603
  of John 216, 701n
  of Luke 358, 561, 710n, 725n
  Job 222, 309, 353
  Leviticus 309
  Revelation 622
  Romans 370, 711n
The Bible Designed to be Read as Literature 304–7
birth 24, 27, 42, 397, 665–6, 713n
  oppression of 582, 584
Blake, W. 110, 167, 172, 204, 279, 312–13, 338, 456, 480, 697n, 699n, 708n, 715n, 718n
blasphemy 217, 701n
Blavatsky, H. P. 240, 346, 604–5, 702n, 707n, 709n
  Isis Unveiled 208–9, 304
blessings xxvii, xxix, 440, 477, 512, 562
blind men and elephant *see under* parables
bliss 405, 588 *see also* happiness
  Nirvāṇa as the highest 106, 111, 428, 697n
Bloom, H. 516, 721n
Bodh Gaya xxi, 13–14, 445, 447, 559, 605–6, 666
bodhi 160, 239, 266 *see also* Enlightenment
bodhi tree 35–6, 39, 52–3
Bodhicaryāvatāra 385, 435, 478, 595, 711n, 717n, 727n
bodhicitta 319, 320 *see also* Enlightenment, will to
  absolute and relative 104
  arising of the 286, 477, 529, 531, 536–7, 545, 723n
Bodhicittavivaraṇa 545, 724n
Bodhicittotpādasūtra Śāstra 723n

Bodhidharma 168, 370, 699n, 711n
bodhisattva 133, 245, 259–61, 334, 545
  Buddha as 53 *see also* Buddha Śākyamuni, previous lives; *Jātakas*
  career or life of 267, 295, 540, 542, 595, 694n, 702n
  irreversible 156, 588
  and play 295–7
  represents time 102
bodhisattva hierarchy 503–4, 509
The Bodhisattva Ideal 681
bodhisattva ideal 63, 146, 239, 267, 347, 529–31, 542–5
  Sangharakshita and 529–31
  seeds in Pāli Canon 63, 533
bodhisattva ordination 530–1, 722n
bodhisattva path *see* path, bodhisattva
bodhisattva vows 239, 529
Bodhisattvabhūmi 542, 702n
bodhisattvas
  archetypal *see* Buddhas and bodhisattvas
  and Buddha-land 652–3
  and five *Jinas* 322, 323
  irreversible 156
  novice 529, 588
'The Bodhisattva's Reply' 527–8
body
  and consciousness 271–2, 455
  contemplation of
    loathsomeness or repulsiveness of 33, 43, 397
  six elements and *see* six element practice
  dream state and 318
  forbearance towards 385–6
  human 29, 427, 515 *see also* human birth
  identification with 30–1, 189
  mindfulness of 88, 402, 409–10
  need for work/exercise 639
  oppressions of 583, 584–5
  psychic centres of 57, 694n
  speech, and mind 184, 267, 431, 436, 461, 510, 558, 576–7, 581
  unskilful action of 266–7
  yoga, t'ai chi and 415
Brahmā 350, 452–3
Brahmā Sahāmpati 45, 55–6, 57–8, 510–11, 720–1n
brahmacariya see celibacy; spiritual life
Brahmajāla Sutta 98, 214, 485–6, 629, 696n, 718n, 728–9n
Bucke, R. M. 91, 696n

INDEX / 733

Buddha 15–18, 67, 102–4, 122, 340, 342–4, 366, 424, 523
  Dhyani- 707n
  figures in wheel of life 326–7, 330–4, 668
  historical, *see* Buddha Śākyamuni
  ideal as uncut diamond 322–3
  images xxii, 34, 50, 165, 218, 273–4, 363, 422–5, 452, 536, 544, 694n
  seeds, *see* seeds, (good/bad/Buddha)
  shines through spiritual friends 506–7
Buddha Day (Wesak) 458, 603–4
Buddha-land 652–3 *see also* Pure Land
Buddha-nature 29, 168, 507 *see also* Buddhahood, potential
Buddha Śākyamuni (Gautama) 18, 50, 67, 85, 225, 654
  attitude to beliefs/teachings of time 67, 212–16, 236, 321, 624, 646
  austerities/self-mortification 12–13, 39, 511, 666, 690n
  and bodhisattva ideal 63, 533, 544
  compassion and kindness of 42, 61, 62–3, 259, 461
  death 60, 251 *see also parinirvāṇa*
  decision to teach the Dharma 45, 55–6, 510, 720n
  disciples *see* disciples, of Buddha Śākyamuni
  and the earth goddess 54–5, 57–9
  effect of praising 508
  Enlightenment 13–14, 36, 45, 52–6, 402, 405–6, 500, 509–10, 588, 713n
    celebrating 458, 603–4
  four sights 7–11, 18–20, 21, 665–6, 688n, 689n
  not a god 16–17, 499 *see also* Buddhism, non-theistic
  Going Forth 11–12, 22, 36–8, 77, 226, 689n
  gratitude of 511–12
  gratitude to 518, 523
  life of 3–15, 21–2, 61–2, 225–6, 251, 311, 453–4, 561, 688n
    archetypal symbolism in 48–60
    biographies xxv–xxvi, 51, 607–8, 613, 687n, 689n, 693n
    legends 4, 5, 8–9, 201, 324, 707n
  as lion 66, 695n
  and miracles *see* miracles
  and the natural world 251–2, 453–4
  as physician 26–7, 144
  previous lives 53–4, 694n *see also Jātakas*
  rebirth 16, 42, 239, 666

  recollecting 536
  response to being abused/criticized 384–5, 486, 722n
  and rose-apple tree incident 4, 13, 405–6, 687–8n
  as shower of the way 119, 227
  teachers 12, 37, 511, 666
  teaching methods 151–2, 214–15, 227, 299–300, 310, 499
  teachings, last 238, 589
  titles 35, 46
  as true individual 37, 226
  victory over Māra 35–6, 40–5, 53–4, 59
  vision
    of beings as lotus flowers 55–6, 87, 252
    of world burning 343
  in wheel of life 327
  words of (*Buddhavacana*) 124, 129, 144, 301, 306, 589
    last 84
Buddhacarita 51, 687n, 688n, 689n, 693n
Buddhaghosa 51, 239, 333, 619, 700n, 708n, 712n, 713–14n
Buddhahood *see also* Enlightenment 18, 67, 161, 168, 322, 337, 354, 574, 596
  potential or immanent/innate 17–18, 263, 334–5, 339, 391, 394, 425, 519, 542, 547, 574
Buddharakshita 249, 444, 645, 647 *see also* Satyapriya
Buddhas
  and bodhisattvas *see also* archetypal forms; *yidams* xxix, 131, 311–12, 323, 417–21, 423, 439–41, 582, 694n
  wrathful *see* wrathful figures
  of confession, thirty-five 582
  'Dhyāni' 322, 707n
  female 322, 323, 596–7
  five, mandala of *see under* mandala
  recollection of the 536
  solitary *pratyekabuddhas* 347, 476, 706n, 717n
The Buddha's Noble Eightfold Path 682
Buddhavacana 308 *see also* Buddha Śākyamuni, words of
Buddhavamsa 689n
Buddhism *see also* Dharma 63, 85, 95–6, 158, 181, 218, 225, 228, 238, 242, 348–9, 430, 437

approaches to
  encyclopedic 129, 130
  fundamentalist 128, 129, 130, 305–7
  ideal 130, 233, 387
  sectarian 128–9, 130, 136, 347–8
  selective 157–8, 431
basic, or original teaching 119, 128, 311
canonical literature see Buddhist scriptures and texts
Chinese 123, 125, 698n see also Chan; Tiantai school
and Christianity see under Christianity
and culture 125–7, 278–9, 334, 617, 640–1
disappearance from India 605, 614
Eastern 49, 65, 76, 123–6
not Eastern or Western 64–5, 123–4, 678–9
essence of 240, 298–9
fundamental principles of 193–5, 240–2, 369–70, 501, 651, 652
and institutions xxi, xxii, 119, 409, 650–2
integration in Western society 650–2
Japanese 123, 125, 623 see also Jōdo Shinshū; Nichiren; Zen;
misunderstandings about see also literalism 34, 49–50, 51, 69, 70, 93–5, 106, 135–7, 212, 231–3, 298–9, 430, 615
  and irregular steps 154–5
non-theistic 229, 439, 651 see also Buddha Śākyamuni, not a god
philosophy of see philosophy, Buddhist
and reason 49, 69, 94, 275, 387–8
and respectability 563–4
schools of 119–25, 128, 130, 132–5, 202, 430–1 see also individual schools
seen through biographies 621
spreading of 151, 215–16, 233, 235, 617, 638
  Theosophists and 604–5
study of see Dharma study
unity of 96, 122, 132–5
Buddhist
  organizations 477, 601
  scriptures and texts 119–24, 128–9, 130, 298–311, 703n see also Mahāyāna scriptures; Pāli Canon
Buddhist Society (London) 75, 435
Burns, R. 591, 727n
busyness 592, 643

Cakkavattisīhanāda Sutta 624, 728n
Campanella, T. 622, 662, 727n, 729–30n
capitalism 362, 634–5 see also materialism
Carlyle, T. 229
Carroll, L. 174, 699n
caste 5, 79, 221, 466, 538, 610–13, 644
  Buddha, his disciples and 593, 624, 637, 646, 728n
  lower 637–8, 688n see also 'untouchables'
caste system 610, 613–14, 624, 626, 645–6, 688n
castelessness 220–1, 637
causality 311–12
Cavell, E. 657, 729n
celibacy 377, 483, 606–7, 616 see also *anagārika*
Ceylon 78–9, 603–6, 608, 616 see also Sri Lanka
Chan school 65, 256, 424, 436, 638, 679, 711n
Chandramani, U 83–4, 530, 615
chanting 75, 279, 416, 433–4 see also mantras
  or recitation, of *sūtras* 431, 638
chastity see celibacy
Chesterton, G. K. 244, 704n
Christianity see also God 57, 203, 216, 217, 234–7, 268, 436, 449, 574
  and archetype, myth and symbols 53, 58, 59, 321, 324
  and Buddhism compared 58–9, 210, 242–3, 252, 299, 350, 358, 359–60
  Catholic Church 223, 436, 581
  and ethics 200–1, 233–4, 551–2
  and faith 69, 93–4, 517
  missionaries 200, 230, 308, 603, 605
  and reception of Buddhism 34, 229–30, 498
Cicero 518, 721n
clarity 147, 149–50, 180, 186 see also thinking and thought, clear
Coleridge, S. T. 155–6, 699n
commitment 65, 67–8, 72, 145, 186, 372, 381, 470, 472, 595
  and confession 579
  and irreversibility 589
  primary, lifestyle secondary 76, 531, 615
  to Three Jewels 46 see also Going for Refuge to the Three Jewels
communication see also language; speech 15, 309, 462, 464–5,

475–7, 507–8, 546–7, 656, 659–60, 674
avoiding *see* concealment
'horizontal' and 'vertical' 493–5, 499
and mutual modification of being 494
and silence *see* silence
communities, residential 478, 650
compassion 43, 56, 120–1, 299, 506, 531–3, 537, 553, 558, 658, 661
  bodhisattva of 118 *see also* Avalokiteśvara
  and duty 574
  and Enlightenment 259, 531
  great (*mahākaruṇā*) 99, 267, 327, 723n
  Green Tārā and xxix, 417, 420, 560
  and kindness, of the Buddha 42–3, 61, 62–3, 259, 461
  and rebirth 239
  and wisdom *see* wisdom and compassion
compassionate action, Buddha of 322 *see also* Amoghasiddhi
competition 335–6, 502, 574
complacency 337–8, 592
concealment 229, 577–81
  confession as antidote 580
conceit 41, 43, 44, 399–401 *see also* pride
  six element practice as antidote 391, 399
concentration 13, 147–8, 161, 391–2, 401, 408, 588 *see also* energies, unification of; *samādhi*
  and happiness 404–6
  writing and 289–90
concepts and conceptions *see also* thinking and thought 49, 51, 97, 132–3, 150, 155–6, 166, 263–4, 454–5
  thinking/feeling through 150, 387–8, 434
conditionality (*pratītya samutpāda*) xviii, xxi, 79, 193–5, 198–202, 206–7, 228, 241–2
  antidote to ignorance of 391, 397–9
  cyclic and spiral/nirvāṇic and saṃsāric 198, 201, 241–2, 575 *see also nidānas*
  four noble truths as example of 32–3
  levels of *see niyamas*
  reflecting on 44, 291, 398–9 *see also* wheel of life, as mirror
  the conditioned, and the unconditioned 20–3, 29, 32, 98–9, 294 *see also saṃsāra*, and *nirvāṇa*

conditioned co-production *see* conditionality
conditioned existence *see* existence, conditioned
conditioning 387, 429–30
  group 37, 648–9
  mental *see saṃskāras*
  psychological 175, 333, 501
  societal/cultural 236
conditions
  dependence on, and independence 426–9
  importance of supportive 589, 650–1
confession 65, 134, 309, 465, 577–82, 583, 586
Confucianism 467–8, 552
consciousness 40, 397 *see also* awareness
  absolute 122, 222, 225, 387, 499
  art and expansion/raising of 273–5, 281–2, 415, 516
  body and 271–2
  cosmic 91, 696n
  in dreams 318
  hierarchy of 244, 493–5
  higher states of *see also dhyānas* xxviii–xxix, 41, 70, 159, 162, 179, 318, 415, 430, 673
    as 'cosmology' 319, 501, 719n *see also under* worlds
  raising the level of 413–16, 499, 571, 587, 651, 673
  reflexive or self- 221–2, 225, 338, 499, 565
  and sacredness or meaning 442–3, 454
  in six element practice 400–1
  smile-producing (*hasituppādacitta*) 294, 706n
  store- (*ālaya-vijñāna*) 401, 713n
  transcendental 217, 222, 225, 246, 499, 704n
  and the unconscious 48–9, 50, 56, 58, 185–6, 370–1, 434, 436
  volitional (*cetanā*) 200, 207, 211
consumerism 398, 563, 564 *see also* materialism
contentment 159, 288, 337, 637, 644, 721n
conversion 22, 76, 169, 537, 625, 684
  four elements of (*saṃgrahavastus*) 479–80
  mass, of Ambedkar and followers 613
Conze, E. 27–9, 128, 332, 618–20, 691n, 698n, 703n, 708n, 711n, 715n, 727n

736 / INDEX

cooperation 336, 338, 574, 576, 589,
    641, 675 *see also* harmony
cooperatives 635–6 *see also* right
    livelihood, team-based, businesses
correspondence, Hermetic 51, 456, 692n
cosmology 41, 501, 719n *see also*
    worlds
craving *see also* desire; greed; lust;
    poisons 19, 43, 190, 259, 362,
    376, 398, 554, 555, 666, 668, 696n
  aversion and delusion *see* mental
    states, unskilful; poisons
  cessation of 106, 165, 544, 666
  countered by contemplating decay
    391, 395–7
  dāna and 384, 538, 540
  image for on wheel of life 397
  Māra's daughters as 54
creative
  activity 411, 561–2
  imagination 618
  inner revolt 677
Creative Symbols of Tantric Buddhism
  683
creativity *see also* mind, reactive and
    creative 143, 172, 184, 189, 216,
    225, 256, 259, 292–3, 661
  Enlightenment as 195, 666
  Sangharakshita and 'creative' energies
    286–92
cremation ground 326, 343, 395–7
criticism 218, 229, 571
Crossing the Stream 683
Cudworth, R. 550, 724n
Cūḷamālunkya Sutta 361, 710n
Cūḷasakuludāyi Sutta 241, 703n
cultural heritage 517, 520
culture 220, 269, 500, 538, 566
  Buddhism and *see under* Buddhism
  Eastern 126, 267, 278–9
  economically defined 244 *see also*
    materialism
  indigenous 452–3 *see also* paganism
  Western 151, 278–9, 320, 409, 452,
    617, 678
Cunda Sutta 555, 725n
cynicism 33, 294

ḍākas 131, 598
ḍākinīs 58, 131, 439, 596–8, 715n
  as esoteric Sangha refuge 507, 596
Dalai Lama, Thirteenth 608, 621
dāna 384, 538–41, 554–5, 723n *see
    also* generosity
Dante Alighieri 253–4, 516, 704n

Darwin, C. 243, 312, 550, 704n, 724n
David-Néel, A. 607–10
Davies, W. H. 255, 704n
De Quincey, T. 309–10, 706n
death 9–11, 21, 23, 25, 27, 118,
    187–90, 193, 195–8, 397, 663–9
  contemplation of 43, 191, 395–6,
    713n *see also* meditation, corpse
  existence after 182, 202–3, 544 *see
    also* rebirth
  forbearance towards 386
  or impermanence, personified (Yama
    or Yamarāja) 326, 327, 339, 663
  intermediate state 312, 364
  Kisāgotamī and 61–2
  Māra as 40–2
  Sangharakshita and 142
  spiritual xxix, 398
  the Deathless 21, 42, 46, 198, 333, 666
    see also the eternal
defilements *see kleśas*
deities, wrathful *see* wrathful figures
Delamare, T. 283
delusion, craving and aversion *see*
    mental states, unskilful; poisons
demon, of death *see* death, or
    impermanence, personified
demons 54, 303, 452
desire 263, 379–81 *see also* craving;
    passion
  neurotic 330, 333, 342
  sensuous, world of *see under* worlds
  views/theories and 97–8, 232
desires, discovering one's real 412–13
Devadatta 519, 722n
devaputta-māra 40–2, 45
devas 41, 287, 654, 692n *see also* gods;
    spirits; supernatural, beings
devotion *see also* faith; reverence xix,
    275, 425–6, 429–30, 435, 449,
    450–1, 508–9, 714n
devotional practice xxviii, 219, 401,
    425, 436, 508 *see also* pujas; ritual;
    worship
Dhamma revolution 614 *see also*
    society, transformation of
Dhammacakkappavatana Sutta 336,
    708n
Dhammapada xxv, xxviii, 33, 35–6, 72,
    106, 119–20, 168, 207, 238, 338,
    369–70, 419, 477, 518, 539, 669,
    687n, 691n, 692n, 695n, 697n,
    699n, 701n, 702n, 708n, 711n,
    714n, 717n, 721n, 723n, 730n
  Commentary 655, 664, 729n, 730n

Dhardo Rimpoche 432–3, 530
Dharma see also Buddhism 85–9, 96,
    129, 167, 173–4, 215–16, 229,
    298–9, 457, 480
  Buddha's definition, to Mahāpajāpatī
    85–7, 213
  Buddha's reverence for 500
  can be lost 48
  and culture see Buddhism, and culture
  doctrine
    and method 33, 118, 593
    not only aspect 60–1, 119, 122, 135
  as duty and religion 574
  embodied in yidam 417, 536
  emotional response to 371–4, 387–8,
    425
  as 'eternal and universal order'
    (sanātana dharma) 211
  greatest gift 518–19, 539, 723n
  holiday 297
  letter, and spirit of 83, 121 see also
    literalism
  misrepresentation of see Buddhism,
    misunderstanding of
  'more and more of less and less' 151
  one taste of see freedom, taste of
  oral tradition/transmission 83, 129,
    150–1, 300–1, 303, 638
  as a raft 218
  realm of (dharmadhātu) 477
  as refuge 66–7, 429
  spreading the xxix, 14, 46
  study or discussion 151, 295, 298,
    302, 379, 390, 457–9, 482, 522,
    592, 595
    ideal student of 232–3
    Sangharakshita's own 78–9, 272
    time for 562, 589, 641, 674
    in traditional civilizations 457–8
  teachings requiring interpretation 32–3
  wisdom through listening to/hearing
    (śruta-mayī-prajñā) 501, 592
Dharma Eye 74
dharmakāya 350 see also trikāya
Dharmapala, Anagārika 601, 603–7,
    613
Dharmarāja 624–5
dharmas, five 553
Dharmasaṅgīti Sūtra 531, 722n
Dhātukathā 309–10
Dhyāna for Beginners 154, 699n
dhyānas xxviii, 5, 161, 405–6,
    411–12, 418, 592, 664 see also
    consciousness, higher states of;
    samādhi

Diamond Sūtra (Vajracchedikā
    Prajñāpāramitā) 65, 73–4, 133,
    174, 175, 218, 251, 371–3, 488,
    529, 619, 679, 698n, 699–700n,
    718n
diamond throne (vajrāsana) 53, 605
diamond thunderbolt see vajra
Dickens, C. 373, 470, 516, 520, 711n,
    716n
Dīgha Nikāya xxv, 22–3, 24, 60, 62,
    88–9, 98, 214, 238, 283, 309–11,
    320, 372, 403–4, 461, 466–7,
    473–4, 478–9, 481, 483, 485–6,
    499, 514–15, 589, 624, 629, 631,
    677, 689n, 690n, 691n, 694n,
    696n, 702n, 705n, 707n, 709n,
    711n, 712n, 713n, 714n, 716n,
    717n, 718n, 719n, 720n, 721n,
    727n, 728n, 729n, 730n
Dīghajāṇu Sutta 723n
disciples, of Buddha Śākyamuni see also
    ascetics, the five 46, 60–1, 86, 89,
    144, 193, 300, 348, 404, 453, 486,
    502, 693n
  and caste 624, 637, 646, 728n
  and teachers see guru, and disciple
discipline 100–1, 130, 144, 345, 592–4
disciplined or regular lifestyle 378, 381,
    415, 592–5
dissatisfaction 7, 108, 676–7 see also
    suffering
distractedness or distraction 41, 43, 44,
    391, 406–8, 653
Dōgen 711n
Doṇa Sutta 15–16, 690n
doubt and indecision 145–6, 183, 579
    see also vagueness
The Drama of Cosmic Enlightenment
    683, 703n
dreams and dream state xix, 20, 59, 104,
    313–14, 318, 319, 493, 622–3
  conditioned world like 251, 272
  truth or vision revealed in 52, 92
drugs 629 see also intoxicants
Dryden, J. 408, 714n
dualism and dualistic approach 365 see
    also subject, and object, polarity
duḥkha (Pāli dukkha) see suffering
duty 573–6, 676 see also responsibility

earth
  connectedness with 237 see also
    animism
  goddess 54–5, 57–9
earth-touching mudrā 55, 322

738 / INDEX

eating *see also* food
  meat 27, 559 *see also* vegetarianism
ecological issues 219, 641–2 *see also* environmentalism
Edman, I. 282, 705n
effort 101, 160, 205, 335–6, 337, 338, 476, 588–9 *see also* exertion; vigour
  different schools' attitudes to 119–20, 122
  perfect 90, 590–1
  problems, difficulties and 490
efforts, four right 89 *see also* exertions, four
ego xxix, 15, 182–3, 363–4, 575 *see also* self
ego-sense *see* conceit; pride
egoism 281, 483, 520–1
egolessness 483, 574–5 *see also* selflessness
elements
  contemplation of six *see* six element practice
  as *mahābhūtas* 454–5
Eliot, T. S. 260, 364, 705n, 711n
emotion, Perfect 90, 371
emotions xix, 142–3, 185–6, 275, 372–3, 643
  dreams and 313–14
  and feelings, distinguished 374–6
  and intellectual understanding 369–71, 378–9, 387–8, 412–13, 424
  positive *see also* faith; mental states, skilful; *mettā* 172–3, 179, 216, 225, 294, 306–7, 338, 451–2, 506, 534, 571
    cultivating 376–9, 401 *see also mettā bhāvana*
  refinement of 279, 377–8, 674
emptiness
  see śūnyatā
  of self *see* self, emptiness of
energies
  concentration or unification of 159, 190, 289–90, 405, 577 *see also* concentration; integration
  ḍākinī as embodiment of Enlightened 596–7, 715n
  emotional 374, 378, 441, 596
  psychic 57
energy 54, 86–7, 145, 173, 177, 213, 259
  blocked and released 294, 371, 373, 412, 598
  cultivating positive 376–9

giving 538
matter as 30
spiritual, bodhisattva as impersonal 543
and spontaneity 410–11
Vajrapāṇi and 417
Enlightenment *see also bodhi*; Buddhahood; Nirvāṇa 3, 34, 48, 65, 85, 97–8, 166, 189, 232, 259, 333–4
  approached from opposite directions 133, 135
  beyond reach of rational mind (*atakkāvacara*) 156, 233
  Buddhas as embodiment of xviii, 424–5, 536
  and communication 462
  compassion and 259, 531
  cosmic 349
  as desire for the Eternal 381–2
  -experience 96–8
  individual or private 239, 347 *see also* individualism, spiritual; *pratyekabuddhas*
  multifaceted nature of 323
  path and 102
  not possible in a 'dead' universe 455
  potential 246, 425 *see also* Buddhahood, potential; seeds
  rūpaloka and 41–2
  and service 506
  seven factors of 89
  three similes for 70–1, 98
  and time 360–1
  will to 245, 534 *see also bodhicitta*
environmentalism 252 *see also* ecological issues; ethics, geo-; natural world
equality 323, 501–2
escapism 69–71, 350–2
the eternal 381–2 *see also* the Deathless
The Eternal Legacy 683, 694n
eternalism 181–2
eternity, and time 102, 361
ethical formalism 120
ethics xix, xxviii, xxx–xxxi, 234, 482, 550–2, 651 *see also* morality; precepts; *śīla*; skilfulness; unskilfulness
  Christianity and *see under* Christianity
  confession and *see* confession
  geo- 656–7
  insight and 553
  karma and 200–1, 576–7
  psychological criterion of 552–3, 556

INDEX / 739

evolution
  or extinction 673
  higher 70, 198, 240, 242–6, 344–5, 349, 366, 503, 676, 696n, 703n, 724n
    communication and 494–5, 499
  lower 504
  theories of 242–3, 703n, 704n, 724n
ex-Untouchable Buddhists, Sangharakshita and 530, 548, 613
exertion *see also* effort
  ritual and 432–4
exertions, four 590–1 *see also* four right efforts
existence
  collective 624–6
  conditioned or mundane *see also* the conditioned; *saṃsāra*; wheel of life 27, 33, 40–2, 98, 182, 198, 332, 333, 339
    as burning house 342, 344
    gravitational pull of 226
    levels of 16, 576 *see also* worlds, three; realms, six
    marks of *see lakṣaṇas*
    oppression of 582, 584
    reflecting on 44, 317, 536–7
    transcending 173, 352
  nature of 241, 382–3, 588, 623
  poetry as 280
experience 96–7, 102, 122, 145, 151, 211, 213, 243
  direct 131–2, 164–5, 177–8, 278, 598
  mundane 97, 107, 331, 588
  mystical 5, 90–1, 269–72, 365
  of reality 175
  spiritual or religious 365, 381
  transcending rational 233
  two contradictory trends of 640
  and *bodhicitta* 534–7
experiment 144, 164–5
eyes
  Dharma 74
  divine 55
  of Enlightenment 443
  inner 417
  Neoplatonic view 313

Facing Mount Kanchenjunga 683
faculties,
  five spiritual *see* spiritual faculties
  higher thinking 244, 429, 715n
  of intuition *see* intuition
faith xix, 120, 134, 175, 423–6, 444–7, 448, 449, 475, 506, 543, 576

Buddha didn't ask for absolute 499
Christian 210–11
and devotion *see* devotion
and observing rules 593
as positive *nidāna* 588
families 25, 37, 185, 403, 472–3, 541, 569–70, 574, 643, 644, 648, 650
  spiritual 509
fear 25, 38–9, 47, 396, 555, 583, 604
  see also anxiety
fearlessness 621
  gift of 538–9
feeling (*vedanā*) 40, 375, 397
  and emotions, distinguished 374–6
  mindfulness of 88, 402
fetters, three 183–7
fidelity 338, 372
  and promises 478–9
Fire Sermon 342–3, 709n
First Council (*saṅgīti*) 300–1, 706n
Flower Ornament Sūtra see Avataṃsaka Sūtra
food 558–61, 627, 628, 635 *see also* alms; eating; vegetarianism
forbearance (*kṣānti*) 384–6 *see also* patience
force
  consciousness, or principle, supra-personal 211, 673
  has no place in Buddhism 228 *see also* power-mode
  or spiritual energy, bodhisattva as 543
forces
  archetypal 313
  of compassion 56
  elements as living (*mahābhūtas*) 454–5
  gods and goddesses as 319, 451
  of inertia 590 *see also* laziness
  or influences, higher spiritual 439
  liberation of creative 144
  represented by Māra and Earth Goddess 35–6, 39, 42, 45, 55
  of the unconscious 54, 56–7
  unskilful 586
forgetfulness 358, 407–8, 521–3
forgiveness 581–2
form (*rūpa*) 40
  world of *see under* worlds
formless world *see under* worlds
four bases of success 89
four foundations of mindfulness 88, 402
four noble truths xxi, 33, 72, 79, 181, 228
four right efforts 89 *see also* exertions, four

740 / INDEX

four sights *see under* Buddha Śākyamuni
Francis, Saint 386
freedom *see also* liberation 98, 100,
    111, 144, 172, 186–7, 209, 216–17,
    222, 259, 509
  ḍākinī and 596
  ex-Untouchables and 613
  modern Western ideas of 372
  religious 541
  of speech 228–9, 231
  taste of 98, 186, 386–7, 697n
Freud, S. 199, 294, 488, 706n
friendliness 43, 44, 104, 446, 451, 661
    see also mettā
friends 372, 578–80, 642 *see also*
    spiritual friends
  evil 585–6
Friends of the Western Buddhist Order
    see FWBO
friendship xix, 374, 495, 562 *see also*
    spiritual friendship
  duties of 478–80, 506–7, 574
Fromm, E. 431, 715n
The FWBO and 'Protestant Buddhism'
    xxiii
FWBO or 'the Movement' xxi–xxiii, xxv,
    xxvii, xxxi, 126, 137, 219, 521–2
    see also Western Buddhist Order

Gadrabha Sutta 476, 717n
Gampopa 337, 504–7, 542, 591, 708n,
    720n, 723n, 724n, 727n
Gaṇakamoggallāna Sutta 227, 702n
Gaṇḍavyūha Sūtra 240, 702n
Gandhatthena Sutta 252, 704n
Gandhi, M. 384, 489, 612
Garava Sutta 500, 719n
The Gateless Gate (Mumonkan) 697n,
    698n
Gautama *see* Buddha Śākyamuni
gender, in Pure Land 623
generosity *see also dāna*; giving;
    precepts, second 67, 159, 239, 340,
    476, 478, 505, 553, 729n
Ghoom 276, 422–3, 616–17
Gilgamesh 196
give what you can, take what you need
    636, 642
giving 54 *see also dāna*; generosity
  and guilt 28
globalization 671–2
Gnosticism 240, 358, 620, 710n
goals 106–11, 133, 135, 166, 295
God 17, 50–1, 98, 200, 210–11,
    229–30, 232, 363, 488–9, 551, 651

god, Buddha not a 16–17, 499
goddess, earth 54–5, 57–9
gods 16, 244, 336, 451, 662–3, 669 *see
    also* devas
  anti- *see* worlds, of the *asuras*
  the Buddha and 17, 37, 453–4
  and goddesses 319, 353, 452, 454,
    615
  pagan 235, 452
  king of (Indra) 340, 452, 693n
  nectar or ambrosia of 283, 327,
    333–4, 662 *see also amṛta*
  realm or world of *see under* worlds
Goethe, J. W. von 156, 279, 516, 699n
Going for Refuge to the Three Jewels
    18, 62, 65–9, 162–3, 287–8, 475–6,
    601, 607, 651
  centrality and significance of 72, 78,
    530–1, 615
  levels of xxii
  and lifestyle 621 *see also* lifestyle
  ritual of 436–7
  Sangharakshita's *see under*
    Sangharakshita
going forth 11, 76–9, 86, 403, 473 *see
    also* homeless wanderers
  the Buddha's 11–12, 22, 36–8, 77,
    226, 689n
  Sangharakshita's *see under*
    Sangharakshita
goodness, beauty, truth and 94, 254,
    267, 277, 285, 474
grasping 108, 397, 540, 573
gratitude xvi, xxx, 473, 509–23, 721n
    see also kataññutā
  and ingratitude 518–21, 721n
  three principle objects of 513–18
  of and to the Buddha *see under*
    Buddha Śākyamuni
Gray, T. 197, 700n
greed 482, 576, 669 *see also* craving
greed type 190–1, 338
the group 37, 46–7, 486–7
  acceptance/disapproval of 563–5, 644
  and the individual *see under*
    individuals
  spiritual community and 79–80, 533
groups, religious 106, 223, 485, 487,
    489, 492, 496, 498
Guenther, H. xxxi, 100, 259, 697n,
    705n, 708n, 720n
guilt 28, 233–4, 296, 358, 557, 579–80
guru 58, 131, 417, 484–5, 487–99, 520
    see also teacher
  choosing a 495–6

guru (*cont.*)
   and disciple relationship 493–5, 499
   distinguished from teacher 487–8, 492–3
   as esoteric Buddha refuge 507
   what a guru is not 485, 487–8, 490–3
gurus
   female 126–7, 489
   three Tibetan 489–90

habit 183–4, 186
happiness 108–11, 172, 198, 242, 308, 477, 669, 723n *see also* bliss; joy
   can be spiritually dangerous 331, 336
   and concentration 404–6
harm 582 *see also* violence
   abstention from 553–4 *see also* precepts, first
harmony 135, 474, 576 *see also* cooperation; speech, harmonious
hate type 190, 332–3, 338
hatred *see also* anger; aversion; poisons 376, 475, 553, 555, 574, 576, 583, 669, 708n
   and wisdom 332–3
heart xxvii–xxviii, 117, 346, 367–70, 388–90, 394, 412, 418–20, 430–2, 436–8, 444, 446–8, 450, 452–4, 462–6, 474, 476–8, 518, 567–8, 574
   as 'higher understanding' 309, 310
   learning by xxvii, 603, 638
Heart Sūtra 418, 619
heavens 37, 106, 119, 156, 162, 206, 719n, 720n *see also* worlds, of the gods
Hegel, G. 129, 243, 698n
hell or hell realm 119, 206, 339, 398, 456, 542, 708n, 719n *see also* worlds, of tormented beings
Hermetic correspondence 51, 456, 692n *see also* symbolic value, of ordinary things
heroes and heroism xix, 34–6, 58, 60, 235, 448, 600, 621
   and bodhisattva 239
   in *Jātakas* and *Avadānas* 303–4, 541, 692n
Hevajra Tantra 134, 698n
hierarchy 243, 501–2, 506
   of aliveness or living forms 455, 503
   of authority *see* authority
   bodhisattva 503–4, 509
   of consciousness 244 *see also* consciousness, higher levels
   false 501–2
   spiritual 244, 500–9
   of persons (*ariya-puggalas*) 501, 719n, 720n *see also* āryas
   of worlds *see* worlds, three
Himalayas 4, 257–8
Hīnayāna xxvi, 544 *see also* yānas
hindrances, five xxviii, 13, 696n
Hinduism *see also* caste 31, 220–1, 258, 343, 345, 350, 415, 612, 614, 670, 691n, 705n, 726n
   Ambedkar and 612–13, 614, 615, 688n
   attitude to Buddhism 615
history 600, 674 *see also* plane, or reality, historical
   and myth 50–2, 56–7, 321
The History of My Going for Refuge xxiii, 73–80, 684
holiness 442–3, 454, 459
homeless wanderers or sadhus 11, 180, 637, 643–4, 666 *see also* anagārikas
   śramaṇas as 194, 511, 700n
Homer 196–7, 353, 516
Houghton Hodgson, B. 322, 707n
Hsüan-tsang *see* Xuanzang
Huineng 65, 73, 424, 679
human
   birth, difficulty of attaining 338
   body *see* body, human
   life, survival of 205, 676
   realm *see* worlds, of human beings
humility 146, 384, 492, 721n
humour 293–5
Humphreys, C. 75, 692n, 699n, 723n
hungry ghosts (*pretas*) *see* worlds, of hungry ghosts
Huxley, T. 550, 724n
'Hymn of the Pearl' 240, 358–9, 703n, 710n

ignorance *see also* forgetfulness; poisons 19, 43, 44, 54, 99, 259, 337, 343, 358, 391, 419, 553
   contemplation of *nidānas* as antidote 391, 397
   image for on wheel of life 397
   of world problems 672–3
imagination 51–2, 179, 244, 258, 275, 282, 319, 324, 373, 436, 516, 715n
   'creative' 618
   and identification with nature 252
   works of 301–2

impermanence 23, 30–1, 43, 150, 187–92, 251, 342, 396, 664–5
  or death, personified 326, 327, 339
  melody of 326, 331
incense xxvii–xxviii, 115, 426, 432, 450–1, 458, 539
The Inconceivable Emancipation 684, 696n
India 125, 450, 608, 610–13, 616, 624–6
  Buddhism in xxi, 77, 85, 605–6, 613–14
  Dharmapala in 605–6
  partition of 77, 646, 729n
  Sangharakshita in *see also* Kalimpong xxv, xxviii, 26, 76–7, 141–2, 220–1, 255, 396, 444, 572, 613, 645–8, 669–70, 726n
    with ex-Untouchable Buddhists 530, 548, 613
individual
  Milarepa as 564–5
  and sexual relationships 472
individualism 68, 520, 565, 575, 594
  spiritual 46, 47, 427–8, 536–7 *see also* Enlightenment, individual
individuality 408, 410, 649, 675, 677
  beyond 543
individuals 87
  āryas as 178–9
  Christianity and 217
  development as 68, 88, 218–19
  great 600, 621
  and the group 37, 46, 78–80, 184–5, 219–28, 644, 648–9, 673, 674–5
  and spiritual community 68, 80, 228, 649, 673
  statistical or 'non-' 221, 223, 225, 485, 660
  true 184, 186–7, 220–3, 225, 565, 621, 675
Indra 340, 452–3, 693n
ingratitude 518–21, 721n
insight (*vipaśyanā* (Pāli *vipassanā*)) *see also* spiritual death 32, 91, 109–10, 191, 244, 275, 332, 401, 482, 673
  breaking fetters and 186
  Buddha's, into *pratītya-samutpāda* 193
  and ethics 553
  initial 20, 90–2, 274, 302, 623
  and Stream Entry 588
  transcendental 150, 159–60, 194
  vision and transformation 509–10 *see also* path of vision and transformation

inspiration xxiv, 11, 60, 206, 234, 301–2, 320, 377–8, 441, 602, 605
  of bodhisattva ideal 319, 529–30, 544–5
ḍākinī as 596–7
integration 57, 59, 366, 434–6, 493, 602, 673 *see also* energies, concentration of
  of Dharma practice in life 456–9
  as individuation 57–8
  mindfulness of breathing and 391
intellectual insight 332
intellectual understanding 32, 49, 150, 155, 436, 440, 617 *see also* thinking and thought
  emotional equivalents for 369–71, 378–9, 387–8, 412–13, 424
  truths beyond 233, 321, 510 *see also atakkāvacara*
interconnectedness 244
interpenetration 261, 574
intoxicants *see also* drugs
  abstention from 555–6
intoxication 410
intuition and intuitive knowledge 32, 52, 233, 310, 455
irreversibility 588–9 *see also* Stream Entry
  bodhisattvas and 156, 588
irreversible, spiritual creativity 666
Isis Unveiled 208–9, 304
iṣṭa devatā 417 *see also yidam*
Itivuttaka xxv, 27, 691n

Jainism 88, 222, 670
Jambukhādakasaṃyutta 106, 697n
James, W. 365
Jamyang Khyentse Rimpoche xxx
Japanese tea ceremony 409, 560
Jaspers, K. 222, 701n
Jātakamālā 539, 541, 723n, 724n
Jātakas 29, 51, 303–4, 340, 540–1, 608, 687n, 688n, 689n, 691n, 692n, 693n, 709n, 723n, 724n
jealousy 482, 489
The Jewel Ornament of Liberation 337, 504–5, 506, 542, 591, 708n, 720n, 724n, 727n
Jina 35, 46 *see also* Buddha
Jinas, five 50, 322
Jivaka 630, 729n
Jiyu-Kennett Rōshi 126–7, 697n
jñeyāvaraṇa see veils, of ignorance
Jōdo Shinshū or Shin school 120, 123, 623

Johnson, S. 512, 566, 726n
joy 159, 198, 242, 259, 410, 509, 588
  see also happiness
  'and pain are woven fine' 338, 708n
  sympathetic (muditā) 507, 508
Jung, C. G. 50, 57–8

Kagyu school 124, 507, 542, 693n
Kālāma Sutta 212–13, 552, 701n, 724n
Kalidasa 258, 705n
Kalimpong
  Mount Kanchenjunga seen from 390
  Sangharakshita in xxii–xxiii, xxx, 50, 180, 257–8, 276, 280, 423, 424, 432, 470, 489, 490, 497, 529, 530, 608, 630, 705n, 712n, 722n
kalyāṇa 474, 517 see also beauty
kalyāṇa mitratā see spiritual, friendship
kāmaloka see worlds, of sensuous desire
Kant, I. 243, 704n
Kapilavastu 4, 86, 654
Karaṇīyamettā Sutta 636, 638, 642–3, 729n
  Sangharakshita's commentary on see Living with Kindness
karma xviii, 198–202, 205–7, 326, 419, 431
  and ethics 200–1, 576–7
  formations see saṃskāras
  fruits/results of (vipāka) 375, 582
  only one level of conditionality 199
    see also niyamas
  and re-becoming or rebirth 42, 98, 197–8, 202, 205–7, 329, 518, 519, 576, 692–3n
Kasauli 77, 80–1
Kashyap, Jagdish (Kashyap-ji) 250, 450, 529
kataññutā 512–13, 519 see also gratitude
Kathāvatthu Sutta 570–1, 726n
Keats, J. 280, 396, 456, 604, 716n
Keble, J. 348, 710n
Kevaddha Sutta 677, 730n
khandha-māra 40, 42
khandhas see skandhas
kilesa-māra 40–2, 44
kilesas see kleśas
kindness 103, 303, 464, 475, 602, 670
  see also mettā
  of Buddha Śākyamuni 62–3, 461–2
Kisāgotamī 61–2
kleśa nirvāṇa 106, 697n

kleśas (Pāli kilesas) 40–4, 106, 697n, 712n see also mental states, unskilful; poisons
kleśāvaraṇa see veils, of passions
Know Your Mind xxiii, 684
knowledge 163–5
  archetypal 244, 715n see also vision
  of benefit gained see kataññutā
  and faith 447
  giving 538
  intuitive see intuition
  and power, literature of 309–11
  and practice 370–1
  rational 244 see also mind, rational
  self- 108–9, 111, 287, 291, 475–6, 591, 602
  vidyā as 259
  and vision of things as they really are (yathābhūta-jñānadarśana) 97, 186, 588
Koliyans 654–6, 658–9, 661, 664, 668–9
Krishna's flute 345–6, 709n
kṣānti see forbearance; patience
kuṇḍalinī or caṇḍālī 57
Kusinārā 82, 320, 444, 664
Kūṭadanta Sutta 283, 478, 705n, 717n

laity or lay people 629, 723n
  and monks, separation of 614, 629, 638–9, 641, 643
  ordination of (dhamma dīkṣā) 614–15
lakṣaṇas (Pāli lakkhaṇas) 23, 30–3, 79, 147, 691n
Lalitavistara Sūtra 51, 510, 607–8, 688n, 689n, 690n, 693n, 721n
Lama Govinda 246, 276–8, 422–3, 616–18, 694n, 704n, 705n
language 150
  of concepts and images 49–50, 151–2, 436
  limitations of 441
  and objective truth 660–1
  of petition or prayer 440
  of poetry and prose 307
  of symbols see symbolism
Laṅkāvatāra Sūtra 166, 272, 488, 559, 699n, 707n, 719n, 725n
Laozi (Laotse) 96, 222, 696n, 706n
Larkin, P. 514
Lawrence, D. H. 279, 514
lay people see laity
laziness 591–2 see also forces of inertia

Lear, E. 174, 699n
legends 51–2, 59, 152, 235, 302–4 *see also* myths
  about the Buddha *see* Buddha Śākyamuni, life of, legends
Li Gotami 276, 422–3, 617
liberation *see also* freedom
  principle of 245
The Life and Liberation of Padmasambhava 151, 520, 596, 693n, 698n
lifestyle 564, 650, 674
  or life, simple 265–7, 674
  monastic, *see* monasticism
  regular or disciplined 378, 381, 415, 592–5
  secondary, commitment, primary 76, 531, 615
līlā see play
literalism, avoiding 33, 56, 97, 101, 281, 294, 298, 324 *see also* Dharma, letter and spirit
livelihood *see* work or livelihood
Living Ethically xxx, xxxi
Living with Awareness 684
Living with Kindness 684, 712n
lotus flowers 252, 417–18
  Buddha's vision of beings as 55–6, 87, 252
Lotus Sūtra see *White Lotus Sūtra*
love *see also* mettā 99, 120, 172, 288, 448, 451–2, 545, 553, 569, 574, 657–8, 661
  possessive (*pema*) 480, 517
love-mode, and power-mode 480–1, 484, 495, 578, 718n
loving-kindness *see* mettā
lust 40, 54, 405, 482 *see also* craving

Macaulay, Lord 573, 726n
maccu-māra 40, 42
Madhyamaka school/Mādhyamikas 134, 693n
Mahā-assapura Sutta 70, 695n
Maha Bodhi journal 606, 704n
Maha Bodhi Society 77, 79, 605
Maha Bodhi temple 605
Mahābhārata 303, 353
Mahāgovinda Sutta 22–3, 483, 690n, 718n
Mahākāśyapa 151–2
Mahānidāna Sutta 709n
Mahāpādana Sutta 689n
Mahāparinibbāna Sutta 60, 62, 238, 309–11, 320, 372, 461, 473–4, 589, 694n, 702n, 707n, 711n, 716n, 720n, 727n

Mahāprājāpatī Gautami (Pāli Mahāpajāpatī Gotami) 4, 85–7, 213
Mahārāhulovāda Sutta 713n
Mahāsaccaka Sutta 198, 687n, 689n, 700n
Mahāsatipaṭṭhāna Sutta 23, 24, 691n, 712n, 713n, 727n *see also Satipaṭṭhāna Sutta*
Mahāsudassana Sutta 320, 624, 707n, 728n
Mahātaṇhāsaṅkhaya Sutta 709n
Mahāvastu 51, 687n, 688n, 689n, 690n
Mahāvīra 88, 222, 696n
Mahāyāna *see also yānas* xviii, xxv–xxvi, 123, 175, 206, 218, 304, 318, 372, 536, 540, 693n, 716n
  and bodhisattva ideal *see* bodhisattva ideal; perfections
  and hierarchy 501
  myth and archetype 311, 319–22, 388
  and vegetarianism 559
Mahāyāna scriptures or *sūtras see also* individual *sūtras* xxv–xxvi, 51, 156–7, 206, 239, 302, 312–13, 324, 558, 619, 623, 722n
  compared to Pāli scriptures 311–12, 320
  Perfection of Wisdom *see under* Perfection of Wisdom
  not to be taken literally 544–5
Maitreya 50, 237, 422
Majjhima Nikāya xxv, 21, 33, 37, 46, 70, 87, 198, 218, 227, 239, 241, 263, 338, 361, 402, 405, 454, 594, 687n, 689n, 690n, 691n, 692n, 695n, 700n, 701n, 702n, 703n, 705n, 708n, 709n, 710n, 712n, 713n, 714n, 718n, 720n, 722n
Mallinātha Sūri 45, 692n
Malory, T. 405
mandala 260
  Buddhism as a xix
  of five Buddhas xvii–xviii, xxiv, 321–3, 707n *see also* wisdom, four or five aspects of
  development of 321–2
  female counterparts 322, 323
  greater, of aesthetic appreciation 259–61, 297
  spiritual practice/life as 423
Maṅgala or *Mahāmaṅgala Sutta* 512, 721n
Mañjughoṣa/Mañjuśrī 96, 334, 417, 419, 702n

mantra-method 134
mantra recitation practice 323, 401, 417, 419–20
mantras 132, 267, 316, 422–3, 431, 467, 559, 612 *see also* chanting
  Avalokiteśvara 444–5
  Mañjughoṣa 419
  Padmasambhava 422
  Śākyamuni 422
  Vajrasattva 420
Māra 35–6, 39, 46, 47, 53–5, 57–9, 226, 693n
Māras, four 40–5
marriage 7, 472, 488, 555, 562–3, 725n, 730n
Marx, K. 550, 724n
Maslow, A. 362, 710n
material things 191, 255–6, 382, 411–12, 440
  giving 538
materialism 106, 124, 203, 205, 255, 451, 715n, 724n *see also* capitalism; consumerism; culture, economically defined; utilitarianism
  and making money 591
  relaxing hold of 382–3
matter, and mind 455
Maudgalyāyana 193–4, 664
Māyādevī or Queen Māyā 4, 687n
meditation xxviii–xxix, 59, 109–10, 238, 331, 377–8, 595, 673–4 *see also* mindfulness of breathing; *mettā bhāvanā*; *samādhi*; six element practice; visualization
  Amitābha and xix, xxiv
  and art *see under* art
  as basis for right view 178
  on body *see under* body
  on Buddhas and bodhisattvas 423, 536 *see also sādhana*; visualization; *yidams*
  collective practice 403–4, 434, 437
  contact with guru through 493
  or contemplation of decay 391, 395–7
  on corpse 43, 190, 192, 395
  death, recollection of 189–90
  different schools' attitudes to 122
  finding a place for 402–4
  five methods and five poisons 391–401, 712n
  and the forces of inertia 590
  forcing 406
  initial motivation for 362–3
  and insight *see* insight
  Māra and 42

methods and techniques 43–4, 401, 413
mudrā 322
on *nidānas see nidānas*, contemplation of
not only way to practise 413–14
perfection of 54, 67
as a plane of existence 319 *see also* planes
poem by Sangharakshita xxvii–xxix, 389, 682
posture 403–4
progress or success in 145, 175, 411–12, 573, 642
and psychic energies 57
by regular and irregular steps 154
  proper preparation 396–7
on retreat 589
śamatha 329, 401
  and *vipaśyanā* xxix, 401
story of Meghiya 481–2
and supernormal powers 160
and temperament 190–1
time for 148, 175, 472, 562, 641, 643
wisdom cultivated in (*bhāvanā-mayī-prajñā*) 501, 592
Meghiya Sutta 481–2, 718n
mental events 199, 694n
mental states 30, 43
  mindfulness and 576–7
  realms or worlds as counterparts of 41, 329
  skilful *see also* emotions, positive 159, 207, 288–9, 552–3, 557, 588, 590–1, 592, 725n
  unskilful 40–1, 207, 288, 290, 553–5, 557, 590–1 *see also kleśas*; poisons
merit 11, 205, 465, 621
  oppression of gaining 583, 585
  rejoicing in 465, 482, 507, 518, 621
metaphors 77, 101, 214–15, 245, 280, 338, 352, 359, 708n
mettā (Sanskrit *maitrī*) *see also* friendliness; kindness; love 22, 192, 259, 432, 506, 514, 517, 554, 578–9, 601–2
  friendship and 480–1, 483–4, 508
  self 192, 393, 560
mettā bhāvanā xxii, 43, 190–1, 391–4, 397, 399, 401, 480, 514, 606
Mettā Sutta see Karaṇīyamettā Sutta
Michelangelo 200, 373
middle way or path 106, 213, 428, 448, 593–4, 666

Milarepa 52, 124, 424, 452, 507, 536, 564–5, 693n, 715n
Milton, J. 253–4, 296, 353, 456, 516, 520, 706n
mind 100
  absolute 596
  absolute and relative 168–9, 172, 401
  and body (*nāma-rūpa*) 397
  body, speech and *see under* body
  Buddhas and bodhisattvas phenomena of 312
  expansion or stretching of 281–2, 302, 401
  illumined 443
  intrinsic, light of 364
  and matter 455
  and mental states *see* mental states
  non-rational 48–9, 319, 370–1, 387–8 *see also* myth
  One 168
  rational 146, 178, 186, 233, 281 *see also* intellectual understanding; knowledge, rational; reason; thinking and thought
  Enlightenment, beyond reach of (*atakkāvacara*) 156, 233
  reactive and creative 100, 167–73, 339, 709n *see also* creativity; reactive patterns
  ultimate 420
  unconditioned 16–18
mindfulness (*smṛti* (Pāli *sati*)) 43, 44, 133, 190, 406, 556, 560–1 *see also* awareness; forgetfulness
  (or continuity) of purpose 147, 408, 576–7, 587, 594–5, 621
  of breathing (*ānāpānasati*) xxii, 44, 391–2, 397, 401–2, 712n, 713n
  Buddha's last words 589
  four foundations of 88, 402
  importance as foundation 192, 397
  and spontaneity 410–11
miracles 5, 676–8, 692n, 730n
monastic code of rules *see* prātimokṣa
monasticism 116, 121, 415, 533, 637–9 *see also* lifestyle, and commitment
  formalistic 78, 80, 120, 564
monk, with dysentery 61, 462–4, 533
monks (*bhikkhus*) 559, 636–8
  'easy to support' *see* subharo
  ethical code *see* prātimokṣa
  and laity, separation of 614, 629, 638–9, 641, 643
morality 54, 67, 120–1, 161, 550–3 *see also* ethics

natural and conventional 237, 556–7, 564
More, T. 622, 662, 727n, 729n
Morris, W. 662, 730n
Moving Against the Stream 684
Mozart, W. A. 264, 271, 283, 517
Mucalinda 56–8, 510
mudrās 55, 267, 321–2, 433, 434, 694n
Mūlamadhyamakakārikā xxx
Muqi Fachang 255, 704n
music 260, 264–5, 268, 269, 326, 331, 346, 373, 381, 415
  Sangharakshita and 270–1, 283–4, 705n
mystical experience 5, 90–1, 269–72, 604
myth xviii, 311, 312–13, 319–24 *see also* archetypes, legends; parables; supernatural beings; symbolism
  Christianity and 321
  and history 50–2, 56–7, 321
  of the return journey 354–66
  ritual and 434
mythology 18–19, 41
myths, native 235 *see also* paganism

nāgā princess xxx
Nāgārjuna xxx, 52, 543, 693n, 724n
nāgas 56, 454, 693n *see also* snakes
Nagpur 613, 615
nakedness 175, 598–9
Nālaka Sutta 688n
Ñāṇamoli, Bhikkhu xxv, 687n, 688n, 689n, 690n, 691n, 695n, 700n, 701n, 702n, 703n, 705n, 708n, 709n, 710n, 712n, 713n, 714n, 718n, 720n, 722n
nationalism 657
natural world xix, 191, 251–2
nature 91, 237, 249, 251, 256, 385, 504
  and animism 450–3, 455–7, 512 *see also* paganism
Neoplatonism 313 *see also* Plotinus
Nichiren Buddhism 136
Nidāna-kathā 687n, 688n, 689n
nidānas
  cyclic 398–9, 663, 709n
    contemplation of twelve links 43–4, 391, 397–9, 713n
  images for 327, 339, 397
  positive xxii, 588, 692n *see also* path, spiral
Nidānasaṃyutta 703n, 713n
Nidanavagga 692n

Nietzsche, F. 270, 279, 578, 726n
nihilism 181–2 *see also* materialism
nirmāṇakāya 350, 505
Nirvāṇa *see also* Enlightenment; the Unconditioned 42, 89, 93–4, 105–7, 110–12, 159, 165, 263, 666
  as the highest bliss 106, 111, 428, 697n
  'without remainder' *see parinirvāṇa*
niyamas, five 199–202, 206–7, 700n
no-self *see anātman*
Noble (or Ariyan) Eightfold Path xxi, 48, 67, 72, 89–90, 228–9, 238–9, 371, 408, 509, 590, 623, 626–8
noble quest 22, 77
non-duality 537 *see also* the conditioned and the unconditioned; subject, and object
non-returner 720n
non-violence 231, 558, 661–2, 664, 667–8, 670 *see also* precepts, first
nuclear holocaust *see* war, nuclear
nuclear weapons 656, 657, 661, 663, 667–8
nuns 62, 274, 424, 533–4, 637–8, 705n
  poems of early *see Therīgāthā*
Nyanaponika 617
Nyanatiloka 616, 617, 697n
Nyingma school 239–40 *see also* Red Hat tradition

offerings xxviii, 105, 117, 131, 343, 432, 433, 434, 450–1, 458, 497, 715n
Olcott, Colonel 604–5
old age 8–9, 21, 24, 27, 189, 192–3, 198, 386, 397, 585, 665–6
once-returners 588, 720n
ordination
  bodhisattva 530–1, 722n
  of Dharmapala 606
  lay (*dhamma diksha*) 614–15
  of Sangharakshita *see* Sangharakshita, ordination
  in Western Buddhist Order xxi
Orwell, G. 660, 729n
other people
  forbearance towards 386, 465–6
  helping 415–16, 533–4, 545–8, 602
  see also altruism; service

pacifism 664
Padmasambhava 50, 52, 151, 422, 452, 520, 693n, 698n
  initiation, Sangharakshita's xxiii, 530

thangkas xxii–xxiii
paganism 233–7, 550 *see also* animism; culture, indigenous
pain *see also* suffering
  and pleasure 198, 375, 588
Pāli, study of 250, 605, 616
Pāli canon or scriptures *see also* Tipiṭaka xxv–xxvi, 214, 312, 320, 384, 453–4, 533, 545
  and Mahāyāna scriptures compared 311–12, 320
Nikāyas of *see* individual *Nikāyas*
Pang Yun (Hōkoji) 317, 707n
parables 388
  of the ancient city 47–8
  of the blind men and elephant 127–8
  of the Burning House 19, 340–52
  of the lute 134
  myth of the return journey 354–66
  of the plants or raincloud 87–8
  of the poisoned arrow 361, 710n
  of the prodigal son 358
  of the raft 218
  story of fish seller 652–3
Paradise Lost 253, 271, 353, 456, 520, 715n
parents 17, 25, 37, 226, 303, 467–8, 469, 473, 488–9, 513–15, 521, 523, 569
parinirvāṇa 14, 42, 320, 488, 664, 697n *see also* Buddha Śākyamuni, death
Pascal, B. 188, 700n
passion 86–7, 213, 582, 583, 598 *see also* desire
passions, veil of (*kleśāvaraṇa*) 98
path 67–8, 100–4, 189, 238–40, 348–9, 677 *see also* spiritual development
  becoming the (*maggam bhavati*) 100–1, 240, 697n
  bodhisattva 101–2, 239, 366, 653 *see also* perfections
  eightfold *see* Noble Eightfold Path
  and goal 102
  and hierarchy 501
  of irregular steps 154–8, 161, 162
  middle *see* middle way
  of regular steps 154, 158–63
  spiral 22, 198, 424, 588–9, 727n *see also* conditionality, cyclic and spiral
  stages of
    and mandala 423
    seven/purification 239
  theoretical previews 150–1
  of thirteen 'abodes' (*vihāras*) 239, 702n

threefold *see* threefold path
  of transformation 90, 92
  of vision 90–2
    and transformation 67, 90, 92, 509–10, 720n *see also* Noble Eightfold Path
The Path of Purity see Visuddhimagga
paths, two, in wheel of life 325, 328, 663
patience 54, 67, 239 *see also* forbearance; tolerance
patriotism 657, 729n
patterns
  archetypal or symbolic *see also* archetypes xvii–xix, 50, 91, 131–2, 204, 244, 260, 293, 316
  for Buddhist living 466, 545, 552–3
  habitual or reactive 20, 99–100, 158, 170–1, 207, 222, 282, 661
  in our awareness 455
Paul, Saint, in Romans 370, 711n
peace 574–6, 656–7, 661, 667
  world 657, 661–4, 667–70
perception (*saṃjñā*) 27, 30, 31, 40, 179
'perfect' and 'right,' use of terms 725n
Perfect Vision 90–2, 177, 179, 238, 371, 626 *see also* view, right
Perfection of Wisdom (*Prajñāpāramitā*) 161–2, 174–5, 259, 297, 309, 332, 418, 419, 448, 693n
  literature xxx, 65, 133, 175, 619, 679 *see also* Diamond Sūtra; Heart Sūtra
Perfection of Wisdom in 8,000 lines (*Aṣṭasāhasrikā Sūtra*) 240, 372, 703n, 711n, 715n
perfections (*pāramitās*) 67, 239, 303, 479, 540, 694n, 710n
  Buddha's practice of 54–5, 693n, 694n
  of skilful means *see* skilful means
philosophies, worldly 179
philosophy xix, xxx, 92–5, 98, 150, 152, 240–1, 249, 250, 674
  Buddhist 150, 152, 240–1, 250, 433, 473, 488, 564
pilgrimage 240, 354, 442, 444–8, 703n
planes 56, 198–9, 202, 239, 319, 719n
  see also realms; worlds
  hermetic correspondence between 50–1
  higher spiritual 493
  material 319, 538
  or reality, historical 311–13, 319

super-rational 281
Plato 222, 468, 498, 622, 670, 699n, 716n
play (*līlā*) 294–6 *see also* spontaneity
pleasure 405
  on bodhisattva path 543–4
  and pain 198, 375, 588
  refinement of 378–81, 405
Plotinus 313, 498, 706n, 719n
poetic inspiration 441
poetry 97, 192, 268, 275, 308–9, 310, 312, 313, 324, 415
  Bible as *see The Bible Designed to be Read as Literature*
  reading Buddhist texts as 301–2, 307
  Sangharakshita and 249–50, 253–4, 271, 280
  written by Sangharakshita xxvii–xxix, 153, 176, 187, 250, 256–7, 277, 285–7, 383, 389, 420–1, 438–9, 441–2, 527–8, 529, 549, 682, 711–12n
poets, and aliveness of universe 456
poisons 19, 342–3 *see also kleśas*; mental states, unskilful
  five, and corresponding meditation methods 391–401, 712n
  three 328, 343, 398, 553, 663, 724n
political correctness 231, 620 *see also* pseudo-egalitarianism
politics 335, 352, 611, 619, 620, 624–6, 718n
  corporate state 223–4
Pope, A. 136, 698n, 706n
power *see also* authority
  aspect of Enlightenment 419
  and knowledge, literature of 309–11
  mode 653
  mode and love mode 480–1, 484, 495, 578, 718n
  other- 120, 210
  self- 210
  of social conventions 565
  structures 220, 485, 487 *see also* groups
powers
  gods and goddesses as 319
  psychic or supernormal 160, 629–30, 677
prajñā see wisdom
Prajñāpāramitā *sūtras see* Perfection of Wisdom
prātimokṣa (Pāli *pātimokkha*) xxxi, 89, 687n, 696n *see also* Vinaya
pratītya samutpāda see conditionality

INDEX / 749

pratyekabuddhas (Pāli *paccekabuddhas*) 347, 476, 706n, 717n
prayer 427, 439–41, 604, 667 *see also* worship
precepts 415 *see also* confession; ethics
 first 553–4, 558 *see also mettā*; non-violence
 second 554–5, 627–8 *see also* generosity
 third 555 *see also* contentment
 fifth 555–6 *see also* mindfulness
 five 75, 553–6, 557–8, 615, 627, 647, 725n
 monks' 557 *see also prātimokṣa*
 refuges and *see* refuges and precepts
 sixty-four bodhisattva 530, 558, 722n
 speech *see* speech precepts
 ten xxx, 134, 478, 558, 717n
  śrāmaṇera 83–4
  Western Buddhist Order and xxi
The Precious Garland (*Ratnamāla*) xxx, 543, 693n, 724n
 Sangharakshita's Commentary on *see Living Ethically*
Precious Teachers xxx, 719n
prejudices 178, 557
pretas see worlds, of hungry ghosts
pride 428–9, 443, 578, 657, 718n, 726n *see also* conceit
a problem and a difficulty 491–2
problems, psychological 205, 349, 362, 491, 547
projections 175, 570
 of authority 301
 psychological 59, 301, 342, 490, 569–70, 571
 religious 58, 111–12, 363
protectors or guardians (*dharmapālas*) 58–9, 131, 323
pṛthagjanas 178
pseudo-egalitarianism 230–1 *see also* political correctness
psychic centres 57, 694n
psychic powers *see* powers, psychic
psychoanalysis and psychotherapy 364–5, 375, 546–7, 642
psychoanalytical regression 360
psychological
 criterion of ethics 552–3, 556
 nature of perfect effort 590
 problems 205, 349, 362, 491, 547
 projection *see* projection, psychological
 states, neurotic introspection and 576–7
 truthfulness 567

types *see* greed type; hate type; temperament
psychology, Buddhist 100, 199–200, 375, 681, 694n, 697n *see also* Abhidharma
 and cosmology 719n
psychophysical states, elements as 454–5
Pudgalavādins 135
Puja book, FWBO 716n
pujas *see also* worship xxvii, 126, 296, 430, 435–6, 518, 522, 536, 559–60, 595
 Sevenfold 435
Pūralāsa Sutta 728n
Pure Land 641, 652–3 *see also* Buddha-land; Sukhāvatī
purification, seven stages of 239, 702n
purity (*śubha*) 259, 417, 420 *see also* beauty
Pythagoras 222, 498

raft 211, 218
Rāhula 7, 688n
The Rainbow Road from Tooting Broadway to Kalimpong 685
Rājagṛha 300, 485
Ramana Maharshi 572–3, 726n
Ramdas, Swami 249
rapture 198, 242, 405, 588, 669
Ratana Sutta 451, 715n
Rathavinīta Sutta 239, 702n
rationalizations 98, 172, 179, 232, 281, 380, 559, 570 *see also* views, wrong
Ratnamāla see The Precious Garland
Ratnasambhava xviii, xxiv, 322
reactive patterns 99, 661
reactivity *see* mind, reactive
Read, H. 281
reality 19–20, 167, 169, 265
 absolute 74, 245, 399
 archetypal (*sambhogakāya*) 311–14
 and hierarchy 503–4
 higher and lower levels of 50–1, 692n
 historical and spiritual 311–13
 of human body 30–1
 is present through true individual 565
 light of 364, 503–4
 metaphorical nature of 280
 non-conceptual nature of 133
 relative 40
 transcendental 165, 243
 vajra as symbol of 693n
realms *see also* worlds
 of the Dharma (*dharmadhātu*) 477

or dimension, spiritual, writing and 287–92
hell *see* hell
six, in wheel of life 192, 287, 326, 329–30, 335, 339, 398, 663
sublime (*brahmaloka*) 483
of undefined meanings 311–12, 324
reason 49, 69, 94, 275, 387–8 *see also* mind, rational
rebirth 16, 157, 164, 193, 197–8, 202–7, 312, 337, 338, 518–19, 542, 544, 576, 616, 666, 684, 686
 bodhisattva and 239, 542–4
 Buddha and 16, 42, 239, 666
 illustrated in wheel of life 41, 344, 397–8
 karma and *see* karma and rebirth
 spiritual *see* spiritual rebirth
receptivity 49, 66, 256, 384, 439–41, 448, 505–6
Red Hat tradition 490 *see also* Nyingma school
reflection 147, 151, 170, 188, 189, 241, 317, 386, 479, 561, 621
 on Vasubandhu's Four Factors 534–7
 wisdom through (*cintā-mayī-prajñā*) 501, 592
refuge(s) 69, 71–2
 being our own 145
 friends as 479
 not escapism 69–73
 three 18, 66–7, 72, 75 *see also* Three Jewels
 esoteric 507, 596
 true and false 72
refuges and precepts, 'taking' 75, 83, 604, 615
 as a formality 68, 476
relationships 330, 372, 465–73 *see also* families; friendship; marriage; parents
 and duty 574–5
 employer-employee 630–4
 sexual/romantic 405, 468–9, 472, 488, 534
religion 94, 135, 143, 349, 365, 366, 443, 456–7, 480, 651, 670
 Ambedkar and 614
 and art 268–9, 274, 281–2
 Buddhism as Eastern 64–5, 123, 678–9
 comparative 365, 486–7, 616, 674
 ethnic 220, 237, 350
 and politics *see* politics
 as revelation or discovery 209–12
 and ritual 429, 431
 transcendental critique of 216–19
The Religion of Art xxiv, 268, 685, 705n
religions
 ethnic 220, 237, 350
 universal 216, 350
renunciation 232, 303, 382–3, 534, 544, 637, 641, 643 *see also* homeless wanderers
responsibility *see also* duty 100, 206, 216, 225, 338, 376, 586, 651, 673, 674, 676
 sharing 635–6
restlessness xxix, 134, 329, 346 *see also* anxiety
retreats 286, 296–7, 377–8, 383, 414, 522, 589, 636, 677–8
 rainy season 390, 712n
reverence 68, 155–6, 157, 449, 556, 719n, 721n *see also* devotion
 the Buddha and 500
 for life 558 *see also* non-violence
'right' and 'perfect,' use of terms 725n
right livelihood
 or perfect, livelihood 90, 414–15, 562, 623, 626–35, 640, 674, 728n *see also* work
 team-based, businesses xxiv, 105, 219, 635–6, 650
rights 573–6
Rilke, R. M. 274, 280, 285, 517
ritual 95, 132, 237, 316, 416, 429–37, 618, 693n *see also* devotional practice
 definition of 431
 gestures *see mudrās*
 resistance to 429–30, 435
Ritual and Devotion in Buddhism 685
robes 76, 81, 83, 279, 284, 594, 607, 646
Rohiṇī incident 654–6, 668
Rongzompa Chökyi Zangpo 260, 705n
roots 53, 162, 234–5, 617
 in the sky 319
Rossetti D. G. 253
Rossetti M. F. 253
rūpaloka see worlds, of archetypal form

Sachin 257–8, 280
Saddharma Puṇḍarīka see White Lotus Sūtra
sādhana xxix, 432 *see also* visualization; *yidam*
Śākyamuni *see* Buddha Śākyamuni
Śākyans 4, 654–6, 658–9, 664, 668

samādhi 46, 134, 159–60, 267, 405
  see also concentration; *dhyānas*; meditation
  in threefold path *see* threefold path
Sāmaññaphala Sutta 403–4, 696n, 714n
Samantabhadra 529
sambhogakāya 311–12, 350, 462, 505, 716n
saṃgrahavastus 479–80
samprajanya 147 *see also* mindfulness of purpose
saṃsāra 41, 47, 218, 245, 263, 428 *see also* existence, conditioned
  and *nirvāṇa* 98–9, 159 *see also* the conditioned and the unconditioned
saṃskāras or mental conditionings 16, 40, 99, 255, 375, 385, 397 *see also* volitional actions
Saṃyutta Nikāya xxv, 30, 87, 106, 134, 181, 207, 252, 336, 338, 342–3, 474, 482, 500, 542, 691n, 692n, 695n, 697n, 698n, 700n, 701n, 703n, 704n, 708n, 709n, 712n, 713n, 716n, 718n, 719n, 721n, 722n, 724n
sangha 68, 474–9 *see also* spiritual community
  early 14, 637 *see also* disciples, of Buddha Śākyamuni
Sangharakshita
  on alms round 655–8
  and the arts 249–50, 253–4, 270–1, 277, 280, 283–4, 286–7, 705n *see also under* poetry
  and the bodhisattva ideal 529–31
  conflict between poet and philosopher 249–50
  different emphases in teaching xxv–xxvi
  early life 253–4, 269–72, 304
  and ex-Untouchable Buddhists 530, 548, 613
  first contact with Buddhism xix, 65, 529, 679, 699–700n
  friendships 77, 141–2, 257–8, 276, 280, 283–4, 432, 497
  in India *see under* India; Kalimpong
  'legacy' to F/WBO xxi–xxiii
  literary work xvii, xxiii–xxv, 74, 250, 512, 601, 619 *see also under* poetry
  memoirs xvii, xxiii, 289–92
  writing as entrance to spiritual dimension 287–92
  ordination
    bodhisattva 530–1, 722n

  śrāmaṇera and *bhikṣu* 78–9, 82–4, 645
  own Going for Refuge and Going Forth 73–84
  realizing he wasn't a Christian 208–9, 304–5
  seminars xvii, xxiii, xxx
  teachers xxix–xxx, 250, 432–3, 450, 490, 497, 529–30, 712n, 719n
  visions 271–2, 437–8, 726n
saṅgīti or First Council 300–1, 706n
Saṅgīti Sutta 719n
Śāntideva 134, 385, 435, 478, 529, 595, 698n, 711n, 717n, 722n, 727n
saraṇa 69, 73 *see also* Going for Refuge; refuge
Śāriputra 193–4, 354, 664, 690n
Sarnath 14, 82, 444, 606
Sartre, J-P. 386
Sarvabuddhaḍākinī 597–8
Sarvastivāda school 707n
satipaṭṭhāna xxii
Satipaṭṭhāna Sutta 33, 402, 454, 594, 712n, 714n *see also Mahāsatipaṭṭhāna Sutta*
  Sangharakshita's Commentary on *see Living with Awareness*
satsaṅgh 416, 505
Satyapriya 77, 82–3, 141 *see also* Buddharakshita
scepticism 212, 444, 447, 593–4
Schayer, S. 210, 701n
Schopenhauer, A. 92, 94, 279, 616
science 30, 211, 212, 240, 334, 457, 674
scientific
  attitude of mind 94, 129–30, 242–4, 246, 312, 455, 459
  truth 51–2
seeds, (good/bad/Buddha) 335–9
seeing (*darśana*) 97, 254–6 *see also* vision
Sela Sutta 508, 720n
self
  belief in reality of unchanging 30, 183, 189 *see also ātman*; ego; habit
  dissatisfaction with 676–8
  emptiness of 31–2 *see also anātman*
  higher and lower 359, 361–4, 366
  mettā 192, 393, 560 *see also mettā bhāvana*
  and other *see* other people
  treating friends as own (*samānārthatā*) 478, 480
self-consciousness *see under* consciousness

752 / INDEX

self-development 673–5 see also spiritual development
self-indulgence 182, 336
self-knowledge 108–9, 111, 287, 291, 475–6, 591, 602
self-mortification or torture 12, 39, 182, 215, 336, 511 see also Buddha Śākyamuni, austerities
self-power 210
self-transcendence 22, 104, 245
  mutual 572
selfishness 483, 533, 574, 576
selflessness 43–4, 91, 282, 537, 575 see also anātman; egolessness
sensation (vedanā) 29, 40, 375
sense-contact 397
sense-organs, six 397
senses
  evidence of 243–4
  five physical 32, 169, 178
sensuous desire, world of see under worlds
service 303, 349, 461, 506, 625 see also altruism; other people, helping
sex 59, 330, 378, 472
sexual misconduct, abstention from 555
shadow 57–8, 59, 60
Shakespeare, W. 25, 188, 305, 312, 353, 454, 516–17, 658, 691n, 715n, 721n, 729n
shame 270, 565
  culture, Japanese 126–7
Shelley, P. B. 280, 604, 704n
Shin school see Jōdo Shinshū
Shiva 192, 257–8, 343, 705n
sickness, or disease 9, 21, 24, 27, 190, 193, 198, 665–6
Siddhārtha Gautama see Buddha Śākyamuni
Sigālaka or Sigālovāda Sutta 466–7, 478–9, 481, 514–15, 631, 716n, 717n, 721n, 729n
Śikṣā-samuccaya 134, 529, 698n, 722n
śīla xxxi, 159 see also ethics
  samādhi, prajñā see threefold path
  translation of word xxxi
silence 105, 163, 166, 264–5, 266, 286, 345–6, 377, 390, 404, 407, 415, 477, 572–3
  on alms-round 645, 646
  of the Buddha 66
  noble 129, 147
  'thunder-like" 96
  voice of the 144–5, 346, 709n
Simeon Stylites, Saint 102, 697n

simple life 265–7, 674
six element practice xxii, xxix, 44, 391, 399–401, 454, 713n
skandha nirvāṇa 106, 697n
skandhas (Pāli khandhas), five 40, 42, 182–3
  emptiness of 31
  unsatisfactoriness of 27
skilful (kuśala), definition 288
skilful means (upāya-kauśalya) 239, 347, 479, 710n
skilfulness see ethics; mental states, skilful
slavery 236, 480, 628, 637
sleep 318, 337, 359, 378
sloth and slothfulness 134, 216, 421
Smaragdine Tablet 456, 692n
Smith, S. 573, 726n
snakes 41, 56, 325, 663 see also nāgas
social service see service
society
  ideal 561–2, 622–4, 632–3 see also utopias
  transformation of xix, 622–4, 626, 641–2, 728n see also Dhamma Revolution
  Western 65, 650–2
Socrates 374, 468, 699n, 716n
solitary 213, 264, 457, 655
solitude 37, 213, 403, 573
Soṇa Koḷivisa 134
Sophocles 280, 352, 601, 710n
soul 203, 281, 288
  and anātman doctrine 157, 182–3, 245–6
  eternalistic views of 182 see also self, belief in reality of unchanging ātman as 31, 343
  Christian 181, 188, 203
space 102, 264–5, 596
speech 267, 465, 478, 566, 573 see also communication
  body and mind see under body
  perfect 90, 566–72
  precepts 478, 555, 566, 717n
    affectionate or kindly 569–70
    harmonious 465, 572–3
    helpful 570–1, 572
    truthful, see truthfulness
spiral path see path, spiral
spirits 38, 252, 450–2, 455, 512 see also devas
spiritual, definition of word 288–9
spiritual ambition 38, 47
spiritual attainment 244, 334, 496, 503

INDEX / 753

spiritual attainment (*cont.*)
  three lamas and 490
spiritual community 473, 498, 578, 580, 633, 650–3, 674–5 *see also* sangha
  Catholic Church no longer 223
  collective memory of 300–1
  described as a movement 219, 319
  differentiated from the group 79–80, 533
  individuals and 68, 80, 228, 649, 673
  team-based right livelihood and 636 *see also under* right livelihood
spiritual complacency 38, 47
spiritual death xxix, 398
spiritual development or growth *see also* self-development 87, 100–4, 145, 337–8, 344–5, 362, 366, 495, 513–14, 570–1, 591, 697n
  miracle of 676–8
  stages of 134, 160–2, 238–9, 503 *see also* path
spiritual faculties, five 89, 133–4, 426
spiritual friends 190, 482, 484, 504–8, 513, 516–23, 579–82
spiritual friendship (*kalyāṇa mitratā*) *see also* friendship xxii, xxiv, xxx, 68, 416, 460, 462, 464–5, 480–4, 636
  meaning of *kalyāṇa mitratā* 474
  the whole of the spiritual life 474, 482
spiritual hierarchy 244, 500–9, 719n
spiritual ideals 18, 34–5, 357, 363, 426, 580, 598, 653
spiritual individualism *see* individualism, spiritual
spiritual life
  as active/militant life 46, 48
  as art 267 *see also* aesthetic appreciation
  different approaches/ways in 134, 349
  and goals/objects 107–9, 588
  involves dependence 426–9
  meaning of *brahmacariya* 483
spiritual practice
  collective or shared 403–4, 431–2, 434, 437, 614, 651
  direct and indirect methods 413–16
spiritual progress 165, 184, 439, 475, 512
  irreversible 588–9 *see also* Stream Entry
  success in, 595–6 *see also* meditation, progress in
  ten levels of (*bhūmis*) 239, 702n

spiritual rebirth 83, 343
  as Young Hero 60
spiritual receptivity *see* receptivity
spiritual significance of confession 580–1
spiritual teachers *see* teachers
Spoken Word project xxiii–xxiv, xxvii, xxx
spontaneity 159, 172, 195, 221, 294–6, 410–11, 508–9 *see also* play
śramaṇa see homeless wanderers
Sri Lanka xxv, 113–15, 118, 430–1, 625, 631 *see also* Ceylon
Stream Entrants 186, 194, 460, 521, 588
Stream Entry 32, 183, 588–9, 720n *see also* irreversibility
'stream of tendency' 350, 710n
study *see* Dharma, study or discussion
stupas 113, 510–11
subharo or 'easy to support' 636, 639, 641–2
Subhūti (in *Diamond Sūtra*) 74, 372–4, 718n
subject, and object
  not different 97 *see also* non-duality; self, treating friends as own
  polarity or duality 168–9, 287, 292–3, 441
subjective, and objective knowledge 454
the sublime 373–4, 483
suffering *duḥkha* (Pāli *dukkha*) *see also* dissatisfaction; four noble truths; pain; unsatisfactoriness 23–9, 32–3, 333–4, 336, 380, 385–6, 495, 535, 548
  Conze's four concealed aspects of 27–9
Sukhamāla Sutta 7, 688n
Sukhāvatī 120, 623, 727n *see also* Pure Land
Sukhāvatī-vyūha sūtras 320, 623, 707n, 727n
śūnyatā 44, 74, 89, 228, 309–10, 574 *see also* emptiness; the Void
superficiality 183, 185–6, 469, 471
supernatural
  beings 16, 454 *see also* Brahmā; *devas*; spirits
  world 453
superstition 426, 443, 447
Śūraṅgama Sūtra 272
A Survey of Buddhism xxiii, 44, 529, 685
Sūtra of Forty-two Sections 384, 711n

Sūtra of Golden Light (*Suvarṇaprabhāsa Sūtra*) 278–9, 309–10, 539, 582–6, 723n, 724n, 726–7n
Sangharakshita's commentary *see Transforming Self and World*
Sūtra of Wei Lang 65, 73–4, 529, 679
sūtras (Pāli *suttas*) 301–2 *see also* Buddhist scriptures
chanting or recitation of 431, 638
Sutta-Nipāta xxv, 307, 451, 508, 512, 624, 688n, 692n, 715n, 720n, 721n, 729n
Suvarṇaprabhāsa Sūtra see Sūtra of Golden Light
Suvikrāntavikrāmi-paripṛcchā 309–10
Suzuki, D. T. 619, 621, 699n, 707n, 724n, 725n
symbolic value, of ordinary things/events 243–4 *see also* Hermetic Correspondence
symbolism and symbols *see also* archetypes 49, 50–1, 131–2, 152, 278, 345, 353, 359, 387, 598–9, 716n
archetypal, in life of Buddha 48–60
Hindu 192, 345
in wheel of life *see* wheel of life

Tagore, R. 188, 616, 700n
t'ai chi 415
The Tanni Shō 120, 697n
Tantra xviii, xxvi, 131–2, 175, 244, 306, 322
Tantric Buddhism 58, 120–1, 131–2, 564, 596–9, 683 *see also* Vajrayāna
Tantric initiations xxiii, 417, 490, 497
Tao-Teh-King 96, 696n
Taoism 261, 297, 552, 670
Tārā xxix, 372, 417, 419–21, 560
The Taste of Freedom 685
Tathāgata 194, 233, 371, 426, 461, 488, 718n *see also* Buddha
Tathāgatas
contemplation of the virtues of the 536–7
five 322 *see also* mandala of five Buddhas
teacher–pupil relationship 471, 581 *see also* guru, and disciple relationship
teachers 59–60, 151, 161, 345, 487–8, 506–7
of the Buddha *see* Buddha Śākyamuni, teachers
gratitude to 513, 515–19, 521, 523
guru distinguished from *see under* guru

rival 212–13
of Sangharakshita *see* Sangharakshita, teachers
technology 224, 289
Teilhard de Chardin, P. 243, 703n
temperament *see also* greed type; hate type 228, 256, 296–7, 299, 347–9, 394, 414, 428, 641
as spiritual affinity 260
Tennyson, A. 281, 662, 730n
thangkas xxii–xxiii, xxx, 136, 261, 422
Theosophical Society 75, 604
Theosophists 322, 605, 607, 707n
Theosophy 618
Theragāthā 251, 460–1, 716n
Theravāda *see also* Hīnayāna
and Mahāyāna xxv, 501, 543, 589, 719n, 720n
modern 119, 156, 320, 436, 557, 606
school 113, 123, 128–9, 239, 430–1, 598, 698n
Therīgāthā 61–2, 694n
thinking and thought 675 *see also* intellectual understanding; mind, rational
beyond reach of (*atakkāvacara*) 156, 166, 233
clear xviii, 142–50, 170, 180, 185, 228–9, 567–8, 593 *see also* clarity; concepts
collaborative 148–9
dualistic 455 *see also* dualism
foolish 582, 583, 584
and initial insight 91
mindfulness of 88, 402
and *samādhi* 267
unskilful 267 *see also* mental states, unskilful
Thittila, U 75–6, 78
Thomas, Saint 358
three characteristics *see lakṣaṇas*
The Three Jewels xxiii, 44, 48, 685
Three Jewels 424 *see also* refuges, three
disparagement of 486–7
esoteric aspect 507, 596
Going for Refuge to *see* Going for Refuge to the Three Jewels
threefold path (*śīla, samādhi, prajñā*) 46, 67, 159–62, 238, 428
Through Buddhist Eyes 685
Tiantai school 154, 698n
Tibet 115–18, 609, 617, 638, 693n
Tibetan Book of the Dead 195, 197, 312, 364, 373, 711n

Tibetan Buddhism *see also* Vajrayāna xxvi, 123, 124, 136, 239, 323, 343, 430–1, 616–17, 630, 693n
tigress 541, 608, 723n, 724n
time 5, 254–5, 263–4, 331, 360–1, 538, 542, 583, 585, 594
 and eternity 102, 361
 kalpas 542, 701n
 and space 96, 179, 245–6, 311, 312, 318, 544
 wasting 19, 662, 674
Tipiṭaka 123, 128–9, 306 *see also* Pāli Canon
Titans, *asuras see* worlds, of the *asuras*
tolerance 135, 227–8, 230–1, 345, 384, 500 *see also* patience
Tomo Geshe Rimpoche 616
Tōyō Eicho 457, 716n
Traherne, T. 204
Trailokya Vijaya 35, 691–2n
tranquillity 43, 91, 401
transcendence 352 *see also* self-transcendence
the transcendental (*lokuttara*) 288–9, 331, 456–8 *see also* the unconditioned
Transforming Self and World 686, 728n
trees
 bodhi 35–6, 39, 52–3
 Buddha's life and 251, 453–4, 664, 666
 magic or wish-fulfilling 325, 329
 oak 195, 452
 pine 255, 457
 World 53
trikāya 350, 716n
truth 74, 91, 129, 170, 177–8, 193–4, 210–11, 216, 233, 698n, 718n
 beauty and goodness 94, 254, 267, 277, 285, 474
 light of 364, 419
 objective and subjective 290–1, 659–60, 668
 two kinds of 51–2
 truthfulness and honesty 149, 303, 555, 566–8, 572, 591, 726n *see also* concealment
Tsongkhapa 592

Udāna xxv, 98, 127–8, 481–2, 691n, 695n, 697n, 698n, 718n, 720n
udāna, meaning 66
Udumbarika-Sīhanāda Sutta 499, 719n
the Unconditioned 22, 29, 168, 172, 291 *see also* Nirvāṇa; the Transcendental

universalism 350, 710n
 pseudo- 228
unsatisfactoriness *see* suffering
unskilfulness *see also* ethics; mental states, unskilful
 bodily 266–7
 oppressions conditioning 582–6
 three roots of 41 *see also* poisons
'Untouchables' or outcastes 548, 610–13, 728n *see also* caste; ex-Untouchables
Upaddha Sutta 474, 482, 716n, 718n
Upaka 690n, 722n
Upanishads 22, 31, 197, 222, 691n
upāya-kauśalya see skilful means
Uposatha Sutta 98, 501, 697n, 720n
uselessness 295–6, 297
utilitarianism and utility 98, 173–4, 259–61, 464, 533 *see also* materialism
utopias 622, 662, 727n, 729–30n

vagueness 183, 185–6, 667 *see also* doubt
Vairocana xviii, xxiv, 691n
Vajjians 473–4
vajra 53, 332, 419, 597, 598, 693n
 chopper 597
Vajracchedikā Prajñāpāramitā see Diamond Sūtra
Vajrapāṇi 417, 419, 693n
vajrāsana 53, 605
Vajrasattva 417, 420, 692n, 693n
Vajrayāna xxvi, 318, 321–2, 507, 691n, 693n *see also* Tantric Buddhism, Tibetan Buddhism; *yānas*
Vajrayoginī 597–8
Vasala Sutta 624, 728n
Vasubandhu
 Abhidharmakośabhāṣya 90, 696n
 Four Factors 536–7, 723n
Vatthūpama Sutta 405, 714n
Vaughan, H. 204
vedanā see feeling
vegetarianism 122, 146, 558–60 *see also* animals, slaughter of; eating meat
veils 12, 255, 438, 504
 of ignorance/false assumptions (*jñeyāvaraṇa*) 98, 419
 of passions (*kleśāvaraṇa*) 98
Vessantara, Prince 304, 540–1, 724n
vidyā 259 *see also* aesthetic appreciation
Vidyadevi xvi, xx, xxiii, xxiv, xxvi–xxvii, xxix–xxx

view, right 177–9 *see also* Perfect Vision
views 148, 175, 177, 214
  Buddha's freedom from 488
  or theories and desire 97–8, 232
  wrong or false 177–8, 179, 180–1, 205, 228, 230, 413, 482 *see also* philosophies, worldly; rationalizations
    extreme 106, 181–2
    fixed-self *see* self, belief in
    sixty-two 214, 696n
    veil of *see* veils, of ignorance
vigour (*vīrya*) 67, 133–4, 239, 275, 447, 602 *see also* effort; energy; exertion
Vimalakīrti 96
Vimalakīrti-nirdeśa 96, 307, 309, 311, 696n
  Sangharakshita's Commentary *see* The Inconceivable Emancipation
Vinaya 86–7, 593, 607 *see also prātimokṣa*
Vinaya Piṭaka xxxi, 55–6, 134, 213, 300–1, 308, 342–3, 463, 511, 687n, 694n, 695n, 698n, 706n, 709n, 716n
  Cullavagga 98, 213, 697n, 701n
  Mahāvagga 66, 194, 390, 511, 533, 559, 694n, 695n, 700n, 712n, 721n, 723n, 725n
  Pārājika 396–7, 713n
violence 225, 553–4, 555, 574–6, 667–8 *see also* harm; non-violence
vipaśyanā (Pāli *vipassanā*) *see* insight
Virupaksha Cave 438, 726n
vīrya see vigour
Vishnu 258, 345
vision 66, 204–5, 241, 244, 398, 544, 677–8, 715n *see also* seeing
  Blake and divine, single and four-fold 312, 456, 715n
  path of *see under* path
  perfect *see* Perfect Vision
visions xxix, 312, 622–3
  Sangharakshita's 271–2, 437–8, 726n
visualization, practice xviii, 174, 323, 401, 417, 423, 536 *see also* archetypal forms; *sādhana*
Visuddhimagga 239, 333, 619, 708n, 712n, 713n
The Voice of the Silence 346, 709n
the Void 129, 162, 168, 364 *see also śūnyatā*
volitional actions 577 *see also saṃskāras*

vows
  bodhisattva 239, 529
  twenty-two, Ambedkar's 615

Wagner, R. 55, 283, 705n
war 575–6, 625, 629, 654–5, 729n
  and weapons, nuclear 656, 657, 661–4, 667–70
Washington, G. 566, 726n
Wells, H. G. 74, 622, 626, 727n, 728n
Western Buddhist Order (or 'the Order') xxi–xxii, xxiv, xxxi, 521
Western culture 151, 278–9, 320, 409, 452, 617, 678
What is the Dharma? xxiii, 686
What is the Sangha? xxiii, 686
wheel of the Dharma, turning of 322
wheel of life, Tibetan 22, 183, 242, 324–40, 344, 398–9, 534, 540, 663, 668, 709n
  as mirror 328–30, 339–40, 398
  origin 324–5, 707n
White Lotus Sūtra (Saddharma Puṇḍarīka) see also myth of the return journey; parable of the burning house 19, 87, 136, 240, 354, 357–8, 388, 695n, 707n, 709n, 710n
  Sangharakshita's Commentary *see* The Drama of Cosmic Enlightenment
Whitman, W. 540, 724n
Who is the Buddha? xxiii, 20, 686
Wilde, O. 24
Windhorse Publications xxiii, xxv, xxx *see also* Spoken Word project
Winternitz, M. 303–4, 706n
wisdom 43–4, 91–2, 120, 134, 160, 164–5, 175, 259, 288, 426, 602, 699n
  bodhisattva of *see* Mañjughoṣa/Mañjuśrī
  and compassion 63, 118, 160, 179, 322, 366, 440, 536–7, 576
  four or five aspects 323, 419 *see also* mandala of five Buddhas
  and hatred 332–3
  passionate aspect 323
  as a perfection (*pāramitā*) 54, 68
  perfection of *see* Perfection of Wisdom
  sword of 327, 332, 417, 419
  three levels of 501, 592, 719n
  in threefold path *see* threefold path
Wisdom Beyond Words xxiii, 686
the Wise 213
Wise Old Man 58, 59–60

Wordsworth, W. 92, 204, 279–80, 456–7, 517, 574, 696n, 710n, 716n, 726n
work or livelihood 89, 238, 295–7, 557, 561–2, 637–40, 643 *see also* right livelihood
  bodhisattva and 261
  'lightweight' (*sallahukavutti*) 642 *see also subharo*
world
  affairs 178, 675–6
  on fire 19, 342–3
worlds *see also* cosmology; planes; realms
  as counterparts of mental states 41, 329
  of dreams 20, 318
  six, in wheel of life *see also* realms, six
    of animals 326, 327, 329, 330, 334, 335, 663
    of the *asuras*/anti-gods/Titans 325, 327, 329, 332–3, 335–6, 398, 663
    of the gods *see also* heavens 246, 325–6, 329, 331, 335, 337, 343, 398, 662
    of human beings 326, 329–30, 334–5, 338, 398, 663, 719n
    of hungry ghosts (*pretas*) 325–6, 327, 329–30, 333, 335–6, 339, 398, 663
    of tormented beings 326–7, 329–30, 335–6, 663 *see also* hell
  supernatural 453
  three 35, 719n
    archetypal form (*rūpaloka*) 35, 41–2, 324, 501, 719n
    formless (*arūpaloka*) 35, 501, 719n
    sense desire (*kāmaloka*) 35, 41–2, 501, 719n
worship *see also* devotion; prayer; pujas; ritual 17, 230, 258, 416, 425, 450–1, 458, 467, 489
  effect of praising the Buddha 508
wrathful figures 312, 323, 343, 373, 419, 597, 691n
writing 149, 287–92, 299–300, 312

Xuanzang (Yuan Chwang or Hsüan-tsang) 240, 331, 510–11, 620, 703n, 721n

yānas
  nine 239–40
  three 124, 239, 347, 350, 530–1
  '*triyāna* system' xxvi, 134, 530–1
yathābhūta-jñānadarśana see knowledge, and vision of things as they really are
Yeats, W. B. 280, 456, 715n
Yeshe Tsogyal 693n, 698n
yidam 58, 416–17, 507 *see also sādhana*
yoga 415
Yogācāra 134, 702n, 707n
Yogi Chen (C. M. Chen) 712n

Zen 102, 151–2, 164–5, 168, 293, 317, 360–1, 424, 692n, 699n, 711n
  schools 65, 123, 165, 404, 431, 638, 679
  stories 151–2, 218, 531–3, 698n, 723n
Zhiyi 154, 698n

A GUIDE TO THE COMPLETE WORKS OF SANGHARAKSHITA

Gathered together in these twenty-seven volumes are talks and stories, commentaries on the Buddhist scriptures, poems, memoirs, reviews, and other writings. The genres are many, and the subject matter covered is wide, but it all has – its whole purpose is to convey – that taste of freedom which the Buddha declared to be the hallmark of his Dharma. Another traditional description of the Buddha's Dharma is that it is *ehipassiko*, 'come and see'. Sangharakshita calls to us, his readers, to come and see how the Dharma can fundamentally change the way we see things, change the way we live for the better, and change the society we belong to, wherever in the world we live.

Sangharakshita's very first published piece, *The Unity of Buddhism* (found in volume 7 of this collection), appeared in 1944 when he was eighteen years old, and it introduced themes that continued to resound throughout his work: the basis of Buddhist ethics, the compassion of the bodhisattva, and the transcendental unity of Buddhism. Over the course of the following seven decades not only did numerous other works flow from his pen; he gave hundreds of talks (some now lost). In gathering all we could find of this vast output, we have sought to arrange it in a way that brings a sense of coherence, communicating something essential about Sangharakshita, his life and teaching. Recalling the three 'baskets' among which an early tradition divided the Buddha's teachings, we have divided Sangharakshita's creative output into six 'baskets' or groups: foundation texts; works originating in India; teachings originally given in the West; commentaries on the Buddhist scriptures; personal writings; and poetry, aphorisms, and works on the arts. The 27th volume, a concordance, brings together all the terms and themes of the whole collection. If you want to find a particular story or teaching, look at a traditional term from different points of view or in different contexts, or track down one of the thousands of canonical references to be found in these volumes, the concordance will be your guide.

1. FOUNDATION

What is the foundation of a Buddhist life? How do we understand and then follow the Buddha's path of Ethics, Meditation, and Wisdom? What is really meant by 'Going for Refuge to the Three Jewels', described by Sangharakshita as the essential act of a Buddhist life? And what is the Bodhisattva ideal, which he has called 'one of the sublimest ideals mankind has ever seen'? In the 'Foundation' group you will find teachings on all these themes. It includes the author's *magnum opus, A Survey of Buddhism*, a collection of teachings on *The Purpose and Practice of Buddhist Meditation*, and the anthology, *The Essential Sangharakshita*, an eminently helpful distillation of the entire corpus.

2. INDIA

From 1950 to 1964 Sangharakshita, based in Kalimpong in the eastern Himalayas, poured his energy into trying to revive Buddhism in the land of its birth and to revitalize and bring reform to the existing Asian Buddhist world. The articles and book reviews from this period are gathered in volumes 7 and 8, as well as his biographical sketch of the great Sinhalese Dharmaduta, Anagārika Dharmapala. In 1954 Sangharakshita took on the editing of the *Maha Bodhi*, a journal for which he wrote a monthly editorial, and which, under his editorship, published the work of many of the leading Buddhist writers of the time. It was also during these years in India that a vital connection was forged with Dr B. R. Ambedkar, renowned Indian statesman and leader of the Buddhist mass conversion of 1956. Sangharakshita became closely involved with the new Buddhists and, after Dr Ambedkar's untimely death, visited them regularly on extensive teaching tours.

From 1979, when an Indian wing of the Triratna Buddhist Community was founded (then known as TBMSG), Sangharakshita returned several times to undertake further teaching tours. The talks from these tours are collected in volumes 9 and 10 along with a unique work on Ambedkar and his life which draws out the significance of his conversion to Buddhism.

3. THE WEST

Sangharakshita founded the Triratna Buddhist Community (then called the Friends of the Western Buddhist Order) on 6 April 1967. On 7 April the following year he performed the first ordinations of men and women within the Triratna Buddhist Order (then the Western Buddhist Order). At that time Buddhism was not widely known in the West and for the following two decades or so he taught intensively, finding new ways to communicate the ancient truths of Buddhism, drawing on the whole Buddhist tradition to do so, as well as making connections with what was best in existing Western culture. Sometimes his sword flashed as he critiqued ideas and views inimical to the Dharma. It is these teachings and writings that are gathered together in this third group.

4. COMMENTARY

Throughout Sangharakshita's works are threaded references to the Buddhist canon of literature – Pāli, Mahāyāna, and Vajrayāna – from which he drew his inspiration. In the early days of the new movement he often taught by means of seminars in which, prompted by the questions of his students, he sought to pass on the inspiration and wisdom of the Buddhist tradition. Each seminar was based around a different text, the seminars were recorded and transcribed, and in due course many of the transcriptions were edited and turned into books, all carefully checked by Sangharakshita. The commentaries compiled in this way constitute the fourth group. In some ways this is the heart of the collection. Sangharakshita often told the story of how it was that, reading two *sūtras* at the age of sixteen or seventeen, he realized that he was a Buddhist, and he has never tired of showing others how they too could see and realize the value of the '*sūtra*-treasure'.

5. MEMOIRS

Who is Sangharakshita? What sort of life did he live? Whom did he meet? What did he feel? Why did he found a new Buddhist movement? In these volumes of memoirs and letters Sangharakshita shares with his readers much about himself and his life as he himself has experienced it, giving us a sense of its breadth and depth, humour and pathos.

6. POETRY, APHORISMS, AND THE ARTS

Sangharakshita describes reading *Paradise Lost* at the age of twelve as one of the greatest poetic experiences of his life. His realization of the value of the higher arts to spiritual development is one of his distinctive contributions to our understanding of what Buddhist life is, and he has expressed it in a number of essays and articles. Throughout his life he has written poetry which he says can be regarded as a kind of spiritual autobiography. It is here, perhaps, that we come closest to the heart of Sangharakshita. He has also written a few short stories and composed some startling aphorisms. Through book reviews he has engaged with the experiences, ideas, and opinions of modern writers. All these are collected in this sixth group.

In the preface to *A Survey of Buddhism* (volume 1 in this collection), Sangharakshita wrote of his approach to the Buddha's teachings:

> Why did the Buddha (or Nāgārjuna, or Buddhaghosa) teach this particular doctrine? What bearing does it have on the spiritual life? How does it help the individual Buddhist actually to follow the spiritual path?… I found myself asking such questions again and again, for only in this way, I found, could I make sense – spiritual sense – of Buddhism.

Although this collection contains so many words, they are all intent, directly or indirectly, on these same questions. And all these words are not in the end about their writer, but about his great subject, the Buddha and his teaching, and about you, the reader, for whose benefit they are solely intended. These pages are full of the reverence that Sangharakshita has always felt, which is expressed in an early poem, 'Taking Refuge in the Buddha', whose refrain is 'My place is at thy feet'. He has devoted his life to communicating the Buddha's Dharma in its depth and in its breadth, to men and women from all backgrounds and walks of life, from all countries, of all races, of all ages. These collected works are the fruit of that devotion.

We are very pleased to be able to include some previously unpublished work in this collection, but most of what appears in these volumes has been published before. We have made very few changes, though we have added extra notes where we thought they would be useful. We have had the pleasure of researching the notes in the Sangharakshita Library at 'Adhisthana', Triratna's centre in Herefordshire, UK, which houses his own collection of books. It has been of great value to be able to search among the very copies of the *suttas*, *sūtras* and commentaries that have provided the basis of his teachings over the last seventy years.

The publication of these volumes owes much to the work of transcribers, editors, indexers, designers, and publishers over many years – those who brought out the original editions of many of the works included here, and those who have contributed in all sorts of ways to this *Complete Works* project, including all those who contributed to funds given in celebration of Sangharakshita's ninetieth birthday in August 2015, and to a further outpouring of generosity after Sangharakshita's death in October 2018. All these donors have made the publication of this series possible, and we are very grateful. Many thanks to everyone who has helped; may the merit gained in our acting thus go to the alleviation of the suffering of all beings.

Vidyadevi and Kalyanaprabha
Editors

THE COMPLETE WORKS OF SANGHARAKSHITA

I FOUNDATION

VOLUME 1 A SURVEY OF BUDDHISM / THE BUDDHA'S NOBLE EIGHTFOLD PATH
A Survey of Buddhism
The Buddha's Noble Eightfold Path

2 THE THREE JEWELS I
The Three Jewels
The Meaning of Conversion in Buddhism
Going for Refuge
The Ten Pillars of Buddhism
The History of My Going for Refuge
My Relation to the Order
Extending the Hand of Fellowship
Forty-Three Years Ago
Was the Buddha a Bhikkhu?

3 THE THREE JEWELS II
Who is the Buddha?
What is the Dharma?
What is the Sangha?

4 THE BODHISATTVA IDEAL
The Bodhisattva Ideal
The Endlessly Fascinating Cry (seminar)
The Bodhisattva Principle

5 THE PURPOSE AND PRACTICE OF BUDDHIST MEDITATION
The Purpose and Practice of Buddhist Meditation

6 THE ESSENTIAL SANGHARAKSHITA
The Essential Sangharakshita

II INDIA

7 CROSSING THE STREAM: INDIA WRITINGS I
Early Writings 1944–1954
Crossing the Stream
A Sense of Direction

VOLUME 8   BEATING THE DHARMA DRUM: INDIA WRITINGS II
Anagarika Dharmapala and Other 'Maha Bodhi' Writings
Dharmapala: The Spiritual Dimension
Beating the Drum: 'Maha Bodhi' Editorials
Alternative Traditions

9   DR AMBEDKAR AND THE REVIVAL OF BUDDHISM I
Ambedkar and Buddhism
Lecture Tour in India, December 1981–March 1982

10   DR AMBEDKAR AND THE REVIVAL OF BUDDHISM II
Remembering Ambedkar
Buddha and the Future of His Religion
The Mass Conversion and the Years After, 1956–61
Lectures in India and England 1979, 1982–92
Wisdom before Words: The Udāna

III THE WEST

11   A NEW BUDDHIST MOVEMENT I
Ritual and Devotion in Buddhism
The Buddha's Victory
The Taste of Freedom
Buddha Mind
Human Enlightenment
New Currents in Western Buddhism
Buddhism for Today – and Tomorrow
Buddhism and the West
Aspects of Buddhist Morality
Dialogue between Buddhism and Christianity
Buddhism and Blasphemy
Articles and Interviews

12   A NEW BUDDHIST MOVEMENT II
Previously unpublished talks

13   EASTERN AND WESTERN TRADITIONS
Tibetan Buddhism
Creative Symbols of Tantric Buddhism
The Essence of Zen
The FWBO and 'Protestant Buddhism'
From Genesis to the Diamond Sūtra

IV COMMENTARY

VOLUME	14	THE ETERNAL LEGACY / WISDOM BEYOND WORDS

The Eternal Legacy
The Glory of the Literary World
Wisdom Beyond Words

15 PĀLI CANON TEACHINGS AND TRANSLATIONS
Dhammapada and other translations
Living with Awareness
Living with Kindness
Living Beautifully
Auspicious Signs
Salutation to the Three Jewels
The Threefold Refuge

16 MAHĀYĀNA MYTHS AND STORIES
The Drama of Cosmic Enlightenment
The Priceless Jewel (talk)
Transforming Self and World
The Inconceivable Emancipation

17 WISDOM TEACHINGS OF THE MAHĀYĀNA
Know Your Mind
Living Ethically
Living Wisely
The Way to Wisdom (seminar)

18 MILAREPA AND THE ART OF DISCIPLESHIP I
The Yogi's Joy
The Shepherd's Search for Mind
Rechungpa's Journey to Enlightenment

19 MILAREPA AND THE ART OF DISCIPLESHIP II
Rechungpa's Journey to Enlightenment, continued

V MEMOIRS

20 THE RAINBOW ROAD FROM TOOTING BROADWAY TO KALIMPONG
The Rainbow Road from Tooting Broadway to Kalimpong

VOLUME	21	FACING MOUNT KANCHENJUNGA
		Facing Mount Kanchenjunga
		Dear Dinoo: Letters to a Friend
	22	IN THE SIGN OF THE GOLDEN WHEEL
		In the Sign of the Golden Wheel
		Precious Teachers
		With Allen Ginsberg in Kalimpong (essay)
	23	MOVING AGAINST THE STREAM
		Moving Against the Stream
		1970 – A Retrospect
	24	THROUGH BUDDHIST EYES
		Travel Letters
		Through Buddhist Eyes

VI POETRY AND THE ARTS

	25	POEMS AND SHORT STORIES
		Complete Poems 1941–1994
		Other Poems
		Short Stories
	26	APHORISMS, THE ARTS, AND LATE WRITINGS
		Sayings, Poems, Reflections
		Peace is a Fire
		A Stream of Stars
		The Religion of Art
		In the Realm of the Lotus
		The Journey to Il Convento
		St Jerome Revisited
		A Note on The Burial of Count Orgaz
		Criticism East and West
		Buddhism and William Blake
		Urthona Interviews
		Madhyamaloka Reflections
		Adhisthana Writings

VII CONCORDANCE

	27	CONCORDANCE TO THE COMPLETE WORKS

WINDHORSE PUBLICATIONS

Windhorse Publications is a Buddhist charitable company based in the UK. We produce books of high quality that are accessible and relevant to all those interested in Buddhism, at whatever level of interest and commitment. We are the main publisher of Sangharakshita, the founder of the Triratna Buddhist Order and Community. Our books draw on the whole range of the Buddhist tradition, including translations of traditional texts, commentaries, books that make links with contemporary culture and ways of life, biographies of Buddhists, and works on meditation.

To subscribe to the *Complete Works of Sangharakshita*, please go to: windhorsepublications.com/sangharakshita-complete-works/

THE TRIRATNA BUDDHIST COMMUNITY

Windhorse Publications is a part of the Triratna Buddhist Community, an international movement with centres in Europe, India, North and South America and Australasia. At these centres, members of the Triratna Buddhist Order offer classes in meditation and Buddhism. Activities of the Triratna Community also include retreat centres, residential spiritual communities, ethical Right Livelihood businesses, and the Karuna Trust, a UK fundraising charity that supports social welfare projects in the slums and villages of India.

Through these and other activities, Triratna is developing a unique approach to Buddhism, not simply as a philosophy and a set of techniques, but as a creatively directed way of life for all people living in the conditions of the modern world.

For more information please visit thebuddhistcentre.com

SANGHARAKSHITA.ORG

You can find out more about Sangharakshita's life, teachings, and the Buddhist movement he founded on his official website: sangharakshita.org